Philipp Spitta

JOHANN SEBASTIAN BACH

VOLUME I

PHILIPP SPITTA

JOHANN SEBASTIAN BACH

HIS WORK AND INFLUENCE ON THE MUSIC OF GERMANY, 1685-1750.

TRANSLATED FROM THE GERMAN BY

CLARA BELL

AND

J. A. FULLER-MAITLAND.

IN THREE VOLUMES

VOL. I

LONDON
NOVELLO & CO., LTD.

NEW YORK
DOVER PUBLICATIONS, INC.

This Dover edition, first published in 1952, is an unabridged and unaltered republication of the Bell and Fuller-
Maitland translation originally published in 1889 by Novello & Company, Ltd. A new bibliographical note was
written specially for this Dover edition by Saul Novack. The
original edition of this work appeared in three volumes, but
this Dover edition is bound in two volumes.

International Standard Book Number: 0-486-22278-0

Library of Congress Catalog Card Number: 52-6022

Manufactured in the United States of America

DOVER PUBLICATIONS, INC.
180 Varick Street
New York, N. Y. 10014

CONTENTS.

PREFACE.

THE work of which this volume is an instalment bears for its title nothing but the name of the man whose life and labours form its main subject. And since it is beyond dispute that no individual character can have full and complete justice done to it unless all the circumstances are laid bare under which it was developed, and worked out its results, this principle must above all be applicable in the case of a man who forms, as it were, the focal point towards which all the music of Germany has tended during the last three centuries, and in which all its different lines converged to start afresh in a new period, and to diverge towards new results. To describe all these can indeed hardly be my present task, all the less because the time is not yet come for saying the last word as to the profound influence exercised by Bach, more particularly on the music of the nineteenth century.

My task is rather to disentangle, in the period that preceded him, the threads which united in that centre, and to trace the reasons why it should have been in Bach that they converged, and in none other; for such a course could not be avoided by a writer whose purpose it was to give even an approximate idea of the grandeur of his personality as an artist. The deeper and more ramified the roots by which he clung to the soil of German life and nature, the wider was the extent of ground to be dug over in order to lay them bare. Hence the reader will find in this book much which he would hardly seek in a mere " life " of Sebastian Bach, but which is nevertheless intimately and inseparably connected with him. And thus, I think, its title will be justified by its contents.

No attempt at such a comprehensive picture has as yet been made; but there is no lack of books which have for their subject-matter the outward events of Bach's life or certain aspects of his artistic labours. Among these, the

most important is the Necrology, which was published four
years only after the master's death in L. Chr. Mizler's
Musikalische Bibliothek, Vol. IV., Part I., pages 158 to 176
(Leipzig, 1754). Its statements would be entitled to our
belief, if only from its having first seen the light at a time
when Bach's memory was still fresh, and in the city where
he had lived and laboured for twenty-seven years; and this
is confirmed by the fact that it was compiled by Karl
Philipp Emanuel Bach, the composer's second son, and by
Johann Friederich Agricola, one of the most distinguished
of his pupils. It is obvious that they combined for this
work, because Agricola had enjoyed the benefit of Sebastian
Bach's instructions at a time when his son had quitted the
paternal roof, and so had personal knowledge of some circumstances which Philipp Emanuel Bach had learned only
indirectly. Agricola also contributed to Jakob Adlung's
Musica Mechanica Organœdi (Berlin, 1768) a number of
valuable notes regarding his illustrious teacher. The
simple picture of Bach's life and artistic powers which the
Necrology contains, with a summary review of his compositions, has been transcribed by almost all the later biographers—so called. Thus, in the first place, Johann Adam
Hiller, in his Lebensbeschreibungen berühmter Musikge-
lehrten und Tonkünstler neuerer Zeit, Part I., pages 9 to 29
(Leipzig, 1784). He was followed by Ernst Ludwig Gerber,
Historisch-Biographisches Lexicon der Tonkünstler, Part I.,
col. 86 (Leipzig, 1790), who does not seem to have known
whence Hiller had derived his information. Still, even in
Gerber, we here and in other places come upon original
observations worthy of remark, founded on statements supplied by his father, who had been Sebastian Bach's pupil.

A curious production in the way of a biography occurs
in Hirsching, Historisch-literarisches Handbuch berühmter
und denkwürdiger Personen, welche im achtzehnte Jahrhundert gestorben sind, Vol. I., page 77 (Leipzig, 1794).
Here the dates given in the Necrology are repeated approximately, and with several errors; then follows a sketch of
Bach's characteristics which is derived from Proben aus
Schubarts Aesthetik der Tonkunst, published by Schubart's

son in the Deutschen Monatsschrift (Berlin, 1793). This fantastic work is of course not to be relied on—not even where some facts seem to shine through of which the inaccuracy is not immediately obvious. C. A. Siebigke, Museum berühmter Tonkünstler, pages 3 to 30 (Breslau, 1801), repeats Gerber and Hiller—that is to say, the Necrology, but adds a few remarks on Bach's style. J. Ch. W. Kühnau, Die blinden Tonkünstler (Berlin, 1810), and J. E. Groszer, Lebensbeschreibung des Kapellmeister Johann Sebastian Bach (Breslau, 1834), have not even any independent musical judgment; and none of these, excepting Gerber in a few passages, can be said to have made any researches of their own.

The first advance that was made in the literature of the subject after Mizler's Necrology is marked by J. N. Forkel's book, Ueber Johann Sebastian Bach's Leben, Kunst und Kunstwerke—Für patriotische Verehrer echter musikalischer Kunst (Leipzig, 1802; a new edition in 1855). Forkel, the most learned musician of Germany of his time, and a passionate admirer of Sebastian Bach, had been personally acquainted with his two eldest sons: he thus became possessed of valuable materials, which he worked up into his book. With regard to the facts of Bach's life, even he has little to add to the contents of the Necrology, though he enlarges on his characteristics as an organ and clavier player, as a composer, teacher, and father of a family. Still, valuable as Forkel's book is as an authority, and little as we can reproach him with mere fanciful inventions, we must use him with caution. For instance, he does not sufficiently distinguish the actual statements and judgments of Bach's sons from his own opinions, but, on the contrary, has worked them up together into a continuous narrative, so that it is often hard to discover the beginning and the end of those passages which give the book its special value. Forkel's own judgment, even as regards Bach, is often strangely narrow. Frequently, no doubt, independent inquiry leads us to a result which coincides so exactly with Forkel's statement as to leave no doubt as to the value of the source whence he obtained his fact; but presently, again, we are startled by some evident inaccuracy, or the discovery that, under the most favourable interpretation, he has misunderstood his authority. Finally, it must be borne in mind that Bach's sons may themselves have made mistakes. For these reasons, though we must necessarily refer to this work at every step, for due security we must accept none of its assertions without testing them.

On the occasion of the centenary of Bach's death, July 28, 1850, two memorial works appeared. First, Johann Sebastian Bach's Lebensbild—Eine Denkschrift, &c., aus Thüringen, seinem Vaterlande; Vom Pfarrer Dr. J. K. Schauer (Jena, 1850). In this is collected all that was then known, briefly, and for the most part correctly; it is conscientious in giving the authorities, and includes a careful list of the published works of the composer, but betrays no profound artistic intelligence. The second centenary writer, C. L. Hilgenfeldt, goes more deeply into his subject, Johann Sebastian Bach's Leben, Wirken und Werke—Ein Beitrag zur Kunstgeschichte des achtzehnten Jahrhunderts (Leipzig, 1850). The book is written with earnest purpose, and is so far a small advance on Forkel that the author has carefully collected a number of dates and of criticisms on Bach from the literature of the last century, and has worked them in with his picture. He too first gave us some detailed information as to Bach's ancestors, and a general review of Bach's compositions, which deserves credit at any rate on the score of industry. Historic breadth of view and scientific method we must not indeed expect to find ; his artistic judgments and his historical purview, like the work generally, are but shallow and amateurish. However, as the author himself is modest as to his powers, it would be unfair to reproach him farther.

Since then a singular literary effort has emanated from C. H. Bitter, Johann Sebastian Bach (two vols., Berlin, 1865). The author has been swept away by the historic current of our time, and attempts to wield the paraphernalia of science, but without being in any way capable of doing so. However, we must be grateful to him for disinterring certain archives previously unknown, for such documents, like books, have their destinies. Unfortunately they are very incorrectly reproduced. The author's own attempts at historical inferences and other reflections could have been omitted with advantage to the author and his book. He has done better in a later work, Carl Philipp Emanuel Bach und Wilhelm Friedemann Bach und deren Brüder (two vols., Berlin, 1868). Here, no doubt, the task was an easier one.

From this sketch it is evident that the only authorities that can be really considered available are the Necrology, Forkel, and parts of Gerber. To procure new material, next to an exact comparison of all the writers contemporary with Bach, a careful search was necessary through all the archives in which any trace of Bach's life as a citizen and official personage might occur. Then it was requisite to produce as clear a picture as possible, not only of the general conditions of the time when he lived, but of the various places where he resided, with his surroundings and duties; to trace all the indications of his wider activity, and follow up the history of those persons with whom he seemed to have had any connection. It is quite certain that Bach rarely wrote letters, most rarely of all to private persons; hence we can reckon very little on this most important source of biographical facts. It has been all the more gratifying to light upon a few valuable discoveries of this kind. An inestimable document is a private letter, full of details, addressed from Leipzig, October 28, 1730, to the friend of his youth, Georg Erdmann, in Dantzig, which I have been enabled to bring to light from among the state archives at Moscow, by the help of my excellent friend, Herr O. von Riesemann of Reval. Erdmann died, October 4, 1736, as " Hofrath " to the Russian Empire and Resident at Dantzig. He left a daughter under age, and her education, with the arrangement of his somewhat disordered affairs, was undertaken by his sister-in-law, a certain Fräulein von Jannewitz. This lady writes, on November 9, 1736 : " Some quite old letters, and papers also, which my late brother-in-law had laid by in a room apart, even before the bombardment, I laid, as soon as I remembered them, in a coffer, and sealed it twice with his seal, which was also used for the other sealing." She herself wished to quit Dantzig, and this property was a burden to her. But among the "quite old letters" was this one from Sebastian Bach, which consequently travelled away to Moscow with Erdmann's official papers, and slumbered there nearly a century and a half, awaiting its present resurrection.

Though such autographs as these, of which the discovery often turns upon a mere happy accident, are extremely rare, we are better off as regards the autographs of Bach's compositions. It may indeed be boldly asserted that the greater number of them still exist, and that a considerable portion are accessible to all. Nor are they only of inestimable value to musicians by reason of their contents; under skilful treatment they yield a mass of biographical data which is sometimes really astonishing; and this source would flow still more readily if the date at which they were written were not usually wanting. Here a field is opened for expert criticism to establish some sort of chronology, in which its utmost skill may be exercised; for, since Bach's manuscripts extend over a period of more than forty years, it would be a by no means impossible task to assign to each period the handwriting that belongs to it by certain distinguishing marks, though in its main features it is curiously constant. The differences in the paper would assist in this, and a third factor would be the investigation of the text for his vocal compositions. The style of the poetry used for these by Bach is for the most part too undefined for us to draw any inferences from it, though sometimes it is possible; but it is a fertile source of information to trace out the writers and the publication of these texts. It was the custom of the time to have the words of the hymns sung in churches printed and distributed to the congregation, that they might follow them, and this contributes to baffle us and to conceal, at any rate, the first printing of the hymns. The various handling which the manuscripts frequently offer to our investigation I shall not, of course, any farther refer to in this place.

The publications of the Bach-Gesellschaft (Bach Society of Germany) have been of immense use in my labours; they

now extend through twenty-seven yearly series, and are
based on the best authorities, and give evidence of the
greatest critical care, especially wherever Herr W. Rust has
set his experienced hand. F. C. Griepenkerl and F. A.
Roitzsch have edited, with no less learning and care, the
collected edition of Bach's instrumental works, published by
C. F. Peters of Leipzig; and A. Dörffel supplemented it in
1867 by an accurate thematic catalogue. Nevertheless, for
the reasons given above, I felt it my duty to examine
every autograph by Bach that I could discover. This, by
degrees, I was able to accomplish with all that are preserved
in public libraries, particularly in the Royal Library at
Berlin. It is, of course, always more difficult to obtain
access to private collections; however in most cases I have
met with a friendly and liberal help. No doubt there are
still several autographs which, lying *perdu* in the hands of
unknown owners, for the present defy research—and, in
saying this, I refer particularly to England. When shall
we recover from thence that which is our own—so far, at any
rate, as regards the matter of its contents?

The mention of Bach's compositions has led us away from
the biographical to the artistic and historical as part of this
work. From the writings of those authors who have already
endeavoured to treat of Bach more or less comprehensively—
Winterfeld, in Vol. III. of his Evangelisches Kirchengesang;
Mosewius, in his discussion of Bach's Passion Music
according to St. Matthew, and others—I could only use a
few details here and there, for it is very clear that they either
under-estimated, or wholly ignored, precisely that very
impetus . which, gathering force during a whole century,
culminated triumphantly in Sebastian Bach. Indeed, it is
always better to see with our own eyes than through those
of others. Besides, all that the seventeenth century produced
in the way of musical forms stands in such close and intimate connection with Bach's art that a somewhat exacter
study of it seemed indispensable. In this, no less than in
considering Bach's own compositions, I have, of course,
attributed the greatest weight to the element of form, in
proportion as an exact scientific estimate of this is more

possible than of the ideal element. Still, I could not regard myself as justified in altogether neglecting this, and so leaving undone a part of my task—the production, namely, of a comprehensive picture of Sebastian Bach and his art. The musical writer must always find himself here in a peculiarly difficult position. He may lay bare the foundations of a certain form, point out the modifications which it has undergone in special cases under the subjective treatment of the artist, but still he will not have conveyed to the reader an essentially musical conception, which is the feeling and purport of the piece. In vocal music the words contribute to bridge over the gulf; in instrumental music he has the option of offering to the reader a mere anatomy, or of attempting in a few words to call up the spirit which alone can give it life and soul. I have selected the latter method, and must trust to the chance that what I find and feel in this or that composition may be also felt by others. I shall not, I think, be accused of having treated this part of my work in too subjective a manner. A homogeneous strain of feeling lies at the base of all Bach's compositions, permeating them so strongly that it must be evident to any one who really studies the master.

Every epoch, every distinct musical form, has its own character and sentiment; nay, every kind of instrument is limited to its own sphere of feeling. Up to this point we walk securely, but beyond this the ground is shifting, the eye is dazzled by the play of hues which at every instant are born and die—none but a poet can find language to convey the effect. Here, however, I must expressly protect myself against the misconception that in order thoroughly to enjoy a work of art it must be possible to transcribe its sentiment in words. Every instrumental composition—like any other work of art—must produce its effect by its own means and by its own nature. I have only attempted to fulfil what I conceived to be an author's duty.

In order to give a broad historical view of Bach as an artist, and of his works, it was necessary first to give due consideration to a circumstance which cannot be a matter of indifference. The hero of this biography was descended

from a family who had already been musicians for more
than a century; Bach himself, and his sons, laid stress on
this long artistic pedigree, and we owe our knowledge of it
to the MS. genealogy of the Bach family, which is preserved
in the Royal Library at Berlin.   It was obtained from the
property left by G. Pölchau, professor of music at Hamburg,
who had it from that left by Forkel, to whom it had been
given by Philipp Emanuel Bach.   It contains fifty-three
numbers, in each of which the parentage and birth and death
days of a male member of the Bach family are recorded;
the first were written by Sebastian Bach himself, according
to his son's statement.   By whom the work was continued
we are not told; still it may be guessed with some degree
of certainty.   In the first place it is demonstrable that it
was drawn up in the last months of the year 1735, since
Sebastian's son Johann Christian, who was born September
5, 1735, is mentioned by name under No. 18.   Philipp
Emanuel was at that time a student at Frankfort-on-the-
Oder.   Besides this, it is clear from certain details that,
with the exception of course of the first number, the
genealogy cannot have been drawn up under the eye of
Sebastian Bach.   The date of his eldest brother's death is
wanting, which he must certainly have known; and, what is
more, in the notice of Sebastian himself a false date is
given (see on this subject Appendix A, No. 9), which relates
to an occurrence so important that Sebastian himself could
hardly have made a mistake in the year.   Now this error is
repeated in the Necrology, and we know that the Necrology
was in great part drawn up by Philipp Emanuel Bach.
The inference is obvious.   When Philipp Emanuel subsequently sent a copy of the genealogy to Forkel, he added
a variety of explanatory notes to extend and improve it;
but copies had already become distributed among the Bach
family, particularly in the line which in the second half
of the seventeenth century had settled in Franconia.   A
copy of it was in the possession of Johann Lorenz Bach,
a cousin of Philipp Emanuel; and his great-grandson,
Johann Georg Wilhelm Ferrich, minister of Seidmannsdorf,
near Coburg, to whom it descended in due course, allowed

it to be published in the Allgemeine Musikalische Zeitung,
Vol. XLV., Nos. 30 and 31.   He erroneously supposed that
Lorenz Bach himself had drawn it up, but a comparison
makes it evident that it is only a copy.   The trifles which
are wanting in the Ferrich genealogy are partly unintentional
oversights, and partly wholly unimportant; some, too, are
easily accounted for by the illegibility of the original MS.
On the other hand it has a series of additions, such as the
dates of Sebastian Bach's appointment to be "court composer" to the King of Poland (1736), and of his death, with
fuller notices of the Bachs of Schweinfurt and Ohrdruf.   In
No. 18, also, the date "1735" is added later, apparently
because the copyist observed that this date was essential for
determining and verifying several others, while at first he
had omitted it as not coinciding with the date at which he
made his transcript.   At any rate these additions must
have been made before 1773, the year of Lorenz Bach's
death, since it is not mentioned; nay, more, we know that
the MS. from which Lorenz Bach copied was not the
original that had belonged to Philipp Emanuel Bach, but
only a copy from that.   This copy also has been preserved,
though only in a fragment, beginning with No. 25; this is
now in the possession of Fräulein Emmert, of Schweinfurt,
who is connected with a lateral branch of the Franconian
Bachs, and who was so obliging as to send it for my
inspection.   From No. 41 in that copy it is plain that it
was made before 1743, and might therefore have had some
more information than Philipp Emanuel's.   Still more interesting is it to note that in No. 39, where Johann Elias
Bach is the subject of the notice, the words "*p. t. Cantor* in
Schweinfurth" are omitted, and instead of them we find
"Born at Schweinfurth, February 12, 1705, at three in the
morning.—*Studios Theol.*"   This Johann Elias Bach was
studying theology in Leipzig during the summer-time of
1759, as is proved by the register of the university, and
during that time became personally acquainted with Sebastian Bach.   From the exactitude of the date of his birth, as
given in the Emmert genealogy, as well as from the insertion
between Nos. 39 and 40 of his younger brother, Johann

Heinrich Bach—who, it is expressly stated, died very young, and who therefore cannot have been known to a very extensive circle—we may conclude with certainty that these details proceed from some member of the Franconian Bach family; from a near relative of Elias Bach, if not from himself. Other additions, again, indicate that it was written under the direct supervision of Sebastian Bach; not indeed the Emmert genealogy, which, as has been said, begins with No. 25, but the additions to the Ferrich genealogy, which is well-preserved. We inferred, from the omission in the original genealogy of the dates of birth and death of Sebastian's eldest brother, that it cannot have been drawn up under his eye; but the Ferrich genealogy has both (No. 22). Now if we suppose that this was transcribed from the copy, it seems to me the probability is as great as possible that Elias Bach was the writer of that copy, and in further corroboration of this view we have the minute details as to his father, Valentin Bach (No. 26); thus the Emmert genealogy would have been written between 1739 and 1743, and subsequently, after it had received further additions, the Ferrich copy must have been made from it. This copy has one trifling omission in No. 43, but it is unimportant, and may have been either intentional or accidental.

Besides these genealogies, the Bachs also preserved the family pedigree. One such family tree was in the possession of Philipp Emanuel Bach, who gave it, with the genealogy, to Forkel; it has disappeared, but a trace of its existence remains in the Beschreibung der Königl. Ungarischen Hauptstadt Pressburg, a work published in that city in 1784, by Joh. Mathias Korabinsky; in this there is a little pedigree with numbered shields and a list appended, containing the names of sixty-four male Bachs; and on page 110 the author remarks that it is the family tree of the famous "Herr Capellmeister Bach, of Hamburg." Its insertion in this work is due to the fact that the Bachs were supposed to be a Hungarian family. Another pedigree was in the possession of Sebastian Bach's pupil, Johann Christian Kittel, Organist of Erfurt; it was published, with ex-planatory notes, by Christian Friedrich Michaelis, in the

Allgemeinen Musik Zeitung, Vol. XXV., No. 12 : where it is now is unknown. Fräulein Emmert, of Schweinfurt, has a genuine original pedigree; it is very carefully drawn and written, and splendidly coloured. From its general plan it must have been drawn up between 1750 and 1760; some supplementary notes have been added by another hand, and in different ink. A still living descendant of the family, Herr Bach, of Eisenach, has exerted himself to have it carried down to the present time.

All these materials have been a valuable contribution to the history of Sebastian Bach's ancestors. The next thing was to reinvestigate all the authorities from which they had been derived, to test the data they afforded—and there was much to rectify—and to exhaust them further; in short, to acquire new materials : for if this biography is to be of any value it must be by working up the more important personages to the most vivid individuality possible, and by giving them for a background as definite a sketch as may be of the times and conditions in which they lived: I have done my best to extract what the materials at hand would afford. In this part of my labours I am especially indebted to my friend, now already dead, Professor Th. Irmisch, late of Sondershausen, who was at all times ready to assist me with his exact knowledge of the history of manners in Thuringia; and I must acknowedge this all the more emphatically because such assistance is less conspicuous in prominent matters than in various suggestions and small information of which the value is hardly perceptible, excepting to the person who has benefited by them. The history of Bach's ancestors has involved me in some places in a considerable number of genealogical details, and while I beg the reader not to regard them as mere useless details, I do so with a lurking hope that the request may be unnecessary. It is evident that, in composing a " picture," a bare enumeration of the unusually numerous members of the Bach family is insufficient; the reader must see them, live with them in the deepest strata of their evolution, and if any should think this dry and uninteresting, it must be remembered that though the beauty of a tree lies in its trunk, branches, leaves, and fruit, the condition of this growth resides in strong and healthy roots. The genealogical matter is therefore worked up into the picture on a definite plan.

As regards the general arrangement of the work, it has been my endeavour to produce a coherent picture, equally elaborated throughout; all that did not directly contribute to this had to be eliminated. This gave rise to two appendices: the one for strictly critical discussions, and the other for quotations of some extent from authorities, and for certain explanations which the plan I had laid down excluded from the body of the book. But it need not therefore be thought arbitrary when some short critical views are introduced into the context, for there are matters which are so closely interwoven with the tissue of a biographical or historical narrative that it is impossible to avoid discussing them without neglecting at the same time a number of things which it is highly desirable, if not absolutely indispensable, to mention. Then, again, is it by mere accident that in so many questions connected with Bach's life we find ourselves thrown back on circumstantial evidence? It seems to me that a reflection of the man's own nature falls across our investigations—of his quiet, modest, and reserved life, absorbed in the contemplation of the ideal of his art. Much in my picture is taken directly from the authorities themselves; this, however, could hardly ever be done without remodelling and smoothing it, so far as to make it homogeneous with the rest. Documentary precision had in these cases to be sacrificed to the requirements of style; however, the characteristics of an antique and original writer need not be thereby effaced. A single unusual expression is often enough to give its tone, nay, even an antiquated form of spelling; it rests with the author to use his tact, and hit the precise limits. The only exception I have made is in the case of documents by Bach himself,[1] or such as refer to his words. When printed works of any rarity are quoted,

---

[1] For these the curious reader must be referred to the original German of this work (Leipzig: Breitkopf und Härtel).

their titles, with the dates, are given in full, in the foot-notes to each chapter; these also contain references to authorities, and such short observations as were unsuited to find a place in an appendix, and which, to have any value, were necessary adjuncts to the text.

The letters B.-G. refer to the publications of the Bach-Gesellschaft ; P. to the Peters Edition.[2]

The book did not all appear at once in its original German dress. The first volume was published in the spring of 1873, the second in the winter of 1879-80. In the interval I was enabled to obtain some fresh materials for the subjects treated in the first volume, as well as to correct certain errors that had crept in. All that I then added as a supplement to the second volume is, in this English edition, worked up into the text. On the other hand, it appeared possible and desirable to effect an abridgment in one or two places. With regard even to the second volume, though so short a time has elapsed since it came out, I have learnt the truth of the proverb, *dies diem docet ;* and the reader who realises the extent of the materials dealt with, and the purely accidental way in which a new discovery is often made, will not be surprised at this. Of course, in this edition, I have availed myself for the second volume also of all the additional information I have acquired. In its English form, therefore, it may be regarded, not merely as a translation, but as a revised and improved edition, and I send it forth with a sincere desire that it may contribute over an ever-widening circle to the knowledge and comprehension of one of the grandest spirits of any time or nation.

PHILIPP SPITTA.

BERLIN, SUMMER OF 1880.

----

[2] The arrangement of this edition is exceedingly confused, there being two different sets of references, one in use abroad, and one for the corresponding English edition, published by Augener and Co. The former, the old method of arrangement, is referred to by the words " Serie" and "Cahier" (as, for instance, " Ser. V., Cah. I." or " S. V., C. I."), and the latter method by the simple number in brackets. In almost every case both references will be found.

TRANSLATOR'S POSTSCRIPT.

A FEW words of explanation seem desirable on one or two points connected with the translation of this book.

In the first place as to the word *Clavier*, which has been left untranslated because, at different dates, it has not had precisely the same meaning. It is a general term for all instruments of the pianoforte kind, such as clavichord, harpsichord, spinet, or pianoforte; in its other meaning of the keyboard of an organ it is of course rendered by *Manual*.

Christian names have not been altered into their common English forms, excepting the familiar ones of royal personages. German titles of musical officials also remain untranslated, the most important being *Kapellmeister*, the official conductor of an orchestra with a fixed salary, as, for instance, the conductor of the opera; and *Concertmeister*, the leader of the first violins, when that also is an official post.

For the explanation of technical terms the reader is referred to Stainer and Barrett's " Dictionary of Musical Terms," or to Grove's " Dictionary of Music and Musicians "; for that of the German terminology of the organ to " The Organ: its History and Construction," by Rimbault and Hopkins.

In rendering the texts of cantatas, &c., rhyme has occasionally been sacrificed to sense and rhythm, as these seemed essential to explain the motive and *raison d'être* of the music. When the words are given in conjunction with their musical setting, they have been left untranslated, except in cases where the meaning has an important bearing on the music, or on the subject in hand. Quotations have been made from translations published in England with the music, where such existed. Texts from the Bible are given in the Bible words.

The German edition of this work is supplied with copious references to the archives and parish registers of German

towns.[1] These have not, for the most part, been copied for
the English reader, since any one desiring to consult such
recondite authorities will no doubt study the original work.
Here and there the authority for important facts has been
given, and every reference to a book is reproduced.

A list is given of those works of which copies are to be
found in the British Museum.

---

[1] Those of Sondershausen, Eisenach, Arnstadt, Weimar, Erfurt, Hamburg,
Mühlhausen, and many others.

BIBLIOGRAPHICAL NOTE

The first American printing of Philipp Spitta's JOHANN
SEBASTIAN BACH comes at a propitious moment in the history
of the appreciation and performance of the music of this great
master of the baroque era. This past year, 1950, the second
centenary of Bach's death, interest in his music was greater than
ever before. Throughout Europe and America leading musical
organizations devoted concerts to performances of his works.
Special festivals celebrated his name. Many new recordings of
both familiar and rarely performed compositions were made.
A number of scholarly studies of special aspects of his music
and life appeared in the leading musical periodicals.

The history of the recognition of the greatness of Johann
Sebastian Bach is an interesting one. During his lifetime he
was known principally for his virtuosity as an organist and for
his amazing keyboard improvisations. During the immediate
generations following his death in 1750, his greatness as a composer was perpetuated only through his pupils, especially his
most famous son, Karl Philipp Emanuel Bach, and the well-
known theorist, Johann Philipp Kirnberger. Some of his key-
board works were known and held in high esteem by a number
of musicians and composers. The "Well-Tempered Clavier"
was regarded by Haydn, Mozart and Beethoven as a model of
perfection in counterpoint. However, his music was almost
completely unknown to the general public.

In 1802 Nicholas Forkel, the founder of modern musicology,
published his ÜBER JOHANN SEBASTIAN BACH'S LEBEN, KUNST
UND KUNSTWERKE. This short work, although filled with inaccuracies because of the author's reliance on second-hand
sources, was the first contribution to Bach research; it was published in an English translation in 1820. The Leipzig Gewand-
haus performance by Mendelssohn in 1829 of the "Saint
Matthew Passion" introduced Bach to the romantic audience.
The performance, with all its romantic colorings and distortions
(setting a pattern for performance from which we have not

escaped entirely today) produced a Bach movement. In 1850
C. L. Hilgenfeldt's biography of Bach appeared. More important was the publication in two volumes in 1865 of Karl
Hermann Bitter's J. S. BACH. The work was the result of
extensive research into the archives of Arnstadt, Mühlhausen,
Halle, Cöthen and Leipzig; a large portion of this material was
used by Spitta, and the work deserves much more credit than
he gives it in the preface to this edition.

The first volume of JOHANN SEBASTIAN BACH by (Johann
August) Philipp Spitta (1841-1894) was published by Breitkopf
& Härtel in 1873; the second volume appeared in 1880. The
English translation was made by Clara Bell and J. A. Fuller
Maitland, and was published in three volumes by Novello,
Ewer & Co., London, in 1883-5. Material that came into
Spitta's hands after 1873, and was published as a supplement
to the German volume of 1880, is here worked up into the main
text with further corrections; so that, as Spitta said in his
preface, the English version "may be regarded, not merely as
a translation, but as a revised and improved edition."

The present edition (1951) is an unabridged reissue of the
English translation, unaltered except that the three volumes
are bound as two.

Immediately after the publication of the first volume, Spitta's
fame spread rapidly. In 1875 he was called to the University
of Berlin, appointed professor of music history and made permanent secretary to the Royal Academy of Arts.

Since the publication of Spitta's monumental work, there
have been many additions to Bach literature. Dr. Reginald
Lane Poole contributed the first important work in English
(1882) that is not a translation from a German original. Most
outstanding among the subsequent studies are those by Albert
Schweitzer (JEAN SÉBASTIEN BACH, LE MUSICIEN-POÈTE, 1905;
German edition enlarged, 1908; English translation by Ernest
Newman, London, 1911), André Pirro (L'ESTHÉTIQUE DE J. S.
BACH, 1907), Hubert Parry (J. S. BACH, 1909), Charles Sanford
Terry, (J. S. BACH, A BIOGRAPHY, 1928; revised edition, 1933).
All of these studies have leaned heavily on the findings of
Spitta. In 1909 Hubert Parry in the preface to his study ac-

knowledged the comprehensive nature of Spitta's work and said that it "seemed to leave little for those to do who come after, but to confess their obligations and to acquiesce in the arguments discussed and rediscussed without stint."

Not to be overlooked are the many invaluable special studies which have appeared in the *Bach Jahrbuch* and in the leading scholarly journals and noteworthy collections of documents such as the BACH READER edited by Hans David and Arthur Mendel (New York, 1945). One must pay homage to the monumenta, the publication of the works of Bach by the Bach Society, which give significance to all these writings. It was a labor of devotion extending over fifty years until all that had been salvaged of the works of Bach was published in 1900. Otto Jahn (the distinguished Mozart biographer) and Spitta kept this gigantic publication free from romantic interpretation and distortion.

Spitta was concerned with all the aspects of German baroque music which were the basis of Bach's art. His work, therefore, was a study of the historical backgrounds of Bach's music. His method of investigation, his predilection for the historical past became a model for all future biographers. In his study of the past, Spitta "discovered" great baroque figures such as Buxtehude, Pachelbel, and Böhm. We are further indebted to him for his editorship and publication of the first fourteen volumes of the works of Heinrich Schütz.

Spitta's study of Bach is still, after more than seventy years, the most impressive, comprehensive and important single work on Johann Sebastian Bach. The freshness of this study becomes apparent when, for example, Arthur Mendel in an article on performance practice of Bach's music (*Musical Quarterly*, 1950, p. 339) says, "Spitta, the earliest writer to treat Bach's performance practice at length, was in no doubt that the continuo instrument for Bach's church music was the organ, and not the harpsichord. Some data have come to light since Spitta's time, it is true—he died in 1894. But they mostly confirm his conclusions."

It is gratifying indeed that this monumental work is again available at a time when more and more of the lesser known works of Bach are being performed—revealing the beauty of baroque musical art.

SAUL NOVACK

New York, N. Y., 1951

BOOK I.

I.

THE BACH FAMILY FROM 1550-1626.

THE family of which Johann Sebastian Bach was a descendant was purely and thoroughly German, and can be traced to its home in Thuringia even before the time of the Reformation. The same constancy which led its members, throughout the seventeenth and during part of the eighteenth centuries, to the pursuit of music, kept it settled in one place of residence for two centuries and a half, multiplying and ramifying, and appearing at length as an essential element in the popular characteristics of the place. It clung with no less tenacity to certain Christian names, and, by a singular coincidence, the first of the family concerning whom we have been able to procure any information bore the name which was commonest among all that occur, and which was owned also by our great master.

This earliest representative is Hans Bach of Gräfenrode, a village lying about two miles south-west of Arnstadt. In the beginning of the sixteenth century Gräfenrode was subject to the Counts of Schwarzburg, but apparently it belonged to the princely Counts of Henneberg, and was held by the Count of Schwarzburg only under a mortgage. The great lords of Thuringia at that time often found themselves in need of money, and would pawn villages or whole districts like mere household chattels. Hans Bach, whom we must picture to ourselves as a mere simple peasant, appears to have laboured with his fellow-villagers—among whom was one named Abendroth—in the neighbouring mines of Ilmenau, of which the management was at that time taken possession of by Erfurt.   Well-to-do citizens of Erfurt took up a temporary residence, no doubt, for this purpose in Ilmenau, and one of these may have been Hans Schuler—whether this Hans Schuler was or was not identical with Johannes Schüler, a tetrach of the council of Erfurt in the years 1502-3 and 1506.   At any rate this Schuler was the cause of an action being brought against Bach—on what ground is unknown—before the spiritual court of the archbishopric of Mainz, and he was taken into custody with the above-named Abendroth.   Not only did Erfurt belong to the diocese of Mainz, but the Archbishop had long had property of his own in the city, and constantly aimed at increasing his influence there.   The prisoners endeavoured to obtain their freedom through the mediation of Günther dem Bremer, at that time Count of Schwarzburg, who seems, however, to have interceded for his subjects without any particular success.   A letter has been preserved which he wrote, in February, 1509, after many vain efforts, to Canon Sömmering, in Erfurt, declaring that he would have the matter decided according to the strictest form of law, in his own supreme court, if Bach and Abendroth were not set at liberty, and this letter is the authority for our narrative of the transaction.[1]   The name of Bach is to be found among the inhabitants of Gräfenrode throughout the sixteenth and seventeenth centuries, and in the year 1676 one Johannes Bach was *diaconus* in Ilmenau itself.[2]

Now, quitting Arnstadt and going a good mile to the north-east, we find ourselves in the village of Rockhausen. Here dwelt in the second half of the sixteenth century Wolf Bach, a peasant of considerable wealth.   When he died he left the life-interest of his entire property to his wife Anna, by whom he had eleven children.   In the

---

[1] See Appendix, B. No. I.

[2] Archives at Sondershausen.   One Bernhard Bach, schoolmaster in Schleusingen, was one of those who signed the Concordienbuch — *i e.*, the volume containing the laws and tenets of the Reformed Church of Luther, before 1580 (Concordia e Joh. Muelleri manuscripto edita a Phillipo Muellero. Lips. et Jenae, 1705, p. 889).   This place is beyond the district in which the Bachs dwelt.

year 1624 she was "a woman of great age," and desired to
divide the property among her surviving children. We hear
of a farm, four good fields and thirty-two smaller ones, valued
altogether at 925 florins, a very considerable estate at that
time; at any rate the most considerable of the place, and
this in itself would indicate a long settlement there. The
children—of whom three sons are named, Nikol, Martin, and
Erhart, and one married daughter—were tolerably advanced
in life. Erhart had been for some years away from home and
was already past fifty, and Nikol in the year 1625 married for
the third time. He, even before the division of his father's
estate, had a handsome property, and it is quite certain that
he was the only representative of the family remaining in
Rockhausen. In consequence of his second marriage he was
involved in all sorts of disputes over money matters; a statement drawn up in his own hand on this occasion has been
preserved, from which it would appear that he was not
unfamiliar with the use of the pen. By the first decade of
the eighteenth century there would seem to have been no
member of the Bach family left in Rockhausen.

Not far from Rockhausen, in a westerly direction, lies
Molsdorf, where also a family of Bachs, with numerous
branches, had its residence throughout the seventeenth
century. The earliest and most important of the parish
registers was destroyed during the Thirty Years' War; those
that remain go back only to the year 1644. According to
them the eldest of the Bach family living there—his name
again was Hans—was born in 1606. But one Andreas Bach,
whose widow died March 21, 1650, must certainly have gone
back to the former century. Ernst and Georg Bach may
have been his sons; the latter was born in 1624. Above
twenty members of the Molsdorf family are mentioned within
a period of scarcely seventy years; the men bearing the
names of Johann, Andreas, Georg, Ernst, Heinrich, Christian,
Jakob, and Paul, all of which, excepting the last, were constantly repeated in the line whence Sebastian Bach descended,
while the female names varied much. Other authorities also
mention one Nikol Bach of Molsdorf, who entered the Swedish
army, and who was buried June 23, 1646, at Arnstadt, having

"been stabbed in a drunken riot on grounds of his own pro-
voking."

Also, we can hardly be mistaken in supposing that Johann
Bach, "musician to General Vrangel," was a native of this
place, a man famous as an "ingenious musician," but of
whom we only know that he was already dead in 1655, leaving
a daughter.[3] He, then, was the first musician of the Molsdorf
line. The above-mentioned Georg Bach had by his wife
Maria (May 23, 1655) a son Jakob, who became a corporal in
a regiment of cuirassiers under the Elector of Saxony, and
was the father of a long line. This branch quitted Molsdorf
at the beginning of the eighteenth century, to settle farther
north at Bindersleben, near Erfurt, where it still exists, after
having produced several admirable musicians, of whom
Johann Christoph (1782-1846) seems to have been the
most remarkable; he, though a simple farmer, enjoyed a
great reputation in his time as organist and composer in
Thuringia.

For a third time we must turn to the south-west, where
we shall find, near Gotha, the home of Sebastian Bach's
direct ancestry. The exact connection between this branch
and those before mentioned is not ascertainable; but it is in
the highest degree improbable that there should be no connection whatever between two families of the same name,
having, too, many christian names in common, and dwelling
near to each other within a comparatively small circuit.
Moreover, we must fix the date of the first common ancestor
in the middle of the fifteenth century, since in the sixteenth
the main stem had already thrown off vigorous branches in
various directions. Even in Wechmar—the ultimate goal of
our wanderings—the Bachs were well settled so early as 1550.
The oldest representative, who also bears the name of Hans,
figures on the Monday before St. Bartholomew's Day in 1561
as one of the guardians of the municipality (*Gemeindevormund-
schaft.*)[4] Such an office required a man of ripe age, so we
may refer his birth to about the year 1520. Veit Bach, who

---

[3] Marriage register of Arnstadt.
[4] According to the records of the Municipal Acts preserved at Wechmar.

is spoken of by Sebastian Bach himself as the forefather of
the family, may be regarded as the son of Hans, and may
have been born between 1550 and 1560 ; apparently he was
not the only one, as will appear from what follows.

He took his christian name from St. Vitus, the patron
saint of the church at Wechmar,[5] thus pointing to an intimate
connection of some duration with the affairs of the place.
He learnt the trade of a baker, quitted his native place, as
his forefather Erhart had quitted Rockhausen, and settled
in some place in Hungary.[6]   It is well known that the
Lutheran religion met with the earliest acceptance in the
Electorate of Saxony, to which, at the beginning of the
Reformation, Gotha and the neighbourhood belonged ; and
in the same way it spread and blossomed rapidly in Hungary
under the Emperors Ferdinand I. and Maximilian II.   The
reaction set in under Rudolph II. (1576-1612) ; the Jesuits
were recalled, and oppressed the Lutherans with increasing
success.   Veit did not wait for the events of 1597, when the
influence of the Jesuits became paramount by one of their
order being made Provost of Thurócz.   " He journeyed from
thence," as we are told by Sebastian Bach, " after he had
converted his property into money, so far as was possible,
and returned to Germany," and, as we may add, to his native
village in Thuringia, where he found safety for himself and
his creed.   Here he seems to have extended his trade as
baker, but certainly not for very long, since by the end of the
sixteenth and beginning of the seventeenth centuries the bake-
houses of Wechmar were in other hands.   The notice written
by Sebastian Bach describes Veit not properly as a baker but as
a miller ; still these two trades were often combined.[7]   Being
a true Thuringian he loved and practised instrumental music.
" He has his greatest pleasure," says his great descendant,

---

[5] Brückner, Kirchen- und Schulenstaat im Herzogthum Gotha. Gotha, 1760.

[6] There is no foundation for stating that it was in Presburg.   This tradition
probably originated with Korabinsky.

[7] The suggestion that the trade of a baker was invented for him, only on
account of his name (Bäcker-Bach), is disproved by the circumstance that the
vowel in the name was pronounced long, " Baach ", and even frequently written
so in the seventeenth century.

" in a small cithara[8] (*Cythringen*), which he even takes into the mill with him, and plays on it while the mill works. They must have sounded sweetly together! He must, at any rate, have learnt time in this way. And this was, as it were, the beginning of music among his descendants." However, the art which Veit Bach pursued for pleasure was already followed as a profession by a contemporary member of his family, possibly his own brother. Veit died March 8, 1619, and was buried that same day. He probably had several children, for the large number of male and female descendants of the Wechmar line can scarcely be all traced back to the sons of whom the genealogy speaks. This names two, or more exactly one, since of the other the existence only is mentioned, while it is silent as to his name. The one named was of course called Hans, and was the great-grandfather of Sebastian Bach. We may very properly suppose that he was born at Wechmar about 1580, since Veit seems not to have married till after his return from his sojourn in Hungary. He showed a taste for music, so his father decided on letting him become a " player " (*Spielmann*) by profession, and placed him at Gotha to learn of the town-musician (*Stadtpfeifer*) in that place. He also was a Bach, by name Caspar, and may have been a younger brother, or at any rate a near relation of Veit's. He took Hans to live with him in the tower of the old Guildhall, his official residence. The sounds of bustle and business came up from the stalls which occupied the whole of the market-place on the ground floor, and from the gallery above he and his assistants must have piped out the chorale at certain hours, according to long usage.[9] His wife's name was Katharina, and of his children we learn that Melchior was already a grown-up man in 1624, that a daughter, Maria, was born February 20, 1617, and another son, Nikolaus, December 6, 1619.[10] After this he moved to Arnstadt, where he died, the

---

[8] The old cithara was a guitar-like instrument, distinct from the modern German zither. The word " Cythringen " is a diminutive.

[9] Appendix A, No. 1.

[10] Register of St. Augustine's Church in Gotha.

first representative of the family in that place; his wife followed him, July 15, 1651.[11]

Hans, "after serving his years of apprenticeship," returned to the paternal village, and took to wife Anna Schmied, the daughter of the innkeeper there. As we very frequently find in those times that the musicians followed some trade besides the profession of music, so Hans Bach commonly practised his craft of carpet-weaving.[12] Still music was his special calling, as is proved by his being called a *Spielmann* in the parish register. This led to his travelling all about Thuringia; he was often ordered " to Gotha, Arnstadt, Erfurt, Eisenach, Schmalkalden, and Suhl, to assist in the town-music of those places." There his fiddle sounded merrily; his head was brimful of fun, and he soon became a most popular personage. It would be difficult otherwise to account for his attaining the honour of twice having his portrait taken. Philipp Emanuel Bach possessed both pictures in his collection of family portraits: one was a copper-plate engraving, of the year 1617, the other a woodcut; in this he was shown playing the violin, with a big bell on his left shoulder. On the left side was written a rhyme to this effect :—

> Here, you see, fiddling, stands Hans Bach ;
> To hear him play would make you laugh :
> He plays, you must know, in a way of his own,
> And wears a fine beard, by which he is known.[13]

and under the verse was a scutcheon with a fool's cap. We shall see presently how this gay temper was transmitted to one of his children.

---

[11] The register of deaths at Arnstadt states that she was eighty-two and a half years old. This does not perfectly agree with the former events cited ; there is probably some clerical error.

[12] The genealogy says that he first learnt the baker's trade, and then devoted himself entirely to music. But a very trustworthy authority is a funeral sermon on Heinrich Bach, Hans Bach's son (Arnstadt, 1692), in which Hans is called a musician and carpet-maker of Wechmar.

[13] Hier siehst du geigen Hansen Bachen,
Wenn du es hörst, so mustu lachen.
Er geigt gleichwohl nach seiner Art
Und trägt einen hübschen Hans Bachens Bart.

Hans did not live to a great age; he died December 26, 1626, in the year of the plague, which snatched away other members of his family. When, nine years after, this pestilence raged still more furiously in the village, so that of the 800 inhabitants 503 died (191 in the month of September alone), his widow followed (September 18, 1635). Of his children only those three will occupy our attention in whom the musical talent of their father reappeared; but that there must have been others which were not remembered in the later genealogies, because they remained simple peasants, is quite certain. Without pausing over the various females of whose existence traces still exist, we must devote a few words to the other sons. It certainly is not easy—often not possible—to find our way with any certainty through the mixed crowd which the parish registers reveal to us; I can only give so much information as was attainable. The authority above mentioned only speaks of Johann, the eldest. of the three sons who were musicians; but besides him we come across six other individuals, who may be supposed to have been about the same age, and to have been sons of Hans Bach, or of his brothers, or of other contemporary relatives in the same place. First, there is one Hans Bach, who is often spoken of as *junior* in contradistinction to Hans Bach *senior*, and who thus must have been his son. He cannot be identical with Johann Bach, since he attended the Lord's Supper with his wife so early as 1621, while Johann was not married till 1635; hence, I consider him to have been an elder brother, probably the first child of old Hans Bach, who, according to the simple manners of the time, married very early.

The son died, still young, November 6, 1636; his widow, Dorothea, survived till May 30, 1678, to the age of seventy-eight. Of the sons of this marriage nothing is known.

Then there is yet another Hans Bach who seems to have been somewhat younger, and who married June 17, 1634, a maiden named Martha. She brought him sons, Abraham, born March 29, 1645; Caspar, born March 9, 1648, who was subsequently a shepherd at Wechmar; and a third son, not named, born March 27, 1656, "who at his birth was scarcely

a span long." The third Hans was also a son of the
" player.' [14] Thus there were three brothers of the same
name, and it is characteristic of old Hans, with the bell,
that he should have taken pleasure in this triumvirate of
Hanses.

Then there was Heinrich Bach, of whom we only learn
that two sons were born to him, in 1633 and 1635, both of
whom died January 28, 1638. The youngest of the musical
trio bore the same name; if he were the brother of the
former Heinrich, the jolly fiddler must have had three sons
named Hans and two named Heinrich.

Next, Georg Bach, born in 1617; his first wife, Magdalena,
was born in 1619, and died August 23, 1669. He married
for the second time October 21, 1670; his bride's name was
Anna, and she died in childbirth, February 29, 1672. But
these folks could not live unmarried : he wedded for the third
time November 19, 1672, and died March 22, 1691 ; his wife,
Barbara, followed April 18, 1698. No sons of his are named,
nor do we know whose son he himself was. One Bastian
(or Sebastian) finally is mentioned, of whose existence we
know only by the date of his death, September 3, 1631. He
may have lived to be an old man, and he is the only one of
the family who bore the name of Sebastian before the great
composer.

As has been said, the genealogy mentions another son
of Veit Bach's without giving his name, nor can he be
certainly identified by any other means; still we learn
from the parish register that there was a contemporary
of Hans Bach, the elder "player," who may have been
his brother. His name was Lips, and he died October 10,
1620; a son of the same name fell a victim to the plague,
September 21, 1626. The sons who continued this family
would therefore be wanting in the register. The genealogy
speaks of three, who were sent to Italy by the reigning
Count of Schwarzburg-Arnstadt for the advancement of
their musical education, and of these Jonas, the youngest,
seems to have been blind and the subject of many strange

---

[14] See Appendix A, No. 2.

stories.[15]   On the other hand, it can be proved that a son of
the nameless brother of Hans Bach bore the name of Wendel,
was born in 1619, and subsequently settled at Wolfsbehringen, a village north-west of Gotha; he seems to have
been a farmer, and died December 18, 1682.   His son Jakob,
probably the only son (born at Wolfsbehringen in 1655), filled
the office of Cantor at Steinbach, and after 1694 at Ruhla,
where he died in 1718.[16]   He was the first master of Johann
Theodorich Römhild,[17] who was afterwards Capellmeister at
Merseburg, and a composer of some eminence.   It is from
him, if the evidence before us is to be trusted, that most of
the musical members of this branch were descended, and the
most remarkable of them undoubtedly was.   This was Johann
Ludwig, the son of the Cantor Jakob Bach, who was born in
the year 1677; in 1708 he was "Court" Cantor at Meiningen;
but three years after, when he married, he was already capell-
director, and he died in 1741.[18]   Since Sebastian Bach established a personal intercourse with him from Weimar it seems
more appropriate to postpone the discussion of his characteristics as an artist.   The great musical talents of this man
survived in his two sons, Samuel Anton (1713-1781) and
Gottlieb Friedrich (1714-1785), as well as in his grandson
Johann Philipp, Gottlieb's son.   All three were at different
times organists at the Ducal Court, and the last-named
belonged to our own time, for he did not die till 1846, in the
ninety-fifth year of his age, and after the death of the last
grandson of the great Sebastian, December 22, 1845.[19]   Besides its musical gifts this branch of the family possessed a
talent for painting, which, in Sebastian's line, showed itself
only in one son of Philipp Emanuel's; and in him it seems
to have been first brought out by the Meiningen cousins, for
they had much intercourse with his paternal home, and

---

[15] Appendix A, No. 3.

[16] Appendix A, No. 4.

[17] E. L. Gerber, Historisch-Biographisches Lexicon der Tonkünstler.
Leipzig, 1792. Part II., col. 309. B.M.

[18] I depend for these details on information kindly given me by Herr Hofrath
Brückner, as well as on the register at Meiningen.

[19] Wilhelm, son of Johann Christoph Friedrich, Conductor at Bückeburg.
Bitter gives the date.

Philipp Emanuel could write in the genealogy, " the son of the Capellmeister of Meiningen still dwells there as organist and painter to the Court; his son is associated with him in both capacities. Father and son are excellent portrait painters; the latter visited me last summer and painted me, and succeeded admirably."

A brother of Joh. Ludwig's, Nikolaus Ephraim, the third son of the Cantor Jakob Bach of Ruhla, had already educated himself regularly as a painter. In 1704 he placed himself under the tuition of a certain Georg Kessler at Weimar, who held the office of Court-painter to Duke Johann Ernst, younger brother of the reigning Duke Wilhelm Ernst. In 1708 he entered the service of the Abbess Elisabeth Ernestine Antonia, at Gandersheim, sister to the reigning Duke of Saxe-Meiningen, and he probably obtained this appointment, which he continued to hold till his death (August 12, 1760), through the intervention of his brother Johann Ludwig. His master, Kessler, testifies of him, in a document drawn up May 5, 1709, that he had with him learnt " something admirable in the art of painting." But what he had to do in the service of the Abbess was by no means confined to this art alone. We soon learn that Nikolaus Ephraim was also a practised musician. On November 30, 1713, he was appointed "lackey"; however, in his appointment it is specially stated : " We hereby give over to him the supervision of our pictures and gallery of statues . . . withal, he shall be of use in music and in incidental compositions; in respect of which we allow him, by our favour, a yearly salary, from Michaelmas last past, of twenty thalers, and from the twenty-second of October last past a weekly allowance of twenty groschen for food, besides the usual two liveries, travelling coats, and winter-stockings." Subsequently he became cupbearer, on May 15, 1719, organist, and "chief butler," and had also to instruct the " abbey servants " in music and painting ; and finally, after the year 1724, he had the control of the Abbess's accounts. It was, no doubt, customary at small Courts, where means were but scanty, to employ one and the same official in various functions. But such a variety of services as must

have been fulfilled by Nikolaus Ephraim can rarely have
been loaded on to the shoulders of a single individual ; it is
plain he was a factotum.[20] Georg Michael Bach (1703-1771),
the teacher of the eighth class in the Lutheran Town
College at Halle, was also probably a son of the Cantor of
Ruhla ; his son again, Johann Christian (1743-1814), was
music-teacher there, and was called for short " *der Clavier
Bach*." He was connected with Friedemann Bach, the
eldest son of Sebastian, when the latter was Organist at the
Liebfrauenkirche at Halle, or perhaps indeed when he was
there no longer. For it was from him that he acquired that
" Clavier-Büchlein vor Wilhelm Friedemann Bach " (" A
little harpsichord-book for W. F. B."), which the great
Sebastian wrote at Cöthen for his favourite child, in great
part with his own hand, and to which we shall presently
devote our special attention.[21]

Finally, we have to mention Stephan Bach, who, according
to the genealogy, must have been connected with this line
without its being stated in what way. He was Cantor and
Succentor on the Blasius Foundation at Brunswick, an office
which he assumed in 1690, and held till his death in 1717.
His first wife was Dorothea Schulze, and therefore Andreas
Heinrich Schulze, afterwards the Organist of St. Lambert's
Church at Hildesheim, whose singing-master Stephan
Bach was, must be regarded as a relative of his wife's.[22]

---

[20] The document presented to Nik. Eph. Bach by Kessler is almost perfect,
and is set forth on two sheets of parchment, of which the back was subsequently used for portraits in pastel. They are at present in the possession of
Herr Brackebusch, Cantor of Gandersheim. The rest I have derived from
documents in the archives of Wolfenbüttel, and the church registers of Gandersheim. The house, which tradition declares to have been built for Nik. Eph.
Bach, as Organist and Intendant, still exists at Gandersheim. It was at one
time inhabited by the father of Ludwig Spohr ; the accomplished landscape-
gardener Tuch now lives in it.

[21] After the death of Johann Christian this book was acquired by Herr
Kötschau, the musical director at Schulpforte, and at his death it passed into
the possession of Herr Krug, Judge of Appeals in Naumburg, to whom I am
indebted for this information. According to the church register of Meiningen
a son of Johann Bach, " Court lackey and hautbois player," was christened
August 13, 1699, and named Johann Christian Carl. This Johann was,
perhaps, a fourth son of Jakob Bach.

[22] J. G. Walther, Musicalisches Lexicon. Leipzig, 1732. B.M.

His eldest son was named Johann Albrecht (born 1703), and was the child of his second marriage. Anything else that might be related of him would be merely a history of the sickness and general misery which this family always had to contend with. These we shall meet with often enough when dealing with the direct ancestors of Sebastian Bach, and we will therefore be silent about them here.[23]

We have been able to discover the roots of the Bach family in various places in Thuringia, and have found them everywhere to be mere village peasants and farmers; so truly did Sebastian Bach spring from the very core and marrow of the German people. And as, before the Thirty Years' War, the whole population of Germany was well-to-do, peaceful comfort was not lacking to the peasant farmer of Thuringia; to industry and capability he added piety. The lists of communicants of Wechmar from 1618 to 1623 give evidence, by their frequent mention of Bachs—male and female, old and young—that their profession of Protestantism was to them a living and heartfelt religion. It must, however, be added, that while Wolf Bach, of Rockhausen, was a freeholder in unusually easy circumstances, a harder lot seems to have fallen to his relatives in Wechmar. In the villages and their neighbourhood there were a number of nobles' estates, and all who depended on them as peasants (or as villeins, as we might say), had to bear a no small burden both in service and in kind; and all the more so because the owners of these estates—the vassals of the Count of Gleichen—had frequently to supply a considerable force of armed men, which, of course, did not benefit those who were left behind.

The death of Hans Bach (*der Spielmann*), in 1626, brings us just to the beginning of the period when Thuringia began to suffer and bleed under the fearful scourge of war. From the year 1623, when the troops first were marched across it, every conceivable horror was wreaked by the wild hordes of war on

---

[23] Register of the Blasius Foundation, Brunswick, and archives of Wolfenbüttel. Griepenkerl, editor of Bach's instrumental works, attributes the series of admirable organists who have lived at Brunswick to the influence of Stephan Bach, as I am kindly informed by Dr. Schiller.

this fair spot of German soil, at shorter and shorter intervals.
The villages were plundered and burnt, the fields laid waste,
the men killed, the women ill-treated—even the churches were
not spared.   Then came the fearful plagues of 1626 and 1635.
Those who could save their lives out of all this misery fled,
for shelter at least, by preference into the towns, or hid themselves in the forests, or like Nikol and Johann Bach of Molsdorf, entered the army, no alternative remaining.   Thus the
Bachs of Wechmar were dispersed ; those who remained died
out by degrees, until, at the end of the last century, a man
of the name of Ernst Christian Bach returned there, and
there ended his days (September 29, 1822) as cantor and
schoolmaster.[24]   Of the three musicians even, the sons of
Hans Bach, not one remained long in his native village.
The time in which they grew up and lived was a time of
terror and bloodshed, a time which deteriorated the gentlest
and best, and wore out the strongest, and which must have
exerted a profound influence on the natures of the three
brothers, according to the natural bent and the special
destiny of each.

II.

THE BACHS OF ERFURT.

JOHANN BACH, the eldest of these three sons, was born at
Wechmar, November 26, 1604.   "Now when his father,
Hans Bach," says the genealogy, "travelled to the afore-
named places (*see* p. 7) and often took him with him, once
on a time the old town-piper of Suhl, named Hoffmann,
persuaded him to give him his son to be taught by him,
which also he did ; and he dwelt there five years as his
apprentice, and two years as his assistant."   After this
he seems to have led a roving life in the midst of the ever-
increasing turmoil of war.   The genealogy states that he
went from Suhl to Schweinfurt, where he became Organist.
But, in 1628, he already appears in Wechmar as " player "
(*Spielmann*), and again in the year 1634; but he can hardly

---

[24] As I am kindly informed by Dr. Koch.

have been settled there, or he would certainly have established a household of his own. The way in which he finally did so leads us to infer a sojourn in Suhl, where he probably for a time officiated for old Hoffmann, who died in the thirtieth year of the century. For the *esprit de corps* which held the guilds together, and prevailed even in music made a young musician choose his bride by preference from among the daughters of the members of his guild, and thus frequently marry into the office held by his father-in-law. Thus Johann Bach, on July 6, 1635, was married to Barbara Hoffmann,[25] " daughter of his dear master," and wedded her in his nátive village. In the same year he was appointed director of the town-musicians at Erfurt.[26] This town, at that time still a free city, could already tell many a tale of the fortunes of war. After the battle of Breitenfeld, in 1631, Gustavus Adolphus had withdrawn thither on September 22, and four days after had left it in the hands of a garrison, who immediately began a pillage and maltreatment of the inhabitants, which, though directed against the Catholics only, soon became general. The houses were broken into and robbed even at night; not a watchman dared show himself in the street, and public insecurity rose to the utmost pitch.[27] Subsequently, indeed, some order was restored, but the heavy taxes and the wild misrule of the soldiery demoralised the citizens more and more, and not least, of course, the guild of town-pipers, or more properly town-musicians, whose principal function it was to perform the necessary music at public or private entertainments, and who consequently were the constant witnesses of the aggravated coarseness of manners from which such occurrences were never free. Shortly before Johann Bach assumed his post, February 27, 1635, it had happened that a citizen, named Hans Rothländer, had taken a soldier into his house with him out of the street. He

---

[25] Parish register of Wechmar.

[26] Raths Musikant, Stadt Musikant, and Stadt Pfeiffer are synonymous, or nearly so.

[27] Falckenstein, *Civitatis Erfurtensis Historia Critica Et Diplomatica.* Erfurt, 1740. II., p. 703. B.M.

"persuaded the town-musicians," as we are told by a manuscript Chronicle of Erfurt, "to play to him to amuse him,
because the master was his godfather—a thing forbidden to
be done. When they were all tolerably drunk the soldier,
who was a cornet from Jena, stretched himself on the bench
and fell asleep. Rothländer's wife roused him, intending to
dance with him. He started from his sleep, crying out,
'What, is the enemy upon us?' snatched up the brass
candlestick, and gave the man nearest to him three wounds
in the head and a gash in the cheek, thus extinguishing the
light. Then he seized his sword, and, stabbing backwards,
pierced another through and through; he clutched a musician
from Schmalkalden, who was a superior player, and stuck
him through the body so that he died twelve hours after, and
was buried in the churchyard of the Kaufmanns-Kirche."[28]
It is possible that the master of the guild perished in this
scene of butchery, and that Bach took his place.

In the autumn of this year the Peace of Prague seems to
have brought better times to the city; the Swedish garrison
was withdrawn and an universal peace festival was solemnly
held. But in the following year the Imperialists, the Elector
of Saxony, and the Swedes already had their eye again on
this important centre for military operations. Bach and his
people were ordered up into the towers of the citadel, "there
to keep watch and ward with due gravity and zeal for the
common weal of the city." Casks filled with brushwood and
straw were placed on the exposed places, and the guard was
enjoined to set them on fire as soon as anything suspicious
appeared; that was to be the signal for the town-pipers to
blow with all their might, so that they might wake all folks
to seize their weapons.[29] Notwithstanding, the Swedish General Banér took the town in December after a short siege, and
the Swedes remained in possession of it till the Treaty of
Westphalia, passing their time in skirmishes and surprises in
the surrounding country. After their final expulsion in 1650,
when the calm so earnestly longed for seemed to have been

---

[28] See, too, Hartung, Häuser-Chronik der Stadt Erfurt, 1861, p. 162.
[29] Falckenstein, p. 716.

restored, the town-council held a festival of peace and thanksgiving, lasting a week, and it was a worthy task for the guild of musicians to contribute their share. We are told that " the most beautiful concertos and splendid motetts by the most famous composers—Praetorius, Scheid, Schütz, and Hammerschmidt—were performed in all the churches." Trumpets and drums rang out from all the watch and church towers, which were decorated with white banners and with branches; troops of children, with garlands on their heads and carrying palm-branches, went to the house of God with songs of praise. A stage was also erected out of doors and decorated with birch boughs, and there, besides an *actus*,[30] "What is brought by peace and war?" was a performance with all manner of musical instruments by a considerable assembly, for every one sang in the chorale " of the citizens, now at last released and breathing out thanksgiving, with trumpets and drums and joyful firing of guns between whiles."[31]

But the burden of war had pressed too heavily on the hapless community; the town was deeply in debt, the richest of its patricians were impoverished, and famine and bitter want, beyond relief, prevailed among the humbler ranks. Worst of all was the utter exhaustion of all intellectual and moral energy. The war itself had for the most part been carried on with a healthy national vigour; the succeeding period found a degenerate and effete race. Instead of combining for determined labour they gave themselves up to thoughtless enjoyment, and, as the disorder of society increased, to a more and more reckless expenditure. At the same time the influence of an insubordinate populace rose in a very threatening way. Men of wisdom and insight were ill-used or expelled from the city, so that in the year 1663 a citizen could write that the city was now in such a lamentable plight " as no pen could describe, nor tongue of man express," and prophecy that Erfurt, like Jerusalem of old, could not escape destruction.[32] At last the Elector of Mainz,

---

[30] Or dramatic performance.
[31] Hundorph, Encomium Erffurtinum, 1651.
[32] Falckenstein, pp. 911, 915.

in consequence of the suggestions of the municipal authorities, asserted his superior rights, and was supported by the
Emperor. The fanatical obstinacy of the townspeople, who
murdered a client of the Elector's and insulted the Emperor's herald, finally resulted in the forcible overthrow of the
city, which, from 1664, lost its independence of the Electorate of Mainz. From that time began a gradual restoration
of its wealth and well-being, and a re-establishment of order.

Johann Bach spent the larger and most important part of
his life in Erfurt. The family he founded multiplied rapidly,
and during a century they filled the office of town-musicians
there so exclusively, that even in the latter half of the
eighteenth century these were known by the name of "the
Bachs," though, in point of fact, no man of that name existed
among them.[33] Next to Arnstadt and Eisenach, Erfurt was
one of the principal settlements of the extensive family of
Bachs, whose remarkable feeling of clanship gave rise to
their having certain home-centres, enabling them to work to a
common end. In the briefly sketched outline of the history
of the city during forty years, we may find also that of the
life of the man whose official position brought him constantly
into contact with the ·unfettered and excited spirit of the
populace. Everything that was astir must have touched
him on all sides, and it must have been a doubly difficult
task to uphold morality, earnestness of purpose, and dignity
in the whirlpool of passion amid which he stood — in
that void and empty turmoil where shouts of revelry and joy
can only have served to stun the ear to the misery they
covered. And the case was the same with all the members
of his family who stood by his side, filling the same functions ; and they too had to sigh in sympathy with others
under the general misery and poverty.

Nor was the private life of Johann Bach unvisited by
misfortune. His first wife gave birth to a dead child, and
died herself immediately after. It was not long before he
married a second wife, Hedwig Lämmerhirt, one of a family

---

[33] Adlung, Anleitung zu der musikalischen Gelahrtheit. Erfurt, 1758, p. 689.
Note *f*.

which we shall presently meet with again. Death visited him repeatedly. In 1639 it snatched a son from his home, probably the first child of the second marriage, and other children followed in 1648 and 1653. Meanwhile, however, he never lost the nature that stamped him as a true Bach. His old teacher and first father-in-law, Hoffmann, the town-musician of Suhl, was dead, leaving a son under age ; a year after the mother followed also, and the child was left an orphan. The brother-in-law came forward immediately, took the young Christoph Hoffmann to his own home, and finding that he took pleasure in music and had a talent for it, he instructed him diligently, and with such success that the youth soon attracted the attention of a wider circle. This, too, is a valuable piece of evidence towards an exact estimate of Bach's own merit and powers. His position, as leader of the musical body of so important a city, of itself points him out as a man of distinguished capacity, and the title of " an illustrious musician " was not denied him even by his contemporaries. At that time his brother Christoph Bach, the grandfather of Sebastian, was in service at the Court of Weimar. This, if we may venture to piece out and combine the fragmentary information we possess, was the occasion for bringing out the gifted pupil at that place. Duke Wilhelm wished to retain him at once for his own band, and offered his teacher one hundred thalers for the instruction he had given him. It speaks well again for Johann Bach and his household that Hoffmann would not consent to this ; he only agreed to appear in Weimar from time to time and to co-operate in musical performances ; but he remained faithful to his brother-in-law for six years as a pupil and for one year more as assistant, and from what we know seems to have trained himself to be an admirable musician.[84] When we are told that at Erfurt he made diligent progress in vocal as well as instrumental music, this chiefly refers only to that uncultivated and naturalistic singing which had to be

---

[84] J. L. Winter, Leichenpredigt auf Joh. Christoph Hoffmann (funeral sermon), preached November 21, 1686. Schleusingen, Seb. Göbel. Hoffmann subsequently carried on a business as armourer in his native city, besides his music, as his father had done before him.

learnt as a part of the mechanical training of the musician, since in the "attendances" (*Aufwartungen*)[35] as they were called, the performance of songs was not unfrequently required.[36] But for this, such readiness in reading the notes and certainty of intonation were amply sufficient, as must follow, almost as a matter of course, on instrumental practice.

Johann Bach, as organist, was only connected with church music in a more indirect, though in a no less essential and important way; he was organist it would seem to the church known as the Prediger-Kirche, and there gave evidence of various excellence. The emolument attached to such an office was but small, particularly in his time, and the salary that was fixed was very often never paid. The organist and cantor were for the most part dependent on payments in kind, and often enough these even failed. From the year 1647, Bach had to demand the annual payment of a measure[37] of grain, and in 1669 he was forced to complain to the town-council that in twenty-two years it had but once been handed over to his family.[38] He died on May 13, 1673, in the sixty-ninth year of his age.[39] As town-musician and as organist he united in his own person both the branches from which, at a subsequent period, the music of Germany, in the hands of Sebastian Bach, developed its noblest blossoms—instrumental music for secular purposes

---

[35] *Aufwartungen*, among the town-musicians, meant attendance at weddings or other solemnities, in order to make music. Jacobsson, Technolog. Wörterbuch.

[36] This custom is expressly spoken of in the "Lustigen Cotala" ("Der wohlgeplagte, doch nicht verzagte, sondern iederzeit lustige Cotala, oder *Musicus instrumentalis*, in einer anmuthigen Geschicht vorgestellet." Frey-berg, 1690. Reprint, 1713.) (*The much tormented, still not dispirited, but at all times merry Cotala, set forth in a pleasant history.*) The author of this work was, according to Adlung, no less a person than Joh. Kuhnau (Anleitung, p. 196). He says, p. 118: "The first day of the wedding all went with much credit, and I got no ill-praise for my singing, for I had with me the very sweetest songs and airs, as well as the very drollest, which were listened to with extraordinary amusement and pleasure by the most illustrious gentlemen and the most worshipful ladies."

[37] *Malter*, equal to four bushels.

[38] Protocol of the Council of Erfurt. June 14, 1669.

[39] Parish register of the Kaufmanns-Kirche at Erfurt.

and religious music. Though he took no direct part as
cantor in vocal church music, even this derived its chief
power of becoming what it did become under his great
descendant, from the development of the art of organ-playing.
His brothers and most of his children and successors preferred to cultivate only one or the other of these two
branches (*i.e.*, secular and sacred) until Sebastian once more
mastered the whole domain of music, though, indeed, the
posts he held did not always warrant this combination.
Through a long period of calamity Johann Bach was the
head of the Bach family of musicians. He lived to see it
spread and thrive, and strike deep root beyond Erfurt, in
Arnstadt and Eisenach. Henceforth began a constant and
busy intercourse between these three towns. Where one
prospered he drew others after him, and by intermarriage
and other family ties they further confirmed themselves in
the feeling of a closely knit and patriarchal community of
interests.

Johann Bach's eldest surviving son, Johann Christian,
born August[40] 2, 1640, studied and worked at first under
the direction of his father, in the " music-union " of Erfurt,
and he then quitted Erfurt for Eisenach, the first of his family
who settled in that place. Here he married, within his
guild, Anna Margaretha Schmidt, the daughter of the town-
musician, August 28, 1665.

The town-council of Erfurt were in no hurry to fill up
his place—he played the viola—their heads were just then
full of other matters. It was not till 1667 that his cousin
Ambrosius was appointed. In the following year, however,
he was again in Erfurt, where his wife presented him with a
son, Johann Jakob,[41] who, as he grew up, rejoined his elder
cousin, Ambrosius, the father of Sebastian, at Eisenach,

---

[40] Registers of the Kauffmanns-Kirche. These documents have been the chief
source of the dates that concern the Erfurt branch of the Bachs, and all that
are not noted as derived from other sources are taken from them. However, they
give, not the day of birth, but that of baptism ; but, as a rule, the baptism took
place within two days after birth, and I have adopted this as the basis of all my
calculations.

[41] According to the genealogy.

where Ambrosius had meanwhile become town-musician, and who died there in 1692, aged 24.[42] He is called in the register *Hausmanns-Gesell*, or musician's assistant, Hausmann being the term in general use at that time for a musician, a player on any instrument.

A second son rose beyond this. Johann Christoph, born in 1673, became Cantor and Organist at Unter-Zimmern, a village north-east of Erfurt, where he married, in 1693, Anna Margaretha König, and in 1698 was appointed to the office of Cantor at Gehren, south of Arnstadt, where his name was already most honourably known through the worthy Michael Bach, then lately deceased, one of whose daughters afterwards became the first wife of Sebastian Bach. He was a cultivated man, had studied theology, and wrote a beautiful flowing hand. Nevertheless, he did little credit to his family. His character was quarrelsome, obstinate, and haughty, and he displayed it in a way highly disadvantageous to himself, even against his superiors ; this led to his being long under arrest, and even threatened with removal by the Consistory of Arnstadt. Much, however, that was due to him on the part of the authorities had been neglected. He died there in 1727.[43] Johann Christian became director of the town-musicians in Erfurt after his father's death. He soon after lost his first wife, and then married a widow, Anna Dorothea Peter, June 11, 1679, by whom he had a daughter, Anna Sophia, and a son, Johann Christian ; the latter was born in 1682, the year of his father's death.[44]

---

[42] Parish register of Eisenach.

[43] Two of his sons lived in Sondershausen, and there kept up their connection with the main branch of the family, and, on the occasion of children being born, called upon their cousins of Erfurt and Mühlhausen to act as godfathers (*vide* the baptismal register of Trinity Church, March 15, 1719). The elder, Johann Samuel, born 1694, was in 1720 a schoolmaster at Gundersleben, and died there n that year. The second, Johann Christian, born 1696, also died young, according to the genealogy. A son, Johann Günther, born 1703, was a good tenor-player, and in 1735 was teacher in the congregation of the Kauffmanns-Kirche at Erfurt. These dates of birth are from the pedigree belonging to Fräulein Emmert, of Schweinfurt.

[44] According to the genealogy.

The place now vacant was filled by Johann Aegidius, the second surviving son of Johann Bach, born February 9, 1645. He had already taken his place in the musical guild of the city, under the direction of his father, for in the autumn of 1671 he had been appointed viola-player in the place of his cousin Ambrosius. He brought home a bride, June 9, 1674, from Arnstadt, where, at that time, his uncle Heinrich was held in high esteem as organist : of him we shall soon speak more fully. But his wife, Susanna Schmidt, was wife's sister to his brother Johann Christian, and her father must meanwhile have moved from Eisenach to Arnstadt.[45] There is something very patriarchal in this incident of the younger brother marrying the sister of the elder brother's wife, and thus walking in this respect in all confidence in the path he had tried ; and similar cases will come before us again. On this occasion Aegidius figures as town-musician and organist ; he subsequently filled the office of Organist in the Church of St. Michael, and in this double capacity trod exactly in his father's footsteps. He died at an advanced age in 1717,[46] after marrying for the second time, August 24, 1684, Juditha Katharina Syring. Of his nine children, whose names could be given—five sons and four daughters—only the former have any interest for us ; of these it would seem only two lived to manhood, Johann Bernhard and Johann Christoph.[47] The former, born November 23, 1676, filled the office of Organist to the Kauffmanns-Kirche at Erfurt, and was called from thence to fill the same post at Magdeburg. This promotion from out of the family circle, of itself indicates some special ability, which is confirmed by the fact that, in 1703, he was accepted as the successor of Johann Christoph Bach, a man of great mark, who will presently attract our particular attention, and who, next to Sebastian Bach, was the greatest musician of the family. Besides his labours as organist, he

---

[45] In the register of Eisenach he is called Christoph, in that of Arnstadt Christian Schmidt. But there is no doubt of their identity.

[46] According to the genealogy.

[47] The others were Johann Christoph, born April 2, 1675, who must have died in infancy ; Johann Caspar, June 7, 1678 ; and Johann Georg, January 6, 1680.

also acted as private musician (*Kammer-Musicus*) in the
band of Duke Johann Wilhelm of Sax-Eisenach, just as his
cousin, Sebastian Bach, must have done at the same time,
for a while, in Weimar.[48] Here, as was frequently the custom
with organists under the same circumstances, he must have
been cembalist.[49] That his merits were duly valued in
Eisenach is proved by the fact that his annual revenue of
sixty thalers—which, though modest enough, was not excessively small for the circumstances of the place and time—
was in 1723 raised to a hundred thalers, and so in fact
almost doubled. He was still receiving this sum in 1741, and
seems to have had it continued to him undiminished till his
death, June 11, 1749,[50] although the band was broken up in
1741, in consequence of the ruling family of Eisenach having
become extinct. Johann Bernhard Bach was not merely a
skilled performer; he was also an esteemed composer.
Four Suites for orchestra remain by him, a few small
pieces for the clavier, and a short series of chorale
arrangements.[51] Judging from these he must, as a composer
for the organ, rank with the most able, though not the
most original, of his time.; for he follows closely in the
path of Johann Pachelbel, of whom I shall have occasion
to say more in a later chapter. An arrangement of the
chorale " Du Friedefürst, Herr Jesu Christ "—" Lord Jesu
Christ, Thou Prince of Peace "—in five partitas, is set in
the mode of chorale-variations, then in universal use; but

---

[48] According to Walther, who would have received the information from
Bernhard Bach himself.

[49] This is expressly stated, for instance, of Vogler, Court Organist in
Weimar, and a former pupil of Sebastian Bach's, in a document *Pro Memoria*
Ernst Bach, November 21, 1755 (State archives of Weimar).

[50] The date of his death is from Adlung, p. 689.

[51] I am acquainted with eight. They are scattered among the collections
which the diligent Organist and Lexicographer of Weimar, Johann Gottfried
Walther, made with his own hand. The Royal Library at Berlin contains
three volumes of such collected arrangements; a fourth is in the Royal Library at
Königsberg (15,839; catalogue by J. Müller, No. 499, p. 71). The fifth, and
most complete of all, comprising 365 pages in oblong folio, is in the possession
of Herr Frankenberger, Musical Director at Sondershausen, who kindly permitted me to make unlimited use of it. The orchestral Suites are all in the
Royal Library, Berlin.

it includes several elegant passages. The *cantus firmus* is treated contrapuntally; between the separate lines of the chorale, and at the beginning of the whole, short figures are introduced, built upon the subjects of the next succeeding line. The least satisfactory are those in two parts (" Wir glauben all," " Jesus, Jesus, nichts als Jesus," " Helft mir Gott's Güte preisen ").[52] The counterpoint moves too much in crude intervals, which are not pleasing. Among the last four (" Wir glauben all," twice over, " Christ lag in Todes- banden," " Vom Himmel hoch ") the melody occurs in the bass, and here especially reminds us of Pachelbel in the treatment of the counterpoint; still it does not proceed with- out some harsh'ness here and there. The most successful is certainly the " Christmas Hymn " (Weihnachtslied), where the chorale, which is given to the tenor and cleverly treated throughout, is accompanied by a flowing and jubilant upper part. A friend of his son praises his works by saying, " They may not be difficult, but they are elegant." [53] There is also another piece of his of the same kind, where a different instru- ment was introduced, to which the *cantus firmus* was given —a method frequently adopted at that time, but which pro- duced nothing of a superior order.[54] But his special talent for that species of composition is exhibited in the Suites for orchestra, or, as they were then generally called, from their opening piece, the " Ouverturen " (overtures). The MSS. in which they are contained have, at any rate for the most part, come down to us with perfect certainty from the possession of Sebastian Bach. He copied the greater portion of the orchestral parts of three of them with his own hand at Leipzig, and at the time of his own greatest powers—a sufficient indi- cation of the value he attached to these compositions. In the " overtures," the introductory portions of these instru-

---

[52] It has not been thought necessary to give the English of German words set to music, excepting when the critical analysis of the work has rendered it neces- sary. The musician can only find the pieces under the indication of the German words, whether in English or in foreign collections.

[53] Adlung, op. cit.

[54] E. L. Gerber, Neues historisch-biographisches Lexicon der Tonkünstler. Leipzig, 1812. Part I., col. 202. Adlung, op. cit., p. 687.

mental Suites, Bernhard Bach displays so much force and
fire that they are in no way behind the best operatic overtures of that time—for instance, Handel's Overture to Rha-
damisto, or Lotti's to Ascanio—while in spirit and variety
they excel them; and in these qualities he is surpassed only
by Sebastian Bach himself. The best by far of the Suites
is that in G minor, for solo violin, accompanied by first and
second violin, viola, and basso continuo. The fugal theme
of the overture—

agrees in a remarkable way, and almost exactly, with the
opening of Sebastian Bach's Sonata for the flute in B
minor;[55] it is carried on through 142 bars with a most ingenious interweaving of the solo violin. In the succeeding *Air*
a lovely independent melody is given to the violin, and it
must be allowed that the closing *Rondeau* has both sense

and character. Besides a *Loure* and a *Passepied*, this Suite
includes an exquisite *Fantasia*, worthy indeed of Sebastian
Bach, written in the flowing and skilful style which is
possible only to the highest development of art.[56]

---

[55] B.-G., IX., p. 3.   P., Series III., Vol. VI., Son. 1.
[56] App. B. II.

Of Johann Bernhard's younger brother, born August 15, 1685, it need only be said that the direction of the "Raths-musik" fell into his hands after the death of Aegidius Bach, and that he still held that office in 1735.[57]

We may pass quickly over the two last sons of old Johann Bach. The third, Johann Jakob, born April 26, 1650, appears not to have been a musician, and only figures once (November 5, 1686) in the parish register. The last, Johann Nikolaus, born 1653,[58] was, on the contrary, town-musician, and a very good player on the viol di gamba. He married Sabina Katharina Burgolt, November 29, 1681, and when, a year later, August 31, 1682, she bore him a son, he selected his father's foster son, Johann Christoph Hoffmann, of Suhl, to be the child's godfather.[59] He died of the plague in the same year,[60] and we have now done with the last offshoot of the lineage of Johann Bach, so far as they play any part in the history of art.

III.

HEINRICH BACH AND HIS SONS.

HEINRICH BACH, Johann's youngest brother, stood in the most intimate connection with him, and we will next turn to him and his descendants; the middle brother, Christoph, will presently lead us in a direct line to Sebastian Bach himself. Of all Hans Bach's children Heinrich is the one who inherited, besides his musical gifts, his father's character, and his gay and innocently jovial nature. It may, therefore, readily be imagined that he was a particular favourite with the old man, who had him care-

---

[57] The genealogy mentions three sons of his: Joh. Friedrich, Joh. Aegidius (both schoolmasters), and Wilhelm Hieronymus. According to the Kittel- and Korabinsky pedigrees, the eldest was born in 1703 (?).

[58] According to the genealogy.

[59] This son was also named Johann Nikolaus; he became a surgeon, and lived in Eastern Prussia. In the same neighbourhood, at Insterburg and Marien-werder, some of the descendants of Johann Ernst Bach, of Eisenach, also settled.

[60] According to the genealogy.

fully brought up, so far as circumstances permitted, and, as we are specially informed, in a pious way.[61] His first teacher in instrumental music was, naturally, his father; and the lad was a diligent scholar in violin-playing. But already he was more attracted by the mighty tones of the organ, which, however, he could certainly not have heard in the church of his native village, since it was not till 1652[62] that Wechmar owned a small organ. When Sunday came round, the boy would not unfrequently run off to the neighbouring villages—Wandersleben, Mühlberg, perhaps even to Gotha—to satiate his ear with the sublime harmonies. He craved opportunities for further culture, and his eldest brother, Johann, was selected to provide for this. Where and when he obtained it cannot be ascertained; but, remembering what we have learnt concerning Johann's earlier place of residence, we are guided to Schweinfurt and Suhl; and the dates suit very well, too, since Heinrich was born September 16, 1615, and the years of his musical apprenticeship must, therefore, have fallen about 1627-1632. In Schweinfurt the brothers suffered severely from the war; the results of the Edict of Restitution drove them out of the town, and thus they may both have moved to Suhl about the year 1629. When the elder subsequently settled in Erfurt, in 1635, Heinrich went with him and played in the Raths-Guild until, in 1641, he at last was appointed to the post which was best adapted to his tastes and his capabilities. He became Organist in Arnstadt, and held this office above fifty years, till his death, July 10, 1692.[63] So soon as he was at home in his new office he began to think of establishing a household; and, as he had all his life long clung to his eldest brother, he now

---

[61a] Joh. Gottfried Olearius, Leichenrede (funeral sermon) auf Heinrich Bach, with the usual supplementary notice of his life. Arnstadt, 1692. The amplest authority as to his life.

[62] Brückner, Kirchen- und Schulenstaat im Herzogthum Gotha. Part III., Sec. 9, p. 8.

[63] The account here given is an attempt to reconcile and connect several contradictory statements and records. That both the brothers lived for a long time in Suhl is clear from the marriages they made.

married the younger sister of Johann's first wife. She
was named Eva, and was born in 1616. The marriage
took place in the year after his appointment. He chose
his two brothers to be godfathers to his first son, Johann
Christoph, born December 8, 1642.

It required some courage to marry in those times, not only
because often enough the husband could defend neither himself, his wife, nor his child against the insolent violence of an
ungoverned soldiery, but also because it was only too often impossible to foresee where the means of subsistence were to
come from. It was not long before the bitterest want knocked
at the door of Heinrich Bach's humble dwelling. It is true
that a salary of fifty-two florins and an allowance for house-
rent of five florins[64] were assigned to him, but it was long since
he had been paid. The petty Government itself, which was
also much weakened by the war, had no money, and so could
give none to its officials and *employés*. At this time the complaints as to arrears of payment were universal. Bach's
predecessor in office, Christoph Klemsee, had once had to
claim for several hundred thalers. Besides, the war-taxes
had to be paid, and if the lowest class of soldiers once fell
upon a man, he was not sure even of the clothes upon his
back.[65] Matters must have come to a very bad pass before a
man of no pretensions or rank could make up his mind to
appear before a Count of Schwarzburg as a petitioner on
such grounds. But, in August, 1644, he knew not, as he
says, "by the strange visitation of God," where to find bread
for himself and his young family, seeing that the salary due
to him had not been paid for more than a year, and that
all he had previously received he had had—to use his own
words—"to sue for almost with tears."[66] It would be quite

---

[64] That is to say, Meissen gülden = twenty-one *gute groschen*. That this may
not be thought less than a fair salary, it may be mentioned that the Conrector of
the school at Arnstadt, even in the latter third of the seventeenth century,
received only eighty-one gülden and ten measures of rye.

[65] See the graphic picture drawn by Th. Irmisch in Der thüringische
Chronikenschreiber M. Paulus Jovius. Sondershausen, 1870, pp. 30, 31.

[66] State Archives of Sondershausen. Documents relating to the school at
Arnstadt. 1616 to 1680.

impossible to conceive how he had lived at all up to this
time, unless we suppose that he had owned a small plot of
ground, and by cultivating it had kept himself at least from
starvation. Some amount of agriculture always was, and
still is, carried on by the schoolmasters, cantors, and
organists in Thuringia. In addition to this, there were certain payments in kind, which, towards the end of the Thirty
Years' War, flowed in all the more abundantly because buyers
were lacking as well as money; two thirds of the population
had perished. The young Count at once issued a strict
command that Bach was to be helped out of his extreme
need, and that he was to have no further cause of complaint; but the keeper of the funds appropriated to such
purposes tendered his resignation, saying that during the
thirteen years he had held his office he had had to submit to
more disagreeables than the meanest servant. It is easy to
see how great the danger was, in such circumstances, of
falling into a dissolute life; and Bach's predecessor had
set him a bad example in this respect, of a life of immorality necessitating the sternest interference of the
authorities.[67] It is, therefore, all the more remarkable that
there is not the smallest record or hint of anything that can
cast a shade upon Bach's character. His life seems to have
been of such innocent simplicity that we may contemplate
it with the sincerest pleasure and admiration.

Johann Gottfried Olearius, standing by the grave of Heinrich Bach, praised the exemplary piety of his deceased friend
with a full heart, and in words which are far from being a
mere form of amiable rhetoric; and though we may be
ready to confirm this verdict, so far as it is still possible to
test its justice, its full value will not be plainly evident to a
superficial consideration. The value of such sentiments
differs with the times. There may be conditions under which
it seems to be no particular merit to be called a pious man;

---

[67] Christoph Klemsee had been educated in Italy, and in the year 1613 had
published (Weidner, Jena) a volume of Italian Madrigals for five voices, as I
learn from a communication by Georg Beckers, of Lancy. (Monatshefte für
Musikgeschichte, IV.)

but there are times, too, when piety is the only safeguard for the highest ideal of human blessings, and the sole guarantee for a sound core of human nature. The German nation was living through such a period during the last years of the Thirty Years' War and those which immediately followed on it. The mass of the people vegetated in dull indifference, or gave themselves up to a life of coarse and immoral enjoyment; the few superior souls who had not lost all courage to live, when a fearful fate had crushed all the real joys of life around them, fixed their gaze above and beyond the common desolation, on what they hoped in as eternal and imperishable, and found comfort and refreshment in the thought that all the deeds and sufferings of men rest in the hand of God. Thus they fostered in silence the germ from which Germany, at its resurrection, was destined to derive new vigour; and we may here observe how culture proceeds from religion.

The first step to freedom was made in the province of religious thought by Spener and his followers, and the first work in which history was scientifically treated grew out of Pietism. Within scarcely a century music was developed by religion—since on the ground of pure feeling there were no external obstacles to be overcome—to a height which afforded an unerring evidence of the indestructible spirit of the German nation, and proved, as no other phenomenon ever has done, the immeasurable depth of its foundations. And as the bias towards instrumental music, with its transcendental ideals, is universal and seated in the depths of our very being, it is quite intelligible why, at that precise time, it was the art of organ music which first soared up on mighty wings, and why all that Germany was then able to produce in the direction of vocal music could only lean on and grow from that. And those men who, during their whole lives, stood in intimate connection with religion, or who were in the service of the Church—which amounts to the same thing, so far as concerns the men whose history specially interests us—we may regard as enjoying particular advantages. The man who, filling such a position, cherished in his soul that precious ideal in all humble and faithful piety, we must, if for that reason only, designate as a foster-father of culture.

Heinrich Bach was so happy as to have preserved in-
effaceable impressions from his childhood, when his own
predisposition for church music had been strengthened by a
pious education; and we learn from the words of the funeral
sermon how full of vitality these impressions still remained
even in his later years, for the preacher can have had no
other source of information than the narratives of the old
man himself. We can, therefore, well understand his horror
when he was once summoned before the Consistory,
because, at some small festivity which he had given to the
carpenters after the finishing of some building, he was said
to have laughed and mocked at the "Paternoster." He
swore emphatically, and by God Himself, that he had heard
and known nothing of it; and, in fact, nothing could have
been farther from him than such blasphemy. It is, too, a
simple but touching trait in his character that he never
omitted to follow a body to the grave, if it were in any way
possible, however poor and mean the social position of the
deceased.[68]   His nature was friendly and helpful to such a
degree that in all the town there was no one who could
speak of him but as "dear and good." From the great
fame he attained as a musical authority he had to examine
the candidates for places as organist throughout the Count's
little dominions, and to pronounce his judgment on them.
When, in the year 1681, a new organist was to be appointed
to Rockhausen, and the candidate had performed before
him, he pronounced that, so far as his organ-playing was
concerned, he was good enough for the salary. Too good-
natured to hinder the musician—who was probably bad
enough—from obtaining the place, he still could not forbear
from reflecting ironically on the smallness of the pay. From
his own experience he could sing a song of lamentation over
the payments of the Government of Schwarzburg-Arnstadt.
It has already been said that he inherited his father's
cheerful temper, and it was so conspicuous a feature in his
character that a century later Philipp Emanuel Bach was

---

[68] Olearius, op. cit., p. 45.

able to speak of his "lively humour."[69] Many disasters befell him in the course of his long life, particularly during the time of war; later again, in family matters; and finally, in his own health. But he always held his head above water, looked at the best side of everything, and preserved his cheerfulness through all misfortunes.

However, fate rewarded this admirable and amiable nature with blessings such as must, above all others, have brought happiness into the life of a man of his disposition. During a married life of more than thirty-seven years, six children grew up around him, of whom three were sons full of talent, nay of genius, whose musical education must have been a joy to him. The eldest son, in all ways the most distinguished, has been already mentioned (Johann Christoph); a second, Johannes Matthäus (January 3, 1645), did not survive his second year. Then followed Johann Michael (August 9, 1648), and Johann Günther (July 17, 1653). The two last were soon accomplished organists, and could, when necessary, fill their father's place. When Johann Christoph, the eldest, was called to Eisenach, and when, in 1668, Maria Katharina, the eldest daughter, born March 17, 1651, had married Christoph Herthum, Organist at Ebe‧ leben, near Sondershausen, the father would often go to visit his absent children, and Michael and Günther had meanwhile to perform the duties of organist. This arrangement, however, which certainly cannot have involved the slightest inconvenience, seemed too arbitrary to Count Ludwig Günther; and in the year 1670, when the choir music on Sundays, which had to some extent deteriorated, was to be improved and raised to a higher level by the appointment of a special hour for practice every Sunday, under the direction of the Cantor Heindorff, while Bach was to play the accompaniment, the Count, in giving him notice, took the opportunity of forbidding him this independence.

In the year 1672 we meet with a modest petition from the artist. He had heard that his predecessor had had a few measures of corn granted to him in addition to his salary; his

---

[69] Postscript to the genealogy.

own perquisites were very small; he still felt sound in health,
it was true, but old age was approaching; hence he prayed for
a similar favour. He had served for thirty-one years before
he even thought of claiming what had been freely given
to his unworthy predecessor; and now that he was a man
fifty-seven years of age, it was, of course, granted to him
also. Then he worked on bravely in his post, and when
occasionally it was too hard for him he was helped by
his youngest son, but, with the consent of the Count,
Michael had meanwhile gone from home.

Ten years later he was an old man, his faithful wife
was dead (May 21, 1679), his limbs were feeble, and
his fingers stiff. He now petitioned (November 9, 1682)
that his son might be appointed his permanent deputy,
for "without vain boasting, he had so learnt his art that
it might be hoped he would serve God and his church
with it, in such wise as that their gracious lordships, high
and low, nay, and the whole community, might approve."
This was granted, and Günther, happy in his appointment,
three weeks later was married to Anna Margaretha, daughter
of *Bürgermeister* Krül, of Arnstadt, deceased. But, before
one year, death snatched away the stay of his old father and
the husband of the young wife (April 8, 1683); Bach had
to sit alone again on the organ-bench, and his home was
solitary indeed. However, his son-in-law, Herthum, had
meanwhile come to settle in Arnstadt, and he combined with
his office of "clerk of the kitchen" the duty of serving the
organ at the castle chapel, while Bach, as heretofore,
officiated in the Franciscan Church of the Holy Virgin.
From the year 1683 Herthum took the old man to live with
him entirely in his house, which was situated in the Leng-
witz quarter of the town;[70] he performed his duties for
him, at first in part and then entirely, and he and his
children endeavoured to cheer and soothe his last days. For
a time Sebastian Bach's eldest brother, who had come from

---

[70] We know this from a list preserved in the Town Hall of Arnstadt. It
would seem to have been the house numbered 308, which for a long period was
the organists' residence.

Erfurt, assisted him in this. Ten years more slipped away, and the old man, now seventy-seven years of age, addressed his last petition to Count Anton Günther. He had been organist for more than fifty years, and was now awaiting a happy death from God; he had never before preferred any petition (of this kind) to the Count; it would be a joy and a consolation to him if only, before his end, his son-in-law was made secure of succeeding to him in his office. He was already blind, and his name stands at the foot of the document, traced with a trembling hand. But his mind was still clear and active, and his grandson had to read the Bible aloud to him. This, his last petition,[71] was presented on January 14, 1692, and granted immediately, and on July 10 he died. Of all his children only Christoph and Michael survived; his two daughters had preceded their father, but he was followed to the grave by twenty-eight grandchildren and even great-grandchildren, and the whole city mourned for him. It will not have escaped the notice of the attentive reader that, in his petition in 1682, Bach desires that his art may be placed at the service not of the Court only, but of the whole community, of rich and poor alike.

His proper instrument was the organ, and, though he is here and there called also "town-musician," we learn from his own statements in writing, as well as from all other sources of information at our disposal, that the only meaning of this was that it gave him the right to perform with the guild of town-musicians, and so opened to him a means of earning something. As a member of the Count's band he also had some duties at court, and may, perhaps, have filled the seat at the Cembalo. It is not now possible to acquire a more accurate knowledge of the kind and degree of his accomplishments as a performer, for very little of his composition has come down to us, and the general admiration of his contemporaries finds expression only in generalities. At any rate, he was certainly one of the most distinguished organists of his

---

[71] This document, as well as the two previously mentioned, is to be found among the archives of Sondershausen.

time. Still he owes his fame, on good authority, to his productiveness as a composer. When Olearius, in his funeral
sermon on Heinrich Bach, mentions Chorales, Motetts,
Concertos, Fugues, and Preludes, he includes nearly all the
forms of musical art employed at that time in church music.
In these Bach poured out his fresh, childlike, and mirthful
spirit; that happy temper which Philipp Emanuel could
praise in his compositions. One of his favourite works was
a composition for church use, founded on the text from
the Psalms, *Repleatur os meum laude tua*, to which Olearius
referred as he stood by his coffin. When the preacher says
that Bach, in his compositions, " of which the purpose is
never certainly discovered till the end, nevertheless fore-
saw and prepared it from the first," he must be understood to mean generally that the artist was able to work
up his composition on a settled plan towards a definite
end. Still we may also trace here a reference to a richer
development of the details and resources of the art, and of
the expression of the words; elements which had been transplanted to Germany from Italy, particularly by Heinrich
Schütz, and left the stamp of their preponderating influence
on the Protestant church music of the whole of the seventeenth century. On the other hand, in a piece for the
organ founded on the chorale "Christ lag in Todesbanden,"[72]
which has been preserved, Bach seems perfectly familiar
with the character and requirements of the old school.
Although worked out for the organ alone, this treatment
of a chorale follows throughout the strict laws of vocal
progression, and it consciously brings into prominence the
most conspicuous features of the Doric mode—intentionally
even, in the last bar but one. It must here be mentioned
that our master had had unusual opportunities for studying

---

[72] First mentioned by A. G. Ritter, Orgelfreund, Vol. VI., No. 14, from a MS.
derived from Suhl, and now in my possession. The piece here, it is true, has
only the initials " H. B.," which may just as well stand for Heinrich Buttstedt
as for Heinrich Bach. In fact, the piece occurs again in a MS. collection of
chorales by J. G. Walther, in the Royal Library at Berlin, under Buttstedt's
name. Still it seems to me to have a certain old-fashioned character, but little
in accordance with that composer's style.

the old church compositions in Arnstadt, for the church library there possessed, in a series of folios, compositions by Orlando Lasso, Philippus de Monte, Alardus Nuceus, and Franciscus Guerrerus, *Liber selectarum* of L. Senfls from the year 1520, and others. These treasures had partly found their way thither by the gift of Count Günther der Streitbare, and they still exist there. On the other hand, there are no doubt to be found in the choir library of Arnstadt compositions of various kinds by Andreas Hammerschmidt, which show traces of much use—an evidence that at the same time full justice was done to the then modern tendency. Heinrich Bach, in the humility of his heart, probably never thought of publishing his compositions, so we must confine ourselves almost entirely to guesses as to his artistic method; these, however, derive confirmation from a glance at that of his sons, whose principal—perhaps sole—teacher he was, and whose works have been preserved by a happier fate.

We have only to do with Joh. Christoph and Joh. Michael, for of Joh. Günther nothing is known but what has already been told. The two brothers resembled each other in character, though not, indeed, in talent. Michael is described by a contemporary witness as of a quiet and reserved nature, and his elder brother, though he remained unknown, alike to his contemporaries and to posterity, in spite of his noble genius and great artistic skill, entirely disdained to assert his pre-eminence—nay, was, perhaps, not fully aware of it himself. What we can relate of the outward circumstances of his life is wonderfully little. It is highly improbable that he should have sought foreign centres of culture with a view to his own education; he could hardly have attempted it with his own small means, and the times were not favourable to obtaining any assistance from the Counts of Schwarzburg. Indeed, at the age of twenty-three we already find him established in an official position; and, finally, his inclinations certainly did not tempt him to distant journeys. The whole family of the Bachs were full of a native and pithy originality, and hardly one of the illustrious musicians it produced, including Sebastian and his generation, ever visited Italy for the development of his

talent, or benefited by the instruction of a foreign master.
They strove assiduously and diligently to make themselves constantly acquainted with every new development and tendency
of their art, but they assimilated it and were not absorbed
by it. If among the elder relatives of Johann Christoph Bach
there had been a teacher at all commensurate with his
talents, his education would assuredly have fallen into his
hands; but at that time his father was undoubtedly the
most distinguished of the family, both as organist and composer, and it was to him that his son first owed his knowledge
and direction. He was appointed to be Organist to the
church at Eisenach[73] in 1665, and he remained at that post
till the end of his life of more than sixty years. Among the
churches where he had to perform the Services, the most
important was that of St. George, of which, however, the
organ must have been dilapidated, or have become useless
on other grounds, for it had to be replaced four years after
Bach's death by a new one, with four manuals reaching to
the e''', pedals up to the e', and fifty-eight stops.[74] Whether,
or when, he was also Court Organist cannot be determined
with certainty; at any rate, this office was filled from
1677 to 1678 by Johann Pachelbel. Bach married on
the Third Sunday after Trinity, 1667, Maria Elisabeth
Wedemann, whose father was town-clerk of Arnstadt.
Seven children were born of this marriage, among whom
four were sons: Johann Nikolaus (October 10, 1669), Joh.
Christoph (August 27, 1674), Joh. Friedrich, and Joh.
Michael.[75] From the year 1696 he was allowed to live free
of rent in the Prince's Mint, where seven living rooms on
the ground floor and stabling for two horses were placed at

---

[73] In a funeral sermon on Dorothea Maria Bach, which I shall refer to again,
in the year 1679, he is spoken of as "the well-appointed Organist of all the
churches here in Eisenach."

[74] Adlung, *Musica mechanica organoedi*. Berlin, 1768. Vol. I., pp. 214, 215.

[75] Of these four sons named in the genealogy, only the second is to be found
in the Eisenach register. The date of birth of the eldest is from Walther, as
also that of the father's death. The daughters were Marie Sophie (March 24,
1674, most likely 1671), Christine Dorothea (September 20, 1678), Anna Elisabeth (June 4, 1689).

his disposal—a tolerably handsome lodging for his position and for the time he lived in.[76] He died March 31, 1703. His successor in office was Bernhard Bach, of Erfurt, as has already been mentioned.[77]

The early life of his younger brother, Michael, was passed, we may be sure, exactly like that of the elder; he enjoyed the advantage of his father's teaching, and, when he was qualified, assisted him in his duties. In 1673 the place of Organist at Gehren, near Arnstadt, became vacant. Johann Effler, who had been intrusted with it till then—and who must have been highly efficient, for great efforts were made to keep him—withdrew in order to take the place of Organist to the Prediger-Kirche at Erfurt, vacated by the death of Johann Bach. Michael passed his examination as organist on October 5, and so satisfied the minister and the town-commissioners that they expressed their special thanks to His Highness the Count for providing the community and the church with a quiet, modest, and experienced artist. At the same time he was made parish-clerk, and received for that office a yearly stipend of ten gülden. His whole income he himself states in 1686 at seventy-two gülden, with eighteen cords of wood, five measures of corn, nine measures of barley, with leave to brew three and a half barrels of beer, and a few other trifles in kind, a piece of pasture land, and free residence. The house in which he dwelt is still standing, and is the deacon's residence.[78] Besides fulfilling his duties and his occupations as a composer, he found spare time in which to

---

[76] The bond relating to this, signed by Bach, sealed and dated April 27, 1696, as well as the only legal document to be found about it, are in the State archives of Weimar. The octagonal seal has the letters " J. C. B." interlaced. The Bach family never possessed a common seal. From the time of his residence at Weimar, Sebastian used a stamp with a rose and crown on it. Stephan Bach, of Brunswick, had a stork, or crane, looking to the left; Johann Elias Bach, of Schweinfurt, a shield with a dove over it, and on the field a post-horn.

[77] Walther, in the manuscript appendix to the Lexicon, mentions that a solemn service was performed in his honour on the verse of Paul Gerhardt. " The head, the feet, and the hands rejoice that labour is ended." Gerber, who was in possession of Walther's copy, repeats the statement.

[78] In the middle of the last century a large portion of Gehren was destroyed by fire. All the municipal buildings which were burnt down were registered by authority; the " City Record Office " was not among the number.

devote himself to constructing instruments; in this he was the precursor and perhaps the instructor of his nephew Nikolaus. We find him in November, 1686, engaged in constructing several clavichords for privy-councillor Wentzing, of Arnstadt,[79] and a violin of his making was, at the beginning of this century, in the possession of the geometrician Schneider, of Gehren; it was given by him to Albert Methfessel, who, himself a Thuringian, at that time was residing at Rudolstadt.[80]

As his brother Christoph had married the elder daughter of the town-clerk Wedemann, it was perfectly natural, from the Bach point of view, that Michael should choose Katharina, the younger. She gave him her hand on the third day of Christmastide, 1675, and in the course of eighteen years of married life brought him five daughters, the youngest of whom became the first wife of Sebastian Bach, and one son named Gottfried, born March 20, 1690, for whom his father selected his first cousin, the town-musician Joh. Christoph Bach, of Arnstadt, to be godfather. But the boy died in the following year, and the father, too, was snatched away in the flower of his manhood by an early death, in May, 1694.

IV.

JOH. CHRISTOPH BACH AND JOH. MICHAEL BACH.

THE devastating war seriously disturbed the Germans in their prosecution of the new musical tendency, which first made its appearance in about 1600, as an introduction from Italy, and which soon found eager adherents and talented artists to develop it in Germany. Those artists, indeed, the roots of whose vitality reached back into the antecedent period, continued to labour during the war; nay, even displayed their utmost power in the worst times, hardly pressed from outside but untouched in their inmost

---

[79] The deeds relating to this are in the archives at Sondershausen.

[80] I have this on verbal but quite trustworthy testimony. What became of this violin after Methfessel's death, in 1869, I do not know.

soul. Even those who were born within the first decade of these years of misfortune could derive their mental nourishment from a national vigour which, though severely tested, was not yet overtaxed ; but during the last fifteen years of the war, and even for some time after, the German nation was sunk in profound exhaustion. It had come apparently to a deadlock, both physical and mental ; and during the whole period from about 1650 to 1675, in which the young saplings of that period might have been expected to bear some fruits, we find throughout the domain of music none but old musicians in any way productive ; no new or fresh growth. It is not until after this that we are first impressed with the feeling that the art is gradually reviving and going forward again, seeking and feeling its way.

Johann Christoph and Johann Michael were born in years falling precisely within this period of depression. But it is most astonishing and profoundly significant, and characteristic of their race, that the common signs of the times were hardly stamped on them at all. They both exhibit a depth and freshness of resource which make them appear as an unique phenomenon in their way. That such a complete insensibility to the influences of the calamities of war, of its outrages, and of the universal degeneracy, should be possible to them, necessarily leads us to infer their descent from a race of the greatest health and vigour, a family of the soundest morality. These influences must also have unfailingly supported them as they grew up amid the life of those days, when every ideal and principle had vanished ; must have hedged them in with shelter, and have so educated them that when they were sent forth independently into the world, any fall from their high moral and artistic standard was no longer possible. Their portion was a reserved and contemplative spirit, which kept their ear open to the deepest stirrings of an unspotted nature, and their eye fixed on the pure images of an unsullied imagination, and which left its mark on their musical creations, as it did, later, on those of Sebastian Bach. Just as Heinrich Bach fostered, in the simple piety of his childlike soul, a spark of that mysterious power which was destined to raise up the crushed

nation to new life, so we may say of these two men, that
that spirit, which in them took the form of art when all
around lay dead and void, was the better self of the German
nation. It is this fact which foreshadows the history of
their works, and which is the real reason why, subsequently,
their compositions were so soon neglected, and those of the
greater of the two forgotten the quickest. While the development of art in Germany stood still for a generation, other
nations, and notably Italy, had progressed rapidly, and
reached the summit by so much earlier. The newly invigorated Germans saw, before them and above them, a blossoming field of art, which they aspired, with true German
instinct, to make their own and to cultivate for their own
profit. They had lost all direct sympathy with what lay
behind them; thus they hurried forward after new ideals.
How strange and tragical are the destinies of the world's
history! In order that the utmost heights of art at that
period might be climbed by two German musicians, their
nation had to lie for a time in a deathlike torpor while other
nations outsoared it, only to place all they had attained at
the disposal of those artists; but they, who held their ground
in the midst of the general decay, who cherished and hid
the precious essence of German national feeling in a pure
vessel—the wheel rolled over them and erased all trace of
them; nay, and soon no one even asked where they had
been.

But they shall not be forgotten for ever! It is not only
as being ancestors of Sebastian Bach that they have a significance for us; their personal merit as artists is considerable
enough for them to deserve that we should assign them a
place of honour in the history of art. Neglect has indeed
suffered the greater portion of their works to perish, and this
is especially to be regretted in the case of Michael Bach,
whose strength must have lain principally in instrumental
music; of all their compositions in this kind only a few
fragments still exist, while those vocal compositions in
which, according to the declaration of the generation which
succeeded him, Joh. Christoph had put forth all his powers,
have been preserved in rather greater number. Still, irrespec-

tive of this disproportion of their surviving works, we may unhesitatingly attribute the greater talent, from a general point
of view, to the latter. His works are of an importance and
completeness which must appear strange indeed to any one
who has made himself familiar with the uncertain, groping
style of the art of that period, if he has not fully realised the
peculiar position held by this master in his own time. An
unresting industry and great technical skill must, in him,
have been allied to a deep, strong sentiment for music—to a
nature which dwelt in solitude, and independently carried
out the ideals of older artists, undisturbed by the appreciation or the indifference of the world, and which would
rather deserve to be regarded as the precursor of Handel
than of Sebastian Bach, if a certain vein of fervent tenderness did not betray his relationship with the latter.

Heinrich Schütz, in the third part of his "*Symphoniae
sacrae*," and Andreas Hammerschmidt, more particularly
in the two parts of his "Musikalischen Gespräche über die
Evangelia" (Musical Discourses on the Gospel),[81] created
a form which was destined to be of the greatest importance in the development of the art of that time, and
finally to culminate chiefly in the Handel Oratorio, although
this derived something, too, from the church music of
Sebastian Bach. This musical-poetic treatment of isolated
biblical incidents arose partly from the impetus towards
dramatic forms of art then developing in Italy, with a certain
leaning towards the type of the sacred *concerto*, as it was
called. The mode in which the Bible text was treated was
sometimes dramatic, so that the speeches of different persons were distributed to different voices, sometimes choral,
narrative, or devotional. Hammerschmidt, for instance, loved
to introduce verses of Protestant hymns. They wished to
make the incident dealt with as vivid as possible by
the means afforded by music—by expressive declamation
and a characteristic use of the instruments, but, above all,
by a constant effort after forms of composition such as had
some musical analogy with the events treated, both as to

---

[81] About the middle of the seventeenth century.

general structure and in details of treatment—all combining
to excite the fancy to reproduce a vivid picture. Since it is
not the character of the oratorio to be actually dramatic,
but only to embody, as it were, in a musical form the feelings
to which an event would give rise, we find that it was already
cast by Schütz and Hammerschmidt in the form which
was brought to perfection by Handel; and the fact that
nearly a century had yet to elapse before this glorious culmination, is owing to the debilitation already mentioned as
having fallen on the German nation in the second half of the
seventeenth century. While at this very time, in Italy, very
important oratorios could be created—as, for instance, the
Santa Francesca Romana, of Allessandri—the above-mentioned German masters, as it would seem, found very few
men of talent able to follow with success in the path they
had opened, and those who could, it is very certain,
worked, at the time, for themselves alone. We possess
only one work of this kind even by Johann Christoph Bach,
but this stands up so far above the works of his predecessors
and the surroundings of his time that, of itself, it suffices to
raise the composer to a high rank as an artist. It is a tone-
picture founded on the mystical strife between the Arch-
angel Michael and the Devil: Revelation, xii. 7-12—
"And there was war in heaven: Michael and his angels
fought against the dragon ; and the dragon fought and his
angels, and prevailed not ; neither was their place found any
more in heaven. And the great dragon was cast out, that
old serpent, called the Devil, and Satan, which deceiveth
the whole world: he was cast out into the earth, and
his angels were cast out with him. And I heard a voice
saying in heaven, Now is come salvation, and strength, and
the kingdom of our God, and the power of His Christ : for
the accuser of our brethren is cast down, which accused
them before our God day and night. And they overcame
him by the blood of the Lamb, and by the word of their testimony; and they loved not their lives unto the death.
Therefore rejoice, ye heavens, and ye that dwell in them."
   In order to meet the requirements of this bold and
grandiose description, Bach summoned to his aid means of

effect which must be considered remarkable, and not merely
for the time when he wrote. Two choirs of five parts each,
two violins, four violas, bassoon, four trumpets, drums,
double-bass, and organ were introduced. Solo voices, of
course, there are not, but occasionally the bass part leads
in the chorus. The introduction is a *sonata* for the instruments without trumpets or drums, which leads by a broadly
conceived succession of chords in common time into an
imitative and more rapid movement in 3-4 time—after a
mode then much in favour, and which reminds us of the
French *ouverture*. Then all the instruments are silent; the
two bass parts of the first choir, supported by the organ
alone, then begin in canon the following strain, which is
declamatory rather than melodic :—

From the seventeenth bar the drums join in with dull low
crotchet beats on the tonic and dominant. Four bars later
a trumpet sounds as it were a distant battle-call; a second
answers it, then a third. The turmoil increases ; it is as if
we saw the armed cohorts gathering from all the quarters of
heaven. The fourth trumpet sounds ; and now the two choirs
attack each other, as it were, like hostile armies. The
whole body of the instruments, with the organ, rushes and
roars above them. From the hottest of the fray the trumpet
rings out in tumultuous passages of semiquavers, challenging

and retiring in a bewildering and unresting double canon.
We can fancy we see the immeasurable vault of heaven
filling with the tumult of battle. A column of sound grows
up, occupying the whole extent of harmonic pitch from CC
to c''', and, except only a quite short passage at the beginning,
remains for not less than sixty bars on the common chord
of C. The contending choirs advance and recede in merely
rhythmical ebb and flow; on neither side will the harmonic
unity give way. But at last the warlike turmoil subsides,
and the choirs come forth triumphantly on the dominant,
with the words, " And prevailed not." A vigorous and carefully constructed fugato for the first choir follows, " Neither
was their place found any more." According to the custom
then in use, and to which Sebastian Bach himself remained
faithful, the violins, by rising independently above the
soprano, extend the structure to seven parts. A motive for
the bass—

continues the description, supported by broad instrumental
harmonies, and soon commands the whole body of the choir
once more, graphically representing in a gradual descent the
overthrow of Satan from Heaven. Then follows a symphony
of victory for all the instruments in a rigid march-rhythm,
and following that comes a new and glorious burst in the
choirs.

The master has given to the words "a great voice" all
the magnificence of the utmost means afforded by the declamatory style, a style which must above all else give free
scope to the musical capabilities of the text itself before it
can venture on any dramatic consideration. The composition extends after this through several numbers, among which
the passage "And they loved not their lives unto the death"
is particularly striking for its fervent sentiment and characteristic stamp; and it closes with a joyful song of triumph
for the choirs alternately. It is also distinguished as a work
of the genuine oratorio character by the great repose which

prevails throughout the modulations and harmonies, notwithstanding the picturesque variety and vigour of the scenes it
depicts; it is no unfettered torrent of feeling that finds
utterance, but the sentiment that flows round and about a
fixed subject.   Inasmuch as most of the composers of
sacred music at the end of the seventeenth century display
this harmonic simplicity, even in their purely lyrical choral
subjects, they must be regarded, in these, as the precursors of
Handel, while Sebastian Bach acquired his style of choral
treatment in a different way, by means, namely, of instrumental music.   A greater variety of modulation might not,
indeed, have proved a disadvantage to the work under consideration.   Though the fertile adaptations of the common

chord of C major with the allied harmonies serve the
descriptive purpose, and though a few startling deviations
stand out all the more strongly—as, for instance, the grand
change from C major to the common chord of B flat major, on
the words " And deceiveth the whole world "—" Die ganze
Welt *verführet*"—still the ear craves a flow of harmony of
a deeper and more penetrating character, particularly at the
close, and especially a more vigorous use of the sub-dominant.
But, indeed, the whole scheme of the work would not have
been what it is, had not Bach worked on a very distinct and
clearly indicated model by Hammerschmidt.   This composer, in his work " Andern Theil geistlicher Gespräche über
die Evangelia" (Second part of "Discourses on the Gospel,"

Dresden, 1656, No. XXVI.), had set the same text for a choir
in six parts, with trumpets, cornets, and organ, and the idea
of making the battle rage round the long held common chord
of C major owes its invention really to him; even in the
musical presentment of the Fall from Heaven, and in the
resounding C major of the close, the originality was in the
older master.   But the power of invention and the genius
with which Bach clothed the image thus presented to him,
and transformed the meagre cartoon into a grand fresco, show
that he so far transcended his by no means contemptible predecessor, that we could hardly realise it without the circumstance of this imitation.   We must not enter on the details
of a comparison which would be highly interesting; still I
may remind the reader how an analogy here suggests
itself between Joh. Christoph Bach and Handel, who in the
same way did not hesitate to work out in the most direct
manner such compositions as took his fancy.[82]

It was impossible that so important a composition should
fail to make an impression on many sincere artistic natures,
in spite of the small amount of intelligent sympathy which was
shown for Joh. Christoph Bach, alike by his contemporaries
and by posterity.   Georg Philipp Telemann evidently became
acquainted with it when, from 1708 to 1711, he was Concertmeister and Capellmeister[83] at Eisenach. He himself attempted
a similar flight, which at any rate dates from that time, for
the festival of St. Michael; but his talents were ill-adapted
to the sublime, and even in this work he dwells in the region
of commonplace, or forces to caricature the spasmodic
treatment of the voices which characterises his earlier work,
and which is objectionable alike in the separate parts and in
the *ensemble* of the chorus.   But the master met with due
admiration from the next generation of his own family.
Sebastian Bach who, as an artist, was in many ways greatly
indebted to his uncle, held this choral work in high esteem,

---

[82] He made extensive use of a " Magnificat " by Dionigi Erba for " Israel in
Egypt." See Chrysander, Händel, Vol. I., pp. 168-177. B.M. A list of these
plagiarisms may be found in the Dictionary of Music and Musicians—Art.
" Israel in Egypt."

[83] For explanation of these words see Translators' postscript.

and even had it publicly performed in Leipzig. Indeed, the stimulus is clearly unmistakable which prompted him to work out a tone-picture of the same poetical subject, which forms the beginning of one of his greatest cantatas.[84] But the all-pervading difference of conception is conspicuous even in this. Sebastian stands supreme on the ground of pure music, and though the uncle's work must retire into the background before the creative genius which speaks in every note of the nephew's work, still it may hold its place by its declamatory character. The text, " Nun ist das Heil und die Kraft," &c., which in Joh. Christoph's work forms a part of the whole, Sebastian has used as the subject of a double chorus,[85] which, of course, admits of no comparison with the work of the older master, and which is, indeed, incomparable as its creator was.

Philipp Emanuel Bach, Sebastian's son, also honoured the " great and impressive composer," as he designates Joh. Christoph.[86] It is from him that we learn that at a performance of this composition by Sebastian Bach at Leipzig, every one was astonished at the effect.[87] This astonishment would certainly be no less at the present day.

We possess no work of this class by Michael Bach ; still, a composition of his with an instrumental accompaniment has been preserved which is purely lyric in style, and hence may be properly called a sacred cantata.[88] It is founded on a hymn in two verses, " Ach bleib bei uns, Herr Jesu Christ "— "Ah, stay with us, Lord Jesu Christ,"—but no sort of chorale melody is used in the composition ; on the contrary, the composer has worked up the separate lines with special reference to the expression of the words and matter of each.

---

[84] " Es erhub sich ein Streit," B.-G., II., No. 19.

[85] B.-G., X., No. 50.

[86] Addenda to the Genealogy.

[87] In a letter to Forkel, dated from Hamburg, September 20, 1775. It is given in Bitter's work, Carl. Ph. Em. Bach, Vol. I., p. 343, where there is also an abridged translation. Ph. Emanuel Bach had preserved the document in his archives of the family (" Alt-Bachische Archive ") a collection of the compositions of the various musicians of the family, before and after Sebastian. It passed from the collection of G. Pölchaus into the Royal Library at Berlin.

[88] In parts, derived from the Bach archives in the Royal Library at Berlin.

Without entering on any detailed discussion of the music, it is easy to see how inadequate this method must be in general. For this mode of treatment can only be applicable when it is desired almost exclusively to give expression to a leading sentiment, which flows like a current through the whole and penetrates every separate part. This piece is half in motett-form and half declamatory; the correct form for such themes had not yet been found, and many a composer was wrecked in seeking it till Sebastian Bach made the thing clear. In other respects the composition is full of interesting details and ingenious ideas; in these Michael hardly stood behind his brother, though he did so conspicuously in his feeling for grand plastic forms. A choir in four parts, two violins, three violas, bassoon, and organ, are employed, and the key of G minor is chosen. An introductory *sonata* of fourteen bars, in which slow progressions alternate with rapid figures, has a somewhat incoherent effect. The first line of the hymn serves as the basis of a structure of sixteen bars, closing with a fermata; there is a passionate accent in the cry, "Ach bleib! ach bleib!" which predominates as early as in the third bar, rising to E flat major and A flat major, then sinking back to G minor, rising again, and finally ceasing in the relative major. The words "Weil es nun Abend worden ist"—"For now the evening closes in,"— are sustained on a descending scale-like passage, which seems to feel its way among the voices, wandering in intermittent tones, not without some harshness in the harmonies—

and six bars later it closes with another fermata on the dominant of G minor.

The soprano now enters with the words "Dein göttlich Wort das helle Licht"—"The clearest light Thy word

divine,"—set to an agitated subject rising by degrees; above
it, two violins have an imitative passage, the first violin
rising to the previously unheard-of height of g''' and a''',
evidently to figure forth the idea of clear, pure light; the
whole choir concludes in a striking manner, " Lass ja bei uns
auslöschen nicht "—" May it in us for ever shine,"—and
carries on the same motive for a time with the instruments,
returning at the end to G major. The second verse is
treated in an analogous manner. The alto sings the first
line alone in chromatic passages, which already, at that time,
was a favourite way of expressing pain and sorrow.

After two subjects, each closing with a fermata, a freely
treated fugato immediately follows, with this pregnant
theme :—

The two upper stringed instruments take part in this in
an independent and skilful way, while in other parts of the
cantata, where the violins have to hold their own above the
voices, they generally behave in a very awkward manner, and
try to avoid a faulty progression of the parts by wonderful
leaps and intervals—a defect to be ascribed less to Michael
Bach himself than to the imperfect *technique* of his time.
A frequent use of the major sixth imparts to this fugato a
stamp reminding us of the Doric mode, which suits it very
well.

    In the treatment of the motett, Michael Bach betrays a
similar uncertainty, but this likewise must be set down to
the account of his time.

    The essential stamp and character of the motett are :

That it is in several parts, that it admits of no obbligato instruments, and that its subjects are set to a text of the Bible or to a verse of a hymn. Hence it follows that the period of its fullest bloom fell within the first great period of art, reaching to about the year 1600, when music was essentially polyphonic, vocal and sacred. Under the succeeding period of the transformation of the polyphonic system into the harmonic, and the swift and comprehensive extension of instrumental music which was inseparable from that change—under the endeavour after some more passionate musical expression that should follow the words more exactly, and the introduction of solo voices, the motett gradually became the neutral ground where the most dissimilar tendencies thought they might tread unhindered. I am here speaking more particularly of Germany, where the impulse communicated by the Protestant Church gave birth to a far greater abundance of forms than in Italy.

Heinrich Schütz, in other respects an important representative of the new school, had, in his *Musicalia ad Chorum Sacrum*, endeavoured to reconcile its requirements with the principles of the old (compare No. IV., " Verleih uns Frieden gnädiglich," and No. VII., " Viel werden kommen von Morgen und Abend "). But it was inevitable that the intrinsically polyphonic character should be more and more neglected, that musicians should strive to compensate themselves for what they thus lost in intrinsic inner fulness by a freer flow of melody, more sprightly rhythm, and more highly spiced harmonies. To make their application possible it was necessary to have recourse to the supporting instruments. Then observation was directed to the novel effects of the body of sound thus produced, and to the possibilities of new combinations. Many of the effects discovered, though purely proper to instruments, were even transferred to vocal music. Many motetts of the seventeenth century are inconceivable without the accompaniment of the organ or other instruments. This may be seen by the progression of the bass part, which not unfrequently lies above the tenor, and would make the harmony quite unrecognisable if it were not supplemented by a sixteen-foot organ bass. It is perceptible, too, in the unchecked introduction of many harmonic progressions which would be unendurable in the delicate organism of purely vocal music, but which escape detection under the rush of the organ and of the orchestra. And many sudden changes of harmony—*e.g.*, that of an eight-part chorus in A major which changes into C minor without preparation—are impossible to perform without firm points of support. Not unfrequently the accompaniment of the organ or of other instruments is indicated by means of a figured-bass or *continuo*. And even where the character of a motett seems to demand the unmixed sound of human voices, it still is easy to perceive that the fancy of the composer was full of musical forms, which vocal music by its inherent nature could not represent. The dramatised biblical scene, which Schütz and Hammerschmidt had introduced, and the custom of placing side by side, in contrast, verses of chorales and scriptural passages, in a sacred concerto or madrigal—of which Hammerschmidt was very fond—were also a reflection from the motett. A four-part chorus (without soprano) begins with the words from the Revelation, which are supposed to be said by Christ : " Siehe ich stehe vor der Thür und klopfe an ; so jemand meine Stimme hören wird und die Thür aufthun, zu dem werde ich eingehen "— " Behold I stand at the door, and knock," &c. After nine bars have been sung, the soprano answers with the melody of the Christmas Hymn, " Vom Himmel hoch "—" From highest Heaven,"—to the words " Bis willkommen, du edler Gast "— " Be thou welcome,"—during which the chorus continues its summons. The contrapuntal working of a chorale tune on the organ had also an unmistakable influence on this form ; nay, it was through this that it gradually came to more artistic perfection, so that, in fact, a hundred years later, instrumental music by the use of its own means reintroduced the polyphonic structure which had so long been set aside in its favour.

But the motett was suited to more complicated dramatisation. An anonymous composition for double chorus, which must be attributed to about the middle of the seventeenth century, lies before us in manuscript. First,

the choruses inquire of each other antiphonally in the
words of Sulamith, "Habt ihr nicht gesehen, den meine
Seele liebet ? "—"Saw ye Him, whom my soul loveth ? "
Cant. iii., 3. Then the second choir changes to the
chorale, " Hast du denn Jesu dein Angesicht gänzlich ver-
borgen ? "—" Hast Thou, O Jesus, Thy countenance utterly
hidden ? "—the first continuing its questions meanwhile and
during the pauses between the lines of the hymn, in which
questioning the second choir joins again, after the conclusion
of the verse. " Da ich ein wenig vorüberkam "—"It was but
a little that I passed from them "—begins the second choir,
and the first, without soprano, repeats it; "Da fand ich!

da   fand ich! da   fand ich!

den meine Seele liebet ! " the soprano now comes in on
rejoicing intervals ; both choirs quickly seize upon this
exclamation and carry it on to the end in exulting cadence ;
and as if filled with beatific assurance, the second choir
enters once more with the last verse of the chorale, " Fahr
hin, o Erde, du schönes, doch schnödes Gebäude, fahr hin,
o Wollust, du süsse, doch zeitliche Freude "—" Farewell,
for ever, oh earth ! for thy joys are but seeming ; farewell
all pleasure—though sweet, thy delights are but dreaming."
The first choir answers, " Ich halt ihn, ich halt ihn und will
ihn nicht lassen ! "—" I held Him, and would not let Him
go,"—and thus at last they are united in broadly developed
harmony. Another motett resembles a dramatised church-
cantata of Hammerschmidt's in poetic aim, and partially in
its plan, and may indeed have been suggested by it. It is the
Dialogue between the Angel and the Shepherds on Christmas
night (Hammerschmidt, Musikalische Gespräche, Part I.,
No. 5.) This master makes the angel announce the joyful
event of Christ's birth with the accompaniment of the organ
and two small cornets, which announcement is interrupted
by the chorus of the shepherds with their joyful excla-
mations. Then the shepherds receive the command to go
to Bethlehem, where they arrive and worship the Christ-

child in the words of Luther's Hymn, "Merk auf, mein
Herz, und sieh dort hin"—"Ponder, my heart, and gaze
herein,"—interrupted again and again by the arousing
summons of the angel; and they conclude with the hymn
"Ehre sei Gott in der Höhe"—"Glory to God in the
highest." The composer of the motett begins with the
chorus of the astonished shepherds, "Ach Gott, was für
ein heller Glanz Erschreckt uns arme Hirten ganz"—"O
Lord, a wondrous shining light Fills us poor shepherds
with affright,"—and the clear soprano voice of the angel
comes in at intervals with the words "Fürchtet euch nicht"
—"Be not afraid,"—and goes on with the subjoined joyful
cry of the chorus, which reminds us of Hammerschmidt—

—"Behold, I bring you good tidings of great joy." Angel
and chorus answer one another for a time, and then unite
in a lively *fugato*, "Die allem Volk widerfahren wird"—
"Which shall be to all people,"—until it ends in a 3-4
arioso movement, "Denn euch ist heute der Heiland
geboren"—"For unto you is born this day a Saviour."
That the words of the angel are, in the course of the
movement, unhesitatingly given without any alteration to
the chorus, is suitable to the declamatory style, since all
that is demanded of it is to indicate the event in the
merest outlines, so that the music may go on its own way
without restrictions.[89]

At last the motett overpowers the chorale in such a way

---

[89] The three motetts quoted as examples are taken from a volume of old
compositions of the kind, which I acquired years ago from a village-cantor of
Thuringia. It contains a great number of good pieces of this kind, of the
end of the seventeenth and beginning of the eighteenth centuries, besides much
of a more modern date. Unfortunately the names of the composers are hardly
ever given, so that possibly some of them may be attributed to Michael Bach.

as to disconnect the individual lines of the melody, distributing and repeating it between the choruses and the solos,
playing round some of the sections in the manner of variations,
or using it for little imitations, and so step by step dissecting
the whole.

Hammerschmidt has treated the last verse of the hymn
"Wie schön leucht't uns der Morgenstern"—"How brightly
shines the morning star"—in this way for double chorus,
and indeed in an excellent manner in the fourth part of his
Musikalischer Andachten geistlicher Motetten und Con-
certe (G. Beuther, Freiberg, 1646), under No. XXII.; by
the addition of a figured-bass, which strictly follows the lowest
voice, the accompaniment of the organ is expressly allowed.
The first and higher chorus begins by delivering the two
first lines in 3-1 time, the second line being already treated in
imitation and prolonged by a bar; then the other chorus,
consisting of the lower voices, takes it up, but extends the
second line by imitations from the original four bars to eight;
the first line is then thrown from one chorus to the other
several times, during which they deviate into other keys;
the second line is repeated, and they unite and conclude with the third line in eight parts. The whole first
section is then repeated exactly as it is in the hymn. The
second section begins with the words "Amen, amen!
Komm, du schöne Freudenkrone," &c.—"Come, thou
fairest crown of gladness,"—in a still richer and more
varied form, flowing on in the last line with massive
grandeur in an artistic and effective eight-part progress,
such as from the middle of the century became rarer in the
German composers.[90] If we add, moreover, that the composers sometimes appended a sacred aria for several voices
to the motett as a kind of *coda;* nay, that even Hammerschmidt once called a collection of songs for one and two
voices, with accompaniment,"motetts," our opinion—namely,

---

[90] An attentive examination should be made of the beautiful motett treated in
the same way, for double chorus, in this collection (No. XXI.), on the chorale
"Ich hab mein Sach Gott heimgestellt"—"I have consigned my care to
God." Michael Bach also set the last verse of the same hymn at the end of
his motett, "Unser Leben ist ein Schatten"—"Earthly life is but a shadow."

that the motett always admitted of accompaniment—would seem to be supported by a concurrence of evidence of the most various kinds. But the form of the motett became by this means a very uncertain one, and when, at the beginning of the eighteenth century, the definitions of Opera, Oratorio, and Sacred Cantata were established, and the art of organ-playing reached its full development, it almost entirely lost its distinguishing characteristics. It carried on an apparent and nominal existence, decked out by further loans from instrumental music and the church‑cantata, and sometimes wholly coalescing with the sacred aria. Had the composers understood how to do anything more with this form, there was special opportunity for it in Thuringia, where the choirs of processional singers have shown signs of vitality even in the present century, and where we might expect to find the proper refuge of the motett, even when the impertinent temerity of the musical world presumed to mock at it as a stage they had left behind.[91] It was here also that the independent songs for two or three solo voices were introduced into the motett. But its time was past. Only Sebastian Bach could still create anything really original and powerful in this branch of music, and yet the full majesty of his motetts can only be appreciated when accompanied by instruments, and especially the organ ; without such an accompaniment, it is only a very admirable performance that can make them appear otherwise than deficient in style.

Of the motetts of Michael Bach twelve have been collected. Much that was in the possession of his great-nephew, Philipp Emanuel, consisting of sacred arias, for solo or for several voices, has not yet come to light again ; but, on the other hand, five pieces have been found which were not

---

[91] F. E. Niedt, Musikalische Handleitung, Part III., edited by Mattheson, (Hamburg, 1717), p. 34 : " I leave the explanation of the motetts to those Thuringian peasants who have inherited them from Hammerschmidt's time, just as the Altenburg peasant girl inherits her boots from her ancestors, or the Spaniards their short cloaks."

known to Philipp Emanuel.[92] Only two of these are without chorales. The one, "Sei nun wieder zufrieden, meine Seele"—"Now again be thou joyful, O my spirit,"—in A minor and in common time, is for double chorus with organ accompaniment,[93] and is one of the less successful works of the composer. A number of clever details cannot blind us to the planless and restless character of the whole, nor compensate for the monotonousness of a persistent homophony. Bach has followed his text sentence by sentence. This proceeding was endurable in the polyphonic style of composition of previous centuries, when the artistic entwining of independent or imitative parts satisfied the demands of art, for unity in variety, by placing them side by side rather than one after another. But the more homophonic a composition is, the more must it satisfy our craving for coherence and harmony, by symmetry in the length of the phrases and by attention to the due connection of the keys, particularly in a work of purely lyrical nature, such as that lying before us. The incoherence of the structure naturally spoils the noble and devout fundamental feeling which the composer evidently wished to give to the whole. Hammerschmidt succeeded in producing a work much more in accordance with the rules of art to the same words (Part IV. of his Musikalischer Andachten, No. 4), of which the end reminds us of Bach, and which was certainly known to him.

The second, a six-part motett in D major, common time, is designed for New Year's Day. The manuscript, which has

---

[92] These hitherto unrecovered compositions are, according to the catalogue of the musical legacy of P. E. Bach, in the Royal Library of Berlin, as follows : "Auf lasst uns den Herrn loben," for alto and four instruments. "Nun ist alles überwunden," an aria for four voices (Arnstadt, 1686). "Weint nicht um meinen Tod," an aria for four voices, 1699. "Die Furcht des Herrn," &c., for nine voices and five instruments. In the three last the composer is not named, but by the arrangement of the catalogue they appear to be by Michael Bach. Two other anonymous compositions will be mentioned below.

[93] So it is, at least, in the edition of F. Naue (Neun Motetten für Singchöre von Johann Christoph Bach und Johann Michael Bach [in three books]; Leipzig, Friedr. Hofmeister. Book I., No. 3), according to a version unknown to me. In the archives of the Bach family it was arranged with four accompanying instruments, supposing it to be identical with an anonymous motett included in that on the same text.

been preserved, has a notice to the effect that the parts for it were to be written in E flat major.[94] Thence it follows, as indeed is probable from the character of the piece, that it was to be accompanied by instruments (probably strings) as well as by the organ. The pitch of the organ differed from that of the instruments by a semitone, so that its D was really E flat. For the chorus it was, of course, a matter of indifference what the signature of the parts might be, since the pitch by which the lead was regulated was given by others; but this was not the case with the instruments, which, according to the custom of the time, had to play from the copies of the singers. The construction of this motett, which sparkles throughout with festal brightness, is homogeneous. It contains seventy-four bars, and is divided into two principal sections, the last of which is repeated, whereby a feeling of roundness is given. Contrapuntal combinations are not exhibited here, but a few charming effects of sound are employed in preference : in the first place, the contrast of a bright soprano solo voice, supported only by a viola, with the full colouring of a deep body of sound, for four-part chorus; then an interesting movement of the upper parts in arpeggio style, of which the full value is brought out by the conjunction of the strings, while the lower voice proceeds in a joyful passage of semiquavers.

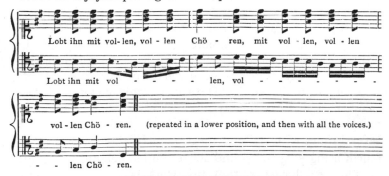

Lobt ihn mit vol-len, vol - len   Chö - ren, mit vol - len, vol - len

Lobt ihn mit vol - - - - len, vol - - - - - -

vol - len Chö - ren.   (repeated in a lower position, and then with all the voices.)

- - len Chö - ren.

---

[94] The collection of ninety-three motetts (in score) of the beginning of the last century, in the Royal Library at Königsberg (13,661), No. 37. The title says " In Stimmen *ex Dis* " (in the parts D sharp), as E flat was still called until the beginning of this century. Similar notices are also found in other pieces.

The echo-like alternation of forte and piano introduced at
the close—an effect of very frequent occurrence in the motett
of the time—betrays the influence of the organ-style; it is
not founded on the nature of the human voice, which is
capable of the greatest variety of gradations of tone.

The ten motetts that are interwoven with chorales are
more developed. First comes a five-part composition with
organ, on the words from Job : " Ich weiss, dass mein
Erlöser lebt "—" I know that my Redeemer liveth,"—after
which the chorale " Christus der ist mein Leben "—"Christ,
who is my life "—enters in the soprano part.[95] For these
ideas Bach had deeply affecting tones at his command. The
four lower voices are alone for the first sixteen bars of the
movement, which consists in all of only forty-one bars (in
G major, common time), the alto, which has the melody,
surprising us by its rapturous intensity of expression, the
free individuality of which is enhanced by the fact that
instead of two phrases of two bars each, which would have
resulted from a naturally simple declamation, here three bars
are contrasted with three bars. The passage to the words
" Und er wird mich hernach aus der Erden wieder aufer-
wecken "—" And He will wake me again from the earth "—
(according to the Lutheran version), ascending and sinking
again with such deep feeling, reminds us of the most beautiful things that ever came from the imagination of Johann
Christoph, his elder brother. At the seventeenth bar the
chorale comes in almost imperceptibly, and moves quietly in
minims above the lower parts, which have more movement,
and which several times, especially in the pauses, soar upwards
with longing to the words " Denselben werde ich mir sehen"—
" Whom I shall see for myself." A certain harmonic combination in great favour with Michael Bach is used here
several times with striking effect, namely, the chord of $\frac{6}{3}$, the
fourth being suspended and its resolution delayed. It must
be admitted, however, that this work is far from absolute
perfection. The melodic progression which is indispensable
in homophonic writing is wanting in the inner parts;

---

[95] Naue, B. I., No. 2.

the tenors remind us of the two viola parts in the five-part disposition of the strings then in vogue, which were only put there to complete the harmonies. It is very awkward when a part, in order to avoid a false progression, suddenly pauses for a whole crotchet-beat, as in bar twenty-three; the obviousness of its purpose makes it all the worse. Moreover, it is not without falsities of intervals: the consecutive fifths in bar thirty-seven, between the bass and second tenor, may indeed easily be altered, but instances of the same kind appear too often in the works of others—nay, even of the most celebrated composers of the time, e.g., Pachelbel and Erlebach—for us to suppose that it did not come from the hand of the composer himself.[96] One principal reason for such licences has been given above. The following generation certainly strove after greater severity; but in the development of great vocal and instrumental masses even Handel and Bach were sometimes self-indulgent.

Another essential deficiency is that the musical contrast between the four-part chorus set to the Bible words and the chorale-melody is not preserved enough. Hence, as both factors are associated, hardly any contrast is discernible but that between the different rhythms of the two sets of words, which of course demand different rhythmical treatment; besides, the lower parts are properly nothing but the meagre harmonic basis of the chorale. We might almost think that the artist had cared by preference for the poetic duality, which certainly can greatly intensify the sentiment even by the simplest combination, because the individual feeling kindled by the Bible words flows in unison with the devotional and congregational feeling. But this assumption is not altogether safe, for though at that time poetic contrasts were in great favour, it was because the musical *technique* was hardly equal to any better solution of such problems. Contrapuntal dexterity among the Germans in the latter half of the seventeenth century was on an average very small, and it is

---

[96] Even Heinrich Schütz did not hesitate sometimes to introduce consecutive octaves in music for many voices: *e.g.*, the fourth bar of the six-part motett, " Selig sind die Todten "—" Blest are the departed,"—between the second soprano and second tenor.

a great mistake to imagine the composers before Bach and Handel as absorbed in those learned intricacies of art, into which these two masters were the first to breathe a real vitality. In this respect they had little to learn from their predecessors. It was otherwise in Italy, where the traditions of the great vocal writers of the sixteenth century had never been cast off, where the transition to the new tone-system proceeded very gradually, and the requirements of the church services, as well as the natural bias of the nation, gave no rest to the incessant elaboration of broad and highly artistic vocal forms, until after the middle of the eighteenth century. It was in this that Handel laid the foundations of his contrapuntal supremacy; while Bach acquired his through organ music, which was already perceptibly showing signs of life, though it was left for him to bring it to full maturity, and then to transfer it to vocal music blended with instruments. If Johann Christoph Bach has done anything of great excellence in the form of the chorale-motett, it is, as we shall soon see, a sign of surpassing talent on the part of himself alone. Amongst a very complete selection of compositions of that style and date, which I have seen, there is not a single one which surpasses Michael Bach in contrapuntal treatment, and indeed all the other defects that might be mentioned do not attach solely to him.

But the striking expression which insures for the last-named motett its full effect, even in the present day, belongs to him alone. He was, indeed, not altogether a complete master, but an artist-soul, full of deep feeling and lofty divination.[97]

Greater praise is due to the motett "Das Blut Jesu Christi, des Sohnes Gottes, machet uns rein von allen Sünden"—"The blood of Jesus Christ His Son cleanseth us from all sin,"—with the chorale verse "Dein Blut der edle Saft"—"Thy blood, the precious wine,"—from Johann Heermann's hymn, "Wo soll ich fliehen hin," for five

---

[97] C. von Winterfeld thinks he finds an affinity, of which, however, I can discover no trace, between Michael Bach's motett, "Ich weiss dass mein Erlöser lebt," and a similar one by Melchior Frank. (See Evangelischer Kirchengesang III., 430.)

voices in F major, common time, containing eighty-three bars on a similar plan to the foregoing.[98] The chorus of the four lower parts is less syllabic, and richer in counterpoint, and the separate parts flow more melodiously ; towards the end we find increasing passion, and a repetition of the two last lines of the chorale, whereby the whole is satisfactorily finished and rounded off. The development of subject, which would give the chorus unity in itself, is very slight, it is true ; the organism of the whole has not yet risen to full existence. But the deep feeling of the composition overcomes us with irresistible power, and one forgets the imperfection of the body in the beauty of the soul which shines through.

A work in five parts, to words that have been often set, and in particular have been used for a very beautiful motett by Wolfgang Briegel, " Whom have I in heaven but Thee, &c.,"—in B flat major, in 3-4 time, 125 bars in length, offers an example of thoughtful, artistic consideration.[99] To this and the following verse of the Psalm Bach has added five verses of the hymn "Ach Gott, wie manches Herzeleid"—" Ah, God! how many pangs of heart,"—in the manner of the former motetts, and in such a way that in the course of the piece the contrast, poetical as well as musical, between the upper and lower voices vanishes more and more, and at the end all are at last united in the last verse of the hymn, " Erhalt mein Herz im Glauben rein "—" Keep Thou my heart in faith unsoiled." The previous verses are arranged in this order: 13, 5, 6, 15. The four-part chorus is at first as independent as possible, with energetic declamation, adorned with different melodic

---

[98] Naue, Book II., No. 5. He has added a figured-bass, which is not indicated in the catalogue of P. E. Bach's musical legacy. The date is here, 1699, which, unless it is a mistake of the transcriber's or printer's, must only mean the year in which the copy was made, for the composer was dead at that time. This circumstance considerably takes away from the authority of the dates which are affixed in the catalogue to the other compositions.

[99] Naue, Book II., No. 6, with a figured-bass, which is absent in the index of the Bach archives. Briegel's motett, which is quite unlike it, has been newly edited by Fr. Commer, in his Geistliche und weltliche Lieder aus dem XVI - XVII. Jahrhundert (published by Trautwein, in Berlin), pp. 80-85.

modifications, indicating already, by some most expressive
entwinings of the inner parts, that breath of ecstasy which
often breaks forth in so overwhelming a manner in the
Chorale hymns of Sebastian Bach; and even some subject
developments are attempted. At the fifty-sixth bar a change
takes place. The words of the Psalm come in: "My flesh
and my heart faileth; but God is the strength of my heart,
and my portion for ever": then comes the simple paraphrase
of the hymn, "Ob mir gleich Leib und Seel verschmacht, so
weisst du, Herr, dass ichs nicht acht," &c.

Six bars before the entry of the chorale the first bar of it
is gone through in the other parts and worked as a separate
subject, as if for a prelude—

Chorale.

Ob   mir gleich Leib   und . .   Seel . . verschmacht,

Treated as separate theme.
wenn mir   gleich Leib,   wenn mir   gleich Leib,   gleich

wenn   mir gleich Leib,   wenn   mir gleich

and is carried on with imitations. A similar passage occurs
before the entrance of the fifteenth verse, which follows next;
then the alto melts away gradually from its own independent
movement quite into the chorale,[100] the rhythmic unity becomes greater, until at last the Bible words end altogether.
The whole of the last verse is taken in a quicker and more
joyful *tempo*, and thus the subjective expression is altogether
swallowed up in the more general feeling of the hymn.
Here we perceive an undoubted germ of the spirit of Sebastian
Bach, a presage of his inexhaustible art in the poetic treatment of the chorale. But the imitations which prepare for

---

[100] The same thing happened before at bar thirteen, but in that place from a
want of skill. The lower harmonising, too, of bars eleven and twelve (and the
corresponding bars thirty-six and thirty-seven) betray an imperfectly cultivated
taste.

the first bar of the melody are exactly like Michael Bach's chorale arrangements for the organ ; under suitable poetic influence he has transferred to vocal music the same method which he had practised in them.

Four motetts for double chorus are worked out on the equally balanced resources of the contrast offered by chorale and Bible words. Two of them are alike even in the details of the plan, and the third agrees in all essential points: all three are in E minor and in common time. The deeper four-part chorus begins homophonically with the words from the Bible, and then the chorale enters, the spaces between its lines being occupied by the second choir. Two verses are gone through in this manner, and then both choirs unite in harmony of from five to seven parts, in such a way that the lower choir repeats the last note of each line like an echo. The poetic combination in one case consists of Hörnigk's hymn, "Mein Wallfahrt ich vollendet hab "—" My pilgrimage is at an end,"—verses 1, 3, 6, with the words from the New Testament, " It is appointed unto men once to die, but after this the judgment. . . . The wages of sin is death; but the gift of God is eternal life through Jesus Christ our Lord." In the second case, the words are taken from verses 1, 4, and 5 of Johann Franck's " Jesu meine Freude "—" Jesu, my joy,"—and the text "Hold fast that which thou hast, that no man take thy crown . . . and be thou faithful unto death, and thou shalt receive a goodly inheritance and a crown from the hand of the Lord "; and lastly, in the third case, the words are from verses 1, 6, and 5 of Flitner's hymn, " Ach was soll ich Sünder machen "—"Ah! what shall I, a sinner, do ? "—and the scripture passage, "Thou, which hast shewed me great and sore troubles, shalt quicken me again. The Lord will not always chide, but He will repent and have mercy upon us according to His great goodness." The fourth is formed on a somewhat different model (in C major, common time, 115 bars long). It has the same contrast as its motive, but it is only employed for one verse, and then the first choir is drawn into sympathy with the freer treatment of the second, so that in this case it comes to pass, as very seldom happens,

that the sentiment is changed from the congregational to the
personal devout feeling—from objective to subjective. And
this tendency is indicated from the beginning. The touching
and beautiful death-chorale, " Ach wie sehnlich wart ich der
Zeit, wenn du, Herr, kommen wirst "—" O how long I for the
time when Thou, O Lord, shalt come "—acquired no extensive
popularity as a congregational hymn, possibly only by reason
of its entirely subjective stamp. Michael Bach harmonises it
in a plain, and even childish, but unspeakably touching way.
In the last verse the individual feeling bursts its bonds in
the recurring sigh, which seems to long for death, "O komm!
o komm! o komm und hole mich!"—" O come, O come, O
come and fetch me!" And now both choruses ascend and
compete with each other on the cry "Herr, ich warte auf
dein Heil"—" Lord, I wait for Thy salvation,"—and come
back at last to the final line of the hymn, to expire in
beatific peace. This is probably the finest of all Michael
Bach's motetts.[101]

The process is almost reversed in another motett for
double chorus, for Christmas (in G major, common time,
seventy-three bars long). The choirs unite in the angel's
words, "Fear not, for behold, I bring you good tidings of
great joy," &c. Then all the altos, tenors, and basses have
a mysterious movement in four or five parts, "For unto you
is born this day a Saviour,"—and at last the chorale
" Gelobet seist du, Jesu Christ "—"All praise to Thee, Lord
Jesus Christ,"—is added in the soprano like a flash of light.
Round this the other voices gather, in fresh, if not very
broadly treated counterpoint.[102]

The motett for double chorus, "Nun hab ich überwunden"—

---

[101] In the Amalien-Library in the Joachimsthal at Berlin. Vol. 116, last piece:
Vol. 326, last piece: Vol. 116, last piece but two: ditto, last piece but one.
The first and fourth motetts have a figured-bass. The entry in the catalogue
of the Bach archives is: "Ach wie sehnlich, &c. Für den Discant, 5 Instrumente und Fundament von Johann Michael Bach." I think that our fourth
motett is intended by this notice, considering the carelessness with which the
index is made. The expression " 5 Instrumente und Fundament " is strange
and suspicious.

[102] Amalien-Library, Vol. 90, first piece. Without figured-bass.

"Now I have conquered,"—(in G major, common time, ninety-two bars long),[103] is characterised by the extension and ornamentation of a chorale-verse by means of the full body of the chorus. That the composer knew Hammerschmidt's arrangement of "Wie schön leucht't uns der Morgenstern" above mentioned, and set it before him as his model, is probable from external and internal considerations. Hammerschmidt's works were widely known, and, as has been already said, existed in the choir library of the Oberkirche at Arnstadt. This very piece has what the others have not — in the figured-bass part direction-marks carefully written in with red ink, besides other proofs of the closest study, for the bars have been counted and their sum noted down at the end. In structure Bach's motett shows an affinity with the older master, particularly in the taking up of the chorale verses, which continually modulate into different keys, by each choir alternately; on the other hand the close is quite different. It is again the lovely melody of Melchior Vulpius, to the no less fervent hymn "Christus der ist mein Leben," that Bach chooses for treatment, here taking the third verse of the hymn. The piece, both as a whole and in detail, is one of the best which have been preserved of this gifted composer. Exception may, indeed, be taken to the declamatory opening (Choir I., "Nun!" Choir II., "Nun!" Choir I., "Nun, nun, nun, nun!" Choir II., ditto): these isolated cries are calculated to increase the musical interest rather than to raise the verbal sense, and the composers of that time were very fond of beginning their motetts in this manner.[104] The

---

[103] Naue, Book III., No. 8. A figured-bass is added, of which the Bach archives say nothing. According to them the motett was written in 1679, when Michael Bach was thirty-one years old and Organist at Gehren.

[104] E.g., "Ich! ich! ich! ich will den Namen Gottes loben" (I will praise God's name), or "Uns! uns! uns! uns ist ein Kind geboren" (Unto us a Child is born), and others. Sebastian Bach, when, true to his family traditions, he began one of his earlier cantatas "Ich! ich! ich! ich hatte viel Bekümmerniss" (translated, in Novello's edition, "Lord! Lord! Lord! my spirit was in heaviness," literally, I, I, I, I was in deepest heaviness), incurred Mattheson's scorn.

feeling of happy confidence is given by the music, which
rises occasionally to the most joyful and martial courage,
particularly in the energetic and intermittent cries, " Kreuz !
Kreuz, Leiden ! Kreuz, Leiden, Angst und Noth ! "—" The
cross, the cross ! sorrows, sufferings, trouble, and fear ! "—
where we are reminded of the bold challenges in the fifth
number of Sebastian Bach's motett " Jesu meine Freude ! "
—" Jesu, my joy." When the whole verse is finished
the two choirs coalesce in a simpler form, and the melody
comes in as a *cantus firmus* in semibreves in the soprano
part, while the other voices have a more artistically worked
counterpoint than we are accustomed to in Michael Bach ;
the counterpoint in the first line is actually formed from the
fourfold diminution of the melody itself, and in the other
lines the formation of real subjects which imitate one
another is attempted.

A last and most remarkable work still remains to be
noticed, in outward form the longest and in inward character the most varied.[105] This is also for double chorus,
but now six parts (two sopranos, alto, two tenors, and
bass) are placed in antithesis to three (alto, tenor, and
bass). The six-part choir starts (in C major, common time)
sternly and gravely with the first two words of the passage,
" Unser Leben ist ein Schatten auf Erden "—" Life on
earth is but a shadow." After six bars the voices are
suddenly seized with an anxious haste ; the first soprano
glides upward with this flying figure—

Un - ser Le - ben ist ein Schat - - ten

a pause, in which there is a long drawn wail in the alto ;
then the restless passage again ; now it vanishes away in an
inner part, like a ghost—one expects to see unsubstantial
cloud-shadows hurrying over a mountain steep. Then the

---

[105] Naue, Book III., No. 7. In the catalogue of Ph. Em. Bach's legacy
the date is 1696. As Michael Bach died in 1694, this cannot refer to the time
of composition.

whole choir begin a perplexing whirling dance, first of quavers, then of quavers and semiquavers together, as when an autumn wind whirls up the dry leaves; now they dance in the air, now again on the ground, then on high again; then all is still and in the interval the death-knells are heard; again the ghostly passage glides before our sight, and once more come the dismal chords of mourning.

Who does not feel in this fantastic picture the romantic spirit of Sebastian Bach? Now, for the first time, the other chorus enters with the fourth and fifth verses of the chorale "Ach was soll ich Sünder machen," the peaceful flow of which is twice disturbed by the intervention of the first choir; its spiritual meaning culminates in the words "Und weiss, dass im finstern Grabe Jesus ist mein helles Licht, meinen Jesum lass ich nicht"—"And know that Christ my way shall lighten, In the grave where all is dim, I will trust and cleave to Him." As if for the confirmation of this trust, the words of Christ Himself are heard in the first choir in three parts, "I am the Resurrection and the Life,"—lasting for twenty-seven bars; and the second choir answers confidently,

"Weil du vom Tod erstanden bist, werd ich im Grab nicht bleiben"—"Since Thou art risen from the dead, the grave can never hold me,"—interrupted by corroborating phrases from the first choir, which is again in six parts. But we shall be mistaken if we think that the motett closes with this peaceful consummation. Deep down in the composer's mind lingers the gloomy picture of universal human mortality. Accordingly the affecting chorale begins again in full harmonies: "Ach wie nichtig, ach wie flüchtig ist der Menschen Leben!" leading up to a marvellous end:

> Ach Herr, lehr uns bedenken wohl,
> Dass wir sind sterblich allzumal,
> Auch wir allhier keins Bleibens han,
> Müssen alle davon,
> Gelehrt, reich, jung, alt oder schön.

> O teach us, Lord, to bear in mind
> That we may die at any hour.
> Here we have no abiding place,
> We must all pass away,
> The wise, rich, fair, old, or gay.

The sad melody is given to two high soprano parts in thirds, which are followed by the lower voices, and three lines are treated in this impressive way, "dividing the bones and marrow." With the fourth line a fearful haste seems to thrill through the whole body of the chorus; they crowd together anxiously, like the souls on the brink of Acheron; "Davon, davon!"—"Away, away!"—is murmured through the ranks, "Davon!" resounds from the depths, "Davon!" is repeated by the two sopranos as they vanish in the twilight.

In this motett Michael Bach, as usual, not seldom came in execution far behind his intentions. It was left for another of his race to bring to perfection that of which he only had an indistinct perception; but possibly a still higher place among the masters of his craft might have been allotted to him had he not in the flower of his years fallen a victim to that universal destiny whose tragic element he had so deeply felt in art. But one thing is very remarkable in this

composition, that it is almost entirely cast in the mould of
the church-cantata ; just as, on the other hand, the single
existing church-cantata of this writer bears upon it the
stamp of the motett. The Church Cantata sprang indeed
from a juxtaposition of separate passages of scripture and of
verses from congregational or devotional hymns. Until the
year 1700 this form alone predominated, and we shall proceed later on to discuss what had been already done in
this way before Sebastian Bach developed it to its fullest
perfection. It was after that date that recitative and the
Italian form of aria began to be introduced into it, and it is
well known how the cantata thus enriched owed its greatest
improvements to Sebastian Bach. We see plainly, even in
Michael Bach, how, in the music of the latter half of the
seventeenth century, the most widely differing germs lay
close to one another, soon to grow apart according to their
individual tendencies. He was one of those phenomena
that are wont to appear as the heralds of a new era in art,
round whom the breath of spring seems to hover, and who
make amends for what they cannot themselves perform by
that which they foreshadow.

But the elder brother, Johann Christoph Bach, to whom
we must readily grant the place of a master in concerted
choral music, also left us a series of specimens in the motett
form. Although it is true that unconditional perfection is
impossible to man, still there is this standard for " mastership," qualified as it must ever be : Whether the artist can
perfectly assimilate with his own conceptions the sum total
of the ideas and means called forth by the requirements of
his time, and can satisfy those demands of art which remain
at all times valid. In the motett it was needful to combine
into a higher unity a multitude of disconnected factors ; to
turn to account the acquisitions of instrumental music, but
with such moderation that only a tempering gleam should be
cast by them on the smooth surface of pure vocal music ; to
recognise the harmonic tone-system, but with constant regard to the fact that the motett form had its roots in the
polyphonic system of past centuries ; at every moment to
refer the movement of the choral masses to the guidance of

the melody which soared above them, and yet not to forget that those inferior parts are individuals with a right to a progression of their own. It was needful to form that musical system which, by means of a law only to be tested by feeling, interweaves the severally divided parts into a rational whole, and, at the same time, to make due allowance for the reasonable demands of the co-operating poem. And, before all else, the task was to gain for that subjective warmth and intensity of feeling which is the art-characteristic of the time, and which appears touchingly, if not very powerfully, in its devotional poetry—to gain for this its due place in the province which was particularly its own, without overstepping that fine and fluctuating line which separates individual feeling from general precision. All these requirements, which to this day continue paramount in sacred vocal composition, were then new; and though their fulfilment seems, in some ways, still harder nowadays, when musical material has so vastly increased—for few, indeed, succeed in moving with artistic freedom in the narrow domain of vocal music— on the other hand this is rendered easier by the amount of experience which has been collected.

But that Joh. Christoph Bach completely solved this problem no intelligent person can doubt; his motetts seem as though they might have been written yesterday. He bears the same relation both in this and in his compositions in the oratorio style to his predecessor, Hammerschmidt, as the latter for his part does to Schütz. Not one of them could have been what he is without his predecessor, and each one in his turn took a step in advance; so much so that in the motett Joh. Christoph Bach seems to have reached a height beyond which even Sebastian could not go, excepting by building up a towering edifice of art; while the Oratorio, the Passion Music, and the Church Cantata did not reach perfection till a generation later, although they presuppose the existence of such remarkable men as this Eisenach master was in his way. If this great master was taken little heed of and quickly forgotten, this is explained by saying that the highest goal which the artistic spirit of the age pursued with quick and happy success was not the motett form. Indeed it could not be, depending as it did on such manifold compromises. That, however, ought not to prevent historical investigation from assigning to him his due position in the development of art, from lamenting the disappearance of the greatest number of the compositions of this master, or from placing the few that remain in the right light as a genuine monument of native art.

In the musical legacy of Sebastian Bach's second son, so frequently alluded to, were seven motetts by Joh. Christoph Bach, or rather eight, since we can with tolerable certainty ascribe one without a name to him;[106] of these four are lost, not for ever it is to be hoped.[107] Five more motetts have been preserved in other ways, and are well known. After the oratorio-like composition already alluded to has been deducted, there remain eight motetts, a still smaller sum total than in the case of Johann Michael. Their internal importance is, indeed, quite different.

First, two small and simple motetts are to be considered, each in five parts, consisting of a moderately long chorus followed by an aria of several verses.[108] The one has for its subject the text, "Man that is born of a woman is of few days and full of trouble." Job, xiv. 1. It belongs to the same category as Michael Bach's "Unser Leben ist ein Schatten," and, although less full of fancy is full of deep feeling. A weary, mournful tone pervades the first movement, which is twenty-two bars long. It begins thus:—

---

[106] This last is the motett in four parts with a figured-bass, "Ich lasse dich nicht "—" I will not let Thee go,"—which can be no other than the end of the original work of Joh. Christoph's for double chorus, "Ich lasse dich nicht, du segnest mich denn "—" I will not let Thee go except Thou bless me,"—which we shall speak of later on.

[107] These are, according to the catalogue, "Meine Freundin, du bist schön," a wedding-song in twelve parts. "Mit Weinen hebt sichs," in four parts with fundamental bass, 1691. "Ach, dass ich Wassers genug," for alto solo with accompaniment of one violin, three viol di gambas, and bass. "Es ist nun aus," a death-song in four parts.

[108] Preserved in an old MS. in the possession of Herr Steinhäuser, Organist of Mühlhausen, in Thuringia.

To the true motett movement succeeds a five-part aria, of the same character, but of more expressive melody, of which this is the first verse :—

> Ach wie nichtig,
> Ach wie flüchtig
> Ist das Leben,
> So dem Menschen wird gegeben.
> Kaum wenn er zur Welt geboren,
> Ist er schon zum Tod erkoren.

> Ah how weary,
> Brief but dreary,
> Full of anguish
> Are our days! On earth we languish;
> Hardly are we born to sighing
> Ere we are condemned to dying.

The two last lines recur as a burden after each of the five verses. At the beginning of each verse, three times over, two short ejaculations alternate with each other; to these the composer has closely clung. The result is a phrase of three and two bars, by which the character of weariness is ingeniously stamped on the piece. I have not been able to discover who was the writer of the hymn, which of course is quite distinct from Michael Franck's "Ach wie flüchtig, ach wie nichtig."

The words in the Revelation ii. 10, "Sei getreu bis in den Tod, so will ich dir die Krone des Lebens geben"—"Be thou faithful unto death, and I will give thee a crown of life,"—are taken as the subject of the other motett. It begins broadly and confidently:—

At the words of the promise the motion becomes more cheerful, and the opening phrase is repeated at the end: the whole movement is only twenty bars long. The aria which follows, "Halte fest und sei getreu"—"Be thou faithful, stand thou firm,"—consists of four verses; its opening intentionally reverts to the beginning of the first movement.

Both these motetts are undoubtedly early works by Joh. Christoph. They have not the grand features and the breadth of structure which mark all the other six, nor does the treatment of the parts display the skill and smoothness which the master subsequently succeeded in acquiring. Still we feel in them the stirring of a peculiar and profoundly meditative fancy; and this, the gift of his nationality, he trained under the

best masters, not merely at his father's instigation, but from
his own inclination as well; since we know that at an early
age he already held an official position, and was consequently
independent.   Nor did he seek to learn only from the two
principal German masters: he went back to the masters from
whom they had learnt—the Italians.   This is proved by his
incomparable superiority to his contemporaries as a skilful
contrapuntist, his more flowing and vocal treatment of the
inner parts, the lovely smoothness of his melodic ideas, and
his harmonic peculiarities, which must be directly referred to
the church music of about 1600, as, for instance, the succession of triads following each other over a descending bass
—a means of expression for which Hammerschmidt seems
to have had no predilection.

As we learn from the master himself, one of his six great
motetts, "Lieber Herr Gott, wecke uns auf"—"Lord God!
Lord God! wake thou us,"—was composed by him at the age
of thirty.[109]   In this he proves himself already a ripe artist.

This beginning

with its beautifully accented melody and admirable declamation, which so exactly hit the expression of fervent filial supplication, could hardly have been invented by any one else.
Bach's motett has no resemblance whatever to Schütz's
composition to the same words (*Musicalia ad Chorum Sacrum*,
No. XIII.).   He must, of course, have known it, and may even
have derived the text directly from thence, for it is not

---

[109] The autograph in the Bach collection of the Royal Library at Berlin bears
the superscription "*Motetta á. 8 Voc:*" at the end is noted " 121 bars "; below
the stave in the right hand corner "Eisenach $\overline{ao}$ 1672, Xbris. Joh. Christo.
Bach *org.*"   Under the vocal parts is a figured-bass; the writing is fine and
elegant, and the bars marked off with a ruler.   This motett has been recently
published by Naue, Book II., No. 4.

biblical but comes from some church prayer; but the suggestion of his having borrowed from it must be altogether dismissed.[110]   It is, nevertheless, interesting to note how, within a quarter of a century, the style of the motett has developed, how it has all become much more plastic and pleasing, how the expression is much more clearly defined, the phrasing more careful, and the progress of the whole more flowing.   Schütz still clings, as is natural from his historical position, in some degree to the traditions of the past, particularly in the uninterrupted connection of the successive ideas of the motett, while Bach, in full possession of the new harmonic tone-system, can dispense with these means in constructing a coherent whole, and proceeds by independent phrases.   Such an arrangement must, of course, be all the more prominent in a composition for double chorus, because this depends essentially on the responsion of the two bodies, and only expands to a simultaneous employment of all the voices at each climax.   After the second chorus has repeated the three bars here given, 3-2 time is introduced, and the composition proceeds in that measure through four sections, to the words " Wecke uns auf, | dass wir bereit sein, wenn dein Sohn kommt, | ihn mit Freuden zu empfahen | und dir mit reinem Herzen zu dienen "—" Rouse Thou us up | that, when Thy Son comes, we may be glad | to receive Him with rejoicing, | and with pure hearts to worship and serve Thee."   The third of these is most broadly worked out ; bar after bar, through thirty-five bars, the body of sound flows up and down between the two choruses, full of vigour and in a glorious stream of movement, particularly in the bass parts, where the direct influence of the Italians is again perceptible.   And in the final fugue, which returns to common time, a warm breath of southern beauty seems to prevail, tempering and illuminating the bold outline of a conspicuously artistic structure.

This is, besides, an interesting example of the fugue form

---

[110] Winterfeld, in his Ev. Kir. III., 429, seems to hint at something of the kind.   Schütz's composition has been lately edited by Neithardt: Musica Sacra, Vol. VII., No. 8.   Bote and Bock, Berlin.

as it was now becoming modified out of the old type. The theme—

durch den - sel - bi-gen dei - nen lie-ben Sohn, die - nen   &c.

when we look at the whole movement, is evidently in the modern key of G major; the answer, however, does not follow according to rule, by which the beat, G, in the first bar would be answered by a D in the corresponding place in the response; but the composer copies the manner of the old school, which attaches the principal importance to an exact correspondence of the separate intervals, and consequently often regards it as unnecessary to give prominence to the relations between the tonic and the dominant. Hence, Bach does not answer his theme thus—

durch den - sel - bi-gen dei - nen lie - ben Sohn,

but thus—

durch den - sel - bi-gen dei - nen lie - ben Sohn,

in the Mixolydian mode; the old and the new schemes of harmony are here mingled to form a very remarkable tonality, which prevails throughout the fugue, with its dependence on the sub-dominant. The close treatment between the upper voices is also in the old style; this is introduced quite at the beginning, and at each return of the subject it is repeated with a definite intention; indeed throughout the motett the principle of close imitation is most ingeniously worked out. The multiplicity of complete or half closes, after which the elaboration begins afresh, are an indication of mere want of development; even the instrumental fugues of that period are still cumbered with this imperfection, and it was precisely by his power of setting free an unbroken stream of melody in the fugue, by constantly and unexpectedly introducing the theme, and intermediate subjects developed from it, that Sebastian Bach was to give glorious proof of his genius, and fulfil the highest conceivable requirements of the fugue.

To return to the artistic construction of the fugue now in question, the theme is adapted not only to a threefold stretto imitation, but in the first stretto (beginning on the third crotchet of the first bar) to a double counterpoint on the eighth and tenth. In order to allow of all the strettos being brought in, the composer in the course of the piece has somewhat altered the theme, and the melodic phrase of the second bar is taken down a third ; still the identity of the theme is not in any way interfered with by this remarkable evidence of episodical modification, while the way is opened for a great richness of combinations. This begins from bar twelve of the fugue, which is steadily elaborated into closer and closer strettos ; it is brilliantly conspicuous in the startling introduction of the theme in counterpoint on the tenth, is confirmed by the majestic doubling of the tenth between the bass and tenor of the second chorus, and flows on in richer and richer harmonies of the whole eight parts to a half close in the twentieth bar, on the dominant of E minor. Immediately the entrance of the voices is repeated as at the beginning, but the similarity is only apparent, because the recently modified form of the theme is here employed, allowing of a different order of modulation ; and the tones soon resolve themselves once more in the splendid *crescendo* just described, repeating it even more elaborately, and closing in grand fulness on bar thirty-four.

The year of composition of another motett is also known to us. It is on the words from the Book of Wisdom, iv. 7, 10, 11, 13, and 14—"But though the righteous be prevented with death, yet shall he be in rest"—(five voices, in F major). This, according to the testimony of Phil. Emanuel Bach, is of the year 1676, and thus four years later than the former one.[111]

---

[111] The MSS. handed down by Ph. Em. Bach are in the Royal Library at Berlin. The same musician has had the voice parts accompanied by stringed instruments and the organ, as is proved by the instrumental parts prepared by his

The relationship to Italian music is here even closer, and
the evident resemblance with a beautiful motett by Giovanni
Gabrieli, "*Sancta Maria succurre miseris,*" can hardly be
wholly accidental. The diatonically ascending motive in the
last movement in Bach—in Gabrieli from bar sixty-two (compare also bars thirty-seven to thirty-nine)—point to a real
relationship; so again do figures such as bars eight to twenty
of Bach (twenty-four to twenty-seven of Gabrieli) with the
identity of key and similar points of agreement throughout
the piece; and finally—though this, to be sure, is less independent evidence, but is supported by other resemblances—
the occurrence of the *proportio tripla* after the diminished
tempus imperfectum in Gabrieli and Bach alike.[112] That the work
of the German master may, in spite of this, be extremely
original, need not be said, and that it is so this very comparison proves. A genius which is capable of filling in a grand
outline displays itself, as Bach has done, in illustrating each
portion of the text. The piece is at once so complete and so
ample, and contains such a wealth of contrasting details,
that the effect of the whole is equally soothing and animating. Unspeakably beautiful is the sentiment of the first
movement—the beatification of the righteous who, by an
early death, are snatched from all the ills and dangers of an
'evil' life, and have attained eternal peace; the softly falling
passages represent the departure of the righteous, with all
that figurative power of imagery which the composer so eminently possessed. But it is not a weary drooping like that of
a withered flower; the full and solemn tones sink like rain-
drops slowly falling and sparkling from the leaves in the last
evening gleam. The second subject is in strong contrast to

---

own hand. The composition has been published by Naue (Book I., 1), with the
organ accompaniment; also by Neithardt, Musica Sacra, Vol. VII., No. 14.
It must be the same which was in the possession of Reichardt, and of which he
praises the power and boldness (*vide* Gerber N. L., Vol. I., col. 207).

[112] The merit of having first pointed this out is due to Winterfeld (*vide*
Ev. Kir. The motett by Gabrieli (a Venetian), here spoken of is to be found
in Winterfeld's book, Gabrieli und sein Zeitalter. Berlin, Schlesinger, 1834;
III., 24-28. We must proceed carefully in finding resemblances at such
remote intervals of time; still in this case the observation seems to me to
be accurate.

the holy peace of the first. It rises in joyful and stirring passages, " Er gefällt Gott wohl und ist ihm lieb "—"He pleased God, and was beloved of Him,"—and it moves steadily onwards through a whole series of various ideas and musical images. Here again we have to admire the expressive power of the composer who could with such certainty reproduce the mental pictures suggested by the words, as at a later period, and in a greater degree, was done by Handel. Observe only the musical subject to the words " Und wird hingerücket "—" Yea, speedily was he taken away "; how it soars straight up into heaven, and how immediately afterwards the wickedness and perversity of the world is stamped on the energetic succession of harmonies, the suspensions and displacements of accent, and after this distressful and sorrowful ganglion of harmonies, the clear triads flash out, " He, being made perfect, in a short time fulfilled a long time." And then comes the perfect pacification of the wild and passionate turmoil in the last movement, which flows on, broad, full, and perfect, a river of gold. The motive which governs it throughout, elaborately worked out, flowing from its source with ever increasing fulness and depth, seems to rush from the dark places of the earth towards regions of light :—

—" Therefore hasted He to take him away from among the
wicked." It is borrowed from Gabrieli, but what with
him is only musical, in Bach's hands—and this was his
original gift—is poetical as well as musical.

If we take the term " romantic "—elastic as it has become
in its application—in its original meaning, and understand
by it a mixture of certain elements of a phase of culture,
complete in itself, with others which have a tendency to
overstep its limits and to reach a dimly perceived goal,
no word can better suit Joh. Christoph Bach, particularly
with regard to his scheme of key treatment. The old
church modes were sometimes combined by him with the
modern system of majors and minors in a quite indefinable
manner, and this gives rise to a series of broken lights,
a singular chiaroscuro, whence these motetts often derive
an undeniable family likeness to the productions of Schubert and Schumann. Even the final fugue of the motett in
E minor, just discussed, is very striking in this respect;
but the romantic character is far more conspicuous in two
other motetts for double chorus. One of them is founded on
the words of old Simeon, "Lord, now lettest thou Thy servant depart in peace."[113] The principal key, or more properly
mode, as regards the more prominent closes of the phrases,
may be termed Æolic, with a plagal commencement and
close; and yet with this the piece is carried out in such a
thoroughly modern style of harmony, and is rounded off into
a cycle, with a return to the beginning so regularly according
to the present principles of form, that it might almost be said
to have no fundamental mode. Mingled with the Æolic harmonies, now and then Doric and Mixolydian intervals strike
the ear; but above all, the wavering between the old and new
systems of key is to be seen in the general manner in which
Bach's harmony progresses. We must use this expression,
since throughout the whole piece the composer deals with
sequences of chords. The raising and lowering of single
notes were regarded by the ancients as *accidentia*—incidental changes which had no further effect on the character

---

[113] See Appendix A, No. 5.

of the key, while with us they sometimes make it uncertain, sometimes entirely change it, and always have an essential influence on the affinities and relations of a chord. Under these circumstances it was a matter of indifference to the older writers whether G minor and E major followed each other directly, or G major and E minor, while to us the last two keys stand in the closest relationship, and the two former are separated by a gap which only the boldest can leap across. Now Bach frequently raises or lowers a note in the old manner, but constructs sequences of chords in the new; hence a series of triads frequently originate, well adapted to rouse in our minds every feeling of a fundamental key. The waves of sound rise and fall in wonderful tremulous motion; they gleam and sparkle in a strange variety and play of harmony; they seem to obey every breath, and often illustrate the expression of the words by modulated turns of extreme audacity, such as we seek for in vain among the composers of the following century, nay, even in Sebastian Bach.

After a close in the common-chord of E major, for instance, Joh. Christoph, with three steps, brings himself into F major, E minor, C major, A minor, F major, and, immediately after, by means of the common-chord of C major, into G major. Another time he introduces the following sequence in eight parts: A major, B flat major, A minor, G major $\left(\begin{smallmatrix}6\\3\end{smallmatrix}\right)$ C major, and then proceeds: A major, B flat major, F major, C major, F major, with which the phrase closes. It is quite amazing how, in spite of this, we never have the oppressive sense of aimless and planless wandering in the modulations, but give ourselves up in perfect confidence as to a trustworthy leader. The musician reveals his idea as a whole with such clearness, and develops it with so much logic, that we receive an image, dreamlike indeed, and floating in mist; but, at the same time, we realise that this is exactly what its creator intended. In fact, when studying other compositions by Joh. Christoph Bach, which betray the definite stamp of a major or a minor key, we can never for a moment doubt that, to him, the mingling of two different systems of harmony was a means of which he availed himself with deliberate purpose to attain a determined end. This of itself stamps him as a master, although not a dozen of his vocal compositions have been preserved to us. In the same way Sebastian Bach, although indeed under quite altered circumstances, handled the old church modes freely as a powerful instrument of expression. We need only recall the overwhelmingly grand use made of the Mixolydian mode in the cantata "Jesu, nun sei gepreiset"[114]—"Lord Jesu, now be praised."

How admirably suited this medium is when the object is to represent and to render in a general and artistic form the frame of mind of an old man, who at last has found the certain pledge of a long looked-for day of redemption, and whose failing eyes see the radiant dawn of a new sun, must be felt by every one. The chorus first sing alternately the initial bars, and then imitate each other at the interval of a bar.

Immediately follows an extraordinarily beautiful passage, part of which has been already mentioned—

[114] B.-G., X., No. 41. Particularly in the opening chorus. The passages on pp. 6, 7, and 18 are indescribably sublime.

and from which it may be inferred that this motett was conceived of with an instrumental accompaniment (perhaps only
with the support of one deep instrument); for in these excessively long-drawn passages in F major, where the bass of the
first chorus descends below the c of the second, the full effect
could hardly have been attained without a sixteen-foot organ
bass. The further course of the composition is difficult to
represent, by reason of its abnormal management, without
extensive extracts, and even then the reader would scarcely
acquire a more vivid idea of the whole than he may perhaps
have obtained from what has already been said.

The long-drawn ascending passage on the words "And to
be the glory of Thy people Israel,"—is full of a mild dignity;
it closes in the true Æolic tone, if I may so say. But now the
real formative power of the artist is first fully displayed. He
first reproduces the whole thirty-four bars of the beginning,
thus arriving at C major, and now, taking a deep breath,
rises again with the original motive from the shadowy
common-chord of F major, brings out again the full volume
of both choruses in imitation, rises twice to the bitter-sweet
D minor chord of the ninth—or as it would then have
been called, from its resting on the third, the chord of the
seventh, an harmonic combination which was just coming
greatly into favour with the Germans—and then sinks softly
down on to A minor—as the head of a dying man sinks on the

pillows. It does but picture the failing eyes before whose last glance all worldly objects float in confusion—the last sigh borne away into infinite space—when, after this, the chorus passes tremulously and dubiously to the major chord of the sixth ; and so the last cry of " Lord, Lord!" floats away, evanescent and faint, on the same notes as the master began the piece with.

The other motett, allied to this in form and feeling, is the grandest of all that remain to us. On the words of Lamentations, v. 15, 16,—"The joy of our heart is ceased; our dance is turned into mourning. The crown is fallen from our head : woe unto us, that we have sinned,"—a grand and gloomy tone-picture is constructed, of no less than two hundred and twenty-five bars of slow movement. We may regard the mode as a transposed Doric, which, as in the previous motett, has a plagal beginning and close. Sebastian Bach proved his admiration of this piece by transcribing part of it with his own hand.[115] For variety, energy, and appealing fervour ot expression—for the development of sound into bold and striking imagery—for the' highest perfection of form as affecting the whole work, it can find no equal excepting among the very best examples of its kind. What deep lament is sounded in this beginning—

Un-sers Herz-ens Freu - de hat . . ein En - de,

Un-sers Herzens Freu - de hat . . ein En - de

---

[115] The score is in the Royal Library at Berlin.   There, too, is another copy in the handwriting of Pölchau.   R. von Hertzberg published the work in Vol. XVI. of Musica Sacra, No. 18.   (Berlin : Bote and Bock.)

and further on, amid the wofullest accents, what a noble strain of melody—

No other composer of that period could have availed himself of such "longue haleine" in uttering the words "The crown is fallen from our head," for thirty-nine bars are devoted to it; and how proudly, how royally, the motive starts!—

None other could have been equal to depicting in so pregnant a manner the pride of ambition and its crushed fall.

When Forkel, the enthusiastic admirer of Sebastian Bach once visited his son Philipp Emanuel at Hamburg, his host, who held his great-uncle's works in high estimation, let Forkel hear some of them. "I still vividly remember," he writes, "how sweetly my friend (Ph. Em. Bach), already an old man, smiled upon me at the most remarkable and boldest passages." Harmonious sequences such as the following—

O,   o   weh,   dass wir, &c.

O,   o   weh,   dass wir, &c.

were indeed calculated still to excite astonishment a hundred years after they were composed; at the end of the seventeenth century they were quite unheard of. Philipp Emanuel
possessed a motett, written about the year 1680, but now
lost, in which Joh. Christoph had used the augmented
sixth, which Forkel very justly terms an act of daring.[116]
The use of this interval was, to be sure, not wholly new; it
occurs before this in Carissimi's oratorio of Jephtha and in
his " *Turbabuntur Impii*,"[117] but, on both occasions in solo
voice parts, while Bach seems not to have shrunk from it
in a choral subject.

The main outline of the motett we are studying approaches far less nearly to the form of the *da capo* air, then
in process of development, than it does, on the contrary,
to the modern *sonata* form, and may therefore be designated
as the product of Joh. Christoph's independent artistic
study. Two quite distinct principal parts are each subdivided
into two, a principal and a subsidiary section. The first principal section is composed of four long phrases (the motives
of three of them are quoted above), and it ends in G minor.
The first subsidiary section begins with a passage, also

---

[116] *Vide* the Necrology in Mizler's Musikalischer Bibliothek. Leipzig, 1754.
Vol. IV., Part I., p. 159. Gerber has somewhat embellished these facts in his
Lexicon, Vol. I., col. 206-7.

[117] For the first example see Chrysander's edition of Carissimi's oratorios in
Denkmälern der Tonkunst, II., 19, in the last bar but one (f d♯, for so the
harmony must be imagined); the second instance is in R. Schlecht's Geschichte
der Kirchenmusik, p. 452, bars four and six, so far as the data are, in this
case, to be trusted.

quoted, " O weh ! dass wir so gesündiget haben," and in its whole character is the most complete contrast, ending with a half-close on the major chord of D. The second part now begins; it repeats the principal section of the first part, but lets the wailing cry of the first subsidiary section now glide along side by side with the most diversified combinations, and now force its way through them, thus including in this grand design, which reveals an extraordinary artistic intelligence, both the development of the sonata subject and the repetition of the principal theme after the close, which, as in the first part, is in G minor. The subsidiary section comes in again in due order, and this time with a wonderfully beautiful effect in B flat major. It is not till the fifth bar that it assumes the same form as at its first appearance. A coda of six bars brings it to an end.

There are still two motetts remaining which, in consequence of the use made in them of chorale melodies, must take a quite distinct place. They are, however, very dissimilar. An example was given above which showed how the dialogue form, worked out with so much predilection by Hammerschmidt in his sacred concertos, had been transferred to the motett. Joh. Chr. Bach's vocal composition in five parts, "Fürchte dich nicht,"[118] in A minor, is of this kind. Alto, two tenors, and bass sing, as if in the person of Christ, the Bible text "Fear not : for I have redeemed thee, I have called thee by thy name ; thou art Mine." Isaiah, xliii. 1.

Against this the soprano afterwards sings the last verse of Rist's Hymn, "O Traurigkeit, o Herzeleid."

> O Jesu du,
> Mein Hülf und Ruh,
> Ich bitte dich mit Thränen,
> Hilf, dass ich mich bis ins Grab
> Nach dir möge sehnen.

> O Jesu! Thou
> My hope and rest,
> With tears I bend before Thee ;
> Help! that I in life and death,
> Ever may adore Thee.

---

[118] It is to be found in a MS. of the last century in the Amalien-Library of the College of Joachimsthal in Berlin, Vol. CXVI., No 1. The MS., which also shows a figured-bass, is unfortunately far from accurate.

When it comes to the last line but one, the voice of
Christ answers with the words, "Verily, verily, I say unto
thee, this day shalt thou be with Me in Paradise." It is
clear that two separate individuals are here represented
in a dramatic dialogue. Thus the composer must have
looked upon the four lower voices as a compact unity,
allowing the soprano to stand out in contrast with the
necessary distinctness; and if we had just now to criticise
Michael Bach's chorale motetts, because the counterpoint of
the other voices is not always treated with due independence
of the chorale melody, any such demand is here to a certain
degree set aside by the general plan of the composition
itself. Bach has, moreover, succeeded in giving the mass of
tone produced by the four voices the character of an independent organism, full of an inner life of its own in its contrast
to the chorale, and has thus produced a real masterpiece of
its kind.

The distribution of the music is, as we are accustomed to
find, clear and masterly, even under these circumstances of
extreme difficulty. It is in three sections. At first the four-
voiced choir sing the Bible words alone for thirty-nine bars.
They begin at once with a vigorous and encouraging shout,
and then work out on this theme—

a fugato for all four parts, allowing sometimes two, sometimes
three, sometimes only one voice to ring out on the word "geru-
fen," with long held chords and notes in a mighty cry, while
the theme here quoted constantly comes in again with small
intentional alterations—a passage well worthy of Handel,
and reminding us of him in its simple grandeur. It closes
with this in C, the relative major, and then leads back to
A minor by a subject constructed on the words "Du bist
mein," which is particularly interesting for the imitation
between the alto and second tenor.

This is the first part; the second extends to the commence-

ment of the fourth line of the chorale, and contains twenty-
four bars.   Here what is highly worthy of admiration is the
way in which the two poetic individualities are kept distinct ;
for example : the soprano coming in on the closing chord of
the chorus carries on the first line of the melody alone ;
the chorus reappears at first only in short phrases and
ejaculations, but presently returns to the motives and
passages of the beginning, already known to the hearer,
and which, though they contrast as strongly as possible
with the melody of the choral, still flow as smoothly
into it as though it had been devised expressly for them.
The grandest dramatic emotion is reserved with ,subtle
foresight for the third part, thirty bars long.   To the
reiterated cry of the soprano for " Help," the lower voices
answer with equal insistance, " Verily, verily," &c., and by
numerous imitations of each give this agitated passage a
fervency adequate to the occasion.   I must resist the
temptation to quote farther details ; it must suffice to say
that all the peculiarities of the master are conspicuous in
this work.

If we compare it with Sebastian Bach's motett, "Fürchte
dich nicht "—" Be not afraid,"—which is in great part set to
the same Bible words, and in which, in the same way, a
chorale melody with poetical antistrophes is introduced, it
is quite clear that Sebastian Bach endeavoured to attain
this art-ideal in quite another way than Joh. Christoph and
his lesser contemporaries, and that his connection with his
predecessors on this point is a merely general one.   The
elder Bach conceived of the two dramatically contrasted
characters as two equally important factors, and endeavoured
to represent their relation to each by musical means only ;
the younger kept the voices which recited the Bible texts in
contrast to the chorale not merely proportionate in volume
but even too independent, since they worked out among
themselves a perfect fugue demanding no supplementary
aid, and to whose calm flow the floating fragments of the
chorale melody might almost seem a mere accidental adjunct,
were it not for the elevated symbolical meaning attributed to
the chorale, which bears no direct proportion to its purely mu-

sical value. But this, as we shall see in the next section of this book, is the view which in fact afforded the standard for the independent treatment of the chorale on the organ; and it was by this route, so to speak—*via* instrumental music, that Sebastian attained a type of art which Joh. Christoph had reached, starting from his own naturally poetic point of view.

But if we here have had to deal with the dramatic contrast of distinct personages, in the other choral motett we find merely a lyrical contrast of emotional moods, such as we have already met with in several of Michael Bach's works. This motett (at first for two and afterwards for one choir) is now the best known of all this master's compositions. The Bible text is "Ich lasse dich nicht, du segnest mich denn" — "I will not leave Thee till Thou bless me"; in the second part the chorale, "Warum betrübst du dich, mein Herz," is interwoven with the third verse of Hans Sachs' hymn; and this is done to such perfection that it might be supposed to be the work of Sebastian.[119] The matter in hand was a contrapuntal treatment of the chorale melody, with independent motives throughout; and we have already seen in Michael Bach's works how little adapted the clumsy style of the German musicians of that period was, on the whole, to the solution of such problems. Johann Pachelbel used the fifth verse of the chorale, "Was Gott thut, das ist wohlgethan"— "That which God doth is still well done,"—as the basis of an elaborate composition of the concerto type, which he worked out smoothly and flowingly, but, for that very reason indeed, quite differently; for there is no contrast of the Bible text and church hymn, by which the fundamental feeling is first depicted in all its depth, while at the same time it necessitates the most complete mastery over the *technique* of counterpoint. It is distinct, too, from the above-named work by Sebastian Bach—irrespective of the dramatic contrast —by this radical difference in the tendencies of the two masters. Sebastian's forms were purely musical; those of Joh. Christoph graphic and oratorio-like. Here, again,

---

[119] See Appendix A, No. 6.

a comparison of the two works, tolerably alike as they are in design, is highly instructive. That of Sebastian is no doubt richer and fresher, but it depends essentially on the organ. Joh. Christoph, on the contrary, still stands on the native soil of the motett—pure vocal style —and gives due prominence to the human voice, with its greater capabilities of expression and all its natural poetic quality. There is, perhaps, no second work of this period in which tendencies, which subsequently diverged diametrically, were so happily and closely combined, and which, nevertheless, stands at the highest summit of art. The treatment of the chorale, with all the technical and æsthetic results involved, points to the way pursued by Sebastian Bach; the graphic tone-imagery of the chief musical ideas points decidedly to Handel. Thus the first principal motive of the chorale counterpoint—which has to serve again in the course of the piece in an inverted form—at once depicts an urgent and instant entreaty—

Ich las - se dich nicht, nicht, nicht, ich las - se dich nicht, nicht, nicht,

while the second, on the contrary, coming in at first in the alto, with a passage of close imitation,

du seg - - - - - - - nest mich denn,

and then with rich modifications, as in the bass in bar eighteen,

du seg - - - - - nest mich denn,

illustrates as by the breadth and fulness of an almost unmistakable expression the mien of one who extends his hand in solemn benediction ; and at the same time all purely musical requirements are fulfilled in the most admirable manner. With what masterly contrast the motives are constructed, and how completely they, and they alone, command the whole composition ! What a perfect adaptation of musical means to poetic beauty in those three bars' rest in the middle, after the artistic complications!—a calm where the parts, hitherto contrapuntal, repose and dream, softly moving in a measure that is now merely declamatory.

This motett, if indeed it is by Joh. Christoph Bach, certainly is one of his late compositions. The connection of the harmonies, particularly in the first deeply expressive part, are, if not bolder, at any rate freer and more subtle. The scheme of the melody is more individual, as, for instance, in the seventh (a′ flat), in the nineteenth and twenty-third bars of the first section, which is taken by the soprano with an upward spring, a very novel venture in any choral composition of that time. Indeed, the key of F minor is unusual in the latter half of the seventeenth century. Finally, the whole bears the stamp of mild contemplation rather than of youthful eagerness or manly vigour, although it cannot be denied that Joh. Christoph, like his brother Michael, and indeed the whole period at which they lived, had a special leaning to the weird and dreamy.

V.

INSTRUMENTAL WORKS OF CHRISTOPH AND MICHAEL BACH.

It has been already said that even less has been saved of the instrumental compositions of Joh. Christoph and Joh. Michael Bach than of their vocal works. In point of fact, only a few fragments remain to bear witness of their undoubtedly great productiveness. But this branch of art is in itself so important—deriving a double significance from its bearing on Sebastian Bach—that we must seek every possible means of throwing light on this aspect of the two artist brothers.

Both were by profession organists, and the art of organ-playing was indisputably the centre of all instrumental music till the middle of the eighteenth century, though it was in Thuringia and in Saxony that it principally flourished and finally even reached perfection; and this was because it found in the Protestant chorale a motive and basis for development, than which it is impossible to imagine one more fit. It was, then, in the treatment of chorales that a master of Central Germany first pioneered the road; and, whether by mere accident or no, all that remains to us of the organ compositions of the brothers Bach are likewise treatments of chorales. The art of writing for the organ, which had been previously confined to a mere ornamental transcription of vocal compositions, in the beginning of the sixteenth century put forth the early buds of a characteristic blossoming, with the first traces of a style peculiar to itself. In Italy Claudio Merulo found in the *Toccata*, as it was called— a kind of composition in which he endeavoured to give full play to the wealth of tone possessed by the organ, by alternating combinations of brilliant running passages with sostenuto sequences of harmonies—a form which, if somewhat erratic and fantastic, was still highly capable of development. The first steps were taken towards the development of the organ fugue in the *canzone* of Giov. Gabrieli; and Sweelinck, a Dutchman, gained great celebrity it would seem, particularly by his elaboration of the *technique* and by a great gift for teaching, and endeavoured to make the heaviness of the organ style lighter and more pleasing by skilful and graceful handling. Samuel Scheidt, the organist at Halle, was one of his pupils. In his *Tabulatura nova* (three parts, Hamburg, 1624), he first succeeded in treating the chorale as adapted to the organ in a very varied manner, and with considerable inventive power. These, the very earliest examples in so extensive and novel a domain of art, show marks, of course, of being a first attempt. A new path is opened out, and abundant means are brought in to level it; but the practical precision and arrangement are lacking which would give the full value to each in its place. In the course of the century a whole series of well-defined and in themselves logical forms grew up for the treatment of chorales. Only a few of these are found in any degree pure in Scheidt, and those the most obvious; among them must be included the method by which the chorale is worked out line by line on the scheme of a motett, and, closely connected with this, the chorale fugue, in which Scheidt still clung

evidently to the vocal style.[120]   In most of the other forms he
had indeed to emphasise the motives, though he applied
them with arbitrary variety to one and the same subject.
Thus the treatment of the first verse of the melody "Da
Jesus an dem Kreuze stund "—"When Jesus stood before the
cross,"—from the first part of the *Tabulatura nova*, begins with
a fugato on the first line; then this first line goes up into the
upper voice, the bass and alto singing it in canon.   The
interlude after the second line is independent; after the
third the interlude is strictly built upon the subject; and after
the fourth there is another independent one.   Pachelbel,
Walther, or even Sebastian Bach would have developed four,
or at least three distinct forms from this abundance of
primary ideas.   On another occasion Scheidt treats the
chorale "Vater unser im Himmelreich"—"Our Father which
art in heaven,"—Part I., v. 1, in such a way as to introduce
the first line *in motu contrario* as a prelude ; but as early as on
the fifth note in a lower part the same line occurs *in motu recto*,
then after four notes *in motu contrario*, at the same distance of
time again *in motu recto* in the upper part, and finally once
more, after the same interval of time, *in motu contrario* in
the tenor.   After this the chorale is carried on in the soprano
part without interruption throughout, but with fresh counterpoint to every line.   It need hardly be remarked that with
such a redundancy of good forms it is vain to look for
clearness or unity of structure.   Still it is evident that this
does not diminish the merit of this master, who in fact created
an epoch and who did all that could be done ; but it is
significant as pointing out his historical position in the art.

Any detailed account of the progress of the art of chorale
treatment, as it was carried out after Scheidt into the second
half of the century, is not necessary here ; nor indeed should
I be now in a position to give it.   The advance seems at
first to have been small, and this is easily intelligible in the
unfavourable circumstances of those times.   Delphin Strunck,

---

[120] Examples of this are the fantasia on "Ich ruf zu dir, Herr Jesu Christ,"
Part I., fol. 239 ; the first verse of "Veni redemptor gentium," Part III., fol. 179 ;
the first verse of "Veni Creator Spiritus," Part III., fol. 179.   The last piece is
also given by Winterfeld, Ev. Kir., II., Musical Supp., No. 214.

the famous organist at Brunswick, and a very popular teacher
(1601-1694), followed in Scheidt's footsteps, without however
arriving at any fixed principle of art from the constant
treatment of chorales, judging from his compositions remaining to us. It is probable that the treatment of the
separate lines of chorales as the basis for motetts continued
to be industriously cultivated ; for instance, the chorale,
" In dich hab ich gehoffet, Herr "—" My hope has been in
Thee, O Lord,"—was set in this way by Johann Theile
(1646-1724), who was almost a contemporary of Michael
Bach's, and who was called, by reason of his great skill, the
father of contrapuntists.[121]   It is in four parts, and displays
great science, for each of the four parts is treated in independent counterpoint, but it is intolerably pedantic and stiff.[122]
According to this, the type of the chorale fugue must have
been established at an early date, if indeed we may apply
the name to a fugal subject, derived from the first line of the
chorale, at the end of which the second line still often
faintly joins in. To this class belongs Heinrich Bach's
admirable treatment of " Christ lag in Todesbanden "
(already mentioned, p. 36).   A contemporary of Joh.
Christoph Bach's, Johann Friedrich Alberti (1642-1710),
Organist at Merseburg, availed himself of the melody of
" O lux beata Trinitas" for a series of three compositions of
this kind.[123] We here find the form already highly developed;
indeed, Alberti is regarded as one of the best musicians of
that period. The first movement takes for the theme of the
fugue only the six first notes, in a dotted rhythm which,
in the course of its development, undergoes a few further
variations. The parts are neatly and skilfully worked out,
as they are in all the movements. The counterpoint, it is
true, is generally note against note, not from want of skill,
but only to reserve an enhanced elaboration for the following
movement, while the return of the stretto, quite at the
beginning of the third section, is, on the contrary, quite

---

[121] Adlung, Anl. zur mus. Gel., p. 184. Note *m*.

[122] Published by G. W. Körner in the Orgel-Virtuos, No. 65.

[123] These lie before me in Walther's handwriting. Comp. Körner's Orgel-
Virtuos, No. 65.

in the old style. The entrance of the theme is each time
distinctly indicated by a pause before it, and short interludes also afford a special preparation for it. Then the
whole first line, in semibreves, constitutes the theme of
the second verse, to which is added a short counter-
subject in crotchets, repeated in double counterpoint. The
theme recurs but four times in the whole movement; it is
heard, slow and majestic, through the stirring busy crowd
of parts; the counter-subject serves for long interludes,
while it also accompanies the theme throughout the artistically managed imitation. The third verse finally owes its
enhanced effect to a fugal arrangement of the first line in 3-4
time. A chorale fugue treated in a similar way to the second
verse, in "Gelobet seist du, Jesu Christ"—"All praise to
Thee, Lord Jesu Christ,"[124]—is no less admirable. The
counter-subject is first gone through by itself before being
combined with the line of the chorale, and it consists of
an idea complete in itself, so that a fully worked-out double
fugue is the result.

Johann Christoph Bach, following his natural bent, pursued his own path through this department of music, and, so
far as we are now able to judge, never departed from it. The
result was the same as with his vocal compositions. The next
generation knew him no more—did not understand him, and
ignored him altogether. Comprehensive collections of chorale preludes made with his own hand by Walther, the
lexicographer, Sebastian Bach's colleague at Weimar, include
not a single piece by Joh. Christoph Bach, and do not even
mention them. Eight such arrangements, some of them with
more than one movement, are contained in a volume which
was formerly in Gerber's possession, but which vanished and
left no trace when, after his death, his valuable musical collection was dispersed.[125] By a happy accident, however, a

---

[124] Which is also extant in Walther's MSS.

[125] Gerber speaks of this volume in the Lexicon, Vol. I., cols. 208-209. The
whole of the collection, however, was not lost. Part was purchased by Hofrath
André, of Offenbach; compare the 'Catalogue CXII.,' 1876, issued by Albert
Cohn, of Berlin; particularly No. VI. Some of his collection is to be found in
the Royal Library at Berlin.

manuscript book of that time has been preserved with forty-four arrangements of chorales.   Its contents were collected by the compiler for a special end, and, if the title it now bears is the original, the little work must have been published.[126] On this we shall have to found our judgment. But first of all it must be said that the case is here quite different to what it was when discussing him as a composer of vocal music.   In that he had a grand tradition behind him, and on its broad surface he could unfold his own essential characteristics; in writing for the organ he was treading on half-tilled soil, over a half-beaten road.   All that he thus created in his isolated position is found, after due consideration, to be neither unworthy of his great talents nor in any contradiction to the praise awarded to him, even as a master of the organ, by the later and greater members of his family.[127] But one single man cannot do everything, and Joh. Christoph is a striking instance of how much we owe to the Italians, even in that most German of all forms of music, the organ chorale.   A yearning after an ideal thoughtfulness, profound care for details—these there was no need to borrow from foreigners; but the sense of beauty as revealing itself in the frankest and grandest forms was needed to sustain and invigorate us ere we could create anything truly masterly.   Such succour soon came flowing in from the south, but Joh. Christoph seems to have shut himself in

---

[126] This is a MS. of about A.D. 1700, in small oblong quarto, now in my possession. The title is " *CHORAELE* | welche | bey wärenden Gottes Dienst zum *Praeambuliren* | gebrauchet werden können | gesetzet | und | herausgegeben | von | *Johann Christoph Bachen* | *Organ : in* Eisenach." (Chorals which may be used as *preambles* during Divine service, composed and published by J. C. Bach.) Below, to the right, is the name, now illegible, of the transcriber and owner. Bach's chorales constitute only the first part of the book, and then, in the same writing, follow a number of other chorale pieces. The book subsequently often changed owners, each of whom busied himself, according to his powers, in filling the pages that remained blank.   Also we may conclude from this title-page that Walther's statement, that nothing of Joh. Christoph Bach's was printed, must be incorrect.

[127] The observation in the Musikalische Bibliothek, Vol. IV., 1, p. 159, that he never can have played in less than five real parts, is a mythical exaggeration. Of all these forty-four chorales, which he certainly must have played, not a single one is in five parts

against it, and so his works remained mere offshoots, unproductive of blossom and fruit.

Bach, indeed, was never in the dark as to the requirements of a chorale treatment from the side of mere *technique*. The organ, with its echoing masses of chords, produced by one man and progressing at his sole will and pleasure, was the most complete conceivable contrast to the ancient chorale music, that rich and complicated tangle of so many individual voices which could never altogether become mere instruments. This, more than anything else, brought about the transformation from the old polyphonic to the new harmonic system. It may, perhaps, seem strange to many readers, and yet it is quite natural, that even the best masters, between 1650 and 1700, showed a much more homophonic spirit, a much more independent treatment of the vocal parts than is compatible with the pure organ style, according to our modern conception of it. Of course the rigid and heavy quality of the organ does not require for its highest idealisation mere external movement—as attained by runs and the spreading of chords—but an inner vitality from the creation of musical entities—for what else can we call melody and motive?—and by their intelligent reciprocity. But this is always a secondary, not, as in polyphonic vocal music, a primary consideration. We admire with justice the organic structure of an organ piece by Sebastian Bach, every smallest detail of it instinct with vital purpose; but the so-called polyphonic treatment, which clothes the firm harmonic structure, is but a beautiful drapery. It resembles a Gothic cathedral, with its groups of columns that seem a spontaneous growth, and its capitals wreathed with flowers and leaves; they call up to our fancy the seeming of independent life, but they do not live, only the artist lives in them. This radical distinction cannot be sufficiently insisted on; without a comprehension of it the whole realm of organ music as an independent art, and all that has any connection with it, including the whole of Sebastian Bach's work, cannot be understood.

When, therefore, Joh. Christoph Bach deliberately widened

the breach, he showed that he knew what needed to be done. The progression of the parts is often quite untraceable; chords occur now in three parts and then in four, in obedience to purely harmonic requirements; only in a few cases can we discern what is intended for the pedal or the manual bass, and in a fugato the very part which had the theme not unfrequently repeats it immediately, a fifth lower. Everywhere the feeling is clearly prominent that the whole conduct of the piece lies in the hands of a single individual. But these concessions made by Bach to instrumental style are but external; he remained a stranger to the essential spirit of chorale treatment for the organ. He now should have boldly ventured to raise the chorale to be an independent motive, as the core and basis of a freely wrought composition; he should have liberated himself from the idea that he must set his arrangement of the chorale in a necessary connection with the congregational hymn that belonged to it, and regard it as a prelude in the strictest sense of the word, leading up to the main subject. This, however, never occurred to him, and so nothing could he originate but feeble vacillating forms without any balance or centre of gravity. If we examine these forms more closely, we find that in twenty-one of the preludes the whole melody is taken up; in ten, a mere *complexus* of the first lines; in the others, the first is used in the way we have seen, as the theme of a fugue, and the second line is heard occasionally, or comes in at the close, but not fugally treated. Arrangements of the whole melody always begin with a fugato of the first line or of the first two, quite short interludes sometimes preparing us for the leads; the following lines are then usually worked out in close canon, for which a pedal-point is used as a favourite basis; but we also frequently find an extension or dissection of the theme, thus forming separate subjects, or a more or less characteristic transformation of the principal features of the melody, and between these again freely invented smaller subjects of a more lively character.

These compositions are far removed from that broad motett treatment which calmly develops each movement of the melody; it is always the chorale *as a whole* which

has floated before the composer's mind as the subject of
his arrangement; the separate lines are briefly and hastily
dealt with, and the hearer, who knows the melody—as he is
always supposed to do—feels at the close as though it had
passed over him, as it were, involved in mist. The counterpoint is usually of very simple construction, note against note,
and running in thirds and sixths; the harmonic principle of
organ composition is often intentionally insisted on when
chords are held in the upper parts and a fugal theme goes on
in the bass. It is easy to see that the composer is struggling
after a form, and in some few movements he may be said
to have succeeded. These indeed are of no great length;
but the arrangement, for instance, of " Ich dank dir schon
durch deinen Sohn," which flows smoothly on in 3-8 time,
reproduces the whole of the choral. He also displays
his feeling for form in the way in which he often entwines
the lines of the melody, bringing in one as contrapuntal to
its predecessor ; or attacks the closing cadence at once, or,
finally, holds the harmonic progression together by the use
of a pedal-point. But, from an excessive consideration for
the conditions of his art, he deprived himself of the right to
construct a musical work in accordance with his own innate
requirements. Now it is the taste of the composer, and
not any inherent law, which demands that here a line shall
suddenly appear in double augmentation, and there be
extended, at least in some of its tones ; that here a section
of the melody is heard in an ornamental and there in its
original form; that precisely in one arrangement the close
shall run off into elaborate passages, and precisely in
another a long episode shall be introduced.[128] If we wholly
set aside the grand sense of unity in these matters of such
a man as Sebastian Bach, it is quite intelligible why even
Joh. Christoph's contemporaries could go no further in this
direction.

The method of chorale treatment, by which only a few

---

[128] One of these pieces which, however, is not one of the most characteristic, is
published in G. W. Körner's Praeludien-Buch, Vol. II., No. 2. A chorale
fugue on " Wir glauben all an einen Gott " is also to be found in Ritter's Kunst
des Orgelspiels, Part III., p. 3.

lines of the chorale are carried through, contains still fewer
germs of development, although the composer here occasionally showed more wealth of resource. For here there is
neither the poetic unity of the whole chorale structure, nor
the musical unity of a composition based on one theme,
and these were in fact the two pillars round which the
whole art of organ chorales clung and grew. In the third
class, finally, which we have called the chorale fugue, he
already trod a more beaten track, and consequently his productions in this department are relatively his best. The
treatment is as facile and unforced as any writer could have
made it who had a perfectly clear understanding of the character of his instrument. At the same time they fully bear out
the character of the "*preamble*," and are precisely light enough
not to throw into the background the musical importance of
the congregational singing that was to follow. Most of them
are quite up to the highest level that could, during that
century, be attained in the solution of such problems, and in
this particular line it can be shown that Joh. Christoph had
imitators. If sometimes their harmonies are somewhat
rigid, and the movement rather too stiff, they may still
be regarded as models—allowance being made, of course,
for the period. It is not very easy to estimate Joh. Christoph Bach justly, and without prejudice, even from the
whole contents of the volume, and it is he himself who
makes judgment so difficult by the great perfection of his vocal
compositions. Any one coming fresh from these upon the
chorale preludes will at first meet with constant disappoint-
ment. The whole distance between a highly developed art
and one in its first stage of uncertainty lies before us, and
to modern feeling seems all the greater because we have
long been accustomed to enjoy the most splendid fruits of
both branches—the vocal and instrumental—side by side and
together. Even the hypothesis that these may be works of
the master's youth is amply refuted by one circumstance :
that the chorale " Liebster Jesu, wir sind hier," is to be
found among the chorale arrangements. This hymn was
not known before 1671,[129] and indeed the whole collection

---

[129] Koch's Geschichte des Kirchenlieds, I., 3, p. 355 (third edition).

could hardly have been made before the middle of that decade, within which Bach had already written some of his noblest motetts.

The meagreness and shallowness which is sometimes characteristic of this (usually) three-part harmony must not lead us to the conclusion that the master was purposely writing easy music for some beginner, perhaps his own musical sons. We may, indeed, readily believe that he has not displayed in them all his powers; but this certainly is not for any educational purpose, but because the character of the compositions, as he proposed to work them out, did not seem to afford grounds for it. Besides, they were published expressly for use during divine service, and three-part movements were customary for such purposes at even a later period. Nothing, in short, can be said but that he could not write them otherwise than as we find them. And if we still must wonder that a man who, as a vocal composer, displayed such wealth and vitality, should here show such poverty of harmony and such halting rhythm, it is because we do not consider the wide difference between a body of singers, which, even with very little harmonic variety, is capable of infinite gradations of light and colour, and can even translate words and phrases into music—a very strong point with Joh. Christoph—and the organ, which within the limits of a single note can never vary in force, and even in rhythm only in an exceptional way, but produces these effects by the succession of different qualities of tone. Once more it must be said Bach understood the full extent of that difference; and he, who in the chorale "Warum betrübst du dich, mein Herz"—"Why art thou saddened, oh my heart?"—treated the vocal counterpoint in so beautiful and striking a manner, could only arrange it for the organ in the form and style which we find at the end of this collection, and with full conviction of its rightness. And we cannot but recognise that he devoted himself to the task, particularly in the diligently worked out and melancholy chromatic motive.[130] That he opened up no new path in this form of

---

[130] See Supplement I.

music is due to his reserved nature, which was averse to
all the influences of his time. Indeed, had it been otherwise
we should not have had his motetts. What else he may
have produced for the organ cannot be determined in the
absence of further evidence.

Five chorale arrangements by Joh. Michael Bach are
before me in manuscript—a very small number, but still sufficient to throw light on his position as compared with his
brother and his contemporaries. Michael was more pervious to
fresh influences, and he also seems to have occupied himself
more with instrumental music in general than Joh. Christoph.
Walther says of him that "he, too, composed sonatas for
instruments and pieces for the clavier." Hence his works
have shown a much longer vitality, and so late as in the
second half of the eighteenth century his chorale preludes
were still known, though they were no longer considered of
much importance. In Gerber's volume of selections above
mentioned, there were no less than seventy-two chorales
treated in various ways, many of them followed by six, eight,
or ten variations. "There is great variety and multiplicity in
these preludes, for the age in which they were written, and
not one is unworthy of the name of Bach." This opinion,
written by Gerber in the first year of our century, is the only
trace of their existence that survives; Walther's four MSS.
may have been written about 1730. But in order to understand the difference between the brothers we must first devote
some attention to the man who, in the last twenty years of
the seventeenth century, helped above all others to advance
the art of organ music, and who was closely connected both
with Thuringia and with the Bach family.

Johann Pachelbel, born September 1, 1653, at Nüremberg,
cultivated his admirable musical and general talents first at
Nüremberg, Altorf, and Regensburg. He was then for three
years Assistant-Organist to the Church of St. Stephen at
Vienna, and came to Eisenach as Court Organist May 4,
1677. Here he remained till May 18, 1678, and then became Organist to the Prediger Kirche in Erfurt, where, as we
have seen, after the death of Johann Bach, in 1673, Johann
Effler had officiated for a few years. He was the predecessor

of Michael Bach at Gehren, and we shall again have occasion
to mention him among the organists of Weimar. Pachelbel
remained longer at Erfurt than in any other place in the
course of his chequered life; it was not till 1690 that he
quitted it to become Court Organist at Stuttgart; from 1692
to 1695 he was again in Thuringia, at Gotha, and passed the
remainder of his life as Organist to the Church of St. Sebal-
dus, in his native city; dying March 3, 1706.[131] As a resident in
two of the chief centres of the Bach family in succession, he
had ample opportunity of coming in contact with this race
(and clan) of musicians. He was on such intimate terms
with Sebastian's father as to be chosen by him to be
godfather to one of his daughters and teacher to his eldest
son, and the chorale treatments which remain to us by
Bernard, son of Aegidius Bach, are of unmistakable Pachelbel
stamp throughout; we shall find other proofs of their intimate acquaintance as we proceed.

His constant changes of residence between South and
Central Germany had an essential effect on Pachelbel's
art, by giving rise in him to the amalgamation of various
tendencies. The style of chorale treatment which was
principally practised in Thuringia and Saxony, found
in the skeleton of the church hymn a form offering, it
is true, a poetic rather than a musical unity; but it
ran the risk of being decomposed by such handling into
incoherent fragments. With that feeling, so especially
characteristic of Italy, for grand and simple forms,
towards which the very being of the organ pointed, and
in far more favourable circumstances, Italy and South
Germany under direct Italian influence, had far out-
stripped North Germany in the art of organ music.
Frescobaldi, Organist to the Church of St. Peter at

---

[131] Mattheson, in the Ehrenpforte, pp. 244-249, has done important service
in clearing up the details of Pachelbel's life; which had got into great confusion
in Walther's Lexicon. Even here his stay in Eisenach is wrongly stated as
lasting three years, while in fact he was there exactly one year and fourteen days,
as we learn from the yearly accounts of the Royal Exchequer, now in the
archives of Weimar. Pachelbel was at first granted a salary of forty thalers
a year, raised in 1678 to sixty thalers.

Rome, had, so early as in the first half of the century, risen to a height of mastery, which, in certain points— for instance, in the skilful contrapuntal treatment of a *cantus firmus*—was scarcely surpassed by any Catholic organ-master of later date. In the toccata, by careful elaboration, a form had at last been worked out which contained in itself nearly all that the art had then achieved— fugues, free imitations, brilliant ornamental passages, and the mighty flow of chord progressions. This summit, fairly represented by Georg Muffat's grand work, *Apparatus Musico Organisticus* (1690), and by the collection of toccatas published by Joh. Speth,[182] had been reached by the end of the century; what remained to be done it was beyond the powers of the Catholic organists to achieve. The motive supplied by the Protestant chorale was lacking to them; the Gregorian chant, which Frescobaldi handled so efficiently and effectively for the organ, founded as it was on solo declamation and the church modes, was opposed in its very essence to that richer development in the new harmonic system, by which alone the full expansion of instrumental music became possible. In the Protestant chorale, on the contrary, that fresh and native growth from the heart of the people, organ music was destined to find the natural element which the Roman nationalities could not supply to it, that pure and unsophisticated essence which penetrated and invigorated all its branches. Nor was it merely an abundant flow of new melodic inventions that sprang from this source; quite new forms of art grew on and from it; an undreamed-of wealth of harmonic combinations was discovered, and possibilities of instrumental polyphony hitherto unknown. Pachelbel carried these achievements of the south into the heart of Germany, took possession of the elements he there found ready to his hand, and from the two constructed something newer and finer. Nowhere better than in Thuringia could his genius have met with

---

[182] Organisch-Instrumentalischer Kunst-, Zier- und Lustgarten. Augsburg, 1693. Republished by Fr. Commer: Compositionen für die Orgel aus dem 16, 17 18, Jahrhundert, Part V. (Leipzig: Geissler.)

men capable of welcoming it with unbiassed minds, and with
a greater capacity for furthering it on its way.   From
this time forth the focus of German organ music lay undoubtedly in Central Germany; the south fell off more and
more; the north, with Dietrich Buxtehude at its head,
preserved its position somewhat longer, and even constructed
a certain chorale treatment of its own, which, however,
lagged far behind that of Central Germany in variety and
depth.   History, however, retains a memory of a personage
older than Pachelbel—J. J. Froberger, of Halle, who no
doubt largely assimilated the southern spirit, and, so far
as I have at present discovered, did not even make any
use of chorales; he nevertheless was held in great respect
by the organists of Central Germany and even by Sebastian
Bach.

How truly Pachelbel stood above all his contemporaries
as a writer for the organ in the southern style is best
shown by his toccatas; and at the same time we may
see even in these that a more powerful and soaring spirit
already possessed him.   For while he leaves their general
character unaltered, which aims at brilliancy, *bravura*, and
the elaboration of broad masses of harmony, he has nevertheless abandoned the motley variety of slow and rapid
movements, fugal and not fugal, simple and ornamental, of
which their contents were commonly made up.   The finest
and best of his toccatas generally run on in constant
movement, built and elaborated on one or more figures,
and usually supported by a few long held pedal-points.
Thus, one of them rests entirely on C for fifteen bars, on
G fourteen bars, and on C again seventeen bars, and is
grandly thought out on this motive—

Another, even finer and more flowing, has first a pedal-
point on C, sixteen bars, then passes by the chord of $\frac{6}{5}$ on
F sharp to G; after remaining there for ten bars it modulates
through F E A to G; here there is a pedal-point for six bars,

and it closes with another on C six bars; the movement of
the upper parts is at first in semiquavers, then it increases to
triplets of semiquavers, and finally to demisemiquavers. Two
more splendid pieces of this kind are a toccata in G minor
and one in F major; the first is on G for seventeen bars, D
for twenty bars, and returns in the last bar to G; the upper
parts at first rush up and down in passages of thirds and
sixths, but presently calm down into arpeggiato chords and
slow waves of harmony. The second is, perhaps, the finest of
all, in its majestic plan and the proud culmination of the
theme; in it we have the precursor of that truly gigantic
toccata in F major by Sebastian Bach.[133]

A chaconne in D minor, of which the bass

is repeated 'thirty-five times, has the same broad character,
full of style, though for inspiration and harmonic richness
it cannot bear comparison with similar works by Buxtehude.

In the field of chorale arrangements Pachelbel deserves
the credit of having brought selection, order, and dignity to
bear on the abundant but uncultured offshoots of organ
music in Central Germany, and of having diverted the tide
of southern beauty to flood the channels of German artistic
feeling. The progress made after his appearance on the
scene is quite remarkable, and perceptible at the first glance.
The direction which this branch of art had to take was that
of every æsthetically constructed form. It had to grow to
independent vitality, freeing itself from those external and
fortuitous conditions to which it owed its existence. Origi-

---

[133] B.-G. XV., p. 154. These two last-mentioned works of Pachelbel are
published by Franz Commer, *Musica Sacra*, Vol. I., Nos. 136, 128 (Berlin: Bote
and Bock). Nos. 48 to 144 of this series are all by Pachelbel, and the originals
used by Commer are partly printed and partly MSS., in the Library of the Royal
Institute for Church Music at Berlin. A few others are published by G. W.
Körner, of Erfurt, in Part 340 of the Orgel-Virtuos, and in Part I. of the
collected edition of Pachelbel's compositions for the organ (no more published).
Besides these a rich mass of MS. material lies before me.

nally intended only as an introduction or prelude suited to the feeling of the congregational hymn, its only value arose from its fitness and connection with that. Separate fragments and concords borrowed from a familiar melody sounded in the hearer's ear; these passages were to him inseparable from the accompanying poetry, and led his feelings in a certain direction, so that when the hymn was raised they blossomed out full and clear.

Art could here produce her result in two different ways. Either a conspicuous feature of the melody might be selected—the first line perhaps—as the theme, and a purely musical composition might be built up upon it; then the chorale itself could only indicate the fundamental feeling which pervaded the whole work. This was the most obvious method; practical usage had already pointed it out. The difference between a fugue designed for a prelude, and a work constructed on a chorale motive is only this—that the former has no meaning nor purpose excepting in connection with the hymn that is to follow, while the latter offers an independent organism, and therefore proceeds to exhaust the thematic source while the former is merely meant to indicate it. Or else the whole melody was transferred to the organ, and was accepted with all the attributes which characterised it in its church function as associated with a religious poem, as a means of general edification, and as an integral portion of public worship, and thus gave rise to a kind of ideal devotion in the region of pure instrumental music of which the melody was really the heart and centre. It is plain that this process is far behind the former one as to universal intelligibility, since too much of what is offered to our perceptions lies outside the essential nature of the melody; and only a very well-defined poetical basis can throw the tone-poet's purpose and feeling into clear relief. But almost infinite room was open for lavish and deeply elaborated development; and the subjective piety of the time found in this form many more and happier opportunities for weaving in its mystical impulses, and following them out to their subtlest issues, than in the bare simplicity of a congregational hymn. The working out of this branch of art, so closely connected with the church, ran parallel to the modification in ecclesiastical feeling; and the less men cared to unite in uttering a strong congregational sentiment in the unction of a church hymn, the more it was left to the organ chorale to express the intimate feeling of individuals. The fact that the chorale even then was practically used as a prelude in divine worship does not alter these conditions. If now the melody of the chorale was to serve as the core—the spirit of such a musical meditation, it was indispensable that it should be conspicuous throughout the music; that it should soar above it all; concentrate it in itself; throw out from itself all its vital germs. These on their part had to develop into members of the melody on every side, however diverse; to group them into constantly fresh and pregnant shades of tone; and, to make all perfect, some consciousness of the feeling of the words had to find a faint utterance through the expression of the musical composition. In order to effect all this they were obliged to move with the utmost possible independence, in obedience to the law that the freer the servant the more honoured is the master.

At the time of his best maturity Pachelbel published eight chorale treatments (apparently at Nuremberg, through Johann Christoph Weigel, 1693) which probably indicate the highest level of his achievements in that line.[134] Most of them are so constructed that the separate lines of the melody are slowly and clearly carried through either the upper or lower part. The subject is rigidly confined to three or four parts, so that at each fresh lead of the melody the richest harmonies arise, and it is thus thrown into greater relief. Every line is introduced by a short passage of imitation deriving its material from the first notes of the line itself, and so preparing us for it; but always in double or fourfold diminution, so that the effect of the chorale may not be weakened by it, but be conspicuously distinct even in rhythm. The contrapuntal figures themselves, however, are not derived from this, but are of independent origin; still, but

---

[134] Fr. Commer, Nos. 48-55.

one or only a few figures are adhered to, which proceed and react by reciprocal imitation. This passage—

&c.

from the chorale "Wie schön leucht't uns der Morgenstern"
—"How brightly shines the morning star,"—representing the last line of the verse, will elucidate this. In the first bar the first three notes of the melody are sounded in preparation, F, E, D; then they recur in the pedal, and the upper parts play above them a passage of imitation in a manner very frequent with Pachelbel; he often repeats even the parallel motion that we find here; the highest grade of contrapuntal free treatment is not yet attained. It is also a defect that the interlude is not of a piece with the counterpoint; otherwise, the flow of the parts is already very easy, smooth, and unforced, and at the same time thoroughly adapted to the organ; and we know that he insisted on a *cantabile* style of composition, even in his pupils, which can mean nothing different from this.[135] The composer rarely goes into the construction of the contrapuntal themes on the material of the text of the melody. The cheerful, pastoral effect of it in the chorale "Vom Himmel hoch" is perhaps unique, and here a field but little cultivated was still left open to the profound genius of Sebastian Bach.

---

[135] As we are told by J. H. Buttstedt, in his work: *Ut, Re, Mi,* &c., *tota Musica et Harmonia Æterna.* Erfurt, 1716, p. 58.

Pachelbel's own manner, indeed, predominates so greatly in his chorales, and where it occurs in the works of his contemporaries the influence of his music is recognisable by so many other tokens as well, that we may unhesitatingly assert that they followed him, and the whole method may with justice be designated as his. For, although attempts in this direction occur at an earlier period, it was certainly he who, by his superior talent and feeling for form, amalgamated the scattered elements to form an artistic whole. He less frequently treated the chorale melody contrapuntally, but still with much mastery, carrying it on in a continuous course without interludes—if we apply the term, as is usually done, to independent phrases however short, but not to a figure which occupies perhaps but a single bar, and only derives its significance from the foregoing counterpoint. Of this treatment—not to go beyond the chorale works above mentioned—the arrangement of " Nun lob mein Seel den Herren "—" My soul, now praise thy Maker,"[136]— may be quoted as an example ; it is also remarkable because the melody lies in the middle part, a task not often attempted at that time. He rarely carries through the chorale in such a way as that the upper part lends play of colour, or with interludes between the lines, and in these respects he is inferior in taste and delicacy of treatment to Buxtehude and his pupils ; but he has enhanced the artistic value of his own manner by the way in which, in a number of admirable works, he graces the chorale with a fugue on the first line of the melody. We see from this how firm a grasp the master had of his ideal—namely, the transfiguration of the chorale, with all its sacred and ecclesiastical associations, to a purely artistic work, regarding it, as it were, as an object of natural beauty to be dealt with by his art. The introductory fugue is in the manner of a prelude, only it is more freely and richly worked out. It bears the same relation to a chorale fugue by Joh. Christoph Bach that an idealised work does to bare realism ; nay, we need

---

[136] Fr. Commer, No. 50.

only compare it with one of Pachelbel's own smaller chorale fugues, intended simply for practical use in the church service, to feel the wide difference between them. The chorale arrangement following the fugue appears by contrast as the main subject, treated with every variety of means at the master's command. The melody is heard in augmentation, often majestically filled up in the bass by octaves, and brilliant and expressive figures entwine and blossom above and around it. Some of the finest are the workings out of " Allein Gott in der Höh sei Ehr," "Vom Himmel hoch," " Nun komm der Heiden Heiland,"[137] and " Christ lag in Todesbanden ";[138] others are more simple but not less admirable.

No more need be said concerning the independent fugues founded on chorales, since they are in all essentials alike, and only differ at the close.[139] But with regard to the fugue form itself, I must take this opportunity of adding a few words. Frescobaldi has been called the inventor of it, but this only really means that he was the first to employ the fugal style of playing on established principles of art. The high position held by this master has already been admitted ; still the form could not be fully developed excepting under a general acceptance of the harmonic system, because it was this which first made the genetic connection between the leading subject and its associates actual and perceptible, and enabled the composer to construct an instrumental work on purely musical lines and possessing an organic symmetry of its own. Then it was that the *Quinten-Fuge* (*i.e.*, a fugue in which the answer is on the fifth above) first grew—undoubtedly the most perfect of those forms—out of all the *canzone, capriccios,* and *fantasias,* by which names everything fugally treated had until then been called, without any perceptible or essential difference. The best things produced by the later

---

[137] Commer, Nos. 122, 143, 144.
[138] Körner, Pachelbel's Orgel-Compositionen, Part I., No. 1.
[139] Such an one may be seen in Commer's edition, No. 53 ; in Körner's, No. 5.

Catholic masters of the organ are to be found in their toccatas. The seventh toccata of the work mentioned above, by Georg Muffat, closes with a fugue in which no less than four extremely pleasing themes are very skilfully worked out; and in the second, fourth, and sixth toccatas, capital fugues occur as distinct portions, not to speak of the free imitative subjects scattered throughout; but the great distance at which they stand from the fugal writing of the later school of Central Germany is at once evident. The harmonic basis of the themes is far simpler; it often can only be termed a system not of counterpoint, but of chords which rather seem to carry the motives than to alternate with them independently. As has been repeatedly said, it was indispensable for the development of organ music that the new tone-system should first be firmly established, and then the nature of the instrument tended inevitably to a scheme of polyphony, which, though radically different from the vocal polyphony of the fifteenth and sixteenth centuries, still seemed to resemble it. But all the means to this end which masters of the organ had been able to derive from the treatment of the Protestant chorales were wanting in the artists of the south—not merely the suppleness of the harmonies, and the intimacy and the independence of the contrapuntal parts, but also a firm and deliberate entrance of the themes which, particularly in the works of Sebastian Bach, always stand forth like a distinct personality with unforgettable features. In Muffat, and other writers, there is something painful in their first appearance, as though they dared not come forth boldly. They seek support from the companion passages which are presently brought in, and so they are soon lost, their close disappearing in a common phrase. It follows from this also that the whole number of parts is not always carried through to the end, and often the parts come in or cease at need, merely to help out the harmony. Pachelbel made great progress in this direction. In the form and attitude particularly of the theme at its first entrance, he already trod the path afterwards pursued by Sebastian Bach and Handel, and his counterpoint is often full of rich vitality, though, no doubt, it is often stiff and unmeaning. The following example will serve as an illustration :[140]—

Pachelbel had a number of disciples in Thuringia, some his personal pupils, others through his influence only. Among the former was J. H. Buttstedt (1666-1727), who succeeded his master at the Prediger Church at Erfurt, and who is known, to his disadvantage, by his lawsuit with Mattheson as to his Neueröffnetem Orchestre; but he was a great master of his instrument, and a remarkable composer of organ chorales and fugues.[141] Then there was Nikolaus Vetter, born 1666, who was still Organist at Rudolstadt (1730), and also did honour to his teacher. In more or less close relation to Pachebel were Andreas Armstroff, who died young (1670-1699), an Organist at Erfurt; Johann Graff, Organist at Magdeburg (died 1709); and of the succeeding generation the more important of those who followed in his footsteps were Georg Kauffmann (1679-1735), a pupil of Buttstedt; the gifted Gottfried Kirchhoff (1685-1746), Organist at Halle; and, above all, Johann Gottfried Walther, of Weimar (1684-1748). His influence made itself felt, by degrees, throughout Thuringia and Saxony, and hence even by the Bach family; indeed, one of its members, the eldest brother of Sebastian, was one of his pupils, and so perhaps was Bernhard Bach, afterwards Organist at Eisenach. Still the Bach family was too innately independent

---

[140] The whole fugue occurs in Commer, No. 124, but the case is the same with many others.

[141] I have sought in vain in Erfurt for his published vocal compositions. mentioned by Walther. It would be worth some trouble to bring them to light again.

ever to give itself up entirely to any external direction, and
this was the very reason why, at a subsequent date, it was
able to produce a still greater and more comprehensive genius.
Indeed, in Joh. Christoph Bach, who lived with Pachelbel for
some time in Eisenach, his influence was never in any way
perceptible; probably the converse may rather have been the
case. Still Michael Bach availed himself of Pachelbel's
method, and certain circumstances point to a personal
acquaintance between these two artists.

Thus, the five organ pieces by Michael Bach remaining to
us are treatments of the chorales " Allein Gott in der Höh
sei Ehr "—" Glory to God alone on high " ; " Wenn mein
Stündlein vorhanden ist"—" If my last hour is now at hand ";
" Nun freut euch, lieben Christen g'mein "—" Sing and be glad,
all Christian folk "; " In dich hab ich gehoffet, Herr "[142]—" In
Thee, O Lord, is all my hope," and " Dies sind die heilgen
zehn Gebot "—" These ten are God's most holy laws." The
two last are quite in the style above designated as Pachelbel's.
Since both Joh. Christoph and Pachelbel himself worked up
the chorale " In dich hab ich," it is easy to see, by comparison, how far behind the other two Joh. Christoph Bach
remained in the flexibility and melody of his counterpoint.
Only the beginning of each arrangement is here given :—

---

[142] I owe my knowledge of this to Herr Ritter, Musical Director in Magdeburg.
It is to be found in the Orgel-Journal of Mannheim, Vol. I., Part 7, and
came from Ch. H. Rinck, a pupil of Kittel's.

In the third piece Michael Bach treats the chorale melody as it goes on, contrapuntally, in a truly fine and flowing manner, striving to keep closely to certain figures, and preluding the whole with a short fugue on the first line.

The two first-named chorales exhibit no clearly worked out form; they are less defined and perfect. The second gives out the first line once, in three parts. After a short interlude the second line comes in without any fugal treatment. Two bars of interlude follow, bringing in the *cantus firmus* of both lines in the pedal, but not in double augmentation. Then comes the first line of the refrain, once imitated, and then the second, followed by the pedal in canon; and finally the third in the same manner. Thus the first line of the second half of the tune does not occur at all in the pedal; the piece has no culminating point and no arrangement. When we compare Pachelbel's treatment of the same melody, which, in his favourite way, has the full and richly figured chorale preceded by a chorale fugue, it would seem as though Michael Bach had produced a not very happy imitation of it. And though Pachelbel does not introduce the *cantus firmus* in augmentation, he has succeeded in giving it value and relief by other means; for instance, by richer figuration.[143] This Michael Bach has neglected. "Allein Gott in der Höh," in short, is so treated that one line is always carried on fugally on the " Rückpositiv ";[144] and then this same line, sometimes in combination with the next, is introduced in the simplest four-part harmony on the " Oberwerk."[144] But even this is not a central idea of form, for what ought to have been effected by truly artistic means is here produced by mere alternations of tone; or, if the simple chorale subject indicates congregational singing, the true significance of a church service has been misunderstood, and it has been transferred to the domain of ideal art, where a quite different standard prevails. This is not to be done by mere realistic copying.

---

[143] Compare, for instance, No. 134 in Commer.

[144] These are the names of two of the manuals in a German organ. The " Rückpositiv " answers in some measure to our " Choir organ," and the " Oberwerk " or upper manual to our swell. *See* Translators' Preface.

Zachau, again, the teacher of Handel, though fifteen years younger, gives us a similar treatment in " Was mein Gott will, das g'scheh allzeit," " Erbarm dich mein, o Herre Gott," and " Vater unser im Himmelreich." So Michael Bach was not singular in his misconception.

The suggestion just now put forward, that Joh. Christoph Bach's peculiar greatness cannot have failed to influence Pachelbel, although he, as an organist, far surpassed the elder master, is founded in the first place on a treatment of the chorale " Warum betrübtst du dich, mein Herz "—" Why art thou saddened, oh my heart? " [145]—in which Pachelbel shows a resemblance that can scarcely be accidental with the above-mentioned work on the same subject, which closes the collection of chorales by Joh. Christoph Bach. At the first occurrence of the sixth and seventh notes of the melody Bach introduces a dotted figure of quavers, in place of which he eventually puts in a chromatic figure, to signify the " saddened " heart. Such playing round his theme is of frequent occurrence with him, while Pachelbel, on the contrary, is wont to leave the lines of the melody unaltered, but to introduce fugal movements. In the arrangement before us he has the transformed figures likewise, and by carrying them consistently through the whole of the chorale fugue he justifies their introduction. Nay, more, even the chromatic motive is turned to account as a counter-subject, though not in the theme ; such references in the chorale fugue to the inner parts of the hymn are not usual with him. Thus the whole work is not only one of the master's finest, but takes a distinct place among others of the same kind and character.[146]

On the strength of this result another conjecture may perhaps be hazarded, namely, that Pachelbel was incited by Joh. Christoph's collection of chorale preludes to attempt a similar work. He did, in fact, collect a series of 160 chorale

---

[145] Published by Körner, Orgel-Virtuos, No. 340. There is yet another and also very beautiful arrangement by him, with the *cantus firmus* in the bass, but which, so far as I know, has never been published.

[146] Walther, too, treated the melody, as based on Pachelbel, with rich chromatic passages, in direct and counter movement with an ornate *cantus firmus*.

melodies, principally for domestic use, with figured-basses, in a *Tabulaturbuch*, and to half of these he added short chorale fugues as preludes.[147] These are quite of the same character as Bach's works, briefly and lightly suggesting the tune, and so forming a very fitting preparation for the congregational singing; only, as might be expected, we find a more free and flowing manner than in Bach. And what is particularly remarkable is, that in the hymn " Warum betrübtst du dich, mein Herz," a chorale fugue is introduced and even the dotted figure. If this view is the correct one, it becomes plain with how little justice it has been asserted on the other hand that Bach learnt of Pachelbel, even in vocal choral music.[148] That this is most unlikely is self-evident, for Bach was twelve years the elder and extremely reserved, while Pachelbel's was a highly receptive and versatile nature. But we have only to look through one of Pachelbel's motetts to find ample proof of the actual inaccuracy of such an assertion. There is hardly the remotest affinity to be detected between the facile and pleasing style of Pachelbel and the bold and thoughtful forms of Bach's work. If the tradition is to be accepted that Pachelbel " advanced the perfecting of church music,"[149] this must certainly refer to his "concerted" vocal pieces (with obbligato accompaniment of instruments,

---

[147] Tabulatur Buch | Geistlicher Gesänge | D. Martini Lutheri | und anderer Gottseliger Männer | Sambt beygefügten Choral Fugen | durchs gantze Jahr | Allen Liebhabern des Claviers componiret | von | Johann Pachelbeln, Organisten zu | S. Sebald in Nürnberg | 1704. | A MS. in oblong quarto in the Grand Ducal Library at Weimar, but not in Pachelbel's hand. Goethe took much interest in this work, and sent it to Zelter, March 27, 1824, who returned it to him eight days after with an opinion as characteristic of himself as of the book (Briefwechsel zwischen Goethe und Zelter, III., pp. 423-426). Winterfeld has given an exhaustive description of it, and five chorale fugues out of it (Ev. Kir., II., 636-642). Those on the melodies "In dich hab ich gehoffet, Herr" (fol. 84 b), and " Erhalt uns, Herr " (fol. 130 b), are only abridgments of longer arrangements. A. G. Ritter has recently proved that it is highly probable that the whole of this Tabulatur Buch is not an original work, but must be regarded as a compilation of abridged organ chorales by Pachelbel, and that these abridgments, or some of them at least, were not made by the author himself (Monatshefte für Musikges. 1874, p. 119).
[148] Winterfeld, Ev. Kir., III., 429.
[149] Walther, Lexicon, p 458. Mattheson, Ehrenpforte, p. 247.

that is to say), and particularly to the use made in them of the chorale.. Here, the *technique* he had acquired by composition for the organ stood him in good stead ; he knew how to avail himself of it with great skill for vocal style, and was in this respect the forerunner of Sebastian Bach. His cantata on the hymn by Rodigast, " Was Gott thut, das ist wohl-gethan "—of which the melody would appear to be his also— is a very remarkable example, as illustrating the state of church music in the middle of the seventeenth century.[150] We should, however, be in error in supposing him to stand alone in these works. We shall presently become acquainted with cantatas by Buxtehude which surpass those of Pachelbel, at any rate in fervency and inspiration.

The melody (in the major) of " Wo soll ich fliehen hin " perhaps affords another example of his labours as a composer of vocal church music—

Wo soll ich flie - hen hin

It must have originated at about that time ; it occurs in Pachelbel's Tabulaturbuch, where it is supplied with a chorale fugue, and it was subsequently worked up with special care by Joh. Gottfr. Walther, which is important circumstantial evidence, since we know his high esteem for Pachelbel. If he was the composer of it[151] we have here grounds for concluding that there was a close intimacy be-tween him and Michael Bach, for Bach has intervoven this tune, then but little known, in his motett " Das Blut Jesu Christi." There is yet another circumstance to be mentioned which seems to prove such an intimacy with tolerable certainty, since it strengthens the hypothesis that the intro-duction of the air into the motett was a friendly attention, and is also a further evidence of the probability of Pachelbel being the original inventor of it.

Pachelbel's versatility led him to direct his energies not only to the organ and clavier (he is said to have been the

---

[150] Part of it is given by Winterfeld, Ev. Kir., II., Musical Supplement, p. 196.

[151] As Winterfeld has already suggested, Ev. Kir., p. 639.

first who adapted the form of the French "overture" to this
instrument), but to other forms of instrumental music, and
among others the *sonata*. Of this two kinds must be distinguished : the secular sonata, adapted for chamber music, and
the sacred sonata. The latter, as a rule, preceded a piece
of vocal church music, and its actual originator was Giov.
Gabrieli. In form, of course, it had nothing in common with
the modern sonata. It was an instrumental piece in several
parts, in which the principal feature was the development of
fuller and finer harmonies, rather than the working out of
a determined theme. A favourite method was the contrasted
use of the instruments then employed in the church—violins,
cornets, and trumpets—in an antiphonal manner. Excepting
in the constantly increasing distinction in the new scheme of
keys, the essence of the church sonata altered but little in the
course of the seventeenth century. In the last decades, to be
sure, the overture form invented by Lully asserted its influence
to some extent. This form consists of a broad introductory
subject in slow time, often graced by brilliant passages, and
followed by a rapid and *agitato* fugal movement. Although
Hammerschmidt had made use of a similar contrast long
before Lully wrote his overtures, which marked an epoch,[152]
still, in later composers, the contrast of the sections is too
evidently intentional and abrupt to leave any doubt as to its
resulting from the application of a deliberate scheme of
form.[153] But even at this later period the writer was often
satisfied with a calm movement full of harmonies and sustained passages, and when a livelier movement follows (often
in triple time) it is by no means always fugally treated, but
quite as often shows only a few passages of free imitation.
This is the form we meet with in Joh. Christoph Bach's

---

[152] See the instrumental introduction to the *Dialogus*, " Wer wälzet uns den
Stein," in Part IV. of Musikalischer Andachten, No. 7.

[153] I may here name, beside Buxtehude, of whom I shall speak presently,
Philipp Heinrich Erlebach, 1657-1714, Capellmeister in Rudolstadt, whose
Gott geheiligte Singstunde (Rudolstadt, 1704), contains twelve sacred pieces
with introductory symphonies. He was expressly celebrated as having considerable mastery in the treatment of the French overture. See Buttstedt as
quoted in the next note.

church sonata, "Es erhub sich ein Streit im Himmel," but the introduction to Michael Bach's cantata (discussed above) is in the former style, though indeed it did not become a model. And the opposition of various groups of instruments is, even now, a very favourite device. It will be our interesting task, in the proper place, to show what attitude Sebastian Bach took up with regard to the church sonata. When we read that Pachelbel wrote sonatas for a double choir, we must—having regard to the period at which he lived—take this to mean instrumental church sonatas, and we know what to understand by the term.

But he also busied himself with secular instrumental compositions, particularly *serenatas*. Serenades were at that time performed with vocal and instrumental music, or with instrumental only. It is highly improbable that any special form of structure should have existed for these; a series of dances and marches were probably played; but we are told of Pachelbel that he composed "a serenata," and as this is mentioned with his sonatas, it may have been planned on the same method, only lighter and gayer. Now this serenata was certainly well known to Michael Bach, and he himself was possibly treated to it on some festival occasion or other. He then took a friendly revenge on Pachelbel on a suitable occasion with a similar composition; and the works of both masters are said to have been of such excellence that Buttstedt mentions them long after the death of the composers, and says that, of their kind, they rank superior to Lully's overtures.[154]

---

[154] J. H. Buttstedt in the work just quoted (see note 153) says: "Art, on the other hand, was more necessary in my late master and teacher, Herr *Pachelbel's Sonatas, in specie* his *Serenate*, Johann Michel Bach's *Revange* and such like" (than in overtures). Thus it would seem that Bach named his piece "Revange" (Retaliation), indicating at once its motive and aim. Adlung appears to have known it, for in his copy with MSS. notes of Walther's Lexicon, now in the Royal Library at Berlin, under the article "Michael Bach" he has written: "Two choral sonatas by Joh. Mich. Bach are engraved and printed." The "Revange" was scarcely known beyond Thuringia, to our loss, for it might in that case have been preserved. Mattheson, who had a tolerably wide acquaintance with musical literature, makes no mention of it. See his Beschütztes Orchestre, p. 221.

Michael Bach's work as a composer of sonatas has already been alluded to; it is mainly in these that it is important to prove the existence of an intimacy between him and Pachelbel. Since Sebastian Bach, by his first marriage, was closely connected with Michael's house—in which, even after his death, the memory of this friend would certainly have been cherished, and his compositions particularly esteemed and probably preserved in considerable numbers—this is of no small interest.

Neither the famous sonatas nor the clavier compositions of Michael Bach have anywhere come under my notice. Three sets of variations for the clavier exist by Joh. Christoph Bach, and going back once more to this Eisenach master, from whom we digressed, we may conclude our study of the musical works of the two brothers. The clavier for a long period played a subordinate part as compared with the organ, though it was nearly allied to it particularly in the form of the clavicembalo, by the lack of subtle shades of tone, and of different varieties of touch. But the quick evanescence of the sound, on the other hand, brought it into contrast with the organ; and in the clavichord this contrast was even more conspicuous, because of the possibility of representing different shades of tone, however soft. While, during the first half of the seventeenth century, music for the organ and clavier was not kept distinct, and as, in Scheidt's *Tabulatura nova*, things were often required of the organ which it was not generally used for, in the second half of the century a special clavier style grew up, based principally on the characteristics of the instrument. Its peculiarities were founded on an increased rapidity in the succession of sounds, adapted to conceal their deficiency in duration and to compensate as far as possible for this defect. For such a style the figured variations already introduced by Scheidt were very well adapted. A subject of simple construction, with a clearly defined and easily recognised melody, was selected for the theme—an aria, saraband, or chorale—and so varied by running passages for the right hand that the salient points of the melody were just touched upon, or so slightly modified that the essential features remained recognisable throughout.

Now and then, for a change, a running passage in the left hand occurred, while the simple theme was carried on above it: The rhythmical proportions of the theme were at the same time not lost sight of. If it was in two sections, so were the variations; and if each section was in four bars, these recurred in the figures. Chorales, in particular, were much used in this way; and so the contemporaries of those writers must often have heard these nimble fancies played even on the organ. Buxtehude, indeed, made a complete Suite out of the fine and solemn chorale, "Auf meinen lieben Gott," by variations on it with a saraband, courante, and gigue, in which the melody is most skilfully retained, in spite of the different measures and the varying character of the dances.[155] Such tasks were undertaken without any thought of frivolity —simply for the delight in the play of sounds. The greatest ingenuity in this species of music was manifested by Georg Böhm, of the Church of St. John, at Lüneburg, a younger contemporary of Joh. Christoph Bach; and like him a Thuringian, who, as we shall see, initiated Sebastian Bach into this form of art. Works of the same kind exist by Buttstedt, and even by Pachelbel.[156] Now and then a more thoughtful and artistic combination crept in from the neighbouring domain of organ music. The titles were "Changes" (Veränderungen), "Variations," "Partie," "Partita," in chorales even "Verses" simply, since it was a favourite plan to make as many variations as there were verses in the hymn, but without any special reference to the text of each verse. These airy and often extremely pleasing structures had a higher result in the progress of art, serving, in the first place, to encourage finger dexterity, besides giving rise to an abundance of figures and subtle variants, which served a later generation as materials for attaining the very highest perfection of clavier music. This variation form was not

---

[155] Thus Mattheson is in error when he attributes to himself (**Vollkommener Capellmeister**, p. 161) the invention of turning chorale melodies into dances by variations of rhythm.

[156] Pachelbel published a work at Nuremberg, in 1699, Hexachordum Apollinis, containing six airs with variations.

capable of any great depth of treatment, for which reason it
proved no longer sufficient for Sebastian Bach's requirements;
and in his variations written for Goldberg he struck out a new
path, worthy of his genius, in which he has been followed by
Beethoven and Brahms. The "Air with variations," however, in its merely "figured" form, has remained in favour
with artists and the public down to the present day.

Joh. Christoph Bach's twelve variations on a saraband,
in G major,[157] are models of fancy and grace. The saraband
consists of three sections, each to be repeated. The first
contains eight bars, the two last each four, and this echo-like
repetition of two such short phrases leads us to suppose that
the composer wrote for a two-manualed harpsichord, on
which the parts were played alternately. It is not deficient
in harmonic subtlety; the theme begins at once, on the
chord of the sixth (it is thus that we must account for the
harmony, although the characteristic E does not come in till
afterwards), a bold attack, worthy of Joh. Christoph. In the
last variation even such chords as these occur :—

The first variation has, in the right hand, a variant on the
air in quavers; the second, a fine flowing quaver bass; the
third gives the melody quite a new character by a pleasing
little variant; in the fourth, the quaver movement is given in
alternate bars to each hand; from the fifth onwards, semiquavers are introduced, but among them, for contrast,
quieter variations come in, as for example in the sixth, of
which the transcendental chromatic harmony is a feature reminding us of Buxtehude; the eleventh variation has quavers
again, and the last closes calmly in grave 3-2 time. Sebastian Bach seems to have known and loved this little work.
In his A minor variations we find a good deal that is
thought out in a similar way, and the beginning of the third

---

[157] In MS. in the Royal Library at Berlin.

Goldberg variation [158] appears to be a further development of Joh. Christoph Bach's fourth :—

Since the grand fourth variation in Beethoven's Sonata (Op. 109) can be pretty plainly traced to its root in Sebastian Bach's composition, we may see in this the indirect influence of Joh. Christoph Bach even in modern times. Beethoven had the highest respect for Sebastian Bach's clavier works, and such a development is by no means extraordinary. Reminiscences of him frequently occur, especially in the earlier sonatas.

Fifteen variations also are extant on an air by Daniel Eberlin, then Capellmeister at Eisenach; it is in E flat major, and seems to be a sort of cradle song. Many of these variations—which treat the melody as a *cantus firmus* with counterpoint, here calm and slow, and there more rapid—have something of the organ style about them. In the eleventh the melody comes out very sweetly in the tenor, and the ninth forms a pendant to the sixth of the series first noticed. But the use of chromatic passages is even more daring, and gives the harmony a strange, intoxicating effect, reminding us of the most modern means of expression used by Schubert and Schumann. It might safely be wagered that no one, unacquainted with the instrumental music of the seventeenth century, would guess at this day that these variations were composed in 1690 ; rather would he imagine from their softness and sweetness that they were by Mozart,

---

158 B.-G., III., 266.

who also knew how to use chromatic passages and motives
with wonderful force of expression. As regards the figures,
they display no great variety, though they are pleasing
throughout, and the grouping of the variations is very much
the same as in the first set. That Joh. Christoph Bach's talent
did not preponderate on this side is confirmed by the third
of these little works—fifteen variations on an air in A minor,
in two sections of four bars each. These have all the pleasing
characteristics of the two others, but give us nothing essentially new. In a few of the variations the organ character is
conspicuous, as in the seventh, where, between the quiet
crotchets of the upper parts a beautiful stream of semiquavers is poured out in the tenor part; in the eighth, where
the same thing happens in the alto; and in the twelfth,
which has the *cantus firmus* in the bass. The counterpoint
is masterly, and makes the loss of all the composer's really
important organ works the more to be regretted. Moreover,
the resemblance to Sebastian Bach's A minor variations
is here still more conspicuous, and cannot be merely
accidental.[159]

It may not only be assumed but can be proved that Joh.
Christoph Bach further cultivated this branch. Gerber
possessed a little paper volume containing an air in B flat
major with variations; the copyist had broken off at the fourth,
but the volume was calculated to contain nearly twenty.[160]
The whole has now been lost, but the air can be restored from
other sources. It appeared in the Geistreiches Gesangbuch, published at Darmstadt, in 1698, and is set to
Neander's hymn, " Komm, o komm, du Geist des Lebens ";
from thence it was transferred to Freylinghausen's
Gesangbuch. It was afterwards used to the words of
Countess Ludämilia Elisabeth, " Jesus, Jesus, nichts als

---

[159] I myself possess the autograph of the second set of variations. Before
the theme of the second it is written: "*Aria Eberliniana | pro dormente
Ca-| millo, | Variata à Joh. | Christoph* Bach. *org : | Mens. Mart. āo.* 1690. | "
The third, now in the possession of Herr W. Krankling, of Dresden, has only
the initials " *J. C. B.*" above, to the right. Both are in small quarto, and
very neatly written.

[160] Gerber, N. L., I., col. 209.

Jesus." Since it is not known to what song—probably a secular one—it originally belonged, no decisive opinion can be pronounced on the merit of this simple melody. As a chorale melody it is neither better nor worse than most of that period. It can, however, scarcely be doubted that it was invented by Joh. Christoph himself, since, if it were not, some remark would have been made as to its origin, as in the case of the air in E flat major.

All has now been told which can be known regarding the two gifted sons of Heinrich Bach. The whole field of their work—a mirror from which their complete identity might have been reflected—is broken up and dispersed; we can only gather the principal features from solitary fragments, and piece them together in imagination as best we may. If I have not succeeded in this, so much at any rate is clear, that they well deserved to survive as artistic individualities in the memory of posterity; while, if I have, it is a clear gain for the comprehension of their own time as well as of the art of Sebastian Bach, their younger and more glorious relative. It will still be necessary to glance at their direct descendants.

VI.

JOHANN CHRISTOPH BACH'S SONS.

THE only son of Johann Michael Bach died soon after his birth. Johann Christoph, however, had four sons, of whom the eldest was the most remarkable. This one, Johann Nikolaus, was Organist to the Town and University of Jena in 1695. He made a journey into Italy shortly after, as it would seem, in the company of Georg Bertuch, of Helmershausen, in Franconia, who had studied for a time at Jena as a talented amateur, and subsequently entered the Danish army, rising at last to be commandant of the fortress of Aggershuus, in Norway. When he returned to Jena, Nikolaus Bach fulfilled his duties there indefatigably till his death—for fifty-eight years in all. He died at the age of eighty-four, November 4, 1753, the last and most vigorous offshoot of a gifted branch, and he had for years been the eldest surviving member of his family.[161]   He married, in 1697, Anna Amalia Baurath, the daughter of a goldsmith of Jena ; she died on April 14, 1713, and he married again on October 13 of the same year, Anna Sibylla Lange, daughter of the sometime pastor of Isserstedt.   Of the ten children which he had by her, five died quite young, and of the sons Johann Christian (1717-1738) alone arrived at maturity ;[162] none survived the father.   Nikolaus Bach was known to his contemporaries as a diligent composer of Suites, and we must be contented with a repetition of their verdict.[163]   A Mass of his, however, remains, which shows that he possessed no inconsiderable talent for compositions of another kind, and that he was a true artist and worthy of his great father.[164]   It is a short Mass, comprising only the *Kyrie* and *Gloria*, the first in E minor, the second in G major, for two violins, two violas, soprano, alto, tenor, bass, organ, and basso continuo : in the Gloria an additional part is added either for a voice or an instrument.   The work is of great interest, both for its substance and its technical perfection.   Its style—melodic, harmonic, and rhythmic—approaches nearly to that of the contemporary Italian masters, especially of Antonio Lotti, both in the considerate and effective treatment of the vocal parts and in the orchestration; two, and on one occasion, four violas being used.   It bears the character of general

---

[161] The dates are from Walther's Lexicon, and from the parish register at Jena.   The date of his death has hitherto been always erroneously given as 1740; and curiously enough, even by his own relations, namely, in the Emmert genealogy.

[162] The Emmert genealogy gives the number of sons as two, but the whole number was really four.

[163] Adlung, Anl. zur mus. Gelahrtheit, p. 706.

[164] The Mass is in the Royal Library at Berlin, and in the Royal Library at Königsberg, in Prussia (No. 13,866).   The latter copy is one made by Schicht in September, 1815, and bears the title: *Messa a 9 voci da Giov. Nicolo Bach*, *figlio di Giov. Cristofforo Bach, e Zio di Giov. Sebastiano Bach*.   There is also another copy, probably made by Joh. Ludwig Bach, in the possession of Messrs. Breitkopf and Härtel, at Leipzig.   This is dated September 16, 1716, so that the date (1734) of the Berlin copy cannot mean the original date of composition.

solemn rejoicing rather than of subjectively religious contemplation. With the Gloria is interwoven the chorale
which represents it in the Protestant worship, " Allein Gott
in der Höh sei Ehr "—" Glory to God alone on high "—of
which one verse only is sung simultaneously with the four
movements, *Gloria in excelsis Deo; Laudamus te, benedicimus
te; Domine fili unigenite; Quoniam tu solus sanctus.* The
fugue *Cum Sancto Spiritu*, at the end, has no chorale. In the
whole work there is an exclusively German and Protestant
element, which could only be fitly treated according to the
method established by the Protestant composers. In it two
entirely distinct varieties of style are therefore fused to form
one whole. The character of the chorale under consideration here facilitated the task which, as we must allow, is
perfectly worked out by Nikolaus Bach, and with the com-
pletest mastery of technical requirements.

The chorale melody is placed in the soprano register, and
may have been originally intended, not for the voice, but for
an instrument, as a trumpet or horn, since a soprano solo
would have been quite inaudible in the midst of the almost
uninterrupted soprano and alto of the four-part chorus.
The actual setting of the chorale for the voice was done
later; it occurs in this way in the score in question, in
which, moreover, a rhymed translation of the hymn into
Latin is given, as well as the original, because the mixture
of German and Latin words would sound unpleasant.
Sebastian Bach has adopted the same method in the *Kyrie*
of his Mass in F, where the chorale, " Christe, du Lamm
Gottes," is given to the horns; this latter instance, however,
is as far above the former as the German style is above the
Italian in depth and intensity of expression.[165] It is curious
to observe the two cousins as representatives of two such
radically different art-tendencies in solving the same problem.
Nikolaus Bach had, like his father, bestowed the most careful
study upon the Italian masters, and, by uniting their charac-

---

[165] In Sebastian Bach's work, the chorale was sometimes given to a soprano
voice, as is shown by a manuscript in the Royal Library at Berlin. B.-G.,
Vol. VIII., p. xiv.

teristics with his national music, succeeded in producing
something in this Mass peculiarly his own.   Still, in general,
it must be said that the Protestant chorale does not coalesce
with the Italian style of sacred music, and that the experiment
probably could only succeed with this particular melody,
considering its character.   To enable Nikolaus Bach to
arrive at the highest point of this branch of art, he must
have opened out the way afterwards followed by Handel,
have disregarded the exclusively Protestant point of view
and its essentially individual nature, and have striven to take
his stand on the freer and more general ground of human
devotion.   But this was denied to him by the circumstances
of his time, and it may be, too, by his natural predilections.
On the other hand, the Italian style could not avail him,
and the only track that could lead to the ideal was that
followed by his great cousin, Sebastian, who engrafted his
own peculiar vocal style on the German art of the organ.
But, as I have said, the masterliness with which this Mass is
written is quite perfect, both in the *Kyrie*, which is not too
much amplified, and of which the excellent fugato at the
end might, as it stands, have been written by Lotti, and
in the *Gloria* with its many movements.   Here we are
especially surprised to see how independently the four-part
choir surround and adorn the chorale tune, how rich the invention is, how different and various the feeling of all the separate
ideas which are so independent, and yet so linked together by
the continual recurrence of the chorale.   A brilliant fugue
crowns the work, which it is to be hoped, if only for its historical
interest, may once more become generally known, and which,
it may safely be said, would not fail of its full effect even in
the present day.

As chance would have it, we are able to contrast with this
composition, which transports us into the world of the highest
ideal, another work by the same master, which is entirely
founded on the most downright realism ; it is a comic *Sing-
spiel*, or operetta.   And this chance is an especially happy
one, because it adds to the portrait we have been endeavouring to give, of the manner of life of the Bach family, a strongly
marked feature, which must of necessity be absolutely true

to nature. However much the minds of these people were devoted to the sublimest and gravest things, they stood on the earth with a healthy firmness, they showed a capability of joining pleasantly from time to time in the trivial amusements of their fellow-men, and had eyes and understandings to enjoy the cheerful and comic side of the ordinary life that lay around them. The more transcendent the flight of genius and fancy is, so much the more does the necessity of mixing busily, and even unrestrainedly, in the world around press upon every properly constituted man. This rule, taught by experience, is confirmed by the lives of all our great artists. The occasional hearty enjoyment of rough and audacious jokes was a special characteristic of the whole Bach family. If we did not know this from good authority, proof enough would be found in the fact that, beside those members of the family who were employed in churches or schools, so many of them belonged to the easy-going body of the "town-pipers." The fact of belonging to, this body presupposes this trait of character, and that it was not absent in other members of the family is proved, even before we learn it from Sebastian Bach's own works, by the burlesque written with such pleasure by his cousin Nikolaus. It is entitled "The Wine and Beer-cryer of Jena," [166] and is a merry scene from student-life, suitable in its form to the German opera of the time, which flourished particularly well in Hamburg. The performance, of course, was by students on some special occasion or other. The simple plot is as follows. Two young students, Peter and Clemon, of whom the second is a "crasser Fuchs" (green freshman), come in singing a song in praise of Jena, the seat of the Muses. They are very much afraid of being cheated by the Jena people, and determine to go to the house of the innkeeper, Caspar, who is a countryman of theirs, and has been known to Peter before. He receives them, puts the timid youths at their ease by singing the

---

[166] *Der | Jenaische Wein- und | Bierrufer. | a | 2 Violini, | Alto, Monsieur Peter. | Tenore 1, Monsieur Clemon. | Tenore 2, Herr Johannes. | Basso, Monsieur Caspar. | ed | Fondamento | von Joh. Nicol. Bach. |* The parts are in the Royal Library at Berlin.

song "Ein Fuchs ist gar ein närrisch Thier" (The freshman is a simpleton), and begins a condescendingly cordial
conversation with them. The " green " Clemon then announces the important news, from his home, that his
"Father's turned his coat, Mother's burnt the fur," when
the crier is heard in the street, shouting out " Good foreign
wine." This attracts attention, and the crier, with comic
dignity, announces in an aria his standing and reputation.
The host adds that he is an "honest Philistine," but that he
has to endure many tricks, and be the amusement of the
company by being insulted and spit upon. After this it
happens that the bold Peter and the frightened Clemon, as
well as the landlord, go to the window and air their wits by
ridiculing the crier, who keeps going by, and who answers
them readily enough in a rough and cynical style. At length
it gets worse, they come to blows, and the crier threatens
to complain of the freshmen to the Rector.[167] They are
alarmed and retire; a charming aria for four voices, treating
of the adventures of the Jena students, is the conclusion.

The joke in its dramatic form may have arisen from some
real scrape; it hits off the rough·life of the place, and the
crier, Johannes, in particular, seems to be intended for a
similar personage well known in Jena at the time. The
same realism pervades the music, especially in the recitatives
that accompany the course of the action. The way that Bach
makes Johannes call out, imitating in a jocular way the actual
intonation of such people, the short insulting phrases, ejacu-
lated by the rogues in the window, are a very successful piece
of " speaking music "; and it is very amusing when the old
fellow replies in a very rapid speaking voice to his assailers,
and then, almost without taking breath, goes on with his
regular business. The enjoyment with which the composer
has here copied the quaint reality is unmistakable, and it is
very evident that he must have lived on the best of terms with
the students.[168] But the whole thing is perfect in proportion

---

[167] The highest academical dignitary.

[168] Compare on this point a remark by the Cantor Caspar Ruetz, who studied
theology at Jena from 1728 to 1730; in Marpurg's Historisch-critische Beyträge,
Berlin, 1754, p. 360.

and form. Bach never for a moment forgets that he is an artist, just as Mozart, in the same kind of jokes, could approach as nearly as possible to truth of nature, and yet make lovely music. The interspersed arias, in which the music assumes its due prominence, are of that small calibre which came into use in the German opera, as intermediate between the German song of the seventeenth century and the fully developed Italian aria. They show great freshness, and frequently a very quaint humour, and are very skilfully constructed.

As to Nikolaus Bach's skill as a performer we have no information, and of his organ compositions there is only to be found a two-part treatment of the chorale " Nun freut euch, lieben Christen g'mein "—" Sing and be glad, all Christian folk,"—in Pachelbel's style ; but it is too small and un-important to found an opinion upon.[169] What went further than his compositions to establish his fame was an extraordinary power and ingenuity in the construction of instruments. When Jakob Adlung, who was afterwards Professor in the Erfurt Academy and Organist of the Prediger-Kirche there, was studying at Jena, Bach sometimes allowed the poor but industrious youth to practise on his organ. By this means it seems that a nearer friendship sprang up between the two, and Adlung has repaid Bach's kindness by frequent mention of him in his writings, and thus, through his agency, many an important trait is preserved to posterity. The Town Church in Jena got in 1706 a new organ, with three manuals and pedal, and forty-four stops in all. This organ was built by an organ-maker named Sterzing, according to Bach's detailed specification, and under his continual supervision.[170] At this time Johann Georg Neidhardt, the musician to whom the demonstration of the equal temperament is due, and who was afterwards Capellmeister at Königsberg, was study-ing theology in Jena. He was even at that time devoting his attention to the most practicable way of distributing the

---

[169] In the possession of Herr Musikdirector Ritter, in Magdeburg.
[170] Adlung, *Musica mechanica organoedi*.   Berlin, 1768, Vol. I., p. 174, and pp. 244-245.   See also Vol. II., p. 37.

ditonic comma, in which he agreed on all essential points with Andreas Werkmeister. He hoped to arrive at the equal temperament on the organ by means of agreement with the monochord, a narrow box with one string stretched across it, on the top of which were marked, with mathematic accuracy, the proportions of the intervals with regard to the distribution of the comma, so that by the introduction of a small bridge at the proper place the required tone could be got with certainty. He now asked permission to be allowed to employ this new method of tuning on the new organ, and obtained leave to make an experiment on it. Bach let him tune the gedackt of one manual by the monochord, and himself tuned that of another manual only by ear. When the result was heard, Bach's gedackt sounded right and Neidhardt's wrong. He, however, would not admit that his method was in fault, but a steady singer was brought in and made to sing a chorale in the unusual key of B flat minor, and he agreed with Bach's tuning. Neidhardt had not taken into consideration the fact that the pitch of the string at the moment of striking is somewhat higher than it is afterwards, nor how easily such a string gets out of tune. The incident shows, however, that Bach, although thoroughly experienced in mechanical matters, still was strictly an artist enough to trust more to his feeling than to an abstract theory. Of course, to tune by the hearing alone is extremely difficult for unpractised ears. And thus it occurred to him to obviate those errors of the monochord which came from the nature of the string, while keeping the mathematical standard. For this he used a pipe of the same width throughout, which he placed over a well-regulated bellows of even action. A cylinder marked according to the distances of the intervals was passed into the pipe, and the required tone was got by pushing it in or out to the corresponding point in the pipe.[171] The practical usefulness of this invention seems, however, to be hampered by the difficulty caused by the greater or less density of all kinds of wood.

Bach had a considerable reputation, as has been said, for

---

[171] Adlung, *Mus. mech. org.*, Vol. II., pp. 54, 56. Anl. zur mus. Gel., p. 311.

knowledge of organ-building, and other organists came to him for advice. When we read of the many complaints that were made of ignorant and incompetent organists, we can imagine that these gentlemen must have stood in no little need of advice and instruction. On one occasion, one of these wanted Bach to agree to the extraordinary view that a sixteen-foot "Principal" on the manual could only be used with a thirty-two-foot "Principal" on the pedal, and not a sixteen-foot. Bach must have shared his enjoyment of this with Adlung, who tells the anecdote.[172] He surely replied to this clever organist that, if he could not combine a sixteen-foot stop on the manual with a stop of the same depth on the pedal, a thirty-two-foot sub-bass would answer the same purpose as a "Principal" of the same kind.

He seems to have inherited his uncle Michael's skill in the construction of claviers, and since the Bachs always went to members of their own family for instruction, he may have received his first impulses in this direction, and even his first instruction, from his uncle. All his instruments were remarkable for elegance, neat workmanship, and easy action,[173] and he was eagerly bent on improving their mechanism too. For claviers with more than one set of strings, he discovered a way by which he could regulate the sounding of sometimes one, sometimes another set of strings, or all together, with greater certainty than by the usual draw-stops. At the back of the key-board,[174] just where the jacks (*i.e.*, those thin pieces of wood at the top of which the crowquills that pluck the strings are fastened) are raised up by pressure on the keys, he cut several notches ; so that, by pushing in the key-board to different distances, the jacks of one or other set of strings, or of both together, came over the notches, and were raised, by pressure on the keys, from, and not with the key-board. In this way Bach could get

---

[172] *Mus. mech. org.*, Vol. I., p. 187.

[173] Adlung, Vol. II., p. 138.

[174] " Palmula," originally the name for the key-board of the ancient organ, afterwards applied to that of the harpsichord or clavier.

seven different changes on a clavier with three sets of
strings, by using either the first, second, or third alone, or
the first and second, first and third, or second and third
together, or all three together.[175] In the usual method of
construction it was so arranged that each time the jacks
were used for all the sets of strings, there was a danger of
their being slightly, displaced, and so not striking the right
strings.

Adlung further praises Bach's excellent " Lautenclaviere,"
or lute harpsichords.[176] He cannot be considered the inventor
of these instruments, which were an attempt to combine the
soft, tremulous tone of the lute with the clavier action. This
honour is rather due to his contemporary, J. Chr. Fleischer,
of Hamburg. The inventive geniuses of the time busied
themselves greatly with projects of this kind, because the
tone of the clavier was felt to be so hard and expressionless.
Sebastian Bach even had one made in Leipzig, according to a
plan of his own. His cousin Nikolaus managed his invention
with such skill that if it were heard without being seen it
would be supposed to be a real lute. He made these instruments of different forms, sometimes with two or even three
manuals, and by the addition of a fifth octave got the effect
of a theorbo, a deeper instrument of similar character with
the lute. A "Lautenclavicymbel," with three manuals,
was sold by him for about sixty Reichsthaler.

His youngest brother, Johann Michael, followed a somewhat similar course ; he learnt the art of organ-building, and
then went off to foreign parts. He went north, and possibly
to Stockholm, where in the second and third decades of the
eighteenth century, Jakob Bach, a brother of Sebastian,
lived as Hofmusicus. His German relations quite lost sight
of him.[177] The dates of his birth and death cannot be given ;
the former seems to have been somewhere between 1680-90.

Johann Christoph, too, the second son, disregarded the

---

[175] Adlung describes this mechanism with diagrams, at Vol. II., pp. 108-9. See
also his Anl. zur mus. Gel., p. 555.
[176] And describes them at length in his *Mus. mech. org.*, Vol. II., pp. 135-138.
[177] According to the genealogy.

old family traditions, and turned his back upon his home and country. He was engaged in teaching the clavier, first in Erfurt and Hamburg, then for a time in Rotterdam, and, until 1730, in England;[178] but, as far as our information goes, he held no fixed office abroad.[179]

Finally, the third, Johann Friedrich, the year of whose birth must be placed between 1674 and 1678, seems to have studied theology ; he took the post of Organist of the Blasius Church at Mühlhausen, in 1708, when it was left by Sebastian Bach. His salary, paid out of the church chest, was 43 thalers, 2 gute groschen, and 8 pfennig, with 10 gute groschen, 8 pfennig on New Year's Day, and, moreover, for weddings with full choral service, 12 gute groschen, and for those with only hymns, 6 gute groschen—an income which has an interest when compared with that of Sebastian. He was at first only taken on trial, but he cannot have had to wait long for the definite appointment. By all accounts he was a highly gifted artist, and of great executive ability, well versed in the art of organ-building —even at the end of his life he provided the specification for the repairs of the organ of the Blasius Church. Heinrich Gerber, who, before going to Sebastian Bach at Leipzig, had been for some time at the Mühlhausen Gymnasium, praised his talents all his life long, and declared that he had learnt all he knew of the organ from hearing Friedrich Bach. He gave no instruction, nor indeed could he, since, alas! he had weakened and degraded his noble gifts by the bane of his life, an inordinate love of drink ; and is even said to have performed the services when in a state of intoxication ; he was incapable, even when sober, of any artistic inspiration.[180] His surroundings were not of a kind to tear him away from these habits, for the time had long gone by when Mühlhausen had been celebrated for its musicians ; this had already been felt by Sebastian Bach. Johann Friedrich was married but had no children. He died in

---

[178] Walther's Lexicon, p. 63.
[179] The Kittel genealogy says that he had an only son, who died unmarried.
[180] Gerber. N. L., I., cols. 208 and 210. Lexicon, I., cols. 490 and 491. See Appendix A, No. 7.

1730,[181] and furnishes evidence of the fact, already proved by experience, that talents transmitted by highly gifted parents are often dangerous and even baleful to the children.

VII.

CHRISTOPH BACH AND HIS SONS.

WE come finally to Hans Bach's second son, the grandfather of Sebastian. He was born at Wechmar, April 19, 1613, and named Christoph. He likewise selected the calling of musician. In the account of his elder brother, it has already been mentioned that he resided for a time at the Grand Ducal Court at Weimar; there he is said to have been in "waiting on the Prince,"[182] by which we must understand in addition some musical duty in the Court band, which at that time was frequently associated with the post of lackey. About the year 1640, he must have removed from Weimar to Prettin, in Saxony,[183] and there lived by his art, for he took to wife a daughter of the town, Maria Magdalena Grabler, born September 18, 1614, whose father was probably a town-musician there.[184] In 1642 we find him a member of the guild of musicians in Erfurt, whence he removed, in 1653 or 1654, to Arnstadt, the residence of his younger brother, Heinrich.[185] Here he died, only forty-eight years of age, as court and town-musician to the Count, September 14, 1661, and his widow followed him on October 8 of the same year.[186]

---

[181] As follows from the document just referred to, which agrees with the statement in Walther's Lexicon, p. 64.

[182] According to the genealogy.

[183] Not Wettin, as it is written in the Ferrich genealogy, and has also been printed.

[184] My attempts to establish this officially have proved fruitless.

[185] In the archives of Sondershausen occurs a small document referring to him, of November 13, 1654, while his name occurs in the parish register of Erfurt on April 16, 1653.

[186] This date, differing from that given in the genealogy, is from the register of Arnstadt.

Of the three brothers, Christoph Bach with his sons most exclusively represent the guild of secular " Kunstpfeifer," as they were called (musicians attached to the town, and with certain privileges and duties), while Heinrich and his sons filled the highest posts in the service of the church as organists and composers, and Johann was capable of filling either. The guilds of musicians were, during the God-forsaken period of the Thirty Years' War, more sunk in barbarism and rudeness than any other class, and were for this reason regarded with very wide-spread suspicion. We have no record to show that Christoph Bach stood forth as a pattern of moral worth and immaculate civic virtue, in contrast to the general reprobateness of his class. But when we consider the incorruptible soundness of a race which, even in such times as these, could produce such worthy men as Heinrich Bach—in whose society his elder brother spent his later years—and which, two generations later, gave birth to a genius of the first order, we are fain to believe in the unspoiled nature of Sebastian's grandfather. It would be an insult to the spirit of the noble grandson, in whom the whole great spirit of the German nation was, in fact, revealed, if we did not also believe that Christoph Bach keenly felt the shortcomings of his class, and had a higher conception of its dignity, and asserted it too, than was at that time generally held with regard to instrumental musicians—for the most part with too good reason.

It may seem somewhat high-flown to seek for such a consciousness of superior artistic dignity among simple fiddlers and pipers; but it is a certain fact that, in the fiftieth year of the seventeenth century, a conviction asserted itself among the best of them that it was their duty to make the most vigorous efforts to raise themselves once more to honour and consideration. It is a token, not to be undervalued, of the great significance of instrumental music in German culture, that the people, even to the present 'ay, have not lost the feeling of its intrinsically elevating power. Above all things it was needful to raise the musician, as such, in the estimation of his fellow-men. The art had then, no doubt, long constituted a guild;

but it was in the nature of the occupation, which frequently led the members to wander through the country, and at the same time could set no fixed limit line between the amateur and the professional, that the protection of the law should prove very ineffectual. In point of fact, complaints as to insults to their calling, on the part of musicians, were extremely common, and increased in number as, during the course of the century, their self-respect and *esprit de corps* grew in opposition to the " beer-fiddlers," as they were termed. If even in time of peace any due control was impracticable, the utmost lawlessness must have prevailed during the thirty years of anarchy. A voluntary association of larger districts, constituted after the fashion of a guild, by which the members pledged themselves to the mutual protection of certain common interests, and to the observance of strict moral principles was, no doubt, a very suitable means to this end. Even if the artist was thus regarded chiefly as an artisan, still some kind of objective counterpoise was provided to that perilous force, tending to disintegrate social morality, which is inherent in music above all other arts.

In the year 1653, the town-musicians of the principal towns of North and Central Germany did actually combine in such a union, under the name of the " College or Union of Instrumental Musicians of the district of Upper and Lower Saxony, and other interested places " *(Instrumental-Musikal-ischen Collegiums in dem ober- und niedersächsischen Kreise und anderer interessirter Oerter.)* They drew up statutes, which they submitted to the Emperor Ferdinand III. for his ratification, and had them printed and distributed. These not only give plain information as to the purpose of the union, but throw so clear a light on the morals and *im*morals of musical life at that period, that they must be here reproduced at length.[187]

---

[187] A copy of this broad sheet, now probably very scarce, is preserved in the town archives of Mühlhausen. The complete title is: " The Imperial *CONFIRMATION* of the Articles of the Union of Instrumental Musicians in the Districts of Upper and Lower Saxony, and other interested places." Folio. The German original is antiquated in style, full of quaint spelling and provincialisms, and the expressions and punctuation are also unusual.

"I. No member of this musical college (union) shall of his own accord settle himself to exercise his art in any town, office, or convent where one of our society is already established and appointed, nor shall he deprive him of any of his 'attendances,' unless it be that he exercises some other branch, or that he is called thither by the authorities of the place; and the musician already established shall be assured that no damage shall ensue to his perquisites, or that at least he may be protected from harm or loss.

"II. Every *sodalis*, when he is actually appointed in any place, shall take pains and care to see that the annual payment previously given to his predecessors *ex publico* is continued to him without reduction or diminution; and because, before now, the noble art and its votaries have fallen into no small contempt, and many honourable men engaged in its service have even been driven out of place, by other men offering themselves to perform at 'attendances' for the bare perquisites, every musician shall guard himself to the utmost against such contracts, which are degrading to him and to the art.

"III. Inasmuch as Almighty God is wont marvellously to distribute His grace and favours, giving and lending to one much and to another little, therefore no man may contemn another by reason that he can perform on a better sort of musical instrument; much less may he be boastful on that account, but be diligent in Christian love and gentleness, and thus walk in his art, first of all to the honour and glory of God most High, to the edification of his neighbour, and so as to enjoy and maintain at all times a good report of his honourable conduct in the eyes of men.

"IV. To the end that every town may at all times be provided with a skilled and duly qualified musician, and that others, particularly assistants and apprentices, may be urged to more industry and constant practice, at all times when one is called in the regular manner to such an office, and subsequently required to give a testimonial to his efficiency, two of the neighbouring teachers, together with a skilled assistant, shall subscribe it, who shall also examine him particularly as to his art, and listen to his proof and mastery

(Meister-Recht) in playing the pieces prepared for that end, and to be found in the library of the board of the society.

" V. No man, whether he be master, assistant, or apprentice, shall divert himself by singing or performing coarse obscenities or disgraceful and immodest songs or ballads, inasmuch as they greatly provoke the wrath of Almighty God and vex decent souls, particularly the innocence of youth. Moreover, in considerable meetings and gatherings, those who serve the noble art of music are thereby brought into the greatest contempt.

" VI. On the contrary, every man who is called upon to serve an 'attendance' shall conduct himself decently, honourably, and becomingly, and not himself alone but also the assistants with him; but still he shall not be weary of cheering and delighting the company present by means of *musicæ instrumentalis et vocalis*.

" VII. Every one shall, so far as in him lies, take special care to have around him pious and faithful assistants, as well as apprentices of good report, so that at public meetings and 'attendances' nothing may be stolen from the invited guests, nor the whole musical college ill spoken of, nor innocent folks led into suspicion and danger.

" VIII. No man shall dare to perform on dishonourable instruments, such as bagpipes, sheep-horns, hurdy-gurdies, and triangles, which beggars often use for collecting alms at house-doors, so that the noble art would be brought into contempt and disgrace by them.

" IX. *In specie* shall every man abstain from all blasphemous talk, profane cursing and swearing; but if any man sin in this matter, he shall be punished for it by his master and fellows, according to their measure and the atrocity and frequency of his sinning; nay, he may even be expelled from the society.

" X. No man shall dare to give 'attendance' with jugglers, hangmen, bailiffs, gaolers, conjurors, rogues, or any other such low company; but, on the contrary, each one shall rather shun and avoid them, and keep wholly and solely with the society, for the preservation of his good fame and report.

" XI. Likewise, no master shall receive an apprentice from

the above-named sort of folks, or from any other unfit person ; but those who are bound apprentice to acquire the art of music shall not only be of respectable birth, but themselves have committed no crime by which they have incurred *infamiam juris;* but each apprentice, when he is bound, shall show his certificate of birth, drawn up according to law, and sworn to by two credible and respectable witnesses, and it shall be preserved by the nearest board of the musical college till he has honestly and dutifully served his apprenticeship, and may so be provided with a good character and testimonials.

" XII. And to the end that a perfect musician, may have been taught many instruments, some *pneumatica* and some *pulsatilia,* and be practised in them, no apprentice shall be free under five years, that he may be experienced in his art and acknowledged as skilled. And at his binding two of the nearest masters of the art and a skilled assistant shall always be present, and in their presence two copies of the indentures shall be prepared (of which one shall be kept by him who is intrusted with the discipline and teaching of the apprentice, and the other delivered to the apprentice's parents, guardians, or other relatives) ; and more particularly they shall remind and exhort the apprentice earnestly and diligently to constant prayer, faithful service, industrious labour, and to pay all due respect and obedience to his master and teacher.

" XIII. To the end that the apprentice, when his time is out and he is thenceforth free, may be all the more perfect, he shall, for the next three years before he settles himself, serve as assistant to other famous masters. But, as among *mechanica artificia* or common artisans, by dint of long custom, the sons and daughters of masters have acquired this privilege and advantage, that they are not always obliged to pass so long a time as assistants, and in travelling; so likewise the sons of the masters in this noble art of music: *item,* also those who may have married their daughters, after they have served one year as assistants, may be exempt from the remainder, and not pass the remaining tests of mastery.

" XIV. So soon as any man shall have served his apprenticeship, and is qualified thenceforth to attend as assistant,

certain articles shall be laid before him and made known to
him, of which he shall make use when he comes into strange
places in making his greetings; whereby masters who are
strangers to him may find out whether the members and
servants of our musical college behave in accordance with
the prescribed articles, and have due and sufficient knowledge of them.

"XV. And when this musical college has been throughout
established and settled with special articles and rules, to the
end that it may be protected against meddlers and bunglers—
as in all other far less honourable *corpora*, as companies, cor-
porations, and guilds—and that, whoever bears love and good-
will to this most noble art of music may be all the more
incited and urged to learn it from the very foundation, all
and each of the members of our college shall banish from
him all disturbers and bunglers, and in the 'attendances'
required of him shall never hold any communication with
them; but during the years of study make good use of his
time, so as to become right skilful and clever in music, and
thus be always preferred and chosen with reason above such
botchers and bunglers.

"XVI. In case of any dissension or strife arising between
the members of the college or their relatives, whereby
any one is hurt by contempt of his honest name and good
report, or is injured in any other undeserved manner, or by
which he may even be deprived of his income, the injured
party shall be empowered to inform six of the masters settled
in the neighbourhood, who then, at a fitting time, shall call
both parties to appear before the district board, and shall
there hear and receive the account of their difference, and
then, with the consent of three assistants, shall commit
the party found guilty, whether the plaintiff or the accused,
to fitting punishment, and hold him responsible for the costs
occasioned by the matter.

"XVII. As concerns the payment of assistants, each one
shall be free to deal with them at each place and on each
occasion as he thinks proper and just, nevertheless, according
to the work in question; and the bargain shall at once be set
on paper and a copy of the agreement shall be taken by each

into his keeping, so that the one party may be bound to pay and the other to serve willingly and faithfully, and that they may have reason to live peaceably together.

"XVIII. Since also one might dare to oust an old master of our art out of his office, by what way or means, or under what semblance or pretext it matters not, and to insinuate himself into his post, therefore any man who seeks his own advancement by the above-mentioned unseemly means, and ousts another, our college shall dispossess him, and his assistants who ought to serve him, and he shall no longer be suffered in it. Inasmuch as venerable age, if accompanied by weakness, easily falls into contempt (all the former long years of great labour, pains, and service being forgotten), and youth generally preferred above it ; if such weakness and impotency in a musician of great age, holding an appointment, should be so great that he cannot fulfil his duties, or only with much difficulty, and that the service of God and other attendances must necessarily be provided for ; in that case some one shall be empowered to serve as a substitute for the old man ; nevertheless, the old man shall enjoy half of the salary and his share of the profits, and all the remaining days of his life he shall be duly respected by the substitute or coadjutor, who shall in all things, if he is not unfit, give the precedence to him, and await the blessing of the Lord ; and all he does well and kindly for the old man shall be highly esteemed and regarded by every one, and God the most High shall surely one day reward him and repay him.

"XIX. And because the labourer is worthy of his hire, and that it may be withheld from none, every man who is bound to hold himself ready in the towns or otherwise to perform music to order, must himself take good care that his assistants and helpmates are justly paid, and to dismiss no man till he has received his arrears of pay ; in the contrary case, no other assistant will be permitted to take the vacant post and service.

"XX. On the other hand, the assistants in a service to which they have once agreed to be appointed must labour diligently, must set a good example to the young apprentices of the decency that beseems them, and, above all, pay all due respect to the Principals under whom they have taken service, and on that account must show no boldness towards them if they should imagine that they are better and more fundamentally experienced in their art than the Principal himself.

"XXI. Since, too, experience proves that many would fain fulfil the service they have undertaken with the aid of mere apprentices, while, on the other hand, sound sense must instruct every one that tyros and apprentices, as in all other matters, so also in musical art, can never bring out any perfect work; and since in consequence hereof, both in public divine service and in other meetings, faults and defects occur, and not only does the director of such music incur all the blame but also great disgrace, and the noble art itself is thereby brought into contempt, no master shall be suffered or permitted to take or keep more than three apprentices at one time to instruct and discipline.

"XXII. Every apprentice shall sign his own indentures when he is bound, or, if he cannot write, they shall be signed for him by his parents, guardian, or relations; so that the bound apprentice shall be pledged to serve truly, entirely, and to the end, all the years of apprenticeship named in the above twelfth article, and not to run away from his master during those years of apprenticeship; but if one should be so abandoned, and run away from his master during those years of apprenticeship, he shall not be taken by any other master under a penalty of ten thalers, nor shall he ever be suffered to be a member of this our musical college, but be held as reprobate. But if it should be found out that the apprentice quitted his master *ob nimiam saevitiam*, and that the master was thus *in culpa*, in that case the master shall be tried by six of the musical elders settled near by, for his neglect and other acknowledged damage to his apprentice, or to his parents or friends, and accounted guilty according to their just award.

"XXIII. To the end that these articles as compiled by us may be the more exactly carried out, and that the *sodales* of this college may meet with the least cost and trouble, and at such meetings transact necessary matters, three boards shall be constituted, one in Meissen, the second in Brunswick, and the third in Pomerania or the Mark of Brandenburg, and established in whatever town may seem most convenient to the members of our college; and these articles shall there be deposited and faithfully preserved, if not *originaliter* at least in authorised and certified copies, so that in all eventualities at the meetings of our college all *actus* and matters which may arise among musicans may be regulated and judged by them.

"XXIV. And though indeed those who already belong to this musical college are not few in number, still admission shall not be refused or denied to any man who after due trial shall be discerned and held to be a skilled and worthy member of our society and union.

"XXV. Now, finally, since evil morals and customs give cause and rise to good and wholesome laws, and since it is not possible so to extend these present articles as to set forth *specialiter* and expressly every case, the remaining cases shall be decided according to the independent judgment of the elders of the nearest place where there is a board, and ordered after the tenour of these articles, and remain decided according to their *arbitrium*, so that in the cases which occur they direct their view to that which is decent and permissible, and for the maintenance of this musical college; that they burden no man beyond what is due and just; that they do not let gross and inexcusable excesses pass unpunished; to the end that all due submission and respect may be preserved for this our college, and above all for His Most Illustrious Majesty the Roman Emperor, and the ratification granted to it by our gracious Sovereign; and that the great and famous end may be attained which the originators of this useful work had in view from the beginning."

If we call to mind what the "evil morals and customs" were against which a resolution is here pronounced—even irrespective of the "special cases not here expressly set forth"—we can form a very sufficient idea of how matters stood at that time among German musicians. It is impossible to overlook the admirable earnestness of this effort to restore discipline, morality, and order; and the conviction that the noble art was worthy of a higher fate than to be universally despised and abused is delightfully prominent in these articles. The list of above a hundred names from the most important towns in the district concerned, which follows the articles, also proves that the desire for an improved state of things was very general ; and other places beyond the district, as Mühlhausen, in Thuringia, allied themselves to this Union of musicians. And though, during the times immediately following, the public estimate of the town-musicians — Kunstpfeifer and Stadtmusikanten — remained on the whole a low one, though it was said to their reproach that their executive practice took the place of all deeper musical knowledge, that they were uneducated, coarse, haughty, and pig-headed ;[188] though petty quarrels did not cease among them, still a few voices were raised to show that "many honourable and skilled men were yet among their number, diligent to walk pleasingly in the sight of God and man."[189] We must never allow ourselves to be misled into forming a too low estimate of the sound inmost core of these men, or of their importance in the history of German art. In every class more inferior and mediocre individuals are to be found than illustrious and distinguished ones ; and, besides this, poverty and necessity pressed pretty equally on all, allowing none but conspicuous talents to expand and blossom freely. Still, they upheld the dignity of art in their own way, and aroused and fostered to the best of their powers the love and feeling for native art among the people, against the foreign influences to which the Courts and upper classes soon, for the most part, surrendered themselves. And the people were not thankless, for they understood their worth and the ideal which gave vitality to their calling. To this day every itinerant musician who wanders round the country from house to house, singing his tunes, is a figure that appeals to the sympathies of every German heart.

---

188 Mattheson, *Critica musica*, II., pp. 217 and 262.
189 J. Fr. Mente, in Mattheson's Ehrenpforte, p. 414.

The regulations for the guild, in Article XXV., were of course not new, but were at any rate based on common custom, which was here merely recalled to men's memory, extended and insisted on. Still, they serve to give us a more general acquaintance with the mode of life of the town-musicians at that time, and consequently with the position of the Bach family.

Christoph Bach must, no doubt, as I have hinted, have come, by his marriage, into close connection with the musicians of the district of Upper Saxony; but there is no evidence to show that he was admitted as a member of their union. On the contrary, we may regard it as decidedly improbable that he, or any member of his family, ever belonged to it. The supposition rather forces itself upon us that they themselves, in their close and clinging intimacy, constituted such a body in Thuringia itself, though lacking countersigns and statutes. It has been already noted that the three towns which were the head-quarters of the Bachs—Erfurt, Eisenach, and Arnstadt—grew into importance at about the same time; and nothing can seem fairer than the hypothesis that these musicians strove, with more or less distinct purpose, to reach the goal which must have shone before them—particularly in those times of demoralisation among their competitors, and especially in Erfurt, as we see it in the fiftieth and sixtieth years of the century—the upholding, namely, of the dignity of art and of their own position, within the pale of a patriarchal and exclusive family circle. And, if it were only to this limited extent that guild interest held them together, it is evident that in their pursuit of the art mere mechanical skill would hold a less important place. This is a circumstance worthy to be noted as raising them above their fellow-musicians to form a little circle of the elect. Since, moreover, the greater number of the family were in the service of churches and schools, as cantors and organists, and so represented, in their way, a portion of the higher culture of the time, their intimate mutual relations must have involved a relatively greater degree of personal cultivation than was then common among men of the same standing. The statement of a contemporary, that among a hundred musicians' assistants scarcely one was to be found who could write ten ordinary words without a mistake,[190] cannot, under any circumstances or interpretation, apply to the Bachs. A further evidence of the spirit that reigned among them is to be found in the " family-days," which, for a long period, were annually observed by all the male members of the family in Erfurt, Eisenach, or Arnstadt. This custom was religiously kept up, even when Christoph Bach's eldest son transferred that branch of the family into Franconia, as late therefore, certainly, as the first half of the eighteenth century. They assembled in one or the other of the above-named places for no other purpose than to revive the feeling of clanship and near connection, to exchange experiences and ideas, and to enjoy a few hours in each other's society. It survived even in the memory of Sebastian's son, Emanuel, how that his forefathers had edified and delighted each other as to matters musical. First they would sing a chorale, then followed secular and popular songs, which, from the contrast with the previous pious mood, would often, by their quips and jests, rouse the mirth of both singers and hearers to a keen and cynical wit. The performance of such songs, be it observed, was part of the calling of the town-musicians. A particularly favourite practice seems to have been the performance of *Quodlibets,* by which, up to the sixteenth century, were understood pieces in several parts in which the voices sang different well-known melodies, often sacred and profane at the same time, and with the words, and endeavoured to combine them so as to form a harmonious whole.[191] The production of a really harmonius result must, however, have been far from the intentions of the jolly musicians ; they would rather

---

[190] Der wohlgeplagte (etc.) Cotala, p. 3. It is evident that Mattheson's reflections on the education of musicians' apprentices in the Neu-Eröffneten Orchestre, p. 14, are founded on the descriptions in this work rather than on his own observations.

[191] Compare Praetorius, *Syntagma musicum*, III., 18. B.M. The instances there alluded to are given, with analysis, in Hilgenfeldt, Joh. Sebast. Bach's Leben, &c. Leipzig, Fr. Hofmeister, 1850. Sup. I. and II. A pleasing account of such sports is given in Winterfeld, Zur Geschichte heiliger Tonkunst, II., p. 281.

have directed their attention to the diversity of the texts, where chance must have ruled and revelled in the wildest contrarieties.[192]

Georg Christoph, Christoph Bach's eldest son, was born at Erfurt, September 6, 1642.[193] At first he was usher in a school at Heinrichs, near Suhl, a position which he probably attained through the connection with Suhl of his father's brother. From thence he moved, in 1668, as cantor, to Themar, a little old town in the neighbourhood of Meiningen, which at that time belonged to the Prince-Counts of Henneberg, but in 1672 was transferred to Gotha, and in 1680 fell into the possession of Duke Heinrich von Römhild. After his death (1710), Meiningen once more took forcible possession of it for a time.[194] Thus, in those times, did men play fast and loose with towns and human beings. Twenty years later Bach was called to fill the same office at Schweinfurt. There he died, April 24, 1697, the founder of the Franconian branch of the Bachs.[195] That he, too, was a composer appears from the circumstance that in Philipp Emanuel's collection of music there was a sacred composition by him, on the text from the Psalms, " Behold, how good and joyful a thing it is, brethren, to dwell together in unity," for two tenors, one bass, one violin, three viole di gamba, and basso continuo. This composition, which is said to have been written in 1689, is at present lost, so it is impossible to guess what his merits as a composer may have been.

---

[192] " The *Quodlibet* is a piece composed of all sorts of pleasing songs, even though they do not regularly suit and fit each other." F. E. Niedt's Musikalische Handleitung, Part II., Ed. 2, edited by Mattheson, Hamburg, 1721, p. 103. See also Forkel, p. 3, and Dictionary of Music and Musicians, art. " Quodlibet."

[193] From data in the genealogy and the register of the Kaufmannskirche, which agree. Ferrich, whose differing statements generally deserve credence when they refer to his own direct ancestors, here, strangely enough, gives the year as 1641.

[194] From documents in the archives of Meiningen. Brückner, Landeskunde des Herzogthums Meiningen, II., p. 239.

[195] The dates from the Ferrich genealogy. In the report of the Council of Erfurt for April 28, 1675, mention is made of the very impoverished condition of one Georg Christoph Bach, who must at that time have been in Erfurt. He thus can certainly not be identical with the G. C. Bach mentioned in the text, but I do not know how to identify him otherwise.

We will go on to his children. The eldest, Johann Valentin, was born January 6, 1669,[196] whence we may infer that his father married when he became Cantor. He was succeeded by Johann Christian (lived from March 15, 1679, till June 16, 1707), and Joh. Georg (from November 11, 1683, till March 13, 1713); nothing certain is known about these two. Valentin became town-musician in Schweinfurt, May 1, 1694, and at the same time, or later, was appointed head watchman. In this position he conceived it to be his duty to marry, and on September 25, 1694, he wedded Anna Margaretha Brandt. He died August 12, 1720. Three sons, the fruit of his marriage, may be mentioned—Joh. Lorenz, the compiler of the Ferrich genealogy, born September 10, 1695, was Organist at Lahm, in Franconia, and died at a great age, December 14, 1773. I am acquainted with a prelude and fugue in D major by him, which shows him to have been a skilled and original composer. The second son, Joh. Elias, whose meeting with Sebastian Bach I shall refer to again later, was born February 12, 1705; he studied theology, and afterwards became cantor and inspector of the *Alumneum* at Schweinfurt, where he died, November 30, 1755. The third, finally, Joh. Heinrich, born January 27, 1711, did not survive his early youth. It is easy to observe how, as they became at home on the Franconian territory, other Christian names occur, as Valentin, Elias, and Lorenz, than those which had been customary among the Thuringian Bachs.[197]

After the birth of his first son, Christoph Bach's wife presented him next with twins, February 22, 1645, which, two days later, were held at the font by Ambrosius Marggraf and Christoph Bärwald, as godfathers, and were named, respectively, Joh. Ambrosius and Joh. Christoph. The former was destined to be the father of the great Sebastian.

---

[196] At three in the afternoon, says the exact register in the Ferrich genealogy. That he was afterwards Cantor at Schweinfurt is an error of Philipp Emanuel's.

[197] These statements are founded on data derived from the Ferrich genealogy, the fragmentary genealogy attached to the pedigree in the possession of Fräulein Emmert, of Schweinfurt, and the parish registers of that town. See Appendix, B. III.

They passed their first childhood in Erfurt; when they were eight or nine years old Arnstadt became the family residence, and there, under their father's guidance, the foundations of their musical knowledge and skill were laid.

When Christoph Bach died, in the prime of manhood, his twin sons were scarcely grown up. Nature had not only tied them by the closest bond of blood, but had bestowed on them a resemblance of both external and mental characteristics that was the astonishment of every one, and that seems to have made them the object of curiosity and interest even in the highest circles. They had the same modes of thought and of expression ; they played the same instrument, the violin, and had the same way of conceiving and performing music. Their outward resemblance is said to have been so great that when they were apart their own wives could not distinguish their husbands, and their unity of spirit and temperament was so intimate that they even suffered from the same disorders; in fact, the younger survived the death of the elder but a very short time. Thus the reciprocal interdependence which was characteristic of all the Bachs, showed itself in its greatest intensity in the relations of Sebastian's father to his twin brother; and since we find little to tell concerning his own life, we will allow ourselves to bring the characteristic peculiarities of the younger to bear—so far as they can be determined—on the person of the elder.

It is probable that after their father's death and the end of their apprenticeship, they both travelled as town-musicians' assistants, but then their roads separated. Ambrosius settled in Erfurt in 1667, and Joh. Christoph received a call, February 17, 1671, to be Hofmusicus to Count Ludwig Günther, at Schwarzbug-Arnstadt. It has already been observed in another place that this nobleman took an interest in church music, which here, as elsewhere, had somewhat fallen into decay. A year before this he had caused a special hour of practice every Sunday to be arranged for the church choir, with the instrumental accompaniment under the direction of the Cantor Heindorff, and he had it carefully kept up. How needful it was is proved by this, that complaint was

still made at the school examination, at Easter of the year
1673, of the bad condition of the singing choir, which consisted principally of the scholars.   Subsequently, on the
appointment of a new town-cantor, the Count stipulated that
the choir should consist of at least four persons in each part,
which, at that time, when single voices were not unfrequently
thought sufficient, formed a tolerably strong choir.   When
the Count appointed a musical groom of the chambers, it
was expressly stated in his appointment that he was " at all
times to be present in the church at the *exercitium musicum*."
We read just the same in the deed appointing Joh. Christoph;
at the same time he was enjoined not to travel abroad without the consent of the cantor and the Count's council, and
" to exercise himself in the graces of violin-playing and
music-making," and " since he would be needed at Court,
alone or with others, to show himself ready and willing."
At the same time the chief directors, the Cantor Heindorff,
and the town-musician at the time, named Gräser, were
instructed on all occasions of municipal solemnity, where
music was required, to apply first to Bach, then to the
watchmen, and then to the assistant-musicians in turn.
It was necessary to specify these subsidiary duties, for
Bach, as Hofmusicus, received a salary of only twenty—
and subsequently of thirty—gülden, with some payments in
kind.[198]

As he was now above want, he ought, in the true Bach
fashion, to have set up house.   His brother Ambrosius had
already set him the example.   He seems, indeed, to have
had some views of this kind; but that they were not at
once carried out, and the reasons why, give us a deeper
insight into the nature of this man than it has been possible
to obtain with regard to any previous member of the family.
The Consistory of Arnstadt, besides its supervision of all
matters ecclesiastical and scholastic, had also a certain

---

[198] From the book of accounts of payments to servants from Michaelmas, 1687,
to Michaelmas, 1688, in the Ministerial Library at Sondershausen, p. 72: " Hofmusicus Joh. Christoff Bach, twenty gülden a year." · The salary of thirty
gülden thus implies an advance.

spiritual jurisdiction over matters connected with religion and morals. On August 19, 1673, there appeared before them Anna Margaretha Wiener, widow, and her daughter Anna Cunigunda, and, as against them, Joh. Christoph Bach; and the hearing of the two parties brought to light certain things which we will reproduce in the characteristic way in which they were then and there recorded.[199]

"After Bach had kept company with Anna Cunigunda Wienerin,[200] and by common report was said to be betrothed to her, both parties appeared before the Consistory, and Anna Cunigunda confessed that she had promised to marry Bach, and he her. And the mother says that he had addressed himself to her, through Hans Lampe, desiring her motherly consent, which likewise she had given, and they had done no less than give each other rings in pledge of marriage, which they still had. She (*i.e.*, the daughter) was minded to keep her word, that her conscience might not be burdened, although she would force herself on no man; and it was now on Bach's conscience and responsibility whether he thought he could withdraw from her under these circumstances without injuring her.

"Christoph Bach confessed, indeed, that he had offered marriage to Anna Cunigunda Wienerin, but they had merely considered the matter provisionally, and he had not in any way considered himself bound. *Negat pure*, that he asked the mother's consent through Hans Lampe; this Hans Lampe was father-in-law to Anna Wienerin and in the closest relationship to her by marriage. With regard to desiring her consent to the completion of the act, he would far sooner demand it through some near blood friend of his own (Bach's), *exempli gratia*, Heinrich Bach, than through any friend of hers. He had given her a ring and she had given him one, but not in pledge of marriage. *In specie* he said she had vexed him about Leuchten's[201] daughter,

---

[199] In this, and in other similar cases, the simplest translation has been thought to be the best. Any attempt at reproducing or imitating the quaint old phraseology would be futile.
[200] The feminine termination added to her surname.
[201] A citizen of Arnstadt.

and had declared he had received the ring from her, to which he replied, in order that she might see that this was not the case, that he would make her a present of the ring.

"Anna Cunigunda abides by what she has said above, and *in specie* that the ring was given in pledge of marriage, so that her constancy was made sure.

"Bach no less abides by what he has said, and denies the circumstances alleged by the opposite party; besides, Anna Cunigunda had asked for her ring back again, and so basketed him.

"Wienerin: After Bach had withdrawn from her and his affection had died out, she had desired to have her ring back, on these conditions: she put it to his conscience that if she were not good enough for him, and if he only meant to make a fool of her, he should return her the ring and answer for it in his conscience before God. She would leave it to him to decide, and have nothing more to do with him of that kind. He, in answer, had sent her word that he had no fear of punishment from God on that account.

"Memorandum: 'Since Bach stands by his statement that he had said nothing binding to Anna Cunigunda, although various reports had been abroad, it is pressingly put before him that he might easily be made to swear to his deposition. To the end that he should diligently try himself, he shall be allowed time for consideration during eight days from this date, when, without further summons, he shall appear again and explain himself. Which shall also be declared to Anna Cunigunda Wienerin.'"

The little romance between the two young people was soon played out. Indeed, neither of them accused the other any further, but the Consistory, when the matter had come to its ears, deemed it its part to take further cognisance of the affair. Although at the next appointed hearing no particular fault on Bach's side was proved, still the Consistory, which in its decision may have had due regard to the personal impression made by the two parties, was in the right not to be immediately convinced by Johann Christoph's defence. The clever and accomplished young artist probably had not failed to win the affections of the citizen's daughter of Arnstadt. He had made advances to Anna Wiener with a view to making her his companion for life, and in the unconstrained fashion of their class he had chatted and talked with her, so that the possibility of their union in marriage had been touched upon. Partly from sincere liking, and partly by inconsiderate conduct, it came to pass that he aroused in the girl a serious affection. The feeling that he did not very warmly return it led to some jealous teasing about the ring, and he, to meet it half-way, gave it to her. I am far from defending such light conduct, but I would not judge him by too strict a standard. Bach was now tired of the half-serious dallying, and left the maiden to the torments of unrequited love. Still her declaration before the Consistory does not betray this alone, but real womanliness and tender feeling also. Too proud to allow him to trifle with her, she had given back the promise, made on her side in earnest, and had given up all intimacy with him; but as soon as she was questioned on the subject she betrayed her real feeling in her repeated appeals to his conscience and to God, before whom he would have to answer for his conduct, and to whose will she submitted her own.

The spiritual court, whose purpose it was to bring about an adjustment, seems on this occasion to have poured oil on the fire. Bach did not feel himself pledged to Anna Wiener, as was already proved by his defiant answer that he had no fear of God's punishment for any breach of faith ; and the fact that the matter had now become public, and probably the talk of the town, only strengthened his recalcitrancy, and turned his indifference into aversion. What further proceedings took place before the Consistory we have no report of; still we can gather this much, that their view was that Bach must marry Anna Cunigunda. If this had, finally, been the result, it would be easily explained by the authority of the Consistory and the custom of the time, for mutual inclination was by no means always the determining cause and motive of a matrimonial alliance ; it was still more frequent then than now to yield to external reasons, and to leave the adjustment, even of serious differences, to time. That a poor musician, wholly dependent as to outward circumstances on the Count's Court and Council, should have resisted this demand with the utmost decision—nay, with much bitterness—is a remarkable proof of a justifiable independence, which allowed of no interference under any circumstances in matters of sentiment and feeling. The Counts of Schwarzburg at that time were dependent on the Dukedom of Saxony, and Johann Christoph, not meeting with justice in Arnstadt, carried his appeal before the Consistory´ of Weimar. This was in 1674, after the affair had already lingered on for much more than a year. He here declared, with a vehemence which must subsequently have been remembered against him, that he "hated the Wienerin so that he could not bear the sight of her." And in Weimar justice was done him. Nothing was then left to the Arnstadt Consistory but to effect a reconciliation, for which Bach showed himself very ready, and so virtually retracted the declaration he had uttered in Weimar. By this time it was the end of the year 1675 ; the worrying contest had deprived him of his freedom of mind for nearly two years and a half. He came out of it triumphant, but all thoughts of love and marriage were marred for him for years. While the others of the Bach family all married early, many by the time they were twenty, he remained unmarried till he was in his thirty-fifth year. He then took to wife Martha Elisabeth Eisentraut, the daughter of the churchwarden of Ohrdruf, about Easter, 1679.

There is a suspicion to be dispelled, which may, perhaps, have arisen from reading the preceding narrative, that it may have been in consequence of some indiscreet conduct that Bach was required to marry Anna Wiener. It is beyond any manner of doubt that their relations were strictly pure and moral; indeed, it is perfectly clear from an attentive reading of the trial given above. Such contingencies as might be inferred or imagined were always discussed with the greatest openness in the transactions of the Consistory, which are our source of information : and in such circumstances the Court of Weimar would certainly not have pronounced in favour of Bach. Moreover, I may here add with great satisfaction, that as regards the relations of the sexes, the strictest principles prevailed in the Bach family, and that in this particular they certainly distinguished themselves as in advance of their time. When, among so great a number of marriages and births as I have had occasion to search out and follow up, not a single instance is to be met with from which an illegal or premature connection can be inferred, this is an honourable testimony of no small import among men of that class, and in times of such general moral confusion and laxity.

Gräser, the town-musician, to whose special consideration on occasions of "music-making" Johann Christoph was recommended, made life and labour bitter to him; not merely damaging him in his earnings, but seeking to hurt and annoy him in various spiteful and contentious ways. He once went so far as grossly to insult not Joh. Christoph only, but the whole Bach family of musicians. This led to a collective action on the part of the Bachs of Arnstadt and Erfurt; but nothing definite can be told as to the outcome, though they seem to have taken proceedings against Gräser. The disputes, however, did not cease; the Government once more took Bach into its service, but at last the old Count lost patience. He saw plainly that, amid eternal quarrelling, music could not prosper, and on January 7, 1681, he dismissed all the musicians from their appointments, "on account of their idleness and disunion."[202] As ill-luck would have it, the Count died shortly after this, and, in consequence of the general mourning, all public music was prohibited. Thus Joh. Christoph found himself bereft of a livelihood, and with his wife and his first-born, a daughter, reduced to extreme necessity. It is not without emotion that we read

---

[202] Documents of March 23, 1680, and January 7, 1681. These and the following statements rest on papers in the archives of Sondershausen : " Concerning Johann Christoph Bach, Hoff-*Musicus* in Arnstadt, 1671-1696." Certain of these and other documents relating to different members of the Bach family were published some years since in G. W. Körner's Urania (Erfurt and Leipzig, 1861.)

that this man, nevertheless, every Sunday sat by the side of
his venerable uncle, Heinrich Bach, assisting him in the
church music without the smallest payment ; how, after the
lapse of a few months of mourning, he craved permission of
the young Counts now reigning, "to perform some quiet music,
so as to maintain himself and his family, however meagrely,"
sometimes in Arnstadt, or, if that were forbidden, in the
remote town of Gehren ; or begged, at the New Year, to be
allowed to " pipe before the doors," in spite of the mourning.
The hardest times were presently past, and in the early part
of 1682 he was reappointed by the young sovereigns " Hofmusicus und Stadtpfeifer."

We may turn from the sadder side of his life and from
the still incessant litigations, over the encroachments on
his office, and other quarrels with his fellow-musicians, to
a consideration of the music performed at the Count's Court.
This will interest us all the more because afterwards
Sebastian Bach had to fill an office at the same Court.

After the death of Ludwig Günther, his dominions fell to
his two nephews. The younger, Anton Günther, acquired the
"Oberherrschaft"[203] with the capital of Arnstadt, where he
took up his residence in 1683, and remained till his death in
1716. He invited Adam Drese to be Capellmeister to his Court,
a man at that time more than sixty years of age. He seems
to have been born at Weimar, about the middle of December
1620, and was sent by Duke Wilhelm IV., in whose band he
was first engaged, for his further education to Marco Sacchi,
Capellmeister to the King of Poland, at Warsaw; he was
then appointed Capellmeister to the Court of Weimar.
Here he presided, in 1658, over a band of sixteen performers,
and received a salary of 275 gülden, besides some payments
in kind. After the Duke's death in 1662, and the division of
his territory, the Duke's fourth son Bernhard took him to
Jena, which fell to that Prince's share. He not only gave
him the post of Capellmeister, but in consequence of Drese's

---

[203] His brother taking the " Unterherrschaft." The Count's dominions lying
up (oben) in the Thüringer wald, and below (unten) in the plain, they were
thus divided between his nephews.

manifold talents he appointed him his private secretary, and magistrate of the town and council. In the year 1667 the Prince made some changes in his establishment, and Drese, for some unknown reason, was dismissed. A petition addressed to Duke Moritz of Sax-Zeitz procured him a flattering recommendation to the Landgrave Ludwig of Hesse-Darmstadt.[204] Whether he obtained any appointment there is not clear; a year later he was back again at Jena. When Bernhard died, in 1678, Drese probably remained at his post, under the regency of the Duchess, and at her death (1682), after a short interval, he entered the service of the Court of Schwarzburg in 1683. In the course of events he had not improved his position; in 1696 he was in receipt of an annual payment of only 106 gülden. He died at the advanced age of eighty years and two months, February 15, 1701.

Drese's musical occupations must have been various and extensive. His principal instrument was the viol di gamba, as it was that of his friend and fellow-artist, Georg Neumark, with whom he lived and worked in Weimar. As a composer he brought out, in 1672, a collection of allemandes, courantes, sarabands, and the like, and he seems to have distinguished himself besides by writing various instrumental sonatas, church-pieces, and theatrical compositions, and especially by his treatment of recitative.[205] Nothing of all these works, printed and unprinted, has as yet been recovered, but fourteen songs by him have been preserved in Neumark's Fortgepflanztem musikalisch-poetischen Lustwalde (Jena, 1657); and an Introduction to the Art of Composition, by him, existed and was in use about the year 1680.[206] Of his "spiritual" melodies, which were composed partly to the hymns written by Büttner, a member of the Consistory at Arnstadt, and partly to his own sacred verses, that

---

[204] The papers are in the archives at Dresden.

[205] Walther, Lexicon, p. 217. Next to Casp. Wetzel's *Analecta hymnica*, I., sect. 4, p. 28, this is the principal source of information as to Drese.

[206] Mattheson, Ehrenpforte, p. 341. This supplements Gerber's quotation, N. L., I., col. 936.

beginning "Seelenbräutigam"—"Jesus, bridegroom of my soul,"—with its interesting setting but somewhat undignified feeling, has remained in use. These poetical and musical productions were closely connected with the change of opinions which took place in Drese in his old age. He had been a light-hearted and jolly musician, who loved to play the "lustige Person" or clown (Mr. Merriman) in the theatrical performances in which he bore a part. After the death of Duke Bernhard he first became acquainted with Spener's writings, and, principally by their influence, became a devoted adherent of pietism. In Arnstadt, besides fulfilling his official duties, he established meetings of his fellow-believers at his own house, in imitation of Spener's example; and in 1690 he published a work at Jena, On the Unerring Evidences of the True, Living, and Bliss-bestowing Faith.[207] Spener himself wrote a preface to it, in which he addresses to Drese the highest praise of his earnest purpose and deep feeling.[208]   But Arnstadt did not afford a favourable soil for pietism ; at any rate the two Olearius, father and son, who enjoyed the highest esteem there, at first together, were thoroughly hostile to it.   It was undoubtedly by their influence that, in 1694, on Cantata Sunday and on Ascension Day, a public warning was preached from every pulpit against the erroneous doctrines of the pietists, and it was not without satisfaction that Joh. Christoph Olearius the younger could write : " Although among others certain Quakerish-minded pietists had hitherto both secretly and openly striven to disturb religious peace, still God had hindered them by the Christian authorities."[209]   He subsequently characterised Drese as a crafty and restless man, full of fanatical whims, and whose house was the " harbour and refuge of all the sleek and subtle pietists"; he objected to include him among the writers of pure evangelical hymns, and expressed his delight " that he and his race have

---

[207] Unbetrügliche Prüfung des wahren, lebendigen und seligmachenden Glaubens.
[208] Winterfeld, Ev. Kirch., II., 603.
[209] Joh. Christ. Olearii Hist. Arnstadiensis.   Jena, Arnstadt, 1701, p. 43.

altogether died out of Arnstadt, and that all his doings
have perished with him." We have no means of deciding
whose judgment of Drese is the more correct, but in general
we cannot help feeling inclined to take the side of the
pietists as against that haughty and overbearing orthodoxy.
It is clear that, under these circumstances, Drese's position
in Arnstadt was not absolutely free from drawbacks, and,
besides this, he frequently found himself in great necessity
through no fault of his own. How little conscience was
exercised in the payment of his salary may be gathered from
a letter, among others, addressed by Drese to the Privy
Council of Arnstadt,.on April 19, 1691 : " I would, besides,
briefly recall that before Michaelmas of last year I was put
off till St. Lucy's (December 13) to draw two quarters (of
salary), so that the arrears might not grow too high. At
the said date of St. Lucy, I was put off till the Holy Festivals (at Christmas), and, after these, till Reminiscere
(February 22). These I waited with patience ; but when I
then again presented myself, I was further put off till Passion
Week, and when I presented myself, as became me, I was
informed there would be no money then. When I should
be put off to, after so many postponements, I knew not."
We must here not omit to notice the facility of expression,
and a touch of individual colouring, in this and other papers
written by Drese,[210] which have a most pleasing effect when
compared with the dead formality of most of the documents
of that time ; and which, even in this unimportant manifesta-
tion of his mind, proves the freshness and vigour which
animated pietism in spite of many perversities. Wilhelm
Friedrich Drese, a son of the old Capellmeister, worked with
him gratuitously in the Count's band' for four years after his
appointment.[211] He then filled some musical post to a Baron
von Meussbach in Triptis, near Weimar, and subsequently
endeavoured to get a place in the service of the Schwarzburgs.
He cannot have remained in it long. Towards the end of the

---

[210] All preserved in the archives of Sondershausen.
[211] He must previously have been Hofmusicus at Weimar, according to documents preserved there.

century the band was temporarily dispersed,[212] and Adam Drese, it is to be hoped, placed in circumstances of befitting ease. After his death, his wife having already died in 1698, the efforts of the pietists soon died out, and when, a few years later, Sebastian Bach came to Arnstadt as organist, hardly a trace of them was to be found. At any rate, Adam Drese himself cannot possibly have exerted any personal influence over him, as it has been thought necessary to suppose, since he was no longer living;[213] and it will presently be abundantly shown that Sebastian Bach's attitude towards pietism was quite a different one to what has commonly been imagined.

Count Anton Günther did much for music, and not the smallest part was at the instigation of his wife, Augusta Dorothea, who was accustomed to the eager artistic life and taste of her father's Court—Duke Anton Ulrich von Braunschweig-Wolfenbüttel. Besides calling a famous master to be at the head of his band, he caused several gifted youths to be educated and sent to travel at his cost, and he brought the band itself to very high perfection as compared with the smallness of his other circumstances. It is true that most of the musicians fulfilled other offices or services, but in their salaries their musical qualifications must always have been taken into consideration. One of the lists of the Court musicians includes the Organist and Cantor of Gehren, the Cantor of Breitenbach, and a bassoon-player from Sondershausen. It happened, too, on special occasions that all the musical forces of the little territory were concentrated, and the sober figure of Michael Bach may often have made its way on foot from Gehren to the castle of Arnstadt, to assist at some exceptionally grand Court concert.[214]

---

[212] On July 12, 1698, Peter Wenigk, of Gotha, petitions for an appointment, in case the Count should " be graciously minded at the dedication of the new chapel in the castle (1700) to establish a small *Capell-Music*."

[213] Winterfeld, Ev. Kirch., III., p. 276, from whom it has been copied by others.

[214] It is hardly possible now to form an adequate idea of what was expected of the German musicians of that time, when Italian singers, male and female, were conveyed in litters to each performance at the Prince's courts. Joh. Philipp

Even without this, a list of the members of the band is miscellaneous enough. The following is the catalogue of the instrumentalists about the year 1690:—Herr Drese, senior, viol di gamba; Wentzing, groom of the chambers, violin; Gleitsmann, groom of the chambers, lute, violin, and viol di gamba; Heindorff, actuary, violin; Clerk of the granary, clavier and violin; Clerk of the kitchen, clavier; Herr Drese, junior, viol di gamba; Heindorff, town-cantor, violin; one fagottist, five trumpeters; Jäger, trumpeter, violin; two oboists, who can also play the violin. Bach and his folks—four persons. These altogether made twenty-one players, enough for the perfect performance of any instrumental sonata. Another list is even more magnificent, giving an account of the vocal forces: it shall be given in its original form. For some inscrutable reason Drese, the Capellmeister, is not named.

Singers.		Instrumentalists.	
Discant:	Hans Dietrich Sturm.	Violin:	[Joh.] Christoph Bach.
Alto:	Hans Erhardt Braun.	Violin:	Christoph Jäger.
Tenor:	1. Clerk of the Chambers.	Violin:	The Actuary.
Tenor:	2. Clerk of the Granary.	Violin:	Wentzing.
Tenor:	3. Hans Heinrich Longolius.	Alto Viola:	} Bach's Assistants and Apprentices.
Bass:	1. Clerk of the Works.	Tenor Viola:	
Bass:	2. The Cantor.	Bass Viola:	
		Contrabasso: Clerk of the Kitchen.	
		Organ: Heinrich Bach.	

Besides Trumpeters, by a gracious special order these have hitherto been admitted to belong to this music:—

For the *Capella* or for *Complimento* [215]
out of the School here:—

Jäger's Son:	*Discant.*
Sauerbrey:	*Alto.*
Müller:	*Tenor.*
Schmidt:	*Bass.*

Weichardt, a member of the ducal band at Weimar, at the time of Sebastian Bach, was a student of law at Jena, and every Sunday he was obliged to make his way to Weimar, to perform in church, and back again.

[215] *I.e.*, for church or banquet music.

Of these persons the following especially may be employed
for instrumental music :—

Jäger, Bach, The Actuary, Wentzing, The Clerk of the Chambers, The Clerk of the Granary, Trumpeter Förster, Trumpeter Herthum, The Cantor, Hans Erhardt Braun, Hans Heinrich Longolius, Bach's Assistant,	Violins.
The Trumpeter's Apprentice, Hans Dietrich Sturm, Müller, from the School,	Alto Violas.
Schmidt, from the School, Sauerbrey, from the School, Bach's Apprentice,	Tenor Violas.
The Clerk of the Kitchen, Bach's Assistant, Bach's Apprentice;	Contrabasso and two Bass Viols.

An exact comparison of the two lists shows that the second
is the earlier, since Heinrich Bach is named in it, and by
the year 1690 he was no longer capable of service. But we
are obliged to attribute the former list to this date by finding
the name of Gleitsmann as groom of the chambers; he entered the Count's service at about that time. The second,
again, can hardly have been drawn up before 1683, or we
should have found in it Günther Bach, Heinrich's youngest
son. From this point of view we further detect, from our
comparison, that the body of instruments had become richer
and more varied under Drese's direction. The stringed instruments have been strengthened by the viol di gamba,
besides the lute, the oboes, and the fagotto. And the
circumstance that, in the second list of instruments, the
cembalist is wanting, justifies the conclusion that the instrumental music at the Court at that time was confined to
simple jingling melodies and dance-music, such as were
quite in place before and during banquets, and also that the
instrumental concerto was introduced by Drese; for it could

not have been performed without the accompaniment of the harpsichord. The clerk of the kitchen, mentioned as playing the clavier, was none other than Christoph Herthum, Heinrich Bach's son-in-law, and the same who in the older list is named as bass-player. Joh. Christoph Bach finally appears with four of his assistants in the first catalogue, but in the second with only three: if any conclusion may be drawn from this, it would seem that he fared better at first in his new position under Count Anton Günther than he did later. But we know from another source that, after the hard times at the beginning of this Count's rule, he never suffered from any prolonged necessity. On the contrary, he was able, at his death, to leave a small fortune to his family.

He, exactly like his father, only attained the age of forty-eight years, dying August 25, 1693. His widow and five children survived him. His widow obtained permission to retain her husband's office, and continue to have his duties performed by the assistants; but she proved herself unequal to cope with these rough and refractory men as regarded their duties, and, at the end of three years, she herself begged to withdraw from the position. The eldest son, Joh. Ernst, born August 8, 1683, had a by no means contemptible talent for music, and for its further cultivation he resided for six months in Hamburg, at his own expense, and afterwards spent some time in Frankfort. He then, undoubtedly, returned to Arnstadt to assist his mother and family by exercising his skill. Unhappily, he was not at first successful in this; and since, in the meantime, all his father's little property had been gradually exhausted by the survivors, and at last a long spell of sickness fell upon the household, Christoph Bach's family were soon in very straitened circumstances. No other branch of the Bach family who might have given them some assistance was then living in the town, excepting the youthful Sebastian, who held his first post as organist there from 1703 to 1707. But even he, as we shall see, did what lay in his power to assist his impoverished cousins. When he was called to Mühlhausen, Joh. Ernst was so fortunate, after a little exertion, as to become his successor. This certainly did not

take place till he had passed an examination under the capellmeister at the time, Paul Gleitsmann, in which Bach won
the precedence over the other candidates by the performance of a prelude on the full organ, and of a chorale with
extemporised accompaniments, and by his skilled and correct
working out of the figured-bass to a piece of church music
set before him at the moment. But that his proficiency at
four-and-twenty was not to be compared with that which
Sebastian had already attained at the age of eighteen is
evident from the considerable reduction in his salary ; he
received the very modest pay of forty gülden and a measure
and a half of corn, and it was also thought desirable to let
a half-year more elapse before he was definitively installed.
Since he remained for twenty years in this post, which could
barely have sufficed to maintain him, it is not astonishing that
he should not have answered the hopes which Gleitsmann
believed he might form of him. At any rate, in 1728, when
he finally was appointed to the Church of the Holy
Virgin, with a salary of seventy-seven gülden, he had to be
warned by the Consistory "to exercise himself still better in
his art, to improve himself as much as possible by due
reflection, not to remain always at one level, but to cultivate his skill by diligent correspondence with one and
another among experienced musicians." However, a weakness of the eyes impeded his studies. He married for
the first time, October 22, 1720, a daughter of the minister
of Wandersleben, named Wirth ; his second wife, whom he
married in 1725, was Magdalene Christiane Schober; she
was the daughter of a law-clerk at Gotha. She, with three
infant children, survived her husband, on whom the sun
of good fortune had so seldom shone.

Of the three brothers of Joh. Ernst, the youngest, Joh.
Andreas, died within a year of his father, aged three; of
another, Joh. Heinrich, nothing is known, but that he was
born December 3, 1686. Joh. Christoph, however, is more
frequently mentioned. He was born September 13, 1689, but
the incidents of his life are as little known to us as the date
of his death. According to the genealogy, he was a dealer
at Blankenhain. On the other hand, a certain Joh. Christoph

Bach, born at Arnstadt, applied in the year 1726 for the place of organist at the girl's school at the village of Keula, in Schwarzburg, where he had for twelve years been in the service of the chief magistrate (*Oberamtmann*) Struve, and had sometimes officiated in playing the organ. As this personage can hardly be any other than the son of Sebastian's uncle, we must either regard the statement in the genealogy as incorrect, or assume that he became a dealer afterwards. This, indeed, is not impossible. He seems to have died in 1736.[216]

Here we lose the line of the descendants of Johann Christoph Bach, the town-musician ; but the case is quite the reverse with those of his twin-brother, Ambrosius. While we do not even know the names of Joh. Christoph's grandsons, the genius of the family continued to blossom even in the children's children of Ambrosius, and though none of them could compare even remotely with the sole and only One, still the spirit of art stirred and lived in them all. The genius of the race, after having diffused itself more or less widely through whole generations, now culminated and exhausted itself in the family of Ambrosius Bach.

We left Ambrosius Bach at the time when he entered the town-council of Erfurt, April 12, 1667, and it was previously stated (p. 21) that he was the successor in it of his cousin Joh. Christian, the eldest son of Johann Bach, who at that time moved from Erfurt to Eisenach. He played the alto viola, as we learn on this occasion. We may certainly extend this so as to include violin-playing in general; and it is worthy of remark, as bearing on Sebastian's musical development, that it was principally violin-playing that he must have heard in his father's house. Only one year after his appointment Ambrosius was married, April 8, 1668. It was in this same year that the outlay at weddings, which had degenerated into extravagance and excess, was restricted

---

[216] According to the pedigree given by Korabinsky. Hilgenfeldt gives the date as 1730, no doubt from an oversight in using Korabinsky's work. The daughter, only once mentioned, of Ambrosius Bach's twin-brother, was Barbara Katharina, born May 14, 1680.

within proper limits by special legislation for the regulation of weddings by the Elector of Mainz.[217] Bach's bride was Elisabeth Lämmerhirt, born February 24, 1644, the daughter of Valentin Lämmerhirt, a furrier, living under the sign of " The Three Roses," in the Junkersande (now No. 1,285).[218] The Lämmerhirt family were not strangers to the Bachs. Johann Bach had already chosen his second wife, Hedwig, from among them—a relation of Elisabeth's, but of course much older. From this marriage issued six sons and two daughters.[219] The first child must have been born between 1668 and 1671, and have died soon after ; then followed the eldest of those that survived their parents, Joh. Christoph, born June 16, 1671.[220] In October of the same year Ambrosius moved to Eisenach, leaving his place among the town-musicians, as has been told, to his cousin Aegidius Bach. Besides the maintenance of his family he now undertook the support and care of his hapless idiot sister, who, however, was released by death from her miserable existence in 1679. It is a genuine trait of the Bach character that the brothers wished to have the funeral sermon preached on this occasion printed as a memorial, as may be seen in the dedication, addressed to the three brothers and Joh. Christoph (their cousin, Heinrich's son). The preacher, taking for his text Luke, xii. 48, " For unto whom much is given, of him much shall be required," pointed out the strange distribution of human wealth and talents, saying : " Our sister, who now rests in the Lord, was a simple creature, not knowing her right hand from her left ; she was like a child. If, on the contrary, we look at her brothers we find that they are gifted with a good understanding, with art and skill which make them respected and listened to in the churches, schools, and in all the township, so that through them the Master's work is praised." This opinion deserves our attention, because it contains the only contemporary

---

[217] Comp. Hartung, Häuser-Chronik der Stadt Erfurt, p. 303.
[218] See Appendix A, No. 8.
[219] According to the genealogy.
[220] According to Brückner, Kirchen- und Schulen-Staat, Part III., sect. 10, p. 95.

judgment now extant of Ambrosius Bach.[221] He never again quitted Eisenach. In the spring of 1684 he was indeed invited to rejoin the Erfurt company of musicians, and showed some desire to obey the call. But Duke Johann Georg would not permit him to go, thus proving how highly he esteemed him.[222] The highly respectable position which he held was, indeed, the reason why other members not only of his own family, but of his wife's, came to settle in Eisenach. The children born there came in the following order : Joh. Balthasar, born March 4, 1673, died in the beginning of April, 1691; Joh. Jonas, born January 3, 1675; Maria Salome, born May 27, 1677 ; Johanna Juditha, born January 26, 1680 (she received her first name from Johann Pachelbel, at that time Organist to the Predigerkirche in Erfurt) ; Joh. Jakob, born February 9, 1682. None of these lived to grow up but Joh. Jakob and Maria Salome, who married one Wiegand, probably of Erfurt, and as early as 1707 she was left the sole survivor of the sisters. The man to whose memory this work is dedicated closed the list, the youngest of Ambrosius Bach's children. We shall enter on a fresh section with the date of his birth.

A comprehensive retrospect over the history of his forefathers and relations, which is here closed, will suffice to show that from no artist have we a better right to expect, at the very threshold of his career, that he should embody the whole essence of the German nation, than from Sebastian Bach. His ancestors had already lived and laboured for centuries in that province of Germany which was his cradle ; they had grown to be one with their native land in a way which results more from tilling and sowing it than from any other form of labour. Thus, deriving their sustenance from the soil, the race had spread abroad as a mighty oak spreads its branches, on all sides, and their common origin

---

[221] The funeral sermon of M. Valentin Schrön on Dorothea Maria Bach, born April 10, 1653, printed at Eisenach, 1679, is to be found in the Ducal Library at Gotha. Another of Christoph Bach's daughters, Barbara Maria, is also mentioned, born April 30, 1651.

[222] From documents in the parish register of Eisenach, first quoted by Ritter in a revised edition of his works on Bach, now coming out in parts, see p. 36.

was never forgotten. For generations they had at once fostered and represented those forms of music which appeal most nearly to the transcendental and metaphysical spirit of the German people, and which were destined to be brought by them to the highest perfection—namely, instrumental music and Protestant sacred music, which chiefly grew out of instrumental music. A constantly increasing sum of musical experience and practice had been handed down from generation to generation, and had at last become an innate portion of the Bach nature; and thus a suitable soil had been prepared for the favourable development of an unapproachable genius. And that modest piety and decent morality which we Germans may specially claim as having been at all times the distinguishing virtues of our nation—though, indeed, they are the necessary conditions of all healthy and vigorous growth—we find faithfully cherished from the first in the Bach family. Indeed, this instinct seems to have constituted a mainstay of that strong family connection which was always closest precisely at those periods when society was most demoralised. During the second half of the seventeenth century, when the rapid growth of the numerous musical bands of the Courts of Germany must have tempted them to more brilliant and profitable occupations, they appear as simple organists and cantors in the service of the Church, or as fostering the national town music-guilds among the people, coming only into incidental contact with Courts. Piety was at that time a precious possession, the Church and the priesthood cherished the highest culture. Hence that feature which is so peculiar to the German character, which was of such conspicuous importance in the time following the war—an ideal standard of life and of its duties, and, consequently, an elevated conception of the nature and ideal import of all Art—could the more easily be developed among them.

There can be no greater contrast than that of German to Italian art at that period. On the one side, with great qualities, brilliant rather than deeply rooted, what arrogance, vanity, avarice, and immorality! On the other a modest and unself-seeking diligence, working in a narrow circle; a life often spent in a struggle against want, but in faithful devotion to duty; and a family feeling which resisted all the floods of the outer world. And with these we find a deeply cherished growth and development of the sublimest forms of art, at first merely dreamed of, veiled as it were in the mists of poetic fancy, modelled with an experimental touch; but then seen and grasped in all their meaning, and brought to life with a warmth and fervency which to this day have lost nothing of their value. Beyond a doubt, such a composer as Johann Christoph Bach had a perfect right to set his exquisite motetts by the side of the most brilliant productions of the masters of Italian art, if it ever could have occurred to him to assert himself in any way; but art was all he cared for, and to serve art was his only pride. The character of the Thuringian land, to which the Bachs clung so tenaciously, also exerted an influence over them in many ways. The loneliness of its woods and valleys—which still, even in these overwhelming times of ours, here and there, arouses a delightful feeling, as though the motley world had been left outside the mountains that hedge it in—whose charms could keep its hold even on the great soul of Goethe for more than fifty years—that spirit of solitude soared over the country with wider and mightier wings a century earlier. It narrowed the outlook and deepened the sources of inward life, the spring from which music, above all, derives its vitality. More particularly it tinged the peculiar religious spirit which speaks to us in the works of Christoph and Sebastian Bach. Beethoven's " Pastoral Symphony," in which Nature appears as a grand temple, and Sebastian Bach's organ preludes and fugues, through which we hear a rush as of the elements through the crowns of mighty oaks, both flow from the same fount of feeling.

It is scarcely possible to name any other artist the roots of whose being can be traced back for two hundred years. A strong stamp of nationality no doubt necessarily involves a certain one-sidedness; and in matters of art it has always been a weakness of the Germans—not often successfully overcome—that they subordinate perfection of form to

the ideal inspiration, while it is only the complete balance
of the two factors that can result in a perfect work of art.
But there was a safeguard, stronger than any other could
have been, against the peril which yawns for every composer who is devoted to instrumental music, of losing himself in that bottomless and introspective subjectivity which
leads at last to absolute artistic and æsthetic demoralisation.
And that was the old tradition of the Bachs—centuries old,
nobly formed, and deeply rooted—which held conquered
acquisition as sacred; this availed to preserve the man in
whom the stupendous flood and torrent of his power would
otherwise have been sufficient to overwhelm all the forms
already extant, and to have left a chaos where, as it is,
works of fabulous beauty rise before us. Thus the good
genius of his race not only raised him, but protected him
too.

The student who desires to appreciate the depth of our
national being, and to do justice to the history of culture at
the beginning of the eighteenth century, must give due consideration to the advent of Sebastian Bach, who, when all
around was dead and void, appeared unhoped for, and as if
called up by a magic word—as a water-lily is thrown up on
the dull and formless surface of a pool, a glorious evidence
of the imperishable vitality hidden in the womb of nature
and of time. Sebastian Bach appeared at the close of a
period of deep dejection for the German people; the first
promise and sufficient pledge of a new spring-time, moral
and intellectual.

BOOK II.

THE CHILDHOOD AND EARLY YEARS OF
JOHANN SEBASTIAN BACH,
1685 TO 1707.

BOOK II.

THE CHILDHOOD AND EARLY YEARS OF
JOHANN SEBASTIAN BACH,
1685 TO 1707.

I.

EARLY DAYS.—EDUCATION.—OHRDRUF AND LÜNEBURG,
1685 TO 1703.

JOHANN SEBASTIAN BACH was born in all probability on March 21, 1685, but the only direct evidence we have is the fact that March 23 was the day of his baptism. His godfathers were Sebastian Nagel, a musician of Gotha, and Johann Georg Koch, a forester of Eisenach.[1] For the first nine years of his life the boy enjoyed the happiness of his mother's care and protection, but on May 3, 1694, Ambrosius Bach followed his wife's body to the grave. Nor need we attribute to indifference to his dead wife the fact that he married again scarcely seven months later (November 27), Dame Barbara Margaretha Bartholomäi, the widow of a deacon of Arnstadt. Married life was almost indispensable to the strong and healthy family feeling of the Bachs, and their vigorous instincts soon turned from the dead to the living; and a woman's presence and orderly superintendence must have seemed doubly desirable in a house full of young children. But Ambrosius was not destined to rejoice long

---

[1] Parish register of Eisenach. It may here be mentioned that the Gregorian Calendar, or New Style, was not used in Evangelical Germany till 1701, and that all the dates occurring before this era must be carried on ten days to make them coincide with the modern reckoning. It would, therefore, be accurate to fix the day of Sebastian Bach's birth as March 31. According to a tradition preserved in a lateral branch of the family, the house in the Frauenplan A 303, at Eisenach, is that where he was born, and a memorial tablet was not long since placed there by the city authorities.

in his newly established household, for he died two months afterwards, and was buried January 31, 1695. The family was now broken up. Johann Jakob Bach apprenticed himself to his father's successor in the office of town-musician;[2] of the other brothers, Johann Balthasar was already dead, as can be proved, and so also, probably, was Johann Jonas. Johann Christoph had already for some years earned his own bread, and it was to him that the care and education of Johann Sebastian, then hardly ten years old, were confided, and the boy never again spent any long time in his native town. So far as we may suppose at this distance of time, this very early period of his life was wholly given up to arousing and cultivating the dormant—or perhaps already active—powers of his mind.

So far as we can judge from the few details and indications we have concerning his own life, and from the character of the twin-brother who so much resembled him, together with the fundamental features of the Bach nature, his father had been a man of moral worth, conscientious and skilled in his art, at the same time of independent views and of good report among his fellow-citizens. That he was highly esteemed by his family is proved by the fact that a large portrait in oil was painted of him, and this also leads us to infer that he lived in easy circumstances.[3]   In this portrait, which represents him as of about forty years of age, we see a strongly marked countenance with the same nose and chin that we find again in his son.   It is still more characteristic, and an unusual thing at that period, that we have here no civic portrait with a curled wig and smug solemnity of face. A frank-looking man gazes out from the canvas in a careless everyday garb ; the shirt, which shows over the bosom, is loosely held together at the throat by a riband, natural brown hair hangs round the head, and a moustache even ornaments the face. Any one who can estimate how much the painting of a picture in oils implies for a man of that rank, will be able to draw the right con-

---

[2] According to the genealogy.
[3] This portrait was afterwards in the possession of Philipp Emanuel Bach, and is now in the Royal Library at Berlin.

clusions from this complete emancipation from all that, at that period, was held to be correct and suitable.

Ambrosius must have noticed his son's great musical gifts at an early age, and have cultivated them, in the first instance, in violin-playing, as his own skill would naturally lead him to do; so that the love for this instrument which Sebastian manifested so constantly must have had its root in the impressions of his earliest infancy. He must also have found an object of admiration in Joh. Christoph Bach, the greatest musician which the Bach family had up to this time produced, with his extraordinary skill on the organ and general musical talents; and he, no doubt, also derived from him much incitement, which for a short period bore outward results in the form of imitative compositions.

Indeed, Eisenach was already generally known for the musical taste and tendencies that were predominant there. So early as in the fifteenth century poor scholars marched through the town three times a week, singing hymns and asking alms. About the year 1600 the perambulating chorus for part-singing was established by Jeremias Weinrich, the master of the school of Eisenach, and soon became the pride and delight of the city and the neighbourhood. Consisting originally of only four scholars, it soon increased to forty and more, and this was the number even about the year 1700, at which period we have information concerning it.[4] As we know that Sebastian subsequently distinguished himself as a fine soprano, we may very well assume that, at any rate towards the later period of his residence at Eisenach, he took part in the performances of the scholars' choir, and marched through the streets singing as he went—just as Luther had done in the same town two hundred years before. Ambrosius Bach had sent his eldest son in his early youth to Erfurt, in 1686, where for three years he

---

[4] *Christiani Francisci Paullini* Annales Isenacenses. Francofurti ad Moenum. Anno M.DC.XCVIII., p. 237. Somewhat further back he says: "Claruit semper urbs nostra Musicâ. Et quid est *Isenacum* χατ' ἀναγρ. quàm *en musica:* vel: *Isenacum, canimus*." ("Our town was always celebrated for music—And what is the anagram of *Isenacum*—the Latinised form of Eisenach —but *en musica*—lo! music. or *canimus*—we sing?")

enjoyed the instruction of their friend Johann Pachelbel. In the last year of his apprenticeship he took the post of Organist in the Church of St. Thomas there ; this, however, did not satisfy even the most modest demands, either as to the organ or as to salary, and he soon gave it up. Joh. Christoph now turned to Arnstadt, where for a time he performed the duties of the venerable Heinrich Bach, and relieved the cares of his godfather Herthum with respect to his old father-in-law.   Since the twin-brother of Ambrosius Bach—whose name was also Joh. Christoph—then living in Arnstadt, had married a daughter of Eisentraut, the parish-clerk of Ohrdruf, we can understand why it should be in this town that Joh. Christoph the younger, in 1690, sought and obtained employment.   He was appointed organist of the principal church of the town.   In the sixteenth century, and to the beginning of the seventeenth, other persons of the name of Bach had already settled in this place; still the scanty records of their existence contained in the parish register do not allow us to hazard a guess as to their connection with the other branches of the family that had flourished elsewhere; and after this time, until the arrival of Joh. Christoph the younger, the name seems to have disappeared there.   He, no doubt by reason of his youth, was installed with the small salary of forty-five gülden a year and a few payments in kind.   He certainly ere long asked for an addition, but though it was refused he still thought his position allowed of his getting married in October, 1694, to the maiden Dorothea von Hof.   This newly established home made it possible for him to receive the young Sebastian on the death of his father, which occurred soon after.   He must have been his first teacher in clavier-playing, and for this reason it would be highly interesting if we could give an approximate sketch of his own works and labours.   But, unfortunately, the means for doing so are wholly wanting.   We are disposed to a favourable judgment of them by the circumstance that he was Pachelbel's pupil during three years.   An invitation to go to Gotha, in 1696—which he refused in consequence of an increase of pay—leads us to infer, though not with any certainty, that his skill was known beyond his own town ; or it may be that Pachelbel, who had quitted Gotha in 1695, had recommended him there; and, from his having made a collection of works by the most famous writers for the organ of that period, we may gather that he strove to reach the highest level of his time. Finally, his sons, who all became cantors and organists in Ohrdruf and the neighbourhood, may be mentioned in evidence of the essentially musical nature of their father.[5] But all the other information we have concerning him has little or nothing to do with music. It was customary then, as it is now, to employ the organists and cantors as elementary instructors in the schools. Johann Christoph at first did not choose to fulfil this double service, which had been performed by his predecessor Paul Beck, but he accommodated himself to it in the year 1700 for the sake of the larger income, which now amounted to ninety-seven gülden, with six measures and a half of corn, six cords of wood, and four loads of brushwood. But he seems to have been ill adapted to be an instructor of youth, and he bore the burden he had taken up with more and more difficulty as the support of his family increased the need for it ; his health began to fail, and he was obliged to own that he was losing his enjoyment and power in the exercise of his proper vocation of organist. He died February 22, 1721, and was succeeded as organist by his second son, while the instruction of the fifth class was given over to a stranger.[6]

---

[5] These sons, or such of them as grew up, were Tobias Friedrich, born 1695, Cantor at Uttstädt from 1721 ; Joh. Bernhard, 1700, Organist at Ohrdruf; Joh. Christoph, 1702, Cantor at Ohrdruf; Joh. Heinrich, 1707, Cantor at Oehringen ; Joh. Andreas, 1713, Organist at Ohrdruf after 1744. Descendants of the third son are still living there.

[6] Melchior Kromayer, superintendent at Ohrdruf, began in the year 1685 to keep a book for entering an account of the life and the salary paid to every priest, teacher, and church official in the town and neighbourhood. This book, which contains, among others, autograph biographies of Joh. Christoph Bach and his sons, Tobias Friedrich, Joh. Bernhard, Joh. Christoph, and Joh. Andreas, was recently found in Ohrdruf, by Herr Staudigel, the town-clerk, and in the politest way put at my disposal. Brückner (Kirchen und Schulenstaat, Part III., pp. 95, 96, &c.) also made use of it, but not without falling into some errors. I am indebted for information from other sources to the kindness of Dr. Schulze, Superintendent at Ohrdruf.

An anecdote attaches to the volume of organ music just mentioned, which is significant as bearing on the instinct for learning of Sebastian Bach. The pieces which his elder brother put before him were quickly mastered and exhausted, as to their technical and theoretical difficulty; he demanded more difficult tasks and loftier flights. Still, pride of seniority made Joh. Christoph withhold this collection from the boy, who every day could see the object of his longing lying within the wire lattice of a bookcase. At last he stole down at night, and succeeded in extracting the roll of music through the opening of the wires. He had no light, so the moon had to serve him while he made a copy of the precious treasure. By the end of six months the work was finished —a work which none but the most ardent votary of his art could ever have undertaken. But his brother soon discovered him with the hardly won copy, and was so hard-hearted as to take it away from him.[1] The perseverance of true genius, with which we shall at a later date still see Sebastian Bach striving after the end on which he had set his heart, is as evident in this story as the fact that he soon had no more to learn from his eldest brother. The most important thing in the matter to us is that he must, while yet a boy, have been acquainted with Pachelbel's creations and with the spirit of his art. How, as a man of honour, he repaid his brother fifteen years later, shall be told in its place.

At Ohrdruf he began at the same time to lay the foundations of a general education. The " Lyceum " or academy there, founded in 1560 by the Counts von Gleichen, enjoyed a by no means small reputation. It was comparatively well endowed, could point to many competent and learned teachers, and could send scholars from its first class to

---

[1] Mizler, Mus. Bib., Vol. IV., p. 161. It is here erroneously stated that Sebastian did not recover possession of the book till after his brother's death, which occurred soon after, and that it was his death which led to his departure for Lüneberg; Forkel, pp. 4, 5, repeats this. But the fact that Sebastian's sons and pupils antedated Joh. Christoph's death by about twenty years is a proof that his influence was not regarded as of special value in the development of Sebastian's talent; otherwise more attention would have been directed to the principal events of his life.

the university. In the course of the seventeenth century it numbered six classes, the lowest three forming the people's school, since those who did not aspire to a learned education were sent home during the Latin and Greek lessons. Still, even in the upper classes those might have a share of the instruction who were exempt from studying the dead languages. However, there were certainly not many branches of study remaining. That Sebastian was not one of those who claimed this exemption is proved by the knowledge of Latin—as peculiar to himself as it was thorough—which is self-evident in his letters and official documents; and, indeed, it may be taken for granted from all the traditions of the Bach family. To judge by the age at which he left his brother's house, he cannot have risen beyond the second class in Ohrdruf (the first class being the highest); and, indeed, what he learnt must, from the divisions of the schools at that time, have been one-sided enough. Theology, Latin, and Greek—the last only on the basis of the New Testament—formed almost the whole of the course of instruction, with a little rhetoric and arithmetic. Of the Roman writers those studied in this class were Cornelius Nepos and Cicero, particularly his epistles. The rest of the instruction consisted in learning grammatical rules written in Latin, with exercises in prosody, in disputation, and in style. French, almost indispensable to the culture of the time, was entirely neglected, as also was history.[8] For music five hours out of the thirty hours of study per week were set aside in the first and second classes, and four in the third and fourth; and the chorus of singers appears to have been at this time an institution of great importance, under the conduct of the cantor. His province included, besides the church services on Sunday

---

[8] Rudloff, Geschichte des Lyceums zu Ohrdruf. Arnstadt, 1845. He gives a scheme of study, p. 20, which I have here followed. It is certainly as early as 1660, but in the course of the century at the utmost the requirements in each branch of learning may have been somewhat raised. Any more extensive variety of branches of learning was not introduced till the beginning of the eighteenth century. Lessons in history were given in Ohrdruf from the year 1716 (Rudloff, p. 14). French was not taught till 1740 (Ibid, p. 17).

and festivals, the performance of motetts and concertos at weddings and funerals, as well as the perambulations with singing, at fixed times, from door to door. The regularity of the school lessons was no doubt seriously interfered with by this arrangement; indeed, it would seem that at Ohrdruf, as distinguished from other places in Thuringia, it was the custom for the scholars to share in the entertainment at weddings, not unfrequently to the detriment alike of their moral and physical balance. How fully the school chorus was occupied is evident from their receipts, which, during the third quarter of the year 1720 amounted to 237 thalers, 11 groschen, and 6 pfennige.[9] Here Sebastian found fresh food for his genius, and it can be shown that he rose to be one of the foremost singers, perhaps, indeed, to be a "concertist," receiving a fixed stipend and a larger share in the subdivision and distribution of the earnings of the choir. From the year 1696 Joh. Christoph Kiesewetter was Rector of the school: a very learned man, who in 1712 went to fill the same office at the academy of Weimar, and there once more met with his former pupil, Sebastian Bach, as court organist and chamber musician. The offices of sub-warden and master of the second class were held from 1695 till 1728 by Joh. Jeremias Böttiger.[10] The religious tone of the school was strictly orthodox, and all the masters, including Joh. Christoph Bach, had to sign the Concordien book.[11] Under these auspices Sebastian grew to be a youth.

When he was fifteen it was his fate to have to stand on his own feet; he was forced into independence by circumstances. His brother's increasing family made the house too narrow; besides, he felt that there was no more to be gained by remaining in that place, and was conscious of sufficient strength to go on without further help from others. What step he should take was ere long settled by a happy accident. It was Elias Herda, who had been Cantor to the

---

[9] Rudloff, p. 25.
[10] Brückner, pp. 83, 86.
[11] Concordia e Joh. Muelleri, manuscripto edita. Lips. et Jenæ, 1705, p. 59.

Academy since 1698, a young musician of four-and-twenty,
who, beyond a doubt, showed him his path.   His father, a
farrier at Leina, near Gotha, had some years before made
a journey to Lüneburg, while his son, then about the same
age as Bach now was, was studying in the Academy at Gotha
and cultivating his musical talents.   There he had heard
from a man of that country that in Lower Saxony boys from
Thuringia were in great favour, on account of their musical
talents and proficiency, and that the Cantor of the Church of
the Benedictine monks of St. Michael at Lüneburg was just
now seeking such a lad, whom he would provide for and
maintain.   Herda remarked that he himself had a musical
son of about the right age, and the Cantor being informed of
it, succeeded, by opportunely representing the case, in getting
young Herda to go to Lüneburg.   There he at once obtained
a free place at the refectory table, and remained for six years.
He afterwards studied theology for two years at Jena, and
soon after received the appointment in which he became
Bach's teacher, perhaps in music only.[12]   It is easy to
guess what followed.   Sebastian had a fine soprano voice,[13]
distinguished himself by his zeal and his performance, and
became a favourite with the young cantor.   When the question arose as to his further progress in life, he recommended
him to the school of the Convent of St. Michael, at Lüneburg, where his own memory was still green, and where the
name of Bach was already well-known, from two of the most
distinguished of those who had borne it.   Indeed, two good
singers must have been needed there at the same time, for
with Sebastian there went thither his friend and contemporary Georg Erdmann, also a young Thuringian of musical
gifts, who, in after years, though his own path of life led in a
different direction, never forgot this youthful friendship.[14]
They set out on their journey about Easter 1700, and

[12] Brückner, p. 88.

[13] Mizler, op. cit.

[14] I have not been able to discover Erdmann's birthplace.   If the parish
register is perfect, he was not born at Ohrdruf.   In the Imperial archives at
Moscow, acts referring to him only record that he was a native of Sax-Gotha ;
nor could I find any account of his parents.

entered the chorus of St. Michael's School in April. They
were at once admitted, on their proficiency, into the select
troop of the "matins scholars," and immediately allowed
the second grade salary given to the discantists at that
time.[15] Erdmann stands above Bach in the list, whence we
may conclude that he was in a higher class. We see that
they can hardly have gone to Lüneburg without some preliminary introduction—that they cannot have gone there
merely at a venture. The matins singers formed the
main body of the choir, and must have been supported by
the Convent. Hence exceptional talents and powers were
looked for, and certainly the requirements must have been
something more than merely a fine voice and practice in
part-singing, when choristers were sought out from Central
Germany. Sebastian Bach, at the age of fifteen, would not
have ventured on his first flight into the world merely on the
strength of his soprano voice ; nay, we learn that he soon lost
it in Lüneburg, and for a long time could not sing at all.[16]
But the opportunity was all the more favourable for showing
himself a skilled instrumentalist. When the cantor was re-
hearsing the singing, an accompaniment was needed on the
harpsichord; in performances with concerted accompaniments
the violin was needed, not to mention other opportunities ;
indeed, we know that the St. John's School instituted a special
band of instruments which, at the New Year, marched playing
through the streets, thus finding a source of profit. The
Thuringians had always had a greater gift for this form of
musical art than for singing, and it certainly was in a great
degree, if not altogether, his proficiency as a violinist,
clavier-player, and organist that procured Sebastian his
admission among the matins scholars of St. Michael.
Whether subsequently, when his voice had completely
changed, he became prefect of the choir—since he remained

---

[15] At my request, Professor W. Junghans, of Lüneburg, has searched out
much information as to the musical affairs of St. Michael's School from the
archives of the convent, with an amount of care worthy of all gratitude, and
published them, with other details as to the practice of music in Lüneburg
itself, in the " Easter programme " of that year.

[16] Mizler.

three years at Lüneburg—is not known; but it may be fairly
supposed in that position he had to undertake a certain
share of the duties of direction, and particularly the leading
of the processional singing.
At any rate his outward needs were provided for. Beyond
a doubt he and his companion Erdmann were allowed seats
at the free board of the Convent, like Herda before them, for
this privilege was granted to all the matins scholars, of which
the average number at that time was about fifteen. The
salary was paid monthly, and for the first two months after
Bach's appointment—of which alone the account has been
preserved—it amounted to twelve groschen a month; the
highest sum to which he could gradually rise was one
thaler a month. If he was able to add to this the office of
accompanist on the harpsichord, this would bring him in an
income of twelve thalers a year. Still the principal revenue
flowed to the whole choir of the college, of which the matins
singers constituted only the nucleus; it consisted at that time
of from twenty to thirty members, and its income was derived
from the processional singing in the streets, and from
weddings and funeral solemnities. In the year 1700 the
receipts came to 372 marks, of which the cantor, according
to custom, took a sixth part; the prefect received fifty-six
marks, and the remainder each a share in proportion to his
standing in the choir. As has already been said, the School
of St. John had a choir which was conducted in precisely
the same way, so it may be inferred how strong the feeling
for music must have been in Lüneburg at that time. A
certain rivalry, which is easily understood, existed between
the two choirs and certainly bore good fruit, though it had
occasionally given rise to conflicts when, at the season for
processional singing—which was only in the winter half-
year—the choirs came into opposition. For this reason the
streets had long been exactly designated in which, each day,
the choirs were to sing.
The employment of the St. Michael's Choir in the services of
the church was tolerably extensive. An order for the regulation of matins and vespers, of the year 1656, assigns a place
and use to concerted church compositions, as well as to motetts

and hymns in parts, and to anthems or *spiritual arias* in one
or more parts.   On eighteen certain festivals of the ecclesiastical year a complete choir and orchestra performed, as well
as on other occasions, not unfrequently by special order.
Thus, in 1656-57, the complete band performed thirty times;
in 1657-58. thirty-four times.   On other Sundays and holy-
days a motett at least was performed at morning service,
and at afternoon service an aria with organ accompaniment.   Indeed, it is evident that the Convent grudged no
means for the maintenance of an efficient choral body, and
for the appointment of noble and worthy church music,
since in the year 1702-3, for instance, it devoted to this
purpose the sum of more than 507 thalers, at that time considerable.   The shelves of the musical library were filled
with an unusual abundance of treasures, and their contents may be seen in the catalogue for the year 1696, still
existing in the archives.   Besides the various important
collected works of earlier composers, as the *Promptuarium
Musicum* of Schadaeus, and *Florilegium Portense* of Boden-
schatz, the seventeenth century was represented by the most
important published works of all the most esteemed German
masters of that period : Schütz, Scheidt, Hammerschmidt,
Joh. Rud. Ahle, Briegel, Rosenmüller, Tob. Michael, Schop,
Jeep, Crüger, Selle, Joh. Krieger, and others.   The Cantor,
Friedr. Emanuel Praetorius, alone (1655-1694) acquired
many more than a hundred volumes.[17]   Besides these there
was a collection of 1,102 sacred pieces, as it would seem
in manuscript only, among which Heinrich Bach and Joh.
Christoph Bach, "*Henrici filius*," were represented each
by one work.   Since Joh. Jakob Löw, a native of Eisenach,
was at that time Organist at the Church of St. Nikolaus at
Lüneburg, it was probably by his instrumentality that the
North German town became acquainted with the two Thuringian masters ; at any rate it is interesting to learn that
the name of Bach was known there before the advent of
Sebastian.   That of Joh. Pachelbel is also to be found.
A few compositions by Georg Ludwig Agricola, the little-

---

[17] Junghans, pp. 26, 28, has given the whole catalogue.

known Capellmeister of Gotha, who died quite young, may have been introduced by Herda.[18]

Thus we see there was ample opportunity for Sebastian Bach to gather knowledge and experience in the province of vocal church music. But the whole course of his life shows that his development was based on instrumental music, too plainly for us not to suppose that he looked on the vocal side of his art as less important, and subsidiary to his training as an instrumental player and composer. To look for his teacher in these branches would be waste of trouble; the only function that any master could fulfil towards this great genius—that of curbing for a time with a steady hand the sportive and soaring exuberance of early youth, until it should have found a sure footing—had been supplied by the traditions and influences of his race. These afforded Sebastian Bach the discipline which Mozart—his peer in native genius—derived from the chastening severity of his watchful father. Thus the young tree grew up, almost of its own accord, in the direction in which it could best spread and flourish; just as a plant turns instinctively towards the sun, so he grew towards the side where he felt that light and space were awaiting him. When the best authorities as to Sebastian's life tell us that he learnt composition, for the most part, merely by study and contemplation of the best works of the most famous and learned compositions of the time, and from his own mental assimilation of them, we may not only be assured of the perfect accuracy of this observation, but may also extend it to his technical accomplishment. His eminent executive talent, when once he had surmounted the preliminary steps, only required to watch and note the performances of good executants in order to acquire all that it needed.

The restless industry of genius—which is rather one of the forces of nature than an outcome of the prompting of our moral consciousness—irresistibly urged him forward and

---

[18] Junghans has also printed the catalogue of this second collection, but in an abridged form, pp. 28, 29. The whole musical library of the Convent of St. Michael has been dispersed and lost.

gave him no rest, even at night, from the solution of the problems he set himself. Hence it is of exceptional importance to our knowledge of his progress that we should be acquainted both with the persons and the artistic influences which can be proved, or even supposed, to have have had a determining effect on it. What the Cantor and the Organist of St. Michael's Church may have done in this way—the former was named Augustus Braun and the latter Christoph Morhardt[19]—can now no longer be even guessed. The musical library contained twenty-four, pieces by Braun, with and without instrumental accompaniment; these are lost, nor is any opinion of either of them by a contemporary to be found. It is equally impossible to state what sort of organ the church possessed; it can have been nothing remarkable, since a new one was constructed in the second decade of the eighteenth century.[20]

Löw, the organist, to be sure, enjoyed a reputation as an experienced and thoroughly sound artist. He had cultivated his talents in Italy and at Vienna, and was a friend of Heinrich Schützen's, who brought him to Wolfenbüttel as Capell-Director in 1655.[21] Bach would certainly not have kept aloof from this his countryman, particularly if Löw, as we may suppose, had been acquainted with Heinrich and Christoph Bach, although he was now an old man[22] and could hardly have had full sympathy with the stirrings of a young genius. But I do not know a single note of his compositions, and cannot venture on any merely general conjecture as to his artistic influence.

However, a fourth musician exerted a recognisable and considerable influence over Bach. This was Georg Böhm, who was also his countryman, and the Organist of St. John's Church. Goldbach, near Gotha, is mentioned as his native

[19] Junghans, pp. 35, 39.

[20] Niedt, Mus. Handleit. Part II., p. 191.

[21] See an interesting letter from Schütz to the Duchess Sophia Elisabeth, written on this occasion, and given by Fr. Chrysander, Jahrbücher für musikalische Wissenschaft, I., p. 162. (Leipzig: Breitkopf and Härtel, 1863.) Compare also pp. 166, 167.

[22] He was born in 1628, as Junghans reckons, p. 39.

place, and 1661 as the date of his birth.[23] He had held
his office from the year 1698, and died at Lüneburg at an
advanced age ;[24] he had previously lived at Hamburg.
This man must have had a special attraction for Bach,
because his method as an organist was nearly allied to
that which Bach was then pursuing. Böhm had endeavoured to elevate and expand what he had been able
to learn or to elaborate in Thuringia as an organist, by
knowledge derived from the masters of North Germany.
The bare statement that he had resided in Hamburg would
certainly be an insufficient foundation for this assertion if it
were not clearly proved to be true by his compositions.
The Lüneburg organist holds a position between the
organ musicians of Central Germany and those of North
Germany, such as they had become about the middle of
the century; a position which corresponds approximately
to that of his place of residence, lying between the towns
of Thuringia on one hand, and Hamburg, Lübeck, Husum,
Flensburg, &c., the headquarters of the North German
masters. The influence of Sweelinck, the Dutch organist,
had gained deeper ground in this district than in any other
part of Germany; and a son of the same soil, Johann Adam
Reinken (born at Deventer, April 27, 1623, died as Organist
to St. Katherine's Church at Hamburg, November 24, 1722[25]),
had aided materially in extending this influence by his remarkable talent and unusually long life. Its distinguishing
characteristics are technical neatness, pleasing ingenuity,
and a taste for subtle effects of tone. As compared with the
calm severity and sunny cheerfulness of the organ-style of
the south, we here not unfrequently find a meandering
looseness of form—no composer has written longer arrange-

---

[23] Walther, Mus. Lex., p. 98. The register of Goldbach does not mention
him, but it was not carefully kept. The year of his birth was calculated
by Junghans, p. 39, from data given by Böhm in a document preserved at
Lüneburg.

[24] Junghans, p. 38, appears to give 1734 as the year of his death. Mattheson,
on the other hand, in his Vollkommenen Capellmeister, published 1739, p. 479,
speaks of him as though he were still living.

[25] Mattheson, *Critica musica*, Vol. I., pp. 255, 256.

ments of chorales than Reinken, Lübeck, and Buxtehude—
and romantic picturesqueness; and this contrast still holds
good, in great measure, even under comparison with the
style of Central Germany after it had entered into its
inheritance of the culture of the South. This school was
in great danger of squandering its strength in mere ingenuity
of external elaboration, but its peculiarities could be turned
to account for delightful ornamentation when wielded by
an artist of deep feeling and learning.

Such an artist was Böhm, and a great musical genius
besides. If he had lived at a period when he could have
had the benefit of that deep-reaching transformation in art
which was produced by Pachelbel's appearance in Thuringia,
his compositions would probably have been greater than
those of all his contemporaries. As it was, the man who
was destined to amalgamate the different lines of art, to
collect in one centre all the forces that had come into play in
organ music, was he who, by his receptive and assimilative
powers, now attached himself closely to the elder master.
Böhm seems to have been on friendly relations with the choir
of St. Michael, since we learn that, at the beginning of the
year 1705, the prefect of that choir went to him with certain
members of the St. John's choir, and had with him "much
reasoning concerning music."[26] Or was this alliance first
formed by Sebastian Bach, who was possibly prefect until
1703 ?

Böhm had learned from Reinken, and it was part of
Sebastian's original nature that he could only drink from the
spring-head. Hamburg was no great distance off, and it is
probable that just at this very time his cousin Joh. Ernst
Bach (son of his father's brother, Joh. Christoph Bach
of Arnstadt) was residing in Hamburg for his musical
education.[27] A holiday excursion thither may therefore
have seemed advisable from family motives, and as it would
enable him to hear Reinken play, and, perhaps, to make

---

[26] Junghans, p. 40, from a document of February 13, 1705.

[27] Joh. Ernst was born in 1683, and it seems unlikely that he should, at his
own cost, undertake such a journey to put the finishing stroke to his education
before he was at least seventeen or eighteen years of age.

his personal acquaintance, Sebastian must soon have regarded it almost as a necessity. If the idea is a correct one, that his cousin in Hamburg—who was two years older than himself—first tempted and led him there, the liberality with which he gave up, at Arnstadt, a portion of his salary to Joh. Ernst, then in great necessity, at a time, too, when he himself had particular need of the money, points to a striking trait in his character. He had the grateful spirit which cannot lightly forget a benefit, and with it the self-respect of independent individuality which makes it a pleasure and satisfaction to fulfil a duty. His conduct towards his elder brother was precisely the same.

After he had once made acquaintance with Hamburg he frequently repeated such excursions, which of course were always made on foot, and with the most humble means of subsistence; but he was accustomed at home to the very simplest mode of living. F. W. Marpurg, who was on the most intimate terms with the circle of the Bachs, had an anecdote which Sebastian Bach used to delight in telling later in life. On one of his journeys to Hamburg all his money was spent but a few shillings. He had seated himself outside an inn hardly half-way on his return journey, and was meditating on his hard fate while sniffing the delicious savours proceeding from the kitchen, when a window was opened with a clatter, and two herrings' heads were flung out. The hungry lad picked them up, and found in each a Danish ducat. This unexpected wealth enabled him not only to satisfy his hunger, but to make another expedition to see Reinken. The identity of his benefactor, however, was never known to him.[28]

Reinken's compositions have become very few and rare. The only one he published is a volume of Suites for two violins, viola, and continuo, entitled *Hortus musicus*. I shall presently adduce evidence that Bach knew this well and valued it highly. For the present this is not important.[29] Only five

---

[28] Simon Metaphrastes, Legende einiger Musik-heiligen; Cölln am Rhein, 1786, p. 74.

[29] Mattheson, Ehrenpforte, p. 517.

more compositions by him in all, for organ or clavier, can be
mentioned as extant ; but it is probable that these have come
to us in a direct line from Sebastian Bach's music shelves, thus
confirming the exactitude of the remark in the Necrology,
that Bach went to Reinken for his models among others. A
chorale arrangement of " Es ist gewisslich an der Zeit (Was
kann uns kommen an für Noth)"—" It certainly is now the
time,"—for two manuals and pedal, in G major, common time,
contains no less than 232 bars.   Every separate line is richly
worked out in the form of the motett, some quite simply, some
with elaborate ornamentation; the independent interludes,
however, are but meagre.   The composition is full of flow ;
changes of time—which were much in favour with most of
these masters—are here disdained; the two manuals cross
each other in a masterly and very delightful way.[30]   The
organ chorale on "An Wasserflüssen Babylon"—"By the
waters of Babylon,"—even extends to 335 bars, in F major,
common time. This attained a certain celebrity from an
incident in Bach's after life, but it fully merits it on its own
account.   The plan and character are the same; single lines
are frequently treated as supplying distinct themes for
counterpoint, but this does not give rise to a rule for the
treatment of every line.   The North German masters rather
looked for the development of grand combinations and various
complicated figures in the widest possible framework, and it
was on this that their peculiar form of organ chorale was
founded.[31]

Very remarkable, too, is a toccata in G major, common
time.   The Northern masters had also worked out a
special form for great independent organ pieces.   They
began with a prelude full of brilliant passages. After it they
brought in a fugue, then introduced an ornate intermezzo,
and finally returned to the theme, now altered both in rhythm

---

[30] This is to be found in a book among the papers left by Joh. Ludw. Krebs,
Sebastian Bach's most distinguished scholar.   This volume, after passing
through the hands of two organists of Altenburg, is now in the possession of
Herr F. A. Roitzsch, musician, of Leipzig.

[31] This composition exists in MS. in the Library of the Royal Inst. for Church
Music at Berlin.

and melodic form, using it for a fresh fugue which closed the whole, and which sometimes had appended to it a showy running passage. Reinken's toccata is precisely after this pattern, and it is particularly interesting for this reason— that we possess a work by Bach formed strictly on this model, which we shall presently consider more in detail, with certain similar works by Buxtehude. But it may at once be said that none of those masters were usually very happy in their invention of themes for fugues. Their ideas certainly appear to flow more spontaneously than those of the southern composers, but they are not melodious, not expressive, not graceful enough. The reason, no doubt, is that this school of composers gave but a one-sided attention to the chorale, and did not go into it thoroughly, so that the complete beauty of true melody was never fully revealed to them. How to combine the greatest brilliancy of ornamentation with the noblest flights of melody was not yet known. Sebastian Bach was destined to show it. All these general reflections apply to Reinken's toccata. It is nowhere grandly conceived, but it is full of grace and felicitous ease, particularly the second half. The same must be said with reference to the two pieces with variations that remain by this master, which, in fertility and variety of figures, are superior to the variations by Joh. Christoph Bach previously spoken of, coming very near them in their spirit, and testifying to a very considerable amount of technical execution.[32] One is founded on a merry air, "Schweiget mir vom Weibernehmen" (altrimenti chiamata: La Meyerin, as the MS. adds)—"Speak not to me of marrying,"—and has eight partitas.[33] The other set are ten variations on a "ballet."

This serves to remind us that at that time German opera

---

[32] They are preserved with the toccata in a book which belonged to Andreas Bach, of Ohrdruf, Sebastian's nephew, and which certainly came to him from his brother, who lived for some time in Sebastian's house. It belonged more recently to C. F. Becker, who bequeathed it with his whole library to the town of Leipzig.

[33] The "Meyerin" must have been a well-known air. Froberger also composed a series of elegant variations on it, which are included in a collection of toccatas, fantasias, canzone, &c., dedicated by the composer to the Emperor Ferdinand III., at Vienna, September 29, 1649.

was flourishing greatly at Hamburg, and that the easy-living Reinken was one of those who, in 1678, had set this undertaking going.[34]   But the opportunity which, some little time later, seemed to Handel the best fitted for the development of his very different projects and ideas, was passed over with indifference by Sebastian Bach.   Handel was in Hamburg from 1703 to 1706 ; Bach probably visited it for the last time in 1703.   The two great geniuses came then and there into closer contiguity than at any other stage of their career. Even Reinken's personal influence could not affect Bach, even if the great difference in their ages had allowed him to regard him with anything but youthful admiration: but more of this when, twenty years later, we shall find Bach, at the climax of his artistic career, meeting for the last time with Reinken, then nearly a hundred years old.

However, it was not from him alone that he could learn in Hamburg.   From the year 1702 Vincentius Lübeck had been working there as Organist to the Church of St. Nikolaus. He was born in 1654, and had previously been employed at Stade ; he likewise was a disciple of Reinken's, and an admirable master in his line.   The same source which supplies us with the above-mentioned chorale arrangement by Reinken also contains others by Lübeck—" Ich ruf zu dir, Herr Jesu Christ " for two manuals and pedal, E minor, 275 bars ; " Nun lasst uns Gott dem Herren," also for two manuals and pedal ; moreover, a grand prelude with a fugue, D minor, 174 bars, exhibiting great technical skill, particularly in the prelude.[35]   So we may surely accept this as a token that Bach did not neglect this opportunity of improving his knowledge and skill.

The statement of the Necrology, that he took as models certain distinguished French composers for the organ, besides the principal North German organists,[36] will serve as

---

[34] Mattheson, Der musikalische Patriot.

[35] Both these pieces are to be found in another organ-book formerly belonging to Krebs, and now to Herr Roitzsch.

[36] Musikalische Bibliothek, p. 162.   Here certainly it is said with reference to Bach's studies at Arnstadt, where he fed upon the store he had laid up during his stay at Lüneburg.

my excuse if, instead of returning at once to Böhm, at Lüneburg, I first follow the indefatigable Sebastian in his journeys
to another centre of art, which he repeatedly visited as well
as Lüneburg.   At the Ducal Court of Celle the instrumental
dance-music of the French had been in great favour ever
since the middle of the seventeenth century, and in
choosing the members of the band great weight was attached
to their being all able, when required, to play this sort
of music.[37]   Without doubt French clavier-music was also
held in preference there.   It had indeed many advantages
over the German, and must always have been regarded
as a model for its elegance and grace.   One of the few
important musicians who were born in Germany in the
fourth and fifth decades of the seventeenth century was a
native of Celle, Nikolaus Adam Strungk, born 1640, who
was prominent as a composer and player on the organ
and violin.   He was installed at the Court of Celle in
1661, with a salary of 220 thalers.   From 1678 to 1683
he directed and composed operas at Hamburg, then held
the post of Capellmeister in various places—last at
Dresden—and died at Leipzig in 1700.[38]   If we had a
more complete knowledge of the skilled musicians who
figured at Celle between the years 1700 and 1703, it would,
no doubt, appear that Bach had some personal acquaintance
or connections there, which made a temporary residence
there profitable to him.   For when we are told that by
frequently hearing the Celle band—at that time very famous

---

[37] An estimate of what " pertains to a rightly constituted band," of the year
1663, exists in the Provinzial-Archiv at Hanover, and runs as follows :
" 1. Director *musices ;* 2. An *alto ;* 3. A *tenor ;* 4. A *bass,* who all three could
at the same time play the violin in French music'; 5. Two violists, prepared
both in ordinary and French music, which we have already; 6. A player on the
viol di gamba, which also we have ; 7. An *organist,* which likewise we have;
8. A *trombonist* or *fagottist,* who can also sing a part and use the violin in ordinary
and in French music; 9. A *cornetist* who can play a violin in French music;
10. Two choir-boys; 11. A blower; in all thirteen persons." All information
is unfortunately wanting as to the time of Duke Georg Wilhelm down to
1705, when the line became extinct.

[38] His compositions for the organ seem to have remained hitherto unknown.
I possess an elaborate and very beautiful arrangement by him of the chorale,
" Ich dank dir schon durch deinen Sohn."

—he had an opportunity of making himself familiar with the French style,[39] this can only have been possible if some acquaintance procured him admission to the rehearsals, for the band never played in public. The only name, however, which has come to light is that of the city organist at the time, Arnold Melchior Brunckhorst, from whose musical efforts and relations to the world of art nothing was to be gained. The presumption is strong that it was the first opportunity that was offered to Bach for acquiring a more thorough knowledge of French music; and that his desire for knowledge should have chiefly included clavier music is probable, both from his own tendencies and from the condition of French orchestral music at that time. Thus the interest which he actually brought to bear on French composers for the clavier, may be, for the most part, referred to the impulse received at this period. A Suite in A major, by N. Grigny, Organist to the Cathedral at Rheims, about 1700, and a similar composition in F minor, by Dieupart, he copied out with his own hand.[40] In collections of selected works, such as were made later by Bach's pupils, we find, side by side with numerous works by their master, pieces by Marchand, Nivers, Anglebert, Dieupart, Clairembault, and others, a proof that Bach directed them to such works. He was, indeed, certainly familiar with the works of François Couperin, the most important of those composers.[41] It cannot, however, be overlooked that even Böhm was more than merely superficially touched by the influence of the French,

---

[39] Musikalische Bibliothek. It is evident, from what has been said above, that the statement that the French style was at that time something new in that neighbourhood, is incorrect in so wide a sense.

[40] The autograph was formerly in the possession of Aloys Fuchs, at Vienna; where it is now is not known. A copy from the autograph, with a superscription by Fuchs, is in the Royal Library at Berlin. Both Suites alike consisted of the following parts: overture, allemande, courante, saraband, gavotte, minuet, gigue. Appended is a list of twenty-nine different ornaments, with directions for performing them. So long as the autograph does not come to light it will be impossible to say whether it was written at the time of Bach's residence at Lüneburg or later.

[41] Forkel, p. 15, ed. 1. This deserves all the more acceptance, since he undoubtedly must have had decisive and complete information on this point from Ph. Em. Bach.

as is proved more particularly by his love for ornate embellishments and florid treatment of melodic passages; and if he did not precisely arouse Bach's desire to make acquaintance with French music, he no doubt must have strengthened it. It is no longer possible to point out any direct effects of that foreign style in Bach's mode of composition, but only, perhaps, because the pieces that might illustrate it no longer exist; for the so-called "French Suites," works of Bach's age of ripest mastery, have no right to the epithet in this sense. Perhaps, however, and this is more likely, such amalgamation as was possible of the German element with the French had already been accomplished in all its essentials, in the individuality of Böhm himself as an artist, so that Bach chiefly imbibed the French element through this medium.

But in order to do justice to Bach's relations to Böhm in particular, it will be necessary to throw a clear light on Böhm's artistic efforts, and on his style in his different compositions. What I have been able by degrees to collect of these consists of three clavier Suites, an overture (and Suite), a prelude with a fugue—these two also for the clavier—and eighteen arrangements of chorales, of which a large proportion are worked out in partitas, besides an air in four parts, " Jesu, theure Gnadensonne "—" Jesu, living Sun of grace,"—a New Year's hymn, no doubt written for the procession choir of St. John's.[42] These only suffice to give us a very small idea of his style of writing, and it is much to be regretted that nothing more has been preserved of the works of so remarkable and admirable a composer. His strength lay rather in composing for the clavier than for the organ, as is not difficult to understand from the extensive influence that was exercised over him, not only by the North German composers, but also by the French. This applies equally to his chorale arrangements, even though he may have intended all, or at any rate most of them, for the

---

[42] Winterfeld, Ev. Kir., II., p. 502, informs us that melodies by Böhm occur in an edition of Elmenhorst's hymns, published about 1700. I have not met with this edition.

organ, and have performed them on it himself. The limit
line between these two instruments seems to have been still
ill-defined, even by the composers at the end of the seventeenth century.   In estimating those intimate reciprocal
relations which the Form and the Idea must bear to each
other in every work of art, we cannot but attribute to Bohm's
chorales a disproportionately smaller measure of ideality than
to those of Pachelbel.   That master set himself the task of
giving an artistic presentment of the chorale with all its significance in the Protestant worship, and in all its bearings
to the subjective sentiment of the individual worshipper.
Böhm's endeavour was to elaborate from the chorale, and on
it, as a basis, pleasing and various forms of tone in which
we can at most detect the general fundamental feeling
of the chorale.   It is tolerably clear from his works that
he was very well acquainted with Pachelbel's method, and
availed himself of it : but he did not follow in his footsteps ;
his genius was far too individual.   The melody " Vater
unser im Himmelreich "—" Our Father which art in heaven,"
—he does once begin to treat just in the manner we are
accustomed to in Pachelbel. The first line is fugal, and then,
in conclusion, is transferred entirely and emphatically to the
pedal, not, indeed, in augmentation, but still with sufficient
stress.   But in the second line Böhm himself appears with
his own characteristics; the theme for the ensuing fugue
does not appear in its simple form—

but modified by a break in the time, by connecting semiquavers and dotted accentuation and grace notes—

   In the course of the piece these fancies gain the upper
hand, leading further and further from the original subject.
The lines of the chorale, which ought to appear as the aim
and crown of each phrase of elaboration, are more and more
thrown into the shade, and only saunter in, as it were, un-

supported in the pedal; nay, in the last line but one, the
chorale seems caught up in the general hurry, and must
submit to be spun out by about six notes. Thus a motley
and fantastic picture is composed, which is not fully justified
either as an organ piece or as a chorale arrangement, but
which, nevertheless, is decidedly attractive from its ingenuity,
its distinctive and truly musical stamp, and the elegance and
skill of the interweaving of the parts. Another time Böhm
pitches on the melody " Allein Gott in der Höh sei Ehr "—
" Honour to God alone most High,"—sets the first line in
opposition to a beautiful *cantabile* counter-subject, and
works both out in a really masterly double fugue. We
here begin to think that no more is coming, or else that
a brilliant treatment in Pachelbel's manner of the whole
chorale will crown the work. No such thing. The second
line follows the fugue in its simplest guise ; then the
whole is repeated from the beginning, as though it were the
unadorned melody, and the remainder is carried out with
equal simplicity. It is a statue with the head and arms
finely chiselled and the rest of it left in the block.

But in setting a counter-theme to a line of a chorale, Böhm
may join hands with Buxtehude, and in such arrangements he
holds a place between the two masters ; *above* them we cannot
say, for the reasons given. Buxtehude, who stands far below
Pachelbel as regards a profound grasp of the chorale and in
calm beauty, still is his superior in ingenuity of combinations
and alluring harmony. There is a chorale arrangement by
Böhm on " Christ lag in Todesbanden," which is so completely in the style of Buxtehude's work, that one might feel
inclined to assert that it must be ascribed to him, if the
versatility of Böhm's talent were not set in the balance.[43]
The essence of this style consists in the motett-like treatment, already spoken of, of the single lines of the chorale, in

---

[43] Such a mistake might easily have occurred, since the names of the organists
above the compositions are often indicated merely by their initials, and " G. B."
(Georg Böhm) might very well have been written for " D. B." (Dietrich Buxtehude). An old MS. copy of Pachelbel's chorale " Erhalt uns, Herr, bei deinem
Wort " (Commer, No. 134), lies before me, signed with " G. B.," but I regard
it as attributable to Buxtehude.

which Buxtehude was particularly fond of changes of time,
rhythmical modifications of the theme, and independent
counter-subjects. More will be said on this matter in its
proper place. The most singular mixture of his own
methods of procedure with those of others occurs in Böhm's
treatment of "Nun bitten wir den heilgen Geist," in which
the manner of Pachelbel and Buxtehude appears side by side
with Böhm's own. This—in which he also wrote whole
organ chorales, and, as he believed, could most freely reveal
his own nature—consists in this : that each separate line is
not worked out polyphonically, but is thematically exhausted
by the disseverance of its principal melodic ideas, and by
their repetition, dissection, modification, and various recom-
bination. Thus an ingenious brain could display its utmost
inventiveness in transforming and modifying a musical
thought, in nimble fancies, and graceful ornamentation.
Nor was he bound as in variations strictly speaking, by
the harmonic and rhythmical conditions of the theme, but
could create new proportions and phrases, building up a
composition all his own, and finding in it opportunities for
contrapuntal elaboration. He must have been the first composer who availed himself in instrumental music of that
development of the melodic constituents of a subject—using
them as independent themes and motives to form the
component elements of a tone structure on a larger scale—
which played a principal part in the musical art of Beethoven's time. In the motett, no doubt, as we have already
seen, similar metamorphoses had been effected with the
chorale which, however, had necessarily acquired a quite
different aspect, from the difference of the materials employed. If we may speak of Pachelbel's and of Buxtehude's
type of chorale, we certainly may also speak of Böhm's.
Böhm must be regarded, if not as the inventor of the
principle (since Frescobaldi, the Italian composer, had
already practised the art of making one musical idea gene-
rate a second), still as the composer who first applied it to
the chorale. He did, in fact, create a new musical form;
and this achievement, of which none but a genuinely fine
talent is capable, assures him a place in the history of art.

He also treated the form he had devised with much wealth
and subtlety of invention.   Thus, in his six partitas on
" Herr Jesu Christ, dich zu uns wend "—" Lord Jesu, turn
Thy face to us,"—he constructs the following image in the
first of them, on the initial line :—

In the third line he begins it as follows :—

The next line is highly coloured, the passages flying up
and down from c′ to c‴ most gracefully, but in almost wanton

sportiveness; the third line again affords a parallel to the first, though worked out quite differently, and the fourth rolls on to the end in rich and vivid colouring, only pausing once, in the middle. The harmony throughout is as simple as in the first line. And there is another *Manier* which Böhm so frequently combines with this mode of treatment that it may be regarded as an expression of his personal idiosyncrasy, quite peculiar to him. He constructs an ornate series of notes, forming two or three bars, to in-troduce the piece, usually in the bass, and then repeats the whole or portions of it as often as is feasible between the lines, using it even as counterpoint to them, and allow-ing it to reappear once more *solo* at the close. An example may here be given of such a "*basso quasi ostinato*" from another arrangement of "Vater unser im Himmelreich," as illustrating the process and as a basis for further remarks :—

This is followed by the three first notes of the melody, interwoven with ornaments in his fashion; then the bass comes in alone, and it is not till then that the real treatment begins, into which fragmentary motives from the melody are thrown as occasion serves. Then, under cover of the long final note of the melody, he once more makes a diversion, and, as it were, closes the door. In the course of this proceeding we are so vividly reminded of certain *tutti* subjects in Italian instrumental concertos that it is doubtful whether a direct imitation was not intended. In one instance the ornate passage lies in the upper part; the melody of "Aus tiefer Noth schrei ich zu dir"—"I cried to Thee in direst need,"—is pitched in the tenor, and then, worked out as a motive, it is carried on in the *Oberwerk* by the left hand alone—a device that could only have been hit upon by a remarkably clever head. What he produced, with this natural bent in the way of chorale variations, may easily be imagined; in fact, his fancy was inexhaustible in novel transformations and new clothing of the melody. He delighted in such labours, but it is true that the chorale

sank to the level of any ordinary secular air. That he
always worked for the harpsichord rather than for the organ
is shown by the fulness of the harmonies which he added to
those simple chorales which commonly preface his partitas;
so that the progression of the parts is undistinguishable, and
chords of five, six, and seven parts follow in succession.
But Böhm could make much more use of the productions
of the French school in independent clavier music than in
the treatment of chorales. In fact, he assimilated its
complete grace without falling into French floridness and
coquetry, though he certainly often leans to these defects.
On the other hand he far surpasses those masters in the
richness of his harmonies and the expressiveness of his ideas.
His Suites (in E flat major, C minor, A minor, and D major)
are beyond question the best which I am acquainted with
of the time before Sebastian Bach. One of these, that in
D major, is preceded by an overture in the French form,
and if the statement is well grounded, that Pachelbel was
the first to transfer this to the clavier, we must regard
Böhm as following his example. But, considering the much
smaller connection which Pachelbel must have had with the
French composers, we might almost imagine the reverse to be
the truth. It is quite certain that the clavier was more Böhm's
instrument, and the organ Pachelbel's; and though Pachelbel left Böhm far behind him in the chorale, still the Nuremberg master wrote hardly anything that can compare with the
prelude and fugue in G minor of the Lüneburg composer.

I have postponed the mention of this work to the last
because in it Böhm's originality is most clearly and convincingly shown. In the first place, as to the whole form of
the piece—which deviates completely from anything we have
yet known, and yet finds complete justification as a work of
art that has grown from and round the musical idea—we
have a prelude in 3-2 time with arpeggio chords that sway
up and down; after a short connecting *adagio* a fugue
worked out at great length; finally, *sotto voce* and *arpeggiato*,
an independent closing subject, of which the semiquaver
movement slowly calms down to *adagio*; and withal a mood
so deep, so purely melancholy—a dreaming and revelling in

keenly sweet harmonies, such as is possible to the German nature alone, and yet, in the fugue especially, a grace such as at that time belonged only to the French, pervade this very lovely piece, which would of itself suffice to set its composer in the rank of the greatest creative talent of his day. We feel in it, in germ and in bud, something which could only open to its intoxicating bloom and perfume in the hands of Sebastian Bach. Those two preludes of the Wohltemperirte Clavier (C major, Part I. ; C sharp major, Part II.), which seem to have hardly any movement except in the harmonies, and yet ebb and flow with such restful pathos, and others like them have, in the beginning and end of Böhm's composition, if not their only precursor, at any rate, so far as I know, the only worthy one. It is significant that it was directly from the family of Sebastian Bach that this piece and the four Suites have come down to the present day.[44] And these Suites, in the same way, form the stepping-stone to those of Bach, in which the light and airy fancies of the French writers are ennobled to forms of undreamed-of beauty. Many details of striking similarity show how highly the great master valued them ; less, perhaps, because they had afforded him an indispensable fulcrum for his own productions than because he felt himself in close affinity to his fellow-countryman, both in their natures and in the character of their training. When he produced the works we are speaking of he was far beyond the need of borrowing from another ; but he must all the more have felt himself drawn to Böhm in his youth, when he craved direction and instruction. In Bach's later life their innate resemblance was conspicuous in the department where Böhm was destined to do his best work. As a youth he imitated him in a branch of music in which, as a man, his deep religious bent led him to adopt very different forms— the organ chorale.

There are among Bach's works a few chorale partitas. An expert in such matters at once detects that they are early attempts. It has been supposed that they were composed

---

[44] They are in the MS. previously mentioned as Andreas Bach's.

in Arnstadt. I have not the smallest doubt that they were
written at Lüneburg, or at least under the direct influence
of Böhm. One series is based on the melody " Christ, der
du bist der helle Tag"—" Christ, Thou that art the star
of day,"—the other on "O Gott, du frommer Gott"—"O God,
Thou righteous God." [45] Here, in fact, there is an agreement
of style such as never recurs, in spite of the various
influences from other quarters that can be proved to have
acted on Bach. Without knowing a note of Böhm's writing
we might, from these variations, become acquainted with his
chorale style, if Sebastian's bright eye did not sparkle now
and then through the mask, and if a certain heaviness were
not perceptible in its bearing. Böhm never harmonised a
chorale melody so solidly—almost clumsily—as his imitator
has done ; as, for instance, the first and fifth notes of the
initial line of the first chorale, which fall on the unaccented
part of the bar, are weighted with a massive six-part harmony
while between these notes it is in four parts. This, and much
else, has under any circumstances a bad effect and is tasteless, even if it is supposed to be played on the harpsichord.
But in general we can but wonder at the astonishing power of
assimilation which deals with the contradictory forms originating in his own mind, and in that of others, with as much
facility as if they were all spontaneous. Such a phenomenon
in a man whose individuality afterwards stood forth in the

---

[45] These are published in the collected edition of Bach's instrumental works
brought out by C. F. Peters, Series V., Cah. 5 (Vol. 244), Part II., Nos. 1 and 2
(quoting from the thematic catalogue of 1867). A third group of partitas on the
chorale " Herr Christ, der ein'ge Gottssohn "—" Lord Christ, God's only Son "—
is to be found with many other of Bach's chorales in a volume formerly
belonging to Joh. Ludw. Krebs, now in the possession of Herr Roitzsch of
Leipzig ; it is not yet published. Bach's name is not expressly given. I nevertheless regard him as the author of these seven partitas, which must have been
composed about the same time as the others. That they were written by Bach
at Arnstadt is a mere arbitrary guess of Forkel's (see p. 60 of the first edition),
who possessed them merely in an old MS. copy. No autograph of them has
as yet come to light. An old MS., containing partitas on "Ach, was soll ich
Sünder machen," and bearing the name of Seb. Bach, was, at my suggestion,
bought some years since for the Royal Library at Berlin. There i no reason
to doubt their genuineness, but their character is so similar to that of the other
two partita works that I cannot think it necessary to describe them in detail.

strongest conceivable contrast to his time, rising before us
as if hewn out of rock, could only be possible during extreme
youth.   Still, it affords us a standard for estimating the way
in which Bach trained himself, and absorbed into himself
everything of value that he met with on his way.   This
mode of energy can be traced in his life, at least up to
the middle of his twentieth year.   The reader is in a position
to compare for himself after reading the foregoing account of
Böhm's mode of treatment.   He will at once find, in the
second partita of each series, the most striking parallel to
that spinning out of the motives of which Böhm must be
considered the inventor.   A highly remarkable thematic
development appears in the four first notes of the fourth line
of the first chorale—

which is worked upon through seven bars in Beethoven's
manner, and in the same way in the other variations also.
Böhm's other characteristics are also to be found in this
work of Bach's.   The chorale opens simply, in the way
which he so often affects, but soon is played round in
various ways, returning, however, again and again to
certain fundamental figures ; then it is wholly dispersed in
running passages in the manner of clavier variations ; the
lines are brought in, one in the upper part and another in
the lower, different principles being mixed in their treatment ; changes of time are introduced, after the model of
the northern masters, and various effects of sound by means
of changes of the manuals—all this we find here, though in
the riper works of the great master it all disappeared again,
almost to the last trace, so far as outward form was concerned.   But a single instance will suffice to show the way in
which these influences continued to affect his mental bias.
Together with these characteristics of Böhm, Bach had also
acquired the use of the *basso ostinato,* just now mentioned.   We
need only look at the beginning of the second partita on
" O Gott, du frommer Gott "—

(*Left hand only.*)

of which it may be said, incidentally, that only the four first
notes of the melody are to be heard, then the bass is repeated,
and not till then does the whole line come in, exactly
as in the chorale by Böhm, previously quoted. We never
again meet with this form in any of his later masterpieces. But if we study the magnificent work on " Wir
glauben all an einen Gott," which appeared nearly forty years
after in the third part of the Clavierübung (Vol. I.),[46] we
find an independent bass, having no internal connection
with the melody, repeated six times in the course of the
piece after proper pauses. Here is the highest development
and glorification of this particular form, and it must be considered as an inestimable evidence of the constant progress
and unity of Bach's mental growth. He never even entered
on any path which he subsequently was forced to admit was
a wrong one, and to quit or return. The young sapling
never struck root in barren pebbles or unyielding rock. The
forces he drank in from every source permeated him with
vigour so long as he continued to create.

As I have said, however, these partitas are not to be
attributed to mere imitativeness. More than once the
player feels himself touched by the characteristic spirit of
Bach, of which the intensity and glow can always be at
once recognised by any one who has once truly felt them.
Such passages are more easy to detect by their direct effect
than to describe circumstantially in words; still, not to deal
merely with generalities, I would direct attention to the last
partita of the first series, and to the eighth of the second,
with their ingeniously worked-out chromatic motives.
Throughout, indeed, in spite of their reliance on an outside
model, these chorale variations bear witness to a quite extraordinary talent. They are by a youth of sixteen or seventeen, and what natural beauty they display! what freedom,
nay, mastery of the combination of parts! not a trace of the
vacillating beginner feeling his way. He goes forward on his
road with instinctive certainty; and though here and there a
detail may displease us, the grand whole shows the born artist.

---

[46] B.-G., III., p. 212 (1853). P., S. V., Cah. 7 (Vol. 246), No. 60.

The fitness for the clavier which we find in these partitas
renders the absence of an obbligato pedal part, nay, of a
pedal at all, less conspicuous. We certainly find in the last
partita in "Christ, der du bist der helle Tag," a pedal-
part marked *ad libitum ;* but this mars the beauty of the
piece, at least if it is played so on the organ. The pedal of
a harpsichord has less duration of sound, and would not so
much conceal the succession of semiquavers in the left hand.
In fact, in a whole series of Bach's compositions, we find
the pedal is only introduced very incidentally, while they
are, on the whole, performed only *manualiter.* This mode
of procedure always indicates an early origin, for at
the height of his powers Bach allowed himself no such
neglect of means of effect. Still, we shall presently be able
to point out further and more subtle distinctions in this
indication.

Here it only may serve to introduce another work of Bach's
which is equally penetrated through and through by Böhm's
method, and which must have been written at the same time
as the partitas. This is the organ chorale, "Christ lag in
Todesbanden," set for two manuals.[47] Again, the left hand
alone begins with the frequently mentioned bass passage ;
the melody is then played on the *Hauptwerk* with more powerful stops, and extended in the first four lines by almost
too elaborate ornamentation. The introductory bass passage
serves as material for both interludes and counterpoint to the
first two lines. For the two next the harmonies are independent, and the interlude to each composed after Pachelbel's
manner ; then the treatment becomes more and more unfettered and fantastic, quite in Böhm's taste. From time to time
the semiquaver movement gives way to triplets of quavers ;
then motives are thrown in on both manuals. We can no
longer tell whether the subject is in two, three, or four parts till
the last line appears, repeated three times in different places,
and closing in calm chorale beats. The relative merit of this
composition, which consists of seventy-seven bars, is much less
than that of the partitas, where it is true the variation form

---

[47] P., S. V., C. 6 (Vol. 245), No. 15.

forbids those wholly unlimited amplifications which indeed
form too glaring a contrast to the essence of the chorale, in
spite of the cleverness which Böhm and Bach may have expended on them.   But its purely technical interest is greater,
both on account of the extraordinary skill and facility which
predominate in it, and for the degree of executive agility
which it presupposes.   The pedal comes in only in the last
seven bars—first, to bring out the last line of the melody, and
then to hold a few fundamental notes.   It is self-evident that
a peculiar closing effect is intended to be produced.   Indeed,
it is tolerably manifest, from one single note, that the composition is intended for a harpsichord and not for an actual
organ.   In the final bar the right hand crosses the left at
the last crotchet, and strikes the low E, although the pedal
has been holding the same note all through the bar.   On the
organ this would be aimless, but on the harpsichord the note
would have already died out before the fourth crotchet, and
as it was indispensable to support the closing chord by a
repetition of it, this is effected by the right hand.   Generally
composers may have attempted to represent the organ pedal
on this instrument by a repetition of the note, and have
contented themselves with this ineffectual suggestion of their
intention, for it could only serve at a pinch in the place of
the organ pedal.   And we, in our treatment of the pianoforte,
must still supply by imagination a great deal which is quite
beyond its powers of presenting.   The inference to be drawn
from this is that Lüneburg is most likely the birthplace of
this arrangement.   Bach had then no organ at his absolute
disposal, and if he desired to hear and perform his own productions without hindrance, and complete, he was obliged
to compose for the clavichord or harpsichord.

It will easily be understood that he as yet made no particular distinction between the organ and the harpsichord as
a medium for his musical thoughts.   It is certainly true
that the two instruments have much in common, but when
it is desired to bring out sequences of long-drawn sostenuto
notes the harpsichord fails ; on the other hand, in frequent
repetitions of the same chord, the flowing character of the
organ, which allows of no staccato, is done violence to.

This last consideration, at any rate, Bach did not always duly regard, and in this Böhm was not a good model; for, unscrupulous as writers might be at that time as to the demarcations of various styles, there still was a certain limit-line which Böhm recklessly overstepped. There is a third arrangement of the chorale " Vater unser im Himmelreich," by his hand, which would certainly be taken for a clavier piece were it not for the express instructions " Rückpositiv. Oberwerk *piano*, Pedal *forte*." The part which delivers the melody is overloaded with ornament; the accompaniment, for the most part, repeats the same chord again and again, is very rarely tied, and generally proceeds in this rhythm—

For example, the pedal begins as follows :—

To this Bach composed a pendant which, from its whole character, can only owe its existence to Böhm's influence, and which is so remarkable that the beginning at least must be inserted here :—

Erbarm dich mein, o Herre Gott.—" Have mercy on me, Lord my God."

Faulty as this is in style, we still cannot fail to discern in it great power of harmony and a deep sympathy with the feeling of the hymn—note particularly bar six : and the whole piece bears the same stamp, though certain harsh harmonies undoubtedly occur.[48]

---

[48] This composition, which has not yet been published, is to be found in Krebs' Organ-Book, which also contains Reinken's chorale " Es ist gewisslich an der Zeit."

It is almost self-evident that the close artistic affinity between the mature and the rising composers must have been supplemented by friendly external relations. Hence we are justified in supposing that Böhm did not hinder Bach from using the organ in St. John's Church, and possibly he may have tried his youthful powers more often on that than on the organ in St. Michael's. Unfortunately it would seem to have been even worse than the latter, for it was replaced by a new one so early as 1705.[49] Thus even in Lüneburg the ill-luck began which pursued the greatest of German organists all his life through ; for he had always to do the best he could with small or bad organs, and never had a really fine instrument at his command for any length of time.

This is all that it is possible to learn as to the musical features of Bach's three years' residence in Lüneburg. Without supposing any intentional negligence on his part, his general studies must have fallen more and more into the background as compared with music. It was to music that he already owed his means of existence, and I have before mentioned how frequently his duties as a choir pupil encroached on his time as an academy pupil, a fact which can be established by other examples at that time. Added to this were the opportunities of employment which a lad of musical acquirements might otherwise find and, under pressure of necessity, make the best of. The subjects of instruction in St. Michael's School did not differ from those in the Ohrdruf Academy. In the first class, to which we may suppose Sebastian to have advanced by degrees, the cycle of Latin authors that were read was rather more extended. We find mention of selected odes of Horace, Virgil's Æneid, Terence, Curtius, and Cicero, with speeches, epistles, and philosophic essays. But besides the necessary Latin exercises, oral and written, Greek also was taught out of the New Testament, religion, logic, and arithmetic—at any rate in the year 1695, and there is no reason for supposing that things were different from 1700 to 1703.[50]

---

[49] Gerber, N. L., I., under the word " Dropa."

[50] Junghans, op. cit., pp. 40, 41.

If the scholars wished to acquire knowledge on other
subjects they might obtain it from the tutors of the
institution, of course for an honorarium ; but those who
had to earn the means of keeping themselves there can
hardly have had much to spend on this object. We may,
however, assume that Bach, when he quitted Lüneburg,
must have completed at least a two years' course in the
first class, for he was eighteen years old, and the university
course was usually entered upon at an earlier age then than
now. That he did not go to the university—though Handel,
Telemann, Stölzel, and so many of his favourite cousins did
—there might be strong external reasons for supposing; but
it is not so as regards internal reasons ; for musical studies
were more compatible with a course of learning at the
high schools at that time than they would be under the
increased requirements of our day. It seems even to have
grown to be a sort of custom—and a good one—that the
youthful musician, if he aimed at higher flights, might not
remain a total stranger to the lecture-rooms of the
high schools; otherwise Johann Bähr, the Concertmeister
of Weissenfels, could not seriously have raised the question
as to whether a composer must necessarily have been a
student.[51] But Sebastian was poor and had no choice, even
if his desire was ever so great to enlarge the circle of his
knowledge—which, indeed, we have no means of knowing.

Still, before we see him depart to struggle onwards, let us
cast a hasty glance on the past. As so great an artist was
living—a member, too, of Bach's family—as late as 1703, as
Joh. Christoph Bach of Eisenach, it may seem surprising
that no distinct influence over Sebastian is referred to him.
Some slight trace of such an influence does certainly appear
to exist, and must not remain unnoticed; only the uncertainty
of the matter postpones it to this place. Three small chorale

---

[51] "Ob ein *Componist necessario* müsse studirt haben." Joh. Beerens
*Musicali*sche Discurse. Nuremberg, 1719 (nineteen years later than the death
of the author), chap. XLI. The author, who writes his name as Bähr, Beehr,
and Beer, had himself had an excellent general education, and gives it as his
decision that, though it was not absolutely necessary, it was better that a composer should have studied.

fugues exist, under the name of Sebastian Bach, on the melodies "Nun ruhen alle Wälder"—"Now silence falls,"—"Herr Jesu Christ, dich zu uns wend "—"Lord Jesu, turn Thy face on us,"—and " Herr Jesu Christ, meins Lebens Licht "—"Lord Jesu, sun to light my path."[52] They have precisely the same character as the fugally treated chorale preludes by Joh. Christoph Bach, lately discussed,[53] and of the similar works by Johann Pachelbel. The second particularly, of which the melody was also worked out by the Eisenach master, has a complete resemblance. It is rather more flowing, and longer by three bars, but otherwise remarkably similar; for instance, in the entrance of the subject at the beginning and the subsequent pedal-point on the dominant. If these little pieces are indeed Sebastian's, the conclusion is almost inevitable that they were written under the influence of his uncle, perhaps even of Pachelbel. It must further be inferred that they are works of his boyhood, before the Lüneburg period even, which would account for their complete insignificance. Consequently we can trace back his impulse towards independent creation to his very earliest years, and this result is at least as interesting as the proof of any direct influence from Joh. Christoph, which in the natural course of things may be taken for granted, but can hardly be regarded as of great consequence to so young a lad, particularly as it displays itself in a branch of music to which the chief powers of the elder master were never directed. If we possessed any choral compositions by Sebastian which suggested his influence, that would be of real importance. But this is not the case at the present time, and it is very doubtful whether any such works ever existed, when we consider the very different path which the nephew struck out for himself.

A further supplement to the stage of his life that we have

---

[52] Published by Fr. Commer: *Musica Sacra*, I., 1-3. He obtained them in 1839 from A. W. Bach, of Berlin, who had had them copied from a MS. by Bach, in the collection of the Counts von Voss-Buch. This entire collection subsequently passed into the Royal Library ; but the chorales in question are no longer in it.

[53] See ante, p. 105.

gone through consists in mentioning a clavier fugue in E
minor, which also deserves to be called a youthful or boyish
work, in the strictest sense of the term.   Since a few fugues
by Sebastian exist of the year 1704, this estimate is not too
severe.   The piece betrays its early origin, not only by the
singular stiffness of the themes, but by the anxious per-
tinacity with which the same counterpoint hangs on to the
heels of the main subject; the persistent clinging to the
principal key through no less than fourteen consecutive
entrances of the theme, the almost total absence of all connecting subjects, and, finally, by a surprisingly unplayable
character, the form not being as yet adapted to the *technique*
of the clavier.   Of all Bach's fugues that are known to me
this is the most immature, and can hardly have been composed anywhere later than in Ohrdruf.   By the time he
quitted Lüneburg he had at any rate gone far beyond so low
a standard in this form of art.

II.

LIFE AT WEIMAR AND ARNSTADT, 1703-4.—INFLUENCE OF KUHNAU.—WORKS FOR CLAVIER AND ORGAN.

In former times Bach's grandfather had had an appointment at the Court of Duke William IV., at Weimar.
This, however, can hardly have been the cause of his
grandson's being invited to the same town.   Other ties must
have existed, of which we know nothing, but which, of
course, would easily have been formed from Eisenach or
Arnstadt.   Sebastian received the appointment to be "Hofmusicus," one of the Court performers, not at the Court
of the reigning Duke Wilhelm Ernst, but to Johánn Ernst,
his younger brother, who therefore must have had a musical
establishment of his own, as he certainly had his Court
painter.[54]   This leads us to infer that he took an eager
interest in all art, and sets the young artist's appointment

---

[54] That it was Joh. Ernst who took Sebastian Bach into his service is
expressly stated in the genealogy (see in Book I., chap. I., what is said regarding
Nik. Eph. Bach).   Further evidence is found in the close relation in which the
musician stood to this Duke's son, Ernst August, although he did not succeed
to the government till long after Bach had left Weimar.

in a pleasing light. For it was obviously a quite different thing to be a member of one of those official bands, which were often kept up only for state, and were in consequence frequently made to subserve all sorts of utilitarian ends, and to belong to a body which had been called into existence by a true love of the art. On the other hand we should be mistaken in our view of the state of things in those petty Courts if we concluded that Sebastian had nothing whatever to do with the Court band proper. It is, indeed, quite certain that though he stood in the position of personal servant to Johann Ernst, he was made of use in the Court band. His place was that of violin-player, and the inference is plain that if he was invited from Lüneburg to take this place in such a band, his proficiency cannot have been inconsiderable. At the same time, as it is quite certain that all his training had hitherto been directed chiefly to organ and clavier playing, it is evident that he accepted this post at Weimar for outside reasons, namely, for a living. Thus, in his own particular line, he made no immediate progress by this first step into the world of art ; however, he at any rate made acquaintance there with a mass of instrumental music, particularly with Italian works, which were much in favour at the Court of Weimar, as we shall see later. There also lived there at that time a violin-player of no mean attainments, Johann Paul Westhoff, the Duke's private musician and secretary, a man who, besides, may have been very attractive from his great experience of the world and general culture.[55] There, too, was the famous organist, Johann Effler, who, as was said in a former place, had been Michael Bach's predecessor at Gehren ; and in fact later evidence would prove, if it were needed, that in Weimar Sebastian was not out of reach of church music. To the musical side of his life these brought him much and various incitement, and the length of his residence there exactly sufficed for him to yield to it so far as at the time he can have thought serviceable. In a few months new prospects were already opened to him.[56]

---

[55] Walther, Lexicon. Westhoff died in 1705.   [56] See Appendix A, No. 9.

Towards the close of the previous century the Municipality of Arnstadt had rebuilt one of their churches, which had been destroyed by fire in 1581, and had consecrated it in 1683 under the name of the New Church.[57] Only an organ was lacking; but the new sanctuary lay so near the hearts of the inhabitants that the Consistory could show soon after, that a sum of 800 gülden had been collected for it, by contributions from all sides, and would still increase to 1,100 gülden. A rich citizen, in 1699, bequeathed 800 gülden more, and now they could take steps for the construction of a really worthy and complete organ. An inefficient builder was passed over, though a native of the town, and Johann Friedrich Wender, of Mühlhausen, was chosen, who constructed and erected the organ between Whitsuntide and the winter of 1701.[58] Wender had built many organs in Thuringia, and had so made a name; but he was not a thorough workman. In a very short time it was shown that four pipes were wanting to the work. Repairs were already needed in 1710, and Wender effected these so carelessly that Ernst Bach, the organist at that time, was forced to explain that the organ required complete restoration to preserve it from becoming quite unserviceable. The same experience was gone through with regard to the organ at the Church of St. Blasius at Mühlhausen, which Wender had also built, and in which there was always something to mend.

Still, the great instrument was for the time complete, and the pride of the municipality. An organist of equal merit and renown was now the desideratum, but not to be found at once. A son-in-law of Christoph Herthum's (the often-mentioned son-in-law and successor of Heinrich Bach) knew how to manage an organ tolerably, and, perhaps at Herthum's application—perhaps, too, because at the moment there was no one else—the place was given to him. His name was Andreas Börner. He took up his appointment at

---

[57] Olearius, *Historia Arnstadiensis*, pp. 52, 55.

[58] The testamentary benefactor was Joh. Wilh. Magen, died May 11, 1699. Documents referring to this organ, of July 1, 1699, exist in the archives at Sondershausen.

the New Year, and was to receive thirty gülden a year and three measures of corn. These were deducted from his father-in-law's income, who, to balance the account, deputed to Börner the duty of performing the early Sunday service at the Church of the Holy Virgin. Börner had also to declare himself willing to rush off to the Franciscan Church as soon as his own morning service was over, whenever the over-busy Herthum was called away at that hour by his duties in the castle chapel. Not much was spent on the man, and very little was intrusted to him. When he had played in the New Church he was required always to restore the key of the organ-stairs to Burgomaster Feldhaus, who had the management of the organ and all that related to it.

This was the state of affairs till the summer of the following year. Meanwhile Sebastian Bach had gone to Weimar, and it may easily be imagined that, once there, he soon proposed to himself the pleasure of visiting Arnstadt, the old meeting-place of all his family, and of seeing his relations still living there. He went, and he played the organ, and the Consistory saw that this was the man they wanted. Small ceremony was made with Börner; he simply had to quit the field. "But, for the prevention of any unpleasant collisions," he had a new place made for him as Organist at matins, and deputy at morning service in the Franciscan Church, and he was allowed to keep his salary, so that in general all was on its old footing. But they thought themselves bound to special efforts on behalf of the young artist of eighteen; he had made a deep impression on the people. As the means of the Church itself were very limited, contributions were raised from three different sources, and the salary was fixed at the handsome sum of eighty-four gülden, six groschen (= seventy-three thalers, eighteen groschen), which was, in fact, considerable in comparison with the salaries of his fellow-officials. He then went through a solemn installation, and received a somewhat sweeping exhortation to "industry and fidelity to his calling," and to all that "might become an honourable servant and organist before God, the worshipful authorities, and his

superiors"; and to all this he pledged himself on August
14, 1703, by joining hands.[59]
Sebastian must have been quite delighted with such a
flattering reception into his new post in the pretty little
town, so full of family memories. His compulsory duties
also were comparatively few, and ample leisure was left him
for his own studies and creations. No burdensome educational duties claimed his energies, no utterly heterogeneous
tasks of a subsidiary kind—such, for instance, as were
allotted to the kitchen-clerk Herthum—could disturb the
collectedness of his mind. His post only required his attendance three times a week—on Sunday mornings from eight to
ten, on Thursdays from seven to nine a.m., and on Mondays for
one church service.[60] With what joy must he have felt himself
for the first time in an independent position, so well adapted
to his inclinations, and have heard the tones of the new
organ resounding under his own hands through the height
and breadth of the vast church. The organ was splendidly
constructed, all the diapasons being of seven-ounce tin, the
gedackt also being of metal, instead of wood, as was more
usual. The character of the "Brust-positiv" must, indeed,
have been somewhat shrill, owing to the preponderance of four-
foot stops; and it was only by using all the stops in combination that even a moderately good effect could be produced;
nor was there on the pedals any deep stop of moderate
strength, still the "Hauptwerk" was well arranged. The
entire specification was as follows:—

Oberwerk (Upper Manual).

1. Principal (*i.e.*, diapason)	8 ft.		7. Mixture ..		4 ranks.
2. Viola da gamba	.. 8 ft.		8. Gemshorn ..		.. 8 ft.
3. Quintatön ..	.. 16 ft.		9. Cymbal		1 ft. 2 ranks.
4. Gedackt ..	.. 8 ft.		10. Trumpet ..		.. 8 ft.
5. Quint ..	.. 6 ft.		11. Tremulant..		..
6. Octave ..	.. 4 ft.		12. Cymbelstern		..

---

[59] All these details are from documents in the archives at Sondershausen. To
form a just estimate of this salary, it must be remembered that Joh. Ernst Bach,
Sebastian's successor, received only forty gülden, and even in the year 1728,
as Organist to the Franciscan church of the Holy Virgin, had no more than
seventy-seven gülden.

[60] Olearius, p. 57.

Brust-positiv (Choir).			Pedal Organ.		
1. Principal ..	..	4 ft.	1. Principal ..	../	8 ft.
2. Lieblich gedackt	..	8 ft.	2. Sub-bass ..	..	16 ft.
3. Spitz flute	..	4 ft.	3. Posaune ..	..	16 ft.
4. Quint ..	..	3 ft.	4. Flute ..	..	4 ft.
5. Sesquialtera	..		5. Cornet ..	..	2 ft.
6. Nachthorn	..	4 ft.	Coupler for the manuals and pedals.		
7. Mixture ..	1 ft. 2 ranks.		Two bellows, 8 ft. by 4 ft.		

The organ still existed until 1863.[61]

Next to the Franciscan or Upper Church, the New Church occupied the second place. It had been originally built as a chapel-of-ease to the former, because the Liebfrauen-kirche was found to be inadequate to the enlarged demands, and there was no room for the large number of Sunday church-goers.

Since Sebastian, in spite of his youth, had taken his place as a musician of many-sided learning, who, moreover, had organised practices of choral music in Lüneburg, the Con-sistory handed over to him the tuition of a small school-choir, which served, as it were, for the stepping-stone to the larger choir that sang in the Upper Church; and with the latter were amalgamated, according to the old Thuringian custom, the "Adjuvanten," or music-loving amateurs of the town. The actual direction, which in the main choir was the task of the cantor, was here the duty of the prefect of the school-choir. Bach had only to rehearse them, to keep the whole together, and to accompany them on the organ. It may be supposed that with these opportunities he would bring his own compositions to a hearing.[62] Finally, it may be assumed with certainty that his violin-playing was occasionally taken advantage of for the Count's band; although historical testimony is wanting, Sebastian could no more have escaped these demands than could Michael Bach in his day, who must have come in from Gehren expressly on stated occasions.

---

[61] Then a new and very fine one was erected in its place, as a memorial to Sebastian Bach; as many of the old stops, however, as could be used were retained. The originator of this worthy project, to which the friends of Bach's art, from far and near, contributed, was the present Organist, Herr H. B. Stade, who devoted himself to managing the matter. The work is now complete.

[62] Evidence of this will appear in the course of the narrative.

Since the band consisted chiefly of native musicians, professional or amateur, it would have been foolish to leave such a remarkable talent unused.

In organ-playing, Sebastian found no one who could teach him anything, much less compete with him. Herthum can only have prosecuted his music by the way, since his post at Court was engrossing and laborious, as may be proved even now by documentary evidence. Johann Ernst Bach quickly lost, in the misery of his domestic circumstances, what he had brought home fresh from his journeys to Hamburg and Frankfort. Sebastian could not learn anything more of importance from him, although the cousins certainly kept up a close friendship. A somewhat greater variety prevailed in other musical matters. The busy life of a gifted artist, Adam Drese, had come to an end some years before. His place had been filled by Paul Gleitsmann, a pupil of the learned Johann Bähr, of Weissenfels. He had already been in the Count's service as groom-of-the-chambers and musician. He was a skilled performer on the violin, the viol di gamba, and the lute; and, judging from the scanty evidence we possess, he seems to have been a cultivated and well-meaning man.[63] He certainly was the man in whom Sebastian could most readily find intelligent sympathy, the only one, perhaps, of the whole band. The Rector of the Arnstadt Lyceum, the learned and energetic Johann Friedrich Treiber, was a great lover of music; and, besides his thorough and wide-spread theoretical knowledge, he possessed practical musical ability, and perhaps had some experience as a composer.[64] His son, Johann Philipp, an imaginative genius, with rare knowledge in all the provinces of the learning of the time, showed remarkable talent for poetry and music, and learned composition under Drese. He had studied at Jena, first philosophy, theology, and medicine, and then jurisprudence: he had obtained the degrees of Master and Doctor, and delivered lectures. His freethinking views on religion compelled him to quit Jena. He then lived for

---

[63] He is noticed in Walther's Lexicon.
[64] For further details, see Gerber, N. L., Vol. IV., col. 384.

a few years in the country, pursuing his scientific labours, but in consequence of these was again prosecuted for atheism, and once even imprisoned for six months in Gotha. After his release he lived with his father in Arnstadt during the years 1704-6. He was forced by disputes with the clergy of that place to go to Erfurt, where he became a Catholic, and obtained high honour as professor of jurisprudence. He died in 1727, in his fifty-third year. While in Arnstadt, in 1704, he published a work, Der accurate Organist im General-Basse, in which he treated the bass part of only two chorales with every possible variety of harmonies; he had previously published in Jena a work to demonstrate the possibility of employing every variety of chords, keys, and time in a single air, and worked out a composition of his own as an example.[65] Later on, in Erfurt, he wrote a "Grand Serenade," in honour of the rector of the academy, and conducted the performance himself.[66] A work which was brought out in May, 1705, at Arnstadt, seems to have been the joint production of both the Treibers. It was a "Sing-spiel" or operetta, according to the title, and was called "Die Klugheit der Obrigkeit in Anordnung des Bierbraucns"— "The wisdom of the authorities in the management of brewing."[67] The plan is that of the biblical school-plays of the seventeenth century, or the sacred musical dramas of Dedekind; i.e., the dialogue consists of Alexandrines, interspersed with songs of several verses and short recitatives, and as many persons as possible (in this instance no less than thirty) are introduced. It is, of course, pervaded with the plain, rough character of the burgher's life, and several of the persons speak in the Thuringian dialect of Arnstadt. The performance of this and other dramatic productions took place in the Count's theatre. Anton Günther did

---

[65] This book, Sonderbare Invention : Eine Arie in einer einzigen Melodey aus allen Torien und Accorden auch jederley Tacten zu componiren, &c., appeared, according to Walther, in 1702. The copy in the Königsberg Library is numbered 1,703 in Jos. Müller's catalogue. I have not seen it.

[66] Hesse, Verzeichniss Schwarzburgischer Gelehrten, Stück 18. Rudolstadt, 1827. Gerber, Vol. II., col. 673. Adlung, Anl. zur Mus. Gel., p. 116.

[67] See Appendix A, No. 10.

not maintain any dramatic or musical company; whatever of this kind was done at Arnstadt, at that time, was due for the most part to the exertions of the citizens. The Count, according to an engagement which he had entered into with Wentzing, one of his privy councillors, and the Capellmeister Drese, had bound himself to found and maintain a theatre, with the necessary appliances; to put the band at their disposal, to provide for the lighting, and to supply the provisions required for the stage banquets. On the other hand they were bound to find the wardrobe, and to play before the Count whenever he liked, provided that fourteen days' notice was given, and to allow free entrance to the Count's suite. This arrangement differed materially from all the other institutions of the court, and approximated closely to the German opera at Hamburg, in that every one "who wanted to see these *Actiones*" could obtain admission "on payment of a certain price." By this means the popular interest was not overlooked. This is proved by the "Beer" operetta, which was followed by a similar "Singspiel" on July 6, 1708,[68] and still more by the actors, some of whom were scholars, and some artisans of Arnstadt. Similar performances took place in other small capitals of Thuringia. Even in Weimar the stern Wilhelm Ernst had an "opera-house," and even court actors.[69] It was a good thing that not many princes had the means of organising such an entertainment wholly without help from the people, or they would gladly have done so. The organisation of the Arnstadt theatre was imitated from

---

[68] At this period all the boys in the first class of the school took part in such performances (Acts in the Raths-Archivs at Arnstadt). The chief part of the theatre contract and a catalogue of the actors was given by K. Th. Pabst in the programme of the Arnstadt Gymnasium for 1846, p. 22. I have not been able to find the interesting original document itself, so must content myself with this.

[69] Operatic performances took place in Weimar from 1697 onwards. Some of the libretti are preserved in the Grand Ducal Library there; also the MS. of a "Lustspiel" or "Vaudeville," called "Von einer Bauren-Tochter Mareien, Um welche zwey Freyer, ein alter und ein junger geworben"—"Of a peasant-girl Maria, who had two suitors, an old and a young one,"—of which part was spoken in the Thuringian dialect.

that of Brunswick, and the plan had been brought from thence by Anton Günther's wife, Augusta Dorothea, daughter of Duke Anton Ulrich. She also had built the Augustenburg at Arnstadt, after the pattern of her father's Lustschloss (pleasure palace) of Salzdahlen, and instituted occasional musical performances in it. On August 23, 1700, she welcomed her parents there with a cantata, the " Frohlockender Götter-Streit "—"The victorious battle of the gods,"—of which the poetry was written by a native of Weimar, with whom Sebastian Bach was subsequently to come into very close relations.[70]

This exhausted the musical resources of Arnstadt at that time, so far as can be ascertained. I have spoken of them, not because they may have exerted a determining influence on Bach, or in order to prove that they can have had any such result ; they were quite inefficient for any such effect on a nature so strongly cast and so energetically self-reliant in its working as his was. But a youth of twenty, just entering on life, must have come into contact with them as the days flew past, and so they might for the moment give his spirit some beneficial refreshment. More particularly the performance of the sportive popular singing may have been a real pleasure to his wholesome Thuringian nature. Thus it is not as bearing on the history of art, but simply from the biographical point of view, that Bach's musical surroundings are here dealt with.

Bach's connection with the choir which was established for the New Church must, ere long, have roused his desire to employ his talent for compositions for their use ; and this must have answered to the wishes of the Consistory. Some of these early attempts in the department of concerted church music he regarded many years later as worth remodelling in Leipzig. It is to this idea of the master's that we owe the cantata for the first day of Easter, " Denn du wirst meine Seele nicht in der Hölle lassen "—" For Thou

---

[70] Salomo Franck, Geist- und weltliche Poesien I., p. 302 ; cf., p. 306. The music was perhaps by a native of Brunswick-Wolfenbüttel. The Augustenburg was afterwards pulled down.

wilt not leave my soul in hell,"—which, as it now stands,
rests on three different sections of the text which did not
originally belong to each other.[71] It is easily observed that
the greater part of it is set to a connected hymn in seven
verses, beginning with the lines—

> Auf, freue dich, Seele, du bist nun getröst,
> Dein Heiland der hat dich vom Sterben erlöst.
> Es zaget die Hölle, der Satan erliegt,
> Der Tod ist bezwungen, die Sünde besiegt.
> Trotz sprech ich euch allen, die ihr mich bekriegt.

> Up, soul! and be joyful, thy comfort is near,
> Thy Saviour hath freed thee, no death need'st thou fear.
> Hell quakes at His coming, who crushes its pride.
> Death trembles in fetters, Sin cowers to hide.
> Peace be unto all who have fought on His side.

The composer has used the first verse for an air for a
soprano ; the second, third, and fourth[72] are set to an arioso
for alto, tenor, and bass ; the fifth is a duet ; the sixth and
seventh arioso again, with a closing air for four voices. This
is exactly on the model of the older church cantatas. At
that time, and until another form gained general acceptance
in the second decade of the eighteenth century, songs
divided into verses were always set in those forms which
had gradually grown up in course of the seventeenth century,
woven in with Bible texts and chorales " to taste." These
even often constituted the principal part, admitting only here
and there an aria in several verses with the same music to
each. Sometimes the text consisted solely of Bible words, or
of a chorale treated in various ways. Recitative was as yet
not used ; instead of it the *arioso* was employed, in which
time was strictly observed, and the instrumental accompaniment was carried on in persistent sympathy, without its falling,
however, into a regular aria. Hence the recitative, " Mein
Jesus ware todt," was most certainly first introduced at the
time when the cantata was remodelled, as indeed is evident
likewise from the free treatment of the rhymed lines—a

---

[71] B.-G., II., No. 15.
[72] Bach composed only four lines of the fourth verse, leaving out the fifth.

device as yet hardly used in sacred verse and very little
known. The duet which follows, " Weichet, Furcht und
Schrecken "—"Vanish Dread and Terror!"—is distinguished
by the very different metrical form of the text, and as having
no connection with the main text, while in its musical
casting it bears the stamp of the earlier time. Since the
contents of the work all bear on the Easter festival, it is
probable that this piece was taken from another cantata—
composed possibly for the second Easter festival—and subsequently combined with the recitative composed later for
the purpose (and in which, indeed, Bach contrived to imitate
his own youthful style in a very masterly way) into a more
important Easter cantata in two parts. The following tenor
solo, "Entsetzet euch nicht "—" Oh! be not dismayed,"—
probably also belonged to the second cantata, and there
preceded the duet. It cannot have been placed immediately after the introductory number, if only because all
poetic connection would then have been wanting. The
whole is most completely welded together, if we suppose
the soprano aria, " Auf, freue dich, Seele," to have immediately followed the introductory bass arioso, and that in
the second cantata the duet, " Weichet, Furcht und
Schrecken," came after the comforting words of the angel.
In this way the proper relation between the Bible words
and those of the hymn is established ; besides, it was the
custom always to preface the verses by a single Bible text,
never more.[73]

We may, with tolerable certainty, fix Easter, 1704, as
the time when the original cantata was composed.[74] Its
character, in details as well as in general, displays the
close adhesion of a young composer to the works of the
same kind by the masters of Central and Northern Germany, particularly the latter. This is easily accounted
for by Bach's three years' residence in Lüneburg, and the
intercourse he kept up from thence with Hamburg. But a
deeply seated feeling of innate affinity also drew him towards them, a feeling to which he, some years later, once

---

[73.] See Appendix A, No. 11.   [74] See Appendix A, No. 12.

again evidently yielded; and we shall then have the opportunity of doing fuller justice to the sacred musicians of the
north, and of illustrating in detail the extent to which this,
the earliest of his cantatas, was founded on them. Here,
for the present, it only concerns us to form some general
conception of its contents. The first number, in C major,
is, as has been said, a Bible text set for a bass voice, " For
Thou shalt not leave my soul in hell; neither wilt Thou suffer
Thy Holy One to see corruption " (Psalm xvi. 11), and is
introduced by a short sonata, in which three trumpets with
drums and stringed instruments are employed antiphonally
with the organ. After five bars *adagio*, where hardly
anything is to be heard but broad isolated chords accentuated by fermatas, comes an allegro of three bars—
a kind of *fanfare*—which leads on at once to the singing.
The antiphonal dialogue is here repeated, but between the
voice and the instruments. When the voice has sung a
phrase *arioso*, it is answered by the violins or trumpets,
or followed up by a short imitation on the instruments.
In the old German aria the Ritornel, or instrumental refrain, plays an important part, and not merely regularly
at the end of each strophe, but between the lines of the
verses. It was then transferred to the informal arioso,
from which it was detached by Bach, who also raised both
the arioso itself and the fully developed recitative to an independent and definite position. The declamatory portions
in the instance before us are somewhat stiff and ineffective;
even the treatment of the bass voice is hardly freer than with
his predecessors, who often knew so little how to deal with
it that they simply used it in unison with the fundamental
bass, or made it move in thirds with it. The recitative
follows, and then the duet for soprano and alto in A minor,
accompanied only by the organ and violins; a most pleasing
little piece, which, though it certainly echoes the sentiment
of the words in only one or two passing details, forms a
contrast to the former arioso by its slender form, moving on
its way unburdened by contrapuntal gravity. The form is
that of the Italian *da capo* aria, which was just then beginning gradually and by stealth, as it were, to gain a footing. It

also lies at the bottom of the following tenor solo, "Entsetzet euch nicht," which returns to the key of C major, and calls out the instruments once more; but here it has to accommodate itself as well as it can to the arioso style. The melodic forms offer us, among many forms common to the period, a feature especially Bach's, at the words " den Gekreuzigten" —" The Crucified,"—where the voice wanders sadly about among harmonies involved in a strict subject in four parts, that marches on as if it could be no other than it is. Among Bach's predecessors, under similar circumstances, this could not always be said. The contrasting passage, " Er ist auferstanden und ist nicht hie"—" He is not here, but is risen," —is full of genuine youthful aspiration, and a still more significant fire—nay, boyish daring—is breathed into the closing aria for the soprano, " Auf, freue dich, Seele." The form again is quite simple ; the lines of the verse are sung one after another with very little repetition, so that the composer still clings for the most part to the type of the old sacred aria; still, since the first thema returns at the close, though briefly and almost as a ritornel, it points in this direction to the Italian form of aria ; while, finally, the sameness of the phrase, which recurs again and again in higher positions of key, with answering instrumental passages between, reminds us of the arioso. The piece is, indeed, a confused mixture of various elements of form, but attractive because it is natural and truly felt. We now come to another grand arioso, in which alto, tenor, and bass take part, usually singly, but sometimes together. Here all the extravagance of an ardent young genius has been allowed full play. The passage which represents the " raving " hounds of hell chases the alto in semiquaver passages, high and low, through storming octaves on the organ pedal, and the parts seem striving to outdo each other in defiant and scornful challenge to hell and death. The bass praises Christ, the Warrior, in a somewhat cut and dried fashion; and, although some attempt at completeness is made by repeating this part, the whole leaves an impression of incoherence.

The second duet in G major, which follows, is also given to the soprano and alto, and shows, like the Lüneburg chorale-partitas, with what uncommon rapidity Sebastian Bach developed his mastery in the art of independent and unforced part-writing. Two quite different motives are here employed side by side, and the greater portion of the duet is developed from this combination. The soprano sings—

Ich jauch - ze, ich la - - che, ich jauch - - ze mit Schall,

while the alto begins only two crotchets later with—

Ihr kla - get mit Seuf - zen, ihr wei - net,

(soprano, "I glory, I triumph, I glory with shouts "; alto, " Ye moan and are sighing, lamenting "). The combination allows of the double counterpoint on the octave, which is very fitly employed, and each time the violins take possession of both motives, the viol di gamba comes in with a third characteristic *agitato* part. But the quaver figure of the first motive is carried on through the whole piece, and keeps it firmly together in all its parts. To comprehend Bach's talent and do full justice to his early maturity, we must always recollect that a flowing polyphonic treatment was by no means the strong side of the German masters of that time, whose conquered ground only he could appropriate; but that, on the contrary, his own genius for construction must have helped him in this to quite an equal degree. Even if we chose to assume that in working through the cantata a second time he greatly improved the duet, which may very well be the case, still the file can only have been applied to details; what is most wonderful in it he cannot possibly have added later, for it is the creative germ of the whole piece. How strikingly these two subjects express the contrast in the ideas of the texts need not be pointed out. Moreover, this chromatic passage is always a favourite motive with Bach, which we shall shortly meet with again in other compositions by him, and which he clung to throughout his whole career.

We now come to the final number. It is prefaced by the introductory sonata, very little altered; then an aria in

several parts gradually grows out of it (an aria, in the old
sense of the word, meaning a subjectively religious hymn in
verses), first given to two and two and then to four voices, but
it is in no respect superior to what we are already accustomed
to in the better composers of this kind of music. It is immediately followed by the chorale "Weil du vom Tod erstanden
bist "—" Since Thou art risen from the dead." The violins
accompany the voices in repeated quavers, and only the first
violin goes on independently, supplying a fifth part above the
chorus; after a few lines the trumpets and drums come in
with a fanfare, and the close works off into free imitation in
all the parts. This all lacks originality, and is elaborated on
well-known models.

In the earlier part of his stay at Arnstadt Bach may have
made many other attempts in the department of church
music, but I have not yet succeeded in bringing to light
any further evidence of his industry. So much, however, is
certain, as that while there his principal efforts were directed
to instrumental music, and that he continued to cultivate his
talents in this direction by technical studies and practice in
composition, as well as by thorough analysis of the best works
of the period. It was at Arnstadt that "he really showed the
first-fruits of his industry in the art of organ-playing and in
composition, which he had in great measure learnt only from
the study of the works of the most famous composers of
the time, and from his own reflections on them." So says
Mizler's Necrology. We will endeavour to make ourselves
acquainted with some of these first-fruits.

Johann Jakob, the second of Sebastian's surviving elder
brothers, had served his apprenticeship as a town-musician
at Eisenach, and then, probably, set forth on his travels "to
inquire what manner of music he might find in other places,"
as used then to be said. In 1704 he may have been in
Poland, then allied with the Elector of Saxony, just when
Charles XII. of Sweden had penetrated so far in his adven-
turous and victorious progress. Spell-bound by the magic of
romance which surrounded the young hero, and tempted
by advantageous conditions—so we may fancy—at the age of
two-and-twenty he made up his mind to enter the Swedish

Guard as oboc-player.[75] He returned home once more, expressly to take leave of his family and friends; and it must have been on that occasion that Sebastian composed a piece for him, which was to serve him as a remembrance of his brother when at a distance. The form was evidently suggested by the personal situation; in five short movements he represented the various moods and scenes which preceded and were occasioned hy his brother's impending departure. To these he appended a fugue, and combined the whole under the title "*Capriccio sopra la lontananza del suo fratello dilettissimo*"—" Capriccio on the absence (departure) of a beloved brother."[76]

This little work is so unique in the whole mass of Bach's compositions that it could hardly be accounted for, even by the occasion above mentioned, if we could not without any difficulty quote a model. This model was presented by Johann Kuhnau's six sonatas on Biblical narratives, which had appeared four years before, and, being the work of so gifted and learned a master, had naturally attracted much attention.[77] In it six incidents derived from the Old Testament were illustrated by a series of tone pictures, an experiment in composition in which, however, Kuhnau did not stand alone at that time. Mattheson, Kuhnau's younger contemporary, tells us — and it has been frequently repeated from him — that Froberger could depict whole histories on the clavier, "giving a representation of the persons present and taking part in it, with all their natural characters"; he also states that he was in possession of a Suite by the same composer, "in which the passage across the Rhine of the Count von Thurn, and the danger he was exposed to from the river, is most clearly set before our eyes

---

[75] According to the genealogy.

[76] No autograph of this is known; hence it must remain uncertain whether the Italian title was given by Bach himself. However, even at his earliest period; he was fond of using Italian designations. It is contained in Vol. 208 (No. 9) of Peters' edition.

[77] Musicalische Vorstellung | Einiger | Biblischer Historien, | In 6 Sonaten, | Auff dem Claviere zu spielen, | Allen Liebhabern zum Vergnügen | versuchet | von Johann Kuhnauen. | Leipzig, | Gedruckt bei Immanuel Tietzen | *Anno* M.D.CC.

and ears in twenty-six little pieces."[78] Allied to this, though
not identical, is the disposition shown by certain French
composers, as Couperin and Gaspard de Roux, to represent
distinct types of character in their clavier pieces. It would,
perhaps, be safe to assert that at all times and so long as
independent instrumental music exists, attempts will be
made, with more or less success, to dramatise definite
sentiments figuratively illustrated, by musical forms, which
can only reflect the world of general emotion. Now the first
and universally typical musical instrument is the human
voice, which can hardly be conceived of apart from articulate
utterance. Hence, it is quite intelligible that Sebastian, in
his nineteenth year, carried away by his genius and technical
skill, should for once have allowed himself to be tempted
into a path which was never fitted for spirits of his mould.
For us it is a particularly happy circumstance, since it
enables us to perceive—which otherwise we could hardly
have done—that Kuhnau as well as so many others had
some influence on Bach; and, indeed, much of various kinds
was to be learnt from him.

Johann Kuhnau was born in 1667 at Geysing in the Erz-
gebirge. From 1684 he was Organist of the Thomas-Kirche
at Leipzig; from 1701 cantor also in the Thomasschule.
He died there in 1722, and Bach, whom he had known
personally so early as when he was at Weimar, succeeded
him in his office. His talent was marked by a versatility
absolutely phenomenal; he had acquired considerable knowledge in languages, mathematics, and jurisprudence, and was
an ingenious writer on musical subjects. In the history of
practical music he made himself famous by being the first to
transfer the chamber sonata, with its several movements, to
the clavier. The first attempt of this kind appeared as the
appendix to the second part of his " New Clavier Exercises,"
in 1695,[79] and consists of a prelude with a fugue in B flat

---

[78] Mattheson, Der vollkommene Capellmeister, p. 130, § 72.

[79] Neue Clavierübung. The first part he had published in 1689, but on
the appearance of the second he had a new title engraved. The first part contains seven suites, " Partien," in major keys; the second, seven in minor keys,
besides the said sonata.

major, an adagio in E flat major, with an allegro in B flat
major joined on to it worked out in imitation, and a repetition
of the two first movements.   He evidently found it approved,
for a year after he brought out a new work containing seven
such sonatas, under the title Fresh Fruits for the Clavier
—(Frische Clavierfrüchte).   Irrespective of this novelty,
Kuhnau had a distinctly creative genius for clavier music,
while the few organ chorales that we have by him seem
insignificant ; his church cantatas must be spoken of in
another place.   In the treatment of the fugue, particularly
of the double fugue, he was regarded as a model by the most
prominent theoretical musicians of the middle of the eighteenth century, such as Mattheson and Marpurg; and deserves
to be considered so still, if lucidity and elegance are looked
for rather than richness and depth.   While comparable to
Pachelbel in the full and expressive form of his themes, he
was led to greater freedom and rapidity by the character of
the instrument for which he wrote.

The Biblischen Historien also contain some capital
fugues, and are throughout so interesting to the musician
that they still must give pleasure to every intelligent player.
Much of what seems odd to us, and which gives a peculiar
flavour to our enjoyment, was certainly not planned to that
end by the composer.   He set about his task quite gravely.
The biblical subject of itself forbade all joking.   At most
might he permit himself a cheerful and whimsical humour
in the sonata on Jacob's marriage.   In the others the
deepest earnestness is expressed, and, when once we have
got over the hybrid character of the music, is really impressive.   This is the case in the piece " Saul cured by David, by
means of music "—" der von David vermittelst der Musik
curirte Saul,"—to which the author has given us the following
argument:—"Thus this sonata represents—1st. Saul's melancholy and madness.   2nd. David's refreshing harp-playing ;
and 3rd. The King's mind restored to peace."   It begins in
the mournful key of G minor, revelling in ingeniously combined and melancholy harmonies.   In spite of the recitative-
like phrases which here assert themselves, all is connected
in sound and form.   Saul's sudden burst of madness is

certainly most energetically expressed by an involved descending passage of demi-semiquavers to a long-held chord of
the $\frac{6}{5}$. A very beautiful fugue is attached to the first movement, with this dimly brooding theme (the embellishments
omitted) :—

The counterpoint consists of an unfixed involved motive in
semiquavers, which is preserved as a second theme throughout the fugue :—

Thus the two images of Saul, as "melancholy" and as
"mad," contain the poetical germ of a truly musical development. Then we hear David's harp striking a prelude,
as it were, and, at intervals, the gloomy meditations of the
King, till David plays on without interruption, in one long
sweep, the following idea—

constantly repeating and varying it. And then, in the
last part of it, the King's restored composure is indicated
by a characteristic finale in staccato quavers. As in
this, so in the other sonatas. Situations are selected
which are characterised by the most simple and unmixed
sentiment. This, for instance, is the programme of the
sixth :—" 1st. The agitation of the sons of Israel by the
deathbed of their beloved father. 2nd. Their grief at his
death, their reflections, and what followed thereon. 3rd.
The journey from Egypt to the land of Canaan. 4th. The
burial of Israel and the bitter lamentation thereat. 5th.
The comforted hearts of the survivors." The prevalent

moods are in parts similar to those which Bach might have
observed in his family at the departure of his brother.   In
fact, a certain musical agreement seems also to betray that this
very sonata, whether consciously or unconsciously, floated in
his mind.   Kuhnau's musical images are throughout more
broadly treated than Bach's; nor can we attribute this to
the score of inexperience in the younger composer, since in
other forms he already knew how to express himself very
effectively.   Rather may we regard it as an indication that
Bach did not set to work with the full musical purpose of
the older man, but, under a sense of doing something only
half-artistic, carried out the composition with a certain
humour, which might easily be associated with his regret
at parting from his brother.   Indeed, the depicting of moods
in which the feelings of the artist are personally involved
is never otherwise possible.   If he himself had actually
lamented and mourned as he represents, the power of composition would have deserted him.   Besides, the objective
musical feeling triumphs so completely in the closing fugue
that no doubt can remain as to the view Bach himself took
of this class of music—Programme-music as it came to be
called.

But we will go through it in order.   The first piece is,
" Persuasion addressed to friends that they withhold him
(the brother) from his journey."   Persuasion is represented
by a very pleasing and really insinuating figure—

which recurs in other compositions of his early time.   The
second number " is a representation of the various *casus*
(casualties) which may happen to him in a foreign country";
a fugue in G minor, nineteen bars long, which soon loses
itself in remote keys—possibly with symbolical intention,
for the modulations proceed softly and imperceptibly—and
terminate at last with an expression as of some one wearied
with talking, on the dominant of F minor.   But, as nothing
makes any impression on the brother, in the third part begins

"A general lamentation by friends." Two basses *ostinati* rule almost the whole movement ; the second of these—

is a favourite motive with Bach, already put forward in this cantata. It occurs again in the first chorus of the cantata "Weinen, klagen,[80] and from thence was adopted into the "Crucifixus" of the Mass in B minor ; the first chorus of the cantata "Jesu, der du meine Seele" ;[81] the first chorus of the cantata "Nach dir, Herr, verlanget mich"; the closing subject of the clavier toccata in F sharp minor;[82] a clavier fugue in A minor,[83] and other works. The upper part associated with these basses has sobbing or chromatically *larmoyant* passages ; as a whole, it is easy to detect in it the form of the *passacaglio*, and the great facility and variety of treatment cannot be sufficiently admired in a composer hardly twenty years of age. The pathetic and solitary bass at the end reminds us again of Böhm, whose influence is also recognisable in the elaborate ornamentation of the first two movements. In the fourth, "the friends seeing it cannot be otherwise, come to take leave " ; for this they have only eleven bars allowed them, for the post-chaise is already at the door. Part five, *Aria di Postiglione*, is a delightful little picture in two parts, in which a cheerful melody alternates with the signal given by the post-horns ; in the second part it lies in the bass, and sounds there as if it never could have belonged to any other place. When the carriage has driven off and the composer is left alone, he takes advantage of his solitude to write a double fugue on the post-horn call.

We must devote some further attention to this fugue. It is the only thoroughly worked out piece in the whole capriccio, and, in a musical sense, much the best. It is evident

[80] B.-G., II., No. 12, P., Vol. 1283.
[81] B. G., XVIII., No. 78, P., Vol. 1294.
[82] B.-G., III., p. 318. P., S. I., C. 4 (Vol. 210), No. 4.
[83] P., S. I., C. 4 (Vol. 208), No. 6. B.-G., III.

that when Bach wrote this clavier-work as a memorial for
his brother, his chief view was to write a good piece of music
in which to show what he was capable of. He prefaced
the parts with descriptions of the situations, because it was
a favourable opportunity for imitating Kuhnau for once
in this branch of art, treating them with that light irony
which does not exclude a true interest in the subject, but
ensures command of it. If we already find reason to admire
a high degree of mastery in the descriptive movements, we
are fairly astonished in contemplating the fugue ; indeed, we
might doubt the early origin of the capriccio if its evident
dependence on Kuhnau did not solve the mystery. The same
phenomenon is observable as in his use of Böhm's chorale-
partitas. Bach had such a wonderful sense of form, and his
assiduity in study was so great, that his youthful receptivity
very soon succeeded in absolutely assimilating the styles of
other masters ; at the same time he in no way renounced
his personal characteristics. If this fugue ever came under
Kuhnau's notice, he must at once have recognised himself in
it, but he also must have discerned from afar the flight of
a spirit other and mightier than his own. To mention the
most conspicuous instance first, the whole technical structure
and mechanism of the fugue is different to Bach's own later
style, which makes the greatest demands on the independence and pliancy of every finger, and occasionally on the
player's skill in runs; and yet its fundamental character is
calm, equable, and flowing, and it is strictly opposed to all
jumps and flying changes. But a player may be thoroughly
versed in Bach's *technique* and yet meet in this fugue with
exceptional difficulties. The themes both mimic the post-
horn, the second recurring to the *Aria di Postiglione* :—

The first part has a new device :—

The combination reminds us of the double fugue in Kuhnau's
"Saul"; then, in some places very decidedly, of a double
fugue in his Clavierübung, for which Bach must have had
a particular liking, since he worked up the first theme of it in
a separate composition. To these two principal subjects he
added a third counterpoint, which may almost be regarded as
an independent theme—it returns with so much regularity, is
so distinct from the others, and yet coalesces with their
combinations as if it had grown together with them. While
the fugue flows uninterruptedly on in a fresh stream, interesting thematic images constantly come out, developing
themselves most naturally from the second theme, so that,
in fact, the whole art of subject-treatment is here brought to
bear. It was a real *Ricercar*, a master-fugue that he would
give to his brother; and if all it contains had been genuinely
his own, we might already call him a master of fugue-
writing.

I have already said that this capriccio is unique among
Bach's works. But it is by no means the only one in which
he has followed the footsteps of Kuhnau, and perhaps a mere
accident has deprived us of the certainty that we possess
a second example of Programme-music by him, for another
composition in imitation of Kuhnau's pieces, with several
subjects, undoubtedly exists.[84] The fact that it is entitled
a "Sonata," a name first applied by Kuhnau to clavier-
pieces in several movements, and at that time not yet universally used, serves to confirm this view.[85] But the internal
evidence is enough to allow of a decisive verdict. The
first subject in D major, 3-4 time, is in construction and
general consistency of character so totally unlike what we
regard as characteristic of Bach, that no one who should
meet with it apart from the movements that follow could
guess that he was its composer. But it is closely allied to

---

[84] P., S. I., C. 13 (Vol. 216), No. 8.

[85] The title which Joh. Peter Kellner has given to the MSS. referred to, in
the possession of Herr F. Roitzsch: "*Sonata clamat in D♯ et Fuga in H moll*,"
is careless and uncertain. It is evident that the name "Sonata" must refer to
the whole work of five movements.

the style of Kuhnau, who, in accordance with his musical
views, produced many consistent and song-like movements;
nay, I do not hesitate to assert that it is constructed on the
pattern of a particular part of the "Historie" of Jacob's
marriage. I mean the section which bears the indication,
"The bridegroom happy on the wedding night; something
warns his heart of evil, but he soon forgets it again and
falls asleep." In time, key, scope, accentuation of the
principal ideas, and in general character, the agreement is
complete. In both the whole is composed of aria-like
phrases, mostly of eight bars, each time resulting in a perfect
and almost always similar cadence, only Kuhnau is shorter
and more lucid, Bach more massive in his harmonies and
almost as long again, though he has on the whole no more
to say. Here we detect the beginner. The similarity goes
still further; just as Kuhnau brings in under the superscription "Jacob's wrath at the deception," a short subject formed
of recitative-like phrases, Bach tacks on a little piece of
fourteen bars in imitation of recitatives, from which a style
is developed of polyphonic combination altogether resembling Kuhnau's (compare the first prelude of the first part of
the Clavierübung), and it leads very beautifully into the
dominant of B minor. The next piece is a fugue with this
theme[86]—

an expressive and remarkably independent piece, only
rendered somewhat confused by the strettos which tread
on each other's heels. We cannot reproach Bach, at any
rate as compared with his contemporaries, for the defects
in the counterpoint, which here and there consists only of a
calm succession of chords; nor for the answers to the theme,
which are occasionally such as would be inadmissible according to those strict laws of composition which he himself
was afterwards the first to observe in all their severity.

---

[86] The almost exact resemblance to the *andante* of Beethoven's Pianoforte
Sonata, Op. 28, must strike every one. Here, of course, there can be no idea
of a plagiarism.

Now comes a beautiful little movement *adagio*, still in
strict style, and showing a depth of feeling which Kuhnau
never had at his command ; then the closing fugue in the
principal key, to which again the other master has contributed his share—perhaps from the first subject of Jacob's
marriage, though in plan it is otherwise quite different.
More interesting to us than the musical value of this slightly
built movement is the indication it bears in manuscript—
"*Thema all Imitatio Gallina Cucca.*"[87]   Thus this light
theme—

is intended to mimic the cackling of a hen, with this other,
which gives the accompanying contrary rhythm throughout
the whole movement :—

It would hardly be too bold to argue, turning to this from the
capriccio, that we here have a connection of similar ideas to
that which subsists between the closing fugue of the capriccio
and the rest of that piece.   The two fugues have considerable
general affinity, but the second dances on more quickly to the
end, which may, perhaps, be attributable to the subject
which was floating before the composer's mind.   That
certain definite ideas did in fact govern its origin is obvious
from the transition from the previous adagio—which is so
devoid of musical motive that it seems to be endeavouring
after some special utterance, from the recitative, and from
its similarity to Kuhnau's "Historie"; which, however, I
am not able to say, and I shall leave it to others to put
forward any guesses on the subject.

At any rate, the dramatic aspect of Kuhnau's compositions
was that which least attracted Bach.   If he ever yielded to

---

[87] Indifferent Italian for "Tema all' imitazione della chioccia."   The post-
horn fugue in the capriccio has the title "Fuga all' imitazione della cornetta
di Postiglione."

it at all there is no lack of evidence that he did so in a far
more humorous vein. Under the relations which exist between instrumental and vocal music, and the many close ties
which at that time existed between these two great branches
of art, as they still did a hundred years later, it would do
his talent no dishonour if he had really for once believed
that this class of art was of some value, particularly since
it was protected by such a name as Kuhnau's. But, unless
some more unknown treasures of instrumental music by
Bach should one day be brought to light, the fact remains certain that, after this juvenile attempt, he never again returned
to this branch of music in the whole course of a long artistic
career extending over nearly fifty years. To a genius so
thoroughly and inexhaustibly musical as his, it must have
been intolerable to see the art limping on crutches, or reduced
to a subordinate position.

The association of a musical composition with the conception of a definite scene, in order to arouse or to represent
its emotional aspect, tends too often to mere platitude and
weariness. It serves to stimulate the composer's inventiveness when the natural energy of his purely musical ideas is
exhausted; and the theoretical composers of Bach's time
who, following the example of the rhetoricians of antiquity,
set themselves a suitable " topic " or subject for invention—
since free invention yielded them little or nothing—found in
this process a means of inflaming their imagination by the
images called up, a *locus adjumentorum*, as it was termed. The
imaginative power of the hearer, however, far from finding a
comprehension of the piece facilitated, is dragged away by
secondary ideas from the main musical conception. The whole
question of course turns on the nature of the ideas which it
is the function of music to deal with. The French, whose
genius for instrumental music is on the whole inconsiderable,
were fond of adopting for their small clavier-pieces—almost
the only line in which they showed any creative talent—
such titles as *L'Auguste, La Majestueuse, Les Abeilles*, &c.,
thus stamping them as portraits or as *genre* pictures, and
betraying their theatrical tendency. With regard to Kuhnau,
a German, it has already been said that he usually succeeded

in expressing situations which were replete with emotion, although, indeed, he sometimes adopts very trivial means, as, for instance, when he assigns recitatives to the clavier; and in the succession of various tone pictures, of which the dramatic requirements are too obviously beyond the conditions of musical art, he really fails as an artist. But when the poetic element is worked out and subordinated to a purely musical conception, so as merely to suggest the limitation to one single and definite scheme of feeling, within which the music can evolve its being, this no doubt serves to concentrate the sentiment, but also to turn the balance between the objective and subjective elements in the work essentially in favour of the latter. For that which is universally paramount in a work of art is Form, in which, in a piece of music, the idea or the image is not included. All such artistic ideas are visions for the solitary soul, and from that aspect are not less justifiable than the lyric form in the poetic art, since Goethe declares that this should properly always be a poem on a given occasion; but to the multitude they are intelligible only in their narrowest development, and even then but rarely sympathetic. If the artist desires to give utterance to such a conception, he must necessarily make use of the human voice, since, in that, Nature has combined articulate speech with musical tone into an unit among the materials at his command.

Bach's development not only bears weighty witness against such musical monologues, but confirms the correctness of the principle just laid down in the most striking way. Take the organ chorale, as written by Pachelbel, blossoming, as it were, from the points of contact where personal feeling meets the church melody, and uttering in mysterious harmonies all the sacred emotions and imperishable memories that were woven round it in the composer's mind. What is it but a subjective picture of his own mood? For a long period indeed Sebastian devoted all the powers of his genius by preference to this form of composition, and opened to us a world of sentiment that is as deep and immeasurable as the ocean. But the true essence of an artist is to be able to give outward form and expression to inward experience;

and, just as all art as a whole is constantly tending to an increasingly objective treatment of the subject selected, so must the individual development of every true artist. The aim and essence of Bach's chorale-choruses and forms of composition allied to them was the raising of the organ chorale to its utmost and highest perfection. Even in Weimar he had already started on this path, and during his residence in Leipzig he followed it up with stupendous energy.

The second movement of the sonata by Bach now under consideration has an independent pedal part, while in the rest of the composition only the hands are employed. A process here recurs which has been briefly alluded to in speaking of a chorale arrangement. In a great number of Bach's works it may be observed how he first gradually educated himself to use the pedals in a thoroughly independent way. No doubt his predecessors, too, had shown much freedom in this respect, since, excepting perhaps in the organ chorale, they had not confined themselves strictly to a subject in which the number of parts was the same throughout; but still the proportions were always such that the pedal had to play an essential part in the composition, as soon as it had once been brought in to take its share in the working-out. But its isolated entrance in the middle of a piece, and its subsequent total disappearance, as in this sonata, is the stamp of a beginner; neither Pachelbel nor Buxtehude would have allowed himself such a licence. Nor is it more mature in style when we find the pedal first introduced towards the close of a composition, whether in the independent conduct of the theme or to give more brilliant effect to a closing cadence; here, certainly, there is an artistic purpose, which however is directed to a superficial effect. Finally, we come upon separate pedal notes serving as "pedal points," or as the deeper bass for a full chord. This treatment, which was known also to other composers of his time, hardly involves the pedal at all in the organism of the piece, and only uses it as an ornamental accessory. Consequently, if we are not completely deceived by the marks, this use of the pedals is still to be seen in the first years of Bach's second residence in Weimar, till it entirely disappears in the course of the artist's advance towards maturity. The other modes of using the pedals are referable only to the earliest period of his labours, and any one who realises the vigorous polyphonic treatment, of which he was master before the age of twenty, will hardly regard compositions of this stamp as still possible in the second half of the Arnstadt period. As a mere external consideration it must be remembered that the frequent practice on the organ, for which he never had full opportunity till he went to Arnstadt, afforded him an opening for the independent use of the pedals, so that his compositions in general may be regarded as a standard by which to measure his technical skill. In the one, as in the other, he went onwards and upwards with gigantic strides; and we know that he would often sit the night out in obedience to the demands of his genius.[88]

One composition thus characterised by an arbitrary use of the pedals has a special biographical interest, because it is connected with Sebastian's eldest brother. As Johann Jakob, when starting with the Swedes, had a musical souvenir written for him, so we find that Joh. Christoph received a composition as a token on some festive occasion. For this, also, the title of "capriccio" was chosen, and, as in the former case, the occasion of the composition was exactly stated. Here it was, at any rate, indicated by the words, "In honour of Johann Christoph Bach, of Ohrdruf."[89] The idea that this was principally intended as an evidence of the artistic skill he had acquired, and of the progress he had made, seems all the more probable since the work was offered to his former master, possibly on his birthday. It can hardly be of later date than 1704, and was probably composed even before he left Lüneburg. The progress of an artist is not invariably straight onward, or the latter date would certainly be the

---

[88] Mizler, Necrology, p. 167.

[89] "*Capriccio. In honorem Joh. Christoph. Bachii (Ohrdruf) per Jh. Sb. Bach.*" Thus in a copy which comes down to us from Aloys Fuchs, and now is in the Royal Library, Berlin. The same title, with a few alterations, is in a copy by his younger contemporary, J. P. Kellner. P., S. I., C. 13 (Vol. 216), No.

correct one, for the merit of the second of these capriccios is undoubtedly less than that of the first. It consists only of one fugal movement, but the title was not then unusual for an informal work of the fugue type. Informal it is, in so far as that all sorts of other elements have a casual existence in subordination to the theme—passages of pretentious counterpoint which come to nothing, transient ornamental effects interspersed with full chords. This incoherent treatment of the fugue betrays the influence of the northern school as strongly as the cleverness of the thematic development, which, indeed, is what lends the piece its chief interest. Otherwise, in spite of its actual length (126 bars, common time), it is not fully and duly developed. The road leads over neither hill nor vale, but through a level plain, not wholly without beauty. The greater part of the blame attaches to the theme—

which, as compared with the brisk fresh post-horn thema, moves on stealthily and almost sleepily. It is in bar sixty-seven that the pedal is suddenly brought in, for no other reason than that both hands may be employed in the imitative passages above the bass. It disappears again after a few bars, returning once more for the same purpose towards the end, where an opportunity is given to the player for exhibiting his skill in brilliant passages of demi-semiquavers. We may assume that the bass was arbitrarily strengthened by the pedal as suitable opportunities occurred. However, it is necessary only in these two places. From its general character the capriccio seems to be intended for the cembalo.

A work, however, in which the adaptation for the organ is unmistakable, and which must likewise be ascribed to this period, on account of the undeveloped form of pedal treatment, is a prelude with its accompanying fugue, in C minor.[90] In this instance the composition may without any doubt be assigned

---

[90] P., S. V , C. 4 (Vol. 243), No. 5.

to the Arnstadt time; the rapture with which the composer
revels in the unlimited wealth of tone in the organ, glows in
every bar.   In the prelude the pedal is, except in an introductory solo of several bars, employed only for the long-held
bass notes, on which is built a splendid flowing movement in
imitation, that is still another proof of Bach's early mastery
of polyphonic writing; in only two places (bars twenty and
twenty-four) does he use the *manieren* of the time, which
he afterwards entirely cast off.   The fugue is constructed
in such a way that the pedal does not enter until quite
the end, when it has the subject, it is true, but with no
counterpoint in   the   manuals, only chords accompanying
it in harmony.   He may not yet have fully conquered
the art of form, any more than that of execution ; but it
is a striking proof of the evenness between the outer
and inner development of Bach's genius, that the impression produced is not in any way that of an idea only partially realised.   His thoughts fell naturally into the form
in which justice could best be done them by his executive
skill; and though this was not yet completely and equally
developed, the composition is homogeneous throughout.
The late entry of the pedal part may practically result from
the fact that Bach was not yet able to use it independently
in the form of an *obbligato ;* it is evident, notwithstanding,
that an intentional climax is obtained at the end by means
of it.   In fact, the true fire of youth burns throughout
the piece with a bright flame ; the semiquaver passages in
the pedals roaring and rushing up and down, accompanied
by the heavy chords in the manual, have a very imposing effect, and one which is particularly suited to the
organ ; and in the rushing torrents of sound, which overwhelm everything at the end, there is much more than
mere striving after executive brilliancy.   If we consider
the structure of the fugue in other respects, we shall
find that the way in which the entrances of the subjects
follow one another betrays the desire not so much to
fulfil the higher and highest demands of the fugue form as
to revel freely in a mighty realm of sound.   That this is a
special characteristic of the period before Bach, which, more

or less removed from the old strict polyphony, strove above all things to bring into use the whole tone material of the organ, has already been emphatically asserted. It was reserved for Bach himself to achieve the most perfect mastery over the outer material as subservient to the loftiest ideal. This was the case at the time of his highest perfection, when, as he became ever stricter and more strict, the traces of the freedom of an earlier time grow very rare. At this time, however, they were of very common occurrence. The C minor fugue is in three parts, up to the entrance of the pedals, where the part-writing ceases. These three parts, however, are not as it were individuals partaking in the development of the piece by the regular alternate delivery of the theme. The theme begins on c, and ascends constantly in the four subsequent entrances into the octave between c″ and c‴; from the third entrance it remains, of course, in the upper part. The rule of fugue construction is not adhered to, except in the changes between tonic and dominant, and their inner relations to one another; in truth, this is the natural foundation for organ fugues, as well as for all branches of instrumental music. The feeling of organic unity, which in other forms is gained in a different way, is here only possible by adherence to a fixed number of parts, which seem, like individuals, intended for one another. The end and aim of form is to vivify its materials, and of all these the organ tone is one of the most inanimate.

Among the most interesting of Bach's youthful works is to be reckoned another fugue in C minor, which seems to be of nearly the same date as the foregoing.[91] It is interesting, too, because themes resembling this one, but more mature and full of meaning, are found in several different fugues, so that it seems to be the expression of an element inherent in Bach's deepest nature. It is brought to marvellous perfection in the three-part fugue in the E

---

[91] P., S. V., C. 4 (Vol. 243), No. 9. Griepenkerl, in the preface to that volume, assigns it, on the authority of a very old MS., to the Weimar period, in which, however, he gives it a very early place. The use of the pedals is also in this case a very plain guide.

minor toccata for clavier, for which this fugue would seem
to be a sketch, so closely allied are they, both in matter
and method. But this one, too, is important enough by
itself, and it may well be doubted if such a theme as the
following had ever occurred to any one else at that time :—

It is true that the harmonic, and at the same time melodic,
figure used from the middle of the third bar onwards was a
favourite and very effective means of uniting rapidity with
breadth of sound on the organ, and dignity with animation; but when we look at the beginning—what a vague
indefiniteness of motion in rhythm and harmony—though
it was, and is, a fundamental rule to make the theme of
a fugue clear both in tonality and in rhythm! In this, at
first, we do not know whether E flat major or C minor is
intended, and even when this doubt is solved in the next
bar, we have the choice, owing to the four semiquavers on
the third beat, of taking it as in F minor or A flat major,
until the entry of the response decides for the major. The
treatment, however, throughout is uncommon and of great
harmonic beauty. The uncertainty of the rhythm continues
still longer; as far as the third beat of the fourth bar the
player or the reader alone could know on which notes the
chief accents lay, and the unprepared hearer would doubtless
conceive of the phrase as accentuated in this way—

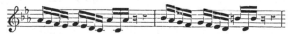

since the organ has no power of accentuation, and the
rhythm is not made clear until the fourth bar. This sudden
plunge from subjective obscurity into objective clearness is
a deeply rooted characteristic of Bach's artistic method. A
glance at the F sharp minor fugue, in the second part of
the Wohltemperirte Clavier, will serve to show how he
yielded to it even in later life. From the theme onwards

the work is pervaded by a feeling of tension and an expression of longing for a blissfulness as yet but dimly anticipated ; a wonderful effect, and one entirely unlike anything then existing, is produced in passages like this—

by the chord of the sixth in A flat major, with the third above and below, and the sad uncertain diminished chord in the next bar. The composer comes constantly back to this counterpoint, as though he could never be weary of it. The flood of feeling with which the whole is permeated is so intense that we willingly forget how little wealth of counterpoint the fugue displays, and how few are the changes with which similar combinations recur in different positions.. It is a restless and delightful drifting to and fro, not designed to carry us to any harbour. At the close a pedal passage comes in, to warn us, apparently at least, of the approaching end ; and this is ratified by an emphatic solo, otherwise we should hardly believe it.

The question here arises what Bach did, at this time of the budding and happy blossoming of his genius, in the way of organ chorales. We cannot suppose him to have now neglected that form of composition to which some of his earliest experiments belong, to which he devoted such indefatigable industry at his greatest period, and to which his inclination continually prompted him. An arrangement of the chorale " Wie schön leucht't uns der Morgenstern "— " How brightly shines the morning star,"—also exists in an elegant autograph, of which the whole character assigns it to the period of his residence in Arnstadt.[92] It is written for two manuals and pedals, and clearly betrays the influence of the northern masters. We must also bear in mind that it was in the path struck out by Pachelbel that the boy

---

[92] Four.leaves in small oblong quarto in the Royal Library at Berlin.

was first led by his brother's hand, and that this influence again met him on all sides when he returned from his three years' sojourn in Thuringia. Since, during his residence in the north, he gave himself entirely up to the influence of the original genius of the masters that were most esteemed there, we should hardly be mistaken in assuming that he would come back with energies renewed and enriched, to the forms of art which he could with truth call those of his native country. These forms were the true soil—the deepest and most productive of all—in which the Bach organ chorale, like a majestic oak, had its root, while all other influences were accessory, serving only as the nourishing water. During these first years at Arnstadt we must think of him as following most of all in the footsteps of Pachelbel. The works that can with any show of probability be pointed out as the result of his studies at this time are certainly very few. A set of seventeen variations on "Allein Gott in der Höh sei Ehr" is ascribed to him in an old MS.[93] The internal evidence against its authenticity is much weakened if we consider it as an early work, remembering how very nearly Bach at this time approached to the style of Böhm and Kuhnau. In many of the variations we perceive a breathing likeness to Pachelbel, but especially in the second, where the *cantus firmus* is in the pedal part, and in the eleventh, where the melody is given to an inner part. The fact, too, of the piece being worked in three parts throughout agrees with Pachelbel's ordinary and usual method. Original features are scarcely to be discerned, and therefore the variations bear no weighty witness to the point of development which Bach had reached at this time. Such evidence can only be derived from compositions which reveal some new matter, even though the form be not original. Buttstedt, Walther, and others wrote pieces all their lives long which might have been written by Pachelbel. Bach's relations to him can have been no more marked than his relations to Böhm, Kuhnau, and Buxtehude. Nay, the more familiar he was from childhood with Pachelbel's method, the earlier must he have learnt to move freely and indepen-

---

[93] In the possession of Dr. Rust, Leipzig, unpublished.

dently in that method ; but this independence, naturally, is not very conspicuous in this production, which was perhaps lightly thrown off and quickly finished.

III.

VISIT TO LÜBECK.—BUXTEHUDE AND HIS STYLE.— INFLUENCE ON BACH, 1704-5.

Two years had slipped away in diligent and secluded labours in his art. If Bach, at the very first, had gained the respect of the citizens of Arnstadt by his conspicuous skill, he had by this time means at his command to rouse them at times to admiration. But whether it fell out so is another question. It is quite certain that only a few suspected his genius ; the majority asked no more than that he should fulfil his duties satisfactorily, which on the whole was not demanding too much. The musician took the contrary view ; to him the aim and end of his official position was the opportunity it afforded him for undisturbed self-improvement. Convinced, for his own part, of what he owed to his own gifts, he found certain parts of his duty displeasing and intrusive. Besides, the supply of artistic experience and inspiration which he had brought with him from the towns of North Germany, had gradually been exhausted. He wanted to find himself free once more, and to enjoy the invigorating and refreshing intercourse with superior artists which he had been deprived of now for some years. He had been able to save the funds for a long journey out of his salary, so, towards the end of October, 1705, after finding an efficient deputy, he petitioned for four weeks leave of absence.[94]

His destination again lay northwards, being in fact Lübeck,

---

[94] Immediately after his return he was summoned to appear before the Consistory, February 21, 1706, and charged with having remained away four times as long as his permission extended. See the document quoted later, which is in agreement with the statement in Mizler, p. 162, that his stay in Lübeck was almost a quarter of a year—if the time for his journeys to and fro and some days spent in Hamburg and Lüneburg on his return journey be deducted.

the residence of Buxtehude. Pachelbel, indeed, was living still nearer to him, but in the south at Nuremberg; and he was sixteen years younger and by so much more vigorous than Buxtehude. But Bach probably, and very rightly, took the view that he could no longer acquire anything in Nuremberg that had not long formed part of the common stock in Thuringia, and become to him part of his very being, while the art of the Lübeck master offered new and peculiar aspects, and had as yet gained small acceptance in Central Germany. His reason for choosing the late autumn season for his journey probably was that between Martinmas (November 11) and Christmas the famous " Abendmusiken," or evening performances, were held in the Marien-Kirche at Lübeck, and he must have wished to hear them. Thus he had no time to linger on the way at Lüneburg or Hamburg, or anywhere else if he was to arrive in time; and the whole fifty miles must be made on foot.

Dietrich Buxtehude was a Northman in the strictest sense—a Dane. His father, Johann Buxtehude, held the post of Organist at the Church of St. Olai (St. Olaf's), at Helsingör, in Seeland, where the son was born in 1637. Nothing accurate is known as to the mode of his education,[95] but it probably was influenced by the school of Sweelinck. In the sixth decade of the century he went to Lübeck, and there he soon attracted general observation by his playing and his conspicuous musical talents. Very possibly he was tempted thither by the prospect of succeeding the Organist Tunder, who had died November 5, 1667, at the church of St. Mary; and he was in fact elected to this office, April 11, 1668.[96] A few months after this he married (August 3) Anna Margaretha, the daughter of the deceased organist. It would seem that a custom at that time made this marriage an indispensable

---

[95] According to Walther, Johann Theile was his teacher, but this is obviously an error, since he was nine years younger than Buxtehude.

[96] H. Jimmerthal, Beschreibung der grossen Orgel (an organ built between 1851-54) in der St. Marien-Kirche zu Lübeck, p. 44. Erfurt und Leipzig: G. W. Körner, 1859.

condition.[97]   The place of organist to this church was one of
the best in all Germany.   At the beginning of the eighteenth
century it was worth 709 marks; the office of receiver, which
was combined with it, brought in 226 marks, and there were
besides various fees and perquisites.   The organ was of
considerable compass, and, as it would seem, tasteful in
construction, with fifty-four stops to three manuals and
pedal.[98]   Hence, a man of genius and energy would find here
a favourable soil for prosperous activity.

Buxtehude had not long been in office when the signs of
his presence were already visible.   His efforts were directed,
not merely to organ-playing, but to grand musical performances, which were only very remotely connected with the
church services.   In 1670, a choir was built in the Church of
St. Mary, close by the organ, expressly for the singers, and,
in the year 1673, we first find mention made of that "evening
music" which Lübeck could at that time boast of as a peculiar institution.   These performances took place every year
before Christmas, on the two last Sundays in Trinity, and the
second, third, and fourth Sundays in Advent, from four to five,
after afternoon service.   Buxtehude must not, however, be
regarded as having instituted them, since he himself wrote in
a church register kept by him, and which still exists, that they
had been customary of old.   As to where they originated and
on what occasion only the vaguest guesses were rife, strangely
enough, even in the eighteenth century.   What, however,
remains certain is that Buxtehude raised them to greater
importance.   On these evenings concerted sacred music
especially was performed, both longer and shorter pieces;
but of course it must be understood that Buxtehude was

---

[97] A passage from his Hochzeitscarmen or epithalamium, in the City Library
at Lübeck, seems to hint at this:—

> True, indeed, it pleased him ill, and he longed to be as free
> As of yore ; but longed in vain—he had lost his liberty.
> For the maiden's fair demeanour—with some unaccustomed fever
> Asking for its satisfaction—got the upper-hand for ever.

In the same song mention is made of the esteem in which the Lübeck citizens
held him as an artist.

[94] The specification is given in Appendix, B. IV.

to be heard between the pieces as an accomplished organist. His brother-in-law, Samuel Frank, a native of Stettin, at first rendered him much assistance. He was cantor at Lübeck, and fourth master in the St. Catherine School, but was already dead in 1670.[99] The municipality showed no less readiness to support the master in his efforts; musicians and instruments alike were procured. Buxtehude attached great importance to a perfect orchestra. Quite at an early date he had purchased two trumpets "constructed in a singular manner, such as had hitherto been seen in no prince's band." In 1680 he organised a grand performance, in which an orchestra of nearly forty persons were engaged besides the singers and the organ. For this purpose the indefatigably zealous musician had himself written out about four hundred sheets, and as the profits did not answer to the outlay, the church allowed him an additional sum of one hundred marks. It might seem from this that the "Abendmusiken" were regular church concerts, to which admission was by payment. This, however, certainly was not the case; entrance was always free, as if to Divine service. But it was the custom to have the books of the words of all five concerts neatly bound together, and to send them to the houses of the well-to-do citizens of Lübeck; and it was a matter of honour on the part of the recipients to send back an adequate honorarium. The *impresario* of the concerts was thus reimbursed for his outlay, and paid himself with the possible surplus. What Buxtehude developed out of the "Abendmusik" proved to be an institution which struck deep root in the life of the citizens of Lübeck, was kept up throughout the whole of the eighteenth century, and was even carried on during part of the nineteenth.[100]

---

[99] The extraordinarily rich musical library of the Marien-Kirche was presented by the town of Lübeck to the Gesellschaft der Musikfreunde, in Vienna, in 1814. See C. F. Pohl, Die Gesellschaft der Musikfreunde (Vienna, 1871), pp. 114, 115.

[100] The principal printed source of information as to Buxtehude is *Johannis Molleri Cimbria Literata, Vol.* II., *p.* 132 (*Havniae*, 1744). There, among others, a passage is quoted from Höveln's Beglücktem und geschmücktem Lübeck, p. 114, where the "Abendmusik of the world-famed organist and

His fame now spread widely and rapidly; he became a centre round which younger talents gathered. The most important of these was Nikolaus Bruhns, born in 1665, at Schwabstädt in Schleswig; Buxtehude afterwards procured him occupation for many years at Copenhagen till he became Organist at Husum, where he died, unfortunately, in the prime of his powers, in 1697. He was also an admirable violin-player, and by his method of double-stopping could produce such effects that the hearers could fancy they were listening to three or four violins.[101] Daniel Erich, afterwards Organist at Güstrow, also deserves mention; and Georg Dietrich Leiding, born in 1664, at Bücken near Hoya, who, like Bach, made a pilgrimage in 1684 from Brunswick to Hamburg and Lübeck to derive instruction from Reinken's and Buxtehude's playing.[102] We may even suspect Buxtehude's direct influence on Vincentius Lübeck, who has already been mentioned. He was in close friendship with Andreas Werkmeister among others, who was Organist at Halberstadt and an excellent theoretical musician, and he took the opportunity of testifying to this friendship by addressing to him, after the manner of the time, two poems in his praise, which were inserted before his *Harmonologia Musica*, 1702; one of these is an acrostic on the composer's name, and shows a more than ordinary facility of diction. A later generation were equally unanimous in his praise, at their head Mattheson, who mentions him with Werkmeister, Froberger, and Pachelbel, as one of the few who, " although merely an organist," still could show intelligent folks that he had something more in him " than merely clanking the cymbals." [103]

---

composer, *Dietrich Buxtehude*," is fully discussed. Other materials are derived from the church registers, account books, and official documents of St. Mary's Church, which I owe to the kindness of Professor Mantel, of Lübeck. Mattheson also, in the Vollkommenen Capellmeister, mentions the "Abendmusik." Ruetz discusses them later and more fully in a work entitled, Widerlegte Vorurtheile von der Beschaffenheit der heutigen Kirchenmusik, p. 44. (Lübeck, 1752.) H. Jimmmerthal has lately discussed the matter in a carefu little work, Dietrich Buxtehude, Historische Skizze. (Lübeck, 1879.)

[101] Mattheson, Ehrenpforte, p. 26.
[102] Walther, Lexicon, under " Erich " and " Leiding."
[103] Mattheson, Grosse General-Bass-Schule, p. 42.

Mattheson, born in Hamburg in 1681, and a resident there throughout his life, had ample opportunity for knowing and hearing Buxtehude. This he did in 1703 ; still the immediate cause of his doing so at that time was the prospect of the possible death of the master, already advanced in years. He had never forgotten the circumstances and conditions under which he himself had obtained his office, and he, like his predecessors, determined that his place should only be filled by a man who should marry one of his daughters. As such a bargain, though not unusual at the time, might not be to every man's taste, it was necessary to look out betimes for a successor. Mattheson at that time enjoyed a reputation as a thorough musician and singer and a skilful player, for which reason Von Wedderkopp, the president of the council, invited him to Lübeck to take a nearer view of the position. In the same year Handel had visited Hamburg and formed a close friendship with Mattheson. By his friend's request he made the journey with him, for it offered various prospects of enjoyment and instruction to the two young men, and it survived as a pleasing memory thirty-seven years after, in Mattheson's memoirs, where he alluded to it.[104] Buxtehude played to them ; then they themselves tried "almost every organ and clavi-cembalo"; and as Handel, notwithstanding his youth, was his companion's superior on the organ, he played that instrument and Mattheson played the harpsichord. But the matrimonial conditions frightened Mattheson away ; and well they might, for the bride proposed to him, Anna Margaretha Buxtehude, was born in 1669, and was thus no less than twelve years older than himself.[105] His comrade of eighteen, who from his previous training was peculiarly fitted for the post, must under these circumstances have had even less inclination for it, even if he had had no other prospect in view. So they satisfied themselves with

---

[104] Ehrenpforte, under " Händel," p. 94.

[105] The church register does not indeed give the name in this particular place, and Buxtehude had six daughters; but as Schieferdecker, the organist who succeeded him, married one of them, named Anna Margaretha, it can only have been this one—the eldest. Her name was the same as her mother's ; besides, it is natural that the office should have involved marrying the eldest daughter.

music and those pleasures which the citizens felt themselves
bound to offer to invited guests and distinguished artists, and
"after many proofs of respect and the enjoyment of many
entertainments," they withdrew from Lübeck.

Two years later Bach was standing before the organ on
which Handel had played. But the very different conditions
in which he found himself throw a strong light on the
difference in the development of the two men. Handel had
come to Lübeck to see whether the place might suit him if
Mattheson should not wish to take it : the evening performances, the fine instrument, and the high salary, might
provisionally seem a temptation to him. He was a very fine
organ-player, but there is no reason to suppose that he was
superior to his contemporary Bach. And yet, with two
years more of diligent study and training, Bach was far from
imagining that he could get a lucrative appointment in
Lübeck. It was exclusively the desire to acquire some
new and important elements of artistic knowledge which
brought him to the side of the great master of organ-playing :
for the organ was the starting-point of his own development—the germ from which, in great measure, his characteristic creations grew and spread. Handel, with a genius
which, if more comprehensive, was far less profoundly laborious, never stood in so intimate a connection with the organ
music of his time, that essentially German branch of art;
and the way in which he afterwards made it subserve his
grand and pregnant artistic ideal, the oratorio, demanded not
so much profound treatment as breadth and brilliancy. The
outward circumstances answer to this. Handel arrives from
Hamburg in the bright midsummer days, in the gay society
of Mattheson, and in obedience to an invitation from the
president of the council ; he enjoys an affable welcome, and
festivities in his honour. Bach comes on foot in the dull
autumn weather from remote Thuringia, following his own
instinct, and perhaps not knowing one single soul that
might look for his coming.[106] But his talent was his best

---

[106] Mizler, p. 162. "In Arnstadt once he was moved by a particularly strong
impulse that he should hear as many good organists as possible. So he went,

letter of introduction. It is beyond all doubt that the venerable Buxtehude must have observed what a genius was here in blossom, and that an affinity in the artistic views of the two men must have bridged over the half-century of years between them, and have drawn them together. Once introduced into this new world of art, Bach soon could think of nothing else. His leave expired without his troubling himself about the matter; he had become indifferent to the place of Organist to the New Church at Arnstadt. Week after week passed by; he outstayed the allotted time—twice the time—three times. It can be to a certain extent ascertained what he heard of Buxtehude's larger compositions. On the occasion of the death of the Emperor Leopold I., and the accession of the Emperor Joseph, Buxtehude performed on December 2 and 3, 1705, from four to six in the afternoon, a *Castrum doloris* and *Templum honoris* at St. Mary's Church. These two works, which were printed at the time, are now unfortunately lost.

A considerable number of Buxtehude's compositions were published at Lübeck during his lifetime. They were principally concerted works for church use, among them the pieces written from 1678 to 1687 for the "Abendmusik," with incidental compositions, large and small. Of these only five wedding arias have been preserved. Nothing has come to my knowledge of his printed instrumental compositions; possibly a work consisting of seven sonatas for violin and viol di gamba, with harpsichord (Lübeck, 1696), is the only one which was published.[107] Mattheson insisted that

---

on foot too, a journey to Lübeck, to hearken to the famous organist of St. Mary's Church in that town—Dietrich Buxtehude." The conspicuous contrast between Handel and Bach led Forkel to interpret the word "behorchen" as meaning "to listen secretly," but it only means to hearken with attention and docility. That Bach, who was already a distinguished artist, should not have ventured to make Buxtehude's acquaintance, while Handel two years previously had boldly gone to work on his organ and brought him pupils from all sides, has really no sense.

[107] Gerber, N. L. I., col. 590, gives a list of Buxtehude's printed works, and inaccurately quotes Moller's *Cimbria Litterata* as the authority, for he has combined with it the notices by Walther (Lex., p. 123) and Mattheson. Moller's list runs as

Buxtehude's chief strength lay in clavier music, and lamented that "little or nothing" of his in that line had been printed. Thus even he knew of none in print. It is therefore doubtful whether a collection of seven Suites for clavier, of which the existence is announced, ever were distributed, excepting in written copies. At the same time, it was almost exclusively to these Suites, now lost, that Buxtehude owed the circumstance that even in later times he was now and then spoken of as a composer. He is said, for instance, to have "cunningly represented in them the nature and characteristics of the planets,"[108] whence we might suspect them to have been examples of the most tasteless "programme-music." On the other hand, it must be remembered that the seven planets —no more were known at that time, and the sun and moon were reckoned in—had special identities of character attributed to them, from which astrologers calculated their influence on the lives and fortunes of men. It is evident

---

follows: "Various Hochzeit-*Arien.*, *Lubecae* 1672, in *fol.*—Fried- und Freudenreiche Hinfahrt des alten *Simeons*, bey Absterben seines Vaters, *Joh. Buxtehuden* [The peaceful and joyful departure of aged Simeon ; on the occasion of his father's death, by Joh. Buxtehude], 32jährigen Organisten in Helsingör (der zu Lübeck am 22 *Jan.* 1674. 72jährig verstorben) in zwey *Contrapuncten musicali*sch abgesungen. Lub. 1674. *in fol.*—Abend *Musick* in IX. Theilen. *Lub.* 1678-1687. in 4.—Hochzeit des Lammes. Lub. 1681 in 4.—VII. *Sonate a doi, Violino & Viola di gamba, con cembalo.* Lub. 1696. in fol.—*Anonymi* hundertjähriges Gedichte vor die Wolfahrt der Stadt Lübeck ; am 1 *Jan.* des Jubeljahres 1700. in *S. Marien-*Kirche *musicalisch* vorgestellt. Lub. 1700. *in fol.*—*Castrum doloris* dem verstorbenen Keyser *Leopoldo* und *Templum honoris* dem regierenden Keyser *Josepho* I. ; in zwey *Musicken*, in der Marien-Kirche zu Lübeck, gewidmet. Lub. 1705. in fol."—To these he adds two works which were ascribed to Buxtehude in the Leipzig catalogue of the Spring book-fair of 1684. "1. Himmlische Seelen Lust auf Erden über die Menschwerdung und Geburt unsers Heylandes *Jesu Christi.* 2. Das allerschröcklichste und allererfreulichste, nemlich das Ende der Zeit, und der Anfang der Ewigkeit, Gesprächsweise vorgestellet."—["1. Heavenly joy on Earth, over the Incarnation and Birth of our Saviour Jesus Christ. 2. The most fearful and most joyful [of events], namely, the End of Time and the Beginning of Eternity, set forth in recitative."] I may here refer the reader to my own edition of Buxtehude, brought out since the first volume of this work was written: two vols., Leipzig, Breitkopf and Härtel, 1875-1876. They include several pieces which were unknown to me at the time when I wrote upon Buxtehude's characteristics.

[108] Mattheson, Vollkommener Capellmeister, p. 130.

that Buxtehude had proposed to reflect these in his Suites, and so to compose seven characteristic pieces; and this, in Mattheson's opinion, he had perfectly succeeded in doing. It is difficult to see why this should be a more unmusical idea than Couperin's, when he called his sarabandes and allemandes " *La Majestueuse*," " *La Ténébreuse*," &c. On the contrary, the suggestion betrays a far deeper comprehension of the essence of purely instrumental music than any Frenchman ever showed. That the art of music is a reverberation of the harmonious order of the universe, and that a mysterious connection subsists between its pure tones in their essence and combinations, and the sempiternal motions of the Cosmos with the heavenly bodies, keeping their orbits in an infinite space which is instinct with life—such thoughts as these have stirred the deepest minds from extreme antiquity down to the present day. Beyond a doubt, that which guided the composer in an attempt which, at the first glance, seems so singular, at a time when it was not unusual to require of music that it should represent a given subject, was a true feeling for what really could be fitly rendered by it.

Between Froberger, Kuhnau, and the French composers on one side, and Sebastian Bach on the other—whose compositions, apart from his organ chorales, are the very essence of pure tone for tone's sake—Buxtehude stands as a compromise, leaning, however, visibly towards the latter. Our hypothesis would be still further confirmed if the seven Suites were based on the seven degrees of the diatonic scale, as Kuhnau, in his " Clavierübung," had gone through both the major and minor scales with seven Suites each, one on each note.[109] Then a direct reminiscence of Greek antiquity might come in : the Pythagoreans taught that the intervals between the orbits of the seven planets corresponded to those of the notes of the seven-stringed lyre. Unfortunately, there is no prospect of this interesting work ever coming to light again. It was greatly due to two

---

[109] Leaving out, however, B major and B flat minor, no doubt, on account of difficulties of temperament.

contemporaneous authorities that any instrumental compositions were even at the time preserved in MS.—the industrious collector Joh. Gottfried Walther and Sebastian Bach himself.[110] The first preserved only organ chorales, but what we derive from Bach, be it observed, are almost exclusively independent organ pieces ; he understood Buxtehude.

In point of fact, interesting and clever as his chorale arrangements are, in this department he cannot stand comparison with Pachelbel and his school. It was, therefore, greatly to the master's disadvantage that, of those few of his compositions which, until quite recently, had been made accessible to the world by being printed, the greater number were chorales.[111] In this way a quite one-sided and often unfavourable idea must be formed of his true importance. His chief strength lay—for we must somewhat expand Mattheson's verdict—in pure instrumental music, uninfluenced by any adventitious poetical idea. In this he is the negative pole, so to speak, to Pachelbel, who marked an epoch by his organ chorales, and by what he wrought out from a thorough and persistent study of popular melody—namely, the invention of expressive musical themes. Buxtehude, by his grand independent compositions, which are full of genius, aided greatly in the culture of one important side, at any rate, of Bach's talent—a side which now might be supposed to be the most imperishable, because it is based on the very essence and nature of music. That he should otherwise have influenced Central Germany very little is easily

---

[110] In the volume of selections before mentioned, Walther wrote out with his own hand a great number of Buxtehude's chorale arrangements together. All that came from Bach's family is in the MS. of Andreas Bach, two remarkably beautiful volumes of writing now in the library of the Joachimsthaler Gymnasium in Berlin, derived from the collections of Kirnberger or Agricola, and in the Krebs volumes.

[111] " XIV. Choralbearbeitungen für die Orgel von Dietrich Buxtehude—herausgegeben von S. W. Dehn. Leipzig: C. F. Peters." A few smaller ones were published by Commer (*Musica Sacra*, I., No. 8), and G. W. Körner (Gesammtausgabe der classischen Orgel-Compositionen von Dietrich Buxtehude. Erfurt and Leipzig, only one part issued.) This contains, in part, the same works as those published by Dehn.

explained, since there almost all effort was concentrated on the chorale, while in the North there was no very great disposition to treat this particular form as a medium for subjective utterance. Between the South Germans, who did not possess the Protestant chorale, and Buxtehude, with his fellow musicians, there was, on the other hand, a closer affinity—as was natural under the more similar conditions—and this is visible in many peculiarities of style, particularly in the construction of melodies. In other particulars, to be sure, as in harmonic treatment, in the employment of colouring, and in pitch, there is all the difference between the noonday and the evening's glow.

There are twenty-four organ compositions, rich alike in matter and extent, on which we can found a more certain judgment as to Buxtehude's high importance in this branch of art.[112] Among them are two chaconnes, a passecaille, one shorter toccata and two longer ones, three separate fugues, and two canzonets; the remainder consists of preludes with fugues, to which we shall first turn our attention. The preludes have generally an ornate subject, carried on in all the parts in a full stream of imitation, of which a good share is given to the pedal, which also becomes frequently prominent in brilliant solo passages. This last feature forms an essential mark of difference from the many similarly constructed toccata movements by the South German organ-masters; and comparison especially teaches us how far (in point of executive quality) these latter works are behind those of Buxtehude and his school, to which a similar impulse had been given by Sweelinck. In these the use of the pedal is chiefly confined to long-held bass notes, or to slow progressions; even in Pachelbel it is throughout almost the same. Georg Muffat put under the eighth toccata of his *Apparatus musico-organisticus* the words,

---

[112] For comparison with the following remarks, see Dietrich Buxtehude's Sämmtliche Orgel-Compositionen, Herausgegeben von Philipp Spitta. Two vols., folio. Leipzig: Breitkopf and Härtel, 1875-76. The figures in brackets refer to this edition.

Dii laboribus omnia vendunt. This piece, which, in his opinion, was of exceptional difficulty, would doubtless have been played straight off by men like Buxtehude and Bruhns. As in the prelude, so of course in the fugue, the pedal has a distinct and independent part, in which, moreover, Buxtehude has, by means of a general plan as characteristic as it is important, made room for a still richer development— that is to say, he usually modifies the theme once, if not oftener, in the course of the fugue, and so gives rise to a fresh treatment. An entire fugue consists in such cases of several separate fugues which, regarded as independent movements, are generally joined into one by short interludes, in which the chief object is *bravura* display. These new forms, in which the first theme only serves as the motive of another, are a very remarkable characteristic of the instrumental music of the time. They show that the fundamental nature of pure music was then perfectly understood, and point onwards to one of the first principles of form in the modern sonata, without departing from the proper ground of fugal form. The cradle in which this form was preserved and fostered was the toccata, and, indeed, we can distinctly perceive as it were the sketch of it in the toccatas of Froberger. But Buxtehude was of course not the only one, even of his period, who adopted this form; a similarly constituted work by Reinken was mentioned above, one too by Bruhns is preserved, and it was this which incited Böhm to write his organ chorales, which are indeed founded on the principle of exhausting each separate line of the tune as a distinct motive. In spite of this, however, Buxtehude must be called the chief representative and perfecter of this form, not only because he has left us the largest number of examples of it, but also because he evinces in it that power of invention which distinguishes the mind of genius. By this he makes up for what his chief subjects lack in beauty or animation.

Thus in one of his greatest organ compositions (Vol. I., No. 6), after a very beautiful prelude of sixteen bars of common time in E minor, he sets off with the following fugal theme :—

When this is gone through he begins afresh with this theme :—

After richly elaborating it and introducing a free interlude, this subject begins :—

We see what rule the composer has followed in the formation of the second and third themes : he takes out the characteristic passage of the chief theme, first the passage from b', the fifth to the tonic e' (first bar), from there up to the octave e", and down to a'; secondly, the passage—as before—from b' to e', going straight to a' without going up to the octave. The skip of the fourth in the second subject (from c' sharp or c' to g sharp), is only apparently anomalous, since Buxtehude intended the last semiquaver but one of the first bar in the chief subject (d"), and not the following e" to be the note of the melody. This last is only an harmonic passing-note, and the melody is considered to go from d" to a', which seems to have rather a harsh effect, but is not foreign to Buxtehude's style. Throughout the whole composition, numbering as it does in all 137 full bars, there moves but one and the same chief musical identity, notwithstanding the various changes of position, mien, and costume ; and the effect is heightened by the change of time. From the regularity with which, in Reinken and Bruhns, a two-time is always followed by a three-time, we see another recognised principle of form manifesting itself ; the organism must change from the grave severity of the beginning to the joyfulness of airy motion, and this form is what is aimed at in these three sections. The first, which although inwardly agitated, yet enters with the external dignity of repose, is followed by the second, with its labyrinth of entanglements and profound

intricacies; beside this subject there are two counter-subjects,
the second of which, with its passages in quavers, impels the
whole to greater animation, and then the first theme appears
in inversion. Such a network of tones, and one in which
each mesh stands out with full and clear regularity, notwithstanding all the complication, could only be woven by a
genius for harmonic invention of the highest order. Between
the second and third sections stands one of those interludes,
without any strict thematic germ or marked working-out,
which serve the purpose of halting-places, and have the
effect of affording a relieving contrast with the strict regularity of the foregoing piece by an unrestricted playfulness,
and of refreshing the hearer and preparing him for what is to
follow. They consist of running passages and broad masses
of chords, in both of which Buxtehude shows such a clearly
stamped individuality that his hand may be most easily
recognised in these interludes. It is he who first introduced
and brought to perfection those passages to be played without
regard to time (a discrezione, or ad libitum), which may be
called organ recitatives; and he, too, was the first to take
pleasure in employing shakes in several parts at once and
even on the pedals, and certain passages divided between the
two hands. It is in the quiet progressions of chords, however,
that he most prominently shows his harmonic individuality,
when some startling harmony stands out from those around
it as a very Fata Morgana, calling up magic imagery, ever
new and ever transient. After such an intermezzo the
conclusion of the tone-drama follows in the last fugal
movement; the theme goes through the different parts in
proud magnificence, assuming in the pedals an expression of
stately grace, and seems to have been intended just for that
position and for no other. It may be remarked throughout
how the organ-character speaks from every note of this great
and remarkable composition.

A fugue in G minor (Vol. I., No. 7) shows also three
forms of the theme, but in spite of this similarity in structure
it is intrinsically quite different. The prelude even is of
another form. In it there is no ornate subject, but a regular
fugue-theme carried on through twelve bars of 6-4 time,

almost the whole of which is on a pedal on G, which only
alters its position quite at the end, and then goes through
the theme once in a more ponderous manner, while the
manual has accompanying chords above. The theme of the
first fugue—which is converted into a double fugue by a
second subject coming in after the first theme has been
once gone through—is this—

and the ambiguity of its harmonies must not be overlooked,
as being a kind of anticipation of Bach. On it, again, is
built a masterpiece of profound harmonic ingenuity, which
can only be found fault with on the ground that it displays
too great a number of combinations in too quick succession,
and so is not quite fitted to the nature of the organ, of which
the majestic character requires constant simplicity up to a
certain point. At any rate, this work of genius demands a
very quiet rendering to make it clear. In one place the
inclination to elaborate passages of rich invention round
about the subject interrupts the calm flow of the polyphony.
Out of the interval of a fourth, between the second and third
notes of the theme, grows a dialogue between the upper and
the two inner parts of four bars long. Then the theme is
given to the pedals and gone through twice running, after
which all the parts work back again in the earlier style.
The melancholy feeling of the whole is carried out by the
interlude that concludes it, which sinks sadly and dreamily,
deeper and deeper, into itself. Then it is awakened by
the first modification of the fugue theme (on the dominant
of D)—

which works itself several times vigorously and recklessly
out of the depths, without regard to the entrance of the
different parts, always rising higher and higher, as in the
C minor fugue of Bach, mentioned above; regardless, too,
of harmonic considerations, for a false relation is repeated

persistently again and again. Then there comes a sudden break; the second modification of the theme begins, and the powerful last movement in 3-2 time:—

Of the same kind is another work on a like principle, and yet how differently carried out (Vol. I., No. 14). The prelude breaks in tempestuously, like the shock of a .wave, and foams wildly about in passages of thirds and sixths. After six bars of 12-8 time there comes in, as though from the depths of the sea, a threatening bass-theme:—

This is repeated five times, while the storm rages above: the waves toss round and over one another, they part and again pile themselves up—truly a fantastical and weird conception. Forthwith the theme appears in the bass—

severe and heavy, as indeed is the whole fugue. In the interlude a bass is brought dreamily in on the manual, while above it are heard broken chords, which under close examination combine to reveal a distinct idea, both as to phrasing and melody, and the melody is heard, like a distant song borne upon the wind. Then the pedals come in with massive leaps of octaves, with an accompaniment of semiquavers; the passages are repeated in the right hand, and at length lead into the last movement—largo, 3-2:—

This time the three-time brings in no cheerful conclusion—indeed how could it?—but, in contrast to the weird monotony of the foregoing movement, a deep and overwhelming sorrow. A fervid and overpowering expression of feeling was at the

command of the composers of that period, which may be
called the youth of the art whose manhood is represented by
Bach and Handel.   Johann Christoph Bach's motetts are
quite steeped in this atmosphere; many things by Kuhnau,
and in a high degree also many arias and songs by Erlebach,
display an intensity of feeling that goes to the heart as
directly even now as it did two hundred years ago.   But
though Buxtehude is steeped through and through with this
element, his way of giving it expression is quite distinct, and
yet not so different but that a resemblance may be perceived.
Although it is difficult to prove this without going into the
smallest details of his peculiarities of style, yet it makes
itself clearly felt, and seems to be accounted for by nothing
so much as by his Danish extraction.   It would be easy to
draw a comparison between him and a distinguished artist of
the present day, his countryman, if references to the living
did not too easily disturb the quiet contemplation of an
historical picture.   Certain it is that this master's manner,
strange and yet familiar, touching us so remotely and yet so
nearly, lends a heightened charm to his art.   The period
before Bach was in its early days a period of musical
romance, and on the instrumental side the greatest roman-
ticist is Buxtehude.   Except his chorales there are very few
pieces by him in which this characteristic is not prominent;
the organ composition in question is quite full of it.   The
movement whose theme was last quoted is especially imbued
with a longing, a striving after infinity, which is the more
striking from its struggling with the stubborn material of the
organ, like Pygmalion's with the cold marble.

In the prelude and fugue in E major (Vol. I., No. 8) the
chief theme reappears three times in different forms.   The
modifications, however, are all shortened, and are constructed
on only the first two notes of the theme, nor is it brought to
a conclusion in three-time, but in common time, by a short
fugue closely connected with it.   The nature of the piece
becomes more energetic and more compact up to the very
end.   In subservience to this idea the first fugue is very
sedate in style, and has its full effect only in conjunction
with the other parts, though even then a certain rigidity is

not altogethcr concealed.[113] As a general rule the theme underwent only one modification, and this must be regarded as the fundamental form which none but such a richly gifted genius as Buxtehude could overstep, and then only occasionally. The greater number of his compositions are confined within these limits, but manifest within them the greatest variety.

Another fugue, also in E minor,[114] with a majestic introductory prelude, has this theme—

which, regarded by itself, seems half insignificant and half peculiar. On playing further, however, it soon becomes clear that, in part at least, this is intentional. The theme charms us but little by its own merit, but interests us by its harmonic uncertainty, which is made use of cleverly enough in the working out. After a short interlude, which, with its semiquavers, reminds us of the prelude, there follows this modification in 3-4 time:—

The counterpoint in the second bar afterwards becomes the motive of some very graceful figures, which gradually extend further and further, until at last they usurp the whole territory and then lead back into common time. Now the semiquaver passage of the prelude reappears, and in addition to this some most charming episodes, formed on a pedal-figure ⟨image⟩ which appeared before as a tributary; and they, by degrees, drive everything else into the background, securing the last word for themselves. Beethoven himself could hardly have done it differently.

---

[113] This first fugue is in the third volume of A. G. Ritter's Kunst des Orgelspiels, and it was afterwards published in a selection of Buxtehude's works, made by Körner. It was, for the reasons given in the text, not the happiest choice.

[114] Vol. I., No. 13.

Buxtehude is very fond of such finales as this, by which the whole work attains a brilliant conclusion; and he makes frequent use of them. The method is referable to the same principle as that by which the rhythmic form resolves itself for the most part into three-time, and which aims at cheerfulness and serenity at the end of the piece. We are not led up to the heights of art and there left alone, but are brought back again to the abodes of men. Since the highest forms of instrumental music require a corresponding height of subjective isolation, we can see in this a healthy and justifiable universal feeling. The same method is followed by Mozart, who always lets the hearer depart with a pleasant impression, whatever depths of feeling may have been previously unveiled to him. Nay, in every instrumental form of more than two movements, this tendency should, to a certain extent, be followed; for at the close it is not the details that should prevail, but the general sentiment; fitness requires this, in art as in life. And this is adhered to no less by Beethoven than by Mozart; no less by the Suite-composers, who always gave the last place to the lively gigue, than by Alessandro Scarlatti in his overtures in three movements. But in relinquishing a form once obtained and made clear, and in returning to an arbitrary and unmethodical style, there is certainly a kind of retrogression. Here it becomes evident that Buxtehude, in spite of all his genius, could not entirely free himself from the fault of the school to which he belonged—viz., the perpetual aiming at effectiveness in performance. That his perorations or finales were often in the highest degree interesting and full of genius, is amply proved by the composition just alluded to. Here, too, he still confines himself within moderate limits, and refers so distinctly back to the prelude that the proper feeling of cyclic rounding-off is well preserved. So is it in the prelude and fugue in D minor (Vol. I., No. 10), where the pregnant theme—

which afterwards reappears in this form—

is clearly announced in the prelude, képt up in the interlude by means of a little imitative passage, and again heard quite plainly in the rhythm of the brilliant peroration. So much unity of subject is not forthcoming in the prelude and fugue in A minor (Vol. I., No. 9), a piece which, in consequence of the remarkable relation which it seems to bear to one of the fugues in Bach's "Wohltemperirte Clavier," will occupy our attention again. In this, however, the peroration is not so long as to weaken, in any important degree, the impression of the foregoing and nobler forms. Of quite different proportions is a composition of the same class in F sharp minor (Vol. I., No. 12). The prelude begins with semiquaver figures, chiefly of a harmonic kind, followed by progressions of chords in Buxtehude's genuine manner; then in a *grave* movement the double fugue makes it appearance, and, in thematic invention, is one of the master's most beautiful compositions:—

As it proceeds it is full of deep expression directly prophetic of Bach. After this lovely movement, the second theme presents itself *vivace*, in this form—

is carried through all four parts, and joins to itself the chief subject in this form :—

Soon it modulates into the relative major, which was not permitted in the melancholy *grave* movement; the groups of three semiquavers begin to develop themselves more and more decidedly as episodes, and the piece, fresh and sparkling with genius, rushes on. In the peroration the composer gives the reins to his fancy. A remarkably free organ recitative is heard, and when at last it returns to a half close on the dominant of the original key, there begins on the phrases—

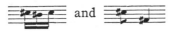

the most charming series of playful combinations, unwearying and inexhaustible, and with ever-increasing brilliancy and wealth of tone. The perfect unity of the ideas, the well-considered changes and progressions of the parts, the high degree of contrapuntal dexterity, the brilliant *technique*, bringing into requisition all the qualities of the organ, combine to make this composition a true masterpiece of German organ music. It cannot be questioned that we here find ourselves on a considerable height : whoso would desire to climb further must possess the strength and breadth of a Sebastian Bach. The æsthetic defect which arises from the form of peroration, and especially such a long peroration, is not indeed entirely removed by even the most inspired treatment, but it is considerably modified.

There are not many organ fugues by Buxtehude which go on their way in one movement without any modification of the theme. There is one such in F major (Vol. I., No. 15), which is introduced by a beautiful prelude, in which, by way of exception, there is one change of rhythm—viz., it is in common time at the beginning and end, and 12-8 time in the middle. But the four-time is at the root even of this, so that the change is almost imperceptible and does not disturb the flow of the piece. The theme is long and characteristic—

and its lively character pervades the whole piece without losing itself in harmonic complications. The semiquaver figure of the first bar gives ample opportunity for pleasing interchanges between the higher and lower registers. The inclination, too, to episodical extensions is very evident. The influence which this work of Buxtehude's has exercised on a great concert fugue of Bach's is unmistakable.

The form of a great toccata in F major (Vol. I., No. 20) is at first sight very varied, but a regular fugue forms the germ which, in some degree, provides the material for the subjects which follow, in so far as they are compressed into intelligible forms, and do not ramble about in fantastic aimlessness. More cannot be demanded of a form which can at most be agreeable and pleasing, though it is fully justified when the higher claims of art are not set aside for it. The toccatas of Buxtehude are naturally immensely superior to those of older masters—such as Froberger—in variety, genius, and effectiveness, and especially in the use of the pedal, as has been remarked before with regard to his productions in general.

But our master knew full well the worth of a composition that increases in purpose and meaning up to the very end. An instance of this is furnished by a great organ composition in G minor—a perfect model of systematic and well-calculated design (Vol. I., No. 5). A short and lively prelude begins the work, coming to a close on the dominant; then follows a fugato *Allegro*, a few bars long, on this subject :—

To this is added a passage which soars upwards and closes in G, the key in which the theme of the principal fugue begins. The meaning of this fugato movement is at first obscure, as it has no connection with the theme of the fugue, which is that subject afterwards so freely used, and which ultimately became common property :—

It is found again in the second part of the " Wohltemperirte Clavier" (No. 20, in A minor), in a string quartet by Haydn, in a Requiem by Lotti, in Handel's "Joseph" and "Messiah," and in Mozart's "Requiem." At the conclusion of the fugue, which, in spite of its interest, contains much that is unwieldy, a new theme appears in 3-2 time, which bears a strong resemblance to the first fugato:—

As it goes on the resemblance becomes more decided, and at last it is confirmed by this pedal passage, which is accompanied by the chord of G minor in the upper parts:—

When the fugue comes to an end, this passage, destined to a twelve-fold repetition, like the theme of a chaconne, comes to light, the offspring, as it were, of the development of the whole:—

This theme is surrounded with a rich counterpoint, which brings the whole work to a close. The expectancy created by the working in of the fugato movement is completely satisfied. The happy thought of developing a fugal idea through a lavish rhetorical treatment as it were, closing on an irrefragable axiom, and so proving his skill in the ever-new relations of the contrapuntal changes, occurred once again to Buxtehude, and was employed in a fugue with a prelude in C major (Vol. I., No. 4); the *Ciacona*, in 3-2 time, stands in the place of the modification of the theme which was formerly in use. Closely allied to the *Ciacona*, or *Chaconne*, is the *Passacaglio*. Both were originally dance forms, in which a short bass theme of two, four, or, at the most, eight bars was incessantly repeated. The opportunities which they afforded for building upon them ever-changing combinations of counterpoint, made them a favourite subject with composers for organ or clavier. What we are told of their characteristic differences by writers of that time is altogether contradictory, and of no authority whatever.[115] Even the composers themselves seem to have held the most various opinions. Buxtehude, however, established for himself a difference between *Passacaglio* and *Ciacona*, which is also noticeable in a chaconne by Böhm—namely, that in the first the theme is always the true bass, and remains unaltered throughout, while in the latter it may go into any of the parts, and be subjected to the most various adornments and variations so long as it remains recognisable throughout. According to this, we must call the concluding movement of the G minor fugue " *alla Ciacona*," since the theme wanders freely about among the parts, and once is even quite lost among the figurations. We also possess two chaconnes and one passecaille as independent works, which for beauty and importance take the precedence of all the works of the kind at that time, and are in the first rank of Buxtehude's compositions. His individual style of harmony unfolds itself here in all its fulness and intensity of expression, and the hearer is overpowered by the melting sweetness of its melancholy. All three works are pervaded with the same feeling, but, in spite of this, they are very different in expression—the very first bars decide this. Of the two chaconnes that in C minor is the more impassioned. It is a work full of wailing longing (Vol. I., No. 2) :—

---

[115] See, for instance, Mattheson, Vollkommener Capellmeister, p. 233, compared with his Neu eröffnetes Orchestre, p. 185, and Walther's Lexicon, under " Passacaglio."

The second chaconne, in E minor (Vol. I., No. 3), is like a ballad, in which the agitation of the speaker, about some mournful or gloomy subject, is concealed beneath the objective aspect of the form in which it is told ; still it is distinctly felt throughout.   The modulation to G major, especially in the second bar, bears the stamp of outward equanimity, and even as the piece proceeds the increasing motion has an external and narrative effect.   But that it is so only in appearance is clear even at the beginning : witness the upper melody with its lovely swing and its well-chosen rhythm and harmony, which is capable of the deepest expression, though it is almost immediately repressed :—

The working-out after the first eight bars is excellently introduced.   From the ninth bar onward it soars bravely outwards and upwards into the world, with so free a flight that the indissoluble chain of the subject in the bass is wholly

forgotten. Later on the feeling resembles more distinctly
an inevitable destiny from whose charmed circle there is
no escape. Though it may sometimes be concealed, or
partially disappear, at the decisive moment it is always in
its place. Of the richness of invention displayed by the
composer in the ever-new superstructures no description can
be attempted ; in the middle there is a series of harmonies,
evolved by chromatic reverse motion between the upper and
lower parts, the possibility of which had been scarcely dreamt
of before Buxtehude.

The warmth of feeling restrained in this chaconne breaks
forth with redoubled strength in the passecaille in D minor
(Vol. I., No. 1). The broad rhythm at once points to this,
and the form of the bass theme—

which transfers itself in so impressive a manner into the
dominant. The passecaille consists of four sections almost
exactly of the same length, of which the first is in D minor,
the second in F major, the third in A minor, and the last
again in D minor. This subdivision gives rise to the
only fault that can be found ; the sections might have
been welded together in a more imperceptible manner by
smoother modulations, while as it is they stand side by
side, only bound together by quite short, modulatory
interludes. For the rest, the composition is above all reproach ; one would fain say above all praise also. It is not
only that the strict form goes hand in hand with melodic
animation, than which none greater or more individual
can be conceived of ; but also there is no piece of music of
that time known to me which surpasses it, or even approaches
it, in affecting, soul-piercing intensity of expression.

What has been said will suffice to make the importance of
Buxtehude's independent organ works very evident. They
are, as they might·be expected to be in a collection put
together by mere chance, of unequal artistic merit, and some
of them have not much more than a historical interest. On
the whole, however, they have no reason to fear comparison

with the highest standard of all ; that, namely, derived from Bach's masterpieces. There can be no doubt that the latter far surpassed Buxtehude, but his advance was, at the same time, a step in another direction, although he used and appropriated the acquisitions of the earlier master. A just estimate demands that, as Mozart's symphonies stand their ground next to those of Beethoven, so too Buxtehude, with his preludes and fugues, his chaconnes and passecailles, should retain his place next to Bach. When an art is approaching its highest stage of development, the relations between its component parts are no longer so clearly defined that one can be said to absorb the others into itself, and so assert its own individual importance. Only the foundations of an edifice are invisible; the building itself rises into the air, and is then adorned with numerous gables and towers. One is wont to overtop the others, but if the architect understands his business he will reach his full effect only with the aid, and partly by means, of all. The *technique* of the organ had already reached such a point of development by the time of Buxtehude's full power, and chiefly by his agency, that it cannot altogether be said that Bach had to open out entirely new paths. He brought what he received to its highest perfection, but it was in that mainly that he found the means of utterance for his inspired ideas. Buxtehude's mental horizon may have been more confined, his talent less prolific ; but what he had to say—and that was of great importance and all his own—he could say in a form utterly perfect, and so reach the ideal of a work of art, so far as it is ever possible to do so. It will be seen later on that Bach, with perfect comprehension of the state of affairs, essayed himself only in a transitory manner in the special forms cultivated with such mastery by Buxtehude, on which, however, he left the stamp of his genius without in any essential degree towering above his predecessor. This is especially true of the chaconne and the passecaille. All that he has of greater profundity and concentration in his famous work of the latter class, the other master makes up for in depth of expression and youthful fervour. Bach, it is true, possessed this fervour

and depth in the highest degree, but it came to the surface
with more difficulty, and for the most part lay hidden in
the depths, pervading and vivifying all.   Still this very
characteristic is the token that both stand on the highest
step of the art of organ music.

It is a constantly recurring phenomenon in history that the
creations of human genius, when they have been developed in
any given direction to the greatest possible perfection, begin
to show some essential reaction, which overpowers and seeks
to ruin them, and so forms the germ of a new and quite different evolution.   Not always, but very frequently, in Buxtehude we meet with forms which seem quite to thirst after
the true soul of music, although it is quite indisputable that
they were intended for the mechanical, soulless material of
the organ.   In the second bar of the chaconne in E minor,
the beginning of which is quoted above, there is no apparent
reason why the composer should not have allowed the upper
part to coincide with the second part on g' on the third beat
of the bar—since it would sound the same to the hearer as
what is written now—unless it be that he wishes to express,
as well as he can, the way in which the melody occurred to
him, and that he had more to say than he could express.
The indications of his having in his mind some instrument more capable of expression are so strong in these
passages that they seem, if played on a modern pianoforte,
as though they were written for it.   If we only attempt
it we shall be convinced that it is utterly impossible
to reflect the deep expression which everywhere rises to the
surface, without the employment of shades in execution, and
even that will scarcely suffice ; we shall feel impelled to call
in the aid of song.   Pachelbel, in consequence of his acquisitions from Southern art, approaches far more nearly to the
true simple essence of organ music; indeed he was the
real inventor of the organ chorale, which by its nature
strives after the most purely subjective expression, and,
although the younger of the two, he more nearly attains
this than Buxtehude.   Their difference of age was equalised,
however, by the enervated state of Germany after the great
war.   Though she did indeed succeed in producing a Buxte-

hude, this was hardly possibly before the time at which
Pachelbel also was born. Thus the only contrast between
them is that between the North and the South, and we
can see, without need of further remark, how they converged,
and met half-way—Buxtehude's restless intensity towards
Pachelbel's chorale, Pachelbel's quiet restfulness towards
Buxtehude's free organ composition. Bach united these
contrasts in himself. But he felt Pachelbel's influence
through the medium of the Thuringian masters, who had
already amalgamated his spirit with their own ; besides, his
nature was German to the core, and more allied to the
romantic than the classic element. For this reason he stands
not exactly between and above them, but somewhat nearer
to the Lübeck master; and, for the same reason, not below
him either, but to a certain extent beside him, and more so
than Pachelbel.

That subjective warmth which a hundred years later was
destined to call forth—in antithesis to this first—a second
golden age of German instrumental music, glowed also in
Bach, and in an infinitely higher degree than in any of his
predecessors or contemporaries. It did not, indeed, gush
forth so unrestrainedly as in Buxtehude's case, but was kept
powerfully in check, influencing and permeating all that he
wrote.

The number of Buxtehude's organ chorales which remain
is almost twice as many, and we are indebted to Walther's
diligence for the greater number of them. To Bach's
collection we can ascribe at the most those three which his
pupil, Johann Ludwig Krebs, has preserved in his two books,
for organ and clavier respectively. It stands to reason, in
the case of so great a master, that his works, even of this class,
are, to say the least, not to be slighted. His natural inclination to pure music led him, indeed, like all the organ composers of the northern school, to disregard the poetic
intensifying of the organ chorale. What there may be of this
poetic feeling is, as it were, only by the way, and is based on
no definite principle. But the organ chorale has become, and
must remain, too closely united with the hymn to be treated
only on musical principles. It is in fact founded on the sup-

position that the melody at least of the chorale shall be plainly heard throughout in its original form, so that the hearer may easily trace it through the more elaborate figures of the organ arrangement, and that what the latter lacks in organic development from its own materials may be supplied by a reference to the original air. Thus it was only the natural outcome of an indwelling germ when Pachelbel extended these conditions, as he could not evade them, by applying them to the poetic meaning of the chorale melody, and thus winning new material for musical forms.

Buxtehude came only half-way to this point, and so all that his inventive genius did in this form must of necessity have a more superficial character. Full of genius, brilliant, effective in the best sense—these are the most just epithets to apply to his chorale arrangements. These qualities are most prominent in the cases where the lines of the chorale are treated in the manner of motetts, as we have before called this method of treatment—an expression which is meant to denote the preponderance of polyphony in contradistinction to Böhm's manner of using the phrases as melodic episodes. To this method belong the three pieces, " Nun freut euch, lieben Christen g'mein," " Gelobet seist du, Jesu Christ," " Herr Gott, dich loben wir," works of the grandest dimensions, resembling those by Reinken and Lübeck, which we have mentioned before. Thus the first of these begins with a movement of 110 bars common time, then 22 bars of 3-2 time, then 18 bars of 12-8, ending with 107 bars common time, consisting of rich semiquaver figures—257 bars in all! certainly one of the longest existing compositions for the organ. The simultaneous employment of two manuals, differing in power and quality of tone, is a favourite device of Buxtehude's in this case—as in others —for he lays great stress on individual effects of tone. This, indeed, is a characteristic of the school. We here meet with the effect used so happily also by Bach, of giving the melody to the pedal in the tenor part, with eight-foot or eight and four-foot stops. In common with Reinken he has made use of the doubled pedal part. This was afterwards turned to account by Bach in the finest forms of his organ music, although in this he had been anticipated in a scarcely less wonderful manner by Bruhns, of whose composition a perfect fugue with two-part *obbligato* pedals has been preserved.[116] Buxtehude is very fond of the double fugue form, so he is wont to oppose independent themes to the lines of the chorale and to work them both together. Especially fine in this respect is a work on "Ich dank dir schon durch deinen Sohn," in which a piece of 154 full bars is developed from a short four-line chorale. The first and third lines are treated fugally with strettos in the old-fashioned way, the latter in double counterpoint; the first gives an opportunity, by a slight chromatic alteration, for the most surprising and genuine Buxtehude harmonies. The second and fourth lines are also treated fugally, but each has two independent themes, with which it undergoes every possible combination in double counterpoint on the octave ; these themes are very characteristically invented, but contain harsh passages which grate upon the ear.

The arrangement of the chorale "Ich dank dir, lieber Herre," is in part more artistic, but in part, too, more simple. The first line is gone through in a quiet four-part movement, as if accompanying the voices for the service; the second follows *allegro*, worked episodically, and then fugally treated, first in two and then in three parts, with a stretto between the two parts. Then the first line in diminution becomes the theme of a fugue which is gone through in the proper way; at the end the pedal is heard through the fabric of the fugue with the subject in augmentation ; this is followed as before by the fugue on the second line but with richer treatment. Then the remaining lines are gone through with their independent themes, the two last being in 6-4 time. It is evident that the composer set himself the task of inventing something outwardly new, as far as possible, for each line, and that he attached more importance to manifold variety than to unity of feeling. For this reason his most

---

[116] Commer, *Musica Sacra*, I., No. 5. There is also given, under No. 6, a chorale arrangement by Bruhns on "Nun komm der Heiden Heiland," which is quite like the great chorales of Buxtehude in style.

successful pieces are those in which he displays the full
brilliancy of his *technique*, which keeps the feeling more
on the surface; for he becomes restless and fatiguing when
he tries to be effective by contrapuntal treatment only.
Buxtehude understood perfectly how to treat a simple
long-drawn-out chorale with uninterrupted counterpoint,
and if he scarcely ever prevailed upon himself to keep
to one and the same figure throughout, like Pachelbel,
yet he took great care that the flow of the work should
nowhere be allowed to stagnate.[117] With a view to a new
effect, he sometimes united the two forms ; as, for example,
in an arrangement of " Nun lob mein Seel den Herren,"
where first the chorale is gone straight through in the
upper part with continuous counterpoint, then treated line
by line, and lastly given to the pedal, and there gone
through without interruption against fine animated passages
in the upper parts.

The same method is followed in the chorale " Wie
schön leucht't uns der Morgenstern,"[118] in which the
melody, beginning in the manual-bass, goes into the upper
part at the repetition of the first section of the tune, and
two sets of ascending passages of triplets soar upwards
between the short lines of the second section. The descending scale of the last line is now thoroughly worked out
in 6-8 time (changes of time are seldom wanting in his
greater organ chorales), then the whole chorale is once
more gone through in 12-8 time, while animated fugal
themes are formed chiefly from the lines of the tune,
and are worked out in uninterrupted connection. It seems
that he wrote but few chorale fugues properly so-called,
preferring to invent his themes for himself.[119] But he
created a special type of shorter two-manual chorales,
which are treated not with a full working out, but with

---

[117] Compare the chorale " Jesus Christus unser Heiland," Vol. II., Part II.,
No. 15.

[118] See Vol. II., Part I., No. 8.

[119] Körner, loc. cit., p. 8, gives one which I also consider genuine, chiefly
because some of the master's little peculiarities appear in it.

a single enunciation of the melody. This is played on one of two manuals, arranged in contrast to one another, and receives grace notes and ornamentations, but no episodical extension as is the case in Böhm's work. With this the other manual and the pedal have counterpoint, which is never confined to a particular figure. Between the lines there are short interludes, sometimes consisting of free imitation, sometimes taking their shape from the beginning of the next line, according to the fancy, and in these the pedals generally lead. Interludes based upon the subject of the following line are also a characteristic of Pachelbel's chorales, but, notwithstanding, the two forms have nothing to do with one another—nay, they are rather in direct contrast. Here there is no attempt at the ideal unity which Pachelbel kept in view, nor any trace of consistent uniformity throughout. Buxtehude aims solely at the adornment of each separate line in an agreeable manner, at ingenuity of harmony, and at giving an especial colour by clever interchange of the manuals, and sometimes, too, by doubling the pedal part. This composer, who was so great in the organic forms of pure music, entirely lost his characteristics when he ventured on the poetic treatment of the organ chorale; for when we do not know the melody which he has treated, it is often quite impossible to discover any plan whatever in his chorales of more than four lines long. Buxtehude only directed his view to details; it was not given to him to find the happy medium, and to show the whole form of the chorale underneath the flowery ornamentation with which he loaded each separate portion. In the organ chorale it must, indeed, be always left to the hearer to supply part of the inner unity, but there are musical means by which even this may be made felt. Apparently Buxtehude did not attempt, in any way, to reflect the chorale organism in his own subjective feeling, and only availed himself of an outward unity in order to give the reins to his inventive faculty for details. It is fundamentally the same as in his greater works, only that in them great independent tone pictures were formed from each line, which, as such, were more readily connected musically with each other ; while here the musical relation of the lines of the melody is interrupted, without any such compensation being offered beyond a cleverly written movement. How similar the radical principle in the two cases actually is we can most easily see where the episodical interludes are somewhat more worked out. In these cases small fugal movements on the separate lines begin as if of themselves, and among these the upper part, which comes in last of all, and to which the melody is always given, appears only as the last among its fellows, and not as the end and aim of the whole development, which should come prominently forward and dwarf all else by its presence.[120] Viewed, however, from the composer's standpoint, even these works afford much refined and artistic gratification. Even in Central Germany this was afterwards acknowledged by competent judges like Adlung and Walther. Adlung did full justice to them when he said " Buxtehude set chorales very beautifully."[121] Walther testified his admiration by writing out more than thirty of them. His interest in Buxtehude, however, has partly a personal foundation, in the intercourse he had, when young, with Buxtehude's friend Andreas Werkmeister. The latter gave him also " many a lovely clavier piece of the ingenious Buxtehude's composition,"[122] which we must envy him, and grieve that he has left us none of them, unless we include amongst them that suite on the chorale "Auf meinen lieben Gott" (Vol. II., Part II., No. 33), which was mentioned before, and which only raises our desires still higher.

Turning now to Buxtehude's vocal compositions, only cursory attention need be paid to the five "Hochzeitsarien" —wedding arias—before mentioned.[123] They are songs in strophes, with ritornels in the fashion of the time ; a harpsi-

---

[120] See, for instance, Vol. II., Part II., Nos. 20 and 22.

[121] Anleitung zur mus. Gel., p. 693.

[122] Walther, quoted in Mattheson Ehrenpforte, p. 388.

[123] In parts, in the Town Library at Lübeck. They date in order as follows : June 2, 1673; March 1, 1675; July 8, 1695; March 14, 1698; September 7, 1705.

chord accompaniment alone is indicated, excepting to the earliest, where two *viole da gamba* with one voice and the spinet-bass compose a subject in four parts. The third and fourth are set to Italian texts, and it is clearly to be seen how the foreign method of singing had at that time begun to influence even these forms. The melodies are very sweet, and particularly well adapted to the Italian words. There is a distinct advance observable in the five pieces, the second representing most purely the old German aria, while the last betrays the sixty-eight years of the composer's age. In the ritornels, too, it may be noticed that those to the two first arias are simply five-part subjects treated as fugues (at the close of the second a *decrescendo* from *forte* through *piano* to *pianissimo* has a very good effect); in the others they are short and in three parts, and in Nos. 3 and 4 a little dance is appended, as was a favourite practice later, namely, a minuet and a gigue.

But his concerted church music deserves more attention, for we already know that an artistic task, to which he attached great importance, was the conduct of the "Abend-musik" at Lübeck; and these compositions played no small part in gaining him fame. The original printed editions are for the present lost, but we have a substitute in the form of beautiful MS. copy, which was written, at any rate in part, under the superintendence of the master. It shows traces of revision more or less important by his own hand, and contains some of the evening music pieces—perhaps actually some of those that were printed.[124]

Hitherto no opportunity has offered for a full investigation of the state of church music generally at that period. Joh. Christoph Bach's great choral work, "Es erhob sich ein Streit," is of quite another stamp, and Michael Bach's "Ach bleib bei uns, Herr Jesu Christ," remained but half developed from the motett. What was before glanced at, as to Sebastian Bach's first attempt, may here very properly be enlarged upon, since Buxtehude's church compositions are not only

---

[124] See Appendix A, No. 13.

interesting in themselves, but admirable representatives of their species; moreover, they will serve as a fitting background to Bach's work.

The form of church music accompanied by instruments—or, as I shall henceforth call it, the older Church Cantata—which was the predominant form from 1670 to 1700, resulted from a combination of the different forms of church music which had previously been in use separately. How the text was commonly constructed has already been told. The musical forms most in use were the *aria*, for one or more voices; the *arioso*, that is to say, the older type of recitative, as it was introduced by Schütz and then preserved nearly unaltered; and concerted choral-singing, in several parts; besides these, certain timid attempts at a few modes of treatment borrowed from organ music. These were used alternately, and it was optional whether an introductory instrumental piece should precede them. Rich polyphony was not much in use; this branch of art had almost disappeared with the extinction in Germany of the old tendencies and views, and could not be recovered till new paths were thrown open. The soft and elementary melody of the time, with its generally homophonous treatment, the poverty of development in the forms in use, and, wherever the sections were of any length, the frequent changes of time; finally, the formless and fragmentary arioso, which grew more spun out, give the older cantatas a sentimental and personal character; and those who seek in the music of the period the reflection and counterpart of pietism must seek it in these, and not in Bach's cantatas.

The first in the collection of Buxtehude's cantatas is founded on the following series of texts—"Whatsoever ye do in word or deed, do all in the Name of the Lord Jesus, giving thanks to God and the Father by Him" (Colossians iii. 17):—

> Dir, dir, Höchster, dir alleine,
> Alles, Allerhöchster dir,
> Sinne, Kräfte und Begier
> Ich nur aufzuopfern meine.
> Alles sei, nach aller Pflicht,
> Nur zu deinem Preis'gericht't, &c.

Thine and Thine alone, Most Holy,
All, O Lord Most High, be Thine;
Heart and soul before Thy shrine,
Here I offer, poor and lowly.
Due to Thee is all I own,
And I bring it to Thy Throne, &c.

"Delight thou in the Lord; and He shall give thee thy heart's desire" (Psalm xxxvii. 4). Then follow the two last verses of the hymn "Aus meines Herzens Grunde," and at the close the text from the Bible is repeated.

No indication as to its use on any Sunday or holy-day is given with either of the cantatas, and the one under discussion seems not to have been composed for such a purpose, but for some special occasion, perhaps a wedding. The instrumental accompaniment consists of two violins, two violas, bass, and organ, for a five-part treatment was more usual than four parts, and when the chorus consisted of four voices the first violin added a fifth part, lying above. The cantata is in G major, and is introduced by a sonata consisting of nine slow bars of common time, with very lovely, soft, and original harmonies, and a *presto* in 3-4 time, which works out the same motive in imitation. *Sonata* and *sinfonia* originally meant the same thing, as applied to an introductory instrumental movement. The former term subsequently fell into disuse for this, as it began to be used for other instrumental pieces. However, it was still retained when the prelude was to display that essential harmonic character which originally distinguished Gabrieli's sonatas, while the name *sinfonia* came into general use, particularly as, with the progress made in time, a more polyphonic animation was introduced. Perhaps the radical meaning of the words may have helped in this, since in the *sonata* the chief importance was given to unity of effect, and in the *sinfonia* to the parts, which by their combination produced the harmonies. And though that form of sacred prelude in two sections, which betrayed the influence of the French overture, was often called a *sonata*, this is perhaps most easily accounted for by assuming that the name was taken from the first movement,

which was always to be broad and sonorous in effect. But
the second portion also frequently preserved this character,
so that the upper parts only carried on a series of imitations
of each other, and the lower ones filled out the harmony.
It was thus that the introductory sonata to Joh. Christoph
Bach's "Es erhob sich ein Streit" was constructed, and
so also is this one by Buxtehude. It may be remembered
that Sebastian Bach, in the same way, prefixed a *sonata* to
the Easter cantata of 1704.

The first text is here sung by the chorus in four parts.
It is almost purely homophonic, and at first each syllable
has a note, but afterwards a few figures and very simple
imitations occur. The somewhat meagre method of spinning out the melodic thread by repeating the same musical
phrase, sometimes in a higher and sometimes in a lower
register, is unfortunately characteristic of Buxtehude's vocal
compositions. Here again, however, we may convince
ourselves to how great a degree the natural conditions
of the instrument employed supply the standard for the
form. The same master whom we lately saw wandering
through the mazes of counterpoint in organ fugues, here
does not venture beyond the simplest combinations. As
we consider these unadorned forms, it becomes clear how
much was left to be done by a genius like Bach in this
very branch of art, and why the greatest organist that
ever lived nevertheless directed his powers as composer
principally to vocal music. The three verses of the hymn
are set to an aria in four parts, with a ritornel for two
violins and a bass; the melody is very pleasing but trivial,
and, like the words, lacking in depth. Then follows an
arioso for the bass, in E minor, on the words "Delight
thou in the Lord," where we at once perceive that speeches
from the Bible, if they were to be given to a solo voice, had
to be treated in this way, since no other available form
as yet existed for them. Thus it is not singular that Bach
should have adopted the same method in his Easter cantata ;
but in the repetition of a melodic phrase in gradual ascent or
descent—as for instance is done in the tenor arioso "Entsetzet
euch nicht," and in the progressions in thirds in the bass voice

and basso-continuo, which come in in the first subject and
elsewhere, and which are such a blemish in part-writing—
we may trace the influence of an earlier master. Buxtehude's
arioso has some analogy to both these, but it is otherwise
full of really consolatory feeling, and its modest beginning,
accompanied merely by the organ, serves as the blank page
for displaying a flash of talent of the greatest brilliancy; for,
after it has closed on the *e*, the whole body of violins come
in at the topmost register, and sinks slowly and grandly
through intoxicating harmonies, like celestial dews on the
thirsty earth, coming down at last on G major below, on
which the hopeful chorale at once begins, "Gott will ich
lassen rathen"—"To God's good counsel leave it":—

The organ must be imagined as playing softly, and particularly as supporting the bass by the use of a sixteen-foot stop.
One verse is then sung by the soprano alone, the second
by four voices, very originally and softly harmonised; for
some time the organ alone accompanies, while the instruments come in with interludes between the lines, till at last
they continue throughout, enriching the subject both in
quality and harmony. In the last bar but two the first
violin soars up in ecstasy and then sinks again; to conclude,

the first chorus is repeated, but is prefaced by a slow introduction full of rapturous feeling, beginning thus:—

Compare bars four to six of the beginning to Bach's Easter
cantata; we here and elsewhere find the prototype of its
separate chords and abrupt harmonies.   There is yet another
sacred *sinfonia* by Bach which quite preserves Buxtehude's
style: it preludes the grand chorale cantata, " Christ lag in
Todesbanden,"[125] but can hardly have been composed for this;
it must have been transferred from some earlier work.   The
final chorus in this instance is somewhat richer, and displays
a pleasing and engaging polyphonic treatment of a thoroughly
agreeable character.

The second cantata is undoubtedly an " Abendmusik,"
composed for the second Sunday in Advent.   It treats of the
Second Coming of Christ to the Judgment, and has a vein of
pomp and mysticism.   The means employed are considerable,
consisting of a five-part choir, three violins, two violas, three
cornets, three trombones, two trumpets, bassoon, double-bass,
and organ.   With this body of sound Buxtehude has constructed one of his grand massive compositions.   A symphony
begins in D major, of which the theme is taken up by a
flourish of trumpets; the violins and trumpets are used for
alternate contrast, but the trumpets are played *con sordini*, an
effect of tone intended to increase the mysterious feeling. [126]
Then the soprano comes in in the same key, with a well-
considered accompaniment of only the stringed quartet and
the organ with bassoon, singing the words of the hymn " Ihr
lieben Christen, freut euch nun "—" Ye faithful Christians
now rejoice,"—but to the melody of " Nun lasst uns den

---

125 Bach Soc., I., p. 97.
126 Walther says of the trumpets *con sordini*, that they sounded " quite soft,
as if they were far away."

Leib begraben "—"Let us now put off this body,"—a deeper sentiment, leading us beyond the gates of death; this selection anticipates an equally significant instance by Bach himself. This chorale is an exact transcript, for the soprano and stringed instruments, of Buxtehude's small organ chorale for two claviers, and its real importance attaches to the application of the organ character to vocal music. For here the principle comes to light which was destined to give to Protestant church music both a new form and a new spirit. In the place of the first manual, which gave out the melody, we have the voice; and in the place of the second manual and pedal, the orchestra. Whatever is praiseworthy in the organ chorale reappears here to greater advantage, beautiful effects of tone from the soprano lying high and clear above the shifting tangle of the instruments and the rich and ingenious harmonies, as the morning rises above the mists of the plain. Moreover, the chorale melody naturally stands out as the principal subject, by means of the voice and words, far more distinctly than it could on the organ, where also its significant simplicity is overburdened with colour; and the passages in canon in the bass, which on the organ are only confusing, here appear as charming subsidiary themes. But the want of plan in the counterpoint, and the want of proportion in the care given to the effects of the body of tone, as compared to the interests of the independent existence of the single parts, remain the same as in the organ piece. At first the rhythm of the theme of the symphony is well pronounced above the varying movement of the instruments, but it soon becomes indistinct and shadowy, and presently vanishes altogether, giving way to vague fancies. To the eye such contrapuntal treatment gives at once an impression of disorder; still, when played and sung, it all sounds well and accurately written, but the real basis of satisfaction is lacking. Pachelbel, who also made an attempt to transfer his organ chorales to vocal music, of course, from his natural temperament, produced something more ideal and profound, as the fifth verse of the cantata on "Was Gott thut, das ist wohlgethan," which may be termed masterly. The succeeding chorus stands in well-considered contrast to the

movement just described. It opens with all the splendour of
the full body of tone in the rousing shout, "Behold the Lord
cometh with ten thousands of His saints, to execute judgment upon all" (Jude, 14, 15). It starts in majestic chords
and then passes into a fugato, which is more important for
the dramatic way in which it is conceived and for the mixture of qualities of tone than for polyphonic art. This
theme, for instance—

is repeated in incessant alternation by the voices, the violins,
and the trumpets, at first in single parts, but soon in two
and three, and still only moving from the tonic to the dominant and back. A picture is borne in on the fancy of the ten
thousand saints riding forth after Christ, hither and thither
from all the corners of heaven, ever more and more rising
above and beyond those in front, and each host more glorious
than the last. A grand effect is also produced when the
choir sings the words " Gericht zu halten," with only the
organ accompaniment, in alternate semi-chorus ; and then,
all at once, the whole body of tone comes in with full force.
Here again we see a prototype of Handel's treatment. A
blaring instrumental symphony of eleven bars follows ; then
we hear a mysterious bass arioso, "Behold I come quickly,
and My reward is with Me" (Revelation xxii. 12), accompanied only by the organ and two trumpets *con sordini*, which
die away in the final passages, so that the mage fades like
a vision. Until now the fundamental key has never been
abandoned. The next movement—for alto, tenor, bass,
three violins, two violas, and figured bass—is in A major,
but it is the weakest in the cantata. It shows how
incapable composers were as yet of animating grand forms
with corresponding spirit. The verses of the hymn which
supplies the foundation are repeated line for line with little
imitations; then each time an instrumental ritornel is
brought in, sounding very stiff and ungainly, however, in

its six parts. The best that can be said of it is that it helps
to produce remarkable contrasts of tone. The solemn peal
of the muffled trumpets follows the union of the subdued
voices with the swaying tones of the violins, and, above the
trumpets, two clear soprano voices sing a fugal "Amen."
Buxtehude always knew how to round off his work; so, to
close, he returns to the chorale of the beginning—

> Ei, lieber Herr, eil zum Gericht,
> Lass sehn dein herrlich Angesicht,
> Das Wesen der Dreifaltigkeit!
> Das hilf uns, Gott, in Ewigkeit!
>
> Yea, Lord, come quickly, judge and seal!
> Thy glorious countenance reveal—
> The presence of the Trinity!
> And guide us through eternity.

It strides on in 3-2 time and in full magnificence; the first
violin throws in a sixth part high above the chorus, and
between the sections of the melody the trumpets come in
with a fanfare. A lively "Amen" ends the chorale, consisting
of a light alternation of imitations between the chorus and
instruments. The reader will at once perceive that we have
here the exact prototype of the closing chorale of Bach's
Easter cantata.

The third, calculated for massive effects, is written only
on three verses of the book of Sirach (Ecclus.), l. 24-26.
It has no solos, and the choral portions again display the
inaptitude of the period for such undertakings. No composer had hitherto dared, Æolus-like, to unchain the spirits
of music and to set them free to rush tumultuously over the
broad ocean of sound; although in Buxtehude's organ-works,
they are heard already hurtling against the door of their
prison. Instead of this, small motives are brought in
which, separately, never dare to contradict or even to assert
themselves, but which show much spirit when all are
working together, though after every little effort they have
to be refreshed by a ritornel. In the middle is a five-part
arioso with the organ, "Which exalteth our days from the
womb, and dealeth with us according to His mercy,"—

of the same type as the three-part arioso in Bach's cantata. In the third part the time is very much varied; 3-2, common time, 3-4, common time, 3-4, 3-2, 3-4, succeed each other, and then the first ritornel and chorus are repeated. This unrest is highly subjective, reminding us of Christian Flor's Musikalisches Seelenparadies,[127] and if the composer were not Buxtehude, we might call it amateurish.

While a quotation from the Bible is the sole text of the third cantata, only hymns are employed in the fifth and sixth. The former depicts the joys of the blest in the next world in the manner of the Song of Solomon, and in the poetically rapturous but sentimental language and feeling of the pietistic hymns. The fifth verse is as follows :—

Die Rosen neigen	The roses bending
Sich von den Zweigen	Are softly twining
Ins güldne Haar	Among her hair.
Der Auserwählten	She is the chosen,
Und Gottvermählten :	The bride and loved one,
Seht, nehmet wahr !	And she is fair.
Sie kommt die Schöne,	Behold, she cometh,
Dass man sie kröne,	And we will crown her ;
Ihr Heiland ist,	It is her Lord,
Den sie zum Lohne,	Who deigns to own her,
Zum Lohn, zur Krone	With bliss to crown her,
Hat auserkiest.	For her reward.

The musician has set all nine verses, but it is only in the first and last, where large masses of sound are handled with but little polyphony, that he has managed the trivial rhythm of the hymn with any freedom. No deep vein is anywhere struck; cheerful melody, facile rhythm, and ingenious combinations of tone, form the whole. In addition to the instruments—namely, three violins, two violas, three cornets, three trumpets, three trombones, bass, and organ—we find—a unique instance—the dulcimer (cymbalo); the chorus is in six parts. We see that the plan of the orchestra is still designed for alternation of effect. After the first section,

---

[127] The Musical Paradise of the Soul. Winterfeld, Ev. Kir., II., 414, and the examples given in notes.

the following verses are carried on in alternate settings for one or for three parts in each, in the aria form and with gay ritornels : happily the same melody is not adhered to throughout, for the inevitable rhythm (of a dotted crotchet and three quavers) in 3-4 time is fatiguing enough as it is.

The sixth cantata, "Bedenke, Mensch, das Ende, bedenke deinen Tod "—" Remember thou art mortal, remember thou must die,"—is far more dignified and grave, but even here the construction is very simple. Five verses of the hymn are fitted to the same music, only the last is richer in detail, and is graced by an "Amen" movement. It is prefaced by a sonata which has quite the form of the French overture in little ; then three voices sing the verses, each finishing with a ritornel on the violins. The "Amen" consists of small subjects fugally treated and taken up by the instruments ; here and there only the first violin ventures on a combination with the other instruments.

The fourth cantata resembles the first and second in its mixture of Bible words, hymns, and independent writing, but musically it is distinct from them by having no chorus on an independent verse ; instead, it has two different chorales. After a short symphony in G minor, plunged in sadness, the chorale strophe is heard handled in precisely the same manner as in the second cantata.

> Wo soll ich fliehen hin,
> Weil ich beschweret bin
> Mit viel und grossen Sünden,
> Wo soll ich Rettung finden ?
> Wenn alle Welt herkäme,
> Mein Angst sie nicht wegnähme.
>
> Ah ! whither can I fly?
> Bowed down and crushed am I ;
> Iniquities upbraid me,
> Whom shall I find to aid me ?
> If all the world stood round me,
> My fears would still confound me.

What was omitted in the former case—namely, the introduction of ornamentation with the melody—is here done to

a certain extent in one of the voice parts; nevertheless, the
solo soprano has not merely a musical, but also a dramatic
purpose, and the small deviations in the melody are only
intended to bring the idea of the tortured heart more
vividly before the mind. To this questioning a bass arioso
replies, "Come unto Me, all ye that are weary and heavy-
laden," &c. Thus we have a dialogue, in which we must
suppose the speakers to be the Believing Soul and Christ,
according to the allegorical form long known in the Protestant Church. The title of the cantata is, indeed,
expressly *Dialogus.* Hammerschmidt, who opened out new
paths in church music in so many directions, had as early
as 1645 published "*Dialogi*, or Conversations between God
and a Believing Soul,"[128] and had followed out the idea in
the fourth part of his Musical Meditations, and in Musical
Discourses on the Gospel, by the alternate response of
hymns and Bible words. But the characteristic feature of
the composers at the close of the seventeenth century consisted in this—that they allowed the chorale to be performed
by a solo voice with an accompaniment, and could thus use
it, with the addition of passion-breathing modifications of the
melody and unexpected harmonies, as a means for expressing
the most subjective feeling, without giving it a polyphonic
form so strict as to counterbalance the subjectivity. It is
in them, properly speaking, as has already been said, that
we most clearly discern the musical counterpart of the
pietistic "spiritual song." Of course, not in the sense
that this style of composition in any way owed its origin
or its tendency to pietism; the direct influence of Pietism
on sacred music and its development was quite insignificant,
for this reason—that it strictly excluded the whole realm
of art.

The two lines of feeling originated side by side, and
from the same root of sentiment; and music, as a fact,
reached that stage of sentimentality and youthful rhapsody
which necessarily ensues on the resuscitation of a nation's

---

[128] *Dialogi* oder Gespräche zwischen Gott und einer gläubigen Seele.

life, and which must first betray itself in music, all the earlier, because—from the very nature of the German people—it was precisely in music that the first vital energy was shown, which budded and blossomed after the miseries of the great war. The beginnings of pietistic verse writing, no doubt, lay within that same musical period. Buxtehude even had more than one opportunity of combining it with his tones, but by the time it was at its fullest blossom church music had long overstepped that stage; partly it had repossessed itself of the religious ideal in its purest sublimity, and partly it had turned in other directions which had no further concern with that ideal.

The bass arioso which responds to the Believing Soul, and which is not wanting in feeling and fervour, is very long, and falls into two parts. The first closes on the dominant of G minor; the second begins again in B flat major, "And ye shall find rest unto your soul," and does not return to the principal key until the last bars. There is no idea of any complete or compact form, but there are in it elements which were of more essential, though of less obvious, importance to the sacred aria formed on the Italian model, and as Bach subsequently developed it. A few conspicuous ones are also traceable. Thus now and then the accompanying violins pass into brief polyphonic combinations with the bass voice; still, the proper treatment of this voice remains an almost undiscovered country—it generally coincides with the instrumental bass. At a later date, Mattheson, speaking of Handel, who, at the time when he went to Hamburg was not yet freed from the manner of the old-fashioned cantata, says: "He composed, at times, long, very long, arias, and positively endless cantatas, which displayed neither true skill nor correct taste, though their harmony was perfect; but the opera, which was a fine school, soon upset all that." [129] Certainly, the church-cantata could not but be influenced in some degree by dramatic music.

---

[129] Mattheson, Ehrenpforte, p. 93.

The Believing Soul now follows the consoling invitation and promises, with the second verse of the chorale—

O Jesu voller Gnad,
Auf dein Gebot und Rath
Kommt mein betrübt Gemüthe
Zu deiner grossen Güte.
Lass du auf mein Gewissen
Ein Gnadentröpflein fliessen.

Oh! Jesu, gracious Lord,
Obedient to Thy word
I bid my weary spirit
Trust wholly in Thy merit,
Some drops of mercy craving,
To bring me peace and saving.

Then, with renewed and more earnest consolations, the bass begins a second arioso in E flat major, "As I live, saith the Lord, I will not the death of a sinner, but rather that he should be converted and live. Ask and ye shall receive, seek and ye shall find, knock and it shall be opened unto you." To this succeeds one of those beautiful slow instrumental movements, several of which we have become acquainted with, and then an aria (*i.e.*, a hymn of four verses with a ritornel) for the tenor, connected with the close of the foregoing passage of Scripture, and meditating on the promises there bestowed. This idea, but in four or three parts, occurs, too, in the first and second cantatas; this again, foreshadows the later church cantatas, and particularly the Bach Passion Music, in which the aria has exactly the same poetic import. The end is formed of the sixth and eighth verses of the chorale, " Herr Jesu Christ, du höchstes Gut," in which it is resolved to approach the Saviour with a petition for grace and a blessed end. The sixth verse is sung by the soprano solo again, with four-part accompaniment of strings and organ; the last verse is given to the chorus with expressive melodic ornaments, deeply moving harmonies which prophesy distinctly of Bach, and several amplifications of the phrases. In the intervals between the lines are inserted interludes, among which one, twice repeated, appears particularly striking and original, even for Buxtehude's style :—

The "Amen" is more elaborate than usual, with beautiful canon treatments and richer and more independent orchestration, so that we may conclude that this dialogue had a special interest for the composer. The tender depth of feeling that makes itself felt in it gives it, in fact, a prominent superiority over the rest of Buxtehude's cantatas, although the feeling is somewhat too monotonous and it lacks animating contrasts.

The seventh cantata is set to Martin Schalling's beautiful hymn of three verses, "Herzlich lieb hab ich dich, o Herr" —"I love Thee, from my soul, O Lord;" it is in the strictest sense a chorale cantata. Buxtehude was not alone among his contemporaries in the employment of this form. The Leipzig cantors Knüpfer and Schelle had worked at it diligently, and a similar composition by Pachelbel has been already mentioned. But in its details, and in the feeling they express, it is a perfectly individual composition. The first verse is again intrusted to the soprano, and is supported by an independent accompaniment in five parts which in part lies above it. This, however, is not thematic, hence it is restless, and without real depth; still, as we have said, the chorale, by being given to the human voice, has the good effect of making itself felt as the principal motive of the work, and of giving unity to the whole. The impression on the senses is captivating, particularly when the two violins soar high up, and the melody is surrounded on all sides with a sea of sound. The poetic expression is rendered very personal by the rapturous harmony bordering on sentimentality, and by the outward means of change of *tempo*, so that the cry, "Herr Jesu Christ!" in the last

line but one, gives the impression of an almost sensuous
desire. On the other hand, Buxtehude's filmy harmonies
have something ethereal in them, so that we seem often
to see a web of silver threads. At the second verse the
motett-like treatment of the melody begins. We do not
see here any mere imitation of Buxtehude's similarly
constructed organ chorales—nay, rather these are themselves imitations of the motett style. But certain features
which occur in them are frequently found again here, particularly the union of the chorale theme with independent
subsidiaries, and the different combinations of the themes
which follow one another in unbroken succession and in
great variety. *Tutti* passages alternate with the polyphonic
movements, and give a beautiful effect of breadth to the
whole. The expression is often made more vivid and
intelligible by a change of *tempo*, or even by a kind of
instrumental tone-painting, which approaches the province
of oratorio. There is a remarkable passage in the second
verse, to the words " Auf dass ichs trag geduldiglich "—
" On which I bear it patiently,"—where the carrying of
the Cross is represented by eight oppressively heavy
chords, of which the harmony scarcely changes at all.
There is deeper feeling still in two passages in the third
verse, the first beginning—

Ach Herr, lass dein lieb Engelein
Am letzten End die Seele mein
In Abrahams Schooss tragen.

Lord, send Thine angel when I die
To bear me up, that I may lie
In father Abraham's bosom.

Timidly, yet fervently, the prayer is begun by two voices,
while all the instruments are silent. In the sixth bar the
violins enter with a whispered *tremolo* in repeated quavers,
and then in semiquavers; the voices go on, alone and forsaken,
as in the lonely death-hour; they are surrounded on all sides
with a fluttering breeze, and we seem actually to hear
the wings of the heaven-sent messengers. A *tremolo* on the
violins, which now has long lost any especial effect, was

then something new; but such is the spirituality with which
it is imagined and worked out, that, even now, one cannot
escape a mysterious thrill of awe at the passage. Later
on, this passage occurs—

> Den Leib in sein'm Schlafkämmerlein
> Gar sanft ohn einig Qual und Pein
> Ruhn bis zum jüngsten Tage.

> The body in its narrow bed,
> Calmly, without a pain or dread,
> Rests till the resurrection.

On the last line the following tone-picture is constructed :
the bass voice, supported by a low instrumental bass, first
takes the word "rest," in 3-2 time, on a long-held e. In the
next bar the second soprano and alto come in on g' sharp
and e', and, finally, the tenor starts on the fifth, b, which,
after the other parts have ceased, is still held softly in the
distance. Then the gradual formation of the chord is
repeated, beginning, however, at the top—b', g' sharp, e', and e
—and as each voice ceases a bar before the next, the chord
dies away dreamily as it descends. In the whole passage
the strings keep up a mysterious whispered rocking motion
in crotchets, in the two octaves from c to c''.

A different method is followed with the hymn by Johann
Franck, "Jesu, mein Freude," in the eleventh cantata. It
is set for only two sopranos and bass, two violins, bassoon,
and organ. After a *sonata*, the first verse is gone through by
the three vocal parts, with a superstructure of two violins,
thus making five parts ; the course of the chorale melody,
which is harmonised very delicately and with great discrimi-
nation, is completely adhered to, and only interludes and a
ritornel at the end are added to it. The second verse is
given to the first soprano alone, supported only by the
organ ; the melody is lost in florid ornamentation, but
any extension of the phrases is strictly avoided, as is
usual even in Buxtehude's small organ chorales. The
third verse is taken by the bass alone, with the instruments.
The effort after the greatest possible individual expression
destroys the rounding off of the phrases, and prolongs the

separate lines by emphatic declamation and the subsidiary development of episodes. The instruments now and then repeat what has been given out by the voices. It is hardly possible here not to be reminded in the liveliest manner of Bach, and convinced that he must have known this piece, and that, consciously or unconsciously, he must have been thinking of it when he wrote his lovely motett, " Jesu, meine Freude." Just as in that, Buxtehude begins (and time and key are identical, too) with the warlike, defiant and intermittent cries, " Trotz! trotz! trotz dem alten Drachen!"—" Death! death! death to that old dragon!"—the rolling passage to the words, " Tobe, Welt, und springe"—" Storm, thou world, and break,"—are precisely similar, and the passage " Stehen und Singen in sichrer Ruh "—" Standing and singing at rest and secure,"— is represented with equal vividness, although by different means. These lines are most characteristically treated—

Erd und Abgrund muss verstummen,
Ob sie noch so brummen.

Earth and Hell henceforth be still,
Rage they as they will.

For " Abgrund " the bass has a phrase of powerful descending octaves (e—E and d—D) and we will give an example of the " brummen " (raging) :—

There is in this tone-picture, although in a much smaller degree, that kind of grim mirth which Bach, like Luther, occasionally indulges in. If we regard more particularly the general scheme of the cantata, we shall see that it is the precursor of those wonderful works of Bach's in which he treats a hymn, such for instance as "Christ lag in Todesbanden," with a strict regard to the original melody throughout. They indeed belong to the period of his greatest perfection ; nevertheless I am inclined to believe that he attempted something of the kind when young, and possibly the *Sinfonia* before mentioned which introduces this cantata, may have been taken from some such youthful performance. We have seen in one striking case, and we shall meet with still more, how the impressions of his youth had their effect on him afterwards, and suddenly rose again to the surface, after many years, in a glorified and transfigured form.

For the fourth verse all three voices are employed, and the instruments come in by turns with them and against them. It begins with passionate cries : "Weg! weg! weg mit allen Schätzen "—"Go! go! go all earthly treasures,"—treated contrapuntally, in the style of Bach's motetts. The fifth verse is given to the second soprano alone, the melody being treated with florid ornamentation and extended, accompanied only by the organ. In the sixth verse all the parts are finally united, and this interesting work closes in rich five-part harmony. Two other cantatas in the manuscript collection are also set to hymns, one to Michael Pfefferkorn's "Was frag ich nach der Welt," the other to the hymn by Angelus Silesius, "Meine Seele, willst du ruhn." Buxtehude has not confined himself, however, to their original melodies, but has regarded them simply as available devotional poems, and has put his own music to them,—a procedure which Hammerschmidt, and even Schütz did not hesitate to employ with the old traditional hymns.

It is a remarkable feature of the period that several cantatas were written for a single voice. To these belong the composition, "Lord, now lettest Thou Thy servant," &c. The first section, which is preceded by a symphony, is remarkable, because in it an attempt is made to mould the *arioso* to a more defined form; and although it is not yct freed from the stiff ritornel, yet a rounding off is attempted at the end by a repetition of the chief melodic theme. It is the same treatment as in the tenor solo and the soprano aria of Bach's Easter cantata. The second section is also interesting in the matter of form, since a very pretty fugue is developed between the tenor and the two violins, in which, however, the supporting bass takes no part. Here a decided attempt to arrive at a new style is perceptible.[130] The cantata "Herr, wenn ich nur dich habe," is also for one solo voice. Here the biblical text is first gone through in an *arioso* manner; then follows an aria in two verses, then an instrumental interlude, and, last of all, a long "Amen," of such a form that the voice has each time a florid passage of several bars on the first syllable of the word, which is then answered by the instruments, and so on to the end. The seventeenth cantata, too, "Ich bin eine Blume zu Saron"—"I am the Rose of Sharon," &c.,—is, curiously enough, set for a single bass voice, although the words—from the beginning of the second chapter of the Song of Solomon—contains the conversation of two lovers.[131]

The other pieces present no essentially new forms to our notice, although they contain many separate beauties and much elegance.[132] The composition "Ich habe Lust abzuscheiden," is particularly remarkable for great tenderness and depth of feeling, and for a very beautiful dying close at the end, in which a feeling is perceived which was to soar to its full height in Bach's cantata, "Gottes Zeit ist die allerbeste Zeit"—"God's time is the best."

---

[130] See Appendix A, No. 14.

[131] After bar thirty-two there is some error in the MS. I presume that the transcriber has only forgotten the conclusion of the voice part (possibly g sharp—e) in the following bar.

[132] They are, "*Lauda Sion salvatorem*," for two sopranos and bass; "Nichts soll uns scheiden von der Liebe Gottes," for soprano, alto, and baritone; "Ich halte es dafür," for soprano and bass; "Also hat Gott die Welt geliebet," for soprano; "*Lauda, anima mea*," for soprano; "Jesu, meine Freud und Lust," for alto. The collection must also have been intended to be continued, since, on Fol. 86b, there is the beginning of another cantata for soprano, in G major, which has been struck through, "Dies ist der Tag, den der Herr gemacht hat."

IV.

WHEN the year 1706 arrived, Bach gradually remembered
that his home was not Lübeck but Arnstadt. Perhaps it
might have happened to him to make a new home in the
old Hanseatic town, since it is scarcely possible that he
would have been refused the post of Buxtehude's successor
if he had married his eldest daughter. What direction his
genius would have taken in that case, and whether he would
have retained the full depth of his character in the vicinity
of the opera at Hamburg, in prosperous circumstances and
surrounded with all the most brilliant accessories of art, it
is impossible to say. But the somewhat mature age of the
daughter deterred him just as much as it had done Mattheson and Handel, and perhaps his affections were already
attached in another quarter. So he left it to another and
an older musician to secure for himself, with the lady, the
reversion of the post of organist in the Marien-Kirche, for
Johann Christian Schieferdecker, previously cembalist (*i.e.*,
maestro al cembalo, or harpsichord-player) in the opera
band at Hamburg, was Buxtehude's successor. The wife
who had been, in the phrase of the time, " allotted " or
" reserved " for him with the situation, cannot long have
survived, since he took a *third* wife in 1717 and died in 1732.
It was probably in the early part of February that Bach
took leave of the venerable master whom he was never to
see again, for on May 9, 1707, Buxtehude was taken from
life and art. On his way home Bach may, perhaps, have
passed by Luneburg and visited Böhm ; he may even have
taken a day at Hamburg, but by February 21, he had been for
some days re-established in his lonely home in Thuringia.

On that day he received a citation from the Consistory.
In matters of business they were in no way punctilious, nay,
they were not so exact as might have been wished. But a

leave of absence extended from four weeks to sixteen outraged even their forbearance. In addition to this, the clerical authorities were not satisfied with Bach's way of playing the service; and they had cause for their dissatisfaction. For though at the present day we may consider that Bach was justified in regarding the free cultivation of his organ-playing as the chief matter, and its employment in divine service as subsidiary, it could not be expected that his official superiors should humour his as yet unrecognised genius in all respects, disregarding the feelings of the congregation. Bach, with his productive power luxuriantly bringing forth innumerable blossoms, would submit to no restrictions even from the congregational singing, in respect to which it ought to have filled a subordinate position. Even during the singing of the tune, he indulged in ornamentations and digressions of a new and bold kind; and doubtless in this irregular habit, from which he subsequently almost entirely freed himself, he was especially confirmed by his close connection with the northern masters, although indeed it was a very general one.[133] He must too, though it was not expressly stated, have given way recklessly to his love of harmonic intensification; and we know how much the character even of the best-known melody can be altered by unfamiliar harmonies. He went so far that the congregation often did not know what they were listening to, and got into complete confusion.[134]

We possess an interesting organ work of his earliest period, which throws a clear light on the style of his playing

---

[133] Adlung could still denounce this practice in 1758 (Anl. zur mus. Gel., pp. 681, 682), "when," he says, "several organists are accustomed to make variations, even while the congregation are singing, as if they were playing a chorale prelude. Now are heard two-part variations and diminutions and playful passages, sometimes on the pedals, and sometimes in the upper part; then they kick about with their feet, they ornament the tune and break it up, and hack it about until one does not know it again. Is this, then, the real way to keep the congregation together? I should think it would rather puzzle them."

[134] The reader will remember an anecdote of Beethoven's youth—that an experienced singer in the Hof-Kirche, at Bonn, was quite put out by his bold modulations. (Thayer's Life of Beethoven.)

at that time. This is the chorale "Wer nur den lieben Gott lässt walten," with prelude, interludes, and postlude, which we see at the first glance to have been intended for divine service, and which must have been written in the first years of the Arnstadt period, since many traces of Böhm's manner can be discerned, and very little use is made of the pedals. The prelude consists of nine bars of semiquaver figures, mostly for the right hand, which anticipate the harmonic progression of the chorale. This follows next, in three parts, with a highly embellished melody, of which the last line but one, for example, has this form:—

The interludes are not introduced regularly between each line, as they ought to be if employed at all; they appear between the first and second, not between the second and third; again, between the third and fourth, and then at greater length before the second section of the tune, but there is none before the last line. It is very possible—nay, even likely—that Bach would not separate those lines that are closely connected together in the form of premise and conclusion; the idea, logically and poetically, was a good one, but quite impracticable as regards the congregation who must have thought it was done in a merely arbitrary manner.[185] He had also overstepped the mark in the free preludes before the different hymns; but when Olearius, the Superintendent, requested him to make them rather shorter, he contracted them to such a degree as to give general offence. The characteristic of an easily aroused

---

[185] The arrangement of this chorale in its pure form, with many improvements and richer adornments, was included in the Clavierbüchlein, made for his son Friedemann in 1720, evidently after he had made the elegant employment of ornamentation a particular study. He was better fitted for that than for accompanying congregational singing. It will be found in its shortened and improved form in P. Ser. V., Vol. V., No. 52; and in its original form as the variant to No. 52 at the beginning of the volume.

irritability and of obstinacy meets us here for the first though not for the last time; it ran in his family, and though we cannot directly point it out in Ambrosius Bach, the reader will remember the affair about the marriage of his brother, whose temper was very similar. Finally, he had completely alienated his choir, and consequently did not care the least about it. In the first place, the choir was too bad for him, and he was too much occupied with composition to take any pleasure in troubling himself with their progress; but he forgot that it was only natural that the best voices of the place should not be allotted to him, since his tuition was only to be a preparation for the chief choir of the Ober-Kirche. He forgot in the ardour of youth that, notwithstanding his extraordinary gifts, he must, after all, fulfil his duty; he forgot, too, the frank kindness with which he had been received, and the great confidence which had been reposed in him. In fact, the Consistory, in exercising their authority, as had at last become necessary, might justly have spoken with much harshness and severity, but they showed themselves mild and patient beyond expectation. But, on the other hand, it must have been pretty hard for a young musician, barely twenty years old, to get on well with the scholars, some of whom were probably scarcely younger than himself. The excellent discipline which had been originally instituted by the energetic and watchful Rector Treiber, had ceased since Johann Gottfried Olearius —who had the interest of the school very little at heart— had been appointed Superintendent and Inspector of the school. Treiber's authority now began to be undermined by arbitrary encroachments on his rights, instigated by his enemies; his influence was gradually weakened and destroyed, and the way was thus left open for disorder in the school, and finally for utter insubordination. In an address from the town-council to the Consistory, presented on April 16, 1706, complaint is made of the disobedient, ungovernable, and lawless behaviour of the scholars. "They have no fear of their teachers, they fight even in their presence, and meet them in the most insolent manner. They wear swords, not only in the streets but in the school too ; they play at ball during service and in school hours, and run about in improper places." [186] When mature and worthy men could obtain no respect from the undisciplined boys, how should an inexperienced and irritable youth succeed?

The report of the examination appointed by the Count's Consistory, to consider the case of Bach, is one of the most interesting documents relating to him. It shall follow here in the exact form in which it has been preserved to us.

Whatever inconvenience may be occasioned to the reader by the antiquated phrasing will be compensated for by the lively view of the time which it gives, for the spirit of an age is reflected in its outward forms. [187]

" *Actum*, de Feb. 21. 706.

The Organist of the New Church, Bach, is required to say where he has been for so long of late, and from whom he received leave of absence?

Ille (*i.e.*, Bach, answered)

That he had been to Lübeck with intent to learn thoroughly one or two things connected with his art, and that he previously asked permission from the *Herr Superintend.*

Dominus Superintendens

That he had only asked such permission for four weeks, but had remained abroad quite four times as long as that.

Ille

Hoped that the organ meantime would have been played by the substitute he had put in, [188] in such a manner that no complaint could be made on that score.

Nos (*i.e.*, the Consistory)

Charge him with having hitherto been in the habit of making

---

[186] Uhlworm, Beiträge zur Geschichte des Gymnasiums zu Arnstadt. Part III., pp. 7-9. (Prospectus of the Arnstadt Gymnasium for the year 1861.)

[187] The report is preserved by itself among the archives of the Principality of Sondershausen, and bears the title: " *Joh. Sebastian* Bachen, *Organisten* in der Neuen-Kirche betr. wegen Langwierigen Verreissens vnd Unterlassener Figural *music*. 1706." (Joh. S. Bach, Organist of the New Church, summoned respecting his prolonged absence and the discontinuance of the part-singing, 1706.)

[188] This was possibly his cousin, Ernst Bach.

surprising *variationes* in the chorales, and intermixing divers strange sounds, so that thereby the congregation were confounded. If in the future he wishes to introduce some *tonus Peregrinus*[189] he must keep to it, and not go off directly to something else, or, as he had hitherto done, play quite a *tonum contrarium*.[140] And then it is very strange that up to this time he has had no "music-making" (*i.e.*, rehearsals), by reason of his not being able to agree with the scholars. Therefore he is to declare whether he will play both part-music and chorales with the scholars ; since another Capellmeister cannot be kept, and if he will not do this, let him say so categorically of his own accord, that a change may be made, and some one who will undertake it may be appointed to the post.

Ille

If a proper Director be appointed, he will play again.

Resolvitur (It is resolved)

That he shall explain his conduct within eight days. And, at the same time, that Scholar Rambach appear,[141] and be reproved for the *désordres* which up to this time have taken place between the scholars and the Organist in the New Church.

Ille (*i.e.*, Rambach)

The Organist, Bach, used to play too long preludes, but after this was notified to him, by the Herr Superintendent, he went at once quite to the opposite extreme and has made them too short.

Nos

Reproach him with having gone to a wine-shop last Sunday during the sermon.

---

189 From the connection, this can only mean a key not proper to the original melody.

140 Meaning a tune harmonised in an unusual way.

141 The name of the choir prefect. In the accounts of the church expenses in the council archives at Arnstadt (p. 63), there appears the entry: "Joh. Andreas Rambach, for chorale singing in the New Church, from Michaelmas, 1705, to Trinity Sunday, 1706—9 months ; 7 fl. 10 ggr. 6 pf." His successor from the second half of the year was Joh. Chr. Rambach (see the same accounts, p. 64).

Ille

Was very sorry, and would never do so again, and their Reverences had already treated him very severely about it. The Organist need not complain of him about the conducting, because that was undertaken, not by him, but by the youth Schmidt.[142]

Nos

He must, for the future, behave quite differently and much better than he has done hitherto, or else the emolument designed for him will be withheld. If he has anything to remember against the Organist he must bring it .forward at the proper place, and not take the law into his own hands, but behave in such a manner as to give satisfaction, as he had promised. The servants of the Court are hereby enjoined to tell the Rector to adjudicate that Rambach be imprisoned on four successive days for two hours each day."

Although the Consistory in their requirements from Bach used, according to this report, very emphatic language, their conduct was patient and forbearing. In his playing the musician may have accommodated himself more to their expressed wishes, and, with regard to the differences with the school choir, they were impartial enough to perceive that there were faults on both sides ; they suggested a change in the circumstances of the case, and they allowed the explanation demanded of Bach within eight days to stand over for a time, hoping that he might of his own accord come to an agreement with the choir. In truth, however, there was little prospect of this, especially since Bach, elevated and replenished with the artistic life he had enjoyed at Lübeck, now, more than before, busied himself with his own productions, and

---

[142] Perhaps Andreas Gottlieb Schmidt, who, in 1728, when Ernst Bach succeeded Börner in the Ober-Kirche, applied for the post of Organist of the New Church, but withdrew afterwards, because he had been " for a long time out of practice," and could not regain his powers in so short a time. He was at that time Registrar (*Acta* " regarding the appointment of the organists at Arnstadt." Fol. 132).

certainly must have found the drudgeries which he had to undergo with the scholars, rough alike in music and in manners, quite intolerable.

The influence of Buxtehude's music clung to Bach all his life, in certain characteristics of form. The ideal side of it swiftly disappeared in the mighty flood of Bach's own originality, because the older master's musical feeling, though much more limited than Bach's, was yet of the same kind. So that all those compositions which, whether in general plan or in particular methods of expression, show an evident leaning towards the style of Buxtehude, may with justice be considered as works of Bach's earliest period, written for the most part soon after his return from Lübeck, partly even before his journey thither.[148] For he could not previously have been unacquainted with Buxtehude's works, or what could have induced him to seek his immediate neighbourhood? On the contrary, he must have made acquaintance with them when he was at Lüneberg, and through Böhm, who had a great respect for them.

I am not able to point out any vocal compositions by Bach founded directly on those of Buxtehude. The cantatas of the following year are indeed in the old prescribed form, but they are, in a great degree, full of his own ideas. Notwithstanding, the impression which he had received from this quarter was certainly an important one, and it has already been pointed out that it unexpectedly appears in some of the later works. We may also believe that the evening performances had affected him deeply. The man who could give such full musical expression to the sweet, elevated yearnings of Advent-tide, and the bright, pure, fulness of joy of Christmas Day, as Bach did in his Advent cantata of 1714 and in his Christmas Oratorio, must have fully entered into the poetry of those performances in the winter evenings in the church, radiant with light and music. A number of instrumental works could be mentioned which seem to have an unmistakable connection with these occasions. The

---

148 Mizler, p. 62. "For organ composition he took (when he was in Arnstadt) the works of Bruhns, Reinken, and Buxtehude for models."

fugue in C minor, before spoken of, betrayed this connection in some measure, especially in the form of the prelude which ushers it in, but much more does a prelude and fugue in A minor[144] from beginning to end, though still in a way which is somewhat immature. The work has the appearance of having been merely a reminiscence, and not a new formation resulting from the assimilation of foreign elements; as if it had been written before Buxtehude's manner had become quite comprehensible, and as it were living to the composer; probably, therefore, before 1706, but at Arnstadt, as we judge from the pedal *technique*. It consists of a short prelude, two fugues separated by an interlude, and a postlude which repeats and dilates upon the movement of the prelude. The second fugue is not based upon the first, but has an independent theme. Thus what was a strict condition of the organism of the northern fugue-form is here wholly neglected, the composition falls into two sections, and is only superficially rounded off and connected by the repetition of the prelude. The first theme bears quite a striking likeness to the models of the northern masters; with mechanical motion and an absence of all melodic expression, it goes round in its narrow circle, and no rich development makes up, as was usual in their works, for its insignificance. It goes steadily downwards without interruption through four entries of the theme, without regard to a fixed number of parts, and then this manœuvre is repeated in a lower position, with a close in C major, and so an end. The second theme has a more individual growth, but strongly inclines to Buxtehude's manner by immediately bringing in a counter-subject, which accompanies it throughout its whole course in simple and double counterpoint, which produces even here an inevitable monotony. From a little appendage to the theme, which appears first in bar fifty-two, an independent figured passage is afterwards generated, which, in detail as in general features, greatly reminds us of Buxtehude; and with this the fugal movement closes, the chief theme not being heard again.

---

[144] P. Ser. V., Cap. III. (Vol. 242), No. 9.

This evolution of a new subject is very clever and subtle. Separate details, in which the true resemblance is often more easily traced than it is in general outline, might be quoted in abundance; for instance, the kind of figuration used, the double shake in the sixth bar from the end, the solo entry of the pedal, the thrice-repeated quaver in the newly formed subject, the false relation twice introduced quite intentionally in the broad harmonic progressions in the interlude, the long-tarrying on the subdominant just before the end, which closes "with the greater third" (*i.e.*, in the tonic major). Nor is there any lack of harsh, unwieldy passages; we are deluded in a particularly unpleasant way, in bars fifteen and twenty-four, into the hope of getting into C major on the third beat of the bar, and in bar fifty-one the sudden cessation of the two upper parts has not an agreeable effect.

On the other hand, a more mature work, and one betraying a greater warmth of feeling, is a fantasia in G major,[145] so called because it neither contains a regular fugue as its germ, nor presents the variety and changing style of a toccata. Although it contains three complete movements, there reigns throughout a perfect thematic unity, such as Buxtehude loved and liked to work out. Nay, more, in his great composition in G minor, which extends into a *chaconne*, or other works of the same kind, we can recognise the progenitors of Bach's fantasia. Kuhnau's subject, already quoted before, serves as the first theme—

and the contrapuntal treatment is very like that of the fugue in the first part of the "Clavierübung." It subsequently appears inverted, and serves in a slightly modified form for

---

145 Unpublished; contained in the Royal Library at Berlin, in an old MS. (in a volume, sign. 287) from the legacy of the organist Westphal, in Hamburg, which came into the market in 1830. The full title is: *FANTASIA. clamat in G ♮ di* Johann Sebastian Bach.

the motive of the second movement (*Adagio*, E minor), namely—

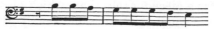

from which is generated finally, for the third movement (*Allegro*, G major), this chaconne theme :—

This form, thoroughly characteristic of Buxtehude, never recurs in any of Bach's later works, and removes all doubt as to the date of composition; we have additional evidence in the unmethodic use of the pedal, in the undefined character wavering between that of the organ and clavier; and lastly, in the expression, which hovers on the surface and seldom is of much depth. The treatment of the subject is free in the antiquated style; the answer comes first three times on the octave, then the theme appears four times in the dominant, then again many times more in the tonic, and afterwards twice in the minor. In the last movement the chief subject lies now below, now in the middle, and now above, its place in the scale varying with each repetition. The way in which it is surrounded on all sides with imitative passages of semiquavers, and yet comes prominently forward with dramatic vigour whenever it appears, is very admirable, and shows how thoroughly the composer had mastered the inherent nature of his exemplar. Just as before we have seen him following Böhm or Kuhnau, so he shows in this instance that his universal talent had the power to assimilate all the different tendencies of the time ; thus he laid the broad foundations on which he was to rear the secure and towering edifice of his own productions. It was not in his character to evince originality of a false and immature kind, but he always infused some individuality into whatever form he used.

To put counterpoint of the most resplendent kind to slowly ascending and descending scale passages in the bass, as is done here, was a favourite style of organ-music with Bruhns and Buxtehude. Bach employed this motive in a broad and fine manner for a piece for the organ, which also has the title of Fantasia, and which is in the same key.[146] But this would not be enough to give it a place here, were it not that the Buxtehude influence in the harmonising of the fantasia, and the kind of feeling it reveals, is prominent to a degree never reached by any other of Bach's works. Here, if anywhere, we find evidence of the fact that Bach must at some time or other have been fully imbued with Buxtehude's peculiarities. It gives the impression that he had resolved for once to revel in the intoxicating wealth of sound which had been brought to him from that quarter. With insatiable enjoyment he repeats those doubled suspensions, chords of the ninth, diminished intervals, wide-spread harmonies, melodic phrases rapturously ascending and outsoaring one another—an entranced delight in the ocean of sound that never pauses to ask what the end will be. Thus throughout the long *Grave* movement the full five parts are almost always kept up, the pedal only ceasing for a short time at bar 102. Towards the end, and especially from this place onwards, the scale subject is more prominent, at first heavy and slow ; and then the expression rises gradually to an indescribable intensity and glow, which soars away far, far above the capabilities of the organ. The pedal slowly ascends with irresistible force from D, through two octaves in semibreves, resting finally in a mighty pedal-point on the note it started from ; then the left hand takes up the subject in thirds, and the counterpoint soars farther and farther above it, until it is interrupted by the chord of the diminished seventh, and then, like a shower of rain in sunshine, down pour the glittering pearls of sound in demi-semiquavers, in groups of six, with many bold intervals and skips from passing notes.

Again he follows his model as regards both form and feeling in a fugue in 12-8 time, and likewise in G major.[147] A comparison of the conclusion of the first great

---

[146] P. Ser. V., Cah. 4 (243), No. 11.

[147] In manuscript in the legacy of the late Musikdirector at Dessau, Herr F. W. Rust; now in the possession of Herr Dr. W. Rust in Berlin.

fugue in E minor with the C major fugue by Buxtehude will confirm this judgment at the first glance, both as to the whole and in the details. Many features exactly correspond: the adornments of the theme, invented with special regard to the pedal, and which are at once brilliant and easy; their repeated accompaniment of chords in short Iambic measure, and much besides. But that a bolder flight and a deeper nature animate this masterly piece, it might just as well have been written by Buxtehude.

A prelude and fugue in E flat major must also be mentioned here.[148] Mention has frequently been made of J. Jakob Froberger, of Halle, who, in the middle of the seventeenth century, was one of the most prominent masters of the clavier and organ, in Germany. Although a native of Central Germany, he had devoted himself chiefly to the southern type of organ-music, just then raised to its zenith by Frescobaldi in Rome. But his performances were known and valued throughout Germany, least of all, indeed, in his own native province—since his education had left him unfamiliar with the chorale form—but much more in the north. It has been already noticed that his toccatas contributed to the formation of the North German fugue-form, consisting of several sections. With regard to free organ composition Froberger stands about half-way between the northern and southern masters. We are told that in the book belonging to Bach's elder brother, which he secretly transcribed for himself in Ohrdruf, there were pieces by Froberger, so that he had made this master's acquaintance when quite a boy.[149] The northern masters, of whom he learnt in later life, had, it is true, long since overtaken Froberger, but they still referred to him, and did not hinder the delight which Bach, determined by his earliest impressions, took in his works. That this was actually the case, is shown by Adlung, a personal friend of Bach, who says: " Froberger was held at

---

[148] In the legacy of F. W. Rust's brother, who lived at Bernburg; now likewise the property of Dr. Rust in Berlin. It bears the date, " Bernburg, 1757."

[149] Mizler, p. 160.

that time in high honour by the late Bach, of Leipzig, although he was somewhat antiquated."[150]   But in the nature of the case, it cannot be thought that Froberger had any important or direct influence on Bach through his own works; the principal elements of Froberger's genius were probably transmitted to him through the northern masters, with whom he stood in closer connection than with Froberger.

In fact the only work where beside or beneath Buxtehude's manner that of Froberger appears at all, is this same prelude and fugue.   It was a favourite device with this master to display at the beginning and end of his toccatas a kind of passage-writing accompanied with chords now lying above and now underneath; these passages consist of notes of different values irregularly mixed, and are easily recognisable by this restless character.   From such a germ grew the prelude of Buxtehude, who, however, added the elements of proportion, order, and development; his "finales" or perorations, ingenious as they are, are allied to the finale passages of Froberger's toccatas.   Bach's composition reminds us strongly of Froberger, not only in the form of the running passages (e.g., the phrase of zig-zag descending semiquavers) and the massive chords, but also in the repetition of the fugue in a form adorned with trivial figures which have no inner connection with it, expanded to a length which in later times the composer never permitted.   On the other hand, the passages have a quieter flow and more connection by means of imitation, as in the works of Buxtehude.   Both influences seem to me less conspicuous in the fugue; the theme has not sufficient motion for the Lübeck master, and the style of contrapuntal invention is not his, while, on the other hand, the harmony is too complicated for Froberger.[151]

Among the most important works of this period, is a great work for the organ in four sections in C major; in it the Buxtehude fugue-form (the extension by means of episodes) is seen in full perfection.[152]   While the technical

---

[150] Anleitung zur Mus. Gel., p. 711.
[151] See App. A, No. 15.
[152] Peters' Cah. 3 (242), No. 7.—B. G. XV., p. 276. See App. A, No. 16.

power of writing in the greater number of the compositions already mentioned leaves scarcely anything to be wished, in this the inherent independence is so great that the work is all but a perfect masterpiece. The additional superscription *concertato* which is found in two manuscripts, shows that it was intended as a piece for the display of execution, and though in this respect it does not come up to Bach's later writings it demands a very high degree of facility both of finger and foot, and its effect is powerful and brilliant. Probably Bach wrote it for himself when, in the year 1707, he was playing in other places besides Arnstadt. We might hesitate to assign such an early date, if the fact that this is the only instance known of Bach's having written a fugue in this form were not clear evidence of his having borrowed it from Buxtehude. In later life he cultivated exclusively the fugue in one movement which concentrates all its strength on internal perfection, and which more fully satisfied his nature; only, in the last period of his working, the older form rose once more from the depths of his musical nature to the surface, in that most marvellous fugue in E flat major in the third part of the Clavierübung. But the theme in its original form is plainly influenced by the northern models, not to mention the running passages of the prelude and of the interlude. But in the fugal working proper we perceive a new spirit stirring its pinions; this lovely, flowing animation of all the parts, none of which is ever used as a mere stop-gap; this bold, free style of counterpoint in the first fugue movement soar high above Buxtehude's more confined and earth-bound nature to new regions. The second fugue movement is remarkable. The triple time, it is true, is retained, but the gracefulness and serenity which should find a share in this part are altogether absent. It is as though such a conclusion were contrary to Bach's nature, that "earnest temperament" which is attributed to him in the Necrology;[153] here at least he has only superficially adopted a form into the spirit of which he did not care to enter; this again assigns the composition to the number of

---

[153] Mizler, loc. cit., pp. 170 and 171.

works of development, and suggests a new reason for his so soon abandoning Buxtehude's fugue-form. In entire contrast to that master, the formation of the theme is broad and heavy, and the working out is the same, nay, almost devotional; but later it is enlivened by counterpoint in semiquavers, and closes with majestic breadth of chords. While Buxtehude, with a dignified smile, bends down to meet the hearer, Bach turns his face heavenwards with a holy gravity.

But we must remember that the complications between our young genius and his authorities were still awaiting their solution. Bach considered this quite unnecessary; and the eight days in the course of which he was to give in his "categorical" explanation had grown into more than eight months, without his having fulfilled the wishes of the consistory with regard to the trial as to the school-choir. This mute resistance, however, was met with renewed mildness, and they contented themselves provisionally with a repeated summons, the short document of which still exists :

"*Actum* d. II. *Novemb.* 706.

It is hereby represented to the *Organist* Bach that he should declare whether, as he has been enjoined to do, he will *make music* with the scholars, or will not ; as, if he feels no shame in keeping his post in the church and receiving the salary, he must also not be ashamed to *make music* with the scholars thereto appointed for the time arranged elsewhere. It is intended that these should *exercise* themselves (*i.e.*, rehearse), so that for the future the music may be better looked after.

Ille (*i.e.*, Bach)

Will make the declaration on this subject in writing.

Nos (*i.e.*, the Consistory)

Furthermore remonstrate with him on his having latterly allowed the stranger maiden to show herself and to *make music* in the choir.

Ille

Has already spoken about it to *Master Uthe*."

The expected written "declaration" should follow here, for the Consistory cannot possibly have left the affair thus only half despatched ; unfortunately we no longer possess it. In it Bach would most probably explain his conduct by a number of difficulties with the scholars, such, perhaps, as their unpunctuality, idleness, insolent behaviour, or their musical incapacity, and perhaps, too, by a reference to his own striving after the ideal, and his compositions. Thus much can be supposed ; but that, in spite of this, the difficulties which embittered his position were not thoroughly remedied is shown by the course of his life during the next year. From that time he endeavoured to get away from Arnstadt into some other position. We shall soon see that it was not for the sake of pecuniary gain, since in that respect he might at that time be considered quite contented, so that it must have been only inward considerations which could drive him away. Whether there were others besides the affair just mentioned is uncertain, but there are no certain grounds on which to found any other suppositions.

The document also mentioned a " stranger maiden," with whom Bach had " made music " in the church. He had certainly not done it without previously informing his clergyman, Master Uthe, [154] but still it was the cause of unpleasant remark. It would, however, be erroneous to conclude from this that the singer had taken part in the service. As long as the form of the old church-cantata was retained—and this was the dominant form at that time at least in Arnstadt—the question of employing female voices in church music would not be even broached. With the introduction of the newer cantata, influenced so essentially by operatic vocalisation, there came the occasional disregard of the command, " Let your women keep silence in the churches." But Bach would certainly never have thought of such an innovation, and Uthe as certainly would not have

---

[154] Magister Just. Christian Uthe (b. 1680), was preacher in the New Church from 1704 to 1709 ; see Hesse, Verzeichniss schwarzburgischer Gelehrten and Künstler. No. 333. Rudolstadt, 1827.

permitted it, so that the question here can only be of some private music in the church. What sort of singer it could have been who could make music with Bach in the New Church, to the enjoyment of both, is a question which we are not without hope of being able to solve. A professional singer might certainly have come over from the Brunswick-Wölfenbüttel opera by command of the Countess. But, considering Bach's nature and musical tendencies, it would even then be impossible to imagine what could lead to an acquaintance, and even to the intimacy of private music-making together, to say nothing of the fact that opera singers would certainly have turned their noses at the simple old-fashioned church singing. An event of the next year puts us on the right track: Bach's marriage with his cousin, the youngest daughter of Michael Bach, of Gehren.

Maria Barbara, as the bride-elect was named, was born in Gehren, October 20, 1684. Her mother is known to have been the younger daughter of Wedemann, once Town-clerk in Arnstadt, where she lived until her death, October 19, 1704. In spite of the scattered nature of the evidence it is pretty clear that Maria, then twenty years of age, betook herself to her mother's unmarried sister, Regina Wedemann, in Arnstadt, where Sebastian made her acquaintance and fell in love with her.[155] Some musical qualifications surely may be presumed in the daughter of one distinguished musician and the affianced bride of another—the most highly gifted of his race—and if it were she who in the case mentioned was the singer in the church, a delightful episode in the courtship of the young couple is disclosed to our view. Her being called a "stranger maiden" quite agrees with the nature of the facts, since she was grown up when she first came to Arnstadt.

The plan on which Bach wished to found his own family shows how he, too, was filled with that patriarchal feeling by

---

[155] The chief ground of this supposition is confirmed by the account of their wedding. As subsidiary evidence may be mentioned the fact that Maria Barbara had several young companions in Arnstadt whom she afterwards invited to Weimar to be godmothers to her children Philipp Emanuel and Gottfried Bernhard; among them was a daughter of the organist Herthum.

which his race was distinguished and brought to such a flourishing condition. Without straying into foreign circles he found, in a relation who bore his name, the person whom he felt to be the most certain of understanding him. If we must call it a coincidence, it is, at any rate, a remarkable one, that Sebastian, in whom the gifts of his race reached their highest perfection, should also be the only one of its members to take a Bach to wife. If we are right in regarding the marriage union of individuals from families not allied in blood as the cause of a stronger growth of development in the children, Bach's choice may signify that in him the highest summit of a development had been reached, so that his instinct disdained the natural way of attempting further improvement, and attracted him to his own race. His second wife, indeed, was not allied with him in blood, but that with the first he found, in some respects, his more natural development may perhaps be concluded from the fact that the most remarkable of his sons were all the children of his first marriage.

In other respects his marriage is a token that by this time he regarded the years of his education as at an end. In the capacity of perfect executive musician, as well as in that of composer, he had gained the topmost height of that time; and in the completely acquired technicalities of his art, he had himself created the forms in which, from this time forth, he cast his surpassingly new and individual thought. This, of course, was shown at different times in different ways, corresponding with the progress of his growth, and vaster, deeper, and more original at each stage; and, side by side with this growth, he perfected also his technical powers, so that his latest works have scarcely anything in common with the earliest but certain general features. The true man never ceases to improve and educate himself; he may be considered as fully developed only when his powers correspond to his demands upon them. That this was the case with Bach is shown plainly by his handwriting. No autograph works of this time can be found, it is true, but there exist still five acquittances for salary received; the dates are December 16, 1705, February 24, May 26, and

September 15, 1706, and June 15, 1707.[156] The writing which these display, and which is of a charming clearness, elegance, and certainty, is substantially the same as that which meets us, full of such characters, in the almost innumerable works of his long life. About the time of the Matthew Passion and the B minor Mass it is rather bolder and larger, but the characteristic features remained so identical, that in the carefully and ornamentally written scores of that period, as, for example, the cantatas " O ewiges Feuer " and " Weinen, Klagen," there is scarcely a perceptible difference from the writing of his twentieth and twenty-first years.

The widely diffused opinion that Bach's development was slow in comparison with that of Handel is shown to be false, by the fact that his powers during the years from twenty to thirty were almost at a standstill, and the reverse would be more near the truth. Bach was much more influenced by his surroundings than his equally great contemporary. It was not only that his extraction and old family traditions led him almost intuitively on the right way; the object which lay nearest to his heart, the perfecting of the art of the organ, was attainable by a much simpler method; he concentrated the efforts of the most remarkable of his ancestors, and, as it were, added the roof to the edifice which they had left but half-finished, completing it with "cloud-capp'd towers." We are not now bringing into consideration the undreamt-of paths opened out, over and above this perfection, by his colossal genius. Handel had to collect the elements of his ideal with much greater labour, and the hewing of the separate stones of his temple of art was a much longer process ; but, as surely as his operas and chamber-music have an eminent artistic value, so surely are they not to be compared with the instrumental works composed by Bach at the same

---

[156] The first four of these are in the Rathhaus at Arnstadt; the last in the Ministerial Library at Sondershausen. The acquittance of December 16, 1705, is naturally dated too soon or too late, since the receiver was at that time not in Arnstadt.

time. In exact agreement with this relation between the two stands their respective estimation with their contemporaries and with posterity. Bach's fame is founded chiefly on the instrumental works of his earlier and middle periods, that of Handel on the oratorios composed in his middle and later life.

Just as Bach's nature was more deep than diffuse, so the years of his "apprenticeship" and his *Wanderjahre* were simultaneous, if indeed there was any period at all which could be designated by the last name. At twenty-two years old he became "master," and according to true German custom the "master" must be married. He must also have "apprentices," and from 1707 onward, such will demand our notice.[157]

Before this, however, his service in Arnstadt must have come to an end. It is related that about this time, in the years 1706 and 1707, different situations as organist were offered to him at short intervals.[158] His fate was decided by a trial performance which took place at Easter in the last-named year, in the Church of St. Blasius, at Mühlhausen.

---

[157] The life of a tradesman or artisan in Germany is divided into three periods :—First, the apprenticeship (Lehrjahre). Second, the period during which he travels and, as it were, "finishes his education" (Wanderjahre), with which the original meaning of our "journeyman" corresponds ; and third, the period from the time of his entering into his business on his own account, onwards—the period called "Meisterschaft," or when he is styled Master. Readers of Carlyle will remember that the first part of his translation of Wilhelm Meister is called "apprenticeship," and the second, "travels." This analogy has been followed in the present work—the book just concluded being called Ausbildungsjahre, or "years of formation," and from the third book onwards, "Meisterschaft." [Translators' note.]

[158] This is related by Forkel, and can hardly be pure invention on his part.

BOOK III.

THE FIRST TEN YEARS OF BACH'S "MASTERSHIP."

BOOK III.

THE FIRST TEN YEARS OF BACH'S "MASTERSHIP."

I.

BACH AT MÜHLHAUSEN.—HIS RELIGIOUS OPINIONS.

THE post of Organist to the church "*Divi Blasii*," in the free imperial city of Mühlhausen, had risen to special celebrity from the many highly gifted artists who had filled it during the last century and a half. From 1566 to 1610 (May 24), Joachim Möller von Burck (born in 1541)—the friend of Johann Eccard, a man who may be regarded as having given the chief impulse to the earnest musical feeling for which Mühlhausen was long distinguished[1]—laboured there. At the end of the year 1654, Johann Rudolf Ahle came to fill the post (born 1625), and was as efficient as a leader of public affairs as he was as an organist and composer, for he became a member of the council, and even a burgomaster of the town. He died in the prime of life (July 8, 1673); from the beginning of the year 1672 his son, Johann Georg, had already officiated for him, and he now succeeded his father. He was equally distinguished for his musical talents, and like him filled a place in the town council, and he also won from the Emperor Leopold I. the title of *poet laureate* "for his virtue and splendid talents, but particularly for his admirable proficiency in the noble science of German poetry and for his rare and delightful style in highly commended music, and his elegant compositions."[2] Both father and son practised musical composition. Johann

---

[1] His less famous successors were Johann Heydenreich (Möller's son-in-law), from 1610 to 1633 ; Rudolph Radecker, 1633-1634; Hermann Schmied, 1634-1649 ; Johann Vockerodt, 1649-1654. These and the following statements concerning the two Ahles depend for their deviations from all previous accounts on the account books of the church of St. Blasius.

[2] See Gerber. N. L., I., Col. 35.

Georg Ahle died December 2, 1706, and was interred three days later with much honour, as became the respect he had enjoyed during his life.[3]

A man to fill the place was not this time easy to find; meanwhilea scholar was intrusted to perform the service as best he might. However, candidates were not wanting for a position of so much honour, and Bach must have cast an eye on it, for in an expression used by his cousin Johann Ernst, who exerted himself to become his successor at Arnstadt, we certainly may trace an echo of his own views. He says in an application laid before the Consistory, June 22, 1707, that it must be known to them that his cousin (Sebastian) had had the vacant post of Organist to the celebrated church of St. Blasius offered to him, and had willingly accepted it on being called." At the same time he was not too forward nor hasty in making the council of Mühlhausen acquainted with his person and his qualifications. The organ-builder, Wender, had wished to induce Johann Gottfried Walther, then residing at Erfurt, to come over and perform on trial on Sexagesima Sunday of the year 1707. He, however, for some reason had not consented.[4] On the other hand a public trial had been made by some others, whom Bach easily drove from the field when he presented himself, which was not till Easter; when the council met, a month later (May 24), they were at once agreed on this point, and caused him to be summoned to appear a second time that they might treat with him as to his reasonable claims in the matter of salary.[5] They feared, no doubt, that so great a virtuoso might make demands they could not satisfy. But Bach's object was not pecuniary advancement, though ere long he had two

---

[3] " Herr Johann Georg Ahle, buried with the whole school and with two tollings, December 5."—Extract from the register of the church of Divi Blasii. The funeral took place three days after the death, as is the custom still.

[4] According to his own statement, in Mattheson (Ehrenpforte), who, however, confounds the younger with the elder Ahle. There was never any question of an invitation to Walther refused by him before the invitation to Bach. Compare Gerber, Lex., II.

[5] The documents relating to Bach are reproduced at full length in App., B. V. of the German edition. They are devoid of interest to the English reader.

to provide for; and when, three weeks later, he treated in person with the council, he obtained only the same salary as he had had in Arnstadt, besides such payments in kind as his predecessor had enjoyed.   It is true that even so his emoluments exceeded those granted to Ahle by nearly twenty gülden, for Ahle had, from the year 1677, only been paid sixty-six gülden and fourteen groschen;[6] and his father had received even less.   Bach's salary, accordingly, was as much as eighty-five gülden,[7] with three *malter* (coombs) of corn, two cords of wood, and six trusses of brushwood, as an equivalent for the arable land previously attached to the office.   The payments in kind were to be delivered at his door.   He also received, according to the custom of the place, an annual donation of three pounds of fish.   He expressly added a hope that he might be assisted in transporting his furniture by the loan of a vehicle; naturally enough the dowry of the young bride he was shortly to bring home lay near the bridegroom's heart.

The council acceded to everything, and all the more readily since it was at the moment sorely pressed by other concerns; for only a fortnight previously a serious fire at night had in great part destroyed the dwellings in the parish of St. Blasius, to which Bach was henceforth to belong; the fire had raged so close to the church and the priests' houses that the books belonging to Frohne, its Superintendent, had been flung into a cellar, where they remained several weeks.[8]   Many members of the churchwardenry were houseless; and when the clerk of the council brought them the agreement to sign, pens and ink were lacking, and they declared that they had just then no thought for music, and that they were satisfied with the decisions of the council. It was the handsomest and wealthiest part of the city that had been destroyed by the fire,[9] and the first impression pro-

---

[6] "70 *schock*" according to the parish accounts.   1 schock = 20 groschen; 1 meissen gülden = 21 groschen.

[7] In Arnstadt he had had only 84 gülden 6 groschen, accurately speaking, for his salary had been paid him in various coinage.

[8] According to a statement made by Frohne himself during the litigation that ensued.

[9] It is thus stated in the penitential prayer referring to this disaster.

duced on Bach by his future home must have been dismal
and comfortless.   That he was nevertheless well content
shows that he was glad to quit Arnstadt; he had no doubt
ample reason: release from onerous official relations, the
acquisition of a post which was doubly honourable by reason
of his youth, and the near prospect of setting up house.

His instalment dated from June 15, thus his new duties
began from the *Crucis* term of the year (ending September
14).   On June 29 he presented himself at the council-house
of Arnstadt, announced what had occurred, expressed his
gratitude for the confidence that had been placed in him,
craved his dismissal, and restored the key of the organ to
the hands of the council.   He did not wait to receive part
of his salary which was in arrear; it often happened that
there was no money in the coffers, then the salary was
simply not paid, and the persons concerned left to manage
as best they could.   On this occasion Sebastian Bach availed
himself of his credit, to obtain assistance for his needy
cousin Ernst, who had lived in Arnstadt for many years
without any appointment.   He had very likely filled his
place during his journey to Lubeck, and had perhaps been
of assistance to him previously in Hamburg when Sebastian
made an excursion thither from Lüneburg, for it may be
approximately calculated that the two had met there at least
once.   This was the desired opportunity for repaying such
services; and the sum was not so trifling as it appears, for
five gülden are an item of some importance out of a whole
income of less than eighty-five gülden, particularly when a
wedding and a removal are close at hand; five gülden indeed
formed an eighth part of the annual salary subsequently
obtained by Ernst Bach.[10]   That Sebastian thought he could
do without it shows what good spirits he was in, and also
throws a clear light on his simple and modest way of life.

He now started afresh, and with youthful confidence in

---

[10] That it was but a quarter of the sum that Sebastian received can be
positively proved from the account-books and receipts in the archives of the
town-council of Arnstadt, in connection with the official statements as to
Johann Ernst's salary.   It is not necessary here to go into the details of the
evidence.

his new circumstances. At the end of three months all was so far arranged that he could fetch his wife home to his own house, and for this purpose he returned once again to Arnstadt. At Dornheim, a village about three-quarters of a mile distant, Johann Lorenz Stauber had, since 1705, filled the place of minister, and had been in close intimacy with the Bach family. His first wife, Anna Sophie Hoffmann, very possibly belonged to the family at Suhl from which Johann and Heinrich Bach had formerly chosen their wives. After her death (June 8, 1707) he married again, in about a year's time, that same Regina Wedemann with whom, as we may suppose, Maria Barbara, Bach's betrothed, was living. This would explain why it was he, who on October 17, 1707, performed the wedding of our young couple. Count Anton Günther gave his express permission, and for them the pre-scribed fees for Arnstadt were remitted; and it is evident from this friendly and courteous conduct that Bach and his patrons had parted without any grudge or ill-feeling. The notice inserted by Stauber himself in the parish register betrays in its details much personal interest. It runs as follows: "On October 17, 1707, the respectable Herr Johann Sebastian Bach, a bachelor, and organist to the church of Saint Blasius at Mühlhausen, the surviving lawful son of the late most respectable Herr Ambrosius Bach, the famous town-organist and musician of Eisenach, was married to the virtuous maiden Maria Barbara Bach, the youngest surviving unmarried daughter of the late very respectable and famous artist Herr Johann Michael Bach, organist at Gehren; here in our house of God, by the favour of our gracious ruler, after their banns had been read in Arnstadt."[11] A particularly fortunate coincidence added to their happiness: Tobias Lämmerhirt, an elder brother of Sebastian's deceased mother, and a well-to-do burgess of Erfurt, had died in September of the same year, and left fifty gülden to each of

---

[11] In the marriage register at Arnstadt the record of this marriage is also preserved. The father of Maria Barbara is there styled Mstr. (Meister) Johann Michael Bach. The title of meister or master probably refers to Michael Bach's skill as an instrument maker.

his sister's children.[12] His will was read September 18, and as nothing stood in the way of an immediate payment of the legacy, this sum must have come in precisely in time for the wedding. Sebastian might perhaps have felt as though his lost mother herself had pronounced a blessing on this union, and the young couple went to their new home joyful and thankful.

Mühlhausen enjoyed a good reputation for music ; at the time, however, when Bach came thither it had greatly degenerated from a past time, in which it could boast of Joachin von Burck and Johann Eccard, Georg Neumark and Johann Rudolf Ahle, and when a " musical society "[13] had collected together the instrumental and vocal forces of the town and surrounding country in great numbers, for regular practisings. Johann Georg Ahle had started on a path which, exclusively followed out, must inevitably result in waste of power. His father, it is true, had also had a predilection, which sprang from his own subjective piety, for sacred arias in the form of hymns divided into verses and set for one or more voices with instrumental " ritornels," or interludes. But sometimes he could hit upon a general and comprehensive musical idea, so that not a few of these evince a fitness for congregational singing; and he was very well acquainted with the greater and more complicated forms of the sacred concerto, and in this had followed up with success the course opened out by Hammerschmidt. Another side of his artistic faculty is shown by some important productions in the way of organ compositions, still extant, with which his skill as an organ-player must have corresponded, and which have hitherto remained unknown.[14] The style of the chorales, which for the most part are treated in the manner of motetts, is, it is true, somewhat arbitrary and lacking in design, as might be expected from the infancy

---

[11] City archives of Erfurt.

[13] I have derived my information respecting this society in the seventeenth century from the documentary sources in the Monatsheften für Musikgeschichte II., pp. 70-76 (Berlin : Trautwein, 1870).

[14] Of his activity as a church composer a complete picture, written *con amore*, is given by Winterfeld, Evangel. Kirchenges., II., pp. 296-328.

of that branch of art at the period. But here and there unmistakable tendencies towards the style of Pachelbel are already apparent, and it is instructive and interesting to observe how a dim and shadowy ideal is here darkly felt for, which, like every genuine truth, seems plain and self-evident as soon as it is found. Ahle's fugues are also remarkable historic monuments. The form of the quintenfuge[15] is not yet brought to its full perfection in them; sometimes the theme is answered first in the octave and then in the fifth, involving another response in the octave; it even occurs that the answer remains for the time exclusively in the octave. Stretto treatment is in great favour even at the very beginning; the character of the key-treatment wavers between the old and new; the use of the pedal is irregular, and presupposes very indifferent technical skill. Two-part writing predominates in the polyphonic sections, and the parts are often repeated in a transposed form, either higher or lower. Notwithstanding all their want of development, these organ works testify to an earnest and thorough dealing with the subject, and bear an unmistakable instrumental stamp.[16]

Johann Georg Ahle had not the musical versatility of Johann Rudolf, but confined himself, so far as we know, to sacred arias and little pieces for several instruments. He was fond of combining the two in short compositions; adding to an air a prelude and a finale, in which he frequently used the motive of the air as the theme, and for this he made pleasing use of the dance rhythms of that time.[17] Compositions for the organ were seldom printed, and it may be an accident that we do not know of any such in manuscript; still the great fertility which he displayed in the aria form points this out as being his chief province;

---

[15] *I.e.*, a fugue of which the subject is answered at the interval of a fifth.

[16] They will be found in the collection (Musikaliensammlung) of Herr Musik-director Ritter, by whom they were copied from the Tabulaturbuch of 1675, mentioned above. Fortunately; for the precious musical legacy of Hildebrand, the organist of Mühlhäusen, was sold by his heirs to a butcher, as I discovered to my sorrow in the winter of 1867-68.

[17] Winterfeld, Op. Cit., 328-342.

and this is hard to combine with the broad objective solemnity of the organ. The sacred aria contained in itself no conditions, either in form or idea, of any richer development. It rose to importance by drawing the deepest feelings of the soul to the surface, and by developing the tone-material in its subtlest details. But in the construction of the great musical forms of Bach and Handel it was only indirectly made use of, and from the beginning of the eighteenth century onwards, its independent importance was lost for musical art, which henceforth, full of a soaring spirit, strove after broad and catholic expression. By constantly mirroring our own mind in the smaller forms of art, we easily lose the sense of proportion, as well as our interest in what lies outside us. Thus was it with Georg Ahle; and the people of Mühlhausen, long accustomed to regard their musicians as ample authorities, had followed him in this, and gave little or no attention to what was passing in the musical world round about them.

Into this situation came Bach, who had perfectly mastered all that had hitherto been achieved in the art of organ-playing and in the " church cantata " form, and was already eagerly striving for something greater, above and beyond these. To this young and ardent soul the fame of his predecessor must have been an additional spur to produce something worthy of his post. According to the terms of his appointment he was obliged to play the organ in the church of St. Blasius only on Sundays, saints'-days, and festivals. But he had already formed the determination to elevate church music in general to a higher grade, and in an address subsequently presented to the council he twice expressly notified this as the end and aim of his endeavour.

A sure and unerring instinct for the field in which the full display of strength will be possible, has been in all times a mark of genius ; and little as Bach may then have thought whither this clearly shown way would ultimately lead him, such an utterance from the lips of an artist of twenty-three years old was very significant. He extended his activity into the province of sacred vocal music, although this properly fell within the cantor's sphere of work ; nay, it seems as though he may have managed it quite alone. Possibly this may have been customary with his predecessors here, and so such an encroachment may have been more easily practicable. With his views of art, he obviously could not endure the preponderance of Ahle's compositions, and as there existed at Mühlhausen very few church compositions besides these, he procured at his own expense, and in a short time, a sterling selection, and had them performed. He tried to complete the church choir as well as the accompanying instruments, and it will be understood that he did his utmost in playing the organ. In all this he was aided by his first pupil, Johann Martin Schubart (born March 8, 1690, in Gehra, near Ilmenau), who lived in close intimacy with him for full ten years, and by this faithful adherence proved how great an attraction Bach's youthful genius and great powers of fascination could exert over other musicians if they approached him without prejudice or vanity. In the year 1717 Schubart succeeded his master in Weimar, but died four years after, in the prime of life. The name also of Bach's choir-leader can be given; it was Johann Sebastian Koch, who was born in 1689 at Ammern, near Mühlhausen, held this post from 1708 to 1710, and died as cantor in Schleiz.[18]

In his indefatigable zeal for his art Bach was not unmindful of the state of music in the immediate neighbourhood, and he must have noticed that often more material of a better kind for the church was available there than in the town itself. Among the surrounding villages Langula, however, has been distinguished from the beginning of the eighteenth century to the present time by having a succession of well-qualified cantors and an active feeling for music. That Bach was known there is plain from a church cantata of his composition which I myself discovered in the "Cantorei" (the cantor's house), and which is recognisable as an early work, apparently belonging to his Mühlhausen time.[19] It is incomplete,

---

[18] Walther, Lexicon, Art. "Schubart" and "J. S. Koch."

[19] Everything of value in the way of old music that had belonged to the Cantor Sachs of Langula came into my hands in 1868. But I only acquired a copy made by him of Bach's cantata, and not the original MS. The first chorus had meanwhile been lost

and is adorned with some certain and other apparent additions by later cantors at Langula; still it offers some genuine
matter for the consideration of the historian. The first piece,
a duet for soprano and bass, in F major, beginning with
the words " Meine Seele soll Gott loben," &c., is still treated,
as regards the bass part, quite in the style of the older church
cantatas, and greatly resembles them in the melodic treatment; it is, however, already cast in the form of the Italian
aria, and has a few interesting passages. The concluding
fugue in B flat major, "Alles was Odem hat," &c., is a
splendid piece, full of fire, of which the bold and soaring
theme may be given as a specimen :—

Al - les was O - dem hat   lo - be den Herrn, lo   -   be,   lo - be,   lo - be den Herrn.

This great advance in melody is displayed also in another
cantata composed at Mühlhausen, which, as it lies before us
in the most perfect state and in an unfalsified form, shall be
subjected to a more exact examination, as befits the first-
fruits of the young master's labours.

The affairs of the city were managed by a council consisting
of forty-eight members (of whom six were burgomasters),
and divided into three sections, each consisting of sixteen
persons. Each of these in rotation controlled the municipality for a year, from February to February, presided
over by two burgomasters. It was the custom that each
change of council should be celebrated with a church festival and a piece of music composed for the occasion, which
was then printed in parts at Mühlhausen at the press of
Joh. Hüter or of Tob. Dav. Brückner. For a long time
it had been the duty of the Organist of Saint Blasius to
compose this music; he, in fact, by ancient tradition was
regarded as the representative of the musical dignity of the
city, and the organist of the other great church—*Beatæ
Mariæ Virginis*—seems always to have been second to him
in importance; his name in Bach's time was Hetzehenn. It
is to the inauguration of a new section of the council, presided
over by the burgomasters Strecker and Steinbach, that a

cantata by Bach, composed for February 4, 1708, owes its origin and also its publication in such a style as, so far as I know, was never bestowed on any other cantata during Bach's lifetime. Not only has this edition been preserved to us, but also the score and the parts, in an autograph of charming elegance and neatness; and in the score the bars are marked, as they often are in the master's earlier works, with lines drawn with a ruler.[20] The performance took place in the church of the Holy Virgin, in which the superintendent of Saint Blasius also had to preach on certain holy days.

The text of the cantata consists of verses from the Old Testament, a few rhymed verses of an occasional hymn, and a verse of a chorale; it first expresses the feelings of a grey-headed servant who longs only to end his days in peace,[21] and who receives benedictions to that effect; it then turns to the governing power of the Almighty, implores Him to protect the city, to grant success to the new ministry, and finally to give health and happiness to the Emperor Joseph. The preponderance of Biblical texts and of the chorale caused Bach to give his composition the title of a *motett*, and not of a *concerto*, the designation which he subsequently most usually adopted. So far as I have discovered, the older sacred cantatas were named only by the first words of the text, and the name *cantata* only came into use with the later form. This title is an instance of the undefined character of the motett at that period; subsequently Bach distinguished exactly between the different classes. By the prefix "*diviso in quatuor chori*" he distinctly indicates the point of view of the older cantatas with regard to the accompaniment, since by this he comprehends the various groups of instruments: three trumpets and drums, two flutes and a violoncello, two oboes and a bassoon, two violins, viola, and bass, used for the most

---

[20] B. G., XVIII., p. 3 to 34. It is evident from what has been said that the cantata should be designated as composed not for an "election" but a "change" of councillors.

[21] Whether among the retiring members there were any very old men, to whom the cantata particularly referred, I cannot tell. The burgomasters for the year 1707 were Johann Georg Stephan and Christian Grabe.

part alternately or *tutti*.[22] The same principle is to be traced in this of a division into a "weaker" and a full orchestra, the full orchestra coming in only in strong passages, and then withdrawing again, and in the score this is termed the *capella*—a recurrence to the terminology of the seventeenth century.

If now we take a comprehensive view of the massive character of the material at command, it is clear how entirely this composition still stands, as to external form, on the same ground as certain church cantatas by Buxtehude; and this makes it all the more interesting to observe how a new spirit pervades the whole. The first chorus ("Gott ist meine König"), C major, sounds at first tolerably familiar, but from the sixteenth bar, where—on the words "der alle Hülfe thut"—"who is our only help"—the voices incessantly follow each other in close imitation, it assumes a new and unusually broad character, which is only weakened somewhat at the close. In the second number (E minor) the tenor sings to an organ accompaniment the words of old Barzillai, II. Samuel, xix. 35 : "I am this day fourscore years old; wherefore then should thy servant be yet a burden to my lord the king? I will turn back, that I may die in my own city, by the grave of my father and of my mother." In opposition to this the soprano gives forth the sixth verse of Hermann's hymn :—

> And should my days be yet
> Extended in their span,
> Should I with stumbling feet
> Tread the last goal of man,
> Then lend me patience, Lord!
> From sin and error save;
> Let my grey hairs go down
> In honour to the grave!

We know that the combination of Bible words with suitable

---

[22] The wood-wind instruments and the violoncello (this last only for convenience) are written in D major, while the cantata is in C major. We see from this that the pitch or the organ of St. Blasius was a whole tone above the ordinary pitch. No transposition was necessary for the trumpets as they were always made to what we should now call concert-pitch (see Mattheson, **Neu eröffnetes Orchestre**).

verses of chorales was no invention of that time. Following Hammerschmidt's precedent, Johann Rudolf Ahle had employed them together with dexterity. Johann Christoph and Michael Bach, with others, had transferred them to the motett; in Buxtehude's cantatas we find an example where Christ and the believing soul converse, though not in simultaneous, yet in alternate musical phrases. All these modes of musical construction are entirely different from the method struck out by Bach. He came to the task, in the first place, approaching the question only from the musical side, his whole development having been derived from the organ; the musical welding of the subject was of the first importance to him, and the chorale-tune naturally the main subject. So little did he direct his attention to the poetical aim of such combinations, that he quite failed to see how the contents of the chorale-verses, chosen in all cases by himself, had properly nothing whatever to do with the feeling of the Bible words. For in one case an old man is speaking, who only longs for a place in which to die in peace, while the other prays that his later years if granted to him may be honourable; the two frames of mind have not much more in common than that they both suit the conception of old age. But still less is there any feeling of dramatic fitness; the fact of the Bible words being intrusted to the tenor voice, and not to the bass, makes it clear that the composer wishes at any rate to give expression to what he himself feels, and not to what would be the emotion of an old man in Barzillai's place. This is borne out still more by the structure of the melody, which, though touching and indeed very expressive, moves up and down in bold steps, nay, even leaps. Even this Bach first conceived instrumentally, and wrote for no technically educated singer, or it could not have escaped him what eccentric expression such a song must acquire when executed by a human voice with all its capabilities of expression at command. It was not long before he detected this great distinction, and in later times his solo songs show the pure gold of a feeling which, though fused in instrumental fire, is still musically poetic, and at the same time he learnt to comprehend the poetic feeling of the interweaving of the words of chorales with passages of Scripture with a depth unapproached by any one before or after him.

Here he offers us at first merely a chorale for the organ constructed on the lines of Buxtehude, but with a vigour and depth of harmony undreamt of by that writer. The piece is strictly speaking a trio for soprano, tenor, and an accompanying organ-bass, in which the parts move with the greatest possible independence—an independence never ventured on before Bach : there appears however another part, in free counterpoint and independent of the harmonies of the general bass, coming in at first in an unobtrusive and echo-like way, and afterwards given out on the choir organ, ultimately forming a quartet. Then comes a double fugue in four parts ; " Dein Alter sei wie dein Jugend," &c. (in A minor), the theme of which, compared with that quoted from the other cantata, is somewhat unmeaning and laboured, and the working-out rather mechanical. The counter-subjects remain tolerably similar throughout the entire fugue, and are only to be distinguished by their position ; the developments[23] are only once interrupted by an episode, and are wound up with a free coda of nine bars long, in which we for the first time trace again the quickening breath of Bach's spirit. This little spot of sterile ground is amply compensated for by a refreshing *arioso* for the bass : " Tag und Nacht sind dein," in F major. Bach deals very arbitrarily with the nomenclatures in the cantata, for the bass solo is a regular *da capo* aria, while the second number, called "*Aria con Corale*," exhibits in the tenor voice an entirely arioso treatment. There may be differences of opinion as to the conception of the words of the text, but the music, as music, is throughout delightful. The treatment of the bass voice in the arioso has still, except in the middle portion, the older stamp, in accordance with which the voice does not move freely through its full compass, but appears for the most part as the basis of the harmonies.

The first part, which returns at the end, has a tender, pastoral character, being accompanied only by the wood

---

23 " Durchführung."

instruments, the violoncello and the organ; a character
which blossomed into full beauty in a charming aria in B
flat major to the words "Was mir behagt," &c., occurring
in a secular cantata composed eight years later. In the
second part the instruments are silent, except the organ;
and the majestic expression of the solo "Du machest, dass
beide, Sonn, und Gestirn, ihren gewissen Lauf haben," forms
a fine musical contrast, and is also well adapted to the words.
Moreover, the arrangement of the whole work bears witness
that the composer knew very well how to produce his effect
by contrasts of sound; and this was no less conspicuous in
his maturer age than in his youth, though from higher considerations, such effects in later times became subordinate.
Now there follows an aria for alto, accompanied only by
three trumpets and drums, without organ, while in the
chorus which follows this, all the instruments except these
are used, the whole of the tone-materials not being reunited
until the final chorus. This alto solo is called "aria"
perhaps because the first phrase with its refrain is heard
again at the close, but it is more strictly an arioso, and
reminds one at last by its superficial melodiousness of the
older German air: we find a hybrid form of similar indefiniteness in the Easter cantata of the year 1704. The
chorus already named (*larghetto*, C minor) is on the other
hand a work full of meaning and individuality. The treatment is homophonic, and its effects are principally due to
the innate expression of the melody and the richly coloured
accompaniment. The semiquavers of the violoncello follow
in arpeggios the harmonic progress of the body of voices; a
running figure in the bassoon part—

gives it the character of weight and coherence, the double-
bass and the organ accompany *staccato*, and the most
expressive phrase of the melody is re-echoed by the flutes
and oboes. In the course of the movement the violoncello
figure is communicated to these instruments, and at last to

all the violins, and they weave rich and fanciful garlands
about the vocal parts, in which—a thought as new it is
effective—all the voices combining in unison declaim the
words first on c', rising then to d' flat, sinking again to b
flat and returning to c', where they die away—the major in
long drawn-out notes.

A terrible expression of suppressed pain is the height to
which the character of the whole piece naturally leads us.
But if we look for the justification of this character in the
text, it is easy to perceive that Bach has coloured the tone-
picture much too darkly.   The words of the psalm: "O
deliver not the soul of thy turtle-dove into the multitude of
the wicked," contains only metaphorically a prayer for protection from the violence of the enemy; and for this prayer,
not less than for the general feeling of the whole cantata, a
calm trustful sentiment is the only fit one. Again, one single
heart, overwhelmed with deep sorrow, expresses itself as a
chorus; the composer has here overshot the mark, and has
so far failed; still, this failure is of the highest psychological
interest, because it betrays unequivocally his own predilection for dark, deeply moved conditions of the soul.   This
chord of his sensitive faculty needed only the lightest touch
to set it in full vibration; the fear of possible danger became
deepened with him (in this case) into the agony of a mind
tormented to the last degree by terror and distress.   Hence
it also follows that no case is found in which Bach's musical
treatment either weakens a really good text or fails to do
it full justice; on the contrary, he is apt to involve himself
too deeply in its meaning, even to the point of abstruseness.
Hence springs his propensity for setting words which have
to do with sorrow and tears, with dying and death; hence
also the faculty by which he is enabled, in a gigantic work
like the St. Matthew Passion, to shadow forth one and the
same feeling in such unheard-of variety of expression.   That
he allowed himself in the chorus of this " Rathswechsel "
cantata to be carried away too far by his subjective bias
must have become plain to him later, when he wrote a chorus
with a precisely similar fundamental idea, nay, with many
similar details (particularly the wailing minor sixths) to the

words, "Weinen, Klagen, Sorgen, Zagen," &c.[24] (Third Sunday after Easter), and afterwards used it again for the heart-rending "Crucifixus" of the B minor Mass. Here, indeed, these tones were in the place to which they had so early and in so startling a manner urged their claim. Even Johann Christoph Bach, rich as he was in earnest and intense feeling, had upon his palette no colours of such glowing fulness. I can only name one who, before Sebastian Bach's time, composed anything approaching this, Philip Heinrich Erlebach, Capellmeister in Rudolstadt (1657-1714). In the first part of his "Harmonischen Freude musikalischer Freunde" (1697), under No. XIV., is found a splendid aria in the cyclic *da capo* form for soprano, with accompaniment of two violins and figured bass, of which the appealing verse expresses the frame of mind of a soul torn by grief. The composition unites broad flowing melody and true German intensity of feeling, and speaks to this day a pathetic language. It comes very near the Bach choruses in expression, resembling the earlier ones in the construction of the principal melody, and the later ones still more in other details.

Circumstances show that Bach may quite well have known Erlebach's collection of arias. On October 28, 1705, the Count von Rudolstadt, commissioned by the Emperor Joseph I., received the homage of the free imperial city of Mühlhausen, and on this occasion the Capellmeister made and performed there a great "Festmusik" (festival composition). Thus Erlebach was known in Mühlhausen, and although we cannot suppose from the character of the inhabitants that he would make many friends there by his music, yet the composition, which contains an excellent chorus, seeming like a prophecy of Handel, was important enough not to be at once forgotten, and it might have had the effect of spurring on Bach to make a nearer acquaintance with Erlebach, if he had not already done so.

But let us turn to the last chorus of the "Rathscantate," to which the direction "*arioso*," intended for only one

---

[24] Cantata zum Sonntage Jubilate, B.S., Vol. II., No. 12.

portion of it, indicates the various changes between the homophonic chorus-passages and the refrains, and between the bars of common time and the others. The most important thing in it is a choral fugue which comes in the middle (the words having reference to the Emperor Joseph), which is so superior to the earlier fugues that they cannot be named together. In those there was hardly anything but scholastic severity—here a fresh, austere vitality reigns. The theme and the counter-subjects—of which two recur so constantly that the piece might even by its musical form be called a triple fugue—are very happily invented; all is united together as if it came from one fount, and increases in richness of sound and in harmonious fulness up to the end. Particularly significant is the co-operation of the orchestra, which shows how clearly Bach even now understood that in the only church style which was possible at that time, the voices and the instruments must be welded together into an essentially coherent whole, so completely that the first should limit and determine the form, as the superior and characterising factors, and yet appear among the instruments, not as masters among servants, but as superiors among equals. He had recognised that the human organ must, as far as possible, divest itself of its personal or, so to speak, dramatic character, and, as much as it can, must become an instrument, without an independent identity, subservient to the lyrical expression of a common religious feeling: with this knowledge all connection with the sentiment and craving for individuality of the older church cantatas was renounced. While others had formerly used the orchestra merely to support, amplify and strengthen the voice-parts and to alternate with them, at the utmost only allowing a high instrument to have an independent part above the choir, Bach gave all the instruments an indispensable part in the fugal working-out. At first the theme is once gone through by the four parts of the semi-chorus, then it is taken by the first violin and oboe, the vocal subject at the same time being carried further; then by the second violin and oboe; now the soprano part of the full choir enters, and the orchestral counterpoint is strengthened, then the remaining parts of the full choir come gradually in, and with them more and more instruments; the harmony meanwhile develops into five and then into six parts, and at last the theme is caught up by the shrill blast of the trumpets, which until then have purposely been kept silent. A more suitable combination of voices and instruments could not be made, nor one more skilfully adapted to increase and heighten the interest up to the end.

The appended coda, which is a repetition of an earlier passage, is, for a composition of Bach's, comparatively uninteresting ; and in estimating this cantata throughout we must necessarily use the standard which the master gives us in his own best works. When compared with the works of his predecessors, it is seen to be 'for the most part far above them and never below them. But in many places we find things of a quite new and original type too decidedly conspicuous for this comparison to be wholly just. That these arose from the only sound and right view we have endeavoured to demonstrate. In the combination of chorale and Bible words Bach disregards everything that is dramatic in order to rise to a general musical idea ; by the reiterated use of strict vocal fugue he indicated that he wished all forms of choral treatment to be centred in this one form, which suppresses as much as possible all personality ; and in the last fugue he endeavours to reduce to a minimum the contrast between the voices and the instruments.

Fugues are very rarely found in the older church cantatas, as is only natural from their character ; and such a fugue as that last discussed was something entirely new, and so were the chorale combinations ; they had only become possible by the fact of their having previously been developed from the art of organ-playing. One must have before one's eyes the vocal fugue-writing of the older masters of that time in order to appreciate properly the immense advance. What little had already been timidly attempted by others before him in this direction vanished before the unfailing certainty with which the twenty-two-year-old Bach comprehended the right and only possible way of treating the subject. Under the decay of unaccompanied vocal music the

organ became the means by which the ideal of devotional art
was kept purest in Germany; from it this ideal was to rise
again with renewed strength, more subjective—since the
musician had had more unlimited command of the dead
instrument than he could have of living men—and so much
the more esoteric and hard to understand as the province
of instrumental music is deeper and more mysterious, but
not on that account the less worthy to express the sublimest religious ideal. The point now was to find the happy
medium, and not to allow the poetic element to be quite
overwhelmed in the waves of pure music.

Directly after the composition and performance of this
cantata, Bach took into consideration a new problem, the
fitting solution of which was of great importance in the
development of church music as he conceived of it. The
organ in the Blasiuskirche—although it had been largely
repaired in the years 1687-1691 by J. F. Wender at a cost of
450 thalers—stood in need of thorough repair—nay, even
of a partial restoration. The number of bellows was insufficient for the size of the organ; the passage of the air into
the wind-chest in the bass had been inadequately fixed;
there was no 32-feet stop, and the pedal trombone had no
strength; in the great organ a number of the stops were
out of order, and the *Brustwerk* had become quite useless.
Bach ascertained all these deficiencies, and presented to the
council a scheme for the repairs mentioned above. As an
entirely new addition he put into his plan a pedal *Glockenspiel* (a peal of twenty-four small bells acted upon by pedals)
invented by himself, in which the parishioners of St. Blasius'
Church took such an interest that they determined to get
it at their own expense.[25] Besides the principal organ
there was in the church a small chamber organ, placed in

---

[25] The subsequent organist of Waldenburg, Voigt, a native of Mühlhausen,
says in his Gespräch von der Musik zwischen einem Organisten und Adjuvanten
(Erfurt, 1742, p. 38): " He (an unknown musician) fell hereupon to talking of
Herr Bach, and if I knew him, as he had learnt that I was a Thuringian and a
native of Mühlhausen, and he, Herr Bach, had been organist of Mühlhausen.
I replied that I well remembered having seen him, though not more than that,
seeing that I was only twelve years old, and had not been there since for thirty

the choir below the organ, which was only used for prac-
tising the choir, or for the unobtrusive accompanying of
motetts, but was not otherwise of use. Bach wished to
employ this in the second theme of the Rathscantate, very
softly, as an echo of the vocal melody, and to introduce it as
a fourth part, probably before he was aware that the performance would not take place in the Blasiuskirche.[26] He
now proposed to give up this little instrument, so as to
obtain the restoration of the large organ, which was the
principal thing, at a less cost. His scheme showed so much
practical knowledge that the council, at a sitting on February 21, not only determined at once to effect the restoration, but charged him in all confidence with the management of the undertaking.[27] As regards the work, it was
again given to Wender, who was prepared to do it for 230
thalers, for which he was also to supply the materials; he
allowed 40 thalers for the little organ. Bach's scheme
testifies to his masterly knowledge of the technicalities of
organ-building, and is also very interesting from its original
and thoroughly artistic style of expression; it is as follows—

Specification of the new Repairs of the Organ of St. Blasius.

1. The defects of the wind to be rectified by three new proper bellows,
   so that justice can be done to the *Oberwerk*, the *Rückpositiv*, and
   the new *Brustwerk*.
2. The four old bellows which still exist must be applied with stronger
   wind power to the new 32-feet stop, and to the other bass stops.
3. The old bass wind-chests must all be taken out and renewed, being
   provided with such arrangements for the passage of the wind that
   a single stop, and then all the stops directly afterwards, can be
   used without changing the wind supply, which heretofore has
   never been done in this way, and yet is very necessary.

---

years. He had added a *Glockenspiel* to the St. Blasius' church, but hardly was
it ready when, to the great indignation of the council of Mühlhausen, he was
summoned to Weimar as Kammer-musicus."

[26] This easily accounts for the fact that in the printed organ part these
passages do not occur. In the Marienkirche they were played on the second or
third manual if there was no separate chamber-organ there; in the latter case
the statement in the text must be modified accordingly.

[27] As is shown by the document as to Bach's demand for his dismissal.

4. The 32-feet wood sub-bass, or the so-called *Untersatz* (support), which gives to the whole organ the greatest weight, comes next. This must have a separate wind-chest.[28]

5. The bass trombone (Posaune) must be furnished with new and large pipes, and the mouthpieces arranged in quite a different way, by which means a much greater gravity of tone can be got.

6. The new *Glockenspiel* on the pedals, which the parishioners wish for, consisting of twenty-six bells of 4-feet tone; which bells the parishioners have already procured at their own cost, and the organ-builder will make them available. As regards the upper manual, there must be put in, instead of the trumpet (which must be taken out) a—

7. Fagotto (bassoon), of 16-feet tone, which shall be available for the new and generally used inventions, and give a very refined tone to the music. Furthermore, instead of the gemshorn, which must be then taken out, let there come a—

8. Viol di gamba, 8 feet, which may agree in admirable concord with the existing salicional, 4 feet, on the choir. Also, instead of the 3-feet quint, which must likewise be taken out, let a 3-feet—

9. Nassat (nason) be put in. The other existing stops of the upper manual may remain, as well as the whole of those in the choir, though they must be newly voiced throughout in the course of the alterations.

10. The following stops will be the essential part of the new front choir-organ (*Brustpositiv*) :—

In the front of it three principal stops, viz.—

    1. Quint, 3 feet,   ⎫
    2. Octave, 2 feet,   ⎬ made of good 7-oz. tin.
    3. Schalemoy,[29] 2 feet, ⎭

    4. Mixture. Three ranks.

    5. Tertia, with which in combination with several other stops, a good full " sesquialtera " tone may be obtained.

    6. " Fleute douce," 4 feet; and lastly a—

    7. Stillgedackt, 8 feet (*i.e.*, a soft gedackt), which may sound well in combination, and if made of good wood will sound much better than a metal gedackt.

11. There must be a coupler to combine these (front choir and the swell) manuals. And last of all, besides the thorough voicing of the whole organ, the tremulant must be so put right that its action may be regular.

Thus Bach displayed on every occasion his earnest

---

[28] *I.e.*, Because there would be no room in the principal chest for this newly introduced stop.

[29] *I.e.*, the Chalumeau.

desire to do his part in the interests of church music.   But
hindrances soon came in the way of his zeal, and these in
the course of a few months must have increased so greatly
that he could already make up his mind, in the summer of
that year, to leave unfinished the work he had begun with
so much ardour.   In his application for dismissal he speaks
of "obstacles which had beset him, and which would not
be removed by any means so easily."   By this we must
understand in the first place the disposition of a portion of
the municipality of Mühlhausen which clung to old fashions
and customs, and neither could nor would follow Bach's
bold flights, and even looked askance at the stranger who
conducted himself so despotically in a position which, as
far back as the memory of man extended, had always been
filled by a native of the city, and for its sole honour and
glory.   In proportion as the inhabitants watched with pride
and delight the acts and deeds of any distinguished fellow-
citizen, they were wont—some of them at least—to be cold
and repellent to anything that came from outside.   It was
noted as a matter of great moment in a MS. chronicle of
the year 1794 that, at the consecration of the church of St.
Mary Magdalen in the year 1704, Johann Georg Ahle had
composed the hymn "Lobt ihr frommen."   But the same
chronicler takes no notice of Erlebach's grand composition
performed in the following year.   And when we read that
Bach's successor, Christoph Bieler, of Schmalkalden, com-
plained to the council of " the strange ways of the people,"
and that " he was met rather as a foe than as a friend," it
seems probable that Bach may occasionally have met with
the same treatment.   The greatest grievance was when the
neighbouring towns were put forward as a model of musical
productiveness, and worthy of imitation; for a certain antagonism existed between Mühlhausen especially and Langula
with the other villages of the jurisdiction—an antagonism
which, as I have been informed, has not altogether ceased at
the present day.   But, after all, these were not essential
matters when the proceedings of a great artist were in question, and Bach on the other hand enjoyed the favour of a
highly estimable council — indeed private friendships were

never lacking to him.[80] Certain occurrences however prove
that all sorts of conflicts arose between him and the spiritual
authority of the city, namely, the Superintendent and chief
preacher of the church of St. Blasius; and that in these
disputes their different views as to church music played an
essential, or perhaps the most important part. If Bach
found himself fettered and hindered in his aspirations by his
immediate ecclesiastical superiors, it is easy to understand
how his position might soon have become thoroughly painful
to him.

It was at this period that the religious struggles between
Spener's pietism and the old Lutheran orthodoxy were
raging everywhere, and were carried on by the Lutherans
with increasing vehemence as, year by year, pietism gained
a broader foothold among the German people. In Arnstadt
it is true it had only struck temporary root, as has been
already said, and after the death of Drese it had not been
able to stand against the hostility of the two Olearius, father
and son; but it was different in Mühlhausen. J. A. Frohne,
Diaconus, or Dean, of Mühlhausen from 1684, and who succeeded his father as Superintendent in 1691, had for many
years, under the influence of Spener, worked eagerly and
without any opposition to rouse a deeply Christian frame of
mind and course of life in himself and others. Spener's
Pia Desideria (1675), which gave the impetus to the whole
religious movement, at first had met with no contradiction,
but had even found full acceptance on the part of many
judicious theologians; it was not till the theory was carried

---

[80] Thus when Friedemann Bach (born November 22, 1710) was baptised, the
godparents were: " Frau Anna Dorothea Hagedorn, wife of Herr Gottfried
Hagedorn, *J.*[*uris*] *U.*[*triusque*] *Candidati* in Mühlhaussen," and " Herr
Friedemann Meckbach, *J. U.* doctor in Mühlhaussen " (Parish-register of
Weimar). Herr Krug, of Naumburg, possesses an interesting relic in what has
been the fly-leaf of a bound book out of Bach's private library ; to the right,
in his own elegant handwriting, are the words, "*ex libera donatione Dn.
Oehmii | me possidet Joh. Seb. Bach.*" The Oehme family, in many branches,
formerly resided at Mühlhausen, and still exist there. This leaf, with the rest
of the book, was in the possession of Herr Koberstein, the historian of literature
at Schulpforte; the fly-leaf he gave away, the book was sold by auction at his
death, with his other books, and it has not been possible to ascertain even
what its contents were.

out vigorously in practice, and the rigidly orthodox were
unpleasantly disturbed in their self-satisfied peace and
unfruitful conceit, that the opposition was begun, with a
combination of small intelligence and great hatred.

This was exactly what occurred in Mühlhausen. In
the year 1699 there came from Heldrungen, where he had
been superintendent, G. Chr. Eilmar, to be *Archidiaconus* and
pastor of the church of the Blessed Virgin; he, though
thirteen years younger than Frohne, was thoroughly inimical
to the eager and active spirit of pietism, and was in a desperate
hurry to prove himself so. In a sermon preached by him, as
a stranger, on Sexagesima Sunday, he had taken up so
offensive an attitude towards Frohne, whose views he must
have known, even finding himself supported on certain
points by the municipal authorities, that Frohne thought
he ought not to look on quietly at such an agitation and
disturbance of men's minds. Eilmar's reproofs had chiefly
borne upon the relation of the pietists to the Bible: that it was
heretical to pray for special enlightenment when reading the
Scriptures, since the Holy Ghost dwelt in the very words of
the Bible; that there was no distinction to be made between
the outward and the inward word; that the pietists held the
word of God to be a dead letter; that those contemners of
the Church and the Bible held that they could be justified
by the mediation of the ministry alone, without personal
conversion and edification. And this certainly was the standpoint of orthodoxy to which they had been driven to subscribe, by the struggle. The first principle of Lutheranism
was already lost to them; the Church was to them almost
as to the Catholics, something perfect and divine, whose
means of grace her children need only receive passively,
and whose ministers considered themselves as the bearers
of a divine official gift which was perfectly independent of
their moral conduct; while pietism, on the contrary, strove to
develop afresh the fundamental idea of Protestantism. When
Frohne came forward to support his views against Eilmar he
could declare with justice that he stood firm on an orthodox
basis, and in his pamphlet of August 12, 1700, could show
reason for repudiating the "false imputation spread abroad

against him, that he was lapsing from evangelical orthodoxy and was given up to Chiliasm and all sorts of innovations." For there was nothing to be found in them, any more than in Spener's *Pia Desideria*, which might not be logically deduced from the fundamental principles of the Protestant Church, and in his official capacity he would certainly never have favoured any separatist extravagances.

The contention which broke out in flames immediately after Eilmar's sermon, and which seems to have caught the other ecclesiastics of the city, soon, however, came to an end for a time, for on May 23 of the same year the council promulgated a very moderate order to the effect that all ministers were to refrain from controversy in their public discourses; and if any one of them noted anything " suspicious " in a colleague, he was to notify it in writing to the consistory, " to the end that such errors might meet with friendly and brotherly correction, and that all other anxious and vexatious proceedings and disorders might be avoided." Most estimable and moderate views, no doubt; and indeed the council throughout this period constantly showed its tact and moderation. But a few years later the squabble broke out again, in speech and on paper. Who began it cannot be decided—each party declared itself to have been first attacked; but, though there may have been faults on both sides, they certainly were not equally divided, and the information derived from the tolerably abundant materials before us is such that the unprejudiced reader cannot doubt to which side his sympathies must lean.

Eilmar stands forth as a worthy partisan of the collective orthodoxy opposed to Spener: hard, bigoted, and sunk in rigid and lifeless formalism. Nowhere can we find a trace of warm religious sentiment; nothing but an unrefreshing and lifeless doctrine, pedantry, scholastic logic, litigious verbosity, and conspicuous coarseness.

Frohne was a man of lively religious feeling, and of great moral courage and severity as regarded both himself and others. This made him obnoxious and hateful to a large number of the citizens, who of course sided with Eilmar, and who had influence enough after Frohne's death to procure him his place. Under any circumstances it rouses us to esteem when we see a man of honest convictions, independently arrived at, contending against the tendencies of his time, and exposed to every sort of insult in return for his conscientiousness ; and to this esteem is added sincere pleasure when in the contest he displays mildness and moderation. This was the case with Frohne—who was by this time old, feeble, and becoming blind—in his written remonstrances to the council, and he had the satisfaction of seeing them take his side very decidedly. Though they twice or thrice admonished him, this only proves their impartiality ; otherwise they entirely disapproved of Eilmar's movement.

The quarrel was ultimately made up by the decision of the disinterested Faculties. Frohne expressly declared himself willing to be pacified in any case if only Eilmar were persuaded to the same. This judgment was pronounced in the council, May 8, 1708, and communicated to the two ministers on the following day ; but no report has been preserved as to how it fell out. Frohne died November 12, 1713, aged 61 ; Eilmar died two years later.[81]

Who that has ever endeavoured to reproduce in his own mind some image of the personal characteristics of the master from his works would not immediately have supposed that in these lamentable dissensions Bach would have stood by the Superintendent and chief preacher in word and in feeling ? And yet the very reverse was the case. In the entry on the parish register of the birth of his first child, which took place in the same year at Weimar, we read first and foremost among the sponsors, " Herr Doctor Georg Christian Eilmar, *Pastor primarius* in the church of the Blessed Virgin, and *Consistorii Assessor* at Mühlhausen."

A careful consideration of the godfathers and godmothers chosen by Bach for his children is of no small importance, because each reveals certain relations, at any rate for the time, to different persons. The principle of selecting near

---

[81] Altenburg, Beschreibung der Stadt Mühlhausen (Description of the City of Mühlhausen) ; and a quatrain in his honour was written by Joh. Gottfried Krause, Poetische Blumen (Langensaltza, 1716, p. 117.)

relations or friends, or persons otherwise trustworthy, has of course always been the same; moreover, in the circle of society to which Bach belonged such events were—and are still—celebrated with special solemnity, and this was the case in direct proportion as the mode of life was patriarchal in its character. That he should, therefore, have regarded the office of first sponsor to his eldest-born child as one of distinguished honour is quite intelligible, and Eilmar figures here by the side of the musician's nearest relatives. As Bach was at this time Court Organist at Weimar, and in no official position as regards Mühlhausen, this step must have resulted from a quite independent decision, and must be considered as an expression of sincere and hearty conviction. Indeed, it is beyond dispute that Bach was an adherent and admirer of Eilmar, and consequently, as things stood, more or less inimical to Frohne. How this could be we cannot but ask with surprise, for is not Bach's leaning towards pietism supposed to be an ascertained fact? It is in fact supposed to be established from certain internal coincidences of evidence. But it never seems to have been duly considered whether the pietistic views of art and life must not from the very outset have counteracted any such bias in his mind. All art, as art, asserting itself for its own sake, in the mind of the pietist fell under the designation of "the world" to which, as they deemed, every true Christian must find himself in primitive, direct antagonism; they declared with more or less unreserve that the artistic pleasures, which orthodoxy regarded as indifferent ($\dot{\alpha}\delta\iota\dot{\alpha}\phi o\rho\alpha$), and in themselves neither good nor evil, but capable of becoming either one or the other according to circumstances, could not be reconciled with a way of life of which every instant should be answered for before God, and that they were therefore to be avoided as tending to seduce and destroy the soul. It was only in so far as art devoted herself unselfishly, so to speak, to the service of religion, and contributed to individual edification and awakening, that it could escape condemnation. With regard to music, therefore, in pietist circles, nothing was encouraged but "spiritual songs" of the narrowest type, which followed the verse as closely and simply as possible, and at the same time were utterly opposed to all sentiment. Every attempt tending to extend the forms of church music as an art, and to combine them into a more massive whole, or to introduce entirely new forms borrowed from the denounced music of operas, must have appeared, from the pietist point of view, absolutely reprobate. For all that in the best instances might be detected in these as an edifying and elevating power was, as they could not fail to see, by no means that contemplative " drawing near " to God which they sought for, and thought could only be found by abnegation of the "world"; it had only grown up as the embodiment and idealisation of historical development. Now Bach saw, as he himself admits, that it was part of his life-task to raise sacred music to a new and higher aim, by fusing all that had been hitherto produced ; and it was precisely in Mühlhausen that he first began to work energetically and with eager inspiration to that end. Since Frohne, according to his convictions, could only endure such an advance to a very moderate degree, he could not but endeavour to suppress the luxuriant productive power of the great musician, and probably never guessed that in so doing he was choking his very life-currents. Here was an antagonism in principles enough of itself to send Bach over from the camp of a noble minister of the church to the side of his opponent. It would also seem that Eilmar had musical tastes, and was in favour of the development of church music on new lines.[32]

But we must go still farther, and assert that Bach had never been of Frohne's party, and had not been forced to attach himself to Eilmar by flying for his life—in the sense of his art. The close connection which he soon established between Eilmar and his own family requires us to assume that they had some feelings and opinions in common ; and

---

[32] Mattheson (Der Musikalische Patriot, 1728, p. 151) mentions a book by Eilmar, published at Brunswick in 1701, The Golden Jewel of the Evangelical Churches (Güldenes Kleinod Evangelischer Kirchen), in which the writer is zealous against the pietists. His defence of the modern church music proved of great service, and he therefore gives a few sentences out of it: this would not have happened amid the mass of writings to which this gave rise unless he had been sure of Eilmar's concurrence.

I need hardly here remind the reader that in the doctrine of regeneration by baptism the views of the pietists and of the orthodox were distinctly opposed. The religious traditions of the Bach family—a simple but deep and living Protestantism, which had been strengthened and rooted by a long course of labours in the service of the Church—had of course been implanted unaltered in the soul of Sebastian as a child. His education under the eye of his elder brother and in the highly orthodox lyceum (or college) of Ohrdruf was not calculated to modify his views. In Arnstadt, in the same way, the atmosphere was wholly unfavourable to pietism; and as the zealots suspected it of being a complete revolution against the pure doctrine that had come down to them from their fathers, Bach must have been strongly opposed to it. He undoubtedly can never have tested its principles, for he can hardly have experienced any religious need which could not be amply satisfied by the creed of his fathers. Everything beyond that he found in art and in his own artist's calling. Beyond question he sometimes expressed himself in these in a way which closely touched on certain aspects of pietism; the mysticism in which he shrouds himself in the texts of his works, particularly in Bible texts, is closely allied to the fervid devotion with which the pietist read the sacred Scriptures. That transcendental vein which made him so ready to dwell on the annihilation of this mortal existence through death and on the joys of heavenly bliss, corresponds very nearly to the attitude taken up by Spener's followers, of "looking for the glorious reign of Christ." Nay, and their craving—at any rate at times—to enjoy a perfect and immediate communion with God, and to feel in themselves the ecstatic consciousness of the infinity of the Divine spirit, has its counterpart in Bach's instrumental music.

It is the proper function of this form of art to give an idealised image of only the most comprehensive and general facts of all human experience; and of all forms of tone-utterance the organ is the least amenable to the stamp of the artist's individuality. A composition of this kind is in truth the symbol of that sempiternal harmony whose mighty waves flow from and to God Himself; to bring this near to and into the human soul without the intrusion of any incidentally associated idea, to grasp it with subjective fervour, and to glow with its inward fire, is the beginning of an impulse similar to that with which the pious soul on fire with devotion seeks to apprehend the unapproachable and incomprehensible divinity of God without the intervention of the Church. How fully Bach attained this is proved by his freely conceived fugues for the organ, which even to this day must appear to every one permeated by devout fervour and a wonderful vitality in spite of their severity, like rocks flooded with a sunset glow. But all these were not the outcome of pietist religious views; they were only the revelation of an analogous tendency, a growth from the same root of German vital feeling, but in the domain of art. And indeed we find side by side with the marks of identity the widest differences; the firmest suppression of subjective demonstrativeness under the severest conceivable forms, a wholesome worldliness in recognising and utilising all that was around him and before him, and in his vigorous enjoyment of his own existence — a characteristic inherited from his forefathers. If all that pietism held of beauty, goodness and truth was most purely embodied—even at that time perhaps —in Bach's music, this could only be because its creator was no pietist. Not indeed that this could have been the case if he had been sternly opposed to pietism; but this in fact can never have been the case. His religious standpoint was above all contentions, something more catholic and sublime, as became so catholic a genius; and though the tradition of his family and the love of his art kept him in the ranks of the orthodox, nothing could be more false than to regard him as a fanatical partisan. Might we not ask indeed whether music so full of vitality and purpose as his ever could submit to an union with the dead and empty semblance of Christianity of Eilmar and his associates?

The pietist mode of expression in Bach's cantatas and in the text of the Passion music is often interpreted as though the composer had here felt himself in the element he loved. But this language, now for the first time appealing with warmth to the heart, had taken general possession of every one who bore in his soul a spark of poetry, and it would be very delightful if all the verse composed to by Bach had been pitched in that tone; we could take into the bargain much redundancy and want of taste, particularly as they would be almost lost in the flood of music or eliminated without much trouble. In point of fact, among the writers of Bach's texts, so far as they have hitherto been identified, there was not one pietist ; nor indeed could there have been, since to them all the new church cantatas were a sinful abomination ; on the contrary, the real originator of this form, so far as it took the aspect of verse, was one of the most zealous champions of orthodoxy. A good authority—in most things highly competent to judge—has attempted to show that Bach had a share in Freylinghausen's hymn-book, both as an original composer and as improving the contributions of others.[33]

Johann Anastasius Freylinghausen, son-in-law and assistant minister to August Hermann Francke (and after Francke's death pastor himself of St. Ulrich's Church, and director of the orphanage founded by Francke at Halle), published, in the year 1704, a "Spiritual Song-book," containing "the substance of old and new hymns, as also the notes of the unfamiliar melodies." Since the end of the sixteenth century, Halle, by the instrumentality of men like Francke and Breithaupt, had become a great centre of pietism, and this book, published "for the arousing of sacred devotion, and for edification in the faith and in a godly mind," was the full utterance of that religious view. It found a wonderfully wide distribution ; edition followed edition, and in 1714, in spite of the virulent attacks of the hostile party, a second part appeared as the "New Spiritual Song-book," which also met with the greatest favour ; in 1741, two years after Freylinghausen's death, this was combined with the first part by Francke's son, forming a collection of above 1,600 hymns, with more than 600 melodies.

---

[33] Winterfeld, Vol. III., pp. 270-276.

The statement that Bach took part in the musical portion of this hymn-book, which, from the master's pronounced attitude from the first towards pietism, we must regard as more than doubtful, rests on a certain "Musical Hymn-book" published for Georg Christian Schemelli, cantor of the castle at Zeitz, by Christoph Breitkopf, of Leipzig, in 1736; in this are sixty-nine tunes which, says the preface, were all either newly composed or partly improved in their thorough-bass by Sebastian Bach. An exact examination proves that forty of these melodies are to be found in earlier sources, and eighteen of them actually occur for the first time in Freylinghausen's hymn-book.[84] Bach's co-operation in this would thus be proved only on condition of proving his authorship of these eighteen tunes, or of some of them. But so far as regards the first edition, Freylinghausen's own words invalidate this attempt, since in the preface he says: "It has been thought unnecessary to add the melodies in notes to the old church hymns in general use; but the new ones are all provided with tunes, partly taken from the Darmstadt hymn-book, and partly newly composed expressly for this work, by Christian and experienced musicians of this place." This preface is dated September 22, 1703, from Glaucha, a suburb of Halle. Bach was at that time eighteen years old, and Organist at Arnstadt; thus it is simply impossible that he should be included as "an experienced musician of this place," i.e., Halle. Thus all the tunes which first appeared in the earliest edition are put out of the question, and these form no less than half of the remaining nine; three occur in the fifth editon of 1710, which in its preface has the general remark repeated, that "all the melodies have been again diligently revised according to the rules of composition by experienced and Christian musicians, and improved in many places."

One of these melodies (No. 436, "Seelenweide meine Freude,") ought then to serve as a chief piece of evidence. To this hymn, by Adam Drese, was subjoined in the first

---

[84] Not nineteen; Winterfeld has by accident counted No. 284 (in Schemelli— No. 94 in Freylinghausen) twice over.

two editions a tune in the Ionic metre (◡ ◡ _ _), probably devised by the poet himself; but its dancelike character had been eliminated by the time it reached the third edition (1706) by a change into common time. The fifth edition gives us an entirely new tune, and as it was erroneously believed that Bach was still living in Arnstadt, together with Drese, and stood in some connection with him, the idea arose that he was the composer. This seemed to be further proved by the fact that the melody occurs in Schemelli's hymn-book almost unaltered, while comparison shows that Bach made abundant changes in melodies which can be proved not to be his, especially in the treatment of the bass; and this in his own composition he might not have thought necessary. But even this criterion turns out to be useless, for it was part of Bach's nature to supply new harmonies to his own melodies as well as to those of others, as often as they came under his hand; among others, this is proved by the tunes of his own invention to "Dir, dir, Jehovah will ich singen" and "Gieb dich zufrieden und sei stille," both of which exist in two different and equally masterly settings; and of melodies by other writers instances innumerable testify that his various modes of setting did not spring from an effort to improve what was defective, but generally from the urgent prompting of his creative fancy. Moreover, it must be added that the other two melodies which remain in Freylinghausen's fifth edition, and occur again in Schemelli's hymn-book,[35] are found in the latter with an entirely different bass and harmonies, and even with several altered passages in the melodies; so that any conclusion we might seem to derive from the former melody is, by this alone, entirely lost to us again.[36]   Finally, it must

---

[35] Nos. 592 and 614 in Freylinghausen, "Die Güldne Sonne" and "Der lieben Sonnen Licht."

[36] Winterfeld is in error in stating that these two last melodies already existed in the first edition of the hymn-book, for there the old tune by Ebeling is given to Gerhard's morning hymn, and Scriver's evening hymn has a melody which is new and quite different from the old one. The index given on p. 271 must be altered as follows: Nos. 108, 121, 463, 475, 522, 572, 580, 700, 779 in Schemelli, correspond to Nos. 363, 278, 349, 461, 659, 515, 405, 353, 412 in

be said that even the style of Drese's hymn in Schemelli shows a few not important deviations.

But even if all these objections are thought insufficient, the following is surely decisive.[37] It was the fifth edition which was to be distinguished from the first edition by the insertion of the melodies. It was not observed that the fifth is merely a word for word reissue of the fourth, which appeared in 1708. The utter impossibility of Bach having, in that particular year—when he was ranged on the side of orthodoxy in a bitter struggle between an orthodox minister and a pietist—taken any part in an undertaking so violently disputed over by the antagonists, must be evident to every one. Thus the whole fabric of conjecture falls to pieces at once. For the probability of his co-operation must be less in proportion as the number of the melodies dwindles in which it seems at all possible. Here one reason supports the other, and now for the last six tunes there is no evidence but on the very untrustworthy ground of resemblance in the harmonies, which indeed, as I have shown, is not even to any extent present. If at the beginning of the work Bach was opposed to it, and always remained aloof from its managers, how could it be possible that they should desire his assistance as it went forward ? And finally, if we reflect that this hymn-book of Schemelli's was publicly said to be a counterpart to that of Freylinghausen, and indeed a compromise between the two parties, since, in point of fact, hymns by the leaders of the pietists as well as of the orthodox party stand in it peaceably side by side—one[38] even is by Freylinghausen himself—it becomes intelligible how Bach got the credit of Freylinghausen's eighteen melodies, and also, how the musical rearrangement of this latter hymn-book might

---

Freylinghausen's first edition, 1704.   Schemelli's Nos. 13, 19, 710, answer to 592, 614, 438, in Freylinghausen's fifth edition, 1710.   The index to the first edition of the second part, 1714, is correct.

[37] Compare Winterfeld, p. 14.   Not twenty-three, but only nineteen hymns have had new tunes set to them ; No. 662 is transposed from major to minor, and some others are set to a more convenient pitch.

[38] No. 496 (" Mein Herz, gieb dich zufrieden ") signed J. A. Fr. It is to be found in the second part as No. 450.   In Schemelli's hymn-book, No. 798, August Hermann Francke's hymn (" Gottlob, ein Schritt zur Ewigkeit ") is introduced.

have been attributed to him, his absence of all partisanship
in religion being well known.   But that he never had the
smallest direct part in Freylinghausen's collection of hymns
may for the future be regarded as an incontestable fact.

Some few months had elapsed since Bach had obtained
permission from the council to repair the organ, and he had
at once set to work with vigour.   During this time it had
become clear to him that he could not remain in Mühlhausen.
A new sphere of action was opened to him sooner than he
could have hoped ; the post of organist in his old and
familiar home, Weimar, fell vacant, and as in any case it
must have been his object to make himself more extensively
known as a musician, he decided on introducing himself
at the ducal court, and made the excursion serve another
purpose as well.   On June 5, Stauber, the minister, was
to celebrate his second marriage, with Regina Wedemann,
the aunt of Bach's wife.   It occurred to Sebastian to grace
the occasion for this worthy man—who a year before had
blest his own union, and who was now entering on a closer
relationship with him—by the production of a cantata. Since
he gave in his resignation at Mühlhausen on June 25, he
must have gone to Arnstadt first, and certainly took his wife
with him ; she then either remained there with her friends,
or else went with him to Dornheim, whence her husband
fetched her again upon his return from Weimar.

The cantata which is here to be discussed, is written to
the words : " Der Herr denket an uns," &c. (" The Lord hath
been mindful of us, and He will bless us "—Ps. cxv. 12-15) [39]
and bears, in its manuscript form, no mark of its destination ; nay, the conclusion that a cantata was written by
Bach at all for that day is only arrived at by combining
several very plain indications.   That the work belongs to
Bach's earliest period will be at once admitted by every
one who has clearly learnt to appreciate certain differences
of style ; as also the fact that it refers to some marriage
festival.   The idea that it is designed for an ordinary marriage is improbable from the words of the text : " The Lord

---

[39] B. G., XIII., 1, pp. 73-94.

increase you more and more, you and your children," and one cannot suppose it was meant for an anniversary festival where there was no religious ceremony. But everything well befits the second marriage of a widower surrounded with children, as Stauber was. And besides, the passage in the psalm applies directly to the house of Aaron, and so is sufficiently appropriate to account for its use in the cantata, and especially finds its exact application to a clergyman from the words, " Ye are the blessed of the Lord which made heaven and earth." The opportunity of composing a cantata for the second marriage of a preacher did not offer itself so often, at all events in the first years of Bach's " master " period, that the exactly fitting conditions in this case can be disregarded. The work is composed of two choruses, between which are inserted an air and a duet. The only instruments used are strings and organ, which begin with a symphony built upon the first subject of the opening chorus; this is gone through on the two violins in short sections, always joined together by two bars of a transitional character. In general two distinct modes of treatment are noticeable in Bach's church symphonies or sonatas. The chief characteristic of the one (which is the older) is, that above the progressions of the harmonies, which sometimes consist of broad chords, sometimes of soft suspensions, two upper parts are written in expressive and *cantabile* imitations. The later form is closely connected with the construction of an instrumental " concerto," and is an ingenious transportation from the province of secular music ; while the earlier method, in which Bach continued the structure begun by his predecessors, takes its rise entirely from religious music. We may regard his achievements in this particular direction as the perfect climax of the Gabrieli sonata-form ; the harmonic masses indeed are still disguised from view, but the vast skeleton is adorned with the blossoms and tendrils of the newer instrumental polyphony. The symphony of the cantata under notice belongs to this older class, although the tenors and cellos have a more prominent share in the counterpoint than has fallen to them in other cases; the part-writing is excellent and flowing.

The four vocal pieces are full of that tender and feeling
expression which is common to the older cantatas, and
may here be accounted for by the purpose of the composition. Both choruses are fugal; the first begins with a
section in free imitation, where the interweaving of the
voices is twice interrupted by the instruments *tutti;* even
from this touch, taken in connection with other similar
passages and the interludes in the last chorus, one can
infer the early origin of this work. The fugue, in which
the theme is answered with a freedom which Bach never
afterwards permitted himself to use, corresponds closely, in
the interweaving of the instruments, to the last movement
of the " Rathswechsel " cantata; at the end the section
with which the number began comes in again like a refrain.
The aria is of a compact *da capo* form and of less importance, the words of the text being too few to serve for a
more extended piece. Much warmer and more captivating is
the duet for tenor and bass: " Der Herr segne euch," &c., a
piece full of genuine evangelic benignity; such Bach never
again wrote. A soft, broadly flowing melody, which carries
as it were in itself the imitation of a second voice, runs, sometimes instrumentally, sometimes vocally, almost through the
whole duet; and though the regular alternations between
the two tone mediums give it an antiquated stamp, they are
interwoven so dexterously and with such genius that Bach's
later manner is plainly foreshadowed in them. The close is
surprisingly beautiful, where, after an apparently final refrain,
the voices give one more last benediction, while the violins
descend in *arpeggio* passages through four octaves on the
chord of C major. The final chorus, which begins with a
homophonous passage, over which there is a brilliant instrumental figure, changes after sixteen bars to a double fugue
(on " *Amen* "), full of freshness and vigour, the effect of
which is indeed somewhat injured perhaps by a few passages
conceived too instrumentally; it is also wanting in breadth
and continuity, since in its development the work is divided
into too short sections between the voices and the instruments used alternately, and the voices and instruments used
together. This was a part of his inheritance from his pre-

decessors, which Bach only appropriated as his own in the course of time, though even now it had begun to yield him good interest. There is a very splendid and bold passage where (in the fifty-fourth bar) both the violins attack the chief theme on *c'''*, while all the other instruments have a rushing accompaniment of confused semiquavers and quavers; it has all the glitter of a knightly hero on a prancing charger. But the gently dying close leads back beautifully into the fundamental idea of the whole. Compared with the "Rathswechsel" cantata, this one has less richness, but a greater unity, and it is a precious production of true religious feeling. And as it was free from the difficulties of most of Bach's works, it was soon taken into favour by the art world, like its slightly younger brother, the beautiful and earnest *Actus tragicus*.

The appointment to Weimar was an auspicious circumstance, and Bach, thankful and overjoyed at this unlooked-for and happy change, hastened to break off his connection with Mühlhausen. The only thing which troubled him was the parting from the council, who had always been well-disposed towards him, and to whom he felt grateful. This is plainly seen in his very polite demand for dismissal:—

Magnifice, High and very Noble, High and very Learned, High and Respected Gentlemen. [40]

Most Gracious *Patroni* and Gentlemen,

This is to represent to your *Magnificenz*, and to my highly esteemed *Patrons* who of your grace bestowed on me, your humble servant, the office, vacant a year since, of *Organist* to the church of *St. Blasius*, and of your favour granted me to enjoy a better subsistence, that at all times I desire to recognise your favours with obedient gratitude. But although I have always kept one end in view, namely, with all good will to conduct well-ordered church *music* to the honour of God and in agreement with your desires, and otherwise to assist, so far as was possible to my humble ability, the church music which has grown up in almost all the parishes round, and which is often better than the harmony produced here, and to that end have obtained from far and wide, and not without

---

[40] This is an approximate rendering of the titles attributed to the patrons, each in his degree, of the office held by Bach: 1st, the burgomaster, who was president of the church committee; 2nd, the town-councillors; 3rd, the literates; 4th, the citizens. In the original all the words in italics are of foreign derivation.

expense a good *apparatus* [collection] of the choicest church pieces, and no less have, as is my duty, laid before you the *project* [estimate] of the defects necessary to be remedied in the organ, and at all times and places have with pleasure fulfilled the duties of my office. Still this has not been done without difficulty, and at this time there is not the slightest appearance that things will be altered,[41] although in the future at this church, even I have humbly to represent that, modest as is my way of life, with the payment of house-rent and other indispensable articles of consumption,[42] I can with difficulty live.

Now God has so ordered it that a change has unexpectedly been put into my hands, in which I foresee the attainment of a more sufficient subsistence and the pursuit of my aims as regards the due ordering of church music without vexation from others, since his Royal and Serene Highness of Saxe-Weimar has graciously offered me the *entrée* to his Court Capelle and chamber music.

In consequence of this privilege I hereby, with obedience and *respect*, represent it to my most gracious patrons, and at the same time would ask them to take my small services to the church up to this time into favourable consideration, and to grant me the benefit of providing me with a good *dimission* [testimonial]. If I can in any way farther contribute to the service of your church I will prove myself better in deed than in word, so long as life shall endure.

Most honourable gentlemen,
Most gracious *Patrons* and gentlemen,
Your most humble servant,
JOH. SEB. BACH.

Mühlhausen, June 25, anno 1708.

[Addressed :]

To all and each respectively of the very high and highly esteemed gentlemen, the ministers of the church of St. Blasius, The memorial of their humble servant.

Unwillingly, but with liberality, the council on the following day granted the dismissal, with the proviso, however, that Bach should promise to give his further assistance in the completion of the repairs of the organ. Since the new "Brustpositiv," as the document quoted above tells us, was not ready till 1709, Bach must during this time have come over from Weimar once at least, but probably oftener. Moreover, the town of Mühlhausen was remembered with

---

[41] Bach's salary was higher than his predecessor's.

[42] Ahle had had a house of his own. Generally rent was paid as part of the salary. Bieler had twelve thalers a year on that account, besides many other small revenues in money and in kind.

pleasure by him all his life long; and even after a period of more than twenty-five years he was induced by the "former favours of the council," to make an application on behalf of his son Bernhard, for the post of Organist to the Marien-kirche. In the post he had given up he was succeeded, as has been said, by his cousin Johann Friedrich Bach.

II.

BACH AT WEIMAR.—HIS FRIENDS AND COMPANIONS.

AMONG the petty rulers of central Germany, as it existed at that time—men who for the most part belied their nationality as much as possible, who had an eye to their own advantage only, and had no conception of the duties of a sovereign—Duke Wilhelm Ernst of Saxe-Weimar stands forth as an independent, conscientious individuality of great depth of character. He had already reigned from the year 1683, and when Bach was called to Weimar by him he was in his forty-sixth year. Separated from his wife after a short and unhappy union, he lived childless and in retirement at Wilhelmsburg, the ducal residence of Weimar. His court was held with much simplicity, his tastes being opposed to all noisy and splendid pleasures; by nine o'clock in the evening in the summer, and by eight in winter, all was silent in the castle. The less time and money he needed for his personal expenditure the more freely he could give himself up to the concerns of his little territory, and he was especially occupied with his care for the affairs of the church and of education. The character of Wilhelm Ernst was eminently that of a religious churchman. Even as a boy he had strongly manifested this feature, for in his eighth year, under the direction of the court preacher, he had preached a regular sermon before his parents and a select gathering, on the text Acts xvi. 33, "with great address and with extraordinary boldness and much grace" as we are told. His reign of forty-five years is full, from beginning to end, of a series of admirable projects and enactments of this character, which to this day have kept his memory green.

In 1713 he had the old ruined church of Saint James rebuilt; in 1712 he transformed the old city school into the gymnasium or college which still exists, and provided it with a new building and benevolent endowments for the maintenance of poor scholars; and again, two years before his death, he founded a seminary for preachers and teachers; on October 30, 1717, the two hundredth Jubilee-festival of the Reformation, on which day he also kept his birthday, he invested a sum of which the interest was to accrue yearly to the ministers, teachers, scholars, and poor; and to commemorate it he had a medal struck bearing on the obverse his own head—a sharply-cut and meagre face, with a retreating forehead, a large prominent nose, and a somewhat projecting chin. He reintroduced the custom of confirming young persons, which for more than a century and a half had fallen into desuetude, and urged on the clergy the teaching of the catechism. He extended the education of the lower classes with vigorous and noble zeal—or rather their training in Christian doctrines, which at that time was the same thing—and often travelled from place to place in his dominions to judge for himself of the condition of the churches and schools.

At the same time a religious bent was conspicuous in his own life. "All in God" was his favourite motto. He performed his devotions daily, and required his suite to do the same; when he proposed receiving the sacrament he secluded himself entirely for some days previously, and limited the proceedings of his council to that which was strictly necessary; and among his court officials he settled from the very beginning of his reign the exact order in which they should communicate by turns. He insisted on their piety and good moral character, but was in other respects known as a kind and considerate master, particularly to old and tried servants. His favourite society were the clergy, whom he liked to see about him in full canonical dress. To meet the requirements of the town, containing at that time above five thousand inhabitants, he increased the number of the regularly appointed ministers to seven at the least, and in the year 1710 he summoned them all at once from the whole country—above a hundred—to a synod at Weimar, where he himself assisted at the proceedings from beginning to end. It was natural that he should be interested by all the discussions on church matters to which pietism as it spread and grew had given rise, but his own convictions were always ranged on the side of the "old church party."[43] For the church of Saint James —so runs the decree—he stipulated for a preacher who must have studied at some university "above suspicion" (of unorthodoxy)—a remark directed against Halle; in 1715 he prohibited private meeting for religious purposes as involving abuses; three years later he required of all preachers their universal assent to the dogmatic proposition that the gifts of even unconverted ministers were saving and effectual by virtue of their office. He caused all the more serious points of difference to be narrowly investigated by the learned men of Jena, and then announced in a full and particular rescript how he would have them decided.

It is pretty clear, however, from all we know of him, that Wilhelm Ernst's interest was by no means directed solely to church establishment and the maintenance of "pure" doctrine, but that a deep vein of living piety ran through his nature. For this reason zealot orthodoxy was repugnant to him; he sternly repressed all controversy in the pulpit, and required that any prevalent religious error should be refuted "humbly and by the light of reason."

Next to this he was well disposed to science and art, and in this he distinguished himself above most of his contemporaries and peers, for he did not merely protect these faculties out of ostentation and for effect, but studied in them himself with honest perseverance. He was in his time a student for three years in Jena, and his very interest in theological matters kept him constantly connected with science. Besides bestowing much care on the archives of the duchy, he laid the foundations of the grand-ducal library, now so extensive, by many valuable and important purchases, and, with his usual businesslike exactitude, placed it in the

---

[43] His younger brother, Johann Ernst, had, in 1691, made an ineffectual attempt to get Hermann Francke as his court preacher and tutor to his eldest son (see Francke's diary in Kramer, Beiträge zur Geschichte. A. H. Franckes, 1861).

charge of a special librarian. He also possessed a considerable collection of coins, and was always endeavouring
to add to it. In spite of his serious character he was
induced in 1696 to allow the erection of an opera-house, and
for a time he even had a " court comedian " (" Hof-
comödiant ") in the person of Gabriel Möller, which, of
course, implies that a permanent troupe of actors enjoyed
the privilege of performing at Weimar and the other towns
in the duchy. In 1709, however, this privilege no longer
existed.[44] The friendly relations which subsisted between
the pleasure-loving court of Weissenfels and that of Weimar
was not without its influence over amusements of this kind.
In 1698 Wilhelm Ernst held here a four days' carnival, with
a great suite ; and even during the last decade of their lives
the cousins were faithful and eager fellow-huntsmen. The
court " capelle," or band, was not inconsiderable for that
period, and even by the year 1702 included some conspicuous
musicians. A sketch of the Duke's life, written in 1735,
narrates ingenuously : " Sixteen well-trained musicians,
dressed in the habit of *heyducs*, at times delighted his ear."
As these were, of course, the best of his band, the conclusion
is forced upon us that Bach himself must from time to time
have presented himself in "the habit of a heyduc"—a
comical figure enough. Meanwhile, the taste for chamber
music was greater in his younger brother, Johann Ernst, in
whose service Bach remained for a few months in 1703 ; and
after his death in 1707 it showed itself in his son (by his
second marriage), Prince Johann Ernst, of whom we shall
hear again presently. Duke Wilhelm's natural proclivities
turned his mind chiefly to church music.[45]

It is clear at a glance that no more favourable spot could
have been imagined for Bach and his great aims. Every
germ of art, however fertile the soil in which it grows,

---

[44] On May 14, 1709, Duke Christian of Saxe-Weissenfels commends, to
Duke Moritz of Saxe-Zeitz, Gabriel Möller, erewhile employed as court
comedian at Weimar (Comp. Fürstenau).
[45] The best sources of information for the life of Wilhelm Ernst is the
sketch given by J. David Köhler's Historischer Münz-Belustigung, Part II.
(Nürnberg, 1730). Gottschalg also gives a large space to this ruler. Some

demands light and air for its full development, and these elements were extremely difficult to find at that time for true sacred music, particularly at courts, which nevertheless were best able to afford the means by which art might thrive. Any real interest in religion hardly displayed itself excepting in the form of pietism, which was inimical to art; for the rest, and for the most part, religious indifference hid behind ecclesiastical formalism, and was best pleased when the church music in common use included a compromise with operatic music, with a leaning, if possible, on that side, since this was now the focus of general musical interest. But it was quite otherwise at the court of Wilhelm Ernst. The Duke had the deepest conviction that the religion of the Protestant Church was the first of human blessings, but that it did not exclude the other aspects of life in all its manifestations and relations, but merely concentrated them and raised them to a purer ideal. Artistic efforts within the jurisdiction of the Church must therefore have seemed to him something exceptionally praiseworthy and deserving of promotion, particularly when he observed what a gifted man this was who applied the greater portion of his splendid powers to this problem. On his views were moulded those of most of the men who surrounded him, and Bach could at once be convinced that his music would meet with sympathetic appreciation, if only because it was church music. He was supported by the favour of a majority, in whose estimation all that was connected with the Church held the highest place. The appreciation and sympathy of our fellow-men is as indispensable as the breath of life to some even of the strongest minds, and to the rest it is at any rate warming and invigorating as the sunshine. The court of Weimar stands forth among those of the princes of that period as Bach himself does among composers for the Church; they seem made for each other.

The new post was twofold, combining those of court

---

details I derived from the archives at Weimar; and quite lately an interesting study by Beaulieu Marconnay: Ernst August, Herzog von Sachen-Weimar-Eisenach (Leipzig, 1872), confirms the view here given of Wilhelm Ernst's estimable character.

Organist and *Kammermusicus*. For this Bach received for the first three years a salary of 156 gülden 15 groschen, which was punctually paid, since the financial administration was very exact.[46] At Midsummer, 1711, he was advanced to 210 gülden 12 groschen; at Easter, 1713, to 225 gülden, and from 1714 still further—an unmistakable sign of how well they knew his value.[47] The church of the castle dated from the year 1630, and had later acquired the name of " Weg zur Himmelsburg "—" The Way to the City of Heaven,"—the Duke had had five new bells cast for it in the year 1712, in order to adorn it still more. How often Bach had to do duty in it cannot be exactly said, since so many extra services were held there. The organ was rather small, but had a strong, full-toned pedal, in which it surpassed that of the town church, while that was superior to it in the number of manuals. It will be interesting to see the specification:—

	Upper Manual.			Lower Manual.	
1.	Principal	... ... 8 ft.	1.	Principal ...	... 8 ft.
2.	Quintatön	... ... 16 ft.	2.	Viol-di-gamba	... 8 ft.
3.	Gemshorn	... ... 8 ft.	3.	Gedact ...	... 8 ft.
4.	Gedackt	... ... 8 ft.	4.	Trumpet ...	... 8 ft.
5.	Quintatön	... ... 4 ft.	5.	Small Gedackt	... 4 ft.
6.	Octave	... ... 4 ft.	6.	Octave ...	... 4 ft.
7.	Mixture	... ... 6 ft.	7.	Waldflöte ...	... 2 ft.
8.	Cymbel	... ... 3 ft.	8.	Sesquialtera	... 4 ft.(?)
9.	Glockenspiel, or carillon.				

Pedal Organ.

1.	Great " Untersatz "		4.	Violin-Bass ...	... 16 ft.
	(support) ...	... 32 ft.	5.	Principal Bass	... 8 ft.
2.	Sub-Bass ...	... 16 ft.	6.	Trumpet-Bass	... 8 ft.
3.	Posaune (Bass Trom-		7.	Cornett-Bass	... 4 ft.[48]
	bone) ...	... 16 ft.			

[46] If he thought it needful the duke assisted his court-officer with advances. *Vide* J. D. Köhler, p. 23.

[47] The collected private accounts in the archives of the Grand Duchy, which give information respecting Bach's salary, are only to be found from Michaelmas, 1710, onwards. Here the following entries occur: 150 gülden of salary and 6 gülden 15 groschen for " 3 cords of driftwood "; besides this, 12 groschen " for coals for the court-organist in the winter." The remaining entries, up to the end of 1713, show a considerable increase.

[48] Wette, who communicates this specification (pp. 175, 176), celebrates the

In the musical capelle (band) Bach was of use both as a pianoforte and violin-player, so that he was afterwards advanced to be concertmeister (leader of the band), which became his customary post, except at the performances in church, when he had his own place at the organ. A list of the ducal musicians employed between 1714 and 1716 numbers twenty-two; it is true that the singers are included in this; but they were all more or less accustomed to play on some instrument as well, and indeed most of the players had knowledge of several instruments. There were always, moreover, some among them who held offices of entirely different kinds; it was the custom, and they were used to it. The four voices of the chorus used to be doubled, and six choirboys added to its strength; also the Stadtmusicus was at hand, who with his company could lend a support if desired.

Bach found a worthy colleague in art and profession in Johann Gottfried Walther, the organist of the town-church of SS. Peter and Paul. He was an "Erfurter" through his mother, whose maiden name was Lämmerhirt, and so he was rather nearly related to Bach; and besides he was connected with the family through his first teacher of music, Johann Bernhard Bach. Born on September 18, 1684, he was nearly of an age with Sebastian, and once already an opportunity had been given to both of trying for the same prize, when the place of Georg Ahle in Mühlhausen was to be filled up. But Walther withdrew from the competition which had been urged upon him, and a few months after, on July 29, 1707, was summoned from Erfurt to the town-church of Weimar, where the town-organist, Heintze, had died shortly before.[49] He remained in this post until his death, March 23, 1748; he had nothing to do with the court band in Bach's time, since he was first called "Hofmusicus" in 1720; while in the year of his arrival he undertook the

---

organ.as " incomparable," which, if any weight is to be given to his judgment, must be referred to the quality of the stops. Its pitch was the so-called cornettone, *i.e.*, a minor-third above the Kammerton or ordinary pitch. See App. A, 17.

[49] A. Wette, Hist. Nach., &c., von Weimar (Weimar, 1737), p. 261.

clavier instruction of Prince Johann Ernst and his sister, Johanne Charlotte.[50] Walther's name is commonly known in the history of art by his Musical Lexicon, which appeared in 1732 at Leipzig, and is the first German attempt to bring the whole mass of musical information into the dictionary form. The book is even now a source of information hardly to be dispensed with, principally owing to the fulness of the biographical notices, which have been collected together with great diligence, although it naturally contains many inaccuracies ; the author, moreover, was always anxious to bring it to perfection, and to publish a continuation, but he died in the meantime.[51] And yet this was only the fruit of this diligent man's leisure hours ; his chief occupation was practical music—playing, teaching, and composition. He was peculiarly fitted for teaching by his precise, indefatigable, and persevering nature, combined with fundamental musical knowledge to such a degree that he could in this well stand his ground beside Bach—at least as a teacher of composition.

His style of playing—judging from those of his compositions which are preserved—must have been broad and solid. Of these a few small examples were engraved on copper in his lifetime,[52] but a large number of them have been handed down to us in autograph—compositions exclusively for the organ or clavier; as to his church compositions, concerning which he himself informs us, I, at least, have never seen them. Five fugues (in A major, C major, D minor, C major, and F major) are respectable, viewed as the further-developed works of his Thuringian predecessors; and still more so the preludes, in the form of toccatas, which are prefixed

---

[50] Walther himself has written the greater part of his life in Mattheson's "Ehrenpforte" (Hamburg, 1740), pp. 387, 390. See Gerber, Lex., II., Sp. 765.

[51] His copy, with many manuscript additions, was in the possession of the lexicographer Gerber, who incorporated the chief part of them in his own Lexicon. After his death the manuscript came into the library of the "Gesellschaft der Musikfreunde," in Vienna.

[52] To those mentioned by Gerber there should be added a book of arrangements of the Advent hymn " Wie soll ich dich empfangen," published by Christian Leopold in Augsburg.

to four of them.[53] His chief interest was bestowed on "organ-chorales"; he was a diligent collector of good chorale arrangements by past, and sometimes by contemporary, composers, and he himself made many hundreds of such pieces. There still exist five more or less comprehensive books of chorales collected by him, in which we find Böhm fairly represented, and also Buxtehude, in whom he had been interested by Andreas Werkmeister. However, his chief model was Pachelbel, by whose genius all the Erfurt organists of the time were influenced, and whose son he went especially to Nuremberg to visit in the year 1706. An entire set of chorale-preludes for a year (*i.e.,* one or more for each service of the year) were composed by him in the manner of that master.[54] One can fully join in the high praise bestowed upon him by Mattheson, who calls him the second Pachelbel, "if not in art the first," and asserts that Walther's chorales surpass in elegance all that he had ever heard or seen, and yet he had heard many and seen many more.[55] In this specialty he must be considered as the greatest master next to Sebastian Bach, if we put out of sight the long-drawn-out form of the North German organ chorale, in which he had only tried his hand. All that Pachelbel had left technically more or less undeveloped was completed by Walther. The counterpoints are worked in freer contrast to the melody, and form an independent and self-contained organism, in which the separate parts move with great freedom; with a like ease the *cantus firmus* now appears in the bass, now in an inner or an upper part; the pedal *technique* is fully developed. Moreover, he has at his command a considerable wealth of inventive combinations, and that facility for the solution of difficult contrapuntal problems which is only acquired by persevering industry.

He was conscious of his powers, and fond of exercising them in artfully devised canons. For example, to the melody of "Wir Christenleut hab'n jetzund Freud," he added a two-

---

[53] In the royal library at Berlin.
[54] Mattheson, Critica Musica, Vol. II., p. 175.
[55] Vollkommener Capellmeister, p. 476.

part canon on the octave at the distance of a crotchet, and put the *cantus firmus* on the pedal.[56] He was very fond of working the melody in canon between the upper part and the pedal in many kinds of alternations, as for example, where the bass enters with the simple melody, and the upper part follows a bar later with it richly adorned (in an arrangement of " Ach was soll ich Sünder machen "), or the upper voice proceeds in minims and the pedal comes in after two bars in crotchets, and so catches it up at the end of each line (" Mitten wir im Leben sind ").[57] Also where it is possible to use two lines of a chorale in close combination, he knows how to discover it ; and accordingly he worked a " chorale fugue " through on the first line of " Herr Jesu Christ, du höchstes Gut," in such a manner that he used the second line as counter-subject and, indeed, in diminution as well as in double counterpoint.[58] Such an experiment, demanding both art and genius, he tried even on the major melody, probably originating with Pachelbel, to " Wo soll ich fliehen hin," which is so worked that it allows of double counterpoint in all four parts, and consequently in the second verse the tenor has counterpoint to the alto, the alto to the tenor, the soprano to the bass, and the bass to the soprano.[59]

But this very facility in counterpoint was the origin of many of Walther's failures. Such a full development of the technical powers is a sword that cuts both ways ; it often turns against him who wields it, since it selfishly makes

---

[56] The autograph is on a loose quarto-leaf in the royal library in Berlin. Mattheson, Critica Musica. In the same place, in the form of a leaf from an album, is a " *Canone infinito gradato à 4 voci, sopra: A Solis ortus cardine* "—

viz., a canon on the fifth, in which the parts ascend at each repetition, so that the soprano and tenor begin the second time on E, and alto and bass on B, and so on.

[57] Both these are in the Frankenberger Autograph, p. 270 and 334.

[58] Commer, Musica Sacra, I., No. 145.

[59] It is in the Königsberg Autograph.

itself too prominent, injuring the composer's conception by its very nature. To curb it properly and to keep it always in subjection to the ideal requires the greatness of genius, which must be denied to Walther, whose scope was narrow, and whose tendency was to trivialities.

The idea of the Pachelbel organ chorales, which was to allow, the choral melody to stand out in its simple grandeur, so that the characteristic religious feeling should spread aloft and around, was often quite obscured by Walther's too artificial method of treatment by canons, in which the attention is given more to separate combinations than to a comprehensive plan. Two examples may make this clear. An arrangement of " Hilf Gott, dass mirs gelinge "[60] is planned quite in Pachelbel's manner ; two upper voices treat in imitation each line of the chorale, which after a time appears slowly and majestically in the pedal part. The composer, however, is not satisfied with this, but, besides the melody in the pedal, brings it in again on a loud great organ a fifth above, and moreover in diminution, adorned and shortened in parts just as it may happen to suit. Every one must feel the painful restlessness of this over-refined combination, since the ear vacillates to and fro incessantly between the quiet simple melody below and the restless ornamented one above ; nay, what is still worse, between the impression of tonic and dominant below and above. A fair and noble picture is thus frightfully distorted. The second instance has to do with the chorale " Gott der Vater wohn uns bei." The two first lines are first delivered by the upper part in minims with beautiful counterpoint in semiquavers. Even with the last three notes the pedal comes in with the repetition, and the attention is urged on to another subject before the goal first suggested is reached. After the pedal is released from its task, the upper voice again takes possession of the lead, but is only allowed to give out two notes before the pedal comes in and drowns it with doubled diminution. The following line is led by the pedal, and the upper part comes after it in canon ; the next is given to the upper part

---

[60] Commer, op. cit., No. 147.

alone, but the one after it is again treated in imitation ; then it is repeated. In the last lines the upper and lower parts are so interlaced that the progression of the melody is almost unrecognisable. Here we are led by the superfluity of art nearly to the point of view of Samuel Scheidt, or a hundred years back.

By an error this organ chorale has come to be included under Bach's name in Griepenkerl's edition of his organ works.[61] But I have no hesitation in saying that Bach never wrote a piece in which the plan and organisation of the whole is so utterly sacrificed to separate interesting combinations. The whole difference between the two composers is clearly shown by such productions, which irresistibly confirm the overwhelming superiority of Bach's genius. Although he had much greater polyphonic ingenuity than Walther, he never allows himself to be carried away by it to the injury of the ideal, but remains grand and simple even through the most complicated forms. In the canonic treatment of a chorale-melody, giving rise to the hardest problems (of which he has given the most brilliant examples among his Weimar chorale arrangements), he hardly ever employs the process in the strict Pachelbel form, evidently because he fully entered into the poetic depth of the chorale. We only know two exceptions, and here the indescribably grand achievement vindicates itself.[62] Thus Bach alone really perfected the Pachelbel ideal, inasmuch as it was he who took that last step with confidence, and reproduced in the counterpoint the poetic essence of the melody, of which only weak indications appear in Walther. A publication, complete as far as possible, of Walther's organ chorales would, however, be the only proper method of judging him, so that their technical subtlety and perfection which Mattheson happily calls "elegance"—should be admired as they deserve.

The personal connection between these two men, already prepared by relationship, soon became a friendly intimacy,

---

[61] P. S. V. Cah. 6, No. 24 (245). It is in the Frankenberger Autograph with Walther's name in full, p. 74.

[62] " Dies sind die heiligen zehn Gebot," and " Vater unser im Himmelreich," in the third volume of the " Clavierübung " (Peters).

and Bach stood godfather to Walther's eldest son Johann Gottfried (September 26, 1712).[63] An album leaf, on which a four-part canon written by Bach, with a dedication, we can certainly refer to Walther, particularly as an exactly similar leaf, on which there is also a canon, but by Walther, is extant. Bach's memento is in this form :—

"Canon à 4 Voc: perpetüüs."

This trifle is here written for the owner (of the book) in affectionate remembrance.

Weimar, Aug. 2, 1713.

Joh. Sebast. Bach.
Fürste. Sächs. Hofforg. u,
Camer Musicus.[64]

A love of the canon form was at that time common to them both ; it is conspicuous, as has been already said, even in some of Bach's organ chorales written at Weimar. We shall presently see them emulating each other in another branch of musical composition. But it is self-evident and natural that men so near in their ages and aims should interchange their views and experience in art. Thus an anecdote, which must have been preserved for posterity by one of Bach's elder sons, most likely refers to Walther. Sebastian had very soon attained so high a degree of skill in organ and clavier playing, and set himself such difficult problems in his own compositions, that he could play the compositions of others unhesitatingly at sight. He once said before a

---

[63] Parish Register at Weimar.

[64] This leaf was in the possession of Herr Clauss, consul-general at Berlin, who allowed me to copy it. The collection was sold by auction in 1872, at Leipzig.

friend—who we suppose must have been Walther—that he believed he really could play anything and everything at sight, and his friend for a joke determined to teach him differently within eight days. " He invited him," says our authority,[65] " to breakfast one morning, and laid on the desk of his instrument, besides other pieces, one which at first sight looked quite insignificant. Bach came in, and, according to his custom, walked straight to the instrument, partly to play and partly to look through the pieces which lay on the desk. While he was turning over the pages and trying them, his host went into another room to prepare breakfast. In a few minutes Bach came, in its turn, to the piece prepared for him, and began to play it ; but not far from the beginning he came to a standstill. He studied it, began again and again, came to a stop. " No," he exclaimed, rising to leave the instrument, while his friend was laughing to himself in the next room ; " no one can play everything at sight : it is not possible."

At a later period some estrangement must have occurred between them ; this is evident from the way in which Walther speaks of Bach in his Lexicon. As we look through the worse than meagre article, it is difficult to believe that its author was the man who had lived with Bach for more than nine years, in a small town, on those terms of equality which result from a community of artistic interests, and the closest intimacy. Not a word in it betrays that it treats of the man who was already one of the greatest organists in all Germany, and not merely esteemed so at the court of Weimar, but famous far and wide. There is no mention of all his numerous compositions written in Weimar —cantatas and pieces for the organ and clavier which Mattheson admired in Hamburg as early as in 1716 ; nothing about the competition—so much talked of and so honourable to all German musicians—between Bach and Marchand in 1717. These were all events amid which Walther had actually lived, and which it was impossible that he could have forgotten by the time when he wrote the Lexicon.

---

65 Forkel, Ueber Joh. Seb. Bachs Leben, p. 16.

Nor can it be objected that in all the biographical articles he confined himself only to the briefest statement of the principal facts; on the contrary, the article on Georg Oesterreich shows how discursive he could be concerning his personal acquaintance. How much more interesting would the narrative of his intimacy with Bach have been! But even his later additions in manuscript refer only to Bach's residence at Leipzig, and are derived from sources accessible to all. His own living interest in his great contemporary must have cooled entirely; and it is difficult to believe, willing as we may be, that the divergence of their paths in life should have been the only cause of it. There is, besides, external evidence that even during the last years of Bach's residence in Weimar the old intimacy between them no longer existed. Bach went from thence to visit his cousin Johann Ludwig Bach, capellmeister at Meiningen, whom he learnt to esteem highly, and he copied many of his compositions with his own hand. If he had still been in intimate intercourse with Walther it would be extremely surprising that he, in his Lexicon, should betray no knowledge of Bach of Meiningen, for he must certainly have heard much in his praise from Sebastian. But as to the cause of his estrangement we can, at most, hazard a guess. Possibly Walther found himself more thrown into the background by Bach's transcendent merit than his very justifiable self-esteem could brook, and when once this form of dissatisfaction has taken root, and the field is so narrow, how easily occasions for sensitiveness and friction arise! It is highly significant that Walther, in his collection of organ chorales—a province of his art in which he had every right to feel himself a master—has borrowed comparatively little from Bach.

Bach was thrown into near relations with yet another personage who held office in connection with the town church, namely, the cantor, Georg Theodore Reineccius. Here again we derive our information from the fact of his having been godfather to one of Bach's twin children (born February 23, 1713). Reineccius was born at New Brandenburg in 1660, and was cantor in Weimar from 1687 till 1726, and also teacher in the Gymnasium, at first to the fourth

class and then to the third.   His colleague Walther testifies
of him that he was an excellent composer, " though he had
learnt to compose merely from studying good scores," and he
adds that Capellmeister Theile, of Naumburg, who was called
the father of counterpoint, had spoken of him as " a learned
composer," for a Mass in E major.   We are in position to
test this opinion, and indeed to confirm it from a motett for
a double choir: " Preise, Jerusalem, den Herrn " (" Praise,
O Jerusalem, the Lord ").   Judging from this, the " good
scores " must have been principally by Italian masters, for
the motett displays so much comprehension of vocal feeling,
so much skill in the treatment both of the double choir and
of eight-part harmony, so much flow in the conduct of the
parts, that a German of that time could hardly have
originated them without an Italian model.   It consists of
several broadly handled movements, and closes with a
" Hallelujah " fugue.[66]   A series of texts for cantatas for
the whole year, founded on the Gospels, and printed about
1700, show him to have been a master of his native tongue
and of rhythm, and the music for these pieces, at any rate
in great part, was also composed by him.   He seems to have
had a manner calculated to engage the confidence of the
young ; for, besides Bach, Matthias Gesner, who was six years
younger and who was corrector (or sub-warden as we may
render it) of the Weimar College from the early part of 1715
till 1729, was devotedly attached to him, and publicly stated
the fact years after.[67]   Gesner was passionately fond of
music, and as the two branches of study were united in
Reineccius, who was a very superior man, it is pretty certain
the learned Gesner and the illustrious artist Bach at this
time had already begun the friendship which after an interval

---

[66] In a collection of 93 Motetts in score (No. 13,661) in the University library
(Gotthold) at Königsberg, p. 203.   This one is only signed " G. T. R.," but as
the collection was apparently made in Thuringia, there can hardly be any
doubt as to the composer.

[67] *Jo. Matth. Gesneri primæ lineæ isagoges in eruditionem universalem.
Tom. II., pag. 553 (edit. alt.): " Vinariæ familiaritas mihi fuit cum præceptore
tertiæ classis (Reinesio) qui simul Cantor erat atque collegii totius senior, et per
XL annos in populosa urbe munere scholastico functus ; et erat vir bonus, cui
fidem habere poteram."*

of more than twelve years they re-cemented in Leipzig, and
which on Gesner's side found enthusiastic utterance in the
well-known note to his edition of Quintilian[68]—an utterance
which does equal honour to him and to Bach.

Bach himself stood in no direct connection with the
Gymnasium, since the scholars engaged in the choir were of
course under the direction of the cantor, and special lessons
in music for the college boys were not instituted till 1733;[69]
still he must have exercised considerable influence over the
choir, at any rate in his later capacity as concertmeister. It
has already been noted that he met again in Weimar with
his old friend the rector of the Ohrdruf College, Magister
Joh. Christoph Kiesewetter, who in 1712 was called to be at
the head of the new Gymnasium.

There is less to say with reference to the members of the
ducal band. The capellmeister was Johann Samuel Drese,
born in 1644, cousin and pupil of Adam Drese, and who,
like him, at first officiated as court organist to Duke Bernhard of Sax-Jena; but at the accession of Wilhelm Ernst in
1683 he was called to fill his office at Weimar, and in 1671
had married a wife of that town.[70] He was, however, feeble
in health, and during the last twenty years of his service
could scarcely fulfil his duties; nevertheless the duke, who
clung much to old and faithful servants, did not allow him
to leave, but gave him the assistance of a deputy. This
assistant, from 1695 till about 1705, was Georg Christoph
Strattner, who is known in hymnology by the melodies he
set to Joachim Neander's " Bundesliedern und Danksal-
men " (" Songs of the Covenant and Psalms of Thanksgiving ").[71] In his installation he was charged with "the
direction of the whole band in the absence of the present
capellmeister, Johann Samuel Drese, when, by reason of his
well-known bodily infirmities, he could not be present, and
in such cases to hold the usual examinations in the house of
the said Drese; also not at any time less than every fourth

---

[68] To the *Institut. Orat.*, I., 12, 3.
[69] Wette, Op. Cit., p. 415.
[70] Walther, Lexicon.
[71] Walther, Lexicon.   Comp. Winterfeld, Evangel. Kirchengesang, II. 516 ff.

Sunday to conduct in the prince's castle-chapel a piece of his own composition, and at all times, whether he were conducting or not, to sing tenor," &c., for which he was to receive 200 gülden yearly. Subsequently Samuel Drese's son, Johann Wilhelm, became deputy capellmeister, probably with the same duties, and after his father's death (December 1, 1716) he filled his place. Nothing can be said as to the artistic productions of either; those of the son seem to have been quite insignificant, since Walther does not even mention him in the Lexicon, and the invalid father during Bach's residence certainly but rarely came into prominence, so that it was easy for Bach to come to the front with his talents and his personal influence. The violinist Westhoff had been dead ever since 1705, and no single celebrity deserves to be named as belonging to the band, so far as I have been able to discover. Still we must assume it as certain that, as a body, it was skilled and competent, from the lively interest taken by the court even in chamber music. Among the musical personages of Weimar who deserve to be mentioned in this place was Johann Christoph Lorbeer, court advocate and poet laureate, who first displayed his taste in the arts by his "Lob der Edeln Musik" ("Praise of the noble art of music," Weimar, 1696), and a year afterwards chivalrously defended his favourite art against the attacks of the rector Vockerodt, who assailed it in a bitter pamphlet. He was on excellent terms with Samuel Drese, who prefaced his friend's "Lob der Edeln Musik" with a poem in eulogy of his "dear friend" ("Herzen's Freund").

III.

THE WEIMAR PERIOD.—ORGAN MUSIC, CONCERTOS, CANTATAS, &c.

BACH'S nine years' residence in Weimar was the period of his most brilliant activity as an organist and composer for the organ, for this particular department was in the first place and above all that which his official position assigned to him. The very competent author of the

Necrology says, " The benevolence of his gracious sovereign inspired him to attempt all that was possible in the art of handling the organ, and here it was that he composed most of his organ pieces."[72] The vigour of endeavour which was characteristic of him, together with gifts of the very first order, left no doubt of his success. His fame soon spread throughout north and central Germany; in the excursions for artistic purposes which he made from Weimar he covered himself with honour of every kind; and Mattheson of Hamburg wrote of him in 1716, "I have seen things by the famous organist, Herr Johann Sebastian Bach, of Weimar, which, both for church use and for keyed instruments, are certainly so conceived that we cannot but highly esteem the man," and at the same time he asked him for a sketch of his biography for his " Ehrenpforte," which he was then planning, but which did not appear till twenty-four years later.[73] How he applied himself to acquire the highest perfection of a peculiar form of fingering *technique*, on which indeed a considerable share of his greatness as a clavier-player ultimately depended, it will be his part to tell us later. With this he combined a certainty, boldness, and versatility in the use of the pedal obbligato, such as had been hitherto unheard of.[74] His works, of which the technical difficulties remain unsurpassed, even at the present day, exist to testify that as time went on he achieved the most unlimited mastery over the mighty instrument; and as with him the external form was always the handmaid merely of an inward purpose, we may conclude that the demands made by them on executive skill never rise to the utmost height of his own technical capabilities, as exhibited in free improvisation when display was the first object, or when trying some new organ.

Even in the knowledge of organ-building—of which the

---

[72] Mizler, Op. Cit., p. 153. Compare Forkel, p. 6.

[73] Mattheson, Das beschützte Orchestre, Hamburg, 1717, p. 222. Probably the first time that Bach is mentioned in literature.

[74] Mizler, p. 172. Compare Gerber, Lexicon, I., col. 90. A fragment, apparently autograph, and a very interesting " *pedal exercitium* " by Bach, are in the possession of Professor Wagener, of Marburg.

project laid before the council of Mühlhausen gives so signal
a proof—he soon had made himself perfect to such a degree
that he was considered as quite the equal of the oldest pro-
ficients. As time goes on we shall often see him called
upon to exercise his keen insight into the subject. This
quality, applied to his own compositions for the organ,
gave rise to one element of essential consequence as
regards the full effect, which element has unfortunately
not been handed down to us in its original form, namely,
a very characteristic and ingenious use of the stops.
Bach's judgment was equally eminent in the combination of harmonies and of qualities of tone, and as in
the former his eye had detected paths which no one had
previously dreamed of, so in the mixture of musical tones he
was inexhaustible in his devices, peculiar sometimes to the
verge of strangeness, but never pedantic or devoid of style.[75]
This art, which was allied to the orchestration of later composers, he displayed especially when a powerful instrument,
fully supplied with stops, came under his hand; unfortunately in his places of residence he never possessed one worthy
of such a master. Since, however, tone-colouring is especially adapted to introduce the expression of a poetic element
into music, skilful management of the stops must be of great
value, particularly in the organ chorales. Whether the
means will ever offer for detecting in a number of these the
traces of his intentions as to the use of various qualities of
tones is in the hands of fate. Bach, at any rate, did not
indicate them in any of the autographs that have been preserved, because the vast difference in the stops of different
organs must determine which are to be used, and at that
time much had to be left to the intelligence of the performer
of organ music.

From the form and character of the compositions only very
general hints can be obtained. But in one single organ
chorale it is possible to arrive at Bach's original way of
using the stops; in an indirect way, it is true, but with
perfect certainty. Walther gives in each of his most compre-

---

[75] Mizler, p. 172.   Forkel, p. 20.

hensive collections an arrangement by Bach of the chorale, "Ein feste Burg," which he must have obtained, as he did all the Bach chorales which he has handed down, at the time of their living together in Weimar; the plan of it points certainly to an early date of composition.[76] In the older collection the direction, "à 3 clav." (for three manuals) is written over it, and over the commencement of the left hand "Fagott," and over the right, which comes in after two and a half bars, "Sesquialtera." Now neither Walther's nor Bach's organ in Weimar had three manuals,[77] nor had either a fagotto stop, so that these directions cannot possibly have proceeded from Walther, nor have been inserted by Bach with reference to the castle organ. But when we remember that, according to Bach's own scheme of the repairs of the Mühlhausen organ, a 16-feet Fagotto was to be put in instead of the useless trumpet; that further, agreeably to his specification, a *tertia* had been put into the "*Brustpositiv*," "with which, in combination with several other stops, a good full 'sesquialtera' tone may be obtained"; and that, lastly, Bach was bound to look after the structure until its completion, and so in some sort was held responsible for it—we can no longer doubt that a composition adapted to the remodelled Mühlhausen organ is before us, in which all the newly introduced stops were to be shown off. Since the new structure was ended in 1709, the composition must be of that date; and the chorale introduced into it more particularly assigns it to the Reformation festival, on which day Bach must have first displayed the powers of the restored organ to the townspeople and the council.

The combination of a reed-bassoon with the sesquialtera is one of those "entirely new inventions" of which Bach speaks in its place in the specification before mentioned, and gives a fairly good idea of the striking combinations of sound

---

[76] These two collections are the Königsberg (evidently the older), and the Frankenberger (the later). The chorale with which we are concerned is P. S. V., Cah. 6, No. 22.

[77] The expression "clavier" refers always simply to manuals when speaking of the organ.

which he was fond of making. The composition shows off
both stops equally well, since the first lines with their
repetitions are almost entirely in two parts, and worked in
such a manner that the right and left hand alternately have
the *cantus firmus*. In the twentieth bar the sign R. (Rückpositiv) shows that both hands are to play on the third
manual, from which point the fifth line of the melody is
treated in Böhm's way, and developed into a subject; and
the pedal enters there for the first time. Although this
bears no direction as to the stops, one can quite see, from
the quietly gliding quavers on the pedals, which demand a
clear intonation in combination with the slighter volume of
sound of the choir-organ (Rückpositiv), that the new 32-feet
sub-bass (see the specification No. 4) was to be shown off.
From the twenty-fourth bar onwards the manuals of the Oberwerk and Brustwerk are once more kept in activity as at the
beginning; they cross each other, possibly with more powerful stops, in semiquaver passages, while the pedal takes the
cantus firmus for the sixth and seventh lines, doubtless to
afford an example of the improved bass-posaune (see specification No. 5); although there is no direction for this, the
whole design points clearly to it.   The treatment of the
eighth line (bars 33-39) corresponds with that of the fifth,
even in the mixing of the stops, since the rhythm of the pedal-
figure ♪♩♪ is very well adapted to the display of a quick
"speaking," on which so much depends in any sub-bass, but
particularly in the 32-feet one. At the last three semiquavers of the thirty-ninth bar we find the direction "Oberwerk" (upper manual), which would hold good in Walther's
Weimar organ; it is not hard to see, from the facility of the
changes of the stops, that from this point the Oberwerk and
Brustwerk were coupled together (see specification No. 11),
and that at last, with the second half of the fiftieth bar, the
full organ enters and continues to the end. Walther, who
very likely accompanied Bach to Mühlhausen as a friend of
the organ-builder Wender, noted down in the copy of the
chorale in his older collection the surprising use of the
stops at the beginning; but in the course of transcription
adapted the changes more and more to his own two-manual

organ (hence the simple direction "oberwerk" in bars 24 and 39), and left out others, as the entrance of the full organ at bar 50; in the later of the two collections he omitted the addition "à 3 clav.," "fagotto," "sesquialtera," because they were without meaning for his own practice.

How Bach himself handled this organ chorale--how he used the rich variety of the organ in beautiful combination and diversity, and yet was able to lose sight so entirely of all these outer inducements, and to forget them in the idea of his composition, that all that was strictly musical held its due and proper place—for this we must feel the deepest wonder. Of course every form was not equally well' fitted for this aim, and Bach, who had at command all possible means, did right in choosing the chorale type of Böhm. Nor need we suppose that he always used such a variety of stops; he allowed himself naturally to be guided in this by the character of the composition, and we may be sure that he never would have fallen into the mistake of adorning the simple grandeur of Pachelbel's chorales with variety of colouring.[78]

We will now turn our attention once more from the technical or external means to their proper end and object, that is the compositions themselves, and must first notice a number of free organ pieces. There is much slighter chronological testimony as to the date of Bach's organ compositions than for his cantatas, or even for his chamber music. What there is to be known, however, gives us, in combination with internal evidence, a pretty clear idea of the works of the Weimar court organist.[79] The free

---

[78] I take occasion here to observe that the Walther manuscript deviates in some points from the Griepenkerl edition. Since there is no autograph of Bach's, Walther's readings have the fullest authority, and this is justified by internal evidence. The two most important differences consist in this, that the second half of the nineteenth bar is thus—

and that the pedal bass is an octave lower in bars 21-28 (? bars 25-32).

[79] See App. A., No. 18.

compositions for the organ fall naturally, even to those only moderately practised in criticism, into two distinct groups, an earlier and a later; but I at least will not venture to carry through such a distinction in the case of the chorale arrangements. It is quite plain that this was the branch of art in which Bach soonest reached maturity, and in which his perfect originality first appeared. In those of Bach's organ chorales which Walther has preserved to us we find in parts a style so extraordinarily large and bold that it is scarcely surpassed by the compositions of the later Leipzig time; and we may remember how perfect those chorale partitas in Böhm's manner seemed, which were written by a youth about seventeen years old. A single piece like the arrangement of "Ein feste Burg," the date of which we are able to discover, is of little service in evidence, since it was written for a particular purpose; for the present we must content ourselves with a collective survey devoted to the close of the Weimar period.

Three independent preludes,[80] respectively in G major, A minor, and C major, standing by themselves, head the list. The first must be one of the very earliest of the Weimar compositions, and may have been written before 1708. A sort of thematic development is indeed perceptible, but the chief motive idea was the setting free of a tumultuous flood of sound, in which the impetuous spirit of the young composer revels with delight; it is expressed in passages of semiquavers that rush tumultuously here and there, and in the full resounding chords. The characteristic of the second is calm, clear sobriety; it is entirely built on the thematic material of a single bar, the separate sections of which go through all the parts with ingenious changes of position and with great variety of harmonies. The effect of the rhythm, continuous throughout and of the same quietness, is at best, however, somewhat monotonous, and only quite at the end is greater animation given by the introduc-

---

[80] P. S. V., Cah. 8, No. 11 (247); Cah. 4, No. 13 (243); Cah. 8, No. 8 (247). The second alone is well-authenticated by the handwriting of Bach's pupils, J. L. Krebs and Kittel; the writing of the others is newer, but from internal evidence there can be no doubt of their genuineness.

tion of semiquaver passages; still the use of the doubled pedal part is especially fine. The third and shortest prelude is partly built on a descending scale-passage treated in imitation, and might, by reason of its neat four-part writing, be assigned to a somewhat later period, did not bars 20 to 26 contradict the supposition, in which the treatment is not of a piece with the strict style of the rest of the prelude, showing an inconsistency not to be found in Bach's later works. A fantasia in C major[81] for manuals alone must next be mentioned, the germ of which consists of the rhythm ♩♫♩ ; it seems to have been written for a technical purpose, since it demands a careful *legato* style of playing and a facility in changing the fingers on the same note. As by this time pupils had begun to collect about Bach, the piece may very well have been written for some of them. Probably a fugue[82] in the same key was originally attached to it, as it is almost entirely for the manuals and is founded on a similar rhythm. Its early date may be inferred from the five concluding bars, to say nothing of all the rest; for one thing, because the formation of the chords in them follows exactly the Buxtehude manner, of which the composer shows no trace in the later Weimar years, and also from the pedal, which only enters at this point. The fugue cannot be called a pre-eminent work of art, though the writing is good and flowing.[83]

Next in order come eight short preludes and fugues which have been handed down together.[84] It is not easily intelligible how these can have been considered as the work of Bach's novitiate, since throughout they bear the

---

[81] P. S. V., Cah. 8, No. 9.

[82] P. S. V., Cah. 8 (247), No. 10.

[83] In the tenth bar I consider the reading incorrect; the F sharp in the alto and tenor should be F each time. Compare the concluding harmonies of the toccata in D minor. P. S. V., Cah. 4 (243), No. 4.

[84] P. S. V., Cah. 8 (247), No. 5. An older MS. of these, from the legacy of G. Polchau, the Hamburg music-teacher, has come into the possession of the royal library in Berlin. The title is: " *VIII PRÆLUDIA* | *èd* | *VIII FVGEN* | *di.* | *J. S. BACH (?)* " On the right side below: " *Poss:* | *C. A. Klein.*" There is in my opinion no reason for the note of interrogation, which is as old as the rest of the title.

stamp of a commanding master of composition, and the
short, simple forms correspond just as little with Bach's
inclination at his earliest period as with that of any other
young genius. On the other hand, with all their general
independence, there are a number of particular features
in them which point plainly to certain mannerisms of the
northern masters: for instance, the form of the themes
in the first and fourth fugues, a great deal of the eighth
fugue, and figures such as those in the thirteenth and fourteenth bars of the fifth prelude. We must therefore suppose
these eight compositions to have been written when the
author had not yet quite freed himself from the influences
of those great organ-masters. We may add to this the fact
that most of the preludes, both in general outline and in
their surprising and irregular figures, show clearly the influence of Vivaldi's violin concertos—a great number of
which Bach was just then engaged in arranging for the
clavier or organ. This influence is so evident that it would be
superfluous to trace it in particular cases, especially as the
arrangements from Vivaldi are published and the comparison
is easy. The suggestion here presents itself that these pieces
too were written for some one especially capable scholar,
or perhaps more; they demand a not inconsiderable *technique*,
especially in the pedal obbligato, but do not display enough
technical difficulty and are not important enough in substance for the master's own use. The second, third, fifth,
and seventh, are especially fine. In the sixth fugue, which
otherwise is very successful, the pedal comes in (in the
thirty-eighth bar) after a long pause, not with the theme, but
only with notes to support the harmony, which is not quite
in accordance with rule, and which Bach never would have
allowed to stand in his later time. On the other hand, the
introduction of the key of C minor (in the thirty-first bar),
quite out of the natural and easy course of things, is a true
masterstroke.

Among the number of compositions of greater extent and
intrinsic merit we must first mention a fugue in G minor,[85]

---

[85] P. S. V., Cah. 4 (243), No. 7.

which, on account of its very beautiful theme and the masterly flow of the writing, has justly become a great favourite. The individual characteristics which make it inferior to the works of the following year must not be overlooked. Of these the most prominent is the counterpoint on the theme, which is always the same, and only in one part, since notes to fill up the harmony and the doubled sixths (bars 41 and 42) cannot be considered as such. It is only from the fifth bar before the end that it is in three parts, while the beautiful free episodes display greater polyphonic animation. The irregular form of the response need not be objected to; the strict rule of fugue which is here transgressed can hardly hold good for so long and melodic a theme, since, although the lead on the dominant should be followed by the lead on the tonic, yet in the next notes the key of D minor ought to be plainly felt, and the ear should only be permitted to rest for a moment in the principal key. Here, however, this is the less necessary since the whole composition inclines not to the key of the dominant, but to that of the relative major; not to mention that the beauty of the theme would have suffered if the rule of the response had been strictly adhered to. Another indication of the date is to be found in the meaningless entry of the pedal in bar 26; and yet another (and a still stronger) in the entry of the theme in the left hand, as if preparing the way for something else, in bar 25, which entry is transferred after a few notes to the right hand. Such features, which, contrary as they are to all objective principles of form, can only be explained by the hypothesis of a momentary freak, would necessarily be more and more cast aside by the thoughtful musician, who, following nature's principle, must endeavour to give definite aim to the several parts of the organism he has created. Now if this arbitrariness and defiance of rule be found elsewhere, it will be a piece of internal evidence of the most certain kind to prove that the pieces in which such characteristics are found were written within a short time of one another.

Appearances then suggest that a prelude and fugue in

C major[86] must have been written about this time. In bar 23 of the fugue, the pedal, which up to this point has been silent, enters with a passage resembling the theme, after which, in the next bar, the theme itself appears in the upper part, and then the pedal is silent again until the thirty-sixth bar, when it has the true theme. Again, near the end, after a pause of more than twenty bars, it starts suddenly once more with a pedal-point. Both the prelude and the fugue, moreover, in their whole form offer us a sufficiently safe ground for assuming the date of their composition in the massive character of the chords, the effective and brilliant close, and the freedom of the part-writing. The effect of this work when well played, and upon an organ of adequate power, is quite extraordinary. Throughout we hear the roar of the wind, as in a stormy night of March, and we feel that such power is irresistible.

A prelude and fugue in E minor is of an utterly different character.[87] In the prelude sullen haughtiness strives against a deep-seated melancholy, which utterly overcomes it in the fugue. The inner connection of the two pieces is altogether much closer than that which usually exists in Bach between the prelude and the fugue. The former begins with broad rolling passages (the shakes in demi-semiquavers in bars 6, 8, 9, 10, and 28 are in Buxtehude's manner),[88] but from the eleventh bar onwards leads up to a quieter climax, in which we seem to see the earnest countenance of the composer without a veil. It is this noble melancholy which is the key-note of so many—nay, even of most—of Bach's compositions; only Beethoven possessed the same degree of power in expressing conditions of the

---

[86] P. S. V., Cah. 4 (243), No. 1. B. G., XV., p. 81. This internal evidence is strengthened by the external evidence of the manuscript, which has come from the legacy of Griepenkerl into the royal library at Berlin. It is in autograph, and evidently a first sketch of the composition, since several passages in it are marked as tentative. From the characteristics of the writing and of the paper, this autograph can belong only to a very early period.

[87] P. S. V., Cah. 3 (242), No. 10.

[88] The numbering of the bars is according to Griepenkerl's (Peters) edition. In the Bach Society's edition bar 18 is struck out, as being at least doubtful.

mind, and these took quite a different colour under his hands.   Like a deep sigh, this phrase—

goes through the different parts, accompanied by chords that come in reluctantly after the notes of the melody.   The pedal indeed ascends with mighty strides at the last, even in tenths, but in vain—it is obliged to yield.   Then the fugue comes in; its meaning as a whole is at once intelligible to every one, but in detail it is full of expression which is quite indescribable, and which yet seems to crave for interpretation.   The theme, at first timid and trembling, and then going on its quiet way, is full of infinite charm ; [89] the counterpoint is in the form of question and answer, and the theme makes its last appearance with resolute calmness in an overpoweringly beautiful pedal entry, and in the same position as the first delivery.

In the case of a musician who feels himself in full and hard-won command of all technical possibilities, it is intelligible that he should seek opportunities of exhibiting his ability from every point of view.   Thus it happens that the compositions of the first year of the Weimar period not unfrequently show, besides the intrinsic importance of the ideas themselves, a strongly marked desire for the display

---

[89] Which, however, is grievously impaired, if the *mordente* (*i.e.*, a trill with the additional note below instead of above) is performed thus—

after which the ear is forced to accept B as the key-note.   The feeling of the wavering fifths which is required throughout is only made clear by this rendering—

It should be noticed moreover that in this fugue too, in bar 19, the pedal, after a moderately long pause, enters with notes which only serve to support the harmony.   Besides the instances of this which have been noticed up to this point, this license does not occur at all again in Bach's later organ fugues.

of execution. The organ compositions in which this is observable constitute even at the present day the most brilliant concert-pieces that exist ; and as Bach's technical skill has been attained by hardly any one since his time, and has certainly never been exceeded, and also because they are based upon and grow out of the most exact and perfect knowledge of the instrument, their effect when performed with full command of the technical difficulties is even now very powerful—nay, often quite colossal, although, it is true, not so deep or lasting as that produced by his later works.

We will first consider a toccata and fugue in D minor.[90] This, even without detracting from the greatness or originality of his genius, shows in its details many traces of the northern school.   Thus the form chosen for the toccata is not that of Pachelbel, simple and quiet, but the varied, agitated form of Buxtehude ; its constituent parts are intermittent recitative-like passages, broadly sounding chords, and running passages on the different manuals, which are arranged in contrast.   The theme of the fugue is one of those of which even Bach is very fond, in which a melody is heard through broken harmonies, thus uniting movement and repose in a way particularly suited to the organ, and more especially effective in the pedal part.   The working-out is free and fanciful ; for long sections the ear, surfeited with sound, is carried restlessly along by rocking passages which have no connection whatever with the chief idea, which appears at the most but once, and is soon suppressed ; while it is impossible to recognise whether there is a definite number of parts or no.   The close leads back into a section of the same character as the beginning, with organ recitative and ponderous, roaring masses of chords ; in bar 137 a figure comes in which Bach made the chief groundwork of an independent clavier piece, and the reader who cares to compare them will not overlook the similarity between the formation of certain phrases (e.g., bars 87 ff., 105 ff.), and some phrases in the G minor fugue before noticed (p. 401).

---

[90] P. S. V., Cah. 4 (243), No. 4.   B.-G., XV., p. 267.

A prelude and fugue in G major will next be considered.[91] Both are treated at great length; the first contains fifty-eight bars of 3-2 time, and the second, after a transitional movement of three bars, 149 bars of common time. The chief importance this time lies in the prelude, which is founded on a subject treated imitatively and episodically with spirit and invention, just as Buxtehude would have treated it, only that this is far richer and more beautiful than he could have made it. A pedal solo of ten bars, which traverses the whole compass of the instrument from top to bottom, gives ample opportunity for display either of individual execution or of the organ (the pedal in the organ of the castle at Weimar was particularly good); and yet it is legitimately built upon the fundamental theme. After this splendid piece there is a falling-off in the fugue which, flowing and brilliant as it undoubtedly is, has an animation of a more purely external kind, and besides is somewhat too long.

Next comes a prelude and fugue in D major,[92] one of the most dazzlingly beautiful of all the master's organ works. The prelude, after a few introductory passages and chords, works out this subject—

with incessant imitations and episodic prolongations; *alla breve* is written over it, but this direction is not to be understood of the pace, but rather indicates only the style, which is strictly sustained, ornamented with many syncopations, and throughout displays full brilliancy of harmony. At bar 96 there is an interrupted cadence in E minor, from which point to the end the treatment is in Buxtehude's manner, in free and fanciful harmony, while magnificent power of tone is obtained by the bold use of the double pedal. In the following fugue, too, the manner of the Lübeck master recurs again and again; it has evidently been influenced by

---

[91] P. S. V., Cah. 4 (243), No. 2.
[92] P. S. V., Cah. 4 (243), No. 3.   B.-G., XV., p. 88.

a fugue by him in F major, before noticed, the theme of which was quoted (p. 272), and near the end, too, by certain figures from the fugue in F sharp minor.   This is a *bravura* piece from beginning to end, but in the best sense of the word. The theme, five bars in length, comes in in semiquavers alone, only once interrupted by a daring pause.   There is not much attempt here at harmonic intensity or ingenious interlacing of the parts.   Skilful pedal-players will find it exactly suited to them, for the theme is quite exceptionally fitted for pedal *technique*.   In this whirling dance of notes, which becomes madder and madder towards the end, we can appreciate the truth of the words in the Necrology : " With his two feet he could perform on the pedals passages which would be enough to provoke many a skilled clavier-player with five fingers."[93] It cannot be doubted that the work was composed for a particular occasion, possibly for one of his musical tours, and this is confirmed by the title *Concertato*, which occurs in an old MS. of the prelude.[94]   It appears, moreover, that Bach afterwards clipped the too luxuriant growth of brilliant executive passages, and greatly condensed the whole, since it also occurs in a form thirty-nine bars shorter, which could scarcely have come from any hand but that of the composer himself.[95]

In complete contrast with this work is a fugue with a prelude, in G minor;[96] the prelude, which in the former work had a homogeneous unity, is here without a definite thematic germ ; it begins with lovely quietly moving harmonic passages, and then chords of the $\frac{6}{5}$ broken up into figures of demisemiquavers rise chromatically in steps, each lasting for one bar, for the first half of which the seventh is always suspended.   The fugue, on the other hand, in which, in the former work, the passages hurried past with their transient brilliancy, is here a well-defined form, full of power, depth, and perfect mastery over the materials ; it is indis-

---

[93] Mizler, Op. Cit., p. 172.

[94] See Griepenkerl's Preface to Cah. 4 (243) of Peters' Edition, p. iii.

[95] This differing version is given by Griepenkerl at the beginning of the same volume.

[96] P. S. V., Cah. 3 (242), No. 5. B.-G., XV., p. 112.

putably the most important of all the works that we have as
yet examined, and in its pure earnestness seems to prophesy
of the works of the later Weimar period. To understand the
advance it marks, it is only necessary to notice how with
each new entry of the theme a fresher and greater life is
brought into the counterpoint, how not a single repetition
occurs which might save trouble of writing, how easily the
episodes come in, and how strictly the four parts are preserved, except in one place (bar 46). But yet the theme,
with its "e'' flat and d'''" four times repeated, and in the
whole of the fourth bar, has not discarded the type of the
northern school, and this is my reason for assigning the
composition to this period. Some other organ works of this
time must be analysed in another connection. We must
here pass them over, with the remark that Bach, who was
fond of remodelling his earlier compositions, sometimes, too,
combined pieces from them with his later productions. The
celebrated organ fugue in A minor[97] has a prelude which
certainly cannot be of the same date, but must have been
written in the period on which we are now engaged; this
will be seen by a glance at its character, which is quite free,
and hardly at all thematically developed; in this it agrees
with the great prelude in C major mentioned above (p. 402).[98]
And Bach went on developing the prelude into organisms
rich in idea and of stricter character.

Of great importance to Bach's thorough development as an
artist was the direction in which he was driven by his post of
kammermusicus, and in which he had up to this time hardly
ventured, if indeed it had not remained entirely strange to
him. Here for the first time he found opportunity for
making himself thoroughly familiar with the chamber music
of the Italians. This knowledge was indispensable for any
man who was to traverse the whole realm of instrumental
music, and build successfully on that soil. And then the
Italian nature, so exceptionally gifted with the sense of
form, had, in music as in the other arts, laid down the principles on which alone a safe superstructure could be built.

---

[97] P. S. V., Cah. 2 (241), No. 8.   [98] P. S. V., Cah. 4 (243), No. 1.

The art of organ and clavier playing had, it is true, freed itself by this time from its influence, and had undergone an independent development under conditions of an individual and a national kind ; but in violin-playing and music, and in all the forms that take their rise from the combined effect of several instruments, the preponderance of the Italian influence was still widely recognised. The chief forms which they had originated were the *sonata* and the *concerto ;* the former determining the arrangement of separate movements in one whole, the latter the formation of a single movement. The principle of form in the sonata agrees with that in the suite, in so far as that pieces of different character are united in suitable succession ; while, however, the suite proper was confined to a set of idealised dance forms, the sonata is chiefly formed on freely invented subjects, and yet without absolutely excluding the dance forms. The standard characteristic of each is the change between slow, sustained, and *cantabile* movements, and those of quick, fugal and ornate character; the so-called "church sonatas," which, however, must not be confounded with those by Gabrieli, but were only chamber music transferred to the church, admitted no dance forms. The three-part form of two violins, bass, and a supporting cembalo or organ was in great favour ; the judicious Italians quickly discovered that a three-part harmony was amply sufficient ; it is true that to deal with so thin a body of sound required some skill, but it also served to show off that skill. The order of the movements was transferred from the sonata to the concerto; but while in the former there were often four or even more movements, the composer of the concerto did not as a rule exceed three, and put the slow movement in the middle.

The form of the separate movements, especially of the first and most important, originated directly in the contrast and contest between the solo instrument and the whole body of sound. A *tutti* subject as important as possible always begins the first movement, and as soon as it stops the solo instrument enters in the same key with a new subject of greater or less prominence, the contrast often consisting

merely in the figures employed. This process is repeated
with modifications and prolongations, and with mutual interweaving in the keys nearest allied to the principal key.
Thus the form is still quite distinct from that of the modern
sonata, in spite of its using two subjects as the corner-stones
of the development; it is not evolved from the intrinsic
nature of the tone system, but superficially constructed by
the combination of two distinct materials of sound. The
slow movement gives scope to the player for the display of
broad tone and tasteful adornments; it is as a rule short, and
then the *tutti* comes back to its allotted task of accompanying,
but in longer movements it interrupts the free solo passages
at stated intervals; or else, by means of a well-marked regular
bass subject, gives support and connectedness to the whole.
The last movement is generally in triple time, and of an
animated and lively character; its form is either similar to
that of the first movement, or it is in two sections, in what
is called "Lied" or song form, with repeats; sometimes
it is in the form of a gigue or courante, thereby reminding
us of the suite, or still more—by reason of the concerto being
in three movements—of the Scarlatti overture.

Bach availed himself of the discoveries and acquisitions
of the Italians, not at first by working in the province to
which they belonged, but by adapting and transferring
them to his own especial sphere, that is to say, to the
organ, the clavier, and the church sonata. He was no
longer a novice in his art, but a master who had come to a
perfect knowledge of his powers and aims, and whose keen
glance immediately recognised the possibility of turning
these forms to good account. It was not till a long time
after, so far as we know, that he first turned his attention
to the sonata and the concerto, and reached the highest
perfection in those forms.

The use of instrumental chamber music at the ducal court
was the more eagerly pursued between the years 1708 and
1715 because a young nephew of the Duke's, Johann Ernst,
showed considerable talent for playing the violin and clavier,
and even for composition. In the two last branches he was
instructed by Walther, who also wrote for the young Prince

a compendium of the theory of music, and dedicated it to him on March 13, 1701; his skill on the violin, his principal instrument, he acquired under the direction of Eilenstein, his gentleman-in-waiting, and probably afterwards cultivated still farther under the influence of Bach. His passion for music was so great that when he was ill Walther not infrequently had to sit with him throughout the night; and that Bach also was closely connected with the Prince as to matters musical, we may conclude from a letter of the master's in which he excuses himself for some delay by saying that he has had to conduct some musical "functions" at court in honour of the Prince's birthday. Walther's instruction in composition—extending over three-quarters of a year—bore fruit in the form of nineteen intrumental works; of these six concertos were engraved in copper and published by Georg Philipp Telemann. Johann Ernst died young, August 1, 1715, at Frankfort-on-the-Main, in his nineteenth year, and his concertos must have appeared the same year—the year before at the soonest. Telemann was at that time capell-meister in Frankfort, but for four years before 1712 he had been capell and concertmeister at Eisenach; he was on very friendly terms with Bach, and in consequence of the intimate relations between the courts must have been in frequent intercourse with Weimar; in 1715 he dedicated to the Prince a work consisting of six sonatas for the violin, with clavier accompaniment. The ducal compositions seem, in fact, to have had some musical merit, for, sixteen years later, Mattheson wrote of them as follows: "The famous master, Herr Telemann, published some time since six concertos, elegantly engraved on copper, composed by the late Prince Ernst of Saxe-Weimar with his own hand and of his own invention. Of these, Concerto V. is in the key of E major, and one of the finest. To find an independent prince who writes musical compositions that can be performed is not a thing of every-day occurrence; still music gives a man particular advantages." [99]

---

[99] Mattheson, Grosse General-Bass-Schule, 1731, p. 409. The matter is mentioned with less particulars in the first edition of the work (Exemplarische Organisten-Probe, 1719, p. 203). Constantin Bellermann says (Parnassus

The Italians having composed the best violin concertos, their favour at court was a foregone conclusion. The musicians who surrounded the prince must have been interested in them, if only out of respect for him ; but they also found ample inducement to a more thorough study of them from the artistic point of view, in their lucid forms and the simple beauty of their ideas. Walther and Bach began to emulate each other in arranging Italian concertos so that they might be played on the clavier and organ. Walther arranged concertos by Albinoni, Manzia, Gentili, Torelli, Taglietti, Gregori, and a few German composers— thirteen in all — for the organ.[100] Bach arranged sixteen violin concertos by Vivaldi for the clavier and three for the organ, besides setting one of the sixteen a second time for the organ.[101]

Vivaldi stands out as one of the most illustrious masters of instrumental composition of the beginning of the last century. From 1713 he lived in Venice as concertmeister to the *Ospitale della Pietà*, after having been for some time in the service of the Landgrave of Hesse-Darmstadt, and he died in 1743. He was an extremely prolific composer, and, as has been said, had achieved distinction by the elaboration of the concerto. He also wrote concertos for two, three, and even four solo violins with accompaniment, he enriched the orchestra by the addition of wind instruments, and devoted himself generally to the adoption and application of new means of musical expression. His great strength lay in the treatment of *form ;* his ideas are often flat and insignificant,

---

Musarum), in enumerating the potentates who have been musical : " *Nec non et Comes de Buckeburg, et Jo. Ernestus Princeps filius Ducis Sax. Vinar. qui modos musicos fecerunt, hanc Poecilen exornant,*"

[100] These exist in autograph in the Royal Library at Berlin. The two concertos by Albinoni are the fourth and fifth of his *Sinfonie e Concerti a cinque, due violini, alto, tenore, violoncello e basso, Op.* 2. In the Lexicon, Walther mentions eleven works by Taglietti, and says they were all published before 1715. That this year (that of the Prince's death) should recur to his mind in writing the Lexicon, conveys an intimation that after that event he ceased to occupy himself more particularly with that kind of chamber music.

[101] P. S. I., Cah. 10, and S. V., Cah. 8 (247), Nos. 1-4. See, too, the Editor's prefatory notice.

though occasionally full of fire and expression.[102] We could only do justice to Bach's method of adaptation of these concertos if the originals were at our command. Only six of these have come under my observation.[103] Still, as they are all very similar in construction, an average judgment of all may be formed from these few. That Bach did not mechanically transfer the different parts of Vivaldi's score to the double stave of the clavier-player will be readily believed; but comparison shows that he not infrequently followed them very exactly, imitating and transforming them, reproducing as it were the abstract idea of the composition, but embodied in the clavier. In the principal themes, of course, for the sake of the whole he could alter nothing, and when they were as utterly meagre and stiff as the *tutti* subject of the first movement of the concerto in G (No. 2), he left the responsiblity to the original inventor. But by giving more movement to the bass, by adding animation to the inner parts, by supplementing the solo passages for the violins with counterpoint, by resolution of the suspensions, and by paraphrasing certain of the violin effects, he has in most cases produced a genuine work for the clavier, and at the same time essentially added to the musical value of the piece. All his additions occur so naturally and inevitably, that the effect is produced of a mere flowing and facile transcription, which in itself proves that none but a skilled artist could have accomplished it.

In this G major concerto Vivaldi gives the solo instrument the support of two violins, violoncello, and harpsichord *concertante;* the *tutti* violins commonly move in unison, while the violoncello supports the clavier bass; the rhythmical and harmonic accompaniment, consisting of the simplest elements, is almost entirely left to the clavier, and the

---

[102] Wasielewski, Die Violine und ihre Meister. Leipzig: Breitkopf und Härtel, 1869, p. 60.

[103] The originals of the first, fifth, and seventh of the clavier arrangements, and of the second of the organ arrangements, are to be found in Vivaldi's Most Celebrated Concertos, Op. 3 (London: Walsh), as Nos. 5, 7, 12, 3, and 6. The original of the second clavier arrangement is No. 2. of Op. 7; that of the ninth is Stravaganza No. 1.

strings are only brought in for special effects. With subtle artistic perception, Bach has reproduced the development of the first movement—which depends principally on the different qualities of the instruments — in the unpliant material offered by the clavier, by constantly filling up the inner parts. The beginning he has left unaltered ; from bar 46 his transforming hand shows itself in the equally flowing quaver bass, instead of the original crotchets with quavers intervening in iambic rhythm, and in the connecting semi-quavers of bars 59 and 67 ; so also he has set free the violin part from bars 60 and 67 in runs of semiquavers, while in the original they alternate with quavers in descending skips. From bars 76 to 90 high chords in quavers on the *tutti* strings come in with the figure in semiquavers of the solo violin ; to indicate this effect of mixed tones Bach has intro-duced demisemiquavers. From bar 91 to the end all the crotchet and quaver movement for the left hand originated with the transcriber; the original composer required merely simple chords, and the final passage through three octaves is developed from a scale three times repeated within the compass of C to *c'*. The *largo* (larghetto in the original) is almost a new composition ; Vivaldi had written a *sostenuto* air for the violin, proceeding only in crotchets and dotted quavers, and as an accompaniment simple chords in crotchets. Bach, detecting the ineffective character of such a melody on the clavier, worked it up in an arabesque movement, supplying the chief notes of the melody with incisive trills and *mordente;* and he also invented an inde-pendent middle part, from whose nobly melodious flow no one could believe that it had not formed an integral part of the original. In the last movement many portions, more particularly of the bass, are newly devised, as in bars 7 and 8 (and corresponding to them 33, 34, and 35), from bars 21 to 28, and especially from bars 43 to 49, where the original writer contented himself with the most meagre structure of chords—a mere scaffolding. Bach also made the finale richer and more brilliant.

If we now transfer the practical results of comparison in this case to the other adaptations, it cannot be very difficult to recognise Bach's share in the work in the general plan, excepting of course a residue of uncertainty in the details. We see his hand in the easy progression of the bass, the melodious middle parts, and in the severer and freer imitative passages. By these many of the concertos have been turned into genuine clavier pieces, to be played with no less delight and pleasure than Bach's original creations. And this is but natural, since Bach took up the work *con amore*, as is proved by the multiplicity of these arrangements. Thus, for instance, the third concerto in D minor must be felt to be entirely interesting—the *adagio* really beautiful from beginning to end—nor must we undervalue the inventive genius of the man to whose mind such a melody could occur; the swift and rushing *presto*, with its truly Italian stamp, was intensified by Bach by lovely imitations. The eighth concerto in B minor appears to owe even more than the others to the German master, and to confirm the observation, so easily verified, that B minor was his favourite key—just as Handel preferred F minor and Beethoven C minor. This concerto indeed differs from the others in the greater number of its movements. The progression in two parts of the first vehement *allegro* beyond a doubt is due to Bach, and the little *adagio* which follows has a remarkably striking effect from its thoroughly Bach-like harmonies ; and in the two other *allegros* the hand of the German is perceptible in almost every bar. The *adagio* of the twelfth concerto is conspicuous by its harmonic richness, and the melody offering in some places an opportunity for imitation in canon, Bach naturally at once availed himself of them. Here and there occur certain rhythmical " manieren " (*i.e.* embellishments) as—

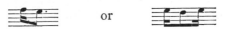

deserving of mention, because they were admired as an invention of Vivaldi's, and eagerly imitated ; they were called " passages in the Lombard style " (" Spielweise im lombardischen Geschmack ").

Bach showed his originality even with greater freedom in his organ arrangements. If in the transfer of concerted

music to the clavier an internal development only seems to
have been introduced, we here find that we have to do with
an expansion or outward development. This may best be
seen by a comparison of the first movement of a concerto in
C major which exists both as adapted to the organ and to
the clavier.[104] For the organ it contains 81 bars, for the
clavier only 66. Vivaldi quite clearly indicated the distribution of the movements in general; it is divided into six
sections, corresponding to the recurrence of the theme for
tutti, and which follow each other in the keys of G major,
E minor, D minor, A minor, and finally C major. But at
the beginning of the second phrase he had introduced the
germ of a form without maturing it, for the theme, which
runs as follows—

he immediately repeats in A minor; and not till then are
the passages combined.

Bach regarded this impressive modification as worthy to
be raised from the position of an episode to that of an
organic feature, by constituting new phrases corresponding
to it; and he therefore added two more sections, each beginning likewise with the modified theme, so that the composition
ceased to lack roundness and symmetry. The first six bars are
alike in both works, then the original, as we might fairly call
the setting for the clavier, passes by a continuous series of
figures extending through three bars to the second phrase in
G major, while the organ piece returns to C major, brings
in the first diminution of the theme, and does not agree
with the original in getting into G major till sixteen bars
after. At the twenty-second bar of the original it again
digresses from the primary arrangement, returns to E
minor, and here brings in the other phrase with the theme
in diminution. After reverting to the first modification

---

[104] P. S. I., Cah. 10 (217), No. 13, and S. V., Cah. 8 (247), No. 4. See App.
A, No. 19.

the two arrangements proceed alike with very slight deviations.   But the much greater variety of means in the organ
involves a quite different handling of the musical ideas; the
contrast between the solo and *tutti* could be represented by
the alternation of the Oberwerk and the Rückpositiv; the
harmonies could be conveniently supported by the pedal, and
the figures could consequently move more freely and more
richly, and in the most suitable position.   Many passages
that were not available for the organ underwent alterations
for this reason; but, even irrespective of external considerations, Bach endeavoured to work out everything more fully
and freshly for this, his own principal instrument, and even the
theme itself underwent a slight modification that essentially
improved it.

The relations which the three other organ concertos
bear to their prototypes we cannot, it is true, ascertain
by comparison, but it is certain at least that the character
of the organ must have involved the same freedom in
handling the musical ideas.   A composition for two solo
violins supplied the foundation for the second of these; and
it is highly interesting to observe how subtly the two concertante instruments are kept distinct from each other, and
what new effects of sound are thus evolved.   The third would
seem, by the extensive compass through which the *concertante* parts move, to be derived from a violoncello concerto;
there are in it a great number of showy passages, particularly
the extravagantly prolonged cadenzas.

Bach now began to avail himself of the new form of
composition, with which he had familiarised himself by
such energetic study, for his own purposes.   It had not
escaped him that the principle of employing two contrasting themes would be fertile in results, though with
certain limitations, even in compositions for the organ and
clavier.   The essential condition of music for these instruments is that it must always be polyphonic; but since a
prelude could be placed before a fugue, it was conceivable
that a piece on the principle of a concerto might be so employed; and, due reference being observed to the character
of each, an adagio might be not unsuitably placed between

them. In his Italian concerto, written at a later period,[105] he proved that under a master-hand the only question is: How? but that the form is not perfectly adapted to the nature of the instrument is also shown by the fact that it remains unique among his compositions. In fact he generally remained faithful to the old accredited forms, but his powerful imagination was now and then irresistibly tempted by any other that he could deem justifiable.

It would seem that the combination of a fugal with a concerto movement had already occupied his attention during his years of study; a composition exists which, from its awkwardness in some parts and want of proportion in others, can only be the work of a beginner. Being entitled a *concerto* in C minor, its evident purpose is to give something of a concerto effect in the first movement, by the juxtaposition of two contrasting groups of notes—for they are hardly to be called subjects; these slide off into a series of undisciplined figures, but towards the close he returns in due course to his *tutti* subject again. Then comes a fugue, very freely treated as to its counterpoint and development; in this, as in the first movement, we find here and there passages which look like badly managed imitations of those *tutti* chords which frequently interrupt the passages given to the solo instruments in the adagio movement of a concerto. This piece may have originated from some impulse given during his first stay in Weimar in 1703; at any rate it must be referred to the very earliest period of his independent efforts.[106]

On the other hand, a toccata and fugue in C major

---

[105] In Part II. of the " Clavierübung," B.-G., III., p. 139.

[106] An old MS. copy exists in the possession of Dr. Rust. What Forkel says with regard to Bach's first compositions for the clavier answers pretty exactly to certain parts of this concerto, so that he perhaps had particular instances in his mind. But when he goes on to assert that Bach was reclaimed from the unsettled character which he for a time exhibited on the clavier, by his study of Vivaldi's works, this may be true as regards that particular class of works, of which he perhaps wrote a considerable number at his very earliest period, but is not so in any general application. Bach had nothing to learn from Vivaldi in what concerns the construction of a polyphonous piece. Hence Forkel attributes his study of Vivaldi's concertos to a much too early time.

stands out as the work of a consciously constructive artist
and these titles are fully justified, for the piece consists of
three independent movements on the model of the Italian
concerto.[107] The first begins with a freely designed prelude ;
an ornate flow of running passages on the manual closing
with a long pedal solo, foreshadowing the two principal
motives of the main subject. One of these is the more
melodic ; the other, as was usual, more ornate. The movement is developed in alternation between them ; deviating
completely from the ordinary type of toccata and prelude, it is altogether concerto-like, but without doing violence to the conditions of organ-music ; it is plain that
here we have no mere imitation, but a masterly adaptation
of another class of artistic work. The adagio in A minor
consists of a very beautiful unbroken *cantabile*, with a perfectly homophonic accompaniment—a piece that has no
fellow in any other of Bach's works, and in which we
nevertheless feel irresistibly that, though in this particular
instance the whole work has been composed expressly for
the organ, the general style of treatment is not of the very
essence and nature of the organ. The pedal figure, in
intervals of octaves, carried throughout, and the chords of
the accompaniment which were to have a manual with soft
stops to themselves, remind us too vividly of an adagio solo
with cembalo accompaniment. An organ recitative leads to
eight bars of harmonic progressions in Buxtehude's manner;
the last subject consists of a quick fugue in 6-8 time which
in its theme, with bold effects of pauses with contrapuntal
passages inserted in them, strongly reminds us of the great
fugue in D major that I have already described.

By the side of this piece for the organ, we may set a composition for the harpsichord, also consisting of three movements[108]; this likewise has the title of *toccata*, which in both
these pieces seems to indicate the final fugue movement by
which alone it is distinct from the complete concerto form.
The first bars of the *tutti* theme are similar in structure to

---

[107] P. S. V., Cah. 3 (242), No. 8. . B.-G., XV., p. 253.
[108] P. Ser. I., Cah. 13 (210), No. 3.

those at the beginning of the second allegro movement in
Vivaldi's concerto in B minor, while the elaborate passages
usual at the beginning do not occur, and the heavy descending groups of chords for both hands remind us of the
methods of execution which frequently occur in the tran-
scriptions of Vivaldi for the clavier. Bars 5 to 7 contain the
solo response, and the movement develops this in the most
careful order through five phrases and the following scheme
of modulation : G major, D major, E minor, B minor,
G major. The adagio, full of melodic sentiment, is also
thought out polyphonically with extreme care; this passage—

in particular being imitated in beautiful variety, so that
German feeling is here amalgamated with Italian form with
an uncommon and delighful result. How completely this
was in fact the purpose of the composer is evident from
his adherence to certain external details—for instance, to the
closing adagio. The conclusion in the fundamental key, and
then the recommencement in order to attain the suspense
of a half-close as a preparation for the last movement, is
altogether in the manner of the Italian composers. Here
again, the 6-8 time and the cheerful nature of the closing
fugue, as well as the mocking phrase borrowed from the
first five notes of the theme, reminds us that it forms the
close of a composition planned on the lines of the concerto.
This gay and brightly dancing movement forms an admirable contrast to the elegiac character of the adagio,
and, like the whole work, was written in an hour of happy
inspiration.

In order to avoid repetition later, mention must here be
made of yet another composition which, though it certainly
belongs to a subsequent period, displays in the same way an
intention of combining the forms of the concerto with the
fugue. All we know with certainty is that it was written before
the year 1725 ; and it appears to me by no means impossible
to show, from internal evidence, that it was probably written
at any rate in the later years of Bach's residence in

Weimar.[109] It consists of a fugue with what is called a
prelude; but this prelude is, in fact, a complete movement,
broadly planned and brilliantly worked-out, on the concerto
model. That this was Bach's purpose is here particularly
clearly indicated by the circumstance that in the later years
of his life he worked up these two movements into a true
concerto for the flute, violin, and clavier, with an accompaniment, inserting an adagio between them,[110]—forming an
arrangement, it may be added, of really dazzling artistic
quality and splendour. A fiery, restless stir runs through
both the movements, and their importance consists in the
incessant waves of new and spontaneous embellishments, in
the fulness of the harmonies—in short, in the conception of
the work as a whole, rather than in the form and character
of the individual motives. That of the *tutti* passage at
the beginning is indeed insignificant in itself, but it acts like
a charm to unloose the spirits of sound; whenever it is
repeated new gates seem to open like sluices, from which
the rushing and sparkling flood pours out. It serves as a
clue through what seems an endless maze of music. The
fugue, which demands no less technical skill and "staying
power" than the first movement, is in 12-16 time, and quite
keeps up the character of a concerto finale. Indeed, in the
arrangement, that form is given to it, Bach having devised a
tutti motive for it; and not only has he inserted this very
skilfully between the sections of the fugue, but has worked
them out side by side without any alteration in the original.

Considering the eagerness with which Bach strove to
derive all the profit he could from the compositions of the
Italians, it would have been strange indeed if he had not
turned his attention to their organ music. Proofs exist of
his having done so; and in particular he turned with just
insight to the works of the illustrious Frescobaldi, a master
whose writings marked an epoch; he succeeded in procuring

---

[109] P. S. I., Cah. 9, No. 2. The piece exists in a MS. by J. P. Kellner, and
bears the date 1725. It has a rather conspicuous resemblance in feeling to that
grand fugue in A minor which is to be found in Andreas Bach's book (P. S. I.,
Cah. 4, No. 2).

[110] P.-G. XVII., p. 223.

a very careful copy of his "Fiori Musicali," composed in
1635, printed on 104 pages of particularly good paper, in which
he wrote with his own hand, "*J. S. Bach*, 1714."[111]   Frescobaldi's importance in the history of fugue is very considerable, although he had already had a remarkable predecessor
in G. Gabrieli.   In Italy the fugue had grown chiefly out of
the *canzone* (*canzone francese*), which were often played on the
organ or clavier, and thus served for the first material for
imitative forms.   Thus even in the course of years certain
rhythmical peculiarities of these chanson melodies remained
clinging to the fugal theme; for instance, it was usual for
the first held note to be succeeded by other rapid ones of
shorter value in a stereotyped form, and not unfrequently
the first note was several times repeated.[112]

Incited to the task by such examples of Frescobaldi's, Bach
now wrote a canzone, in which he preserved to the utmost
the Italian type, though he could not escape infusing his
own mind into the whole work.[113]   No one can fail to feel
the singular charm of this lovely piece; even at a superficial
glance the construction of the theme cannot but be striking,
and closer observation soon reveals the typical canzone
rhythm.   A second theme, chromatic in structure, is contrasted with the first, and the subject proceeds deliberately,
strictly in four parts, without any concession to executive
effect, or any attempt at instrumental brilliancy.   After a
steady course of seventy bars in common time it comes to a
half-close, and a new section begins in 3-2 time, the *prolatio
perfecta* in the terminology of that day.   This change of beat,
well-known in the works of the North German organists, was
also a common feature with the Italians of the first half of
the seventeenth century, and appears to have arisen in

---

[111] This remarkable relic is in the library of the Royal Institute for Sacred
Music, Berlin.

[112] This interesting observation was first made by Ambros (Geschichte der
Musik, Vol. III.   Breslau, 1868, p. 533).   Compare also Vol. II., p. 506.   A
selection from Frescobaldi's *Fiori Musicali* was published by Commer (Compo-
sitionem für die Orgel aus dem XVI., XVII., XVIII. Jahrhundert.   Leipzig:
D. H. Geissler, Part I).   Among them are two canzone which enable us to
make a comparison with Bach.

[113] P. S. V., Cah. 4, No. 10.

imitation of vocal music, in which Giov. Gabrieli, for instance, was fond of using it.   Nay more; Frescobaldi had already employed that melodic transformation of the theme, by altering the time, which had acquired almost the dignity of a principle of construction with Buxtehude and some others.   And thus Bach also made use of the materials of the first subject to make a new and highly ingenious one, following the rhythm of the canzone in altogether a different manner.   But a comparison, not with Buxtehude's work only, but with the closing movement of one of his own earlier works (see *ante*, p. 321) suffices to show how well aware he was of the difference of style which existed between them. Here the character is freely and purely musical, there it is smooth and sacred, so far as Bach's individuality would permit.   For he could no more belie his own nature than he could ignore the advance of his art; and his own craving for a nobler musical vitality, richer in individual colouring, led him in the quicker rhythm of the second section to supply a deeper harmony, and to demean himself more boldly in the progression of the parts.   Nevertheless, a thorough study of the details reveals a number of harmonic peculiarities, which are best explained as the results of a leaning towards Frescobaldi's style; thus, only to mention one—the attacks of the theme throughout the first section succeed each other exclusively in the principal key of D minor.

This canzone is not the only one of this character among the works of Bach.   An *alla breve* in D major is likewise clearly recognisable as being in Frescobaldi's manner, or rather in the manner common to the Italian organ composers of the period.[114]   It is an undivided fugue in an unbroken flow of four parts, and the peculiarity of this composition lies in the very method of the fugal treatment.   The main theme is immediately joined by an answering theme which accompanies it for the most part throughout the piece; close imitation is employed by preference; the entrance of the theme is but slightly marked, often not at all; the counter-

---

[114] P. S. V., Cah. 8 (247), No. 6.   It is interesting to compare a similar work by Pachelbel in Commer, Mus. Sac., I., p. 137.

point overflowing, as it were, into the theme, which moves in
the simplest diatonic intervals.   All this is calculated not so
much to preserve the vital and formative power of an in-
dividually characteristic idea through a series of diversified
aspects, as to present a grand organic whole, of which the
fundamental principle is laid on broad, general lines, while
its progress is always fettered by external conditions or by
its very essence.   That a composer has a perfect right to
distinguish between the Protestant and Catholic styles, and
that Bach here felt the distinction, is easily proved by
comparing this with other pieces for the organ.   The
solemnity of the general effect is farther heightened by the
breadth given by using nothing quicker than crotchets, and
by the preparation of the discords, which remind us of the
old vocal style whose true home was always the Catholic
Church.   But indeed no one but Bach could have written
this piece; the very magnitude of it, extending like a vast
arch, through 197 bars, could hardly have been constructed
by any other hand; and then those vigorous introductions
of new motives, as in the alto part, bars 32 to 46—those
grand organic superstructures, as the interlude bars 113 to
134—those imaginative and brilliant series of harmonies!
Though we may call the canzone a romantic child of German feeling and Italian mould, this *alla breve* will always
remind us of a deep blue sky whose image is reflected from
the calm face of a translucent flood.

Nor were the writings of Giovanni Legrenzi—who lived in
the second half of the seventeenth century, and was known
as an eminent organist and composer, and as the teacher of
the great Venetian Antonio Lotti—unknown to the German
master.   This is proved by Bach's having arranged a thema
by Legrenzi as an organ-fugue.[115]   A striking feature in
this is the constant recurrence of a full close before each
entrance of the theme, by which it acquires a somewhat

---

[115] P. S. V., Cah. IV., No. 6.   The autograph, which for the present has
disappeared, did not, according to Griepenkerl, name Legrenzi as the inventor
of the thema; but Andreas Bach's MS., a trustworthy authority, has the superscription: *Thema Legrenzianum elaboratum cum subjecto pedaliter.*   By *sub-
jectum* is meant the independent counter-subject.

fragmentary and short-breathed character, while usually Bach devoted so much industrious care to bringing in the repetitions of the theme as a surprise or, as it were by accident, against the background of continuous sound. This and the brilliant display of the close, in the manner of Buxtehude, make it seem probable that the fugue was written not later than 1708 or 1709. We must not, however, attribute to its early origin the simplification of form to which the second theme is subjected in bars 43, 49, 66, 77, and 88; at any rate this cannot have arisen on technical grounds, since the theme is not difficult to perform on the pedal in its proper form. The imitative counterpoint at the beginning must certainly be referred to Legrenzi ; Bach's own method of treatment is only evident from bar 34. The broad independent scheme of the double fugue form was new at that time—both the themes being independently and completely worked out before they unite—for, though before this the double fugue had been preferred to the simpler form, this was not for the sake of the greater richness, but for convenience and simplicity ; the second theme accompanied the first from the beginning, like its shadow. Here we have a full and mighty organism, whose abundant beauty far outweighs the deficiencies we have mentioned.

From which of Legrenzi's works Bach derived this idea we cannot say ; the matter is clearer in the case of three other fugues to which certain violin-sonatas by Corelli and Albinoni have supplied the themes. Arcangelo Corelli (born 1653, died 1713) was equally distinguished as a composer and as a player and teacher of the violin, and was properly speaking the originator of the violin sonata and the head of the Roman school of music. Tomaso Albinoni lived about 1700 at Venice, a musical dilettante who gained celebrity not only as an instrumental composer, but as the author of several operas, and as a singer and violinist. Corelli published as *opera terza* twelve sacred sonatas in three parts, of which the fourth was considered one of the finest.[116] The second subject is a fugue with the following theme :—

---

[116] Gerber, N. L., I., col. 786.

Bach borrowed this for an organ fugue in four parts which has nothing in common with Corelli's piece, excepting the stretto treatment of the first movement.[117] Though Corelli had by the end of thirty-nine bars exhausted all he could find to say on the two themes, Bach required more than a hundred to develop all the wealth of his flow of ideas. Of course he could make no use of the same structural arrangement as that employed by the Italian. He begins the stretto at the seventh bar, and remains constant to this intricate form till the very end; while the German writer, on the contrary, does not adopt this means of enhanced effect till the ninetieth bar, and works out the whole spirit of the theme fully and freely, grouping and linking the principal phrases by means of well developed episodes With what special ingenuity and facility these are developed is shown in bars 25 to 30, among others; here the minims of the first theme are steadily taken down by degrees deeper and deeper, while above and among them a delightful alternation is worked out in semiquavers, and leads gracefully back to the theme again. The fact that Bach should have used Corelli's theme for the organ especially, probably indicates that the Italian use of sacred violin sonatas had been accepted as a custom in Weimar. And we shall indeed presently see that he even adopted a form borrowed from that type of music in one of his cantatas.

Bach must have had an especial liking for Albinoni's compositions. Even in his later years he was accustomed to use bass parts of his for practice in thorough-bass; and Gerber tells us that he had never heard anything more admirable than the way in which his father—a pupil of Bach's—em-

---

117 P. S. V., Cah. 4 (243), No. 8. The sonata is to be found in the new edition of Corelli's works, by J. Joachim (Denkmäler der Tonkunst, III. Bergedorf bei Hamburg, 1871, pp. 142-147).

ployed these same basses in the manner of his master, and
that the accompaniments thus worked out were of themselves
so beautiful that no leading part could add to the charm he
felt in them.[118]   And this is quite in agreement with the fact
that we possess two fugues in which Bach made more or
less use of compositions by Albinoni.[119]   The Italian pieces
are in three parts, and Bach's—both for the clavier—are
this time the same; thus the scheme is alike in both.   The
first fugue is in A major;[120] Albinoni had considered the
matter at an end, and thought he had done enough when
he had supplied one counterpoint to the theme—

which he always repeats exactly in the proper transpositions
of key.   Nor does he trouble himself much with development, and in his piece, which is 48 bars long, he only
recurs to the theme eight times; the remainder consists of
free passages, not always above triviality.   Bach could use
but little out of the whole material of the composition.   The
counterpoint quoted he employed but once, in the first
entrance of the response, and even there with essential improvement; afterwards throughout the hundred bars which
constitute the piece he never recurs to it, as though plainly
to point the lesson that a regular fugue was something more
than a series of mechanical transpositions of the parts upwards or downwards—that it ought rather to throw off a
number of new shoots from the same stem.   He also borrowed an idea from a subsidiary phrase in bars 8 and 9—

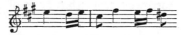

with which Albinoni could do nothing farther, but which in
Bach's hands blossoms out into the loveliest episodes (com-

---

[118] Gerber, N. L., I., col. 492.

[119] Both are to be found in the *Suonate | a tre | doi Violini, e Violoncello | col
Basso per l'organo da | Tomaso Albinoni | Musico di Violino diletante Veneto. |
Opera prima |*.   They are the two movements of the third and eighth sonatas.

[120] P. S. I., Cah. 13, No. 10 (215, p. 57).   Though it also occurs in G major,
this must be regarded as a transposition.

pare bars 24-27 and 44-47). Everything else in this remarkably beautiful composition is original; a keen freshness like
that of a fine autumn morning pervades it, and the figures
flow on as from an inexhaustible fount—healing and consolatory. The tempo, given as *allegro* by Albinoni, must be
the same in Bach. The richness displayed at the close, with
the introduction of the pedal, still has a flavour of juvenile
redundancy; but it is so completely of a piece with the rest
that even in later years, as it would seem, the composer made
no further alterations. In the other fugue in B minor, on the
contrary, he deemed them necessary, as two rearrangements
prove. There is in fact a great charm in noting how Bach
digested in his imagination all the prominent features of the
work, and here elaborated as it were a new combination of
the elements, so that they all reappear again in the new
work, but in a very different and far more effective connection.[121] A middle passage of the counterpoint of the
response is more frequently resorted to :—

This, which is the last quaver of the third bar and the first
half of the following bar in Albinoni, is used by Bach at first
in bars 12 and 13 of the upper part, in bar 58, and again in
bars 80 and 81 of the middle part. In the fifth bar this
passage of three quavers—

repeated in bar 29, is rendered surprisingly expressive by the
use made of it by Bach in bars 59 and 60; it flashes from
the depth of his soul with a fearful effect. The chromatic
passage given to the second violin in bar 20 appears in bar
40 in the clavier fugue, likewise for the middle part, then it
reappears at bar 50 in the upper part; a little *staccato* figure

---

[121] The second arrangement of Bach's fugue is to be found P. S. I., Cah. 3,
No. 5 (214, p. 48), the first in the appendix to the same volume. Albinoni's fugue
will be given at length in the Musical Supplement to this work.

in semiquavers from bar 22 slips in lightly and unobserved at bar 25 of Bach's work, and maintains its existence for some time. The chromatic ascending passages, bar 33, distributed between the second and first violins, are distinctly introduced as early as bars 14 and 15 in the clavier piece, and, after some restless turns in broken and divided semiquavers in bars 34 and 35, are at last worked out completely on the high notes. Such a palingenesia is certainly one of the rarest phenomena of the world of art; in it the composer has so completely assimilated in his own work that of another writer, that its farther existence seems thenceforth superfluous; and yet he has produced something so fundamentally different that, irrespective of the theme, the two compositions can scarcely be compared.

Still a certain hardness and stiffness clung here and there to Bach's first arrangement;[122] the process was not altogether perfect till the second was written, when Bach worked only upon his own first composition, without any reference to Albinoni's. Here all the seams were closed, all the contours rounded off, and all the parts were reduced to proportions of the most perfect beauty; at every bar we cannot but admire the master's consummate judgment. Consider, for example, only the transformation in bar 30 and the way in which its counterpart appears in bar 94; how in the phrase from bar 34 on to the next attack of the theme every part is stretched and expanded, while at the same time the chromatic figure of the bass is long drawn-out, like the enfolding sheath from which the living germ at last comes forth. From bar 68 of the second arrangement the development is quite different to that of the first, overflowing those limits by a long way, and never receding to a calm till bar 102. The general sentiment of this fugue is quite different from that of the former one: it floats in that mysterious twilight of feeling in which Bach is more at home than any other composer, and

---

[122] The b' as the third note of the response (bar 3) I regard as an incorrect transcript in the written copy for $c'\sharp$. There was no reason for altering this $c'\sharp$ which exists in Albinoni, and which Bach himself retains in bars 12, 37, and 68, and throughout in the second arrangement; the b' is a particularly unpleasant discord with $c'\sharp$ in the counterpoint.

which evades all verbal expression as completely as a vision. The Italian original has nothing of this ; and this radical difference would justify us in a corresponding moderation in applying the *allegro* of the Italian fugue to the tempo of Bach's. Besides, the second arrangement must certainly have been the product of Bach's fullest maturity, for the work undoubtedly is one of the master's finest and best. He himself had a great preference for it, and added to it, as it would seem, a grand imaginative prelude.[123]

When speaking of Joh. Adam Reinken and his influence on Bach, mention was made of that master's *Hortus Musicus* (see p. 197).[124] This work contains six sonatas, each for two violins, viola (di-gamba), and basso continuo.[125] As they are quite on the model of the Italian violin trios, particularly Corelli's, we may here discuss them in connection with the original Italian music. There are in existence two clavier sonatas, in A minor and C major, which have hitherto passed

---

[123] This prelude, which occurs together with the fugue in two MS. copies, has lately been ascribed to Wilhelm Hieronymus, the son of Joh. Pachelbel, and it has therefore been suppressed in the Peters edition. It should however be restored to Bach, since in what is known as the Fischhoff autograph of the first part of the Wohltemperirte Clavier (in the Royal Library at Berlin) after the last fugue, the first fourteen and a-half bars of the prelude are written by the same hand on the last four staves, with the title "*Prælude di J. S. Bach.*" Even if the Fischhoff autograph is not genuine—and I must confess to some well-founded suspicions—we may credit a very careful copyist of twenty-four of Bach's preludes and fugues with having assured himself of the genuineness of what he transcribed.

[124] *Hortus Muſicus | recentibus aliquot floſculis | " SONATEN | ALLE-MANDEN, | COVRANTEN, | SARABANDEN, | et | GIQVEN, | cum 2 Violini, Viola et Baſſo | continuo, conſitus | à | JOHANNE ADAMO REINCKEN Daventrienſe tranfisalano, | Organi Hamburgenſis ad | D. Catharinæ celebratiſſimi | Directore " |*. Hamburg, no date. Five parts in separate score engraved in copper ; folio. The only copy known to me of this now very scarce work is in the possession of Professor G. R. Wagener, of Marburg.

[125] Reinken in each instance has entitled the first *Adagio*, the second *Allegro Fuga*, and the second *Adagio* which follows this, the *Sonata*, combining the three under one number; to the dances which follow he gives a distinct number. But as these are always in the same key as the previous movements, and are conceived in the same vein, we may be allowed to give the name of Sonata unhesitatingly to each set, including the dances, and are supported in doing so by the practice of the Italians.

for Bach's compositions, because in the manuscript, which is
certaintly not his autograph, they are simply designated as
" *di Signor J. S. Bach.*"[126]   A glance at Reinken's *Hortus
Musicus* shows us that they are not altogether original compositions by Bach, but clavier arrangements of Reinken's
first and third sonatas. The first sonata is indeed completely
preserved in all its parts in the clavier piece; the third only
as far as the allemande, inclusive.   Nothing can throw a
clearer light on the sincere sympathy which Bach brought
to bear on Reinken's music, and nothing can more clearly
prove a certain intrinsic affinity between the masters, than
the circumstance that hitherto no one ever had a suspicion
of their not being genuinely and originally by Bach.   The
material supplied by Reinken has actually become Bach's
property by his treatment of it, though he has in most
of the movements done no more than paraphrase them
more freely and richly in a highly admirable and masterly
way.   Only in the fugues do we see him follow somewhat the same method, as with Corelli and Albinoni.
The second subject of the A minor sonata in Reinken
contains fifty bars, in Bach eighty-five; the giga of the
same sonata has nineteen bars in each part in Reinken, in
Bach thirty.   The second movement of the C major sonata
has in the original forty-seven bars, in the clavier arrangement ninety-seven. In this latter piece Bach disports himself
most freely; he hardly avails himself of anything of his
predecessor's but the theme.   He keeps more closely to the
structure of the original in the fugue movement of the
A minor sonata ; particularly in the theme response, which
he leaves unaltered, excepting the final fifteenth bar, although
he distributes it differently among the parts and introduces
very ingenious free interludes.   There can hardly be a more
interesting study than that of the process of modification
which has here been effected by Bach's genius, by which he
has produced works which are equal to his finest original
compositions.   We can see at a glance that these arrangements were not written at this early period, since Bach

---

[126] P. S. I., Cah. 3, Nos. 1 and 2.

endeavoured to learn from Reinken in Hamburg. Only a man who was himself a master could have allowed himself to undertake such a task, or have brought it to such a splendid result.[127]

To conclude the subject of Italian influence, as shown in Bach's compositions of this period, we must still mention a piece with variations, *alla maniera Italiana;*[128] these, which are arranged for the clavier on a delicious thema in song form ("Liedform"), resemble the Italian variations for violin. The figures, with hardly an exception worth mentioning, lie in the upper part: the bass simply goes on as a support to it, though it is not devoid of independent movement; the subject is principally in two parts, and so undoubtedly forms a strong contrast to the splendidly harmonised thema, which recurs somewhat altered as the last variation. Many passages reproduce the style of violin music, no doubt intentionally, and the modes of execution frequently recur which we saw in the arrangement of Vivaldi's concerto.[129] Compared with the "Goldberg" variations, in the fourth part of the "Clavierübung," these certainly fall into the shade; they are like neat and delicate pencil drawings by the side of richly coloured paintings. But the spark of Bach's fire is not wanting; it glows with intensified strength in the sweet

---

[127] J. P. Kellner has given us yet another anonymous fugue in B flat major which proves to be an arrangement of the first allegro of the second sonata from the *Hortus Musicus*. (See Dörffel's thematic catalogue of Bach's instrumental works, App. I., Ser. I., No. 11.) Most probably this arrangement also is by Bach. Reinken's Sonata in A minor will be given entire in the musical supplement to this work. It will be observed that Bach has disregarded the repetition in the second adagio, and he has done the same in the C major sonata. With regard to the cross ×, a sign that constantly recurs, we may note what Reinken thought proper to prefix as an *admonitio* to the viola part " *Si quis forte ignoravit, quidnam simplex × sibi velit, is sciat tremulum significare, qui inferne tonum feriat quemadmodum, hæ duæ* || *tremulum notant, qui superne tonum contingit.*" (" If any one be ignorant of the signification of the sign ×, let him know that it means a trill, in which the note immediately below the principal note is used as the assistant grace-note, while these two marks || indicate a trill in which the note immediately below is employed.")

[128] P. S. I., Cah. 13, No. 2 (215, p. 12). The number of variations differs in the original copies. Andreas Bach, our best authority, has ten.

[129] Compare, for instance, the B minor concerto, No. 8, particularly the beginning of it, with Var. 9.

and melancholy theme, which seems to wander like a shade
through the variations, but blossoms out again in the full
beauty of intoxicating harmony in the last.

The third group consists of such instrumental compositions as do not owe their origin to the influence of Italian
art, and are intended exclusively for the clavier. Since, as
has been said before, in the cases where Bach followed the
Italians, he did so not with the uncertain steps of a novice,
but with the deliberation of maturity, he could produce, in
addition to the works we have been enumerating others, of a
quite different kind, and of a masterly character. In the
course of our examination of these, elements of French as
well as of Italian art will several times be observed, the
employment of which only exemplifies his unfettered control
of all means and materials.
  Bach begins a small suite in F major with a complete
overture in the French style.[130]   The whole of the little
composition, which only contains three dance-pieces of the
most meagre proportions—a minuet, a bourrée, and a gigue—
acquires a heightened interest when compared with the later
suites, which are just as remarkable for the boldness and
ideality of their treatment as this one is for the unpreten-
tiousness with which it confines itself to the simple dance
forms.   After the overture there follows, by way of interlude,
an "*entrée*," which was designed to prepare the way for the
other movements; in character the *entrée* generally was
similar to the opening movement of the overture, but was in
two parts, each of which was repeated just as in the present
case.   The most valuable portions of the suite are the
charming fugue movement of the overture, and the minuet
with its lovely trio.
  Of the separate clavier fugues one particularly fine one in
A major must be mentioned before all the others.[131]   In outline it bears an unmistakable likeness to the one on a theme
of Albinoni's in the same key, although in detail it is quite

---

[130] P. S. I., Cah. 13, No. 4 (215, p. 27).
[131] P. S. I., Cah. 13, No. 9 (215, p. 52).

different to that, both in theme and in construction. From bar 35 onwards the development is achieved by the inversion of the theme, with which the counter-subject—

is now and then intermingled, after which the two motives are ingeniously worked together. At the end there are several of those pedal effects which, in their striving after technical display, point to a more or less early date of composition.

Another fugue in A major[132] is of less importance ; in this the strettos are hurried and yet slack, both in direct and inverted motion, and the theme is answered in bar 3 in such a way as to lead us at first to think of E major as the tonic. It must have been written at a very much earlier period than the others, or else in an unpropitious moment.

A fugue in A minor[133] in free form, and of an early date, has a charmingly arch and playful character; in it we seem to hear the elves chattering and tripping to and fro; it sounds like a scherzo of Mendelssohn, anticipated by about a hundred years. Another in the same key resembles it in many ways, and on that account may have been written about the same time, but further chronological testimony is wanting.[134]

We have previously mentioned several independent organ preludes. Whether they are really to be considered as independent pieces, or as belonging to fugues now lost, it is impossible to decide. The first of these hypotheses can be asserted with greater certainty of two clavier preludes, which have an unusual form that is common to both, and which, although they fail to become firm, distinct formations, yet reveal a certain condition of mind, dreamy and vague, full of passionate longing and unsatisfied aspiration. Until evidence to the contrary is produced, I must regard it as ex-

---

[132] P. S. I., Cah. 9, No. 13 (212, p. 66).

[133] P. S. I., Cah. 9, No. 15 (212, p. 70).

[134] In MS. among the legacy of Westphal, now in the Royal Library at Berlin (sign. P. 291, 34, piece 1). I know nothing against its authenticity. It is stil unpublished ; its theme is given in the Berlin thematic catalogue of the instrumental works, App. I., p. 19.

clusively characteristic of Bach to content himself with subjective tone-pictures such as these, without intimating the
connection between individual and general feeling in a piece
in strict form which should follow ; this characteristic, however, is naturally less observable in his more mature years.
The prototype of such compositions is found in a work for
the clavier by Georg Böhm before mentioned, in which, it is
true, the dreamy prelude is followed by a fugue; but after
this the character of the beginning is resumed, and the composition dies away in melancholy, murmuring chords.   Now
we know a copy of one of these two preludes by Bach, made
in the year 1713 by another musician, we may therefore
suppose the date of composition to be somewhere about the
year 1710.[185] That the other must be of about the same
date is probable from the similarity in form, and the fact,
which may be observed throughout Bach's works, that when
he essays the employment of a new form, he never contents
himself with a single attempt, but endeavours to exhaust it
as far as possible by repeating the experiment.[196] Both
are lacking in melodic charm, and present only harmonic
progressions which are strictly confined to a stiff and
unchanging rhythmical figure.   This rhythm indeed divides
their form into two chief sections, which are limited by
chords and passages of preparation or cadence.   The key of
the first is C' minor, but the entirely subjective character is
clearly seen in the fact that, except in the first and last
phrases, the key scarcely makes itself felt at all.   Even the
melancholy *arpeggios* of the introductory chords lead directly
into G minor, and in G minor the first chief section begins—

---

[185] The copy is in the Royal Library at Berlin, and has this title : " *Jova
Juva | Praeludium ex c dis* [= E flat, *i.e.* in C minor] | *di Joh. Seb. Bach.* | "
Below, on the right : " *Joh. Ch. Schmidt* | Hartz *p. t. org.* | d. 9 9br., 1713. | "
" Hartz "   may signify *Hartzungensis, Hartzburgensis, Hartzgerodanus,* &c.
I have not succeeded in discovering anything about the writer, who, moreover,
has copied it very incorrectly. This piece also occurs in Andreas Bach, fol. 71ᵇ
and 72ᵃ, carefully written, but without the name of the composer, and in a
different handwriting to that of the other works of Bach.

[136] The second is published in P. S. I., Cah. 13, No. 1 (215, p. 5), under
the title *Fantasia,* although in two MSS. it also bears the superscription
" *Præludium.*"

which, by modulations through the allied keys on the full subject in E flat major, leads into the second chief section, in 4-8 time. The semiquavers in the left hand yield to a quaver figure, and the upper phrase is replaced first by crotchets, and then by quavers intermingled with semiquavers; at last only semiquavers are heard. The close consists of two small episodes, in common time and 24-16 respectively, the last of which rushes up impetuously with short pedal-points, almost entirely on the subdominant, the tonic key recurring for the first time with these questioning chords :—

The other prelude is more broadly treated. Its introduction is made up of figures in demisemiquavers, and clavier recitatives. The first section begins at the fourteenth bar; the rhythm expresses an inward and ever-increasing restlessness, in accordance with which the harmonies are worked up from dim regions, higher and higher, till they reach their climax in one passionate outburst (bar 32), and then sink back into the depths. The rhythmic figure that pervades the second section is the same as that which we noticed at the end of the organ toccata in D minor;[137] there it vanished before it was thoroughly played out; here it is almost over-exhausted in fifty-two bars. From the epilogue (bars 87-106) one passage must be selected of marvellous effect; after stormy ascending semiquaver passages, followed by a short pause, we come suddenly to this :—

[137] P. S.. V., Cah. 4 (243), No. 4.
[138] A harmonic progression of exactly similar character occurs in the last of

With these two preludes we must contrast four fantasias. It is a complete mistake to imagine that Bach signified by this name rambling improvisations, to which he was in general little addicted. The fantasia, in the sense in which he employed the word, comprises regularly constituted forms evolved from melodic subjects, and not unfrequently consists of such forms alone. The question is quite decided by the fact that Bach originally gave this name to his " clavier symphonies " [139] in three parts, which are sustained throughout in the strictest style; and this is confirmed by a comparison of his works which have this title. But the opportunity for the free display of an inventive talent is by no means entirely cut off; the name seems to be ascribed to those pieces whose construction was not perfectly analogous to the customary forms, but always presented some few features of a free character. Such is the case with the fantasias under consideration.

The first, in G minor, [140] is built on three subjects fitting into one another, which all admit of double counterpoint on the octave; by means of their transpositions and developments the powerful flow of the piece is kept up. In the second, in B minor, [141] the first movement is ingeniously evolved from the germ—

and the second is freely developed on this subject :—

The third again, in A minor, is different in form.   It begins

the Italian variations (last bar but one); a new proof that both works were composed at the same period.

[139] In the autograph " Clavier-Büchlein vor Wilhelm Friedemann Bach." (" Little Clavier-Book for W. F. Bach.")

[140] P. S. I., Cah. 13, No. 5 (215, p. 32).

[141] P. S. I., Cah 13, No. 7 (216, p. 41). I cannot agree altogether with Roitzsch's theory that the B minor fantasia was intended for the organ. At the time of Bach's maturity—and to that time the piece must certainly be assigned—the employment of isolated pedal-notes, as in bars 15-24, occurs only in clavier

with a very brilliant toccata-like movement, followed by a
very lively though somewhat shallow fugue on the theme—

Presto.

at the end it returns to the toccata, which this time is
kept up by means of changes in *tempo* and recitatives to
thirty-five bars.[142]
The fourth is the longest and most remarkable of all, and
displays the most wonderful variety of forms.[143] After a few
preluding bars the first movement begins in D major on this
subject—

which is at first answered quite regularly on the fifth as if it
were a fugue, but soon is carried farther and worked out in
the left hand with free repetitions, while the right has short
chords, until this group of notes

interrupts it, forming a new subject, which is continued for
some time, the quavers being alternately above and below.
At the thirteenth bar the two groups are set in opposition to
one another, and from this opposition is evolved all the
subsequent progress of the piece. It is obvious that the
concerto form is at the root of this. This is followed by a
varied *adagio* movement in true toccata form; a short phrase
of four notes is prominent in it, interrupted by tremolos,

---

works; at least, my observations have always led me to this conclusion. The
light and minute character, too, of the first movement seems to me to be unfitted
for the organ.
142 The MS. is in Fischhoff's bequest in the Royal Library in Berlin.
143 P. S. I., Cah. 9, No. 3 (211, p. 28).

leading to figures in bars 4-7, which exactly correspond
to a passage in the A minor prelude (bars 87 ff.) already
described (see p. 430), showing that both pieces must have
been written within a short time of each other. We now come
to a third movement of more animated form again, which in
construction exactly resembles the G minor fantasia just
mentioned; here also there are three interwoven themes
arranged in double counterpoint on the octave; by giving
opportunity for the formation of episodical interludes they
provide the means for the development of the whole movement. Their first entrances follow the rule of answering on
the fifth, so that a regular triple fugue is the result. The
key of this section was F sharp minor, so the next movement has to lead gradually back to the original key; it is
even more varied than the first interlude, and is full of
pathetic clavier recitatives (to be played *con discrezione*, as
is remarked in some of the manuscripts) and broad uniting
harmonies; the progression from the A minor prelude,
which was illustrated above (p. 435) by an example, occurs
also here (bars 9, 10). At last we come to the concluding
fugue, in 6-16 time, which flutters away on wings as light
and airy as those of a butterfly. This last fantasia is in its
form a combination of the before-mentioned toccatas, in three
movements, of which the first is in the style of a concerto,
with another kind of toccata, of which also Bach has left
several examples. It is called a fantasia undoubtedly because it corresponds to neither one model nor the other
entirely.

For the proper estimation of Bach's artistic nature it is
by no means unimportant to observe how, even in a form
which allows of the most arbitrary formlessness, he endeavoured to construct great organisms in accordance with
fixed principles, and yet kept them utterly free from eccentricity. All that he did was controlled by the greatest
severity of form. And it was for this very reason that,
when he conceived himself to have hit upon a good scheme
of form, he sought, by repeating it in another work, to assure
it to himself anew, and to test the fertility and worth of the
scheme thus evolved. He did so with the toccata form,

which has considerable affinity with the D major fantasia.[144]
It is in four movements, of which the second and fourth are
fugal, while the others are in freer form.

The toccata in D minor must, according to the tradition
in the family of Kittel, Bach's pupil, be the master's first
toccata, and we have no right to doubt the statement.[145]
The first movement is very animated until bar 15, when,
according to the oldest style of the toccata, it alternates
with sustained passages in the strictest four-part harmony,
and full of warm, deep feeling. The second movement consists of a double fugue, in which the only peculiarity is that
both themes are almost exactly alike in melody and rhythm,
the only essential difference being that the first contains a
skip from d to d', and the second a skip from d' to b' flat.
What purpose the composer had in this remarkable construction, which occurs nowhere else in his instrumental works,
cannot be imagined; the result is naturally somewhat
monotonous in effect. The part-writing is in a high degree
flowing and elegant, with two exceptions, where the inner
parts are tossed about in an utterly aimless and unmelodic
manner (bars 10-12 and 73-74). This is followed by an
adagio of tender, wailing character, founded on a subject of
one bar long, which wanders restlessly from one key to

---

[144] I use the simple title " toccata " and " fantasia," for the addition " con
fuga " has no justification, as all these pieces contain several fugues, and
indeed appear to be nothing more than introductions to the concluding
fugue. I am convinced that such was Bach's intention, since, for example, in
the autograph of the toccata in F sharp minor (which we shall consider further
on) this is the whole title. See P. S. I., Cah. 4., No. 4, with Griepenkerl's
remark.

[145] A copy which came from Kittel's sale, and appears to be in his writing, is
in the Royal Library in Berlin, and bears the title : *Toccata Prima. ex Clave D.
b. manuliter. per. J. S. Bachium.* (D. b. signifies D bemol = D minor). By
the order of the words and the punctuation, *prima* can only apply to the
Toccata in general, not to the indication of the key. The work is published in
P. S. I., Cah. 4., No. 10 (210, p. 68), but in a form which seems to be a second
recension by the composer himself. The old edition, corrected by C. Czerny,
and published by C. F. Peters, seems to exhibit the first recension. This follows
from bars 18 and 19 of the first fugal movement, which are wanting in the present
edition, and yet are so very necessary for the clear understanding of the development. Czerny's evidence is valuable, while Griepenkerl's omission is
probably due to a printer's error.

another, and at bar 25 comes to a standstill on the dominant
of D minor. The changing of the harmonies is apparently
the chief object; it has the effect of giving relief and vigour
for a new effort, and in the economy of the whole work this
section holds the same position as do the free interludes
in Buxtehude's organ fugues, only here there is more connectedness. The last movement again consists of a double
fugue, of which the themes—

are certainly petty and unimportant when compared to what
we have been accustomed to in Bach, and even to the themes
of the other double fugue of this work. The composer could
not have made the first working-out follow immediately upon
the entrances without any episodes had he not intended to
produce the impression of breathless haste. On the other
hand he was in danger of entirely stifling the insignificant
themes by using episodes, so he chose an expedient which
seems strange, but is justified by the want of definiteness
in the whole piece, and before the real beginning of the fugue
he ushers it in with eleven bars of free treatment based on
the subject material. The themes are given out, and in
bars 3 and 4 are treated in double counterpoint on the
octave; in the remaining bars is stored up the material for
the episodes. After this the working-out begins, and has
many beautiful points; but in spite of its 140 bars it shows a
great want of breadth and fulness. The phrases are all too
short and breathless, and the themes too are so unfruitful
that one has soon heard enough of them. The constant
uniform rhythm is also very wearisome.

Nor is there much more to be said about the second toccata,
in G minor.[146] It is of exactly the same form as the one just
noticed. The first movement begins with a rush of descend-

---

[146] P. S. I., Cah. 9, No. 1 (211, p. 4).

ing passages, followed by an adagio in "free fantasia" form, in place of the beautiful four-part section in the D minor toccata. The second movement is a double fugue in B flat major, with a firm, soldier-like bearing, the themes of which come in together, but are kept more distinct from each other; the first entrances are again remarkable, for the themes are answered in the octave, as at the beginning of the last movement in the former toccata, but with several modifications that give rise to new harmonies. Here again a moderately long adagio without any regular thematic germ serves for the third movement; and the last place is occupied by a broadly treated fugue, with this splendidly energetic subject—

which is also treated in inversion, and by this means produces an impression of defiant fierceness, though it fails of its full effect by never appearing with sufficient freedom. The close refers back to the opening of the first movement, thus giving a cyclic form to the work.

The third toccata, in E minor,[147] differs in form in so far as that in the first movement there are no long-drawn-out harmonic progressions, and its general character is short and like a mere prelude. All else is of similar form: the double fugue for the second movement, the adagio with its fantasia-like recitatives for the third, and the concluding fugue. In substance, however, this toccata ranks distinctly above its fellows, and is one of those pieces steeped in melancholy and deep yearning which Bach alone could write. Thus the exquisite short double fugue is full of agonised longing from the beginning, where the first sigh is heard in the suspended seventh, to the close, where the themes repeat themselves twice over in the same position, as if they never could be satisfied. And then the last movement, so light and slender, like a fair vision passing by, yet with so pale and tearful a counte-

---

[147] P. S. I., Cah. 4, No. 3 (210, p. 23). Griepenkerl, not recognising the form from which it took its rise, names it incorrectly in his preface to the work.

nance that it can only be fully appreciated by those who, experienced in sorrow, have lived through the whole cycle of grief.   It should be noticed that this same frame of mind, which was represented in an earlier fugue[148] here attains its most perfect utterance ; the similarity between the two shows itself also in the subtlest details, especially in the faltering and intermittent character of the counterpoint to the theme, which has an essential part in giving it its unspeakable charm.

We cannot doubt that in the whole of the first half of the Weimar period, which, in brief, brings us to the year 1712, Bach's interest in vocal church music had withdrawn into the background, and no important losses are to be deplored, though we can only specify three cantatas written during this period.   Their characteristics are the same as those of the older church cantatas, and, as will be shown immediately, it was not till after 1712 that Bach decisively adopted the newer cantata form ; so that the period of their composition is indicated with more or less certainty.   They are, within the limits of their plan, as we might expect from the power of their creator, the most perfect cantatas of this kind extant.   But, moreover, Bach's individual cantata style, which has its roots in the full breadth of instrumental music, breaks forth here with far more power than in the Mühlhausen festival music and the wedding music, which is perhaps of the same date.   The composer had not only attained a higher level in the art of the organ, but had also received quite new impulses from chamber music, especially that of the Italians ; both these influences were turned to account in the cantatas.   The exact chronological order in which they stand among themselves cannot be decided except by internal evidence ; viewed collectively, however, they have many features in common, and are about on the same level as regards technical display.   One has no chorale ; it does not, however, take its text exclusively from the Bible, as in the wedding cantata just spoken of, but includes rhymed poetry,

---

[148] P. S. V., Cah. 4, No. 9, in C minor.

according to usual custom.   Even on first glancing at the
score we see the influence of the Italian chamber music;
the cantata begins with a *sinfonia* in B minor, on the pattern of the Italian three-part violin sonatas.   Two violins
and continuo—that is to say, the organ accompaniment, the
bass of which is reinforced by a bassoon—constitute the instrumental portion of the material; this is not increased in
the course of the cantata, but the bassoon has an occasional
obbligato passage.[149]

In this, as in the "Wedding" cantata, the opening theme of
the first chorus is gone through at first as a kind of preparation.   This chorus is set to Ps. xxv. 1, 2, the four clauses of
which are treated with as many corresponding musical ideas,
"Nach dir, Herr, verlanget mich"—"Unto thee, O Lord, do
I lift up my soul. O my God, my trust is in thee; let me not
be ashamed, let not mine enemies triumph over me."   The
external form of the chorus is fixed by this correspondence.
At a later period Bach would have contented himself with a
smaller quantity of words, probably with the first two clauses
alone, and would have built upon them two contrasted movements, but the whole was not too much for his present ideal
of form.   He makes it into one movement, with strictly fugal
sections at the beginning and the end, set respectively to the
first and last clauses of the text, for which he uses the same
theme in different forms; between these two sections is
inserted a middle section in free form on the second and
third clauses.   It is unmistakable that here Buxtehude's
fugue form has been transferred to vocal music.   The first
theme is this, with some modifications at the end:—

Nach dir, Herr, ver - lan - get mich.

It is briefly worked out in three divisions, with strettos in
the old style, and between the divisions there come in short
passages from the introductory symphony, in the style of the
ritornel which was usual in the older church cantatas.   The

---

[149] My knowledge rests hitherto upon the authority of a MS. in the Royal
Library in Berlin; another MS., apparently older, is still in Hauser's legacy.

theme appears in a more animated form and in quicker time
in the concluding fugue :—

dass sich mei - ne Fein - de nicht freu - - - en ü - ber mich.

It goes on for twenty-one bars without interruption, at first
with close strettos, and gradually with more and more
freedom. The relation between the quiet and animated,
the weighty and light portions, is just the same as in the
two fugal movements in Buxtehude's organ works, and
so too the interlude in this work agrees exactly with its
prototype in its abrupt and aphoristic nature. The words,
"Mein Gott!" which sound out on a fermata, lead into F
sharp minor, when the words, " Ich hoffe auf dich "—" My
trust is in Thee "—are set to an allegro of three bars long,
with semiquaver movement in the soprano part and supporting quavers in the other parts. Then, after a few chords
on the instruments, comes a passage of four bars long, with
strict imitations and interesting harmonic progressions, *un
boco allegro*, to the words, " Lass mich nicht zu Schanden
werden "—" Let me not be ashamed." This is followed by
a repetition of the word " ashamed " for a few bars more,
adagio, with alternating accompaniment of the instrument,
until at last a short ritornel leads into the last fugue. The
polyphonic treatment is very rich and skilful; the two
violins are always, the bassoons very frequently, obbligato;
one figure in the accompaniment—

may be especially noticed, for it occurs in all three cantatas
in more or less the same form. If any further evidence for
the thoroughly instrumental origin of this first choral
number were required, it would be found in the fact that
Bach used the idea created here again in his toccata for
clavier in F sharp minor, and altered its form in order to
suit the requirements of that instrument. This also must
have been done in Weimar; still, judging from the evidences

of maturity in the toccata, not immediately after the completion of the cantata. It would have been psychologically
curious if it had been, since the composer must have felt
that his material was exhausted for the moment.

The second number consists merely of a short aria for
soprano, accompanied by the violins in unison and the
organ; the words, which are in rhyme, express a firm confidence in trouble. Its form corresponds neither to the
Italian nor to to the German aria, nor even to the arioso,
although it bears several traces of this latter form. It is
restless and transitional in its character. The soprano aria
in the "Wedding" cantata, though on the plan of a trio, had
a much more distinct form. After this short interruption
the chorus goes on with the fifth verse of the psalm : " Lead
me in Thy truth, and teach me, for Thou art the God of my
salvation ; on Thee do I wait all the day." Its form is that
of the motett, in so far that each of the four leading thoughts
of the verse is gone through briefly by itself, and there is no
interruption of the instrument between them ; the instruments are only independent when they add higher parts to
the harmonic structure. Bach has a new and beautiful
leading idea for each section of the verse. First the words
" Lead me " give rise to a scale passage, which ascends in
crotchets from B to d''', in which the parts relieve one
another at every bar, beginning with the bass; the other
parts meanwhile declaim the words " Lead Thou me " in
full chords, and grand, restful alternations of harmony, in
this rhythm : ♩. ♪♩ At last each separate part takes up
the phrase—

Dai - ly wait I on Thee.

in different positions, while the other parts have hurried
semiquaver figures. At last the cry is heard in the bass part
on b, lasting for several bars, while the other voices press
upwards from above and below, with an intensity of passion,
like entreating hands stretched out towards the Saviour.
This is followed by an aria in D major—the principal key
being now left for the first time—for alto, tenor, and bass,
in the form of a simple chorale verse. As the subject of the

verse is a storm, the basses have a graphic figure in semi-quavers and quavers. A bar of instrumental symphony is occasionally introduced between the lines of the verses, which are here and there slightly extended by short imitations; with these exceptions the course of the whole is quite symmetrical.

The next chorus goes back again to the Bible-words, being set to verse 15, " Mine eyes are ever towards the Lord, for He shall pluck my feet out of the net." It begins in D major, but soon works back to B minor through F sharp minor. The first section is homophonous, but is interwoven and surrounded with an ingenious piece of orchestration, which represents in a manner as new as it is beautiful, a longing, heavenward glance in the passionate upward striving of the violins, supported by the gently flowing semiquavers of the bassoon. The second section—a fugue with an independent accompaniment for the violins—takes its character from the image called up by the text. The complicated interweaving of the parts is like a compact net; the escape from it is fitly enough represented by an upward leap of an octave on the word " ziehen "—" He shall pluck,"—and at the close by the forcible rush of the harmonies :[150]—

The last chorus shows in a decisive way the direction

---

[150] I may, however, mention that Johannes Brahms, to whom I showed this cantata, supposes the passage to have been wrongly written, and to run as follows :—

taken by Bach at this time.   It is nothing less than a
ciacona transferred to the accompanied body of voices.
There was no necessity for Bach to hesitate to use this
form because it had been originally a dance, for it had
been for a long period so frequently and freely employed by
composers for the clavier and organ as a form suitable in
the highest degree for the display of polyphonic art and
inventive faculty, that a disturbing remembrance of its
original purpose would scarcely occur to any one.   It was
frequently used even in organ chorales, as, for instance, by
G. Kirchhoff in his arrangement of the melody, " Herzlich
lieb hab ich dich." But its adaptation into the realm of
vocal church music was at least as great an innovation as
was the Buxtehude fugue form.   Bach solved the hitherto
unheard-of problem, which was that of also letting both
choir and orchestra have their full effect in contrast to and
in combination with one another; and this with wonderful
musical skill and judgment.   The chaconne theme is this—

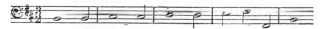

and it is set to the following words :—

> Meine Tage in den Leiden
> Endet Gott dennoch zu Freuden ;
> Christen auf den Dornenwegen
> Führen Himmels Kraft und Segen ;
> Bleibet Gott mein treuer Schatz,
> Achte ich nicht Menschenkreuz,
> Christus, der mir steht zur Seiten,
> Hilft mir täglich sieghaft streiten.

> Though my days are full of sadness,
> God shall make them end in gladness;
> Pierced with thorns, our feet are bleeding,
> Yet the way to heaven is leading ;
> God shall be for ever mine
> At the cross I'll not repine ;
> Christ, who ever art beside me,
> On to daily conquest guide me.

In the first section, in which the first six lines are treated,
the instruments, with quieter or more animated passages,

alternate now with the full choir, and now with the separate parts of it; and by means of skilful digressions into D major, F sharp minor, A major, and E major, all trace of monotony is dispelled. In the second section (from bar 53 onwards) we never again lose sight of the principal key, but on the simple bass theme an imitative structure in six parts is raised, of the greatest beauty and breadth; victorious ("sieghaft") as well in its expression as in the conquest of all technical requirements, so that a surpassing climax is attained, not for the final chorus alone, but for the entire composition. There can be no greater pleasure to the historical critic than, while examining the older church cantatas in their order, to come at last to works such as this and the one which we shall next consider by Bach. We feel the same ground beneath our feet, but all around us is transformed as with the wand of a magician. An undreamt-of wealth of new phenomena meets our gaze on all sides; grand tone-pictures in new, strange, and diversified forms, single ideas of stalwart growth, and of free and noble birth; poetic inspirations of such unspeakable depth, that we are impressed with an unearthly awe. The wonderful individuality of these cantatas is a circumstance which, occurring as it does hardly anywhere else in the history of the art, would be perfectly inexplicable and marvellous were it not that we can point out its instrumental sources, as we have already sought to do, and as will be done still more farther on. The accumulated results of experience which had been stored up in another sphere of art were suddenly and with a powerful hand directed into a new and only scantily fed channel; what wonder if a mighty flood rushed into it? It is true that after this account of the phenomenon, enough remains which can only be considered as flowing from Bach's own nature; and he must, indeed, at first have produced in the instrumental branch of the art the greater part of what he afterwards ventured to employ as material for his sacred compositions.

The poetic foundation on which the second of the three cantatas is built is the whole of Psalm cxxx., with which is interwoven the second and fifth verses of the hymn, " Herr Jesu Christ, du höchstes Gut "—" Lord Jesus Christ, Thou

chiefest good."[151] The cantata is in G minor, and contains five
long movements; the chorus is in four parts; the instruments,
besides the organ, are one violin, two violas, double-bass, oboe,
and bassoon. The words of the opening chorus are : "Aus
der Tiefe rufe ich," &c.—" Out of the depths have I cried
unto Thee, O Lord: Lord, hear my voice ; let Thine ears be
attentive to the voice of my supplications." It falls naturally
into two sections, a slow section (*adagio*, 3-4), and an
animated one (*vivace*, common time). It is preceded by a
symphony of a kind described before, in which Bach perfected the "church sonata" of Gabrieli, according to which
two upper parts—in this case an oboe and a violin—carry
on an imitative movement supported by the broad harmonies
of the other instruments. The subject of the symphony is
in this instance the same as the chief subject of the chorus
that immediately follows it :—

Aus der Tie - fe . .

This chorus has a tender and melancholy character, and is
doubly interesting in the consideration of Bach's emotional
history, when it is compared with the tragic majesty of those
colossal choruses on chorales : " Ach Gott vom Himmel sieh
darein," and " Aus tiefer Noth schrei ich zu dir," which
were the productions of his later years. In its form it corresponds in essential particulars to the older manner ; there is
no great extension; it is homophonous, and keeps up an alternating dialogue with the instruments. But in the fifth bar

---

[151] A copy which has come to us from the collection of Count von Voss-Buch
is in the Royal Library at Berlin (press mark, p. 49). The autograph was formerly
in the possession of Aloys Fuchs, of Vienna. A copy of his autograph catalogue
is preserved in the City Library at Leipzig. Here the title is : " Motett '*Aus
der Tiefe*,' 4 sings. u. Instr. (Partitur) 1715." If the date is correct this
cantata must reach back to another period of Bach's labours. A few very deep
notes in the bass voice, as D and C, are accounted for by the high pitch of
the organ at the castle of Weimar.

from the end the unprepared seventh on *e″* flat is for that
time a very bold stroke.

The *vivace* which follows gives the effect of impassioned
excitement, and at the same time is of the greatest interest
in its form because in the fugal writing it presents a most
striking likeness to the D minor clavier toccata in four
movements before mentioned (p. 439). As in the last
movement of that work, so also here, we find that the
materials of the fugue are set out in order before its commencement, while the theme is twice delivered by one part
in different positions, and is each time interrupted by the
full choir coming in. But, more remarkable still, the method
of procedure here is the same as in the second movement
of the toccata, where a double fugue was evolved from one
theme, only slightly modified for the second subject—a phenomenon that occurs nowhere else in Bach's instrumental
works. Thus from bar 12 onwards :—

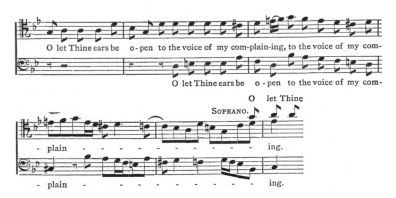

And, finally, as in the second movement of the G minor
toccata spoken of at the same time (p. 440), the themes of
the double fugue are answered at the octave, so also here the
first theme does not take the dominant until its third entry,
and after that the answer goes back to the octave again.
Such observations as these, instructive as they are as to the
formative working of Bach's creative genius, seem to me
also to offer the strongest internal evidence for the same
date of composition of these works. It is the same thing

as in the case of the preparatory entrances of the theme in several fugues that were mentioned earlier. That Bach should at different periods of his development, which never was stationary, have come back to such arbitrary experiments as these is in the highest degree improbable.

In the second movement, in which verses 3 and 4 of the Psalm are combined with the second stanza of the chorale before mentioned, we see Bach following out the method adopted in the " Rathswechsel" cantata, namely, that of transplanting the organ chorale into the soil of vocal music. There the pure musical element was too conspicuous; but here due allowance is made for the requirements of poetry. The apprehension which marks the words of the Old Testament poet, "So du willst, Herr," &c.—"If Thou, Lord, shouldest mark iniquities, O Lord, who shall stand?"—is dispelled by the Christian confidence of the lines—

> Erbarm dich mein in solcher Last,
> Nimm sie aus meinem Herzen,
> Dieweil du sie gebüsset hast
> Am Holz mit Todesschmerzen.

> Have mercy, Lord, upon my sin,
> The load 'neath which I languish;
> Its expiation thou didst win
> Upon the cross of anguish.

The words of the Psalm are sung by the bass, the chorale by the soprano, each solo; an oboe part is added to these two, and has a wonderfully pathetic, and yet consoling, effect, as it hovers around and above them; the whole is supported by a *basso continuo*, which proceeds in quavers, so that the result is in fact a quartet. It is not every one who can at once enter into the style of such of Bach's pieces as this; the only safe key to a thorough understanding of it is to consider how he developed it from the organ chorale. The ruling idea is the chorale melody, and the end in view is to develop this, poetically as well as musically, to a more tangible objectivity than is possible with pure instrumental music. So the contrasting Bible words, or whatever else might be used, only served the purpose of reaching a deeper feeling and bringing it up in a swelling flood to the surface, but did not serve that of dramatic contrast. This is moreover unmistakably shown in this case by the oboe obbligato, which musically has just as much importance as the bass voice; and the whole character of the work, while it reaches to the very depths of intensity, is as broad and general as possible. Bach achieved the combination of two apparently inconsistent objects: that of making the chorale the receptacle for the most subjective feelings, and that of preserving its congregational value and importance. He grounded his style entirely upon that of the older church cantatas, but succeeded in introducing individual sentiment in a masterly way into the general connection, and so giving strength to its delicate and tender nature. The contrapuntal web of the parts is so closely woven that no one part can have the pre-eminence without risking its coherence. The singer has to adapt his rendering to correspond to this. He must not simply sing his part mechanically, which indeed would hardly be possible with the extremely impressive changes, but must keep his place as the fulcrum of the whole, and make his style resemble the equable strength of the organ tone, avoiding all passionate demonstrativeness. The same rule must be observed in singing the chorale itself, although here the danger of attempting dramatic delivery is less, as long as the real meaning of the chorale is kept in view; in order to understand Bach's intentions thoroughly we must remember, especially in pieces of this kind, that the soprano and alto parts were taken by the unimpassioned voices of boys. Whoever blames such a contrapuntal treatment of the voice parts as wrong in style must abjure every kind of vocal chorale writing, except those where the chorus is treated either as a mass or in unison with instrumental accompaniment. It is evident that in that case certain classes of expression must be entirely given up. It is true that Bach himself must have made such reflections as these, for he soon found another and in certain respects a preferable form; but in his later years he returned more and more to the two methods of treatment just mentioned.

The comfort so anxiously prayed for in the second number is expected in the third, although not yet found : " I wait on the Lord, my soul doth wait, and I hope in His word." After the sad key of G minor the quiet beginning of the chorus in E flat major has a striking effect, since that key has scarcely been heard at all in the foregoing section. This key is not retained for long, for the fugue that sets out in bar 6 is only in minor modes. Beginning in F minor, *largo*, it goes through the keys of C minor and G minor to D minor, from whence it goes back for a close to G minor. This ingenious soaring up from dim melancholy to brighter regions is, however, only one trait of this piece, which, look at it from what side we may, must astonish and touch us. It is one of Bach's sublimest productions; nobler or more fervent tones of longing have never been sounded, nor could any spring of music well up to more perfect or satisfying fulness. Of certain of the earlier pianoforte sonatas of Beethoven it may be said that, although they are surpassed in boldness of imaginative flight by his later works, they yet bear the stamp of the master's pure and lofty soul in its fullest originality and most perfect form, so that we know not what there is to be wished for beyond them. So it always is with Bach; his later choruses are indeed loftier and more majestic in structure, but no one of them shows more mastery, nor speaks more directly to the heart. The following example (the opening bars) will give some idea of the theme and its lovely accompaniment :—

As this is more and more elaborated the entrances of the theme become ever more surprising and more impassioned, so that in order to give a perfect idea of it the whole fugue would have to be quoted.

The fourth number corresponds to the second; the fifth verse of the chorale is given to the alto, the sixth verse of the Psalm to the tenor, accompanied by a *basso quasi ostinato*, such as we became acquainted with in Böhm's organ chorales. The tenor part is very melodious, and the feeling of the whole is less troubled than in the second number, as suits the requirements of the text; but the movement seems somewhat too much spun out, and the interludes between the lines of the chorale are so long that the sense of its continuity is lost. As to the choice of the chorale verse, it strikes us that in its place in the hymn it forms only the antecedent to the following verse; unless it is to be considered as something apart and unconnected we must take it as a sequel to the text of the previous chorus; even then the word "and" is quite unintelligible.

The fifth number is naturally choral again, and is set to the closing verse: "Let Israel hope in the Lord; for with the Lord is mercy and plenteous redemption. Redeem Israel, O God, out of all his troubles." Since the last sentence is the most important, Bach treats the foregoing one in three little subjects, kept distinct by changes of time, among which the middle one is especially prominent for its beautiful expres-

sion, while the first, with its echo-like *pianos* and short
imitative passages, moves more in the older and more con-
ventional forms, and the last has an instrumental character
about it. On these chief ideas, however, is formed an
excellent and compact triple fugue, of a grave character :
no doubt the composer felt that a bright and joyful chorus,
after what had gone before, would not have formed a fitting
conclusion. In the treatment of the three themes, however,
it is the nature of the instrumental composer that shows
itself, for the text does not suggest such treatment. If the
demand that in a vocal fugue each theme should represent an
independent poetic idea is a reasonable one, Bach has here
committed an'error in æsthetics. If however his ruling principle was to merge the individuality of the voices in the
general effect, he is only consistent in this case. The justification of this principle in church music is self-evident ;
and it is Bach's special and peculiar merit, at a time when
the greatest egoism of feeling prevailed in church and the
theatre alike, that he succeeded in bringing the individual
will into subjection to the lofty aims of religion. Still,
human beings ought not to be simply regarded as singing-
machines, and there is a limit which should not be overstepped. Bach, however, begins the fugue thus—

and by the simultaneous sounding of words which should be
heard after one another impedes the clear recognition of
the predominating poetic idea. This is an excess of instrumental arrangement which cannot be approved of, and it

is significant that Bach's pupils and admirers took pleasure in performing this fugue as a mere organ piece.[152]

The third cantata is generally known under the name *Actus tragicus* or, from its commencement : " Gottes Zeit ist die allerbeste Zeit "—" God's time is the best."[153] Judging by its contents it was designed for the mourning for some man, probably of advanced age, to whom the song of Simeon could be suitably applied. No such death took place in the ducal house at this time, for Prince Johann Ernst died when a youth, and also when Bach's style of composition had reached a different stage. Possibly the cantata has reference to *Magister* Philipp Grossgebauer, the rector of the Weimar school before its reorganisation, who died in 1711 ;[154] at least I can find no other suitable occasion. The contrast between the spirit of the Old and New Testaments—between the wrath of an avenging God and the atoning love of Christ—which had already appeared in Psalm cxxx., is the germ and root of this cantata to such a degree that it is evident that Bach had fully realised by this time how fertile a subject for treatment it was. It contains no chorus of such depth and force as those of the 130th Psalm. Its character is much more entirely individual and personal, and so it has a depth and intensity of expression which reach the extreme limits of possibility of representation by music. The arrangement of the poetic material is most excellent ; it does not wholly consist of Scripture texts and verses of hymns ; and in several fit and expressive thoughts which are freely interspersed we can almost

---

[152] Published in that form from the MS. of Kittel and Dröbs in P. S. V., Cah. 8 (247), No. 12. This meagre arrangement cannot possibly have come from the hand of the composer, for it only gives the voice parts, and often not even all these without alteration ; while in the original not only is the figured bass quite independent, but the instruments take part in the fugue in a striking manner. In the four concluding bars—which are wanting in the original—the arranger has gone back to the introduction.

[153] Kirchen-Musik von Joh. Sebastian Bach, edited by A. B. Marx. (Bonn : N. Simrock), No. 6. B.-G., XXIII., No. 106. Also with German words in Peters' edition, No. 42, and with English words by Rev. J. Troutbeck, published by Novello, Ewer & Co.

[154] A. Wette, Historische Nachrichten, p. 418.

recognise Bach's own hand.   If such be the case the whole
arrangement of the poetry may, with reason, be ascribed to
him.

A tender, flowing sonata (E flat major, *molto adagio*,
common time), for two flutes, two viol-da-gambas, and
figured bass, forms the introduction, in which certain phrases
in the middle movement of the cantata are anticipated ; these
instruments are not replaced by any others during the whole
course of the work, and they impart a muffled and dreamy
effect to it.   The first chorus, " Gottes Zeit ist die allerbeste
Zeit," &c.—" God's own time is the best, ever best of all.   In
Him live we, move and have our being, as long as He wills.
And in Him we die, at His good time,"[155]—expresses at first
only the feeling of dependence upon God in life and death ;
and the greatest stress is laid on this first phrase, since after
a few beautiful bars of slow movement a lively fugue is
formed on the second sentence, depicting in the most vivid
manner the varied agitations of earthly life.   It is with the
last sentence, to which are allotted seven deeply expressive
bars and no more (*adagio assai*, C minor, common time),
that thoughts of death first begin to sink down upon us like
obscuring mists, and after the anxious half-close, "when He
wills," we wait, uncertain what is to follow.   In the same
minor key (*lento*, common time) the tenor now turns our
thoughts in an impressive way to the common lot of mankind, in the solemn words of Psalm xc.: " Ach Herr,
lehre uns bedenken," &c.—" O Lord, incline us to consider
that our days are numbered : make us apply our hearts unto
wisdom."   A mournful passage on the flutes, supported by
the other instruments—

is repeated again and again—like an inverted chaconne, as
it were—always in new forms, like an unceasing reminder ;
it remains some time in the original key, and then goes into

---

[155] The middle sentence alone is biblical for the most part (Acts xvii. 28).
Whether the others are original, or have their source elsewhere, I do not know.

G minor, and thence (omitting E flat major) into C minor again, and is the leading idea of the whole movement. The *arioso* voice-part goes on, frequently interrupted by pauses. And now comes the message so anxiously expected : " Set in order thine house, for thou shalt die, and not live," the words once spoken to King Hezekiah by Isaiah, are now heard in the gloomy tones of the bass voice, and the fearful and expressive close demands instant results. And if we dare to look in the face of the destroyer and ask " Why ?" the psalmist tells us : " For we are consumed by Thine anger, and by Thy wrath are we troubled."

With reference to this gloomy vision the choir begins a new movement—for the bass solo is in its form the second part of the tenor solo—on the words of Jesus, the son of Sirach (Ecclus. xiv. 18): " It is the old decree : Man, thou art mortal" (F minor, *andante*, common time). We have here the chief movement of the work. It contains three con-stituent musical parts. First the three lower voices have a double fugue on the text just quoted, supported by a figured bass of steady, even character. In contrast to them the soprano sings alone the words of resignation and longing : "Yea, come, Lord Jesus!" Lastly, the flutes and viol-di-gamba, in three parts, have the melody of the old death-hymn :—

> Ich hab' mein Sach Gott heimgestellt,
> Er machs mit mir, wies ihm gefällt ;
> Soll ich allhier noch länger leb'n,
>   Nicht wiederstreb'n,
> Sein'm Willen thu ich mich ganz ergeb'n.[156]

> I have cast all my care on God,
> E'en let Him do what seems Him good ;
> Whether I die, or whether live
>   No more I'll strive,
> But all my will to Him will give.

---

[156] It is not the melody in its usual form, but a modification of it that is here introduced, which is also quoted by Dretzel (Des Evangelischen Zions Musica-lische Harmonie. Nuremberg, 1731, p. 689, third stave) ; its first lines agree exactly with the tune of " Warum betrübst du dich, mein Herz." There is an error in Mosewius, Joh. Seb. Bach in sienen Kirchencantaten and Choral-gesängen (Berlin : T. Trautwein, 1845, p. 13.)

The design is clear ; the curse of death has been changed
into blessing by the coming of Christ, and that which mankind dreaded before, they now stretch out entreating hands
to; the bliss of the new condition of things shines out in
supernatural glory against the dark background of a dis-
pensation that has been done away. This is the idea of
the concerted vocal parts ; and the fact that thousands upon
thousands have agreed in the joy of this faith is shown by
the chorale tune now introduced; for to the understanding
listener its worldless sounds convey the whole import of
the hymn which speaks so sweetly of comfort in the hour
of death; sounds which must recall to every pious heart all
the feelings they had stirred when, among the chances and
changes of life, this hymn had been heard—feelings of
sympathy with another's grief or of balm to the heart's own
anxiety. These are the sounds in which all the deep
emotion of the piece is concentrated ; they raise an invisible
temple above and about us, among whose lofty arches the
song is prolonged and re-echoed a thousand-fold. At the
same time there is a proportional falling-off in clearness
and intelligibility. This form has this advantage over
that employed in Psalm cxxx., where the chorale is given
to a single voice, that the contrapuntal voice-parts are not
so completely lost among the instruments, since they can
assert themselves much more easily against the flutes,
violins, or oboes. But the principal thing, the chorale,
becomes mystical and indefinite, especially when, as here,
it departs from its normal course by means of ornamentation
and prolongation, and with it the import of the work is
obscured. But for moods in which we are made to feel the
deepest mysteries of existence this form is wonderfully
suitable; and, truly, who would not bow before the greatness
of the genius evinced by the youthful composer? Considered
from a technical point of view, what is it but a transcription
of an organ chorale in Böhm's manner, with interludes on
independent motives? And yet how entirely the form is
made subservient to a new and lofty idea! and, on the other
hand, how perfectly the idea inspires the form! This form
demands, for the sake of a consistency which can be least

dispensed with in organ pieces, that the episodical material shall be repeated after each line of the chorale, and by this the work, even in its vocal form, preserves the characteristic of its genus.

We might have expected that Bach would have treated the contrast between the two aspects of death, under the Old and New Covenants, in such a way that, as the former was in truth conquered by the latter, so in his artistic representation it would gradually retire till it was reduced to silence. This would have been a dramatic representation of the conflict between the two powers; but all dramatic modes of treatment lie wholly outside the province of Bach's church cantatas, and indeed are foreign to the spirit of genuine church music in general. Gluck makes the furies retreat gradually before the song of Orpheus, and leave the field to him; in Bach the threatening image of the " old decree " survives to the last. The representation of the contrast is purely lyrical, just as it is in the choral numbers of the " Rathscantate," of Psalm cxxx., and in many other places. In his striving after the greatest possible emotional intensity Bach is not content with the ordinary means at his command; some factor or other, which need have no obvious connection with the musical materials, must be added to complete the intended effect. To this end the words of the soprano part are taken from the Revelation (xxii. 20), that production of the most ecstatic religious devotion, and by this means the whole feeling of that book, with all its mysterious awe, is brought before the imagination of the hearer who is versed in the Bible.[157] And what is that curious fluttering produced by the low flutes after the last note of the chorale, and the strange shake that dies away before coming to the end of the note?—

---

[157] That these four words may have been inserted here, without regard to the context, is of course not impossible, and I cannot prove my assertion except by appealing to my own personal idea; yet I am almost convinced that such is the case. Let any one read the two last chapters of the Revelation with regard to the general poetic impression alone, and then turn to Bach's music, and let him judge for himself.

Wenn mein Herz und Gedanken
Zergehn als wie ein Licht,
Das hin und her thut wanken,
Wenn ihm die Flamm gebricht—

When heart and flesh are failing
Like to a flickering light,
Which wavers in its waning
Ere it be lost in night.

These words, from a glorious old hymn,[158] to which the
melody had been put more than a hundred years before,
by a cantor of Weimar, Melchior Vulpius, give the fitting
answer. Doubtless they were in the composer's imagination, and inspired that unique tone-picture where the lower
parts, still muttering the stern decree of fate, at last mount
gently in triads (while the strings have a passage in contrary motion) and vanish like clouds into the air, while the
soprano—supported by a bass, the pulsating rhythm of
which grows ever fainter and fainter—hangs alone over
the abyss like a fluttering spirit, and when at last all has
become still as death fades away, gently murmuring the
name "Jesus."

Let us consider once more the number of sources from
which Bach has drawn the feelings which make up the
whole emotional material that filled his imagination. Old
Testament dread, Gospel consolation, exaltation of a general
devotional kind, ecstatic hope in an ineffable splendour, the
powerful picture of mortal frailty vanquished by the spirit;
and, as a more solid element in this sea of inconstant, ever-
varying colours, a strict and simple musical organism is
added. The man who can feel all these diverse elements in
a comprehensive whole is capable of wonderful experiences.
But it is certain too that when such various and intensely
subjective feelings are brought to bear on the construction of

---

158 "Christus der ist mein Leben," by an unknown author.

a work of art, general effect is out of the question. If Bach wrote no second work of this kind, he knew the reason why.

The way of Christian consolation has been pointed out ; now confidence takes deeper hold on Christ's redeeming work. The alto sings a paraphrase of the words spoken by Him on the cross to an indescribably quiet and deeply touching air : " Into Thy hands my spirit I commend ; Thou hast redeemed me, O Lord, thou God of truth " (B flat minor, common time). It is accompanied with the figured bass alone, and exhibits—in a bass subject which recurs five times —a form compounded of the chaconne and Böhm's organ chorales. The soul praying thus fervently hears the words of the Redeemer addressed to it, as the bass comes in as if in reply, also *arioso :* " Thou shalt be with Me to-day in Paradise." After this promise, " Simeon's death-hymn" (a well-known chorale) flows forth as it were involuntarily from the comforted heart : " In joy and peace I pass away whene'er God willeth," which is sung by the alto, while the bass continues its beautiful and expressive solo; and two viol-di-gambas are brought in independently to complete the picture. Thus individual emotion is once again sublimated to general devotional feeling, and this is brought into prominence by the bass only accompanying the chorale through half its length, and then keeping silence and letting the chorale finish alone, as if nothing remained to say but what the chorale implied in itself, with its thoughtful interpreting instrumental accompaniment. With this the fourth movement concludes, having returned to the key of C minor at the beginning of the chorale—before that it was in B flat minor—and in the final chorus it goes back to the original key.

The whole plan clearly shows that the chorale was originally intended for a solo voice, although of late the contrary opinion seems to have come into favour. In such questions it should be remembered that the noticeable difference in tone between a solo and a chorus, such as we are accustomed to nowadays, did not exist for Bach. The choir proper could only double the parts ; and even when the ripieno chorus of the schoolboys, and perhaps some of the "Adjuvanten" (see p. 225), were added, which was only the case in full choral movements, each part certainly could not have numbered more than five representatives. Even if Bach had allowed this multiplying of voices, a performance by a chorus on the modern scale would not be justified; there would however be no æsthetic objection to the addition of two or three voices, in such a way as not to disturb the acoustic balance. The *vivace* for bass, "Set thy house in order," is certainly also designed only for solo, or else we must assign to the chorus the preceding tenor air, which agrees with it exactly in form. It is plain that the relation between the voices is the same as it is in the fourth movement between the alto and bass. In general the character of the cantata is unsuited to large masses, with the possible exception of the principal movement, in which, if anywhere, the ripieno choir may have assisted.[159] These two movements correspond to one another in the same way that the second and fourth do, so that the movement in F minor, the true centre of the whole, is inclosed by double and corresponding numbers. The last chorus consists of the so-called "fifth Gloria" to the melody "In dich hab' ich gehoffet, Herr"— "In Thee, O Lord, is all my hope":—

All glory, praise and majesty
To Father, Son, and Spirit be,
The holy, blessed Trinity;
Whose power to us
Gives victory
Through Jesus Christ. Amen.

The treatment of the chorale, with its melodic adornments and interludes, and the form of its prelude, is in that still older style which is known to us from Buxtehude's cantatas. The lines are given out in broad four-part harmony, the last serving as the theme of a fugue; the counter-subject comes in on the word "Amen" in semiquavers, and the brilliant number rushes by, *allegro*. The late entry of the instruments, and the augmentation of the theme in the soprano near the

---

[159] It is a great pity that we have no autograph remaining which might possibly tend to clear up this point.

end, give it constantly increasing interest. After that there is a remarkable effect; the last two chords in the chorus vanish away with an echo on the instruments, *piano*, which was at that time a favourite kind of close, owing its origin to an organ effect; it also occurs in the " Wedding " cantata. In this case these chords, which, to attain their proper effect, should be rendered very broadly, and slightly *rallentando*, are intended to keep up the feeling of the whole in the hearer's mind.[160] It is obvious that in feeling and sentiment this chorus is the companion picture to the first. There the idea is that of life committed into God's hands, here it is that of the final victory of life through Divine assistance, although it is solemnised by the subject of death. And so it must be; we have to learn to repress by the customary duties of life the thoughts stirred up at the grave of a beloved one; thoughts which lead us away from life and the world.

So we have before us a work of art, well rounded-off and firm in its formation, and warmed by the deepest intensity of feeling even in the smallest details. It fully deserves the universal admiration it has gained since its re-emergence to the light of day. This and the cantata " Ich hatte viel Bekümmerniss"—" My spirit was in heaviness,"—which is nearly allied to it both in date and feeling, have become the most popular out of about a hundred and fifty cantatas by Bach already published. It was quite natural that the musical instinct should be attracted by this more youthful and tender religion which speaks so plainly to the soul, rather than by the stern heights of his later compositions. For it was not through the medium of the Church that our age again found access to Bach, but through music in the abstract; his instrumental compositions had never been entirely forgotten. A similar road was taken by the master himself when, starting from the organ and clavier, he first improved the older church cantatas originated by individual

---

[160] In the editions the *piano* is only put for the instruments; of course it applies equally to the last " Amen " of the chorus, if analogy and internal considerations are to have any voice in the matter.

feeling, so as to infuse into them some universal import, and then soared steadily upwards to the heights of devotional sublimity. In this similarity of progress lies the ground for hoping that in our time an ever-increasing interest will be taken in the later church music of Bach, to which these earlier cantatas lead up gradually. It is true that, as these are more than mere stepping-stones—nay, perfect works of art in themselves—they have certain individualities which are absent from the works which follow. The words have the great advantage of consisting of texts of Scripture full of deep meaning, and church hymns; while in the later cantatas, rhymes—often of the most washy description—take their place. The music is easier of performance, particularly because of the very limited employment of wind instruments.

More than all, however, there is in these a fresh originality which is impartially applied, even to the most minute details; which sometimes goes perhaps too far, but always gives the feeling of an inexhaustible power. Not only the individual ideas, but the general forms—all alike are entirely new. Only consider the fabulous variety and fulness of the forms comprised in these three cantatas, and how these forms contain nothing which strikes us as forced, but are thoroughly and perfectly formed with admirable power. When, soon after this, Bach had made himself familiar with the Italian *da capo* aria, he became conscious of his waste of power, since he could do much with that form, of a simpler, and therefore better kind, without foregoing his originality in any degree; while ample field was left in other directions for the exercise of his gift for creating new general forms. Though production was rendered easier by this means, yet there was at least the possibility of his lapsing into formality, which in truth occurred very seldom indeed, but for which the opportunity was entirely wanting in the older cantatas. Whoever will compare these with those, and seek to comprehend them thoroughly, will find that these earlier works seem to soar up into a world of their own, as if released from all material bonds. If we can, however, point out passages in which the roots are let down to the realm of earth, the works are exonerated from the reproach of formlessness; nor could it ever have been raised but from a misapprehension of their place in the history of music.[161]

IV.

CHURCH MUSIC.—ANALYSIS OF THE CANTATA FORM.

WHILE Bach was striving contemplatively after his pure ideal in quiet and calm activity, outside in the world the murky flood of an aimless artistic struggle was rising higher and higher, and approaching with its threatening tide even the domain of music which still remained the stronghold of earnest endeavour, the last and highest goal of human effort. It was now the opera which, being more and more cultivated by both German and foreign artists, was attracting all attention to itself. Invented, to a certain extent, at the beginning of the seventeenth century by the Italians, it had soon been transplanted as a luxury for courts into Germany, then again it was checked in its growth by the great war; but during the last decade it had shot up luxuriantly, not without acquiring some national peculiarities, particularly since the citizen class had taken possession of it, following the example of Hamburg. Ere long, however, it was again wholly dependent on the foreigners who had originated it, and who were by nature so well qualified for it, and in this form it retired

---

[161] In a letter to O. Jahn (Mitgeth. Grenzboten, Jahrg. XXIX., p. 95), Hauptmann says, mixing deserved praise with undeserved blame: "Yesterday at the Euterpe Concert Bach's 'Gottes Zeit' was given. What a marvellous intensity pervades it, without a bar of conventionality! Of the cantatas known to me, I know none in which such design and regard is had to the musical import and its expression. Were we able and willing, however, to disregard this side of the beauty, and look upon the whole as a work of musical structure, it is a curious prodigy, composed of movements which jostle one another and yet grow out of one another, put together by accident, just as the sentences of the text are, without any grouping or climaxes," &c. Other utterances of Hauptmann's on the cantatas occur in his letter to Hauser (Leipzig: Breitkopf and Härtel), I., 86, and II., 51. It is remarkable that Mendelssohn's artistic feeling led him to judge rightly of the relations between this and the later cantatas (Letters, II., 90).

completely, during the first half of the eighteenth century, to the courts of princes, as being its most suitable refuge, there to minister to their splendour, extravagance, and amusement—a foreign growth on German soil, rich in foliage but barren in fruit.

What we did to advance the cause of opera is, on the whole, but little to boast of. An enervated and powerless generation, lacking any lofty common aim and incapable of any serious artistic enjoyment, found only the means of forgetting the deplorable conditions of actual life in these gaudy and uninspiring phantasmagoria, of which the material was for the most part both foreign and indifferent to them. But there were still some noble and genuine spirits of true metal who dug once more into the uncorrupted depths of humanity and strove to extract from them something fresher and better; as a sign of resuscitating life there were a number of vigorous and highly endowed artists, who would have laughed to scorn existence itself if they had been desired to fritter their talents for nothing better than the trivial amusement of a heartless crowd. But since in spite of all this the liking for opera was almost universal, there must have been some deeply rooted reason for this preference; and in fact it is easy to detect. The tendency of all the musical art of the last two and a half centuries had been increasingly towards the expression of individuality, corresponding in fact to the general spirit of the times; personal feeling, which had been kept in the background by the many-voiced music of the preceding period, now asserted its right to the most vehement and express utterance. The Germans indeed were not equal to inventing means and forms for this; they were hindered alike by the character of the national mind and by the unfavourable circumstances of the times. But when once the Italians had set them the example, none but the Germans could carry on the development of it in the right direction, since the impulse towards individualisation is inborn in them more than in any other people; and from the beginning of the eighteenth century Germany took the lead among the nations in matters musical, and has held it to the present day.

Now it was in the opera of that period that this craving found the most unlimited gratification, since it consisted almost entirely of solo singing; the dramatic element was degraded to a mere framework on which to hang personal incidents, and so imposed neither musical nor poetic limitations on the egoism of the parts. Indeed, as everything in it aimed merely at satisfying the vanity of individual executants, no work could originate possessing any artistic vitality or elevating influence. But it was only the way in which the ruling impulse expressed itself that was in fault, and because it displayed itself in needless imitation of the work of others; in itself it was healthy and justifiable, a natural outcome of historical progress. Hence, though the opera of that date was incapable of producing any enduring work on its own lines, it exerted an influence on those branches of art in which the vocal and instrumental music of the time presently culminated—the Cantatas and Passion-music of Bach and the Oratorios of Handel, so that the clearest results of that influence, mingled of course with other elements, are recognisable in those works.

Personal sentiment had acquired a very conspicuous hold even in sacred music from about the middle of the seventeenth century. But the occasion was at the moment unfavourable to any radical transformation; both on historic grounds— since church music still clung to its past traditions of noble and beautiful chorale singing—and on æsthetic grounds, since the sacredness of the feelings involved seemed to forbid the expression of individual emotions. It was not until this new development of music had drunk its fill of vigour in that current where solo singing constituted a determining factor and had roused a sympathetic echo in the hearts of men throughout Europe, that it knocked insistently at the gates of the Church, and had not to wait long for admission, being recommended by universal favour.

Its captivating effect rested principally on two main features—the recitative and the aria. The Church had already accepted recitative in its older and still very limited form. The *arioso* had grown out of this, and had been frequently used in the solo declamation of Bible words; and, being supplemented with a certain richness of instrumental harmony, produced an effect which, though informal, was not altogether undignified. On the other hand the recitative was gradually developed in the theatre into great pliancy and movement; it grew to be what it ought to be, a discourse in certain registers of tone, founded on the simplest harmonies, capable of expressing the most passionate emotion without teaching it objectively in the narrative form. The aria—hitherto synonymous with a song in verses for one or more parts, and graced with a ritornel—in spite of its sentimental character, had been to a certain degree hedged in from subjectivity by the necessity of fitting all the verses to the same melody. But now the Italian arias gained by degrees methods by which were formed compositions rounded off in a broad cyclic form of three sections, and representing a particular emotion in a dialectic way. These two new forms of solo-singing, suitable as they were to serve in the most perfect way for the freest emotional expression, still needed for their full development a corresponding and fitting text as a foundation. The German of the Lutheran Bible was too terse and ponderous for the blandishments of recitative, and indeed its sacred purport seemed hardly reconcilable with the rapidity of declamatory solo. It was not sufficiently susceptible of the three-verse form for the aria, and in fact its grandiose sentiment generally was adverse to solo singing. The sacred poetry of the time, with its diffuse character and strict scheme of rhymes, with the short-breathed lines of its verses or its lengthy Alexandrines—now met with only in dramatic poetry—were perfectly unsuited as a medium for the outpourings of personal feelings.

Since the Italians had supplied the musical form they were now referred to for the poetical framework as well, and it was found in the *madrigal*. The first reference to this form of verse was by Heinrich Schütz, whose brother-in-law, Caspar Ziegler (a theologian of Leipzig with a taste for music, who subsequently studied jurisprudence, and died in 1690, at Wittenberg, as professor of legal science), first introduced the madrigal into German literature by a treatise on its nature, with specimens appended. He caused a letter by

Schütz to be printed, as introductory to his work, from
which the elder master's influence in the undertaking is
plainly discernible.[162] Ziegler, who had made a profound
study of the Italian madrigal, defines it as an epigrammatic
poem, " in which we often find more to reflect on and more
to understand than appears in the words or meaning," and of
which the main subject reappears in the last line of each
verse ; but as to form it is the freest of any.

It is not limited to any particular number of lines as the
sonnet is, still from five lines to sixteen formed the limitations between which the Italian poets were content to move.
The lines too must not be of equal length ; on the contrary,
the poet might mix long and short at pleasure, though
the Italians preferred those of seven and eleven syllables ;
finally, it was permissible that all the lines should not
rhyme, " since the madrigal can endure so little coercion that
it even often resembles a plain discourse rather than a poem."
Of all species of verse in the German none lends itself more
readily to music ; and the form of language which was employed by the Italians in their musical dramas was no more
than a prolonged madrigal, " but yet so constructed that an
arietta or even an *aria* with real verses was inserted here
and there, to which both the composer and the poet had to
pay particular consideration, so as to alternate them at
appropriate periods, and in a sweet and pleasing manner."
To what extent Ziegler's recipes were followed in the other
musical departments at that time I know not. In church
music it was not till nearly fifty years later that the Italian
system took root, and it then became at once almost
universal.

The man who by his energy conquered the numerous
prejudices that opposed it, was Erdmann Neumeister. His
home was in central Germany, where he was born at Uech-
tritz, near Weissenfels, May 12, 1671, the son of an humble

" Caspar Ziegler | von den | Madrigalen | Einer schönen und zur Musik
be- | quemesten Art Verse | Wie sie nach der Italiener Ma- | nier in unserer
Deutschen Sprache | auszuarbeiten, | nebenst etlichen Exempeln | LEIPZIG, |
Verlegts Christian Kirchner, | Gedruckt bey Johann Wittigaun, | 1653. | "

schoolmaster. The healthy vigour of the lad at first found more pleasure in a country life than in books ; not till he was fourteen did his taste for learning and study declare itself, hand in hand with excellent talents. After living for four years at Schulpforte he went in 1689 to Leipzig to study theology, and there August Hermann Francke made a deep and permanent impression on him. As subsidiary to his main studies, he here already occupied himself with the art of poetry, and in 1695, having taken the degree of *Magister*, he gave a series of readings on poetry, based on a dissertation on the poets and poetesses of the seventeenth century.[163] Two years later he entered on his first post as preacher at Bibra, and shortly after was called to be colleague in the superintendency of Eckartsberge, and in 1704 to Weissenfels, as court deacon. He was already connected with this town, having eight years previously married a wife from thence ; he soon became a great favourite with the Duke, and was intrusted with the education of his daughter. His eloquence and lucidity, and a manly and unflinching demeanour, distinguished him as a preacher. Although he did not reside long at Weissenfels—for in 1706, after the Princess's marriage, he retired with her to the court of the Count of Sorau —he kept up a lasting connection with the ducal house, as is proved by a series of congratulatory epistles of the years 1736 to 1741, which were regularly answered by the Duke.[164] His theological views, meanwhile, had become sternly orthodox, and he accordingly began in Sorau his contests with pietism, and maintained them throughout his life, as one of the most valorous, respected, and learned leaders of his party. From Sorau, where his independent courage incurred the Count's displeasure, he went in 1715, in obedience to a call from thence, to be head minister of the church of St. James (Jacobi-Kirche), Hamburg. Here he laboured with

---

[163] "*De poetis Germanic is hujus seculi præcipuis Dissertatio compendiaria. Additæ et sunt Poetriæ, haud raro etiam, ut virtutis in utroque sexu gloria eo magis elucescat, comparebunt Poëtastri Erdmann Neumeister et Friedrich Groh-mann. Lipsiæ, 1695.*" S. W. Klose, in his Lexicon of Hamburg authors, Vol. IX., p. 497 ; he also gives (p. 496) a careful list of Neumeister's writings.

[164] These documents exist in the archives of Dresden.

undiminished vigour up to a great age, preaching himself on
the fiftieth anniversary of his call to the ministry; and he
died at the age of eighty-five, surrounded by a numerous
family of children and grandchildren (August 18, 1756).[165] His
literary works were only in part theological and polemical;
he published by degrees a great number of collections of
sermons, which were much read, and a considerable number
of his hymns were adopted for use in churches; indeed,
many of them, as the hymn for the Epiphany "Jesu, grosser
Wunderstern"—"Jesu, Star of glorious light,"—are among
the best hymns, not only of his time, but of the Lutheran
church at any period.

Neumeister's first appearance as a writer of cantata texts
occurred precisely in the year 1700.[166] Since he himself was
deficient in any intimate knowledge of music[167] the suggestion
must have come to him from outside, and as it was for the
court band at Weissenfels that he wrote the first cycle, what
gave rise to it is quite clear. The opera then flourished at
that court under the conduct of the capellmeister, Johann
Philipp Krieger, a talented man of experience both in art
and in the world; thus it exercised a direct influence on the
style and construction of these texts which, by Neumeister's
own statement, Krieger was fond of using for his own compositions, and which procured the poet the name of the
"Chenaniah[168] of Weissenfels," who bore the palm among the
executants of church music. The hymns refer to the Sundays and holy-days of the Christian year; they were printed
separately, and distributed to the congregation for reading
from. When Neumeister came as preacher to Weissenfels
in 1704, they were collected into a small octavo volume, and
he wrote a new preface to them.[169] In this he first enlarges

---

[165] Koch, Geschichte des Kirchenliedes I., 5, 471 (third edition).

[166] G. Tilgner, in his preface to Neumeister's Fünffachen Kirchen-Andachten.
Leipzig, 1716.

[167] As we are expressly told by the writer of the preface to the Fortgesetzten Fünffachen Kirchen-Andachten (Hamburg, 1726), a certain J. E.
Müller.

[168] "And Chenaniah, chief of the Levites, was for song; he instructed about
the song because he was skilful."—I. Chron. xv. 22.

[169] Erdmann Neumeisters | Geistliche | Cantaten | statt einer | Kirchen-

on the term cantata as generally applied, and then goes on :
" To express myself shortly, a *cantata* seems to be nothing
else than a portion of an *opera* composed of *stylo recitativo*
and arie together ; and any one who knows what they both
required will not find it difficult to work out such a *genus
carminum*. However—to be of use even to beginners in the
poetic art, and to say somewhat of each—for recitative
the iambic measure is suitable ; but the shorter the verses
the more pleasing and commodious are they to compose to.
Nevertheless, in an *affettuoso* phrase now and then a few
trochaic or even dactylic lines may be very fitly and expres-
sively introduced. Indeed, as in a madrigal, the writer is
at liberty to alternate and mingle the rhyme and metre at
pleasure. Only the ear must be constantly consulted so as
to avoid all forced and harsh combinations ; on the contrary,
a flowing grace must be observed throughout. With regard
to the aria, it should consist of one, or at most two strophes—
very rarely of three—and always turn upon a sentiment or a reflection complete and proper to it. And to this end it must be
led up to by a fitting situation, according to the circumstances.
And if in such an aria, the *capo*, as it is called—the beginning—can be repeated with perfect fitness at the end, it has
a very excellent effect in the music." To all this he adds
the observation that recitative and aria may be intermingled
according to taste, and then points out the great advantages
offered by such a poem to the composer.

With reference to the hymns in his volume, he remarks
that the ideas expressed in them have reference to his own
sermons. "When arranging the regular services of the
Sunday I endeavoured to render the most important subjects
treated of in my sermon in a compact and connected form
for my own private devotions, and so to refresh myself after
the fatigue of preaching by such pleasing exercises of the
mind. Whence arose now an ode, now a poetical oration,
and with them the present cantatas." They were published,

Music. | Die zweyte Auflage | Nebst | einer neuen | Vorrede, | auf Unkosten|
Eines guten Freundes. | 1704. This is to be found in the Wernigerode
library ; it is omitted from Klose's list.

however, in accordance with the desire of certain artistic and musical friends to whom they were known—and, in fact, a pirated edition[170] brought out so early as the following year by Renger, of Halle, shows what approval Neumeister's innovation met with. And the publication, in 1707, without his consent or knowledge (by Chr. Fr. Hunold) of a *Collegium Poeticum*, held at Leipzig, was also a result of the universal notice which he now attracted; his volume, entitled " Die allerneuste Art zur reinen und galanten Poesie zu gelangen,"[171] came to several editions in the course of the year.

In 1708 this first attempt was followed by a second series of cantatas for the year, on the Gospels, and this went to the court of the Count of Rudolstadt, and was set to music by Erlebach. A third and fourth cycle were written in 1711 and 1714 for the church of the Duke of Sax-Eisenach, where Telemann was then capellmeister.[172] They were all republished —together with a new fifth series, in 1716—with the consent of the author, by Gottfried Tilgner, and dedicated to Duke Christian in Weissenfels; a neatly executed copper plate, representing Neumeister in his study, ornaments this edition, and in the preface Tilgner speaks of him as "the man who, without contradiction, deserves the fame of being the first among us Germans who brought church music to a higher standing by introducing the sacred cantata and bringing it to its present perfection."[173] This collection of poems, in the course of time, had two supplements published; the first called Fortgesetzte fünffache Kirchen-Andachte, Hamburg 1726,

---

[170] That it was one is clear from the preface to the Fünffachen Kirchen-Andachten.

[171] " The very newest method of attaining a pure and polite [style of] poetry."

[172] The third has no author's name, and was printed at Gotha, with the title: "Geistliches | Singen | und | Spielen, | Das ist: | Ein Jahrgang | von Texten, | Welche | dem Dreyeinigen GOTT | zu Ehren | bey öffentlicher Kirchen-Versammlung | in Eisenach | *musicali*sch aufgeführet werden | von | *Georg. Philip. Telemann*, | F. S. Capellmeister und *Secr.* | GOTHA, gedruckt bey Christoph Reyhern, | F. S. Hof-Buchdr., 1711." A copy is in my possession.

[173] *Tit.* "Herrn | Erdmann Neumeisters | Fünffache | Kirchen-Andachten | bestehend | In theils eintzeln, theils niemahls | gedruckten | Arien, Cantaten- und Oden | Auf alle | Sonn- und Fest-Tage | des gantzen Jahres. | Heraus gegeben | Von | G. T. | LEIPZIG, | In Verlegung Joh. Grossens Erben. | Anno 1716. | "

the second, Dritter Theil [third part] der fünffachen Kirchen-
Andachten," Hamburg also, 1752. Neumeister was besieged
for texts on all sides, he gave away many copies, and
they were often printed without his knowledge. The collection of 1726 contains, besides the appendices for public
services and private meditation, three complete series for the
year, of which the first had appeared as early as 1718 at
Eisenach, under the title of " Neue geistliche Gedichte "—
"New Spiritual Songs,"—and several cantatas out of this
series occur again in a collection anonymously printed in 1725
at Weissenfels. The cycle contained in the third part had
music composed to it throughout by Telemann, in whom
Neumeister found at all times an industrious and grateful
fellow-artist. For Mattheson also he used his pen when at
Hamburg, writing for him the oratorio, " Die Frucht des
Geistes"—" The Fruit of the Spirit"—1719, and "Das
gottselige Geheimniss " — " The Blessed Mystery." [174] A
poetical flight of another kind, but relating to the Christian
year, occurs in the second part of the " Evangelischen nach-
klangs"—" The Echoes of the Gospel"—(Hamburg, 1718 and
1729), but although these were only hymns in verses, they
were also employed for church music ; at any rate certainly
the second part, which was produced for the Castle chapel of
Weissenfels. Imitators now appeared in troops ; this form
seemed a positive revelation of the very thing which had
been the desideratum ; and since any depth or breadth of
thought was not necessary, the composition of a cantata text
was a not very difficult task. But there were very few that
could rival Neumeister's productions, for the most part they
stood far below the model.

The Fünffachen Kirchen-Andacten continued to be the
principal work of this kind, and it is now our duty to examine
its character somewhat more closely. Neumeister himself
called the first series the poetical duplicate, as it were, of
his sermons. But it would be a mistake to imagine that
they in any way reflect the sermon form, and still more
erroneous is the idea that the form of the new church

---

174 Mattheson, Ehrenpforte, pp. 205 and 210.

cantata was in general borrowed from the sermon, or always
an idealised reflection of the whole cultus of Protestant
Christianity.[175] Its standard was on the contrary derived
from quite other and different principles : first of all the
imitation of the operatic form, which met the spirit of the
times ; then a simple consideration of the means of expression that church music had at its command. In the two
first cycles and in the fifth, neither Bible text nor verses of
chorales were turned to account; the last indeed consists
wholly of songs in verses, each prefaced by a motto of three
rhymed lines.   The cantatas of the first cycle consist of
recitatives and arias.   We must however always remember
that, at the beginning of the century, the word *aria* was
employed not exclusively for solo songs, and much of his
work is so constructed as to demand the German form of
aria, and to be adopted for singing in several parts; still by
far the greater portion is intended for solo singing. The recitatives are in iambic verse, as the author himself enjoins, and
the arias generally in iambic or trochaic metre, with greater
uniformity in the length of the lines.   Still, as compared with
the hymns of that period, a very remarkable freedom prevails
in the arrangement of the rhymes, and in the number and
length of the lines, so that the influence of the madrigal
here too is perceptible.   A *da capo* is not always possible, and
often only a very brief one ; here and there too the verse
form still appears, though divided by recitatives.   Dactyls
are more rarely used, sometimes only at the outset of one
aria ; twice we even find Alexandrines ; and once again they
occur, mixed with iambics and trochees, but the verse always
begins on an accented syllable.   An aria introduces the
cantata and closes it—seldom a recitative ; sometimes short
arioso lines are introduced into this separately—lines which
might have some connection with each other; this method
was still farther worked out at a later date.   Usually each

---

[175] Winterfeld, Evang. Kircheng. III., 61.   The opinion of this investigator
that from this period a text from the gospel of the day was taken as the germ
of these musical and devotional compositions, is quite incorrect. On the
contrary, the words of Scripture were employed much less frequently here than
in the older church sonata.

cantata contains three arias with the corresponding recitative, sometimes even more.

The second cycle shows a marked advance, inasmuch as Alexandrines have altogether disappeared, and the parts intended for the chorus are indicated. Since church choirs were now universal, they could not be altogether ignored. The employment of the chorus is in every case the same: three rhymed lines begin the piece, and are repeated at the end, and in the middle four lines are again given to the choir. These *tutti* phrases are almost altogether wanting in that force and generality of purpose which the words for a chorus require; but Neumeister either detected this himself or his composers pointed it out, for in the third and fourth series chorales and Bible texts are introduced, and with this we may consider the form of the modern church cantata to have become established. No other principle but that of alternation is discernible in the arrangement, and it is no more the rule that a verse of a chorale should constitute the close than that a sentence from the Bible should stand at the beginning. The idea which gave it unity was derived from the ecclesiastical meaning of the Sunday or festival to which it belonged; the text did no more than throw light on this in various aspects; all the rest was the concern of the composer. If we look at Neumeister's work in detail what we find to praise above everything is the easy smoothness, nay, elegance of the language. Not unfrequently we meet with a really melodious cadence, but at the same time we cannot overlook a certain straining after graphic and picturesque expression. The recitative and aria are for the most part distinctly defined—the former being applied as far as possible to reflections and meditations, the latter to expressing unmixed and untroubled sentiment. The imminent danger of falling, in recitative, into a prosaic and diffuse moralising tone, certainly often beset Neumeister; a dreadful example occurs in the cantata for the Fourth Sunday after Trinity in the first series. Occasionally he sinks to astonishing platitude, as in the cantata for the Fourth Sunday in Lent of the second series, where the first recitative goes through all the four rules of elementary arithmetic; while here and there the expression is intolerably dry and tasteless, as in the cantata for Sexagesima of the first series. His arias often lack even the moderate amount of fervency and aspiration which was required; he had in fact no sufficient fount of poetical fancy, and wrote too much—and to order. Still he not unfrequently finds warm and stirring words. Taking them for all in all, we cannot think meanly of these works; they not only fulfilled their end, and were well suited for musical treatment, but they display a feeling for form which, in the then state of German literature, must not be undervalued; and many of them are really models of their kind, and might well satisfy even our present much enhanced requirements —as, for instance, the Advent cantata, used also by Bach: " Nun komm, der Heiden Heiland "—" O come, Thou Saviour of the heathen."[176]

No innovation has ever escaped antagonism—violent in proportion to its extent and importance. The transference of the dramatic style to church music was a kind of revolution in art, and the fact that it could be set on foot by an eminent ecclesiastic who had testified throughout a long life, by word and deed, how dear to him was his Church, proves that it answered to a real and deep need of the spirit of the time. Neumeister himself had not been wholly free from doubts, but he had crushed them. " I have already said," he wrote in the preface to the first year's cycle, 1704, " that a *cantata* has the appearance of a piece taken out of an opera, and it might almost be supposed that many would be vexed in spirit and ask how sacred music and opera can be reconciled, any more than Christ and Belial, or light and darkness. And therefore it might be said I should have done better to choose some other form. But I will not strive to justify myself in this matter till first I am answered: Why certain other spiritual songs are not done away with

---

[176] Among his contemporaries he was universally regarded as a great poetic artist. Gottfried Blümel speaks in one of the collections of his own cantatas (Budissin, 1718) of Neumeister's little metrical vagaries as merely *nævi in pulchro corpore.*

which are of the same *genus versuum* as worldly, nay, often
profane songs ?   Why the *instrumenta musica* are not broken
which we hear in churches to-day, and which only yesterday
were performed upon for the luxury of worldly pleasure ?
And hence, whether this kind of poetry, though it has
borrowed its model from theatrical verse, may not be sancti-
fied by being dedicated to the service of God ?   Whether
the Apostle's words may not be applied to this case, as it is
written in I. Cor. xiv. 7 ; I. Tim. iv. 5 ; Phil. i. 18, and
whether such an application is not a sufficient answer on
my part ?"   However, there were many who were not to be
thus convinced, who saw in this innovation a profanation of
the sanctuary, and opposed it with anger and disapproval.
Unsuccessful as was this opposition—for the new church
cantatas gained ground every year—so much obstinate dis-
like was manifested, and the champions of the new principle
were so little satisfied to hold their own merely by artistic
effort, that ere long a bitter literary war broke out along
the whole line, which declared itself in endless paper
missiles on both sides.

The Pietists were of course its most determined foes ; even
the earlier forms of church music had been an abomination
to them—nothing would they endure beyond the simplest
verse hymn.   It is often strange how little mutual understanding exists between tastes and tendencies which are
really identical in aim and feeling.   As if, in point of fact, the
endeavour to express personal emotion on the boards of a
theatre differed in essence from the transcendental subjectivity of the hymns in the devotions of the Pietists themselves!
But with them it was useless to discuss the matter, as Neumeister well knew, and he did not hesitate to hit them a
direct blow when he put these words into one of his cantatas—

> Then let us trust His faithful saying
> Living in faith, and praying
> And bringing forth the fruits of holiness and truth
> In humble, Christian seeming,
> Not pietistic dreaming—

and by coupling them in a not very flattering manner with
the Pope and the Turks in the first verse of the hymn " Erhalt

uns Herr bei deinem Wort "—" O Lord, maintain us by Thy word."[177]

A second, but certainly not a numerous, host of antagonists consisted of certain musicians of the old stamp who were possessed by an antipathy towards theatrical music in general, though in fact they could not have said in what other way an effective sacred cantata was to be constructed; but as for the most part they could not wield the pen their position was not a strong one. To them belonged Johann Heinrich Buttstedt, the organist of Erfurt, and a distinguished man in his way, whose misfortune it was that in his *Ut, re, mi,* &c., he should have undertaken to defend a cause already lost against so skilful a writer as Mattheson. A third camp of foes consisted of the more serious-minded laymen and dilettanti, such as the pastor Christian Gerber, who pointed out the abuses in church music in his book Unerkannte Sünden der Welt—Unrecognised sins of the world,—and Joachim Meyer, a professor of jurisprudence at Göttingen, who also involved himself in a squabble with Mattheson.[178] Associated with Meyer in this contest was Guden, a theologian of Göttingen, who, unlike Meyer, was a dabbler in music: between these parties the strife was a fierce one.

Those who make assertions have to prove them, and the innovators gave themselves infinite trouble. It cannot, however, be said that Mattheson, Motz, Tilgner, and the rest adduced anything more or newer than what Neumeister had already said in fewer words; and he himself only revived old weapons of defence, for long before this the older church cantatas had been accused of worldliness.[179] Above all it was

---

[177] Fünffache Kirchen-Andachten, Jahrg. IV., Eighth Sunday after Trinity. Constantin Bellermann puts it forcibly in his " *Parnassus Musarum,*" p. 5: "*pii quidam homines—qui—omnem externum musices usum aut ex templis eliminant aut minaci lege circumscribunt: faciamus hos missos, quos neque herba neque pharmacum restituet.*"

[178] By his book Unvorgreifliche Gedanken über die neulich eingerissene theatralische Kirchenmusik und die darin bisher üblich gewordenen Cantaten (1726)—Unauthoritative considerations as to the newly introduced theatrical church music, &c.

[179] So, for instance, the cantor of Lauben, Christian Schiff, was accused by

sought to prove out of the Bible that the forms and instruments attacked were pleasing in the sight of God, and were commanded by him. The permission to use noisy instruments was derived, for example, from II. Chron. v. 12, where it is related that at the dedication of Solomon's temple the Levites sang to cymbals, psalteries, and harps, while a hundred and twenty priests blew trumpets. Miriam's song of thanksgiving and Zachariah's song of praise were held to sanction a cheerful and lively form of expression. The frequent repetition of the text in the aria was supported by the parallelisms which characterise the Hebrew poetry, and Tilgner referred even the *da capo* to Psalm viii., of which the first verse is repeated at the end.[180] Weapons were borrowed too from the old type of church music. Those who demurred to recitative were reminded of psalmodic singing at the altar; those who objected to the adoption of the operatic style were asked whether, after all, many sacred airs had not been originally secular, and often of very doubtful purport; and finally they were appealed to as to whether, as all was done to the honour of God, it were not a matter of indifference by what means the mind was attuned to devotion so long as devotion was the outcome, and reminded that the religious words in themselves ought to divert the thoughts from all worldly subjects.

Neumeister had besides laid down the principle of adhering as far as possible to the phraseology of the Bible and of theological writings. For this reason the theatrical and the sacred dramatic style of music could never be exactly alike. Opponents like Buttstedt, it is true, declared that no judicious musician could deny their intrinsic identity, nay, that "all sorts of singable stuff was brought into the

---

his clergyman, Joh. Muscovius, in 1694. The substance of his defence is given by Mattheson, Ehrenpforte, p. 317.

[180] In Mattheson's reply to Joachim Meyer (Der neue Göttingische, &c., *Ephorus*. Hamburg, 1727), he copied all the account relative to this question from Tilgner's preface to the Fünffachen Kirchen-Andachten, and added supplementary notes (pp. 101-108). For the *da capo* form he quoted sixteen passages from the Psalms as authorities, among which two, he says, must have been quite in the *rondo* form.

church, and the gayer and more dance-like it was, the better it pleased, so that sometimes for a very little more the men would join hands with the women and dance among the chairs, as sometimes at a wedding they would go over tables and benches."[181]   But Mattheson replied that it would be bad indeed if no distinction were made between a sacred and an operatic recitative, and that "it would be a sin and shame if unskilled scribblers of music were to bring all sorts of singable stuff into the church; but that the true church style remained nevertheless an independent style."[182]   But then if it was further asked wherein its independent character was discernible there was the difficulty.   Mattheson said that all intelligent musicians knew very well how to treat it, and keep the "happy medium"; Tilgner, that "the composer must make his work plain and devotional, without offering to God the old leaven of misplaced fancies, but preferring the choicest ideas to sinful pastime."   Niedt[183] advised the composer to accommodate himself to the taste of the congregation, whether they preferred motetts, concertos, or arias; to set recitatives and arias as simply as possible, and to work out all fugues "on an 'Amen,' 'Hallelujah,' or the like," because they resembled nothing so much as a "mirthful juggler's trick, and in general would only be listened to by the folks in church with disgust and annoyance," and advised that the singers should be constantly admonished to sing "from the heart, and so to touch the hearts of others.'   And he himself worked on these principles; to be sure he was in consequence regarded as a Pietist, and almost driven from the town and country by an inquisition; in point of fact, to ˙his day no man can say what is the strict and true style of church music.

Thus matters stood; and no one attempted to get at the bottom of the affair on grounds of independent and unprejudiced judgment.   The defendants took too great a per-

---

[181] Buttstedt, Ut, re, mi, &c., pp. 81 and 64.

[182] Mattheson, Das beschütze Orchestre, p. 142.

[183] Friedrich Ehrhardt Niedtens Musicalischer Handleitung, Part III. (Hamburg), 1717, p. 37.

sonal interest in the subject; some of them, and Mattheson at their head, were musicians fighting, so to speak, for hearth and home, and the practice of highly intelligent men like Keiser, Telemann, and Stölzel, was arrayed convincingly on their side. Even if any one could have brought forward irrefutable proof of his error, the creative artist would have gone on with an incredulous smile, and have finished his dramatic-sacred composition undisturbed; the rest would very likely have wavered until the next performance of sacred music, and then have been entirely reconverted to their former opinion.

The course of great movements in the progress of culture is at all times mightier than the will of individuals, and any attempt to judge an impulse which is felt to be a condition of existence would be out of place here. Otherwise it would not have been difficult to point out the fact that the growth of each branch of art presupposes a definite impulse in the progress of the human mind, and that the mental forces which led to the production of the opera were quite different from those which found expression in the art of sacred music. Each growth of art bears deep in itself, and not on its surface only, the character of the soil from which it grew; and it was indeed utterly to undervalue the power of music—as distinct from that of speech—when men supposed that its nature could be essentially modified by its application to sacred texts. This was merely a plausible view calculated to encourage self-deception; and those who asserted that they were inspired with sentiments of devotion as much, or more, by religious opera music as by any other, mistook in their own minds the romantic art-afflatus for sacred aspiration. The restless "scriblomania" of the various apologists for the new style, which kept them in a constant stir, round and round the same circle, also betrayed very sufficiently their own indecision in the matter; and naturally enough, for intelligent reflection must sometimes sit silent, while the hasty judgment of feeling does not.

Thus their opponents found ample justification for their energetic disapproval; in this only were they unjust: in demanding that every suspicion of worldly art should be

eliminated for the sake of purity in church music. What is
church music? The question has been asked again and
again during nearly two hundred years, and if we consider
it closely we find that the answer with most of us is at the
same stage as it was with Mattheson and his contemporaries.
And yet the answer is simple enough : Church music is
music that has grown up within the bosom of the Church.
But while, in the first instance, all musical art belonged to
the Church, and to it alone, in the course of time and under
the extension of culture many branches of it have blossomed
freely out in the world. And unless the Church insists on
shutting herself up in the fatal idea that she is the one
and only fertile parent of all intellectual effort, needing no
helping hand — thus choking the wellspring of her own
vitality—she cannot but direct her attention to the fruits
of a free development in this art. In the sixteenth century
the secular songs of the people had brought a renovating influence to bear on sacred music, in spite of its light or even
obscene verbal texts ; why should not something of the same
kind be possible to operatic music? There was still, surely,
an actual living art of sacred music, capable of absorbing
a foreign element, of purifying it, and of assimilating it as
nutriment. But the only branch of art which throughout
the seventeenth century could grow up to an imposing
height within the limits of the Church, and blossom into
splendour, was organ music. It alone was true church
music at the beginning of the eighteenth century ; and any
element that hoped for more than a mere temporary admission to that sublime realm of art had to blend itself with that.
Its very nature seemed, indeed, to tend to this ; for its principal form, the organ chorale, already had a hold on ideas both
purely musical and dramatically musical, and was distinctly
tending—with an impulse common to every natural growth
—to escape from the dimly lighted region of abstraction
and sentiment into the clear light of day. Nay, all organ
music imperatively required to be associated with a flow of
music linked to a poetical form of words if it was to fulfil
all the requirements of church music. Instrumental music
of a purely ideal nature is too catholic to satisfy the needs

of any Church; it may be *religious* in the highest sense, but the essence of a Church as a body lies in a creed common to its members, and this can only be indicated in its music by the words sung. So, as natural means to an end are always the fittest, the severely sublime and apparently passionless style of organ music—a consequence merely, in the first instance, of the mechanism of the instrument—proved spontaneously, as it were, to be a corrective of the erratic individualism of the opera. Still this could not be altogether rejected so long as men's thoughts were directed to evolving a living type of church music. For every art must solve the problem of how best to grasp and embody the spirit of the period as it passes by.

Thus both the contending parties overshot their mark, as is always the case on such occasions. The only one who did not struggle and theorise, but acted in the only right way, with all the confidence of genius, was Sebastian Bach. His intellect, which with a kind of centripetal force drew towards itself all the forms of which the air just then seemed full, seized also on the opera; and the fact that throughout his life he encouraged it proves that he understood its real value. But he altogether eliminated its emotional sensuality by the chaste translucent flow of his organ music. Bach undertook to amalgamate the two styles, dissimilar as they were, and so created the only possible form for the church music of that period. It was he, and he alone, who undertook this task; and the innumerable sacred compositions of his gifted contemporaries fell, without exception, stillborn, like barren blossoms from a tree, while his works are to this day a living power with an ever-increasing procreative influence. That he should have been reproached for availing himself of theatrical forms and his works condemned as not fitted for church use, shows a not very Protestant spirit, and still less a rational historic sense; it might indeed be called quite incomprehensible, if people's views were not so confused about Bach's cantatas, and so obscure even now as to the mode of executing them. Of course, if we insist on performing them without an organ they resemble some artificially galvanised body from which the heart has

been removed ; while with an organ all our puzzles and
doubts solve themselves—at any rate, for any one who has
set up no fanciful ideal of evangelical church music, but
accepts as such the form which has evolved itself spontaneously from the very being of the Church. It is true that
organ music was the latest independent offshoot that the
Church produced, and so Bach has remained to this day the
last church composer ; since his time we have had *religious*
music only. It would be a great mistake to regard its development into the church cantata as the final and only
aim to which, as independent instrumental music, it served
merely as a stepping-stone. It was a branch of art complete in itself—if we except the organ chorales with a
certain reservation—and thus, without quitting the province
of church uses, it was able to outgrow its limits and to infuse
a certain religious catholicity into the church ideal. Thus
while with one hand it pointed out the way to true sacred
music, with the other it pointed from it to another road.
This path led, first and foremost, in the same direction as
the popular feeling of the time, and so it came to pass that
Bach remained without an imitator in his church cantatas;
nay, that even during his lifetime they had, to a certain
extent, ceased to be understood. It would almost seem as
though we were now to gather up the clue which then was
dropped.

Bach became acquainted with Neumeister's verses for
cantatas through the Count's court at Eisenach. The third
and fourth series were written, as has been said, for the
capelle there in 1711 and 1714. Under the circumstances
of relationship between the families of Saxe-Weimar and
Saxe-Eisenach, and more particularly of the friendship that
existed between Telemann of Eisenach and Bach (Telemann
was indeed godfather to Bach's second son, Philipp Emanuel),
it was easy for him to obtain a copy. Judging from the
music now extant, Bach seems to have composed four out of
the fourth series, two out of the third, and one out of the
first. Of the fourth series it can be proved that two were
written later, at Leipzig, and they will not come under con-

sideration here.[184] We know that in the year 1715 a cycle of cantatas, written by a poet of the place, was prepared especially for the capelle at Weimar by command of Wilhelm Ernst, and two consecutive series from the First Sunday in Advent of 1716; and Bach, so long as he remained in Weimar, had to bear a part in composing music for them; so the date of composition of the other two is quite certainly established. With regard to the last three we have a choice between the ecclesiastical year of 1712-13 and that of 1714-15.[185]

We will study them in their probable order, and begin with a cantata for the first day of Christmas-tide.[186] Its superscription—"*Concerto Festo Nativitatis Christi*"—gives it the designation which Bach was accustomed to bestow on his church cantatas when he did not otherwise distinguish them by the initial words of the text and the day for which they were intended, or did not call them "*dialogi*," from the character of their contents. He avoided the Italian word "*cantata*," by which in his day a dramatic scena for one or more solo voices was understood, and clung to the custom of the seventeenth century in using the name "*concerto*," which at the same time served to indicate the necessary distribution of the instruments. Happily Telemann's composition on the same text has been preserved,[187] and we can compare them. The difference is as great as that between the characters of the two musicians, and extends to every particular, even to the key. Telemann's composition is C major. He sets the text from Isaiah, which introduces it—"Unto us a Child is born," &c.—to a chorus in five parts, homophonic throughout, with violins and trumpets introduced alternately, and by the end

---

[184] "Ein ungefärbt Gemuthe"—"A spirit faint and failing,"—for the Fourth Sunday after Trinity (B -G., I., No. 24); and "Gottlob nun geht das Jahr zu Ende"—"Now that the year is near its ending,"—for the Sunday after Christmas (B.-G., I., No. 28). The evidence will be given later. Perhaps the first may be based on an earlier work, though there are no distinct traces of this.

[185] See App. A., No. 20.

[186] Extant in MS. in Fischhoft's bequest to the Royal Library at Berlin.

[187] I obtained it from the Cantor's Library at Langula, near Mühlhausen; it had no doubt gone there from Eisenach, which is at no great distance. It is a MS. written about the year 1750, score and parts.

of forty-two bars in 6-8 time has performed his task, greatly
aided by the use of a *da capo*. This piece, probably written
in half-an-hour—to judge from the swiftness of the writing—
shows us the worst side of the church music of the time ; it
has all the meagreness and meanness of the older cantata,
with all the pretension to filling a broader form. Bach chose
the key of A minor, prompted to this selection chiefly by the
fact that he set the text of the altered form, associating
with it the Æolic chorale, " Wir Christenleut hab'n jetzund
Freud "—" We Christian souls may now rejoice,"—instead
of the Mixo-Lydian " Gelobet seist du, Jesu Christ "—" All
praise to Thee, Lord Jesus Christ." [188]   But this idea apparently pleased him, for he has adhered throughout the
cantata to the subdued minor key, which offers so singular
a contrast to the bright joyfulness of Christmas. It gives
a tone as of melancholy reminiscences of the pure Christmas
joys of our childhood, as they float before our "mind's eye,"
in a tender and changeful glow; in contrast to this Telemann's
eternal C major is often unutterably shallow and flat.   Bach
moreover does not begin at once with a vocal part ; he introduces it by an independent instrumental piece for a quartet
of strings, two flutes, two oboes, and basso ; this is kept
strictly to the form of the Italian concerto—an evidence of
the stage of development he had then reached—and ends
with a picturesque preparation for the succeeding chorus.
This is a double fugue with the following theme :—

The commencement offers a fresh example of that remarkable
method of construction which we also meet with in the last
movement of the toccata in D minor for the clavier (see
p. 439), and in the first fugue in Psalm cxxx. (see p. 450), the
theme is distinctly set forth before the fugue itself begins.
The two ideas are at first stated, as quoted above; but when

---

[188] See App. A, 20, for further details as to the alterations in the text.

the fugal treatment proper begins (at bar 4) the second theme enters immediately after the fourth note of the first, and thus they proceed together for the greater portion of it. But it is perfectly clear that this exposition of the theme has some other reason than a purely musical one ; the two verbal texts, so to speak, of the musical discourse are distinctly spoken to begin with.   Thus a fault which we had to point out in the closing fugue of Psalm cxxx. is here avoided by a means so simple that none but a genius could have devised it.   The choral movement goes on without a break for nineteen bars, with a complication of strettos; it is then relieved a few times by instrumental episodes, and from bar 29 once more proceeds uninterruptedly to the end, but with a preponderating emphasis on the second theme, which continues to be heard for a while in the coda.   Only compare with this massive subject the principal motive of Telemann's chorus:—

5 parts.   C major chord.

To us a Child is giv - en,   to us a Child is giv - en.

This is succeeded by a solo movement: "Dein Geburtstag ist erschienen"—"Hail, O Saviour, born this morning,"— composed by Telemann in C major for two soprano voices with figured bass accompaniment, by Bach in E minor for bass in the Italian aria form, with two violins and figured bass.   Telemann's duet indeed is not one, properly speaking, but with rare exceptions a song for two voices, and superficial throughout; while Bach's aria is full of tender feeling and melody, and most carefully worked out as to *technique*. The aria style proper to Bach declares itself plainly even in the working-out of a small motive for the bass, although a too frequent repetition of the ritornel cuts up the vocal part too much, and his wonderful melodic interweaving of the instruments with the voice is as yet but little developed. The next movement consists in each composition of a chorus in C major, on the text of Psalm lxix. 31: "Ich will den Namen Gottes loben"—"I will praise the name of God with a song, and will magnify Him with thanksgiving." Telemann here gives us the best he has to offer

in a double fugue; the first theme, it is true, is not worth
much, but with the second a little more spirit is infused,
and this composer never lacks a certain facile flow. In
Bach's work this movement is the least good. The figuration, at first started between the two parts in close imitation,
soon gives way to an antiquated homophony, and the rest
of the section is quite insignificant. It bears stamped on
the face of it that Bach wrote it without sympathy—nay,
with more than indifference. He thought a bright and
splendid chorus was due to the Christmas festival and could
not then put himself in tune for it. It is not till we come to
the following aria, where he again strikes a minor key, that
we find him his true self again. The poet has here given the
words for three arias which bear a relation of rhythm to each
other, though two are divided by a recitative. Telemann
has composed the whole of this for alto, bass, soprano, and
then bass again, all three to arias in C major, and we cannot
but confess that they are very skilfully contrasted as to rhythm
and melody. The form, in accordance with the poem, had
to be Italian. Violins are employed to accompany the two
first tunes, but they have scarcely any interludes to execute;
the second part of the aria has only a figured-bass for the
sake of contrast—this was customary. The third is set to
a species of chaconne-bass, and has at any rate a somewhat
graver effect. Indeed the combination—

Lord, to Thee be glo - ry giv - en,

is worked out with all Telemann's skill on paper, but it
cannot sound equally well, because the bass voice and the
instrumental bass are perpetually interfering with each
other. The recitative as set by Bach is shortened by more

than half; also he has made use only of the first and third
verses, and both to the same music, only first it is in A
minor for the tenor, and then for the alto in D minor. The
words, which are full of a sentiment of gratitude and praise,
are pitched in a very melancholy strain :—

Oboes (*Flutes the second time*).

Praise to Thee, O Lord,   Lord, to Thee all thanks be giv-en,

Here again we miss the grand flood which in Bach's
most highly developed arias enables the song to flow on, with
only a ritornel to mark the principal divisions of it; here
again the skill and power won in the school of organ-playing,
and which would have supported the voice with the instruments—answering, echoing, amplifying, and spiritualising it as
they mingled with it— appears in a very moderate degree. It
is only when we compare it with Telemann's production that
we instantly detect that their two courses are already widely
different. A simple four-part chorale forms the close in both
compositions ; the parts being treated in an interesting
melodic style by Bach, and by Telemann in an off-hand way
on mere harmonic principles. Bach has added an accompaniment in semiquavers, which is limited, however, to an
adornment of the melody ; so there is still a long distance
from this to those chorales for a choir in which the instruments follow out an idea of their own, through which the
chorale itself shines, as it were, by its own magic light.

The second cantata of Neumeister's third cycle is devoted
to Sexagesima Sunday, and must therefore have been performed either on February 19, 1713, or on February 4,
1714.[189] Here again we have a composition by Telemann

---

[189] Published by the Bach Society (B.-G., Vol. II., No. 18) from the parts in
the Royal Library at Berlin, which are for the most part autographs. With
respect to the style of writing and of the paper, most of them correspond with
the autograph of the cantata for Advent, written 1714.

for comparison.[190]   The text, founded on the closing portion
of the Gospel for the day, treats of the miraculous power of
the Divine word.   It starts with the passage from Isaiah
lv. 10, 11, where the word of God is compared with " the
rain that watereth the earth and maketh it bring forth
and bud," and then in a recitative it beseeches God to prepare the hearts of men to receive it.   Between the phrases
of the recitative two appropriate lines from the German
litany are inserted here and there, and the recitative closes
with the same words.   Then follows an aria, praising the
sacred word as the highest and only precious possession, and
it ends with the eighth verse of Spengler's hymn, "Durch
Adams Fall ist ganz verderbt "—" Through Adam's fall the
world was lost."   Bach again begins with an instrumental
sinfonia for two flutes, four violas, bassoon, stringed bass,
and organ ; key of G minor, 6-4 time.   This grand and truly
inspired composition has something of the character of a
chaconne ; a powerful theme for all the instruments, except
the flute, is carried all through it—

repeated strictly for the most part, but sometimes interwoven with other subjects with the freedom characterising
the chaconne ; once even it comes up from the bass to the
middle part.   A few details are derived from Italian concerto movements : thus, just at the beginning, the interlude
before the second entrance of the theme, after which we
expect a development between two ideas; then the unaltered
return at the close of the first twenty bars ; and the general
structure of the theme, which strongly reminds us of the
concerto *tutti* in unison.   As Bach introduced the forms of
Italian chamber music into organ composition he might very
well make use of them also for the church cantata; only the
organ had to stand out as the predominant factor, for the
sake of unity of effect, and this is not yet altogether the case

---

[190] In parts, in the library of the castle-chapel at Sondershausen ; only the
soprano part is wanting, but can be supplied from that of the first violin.

in the *sinfonia* to the Christmas cantata. The chaconne, on the other hand, as has already been remarked, had already been long regarded as a true organ form; and it is from this point of view that Bach composed the piece under discussion, without at the same time disregarding the peculiar character of the wind and stringed instruments. The organ is taken as the standard for the instrumentation; for instance, the flutes always double the parts of the two first violins an octave higher, as though a four-foot stop were used to supplement an eight-foot. This effect is often found in Bach's works, as in the lovely air for an alto voice in the cantata for Whit-Sunday, "O ewiges Feuer, O Ursprung der Liebe"[191]—"O fire eternal, O fountain of love,"—and it is highly instructive as to the principles which guided him in instrumentation.[192]

It still may be a question whether the composer intended to express some definite idea by this *sinfonia*—perhaps to give a musical presentment of the abundant power and effectual working of the divine word. I myself do not think so, for in all his instrumental introductions Bach merely gives us general preparation for the feeling of the piece, and never has any descriptive aim in view, which is one reason why he so frequently employed detached pieces from independent instrumental works as introductory to his cantatas. He only intended to compose a movement answering to the solemn character of the cantata; and it was only owing to his great affection and natural bent for instrumental composition that he did not in general begin at once with the vocal portion.

In the treatment of the words the two composers to a great extent agree, if we consider the general structure; but in the details the greatest dissimilarity appears, as might be expected from the difference in their standpoint and dispositions, above all in the recitative. The introductory words from the Bible are thus treated by both, but with an early transition into the arioso, which from its greater expressiveness seemed the fitter form in cases which were unsuited to the introduction of a chorus. Telemann's work has beyond a doubt the

---

[191] B.-G., VII., No. 34, P. 1291.   [192] See App. A, No. 21.

advantage of the most natural and obvious conception: he
gives the first clause, (verse 10), to the tenor as a recitative,
and the second clause, (verse 11), to the bass, but turned into
an arioso; here only the organ and bass viol accompanying
the voice, while in the first section a rushing intermezzo on
the stringed instruments represents the words " As rain and
snow fall from heaven." Bach gives the whole passage to
the bass voice, accompanied by the organ and supported by
the bassoon, and it is only at the recitative of the hymn that
another voice and the full body of instruments are brought
in. He thus marks a stronger contrast between the Bible
words and those of the modern poet, while on the other
hand he weakens the contrast which exists in the Bible text
itself; he treats both verses in the same way, beginning them
in recitative, and deviating into the arioso. It is not that the
picturesque element is lacking, but it here lies in the voice
part, while in Telemann it is given to the instruments.

Strictly speaking, it is inexact to speak of the *picturesque*,
though the music no doubt mimics the movement of a tangible
visible object. In every movement of the phenomena of
nature man may discern the image of a certain phase and
flow of feeling in himself, and feeling is to us the most cogent
token of life. Now life—that mysterious current that flows
deep below the surface, in which every phenomenon of the
visible world dips its roots—life is the fundamental idea which
it is the function of music as an art to set before us. This
is what justifies imitative music—the reproduction of the rip-
pling of a brook, the surging of the sea, the downrush of the
rain, the sweeping march of the clouds, the whisper of the
leaves; nay, even the busy hum of birds and insects; it represents the indissoluble bond which makes us really one
with all that seems external to us—the power which pervades
the whole world with the same intensity as it does our own
being. But since the justification of such attempts can only
be found by reference to the inmost soul of musical meaning,
they naturally fall strictly within the province of pure music,
i.e., instrumental music. That Bach should have paid no
heed to this shows what was the governing principle in his
essentially creative nature: namely, that catholic feeling for

music as music, which regards the human voice as first in the whole order of instruments. This principle was in fact the standard of his treatment of recitative in general, although the nature of this form was apparently contrary to it. The recitative was in its origin a dramatic form of art, and its function is to facilitate the presentment of a transitory incident either by narrative or by dialogue. Hence the important point is what is said in singing, and not what is sung in the saying; in other words, the meaning conveyed rather than the melody which is engrafted on it. Still it had an eminently musical side, and it must soon have been detected that with the means at its disposal and an impassioned text it could rise to a high pitch of pathos and impressiveness—nay, all the more so from being devoid of all equalising uniformity. In consequence of this it was, on the other hand, peculiarly fitted to prepare the hearer, by exciting and attuning his attention (musically), for a composition presenting itself in a more complete and symmetrical form. From the former point of view it could have no application in church music, and even in the latter no immediate justification; for it is impossible to say that the self-assertive display of personal passion is appropriate to the Church. Hence the dramatic factor was set aside in the words, while the composers absorbed the musical element unchanged into church music. They treated recitative, exactly as in opera, as speaking in a singing voice: a kind of chant, with here and there a stronger musical accent, as the poetry admitted; the utmost they demanded was that the singer should to some degree efface himself in performing it, but it did not always occur to them that the same moderation might be needful in the composer.

Bach is the only one who even here borrowed nothing from outside, but created much that was new. Expressive declamation was by no means all he aimed at. A general principle of music governs his compositions for recitative, a law above and beyond those which rule over mere declamation, which sometimes is identical with them, but not unfrequently defies them and forces them to give way; and it is precisely this which fits his recitative to the style of church music. We instantly feel that the arbitrary subjective feeling is

subdued to a sublime artistic conception, which confines it
within invisible limits. The stream of melody in Bach's
recitative is sometimes so full and equable that we can unhesitatingly disjoin it entirely from the words of the text. The
beginning of the second recitative in this very cantata (238
and 239) is the most striking instance of this, with which
compare Telemann's setting of the same passage :—

In this way are evolved in due course all the wonderful
features which strike us again and again in Bach's recitatives.
Thus in the cantata, "Aus tiefer Noth schrei ich zu dir"—" I
call to Thee in woful need," [193]—we find a recitative against
which the bass part of the organ accompaniment performs
the whole of a chorale, and we meet with a similar combination with an upper instrumental part in the cantatas,

---

[193] B.-G., VII., No. 38.

"Du wahrer Gott und David's Sohn "—" Thou very God,
yet David's Son,"[194]—and "Wachet, betet, seid bereit"—
"Watch and pray, and be prepared."[195] And how would it
have been otherwise possible to write a recitative with fugal
treatment in four parts, such as we find in the sixth section
of the Christmas oratorio,[196] or a duet in recitative such as
that in the cantata for Trinity Sunday for the year 1715?

We hear people criticise the *unrest* of Bach's recitative,
but it only appears restless so long as singers insist on
declaiming it in the usual manner. As soon as its intrinsically melodic character is clearly realised and expressed
all that seems forced becomes natural and harmonious,
while the sharp and angular accentuation is softened and
rounded off under the light of a purely musical standard of
plastic, as distinguished from dramatic beauty. This is the
only mode of performance indeed which is not in glaring
contrast with the sustained flow of the organ accompaniment.
As this view as to Bach's recitative is, however, somewhat
antagonistic to that usually received, I must here repeat
that an impressive accentuation of the words is by no means
absent; on the contrary, we find in his work, no less than in
that of other masters, those emphatic tones which light up
the deep places of our inmost feeling as with a lightning
flash, revealing the idea to its very roots; and any one who
knows Bach, even but a little, will readily believe that in him
these flashes are of magical brilliancy and colour. But it is
undoubtedly an error to suppose that Bach watched and
imitated the accents of ordinary speech in arranging the
tones of his recitative, and had no end in view but the
utterance of the text. It would be quite easy to name
examples in abundance which in the common acceptance
are simply failures so far as declamation is concerned.[197]
Of course they are not so in the least when considered
from the right point of view, and any one who might be

---

[194] B.-G., V., 1, No. 23, P. 1651.

[195] B.-G., XVI., No. 70, P. 1666.

[196] B.-G., V., 2, p. 255, P. 26 (full score), 38 (piano score).

[197] This has been already done, and with the same purpose, by Lobe, in his
Lehrbuch der Musikalischen Composition, IV., p. 58.

tempted to try to alter them would at once perceive that
it was impossible without seriously injuring their melodic
character. We must therefore pronounce that his recitative
bears the most perfect relation to the style of his arias. It
leads up to and beyond them just as in organ music a
prelude does to a fugue; and just as these are often set in
contrasting qualities of tone, so, to meet the dramatic conception, one voice may sing the recitative and another the aria.

To return to the cantata for Sexagesima Sunday—every
recitative runs into an arioso, often with a very complicated
accompaniment and a picturesque and varied treatment of
the voice part, appropriately leading into the recurring
transition into a verse of the litany. This feature too must
be referred to the conditions just mentioned ; it is almost an
established rule in the cantatas of that period ; and the
instrumental bass usually imitates the phrases of the arioso.
Moreover, Bach invariably gives the first line of litany to
the soprano alone, with a busy accompaniment on the
organ ; and it is only on the cry, " Erhör uns, lieber Herre
Gott"—"O hear us, Father, hear our cry!"—that the chorus
and all the instruments come in. Telemann makes shorter
work of it, and brings his full chorus in immediately after
the recitative. The text throughout is on too large a scale,
and in parts full of the dryest moralising. For this reason
Telemann certainly achieves a more pleasing general effect
by passing more rapidly over the solo passages than Bach,
who revelled and lost himself in musical depths. Telemann
set the next aria to a pleasing composition for the tenor in
D minor (the leading key is A minor), which has more
value and purpose than any aria in his Christmas cantata,
though it is merely a simple melody, with only violins to
accompany it. This is how it begins :—

Mein See - len - schatz ist Got - tes Wort.

Still it sinks into nothingness by the side of the extreme
originality and sparkling freshness of Bach's music.   He

selected the soprano voice and the key of E flat major, which after the persistent minor of the foregoing section is doubly refreshing. The accompaniment rests with the organ and all four violas in unison, an effect which Bach did not invent,[198] but to which he gave peculiar piquancy by four-foot stops—that is to say, by requiring the flutes to carry it out in the higher octave. This complicated accompaniment is combined with a splendid melody for the voice, full of joy and assurance. Here the soprano lightly breasts the dark waves of the swaying violins and flutes. Here again they seem to give a tremulous reflection of its form— now the parts fly asunder in joyful haste; then again they combine in a happy rocking motion. We shall yet learn something of the sentiment of similar arias in the Easter cantata, to be spoken of shortly, and the Advent cantata of 1714; but any one who has in some degree familiarised himself with the character of the different periods of Bach's career as a composer cannot overlook the fact that here again we have that spring-tide freshness which comes but once in a man's lifetime ; in later years the master com pensated for its loss by greater breadth, depth, and maturity, but he could never return to it.

The final chorale is harmonised by Telemann with simplicity and dignity, and is only marred by this incomprehensible and impish figure in the bass :—

Bach's setting, simply in four parts, and supported by all the instruments, displays that marvellous wealth and bold independence in the progression of the parts which must have grown out of his mastery of the organ, and by which he is at once distinguishable from all the composers who at that time set chorales for voice parts. While they generally added the chorale for mere custom's sake, slightly and super-

---

[198] Mattheson, Neu eröffnete Orchestre (Hamburg, 1713), p. 283 : " There are many whole arias with accompaniment of *Violette all' Unisono*, which sound very strange, because of the depth of the accompaniment."

ficially treated, we find Bach throwing himself with fresh
vigour and delight into the work of elaborating the simple
subjects of a chorale. Others, who could only effect a superficial union of the secular types of music with the uses of
the church could, of course, neither fully understand nor
care for the chorale, with which it soon became the universal
custom to close all sacred cantatas. Indeed, viewed from the
musical standpoint alone, it was somewhat dry and devoid of
artistic effect, when a work claimed to avail itself of all the
various forms at that time known—more or less—only to
dwindle off into a commonplace hymn-tune in four parts.
But to the hearts of the congregation the chorale, simple as
it was, was still the most significant and important form of
vocal music; and Bach, by devoting to its development his
utmost care, proved by that how truly he, and he alone, had
the right feeling for church music. The closing chorale was
the modest vessel in which the whole essence of the cantata
was to be collected; and it was a labour of honour, and worthy
of the artist, to preserve it with loving care, and fo cover it
with emblematic decorations. Strangely enough, in these
later days many critics have opined that the congregation
joined in the final chorale. Then, indeed, Bach might
have. saved himself his artistic labours. To any one who
can appreciate the church cantata as a real form of art, it
will be inconceivable how any one can even imagine the
possibility of such a naturalistic travesty. It cannot even
be admitted that the choir of singers represents an ideal
congregation. In church music it does not signify in the
least who it is that sings; what is sung and how is the only
question. We may here also contravene the error—which,
indeed, Bach's own son helped to establish by editing his
father's chorale treatments separately—and which regards
these chorale settings as complete and independent masterpieces somewhat analogous to Hassler's four-part hymns.[199]
They were merely conceived of as the keystone of the

---

[199] " Kirchengesäng : | Psalmen vnd geistliche Lieder, | auff die gemeynen
Melodeyen mit vier Stimmen simpliciter gesetzt, | durch Hanns Leo Hassler,"
&c.   Nürnberg, 1608.   A new edition by G. W. Teschner.   Trautwein, Berlin.

cantata, giving to it its full significance, and demanding, as such, the brilliancy and support given by the association of instruments. They are altogether too bold in the treatment of the parts for *a cappella* singing, and sound forced and heavy, although individual movements, if well performed, might have a very striking effect.

The text which Bach chose from Neumeister's first series is intended for Easter Sunday. That it should have been written earlier than when he was in Weimar is extremely improbable, and certain particularly fine passages and remarkable features seem to indicate that it was written even later than the two cantatas of the third cycle.[200] If so, the performance must be dated as April 16, 1713, or April 1, 1714. It is throughout a solo cantata for the tenor, and probably the first of the kind that Bach composed.[201] No instruments are employed but the organ, with a bassoon to strengthen the bass, and a solo violin. The text, like all those of the series for that year, is exclusively Neumeister's own writing, and consists of three arias and two recitatives. The first two arias are written in the same metre, and separated by the first recitative, and Bach has set to each a different air, unlike the Christmas cantata. The whole composition exhibits that union of tender sentiment and fresh vitality which we have already admired in the Sexagesima cantata. The first aria has a particularly sustained character. It is an elegant detail when the principal motive, brought in again by the ritornel—

recurs, as at first in the voice part, in augmentation—

Ich weiss dass mein Er - lö - ser lebt.

---

[200] See on this subject App. A, No. 20.

[201] The owner of this precious unpublished MS. is Dr. Rust, of Leipzig. It is an autograph copy by Bach's disciple, Heinrich Nicholaus Gerber, but shows

a real flower opening from the bud, and suggested perhaps
to the master by the words of the text—

> Faith blooms into assurance:
> I know that my Redeemer lives.

The second time the subject appears in its simple form
again ; but in its farther progress it gives rise to turns and
subtleties of every kind.   The poet had supplied very suitable words for the succeeding recitative, having once more
briefly recurred to all the history of the Passion of our Lord
from the beginning till the Resurrection, in phrases of admirable significance and brevity, indicating at the same
time the reverent pity of the Christian soul.   What Bach
made out of this is a real gem of stirring declamation and
glorious melodic flow.   In proof of this we here give just
the beginning.   No one can listen unmoved to the expressive
character of the last two bars, with the suspended seventh,
and the transition into F major :—

The accents of creation, "travailing and groaning," are hit

---

no great care ; from bar 33 of the first aria two bars are missing ; however, it
is very easy to reconstruct them from the ritornel at the beginning; but in many
places the text is wrong or unintelligible.   Two deviations from it seem,
however, to have originated with Bach himself, namely, those in bar 37 of the
first recitative and the beginning of the second.

with wonderful realism on the words " folgt ich halbtodt bis
Golgotha im nach "—" Half-dead, I followed Him to Golgotha,"—and the very expression of piercing anguish is found
in the emphasis on the lines " Hab ich So manchen Stich Mit
Ach und Weh empfunden, Da man sein Haupt mit Dornen
stach "—" And when His brows were pierced with thorny
crown of anguish, I felt as many pangs as He," and all
merely by simple contrivances of melody and harmony,
without any special aid from the instruments. Once only
is a certain richness of colouring given to the idea of " tears
of joy " by musical appliances, and in fact this is a true
climax. Arioso settings there are none, perhaps because
the composer did not wish to extend any farther the already
long recitative. The second aria, which, as well as the third,
is in C major, sings in ardent tones of the saving power of
the resurrection of Christ, and already shows a broader
stream of melody than other airs of the same kind in the
earlier cantatas. The voice part already bears to the instrumental parts a relation approximate to that of a first among
equals, which is the ideal of Bach's sacred aria. It was not
customary to devise any prominently new idea for the middle
sections of the aria, and even Bach followed the rule, and in
this place used some of the previous material for new elabo-
rations. It is interesting to note how, in this part of the air,
the motive from which, properly speaking, the whole aria is
developed—

lies in the bass, where it is busily worked out, though the air
itself scarcely refers to it at all.

There is still another passage worth noticing, where the
voice part, after a full close on the dominant, returns to the
leading key through a jubilant passage, helped out by the
chief phrase :—

(mein Erlöser) lebt ! . . . .

A perfectly similar passage occurs in the cantata " Ach ich

sehe, jetzt da ich zur Hochzeit gehe," of the year 1715
(duet, bar 25); and as this transition is very unusual with
Bach, it seems to suggest the idea that these cantatas must
have been written at no very long interval of time. The
following recitative shows at the beginning how admirably
Bach knew how to avail himself of the contrast between
recitative and arioso for purposes of expression :—

The final aria is equal to the others in merit. We might
perhaps have expected, and particularly from Bach, a deeper
expression of feeling in music written to words which express
the desire to be united to Jesus in heaven; but the idea of
producing a steady intensification of vehemence running
through all the arias appears to have governed throughout.

We may regard these three cantatas for Christmas, Sexagesima and Easter as so many successful attempts by Bach
to master and appropriate the forms of the newer church
cantata. Not that they have no other value! At the
eminence where Bach was already standing there could be
no further question of mere experimental study. Still,
neither of the three shows us all Bach's mastery over every
aspect of the requisite *technique*. The first is still defective
in the treatment of the aria and chorale, and is generally
the least important; the second starts with a strong flight,
but no broad choral forms are developed; the last is in
every respect admirable, though merely a solo piece.

We shall soon, however, make acquaintance with a sacred
composition which not only exhibits a masterly combination

of all forms, but also proves that by the year 1714 Bach had already perfectly established the style which we must call his own, and which at the same time stands by itself as the sole representative of the sacred style of the period. By this we must understand the perfect amalgamation of all vocal music with the methods derived from organ music, after the organ had itself extended its domain by contributions from chamber music. Its influence is most directly traceable in choral music—both in that which is freely treated, generally fugally, and in the chorus with a chorale; less as establishing its proportion than as determining the specific characters in the aria and its allied forms for several solo voices, where, as a result of its polyphonic association with obbligato instruments, the human voice is compelled to renounce its individuality to the utmost. Again, in the arioso, by the canon treatment of the bass, which has become almost a rule; and finally in the recitative, by asserting and upholding the laws of instrumental—that is, pure music in the strict sense. Even in the instrumental *sinfonia* the organ style asserts its invigorating spirit; in the forms borrowed from chamber or operatic music, as well as in that which was the last offshoot of Gabrieli's sacred sonata. With regard to solo-singing, the difference we find between the last noble cantatas of the older type and those of the new is that between a less and a greater perfection of form; but this must be considered as referring not only to Bach's productions, but to the general ideal of form at the period.

The medium which the master had by this time created for the utterance of his ideas underwent no further essential modification during the remaining thirty-six years of his life. Those differences which we may yet observe in the distinct periods of his work proceed from the constantly expanding scope of the artist's sentiments, sympathies, and views of life; they are differences of import, and as the thing he had to say constantly expanded the form in which it had to be said, it always found the fittest to meet its requirements. If we reflect that Bach's indefatigable energy had only just begun really to work in the field of sacred cantata-writing, we shall recognise in this rapid evolution of a form so ample and perfect—every member of which he had to mould afresh from insufficient and heterogeneous models—a revelation of a marvellous creative power, comparable only to the thaumaturgic forces of nature. Since, however, a form without substance is inconceivable, and since the two exist in inseparable reciprocity, we see the reason why the cantatas of the later type bear a relation to human feeling so different from those of the earlier. They speak a clearer and more emphatic language ; the will asserts its rights as well as the emotions. At first we still meet here and there with accents of that earlier speech ; its echoes often float past like the tones of a harp from some vanished land of enchantment ; but soon these romantic chords are hushed, and the music marches steadily on without any melancholy regrets towards the solemn goal of riper manhood.

The cantata here indicated is the first of the fourth cycle of Neumeister's poetry, and intended for the First Sunday in Advent. The date 1714 is moreover written by Bach himself on the title-page ; so, according to this, it must have been performed on December 2.[202] Connected with this cantata is an interesting biographical incident to which I shall recur presently. Also, in order to come to a musical analysis of this composition, we must for the present pass over another cantata written earlier, and which has all the technical merits of the Advent music, but which from many points of view belongs to another place.

The text is in every respect admirable ; it is one of the best that Neumeister wrote. Two chorales begin and end it : at the beginning we have the first verse of the Advent hymn of St. Ambrose, "Veni, Redemptor genitum"—"Come, O Saviour of the nations." The close consists of the second section of the last verse of "How brightly shines the morning star !" The first recitative reminds us of the importance to the Church of Christ's incarnation, the final aria implores

---

[202] B.-G., XVI., No. 61. The original MS., for the most part autograph, is written with extreme care, and all the bars are marked off with a ruler. In the Royal Library at Berlin.

His merciful presence during the new ecclesiastical year. The feeling of the piece is diverted into personal sentiment by the beautiful mystical words from the Book of Revelation (iii. 20); in a new aria the heart of the worshipper opens to receive the coming Saviour, and this idea is then expressed by the whole congregation in the chorale which immediately follows. Thus the whole poem falls naturally into two contrasting groups of three sections in each. How clearly Bach had seized the suggestion thus offered is at once proved by his choice of keys; in the first group A minor and C major, in the second E minor and G major. The separate images are planned and worked out with the utmost care and tenderness. The first chorus is an instance of the unusual combination of a chorale with the French overture; it is evident that this could only be possible after the transition of this strictly instrumental form through the medium of the organ; and in fact the first part corresponds very closely to an adaptation to the organ of a *cantus firmus;* while in the second part, which is fugal, the overture was appropriate to the organ as it stood. Only quite distinctly constructed verses could be suited to such a mode of arrangement; but Bach must have seen very plainly that the results reached would bear no proportion to the trouble to be expended on it, and that the French overture had no special feature which the organ did not already possess in a better and more fertile form in the prelude and fugue. However, the combination is carried out with remarkable skill. The two first lines, "Nun komm der Heiden Heiland, der Jungfrauen Kind erkannt"—"Come, O Saviour of the nations, the Virgin-born art Thou,"—come in with the grave and ponderous first part of the overture; the upper instruments march on in a dotted rhythm; the organ, bassoon, and double-bass play the melody, which is next transferred to the soprano, and from thence to the alto in the fifth above; then again, after a moderately long interlude, to the tonic in the tenors, and again to the fifth in the bass. The parts then combine on the second line, and bar 32 passes on to the next section, "Des sich wundert alle Welt"—"Wonderful to all the world." The melody set to this serves as the theme for an effective and flowing fugue in 3-4 time,[203] full of a grand and healthy severity, and reverting according to custom to the first subject, supplemented by the last line of the chorale, " Gott solch Geburt ihm bestellt." Bach has given the melody a singularly modern cast by raising the third note of the first and last lines, by which means the key of A minor is sharply insisted on from the very beginning; but a melodic interval, forbidden in all laws of diatonic writing— the diminished fourth—is the result:—

The same feature recurs in an organ arrangement of this chorale by Nik. Bruhns, which Bach probably knew.[204] The G sharp, however, so took possession of his ear that it led him into a fresh piece of daring in the fugal movement, where he introduces this imitation :—

In a later cantata he returned to the original form in treating this same chorale. [205] The matter finds a real explanation in Bach's personal attitude as regards the church tones, to which reference will be made later on.

The first recitative, which passes into a melodious and highly developed arioso, gives us at the beginning a conspicuous proof of how completely the musical spirit predominated in Bach over the dramatic. Neumeister wrote :—

> Der Heiland ist gekommen,
> Hat unser armes Fleisch und Blut
> An sich genommen.
>
> On earth, with man abiding,
> The Saviour comes in flesh and blood,
> His Godhead hiding.

Bach treats the first period in the regular manner, but ends the second after the word "Fleisch," and gives "und Blut"

---

[203] With the indication " *gaij*," probably an abbreviation of " *gaiement* " or " *gayement*."

[204] Commer, Musica Sacra, I., No. 6.   [205] B.-G., XVI., No. 62.

to the following phrase—altogether wrong as regards declamation. But if we consider the sequence of the notes we
perceive that this method gives rise to three *musical* phrases
of equal magnitude, of which the first and third have a softer,
gentler flow, while the middle one is stronger and more
vigorous, so as to constitute a small cycle of beautiful symmetry. The faults in declamation may be easily altered
and then the charm is thrown into relief, which the ear
confesses in hearing a due balance of parts. It is the
singer's duty to mitigate the defective declamation by a
certain subtlety in the rendering, without disturbing the
musical structure. The tenor aria, " Komm, Jesu, komm zu
deiner Kirche "—" Come, Lord, O come into Thy temple,"
—is full of exquisite melody. The voice part is supported
by an independently flowing continuo with four strings in
unison (two violins and two violas), and their yield-
ing body of sound fitly clothes the tender gravity of the
subject. Bach, led astray perhaps by its charm, has let the
voice sink more into the background than it ought; a ritornel
of noble breadth first displays the real melodic material,
even while the voice is employed almost all the chief portion
of the melody is given to the violins, although the poetic
element is so far respected that the words of the text are
quite clearly distinguishable ; and then the whole ritornel is
once more repeated, so that it recurs four times including
the *da capo*. In the second portion of the aria certainly the
oversight is made good—still it is not important enough.
Apart from this deficiency it is a masterpiece in Bach's
own style. It may give some idea of the fulness of the
melodic flow to say that through fifty bars in 9-8 time, as
far as the beginning of the second section, there are only
three real full closes.

With the next recitative a fresh mood is struck: " Behold,
I stand at the door and knock," &c. (the words of Revelation iii. 20). Christ is at hand, and blessedness awaits those
who welcome His coming. But Bach did not mean to
express this Advent thought alone ; he goes deeper than this,
and has infused the whole import of the Apocalypse into the
ten bars set to these words. Anxious waiting breathes out

of the *pizzicato* chords on the violins, which mark the passing
of time with steady regularity, like the swings of a pen-
dulum, and measure the hours till the expected One shall
come; they begin, too, in a very characteristic manner on
the unprepared chord of the seventh, as if they had gone on
so from eternity. The words are sung by the bass—in no
sense a dramatic impersonation of Christ, any more than in
another cantata the bass singer is supposed to represent the
Holy Spirit.[206]   It is only the medium of utterance: the
instrument best fitted to the purpose here aimed at.   How
peculiar and picturesque is this phrase, as embodying a feeling
above all others transcendentally superhuman :—

Und   klo - - pfe   an

Tasteless as it might perhaps have been if Telemann or
Stölzel had taken it in hand, here it is grandiose, standing
as it does in the foreground of such a stupendous per-
spective of feeling.   Bars 4 and 5 again would be a failure
in the declamatory sense, with the emphasis—

So   Je - mand mei - ne Stim-me   hö - ren wird

if the pen of the master had not infused into it an ideal
quite apart from the logical distribution of the accent in the
words; if it were not treated as a watchman's cry, sounding
awfully and mysteriously through the night with a warning
to wake up from sleep, and stand like the five wise virgins
ready for the moment of departing.   Thus a sinister and
lurid glow as of the Last Judgment is cast over the joyful
glory of the festival.   But it soon turns to the purest radiance:
the Lord is welcomed with childlike devotion.   This is
expressed in the aria in G major, " Oeffne dich, mein ganzes
Herze "—" Open wide, my joyful Spirit,"—which contrasts
with the recitative.   Yea, that is the true Advent blessedness
which no human being can ever forget whose childhood has

---

[206] B.-G. XII., 2, No. 60.

not been absolutely bereft of all religious influences; that is
the feeling with which the soul filled with the tender and
mighty images of the Gospel of the Advent looks forward to
Christmas! The soprano alone utters its childlike rejoicing
in a triumphant melody, to the accompaniment of the organ
and a supporting violoncello; the simplest means alone could
be admitted here. This motive, however—

is treated with a subtle delicacy which may be divined from
the bass. Bach, as usual, has not left us the organ ritornel
and the figured-bass accompaniment to the vocal part. It
was usual to derive the materials for the ritornels exclusively
from the motives of the songs, so that their main features
were never difficult to recognise, and this is the case here;
the details are left to the good taste of the writer who undertakes their restoration. The chorus comes in emphatically:
"Amen, amen! Komm, du schöne Freudenkrone"—"Amen,
amen! Come, thou glorious crown of blessing, do not tarry.
I await thee full of longing." This is the first chorus on a
chorale in Pachelbel's manner which we meet with in Bach.
When this flood of sound poured forth from the body of the
organ it must have seemed as though the church were filled
with a glory of pure light. The violins in unison take an
independent course; from the eighth bar onwards they wave
their wings up and down in semiquavers, and rise at last to the
g'''—a height at that time rarely hazarded—as if soaring into
the empyrean: an anticipation of one of the most famous
points in the Credo in Beethoven's Missa Solemnis.[207]

There still remains a second cantata which Bach set
to music, taking the text from the fourth series of the
Fünffache Kirchen-Andachten. It belongs to Whit-Sunday,
May 31, 1716.[208] Bach did not set the whole of Neumeister's

---

[207] Mattheson (Neu eröffnetes Orchestre, p. 281) says of the violin that it has
a compass of three and a half octaves, "excepting in some few cases when it is
carried up to the g''', thus making three octaves, which however no assistant
can do"—i.e., none but a master.

[208] B.-G., XII., 2, No. 59. See App. A, No. 2.

poem, but he thought a part of the music worthy of extension and elaboration so long as nineteen years later. The first movement consists of a duet for soprano and bass, " Wer mich liebet, der wird mein Wort halten "—" He that loves Me, he will keep My saying,"—and it is interesting on account of its highly artistic polyphonic treatment, though it is not marked by strong melodic feeling. Of all the instruments, namely, the organ, string quartet, two trumpets and drums, it is only the last and the viola that do not work out independent passages on their own account. The form is taken from the Italian concerto, and we must be familiar with this, or the repeated closes and recommencements with the same leading idea will seem strange and unpleasing. In dealing with the Bible text the *da capo* form was hardly possible; that here selected offered the opportunity for enhancing the idea it expresses as a whole by a succession of new combinations and richer harmonies up to the very end, and this was undoubtedly the most proper method. A recitative follows, to which the stringed instruments, as well as the organ, play an accompaniment in long-drawn chords. This method, which we have already met with in the Sexagesima cantata, is very remarkable in Bach's recitative. It hinders the primary and dramatic purpose of recitative, which, as such, only requires a musical fulcrum in the form of short chords, or at most, in emotional passages, an harmonic modulation, with perhaps some illustrative interludes. But this accompaniment wraps the voice in a close veil of harmony, so that it cannot for an instant forget that its final cause is pre-eminently musical. It is, as we cannot fail to see at once, an imitation of organ *technique*. The recitative finds an issue in the Whitsuntide chorale, " Komm, heiliger Geist, Herre Gott"—"Come, Holy Spirit, God and Lord,"--magnificently set, and the only chorale number of the whole work. Then follows a bass aria, with a violin, of a warm melodious character, which in its trio-like plan is more perfect in style than the tenor aria of the Advent cantata, since the voice part has the prominent position that is due to its importance. A particularly pleasing effect is produced when the melody of the two first lines is repeated to other words in the first section of a hymn in verses; it is a delightful amalgamation of this form with that of the Italian aria. Bach's cantata ends here, though Neumeister supplies the text for three more numbers—a verse of a chorale, a Bible verse (Rom. xv. 13), and words for an aria. It seems to me doubtful whether Bach did not end the chorale with the third verse, from " Erhalt uns, Herr bei deinem Wort "—or at any rate intend to end it there; there exists in MS. some slight trace of such an intention. The reason why he left the rest unset lay undoubtedly in its indifferent adaptation to musical purposes; for the condition of the autograph gives no ground for believing that any part of it has been lost.

V.

BACH'S VISITS TO VARIOUS TOWNS.—SOME OF HIS PUPILS.

THE journeys made by Bach with a view to his advancement in art brought some variety into the quiet and monotony of his labours as a composer and the fulfilment of his official duties. If I am not mistaken, he was wont for some time to make a longer or shorter excursion in the autumn of every year, in order to play on the organ at different courts, or in the larger towns, and also to conduct in person performances of the cantatas he had composed. We have proof of several such journeys; one was to the court of Cassel. The opera was at that time flourishing greatly there, under the patronage of Karl, Landgrave of Hesse Cassel; in 1701 Ruggiero Fedeli had been appointed capellmeister; Lucia Bandarini, Cristina Maria Avolio, A. Noleati, Laura Valetta, are the names of the female singers at the time; of the men we find the names of two—Albertini and a certain Pierri. The salaries of the singers were fairly good, though not to compare with those given in Dresden,[209]

---

[209] One named Salbey received about 1,300 gülden. It was probably in 1710 that Madelaine du Salvay was appointed in Dresden, where she had a salary of 2,000 thalers (Fürstenau, Geschichte der Musik und des Theaters zu Dresden, II., p. 135).

and the ladies had, besides, sedan-chairs provided to take them to the opera-house, delicacies for the table, presents in money, hundreds of thalers in compensation for travelling expenses, residence rent-free, furniture for their apartments, &c. The capellmeister's income amounted to about 1,000 gülden, and to this 600 thalers were added—later indeed 700 —for two male sopranos. The court organist, Karl Müller, on the other hand, received, besides his court emoluments, only 140 gülden, which was not raised to 200 thalers until ten years later. One of the best German violin-players of the time, Johann Adam Birkenstock, in whom the court took a particular interest, and who was concertmeister at Cassel from the year 1725, nevertheless received no more than 200 thalers and emoluments.[210]

It would appear indeed that it was less the Landgrave him-self that attracted Bach to Cassel than the Crown Prince Friedrich, afterwards King of Sweden. A basis was afforded by the relationship existing between the two courts; the mother of the musical Crown Prince was a Princess of Hesse Homburg. In 1695 the Landgrave Karl, with the Crown Prince and some Princesses of Hesse, had paid a visit of several days to Weimar,[211] and in July of the same year August Kühnel, at that time deputy capellmeister to Duke Wilhelm Ernst, was invited to be capellmeister at the court of Cassel.[212] Bach's journey must have taken place before the end of the year 1714, his primary object being the trial of the newly restored organ. On this occasion, in obedience to the wish of the Crown Prince, he played the organ to him alone, and so filled him with astonishment and admiration by his marvellous execution of a pedal solo that the prince drew from his finger a ring set with precious stones and presented it to the master. " His feet flew over the pedal-board as if they had wings, and the

---

[210] I derive this from data in the Acts preserved in the royal archives at Marburg.

[211] Gottschalg, Geschichte, p. 286.

[212] Document at Marburg. He must have been deputy, since the office of capellmeister was held by Samuel Drese, and another deputy was appointed in 1695.

ponderous and ominous tones pierced the ear of the hearer like a flash of lightning or clap of thunder; and if the skill of his feet alone earned him such a gift, what would the prince have given him if he had used his hands as well?" So writes an intelligent admirer of art in 1743, when speaking of this incident. We know no more, however, of Bach's stay in Cassel.[213]

In the autumn of 1713 we find him in Halle. It is doubtful whether he did not stop there on his way back from some longer expedition. Just at this time a large organ had been erected there in the church of the Holy Virgin—Liebfrauenkirche—by Christoph Cuncius, of Halberstadt, after the old organ had fallen into utter ruin. The new one had sixtythree sounding stops. Bach had probably heard of it, and the great interest he took in organ-building may have led him to Halle principally on that account. At any rate it is certain that he performed there with the greatest success. The post of organist at this church had remained vacant ever since the death of F. W. Zachaus (August 14, 1712), and it seemed only waiting for Bach to offer himself. the prospect of working on this fine instrument, so infinitely superior to that at Weimar, must have been tempting. A part of it was to be ready for use by the following Easter; he therefore presented himself at once, before leaving the town, before the church authorities, and announced his willingness to accept the appointment. They, on their part, did not hesitate to seize the opportunity, and as part of the organist's duties consisted in composing music and conducting church music, the chief preacher of the church—one Dr. Heineccius—pressed him to submit at once to the prescribed tests. Bach arranged for a prolongation of his stay, composed a cantata forthwith, and conducted the performance; then he set out homewards, for time was pressing.

The elders of the church of Halle were very polite to the Weimar organist, and they never doubted but that, under the circumstances, he would esteem himself lucky in the possession of such a post. Although they separated without any

---

[213] See App. A, No. 24.

decisive agreement, they sent him before Christmas a "call" regularly drawn up in duplicate copies for his signature. Meanwhile Bach had notified to the Duke that he was in treaty with Halle. The Duke would have been sorry to see him depart, and indeed Bach himself was not altogether satisfied with the salary and conditions of the new appointment. Still he clung to the idea, expecting that the Chapter would take his personal wishes into consideration ; he therefore returned one copy unsigned, at the end of a few weeks, keeping the other, however, in sign that he was in earnest about the matter, and promising to formulate his demands precisely as soon as possible ; and if they could come to an understanding to return to Halle, and sign and seal then and there.   This is the letter he wrote :—

Most Noble, Most Respected Sir,[214]—

I have duly received your favour with the *vocation* in duplicate ; I am greatly obliged to you for sending it, as I esteem it a happiness that the whole of your most noble *Collegium* condescend to call me, your humble servant, who had determined to follow the guidance of God shown in this *vocation*.   Still, most honoured sir, I beg you not to take it amiss that I could not hitherto notify to you my final *resolution*, by reason that I have not yet received my final *dimission*, and (2) because in one or two things I should be glad of some alteration both as to the salary and also as to the service, all of which shall be specified in writing this week.   Meanwhile I remit to you one *exemplar ;* and since I have not yet received my entire *dimission*, I pray you, most honoured sir, not to take it ill that still, at this time, I cannot engage myself, by subscribing my name or otherwise, before I am actually out of service.   And so soon as we shall be agreed as to my *station* [work and pay] I will present myself in person, by my signature to prove that I have really and truly intended to bind myself to your service.   Meanwhile, most honoured sir, I would beg you to commend me most respectfully to all the elders of the church, and to make my excuses for that want of time has hitherto not possibly allowed of my giving in any categorical resolution ; for certain preparations at court for the prince's birthday,[215] and also the regular church services, have not suffered it ; but it shall, without fail, be done circumstantially this week.   I received your favour with

---

[214] The address of the letter is wanting, but it was undoubtedly sent to A. Becker, Licentiate, to whom Bach's other letters on this occasion were addressed. He was a member of the church committee.

[215] Johann Ernst, born December 26, 1696. The *vocation* was dated December 14, 1713.

all due respect, and I hope the illustrious *Collegium* of the church will be graciously pleased to remove certain difficulties which appear. In the hope of an early and happy issue, I remain, most noble and most honoured sir,

Your devoted servant,

Weimar, January 14, 1714.   Joh. Sebast. Bach.[216]

The second and more explicit letter must certainly have followed this very shortly, but the church committee would not hear of any alterations in the conditions of the appointment, and desired Bach to send back the document of *vocation* if he was not satisfied with its contents. This he did ; and the citizens of Halle were now mean enough to declare that he had only opened the negotiation in order to extort some additional advantages in Weimar. Such treatment must have infuriated Bach all the more because his salary at the ducal court had for a long time been higher than that offered to him in Halle. The income from the Liebfrauenkirche amounted in all only to 171 thalers 12 ggr. —irrespective of unestimated perquisites—while in his old place Bach had been receiving ever since the previous Easter the sum of 225 gülden (=196 thalers 21 ggr.). It was by abstract advantages that he had been tempted, as he had been once before from Arnstadt to Mühlhausen, and his conditions seem to have been modest enough on both occasions. But that a man should have an ideal, or any but sordid motives, seems to have been incomprehensible to the elders of the church : they judged Bach by the standard of an avaricious artisan. However, he was not the man to swallow such an affront in silence. He wrote an answer which leaves nothing to be desired as regards clearness and a determined attitude :—

Most Noble, Illustrious, and Learned, Most Honoured Sir,—

That the very worshipful *Collegium* should be surprised at my refusal of the post of organist, of which—as they suppose—I was ambitious, does not at all surprise me, for I perceive that they can have considered the matter very little. They suppose that I greatly desired the above-mentioned post of organist, while nothing could be farther from my mind. This

---

[216] The reader who is interested in the quaint originals of Bach's letters is referred to the German of Herr Spitta's work.

much I know, that I offered myself, and that the most worshipful *Collegium* much desired me ; for I, after having presented myself, was minded to travel away at once, when I received Dr. Heineccius' command; and politely remained, though I was not compelled, to compose and conduct the piece you know of. Moreover, it is not to be presumed that a man should go to a place where he injures his position. This, however, I could not accurately ascertain in from fourteen days to three weeks, for I am quite of opinion that a man cannot ascertain what his wages are in any place—as the perquisites must be reckoned as part of the pay— even in a few years, much less in fourteen days ; and this is in some degree the reason why I accepted the nomination, and on the ground of my (unsatisfied) desires gave it up. Still, from all this, it is a long way to concluding that I have played a trick on the worshipful *Collegium* in order to move my gracious master here to increase my salary, since his highness has already shown so much favour to me and my art that I had no need to travel to Halle for an increase of salary. Thus I regret that the certain conviction of the most worshipful *Collegium* should have led to such a very uncertain issue ; and to this I would add : Even if I were to get as good payment in Halle as here in Weimar, should I not still be bound to prefer the former service to the new? You, who understand law and equity may best judge of this; and I would venture to request you to lay this my justification before the most worshipful *Collegium*, and remain, most honoured sir, yours obediently,

JOH. SEB. BACH,

Weimar, March 19, 1714.   *Concertmeister and Court Organist.*

[Addressed]

A Monsieur | Monsieur A. Becker | Licentié en Droit. Mon | tres honore Ami a | Halle | [in the lower left-hand corner :] p. couvert.

That he was fully justified in boasting of the duke's benevolence we already know, from the steady increase in Bach's salary during many years. At the beginning of 1714 his income was again increased, so that it now amounted to 264 gülden.[217] The words that " he had no need to travel to Halle for an increase of salary " prove that without this cir-

---

[217] The whole expenditure for chamber music from Michaelmas, 1713, to 1714, " 232 florins 10 ggr. 6 pf. To the concertmeister and court organist, Joh. Seb. Bach :—

53 fl.	15 ggr.	9 pf.,	to Crucis	⎫	1713.
53 ,,	15 ,,	9 ,,	,, Luciæ	⎭	
62 ,,	10 ,,	6 ,,	,, Reminiscere	⎫	1714."
62 ,,	10 ,,	6 ,,	,, Trinity	⎭	

And besides this 12 fl. for wood and 2 fl. from the foundation. In another list of payments (under " Court and household expenses: *Miscellanea* ") we find this notice, " Concertmeister Bach, 18 bushels of corn."

cumstance a further increase of payment was in view, and
indeed must have been in consequence of the addition to his
duties. For at the same time he took the place of concertmeister, whose place it was then, as it is at the present day,
to lead the orchestra, playing the first violin. Drese's advanced age and infirmity must have obliged him altogether
to give up this post, and with it the lead in chamber music ;
for Bach subsequently had to take part of the duties of the
capellmeister as well.

At the beginning of December we find him in Leipzig,
where, on the First Sunday in Advent, being the second day
of the month, he conducted a performance of the cantata,
"Nun komm, der Heiden Heiland," in the church either of
St. Thomas or St. Nicholas, and led the whole service as
organist. This journey, like the one he made years before
to Halle, was undertaken from purely artistic motives; he no
more thought of seeking a new appointment now than he had
then. He may have been more particularly prompted by a
desire to make acquaintance with Kuhnau, whose works had
not been wholly without influence on his mind and its development, and perhaps to make known to him the full extent of
his own powers. In order not to lose his way in the involved
order of the service, he noted it with his own hand on the
inside of the cantata score.[218] Here he found ample opportunity
for showing his skill on the organ. He opened the service
with a prelude, followed by a motett; then came a prelude to
the Kyrie. After the intonation by the preacher in front of
the altar, the reading of the epistle, and the singing of the
litany, came the prelude to the chief chorale, in which he
could display his skill in chorale arrangement. Then the
gospel was read ; and next Bach introduced the chief music
(Hauptmusik), which on this occasion was his own cantata,
by a prelude on the organ. After the sermon followed the
communion, with another prelude to a chorale, and finally he

---

[218] The note is given in the preface to the cantata; it is by this alone that we
know of Bach's journey to Leipzig. It is evident that it was not inserted later,
when Bach was cantor at Leipzig, because he entered on his office there in the
spring of 1723, and by Advent of that year could certainly no longer have
needed to make any note as to the order of the service.

had to close the service, and here, again, could put forth all his powers in an organ piece on the grandest scale. This was the first visit he paid to the town where he was destined to spend twenty-seven years—the most laborious of his life.

Meanwhile, it began to be understood in Halle that the accusations brought against Bach were wholly unfounded. When at Easter, 1716, Cuncius had finished his work, after three years labour, Bach was invited to try it. It does the elders of the church much honour that they should have endeavoured to make amends for their injustice; and the fact that they trusted to his impartiality in spite of all that had taken place shows the high opinion they must originally have formed of his character. He was to be assisted in his judgment by Kuhnau, from Leipzig, and Christian Friedrich Rolle, of Quedlinburg, the father of the well-known church composer, Johann Heinrich Rolle. The invitation was transmitted by Becker, the licentiate, and the master was greatly pleased and touched by it. He wrote a polite reply, which runs as follows:—

Most Noble Gentlemen,
And you particularly, Highly Honoured Sir,—
I am deeply obliged by your honour's very particular and gracious confidence, and by that of the whole very most honoured *Collegium;* and, as I always find the greatest pleasure in waiting on your worship, I shall now more than ever endeavour to make my services acceptable to your worship, and to give satisfaction to the utmost in the *examine* required of me. I would beg you accordingly to communicate this my resolution to the most honoured *Collegium* without delay, and at the same time to offer to them my most humble greeting, and my dutiful respects for the special confidence with which they have favoured me.

I also beg to acknowledge with obedient gratitude all the trouble your worship has been pleased to take for me in many ways up to this time, and will take again; and I shall have the greatest pleasure, so long as I live, in subscribing myself, most honoured Sir,
Your worship's devoted servant,
Joh. Seb. Bach,
Concertmeister.

[Addressed to]
Herrn | Herrn *Augusto Becker* | Best*meritirten Licentiato Juris,* | Wie auch der Kirchen *B. M. Virginis* | fürnehmen Vorstehern. Meinem| insonders HochgeEhrtesten Herrn | in | Halle. |

The examination of the organ was fixed for the second week after Easter, and was to begin on April 29. Kuhnau wished it postponed for four days, for he was just then much pressed with official duties; but the authorities at Halle would not agree to this. The testimonial in writing which was given by all three experts was altogether to the credit of Cuncius, and the only essential defect pointed out was in the arrangement of the bellows. The specification had been exactly carried out in all essential points, and Halle could henceforth boast of possessing one of the largest organs in Germany.[219] What effects Bach may have produced with such an abundant variety of stops of course we cannot even imagine; but even less able organists found themselves helped and improved by the intelligent care bestowed on the instrument—the three manuals being quite different in character without either of them suffering any loss of fulness and roundness of tone. It cost the church authorities much trouble, however, to engage an organist worthy of the instrument—the post was too ill-endowed. Melchior Hoffmann, of Leipzig, who was treated with after Bach had left, likewise refused. At last, by the middle of 1714, they came to an understanding with Gottfried Kirchhoff to take the post. He was a contemporary of Bach (born in 1685), a pupil of Zachaus, and at that time organist at Quedlinburg. He followed in the footsteps of Pachelbel as a composer of organ chorales, but with much talent and independence.[220]

---

[219] The sketch of the specification in Cuncius' writing is still extant. Adlung gives us a list of stops in working order in 1768 (Musica Mechanica, I., p. 239), with some little differences. Some alterations must have been made already.

[220] The documents concerning the Halle appointment are preserved in the church. It is Chrysander who deserves the credit of having first directed attention to them (Händel, I., p. 22). He subsequently published a paper on them in the Jahrbüchern für Musikalische Wissenschaft, II., p. 235. He has, however, fallen into the error of regarding the specification as written by Bach himself, and infers that it was his ideal of what an organ should be, and that he and Cuncius were on intimate terms. Bach did not write the specification; it was copied from a sketch-specification by Cuncius, who signed it. The faults of spelling are of themselves sufficient evidence, and Chrysander's error sets Bach in an unfavourable and undeserved light. I take this opportunity of expressing my thanks to Herr Karmrodt, of Halle (music-dealer), who materially assisted me in collating the documents in question. Mizler

As Bach's fame grew and spread the number of his pupils grew in proportion; it was his executive skill, of course, which most struck the public, so at first his instruction was more sought for organ and clavier-playing than for composition. I have already spoken of his first scholar, who for many years was also his amanuensis, Johann Martin Schubart. The next to be mentioned is Johann Caspar Vogler, who was born at Hausen, near Arnstadt,[221] in 1696, and is said to have had the advantage of Bach's teaching as a boy, when Bach was still organist at the New church.[222] He subsequently went to the musical training-schools of Erlebach, and of Petter, the organist at Rudolstadt; then he went again to Bach at Weimar, who made of him, as he himself declares, one of his best organ pupils.[223] In 1715 he was organist at Stadtilm, and after Schubart's death he succeeded him. After that he did not again quit Weimar, although (1735) at a competitive examination at the Marktkirche at Hanover, he triumphantly beat ten candidates out of the field; but, in order to retain him at Weimar, Duke Ernst August gave him the title of vice-burgomaster. He died about 1765. He himself published one of his compositions, a choral work, entitled Vermischte Musikalische Choral-Gedanken, 1 Probe (Weimar, 1737)—Miscellaneous Musical Chorale Subjects.[224]

---

alludes very briefly to the matter, and is not quite accurate as to the order of events, in the Necrology, p. 163 : "After the death of Zachaus, director of the music and organist to the Marktkirche (Market Church) in Halle, our Bach received a call to the office. He did, indeed, go to Halle, and there went through his tests. But he found reasons for refusing it, and it was given to Kirchhoff."

[221] According to the trustworthy statement of Hesse in his list of the worthies and artists of Schwarzburg, No. 388 (Rudolstadt, 1827).

[222] So Forkel says (p. 42), and there is no reason to doubt him.

[223] Gerber, Lex., II., col. 746. An expression of Kirnberger's contradicts this statement strangely (Die wahren Grundsätze zum Gebrauch der Harmonie, 1773, p. 54). Some critic in the Zeitung von gelehrten Sachen, of Jena, had set Vogler on the same level with Bach, on which Kirnberger writes: "If we ask, 'Who is this Vogler?' after much inquiry we discover that he is a burgomaster and organist of Weimar, and a pupil of Bach, but not the most eminent by a long way." Had Kirnberger, himself a disciple of Bach, really never heard of Vogler, or is this merely his sarcastic manner ?

[224] A copy of this rare work exists in the library of the Institute for Church Music at Berlin.

Somewhat older than Vogler, though he emancipated himself later from his master, was Johann Tobias Krebs. He was born in 1690, at Heichelheim, near Weimar, where he got his schooling, but in 1710 was organist and cantor at Buttelstadt. He did not achieve his musical acquirements till he was already in office and married. As late as in 1717 he visited Weimar on foot from Buttelstädt, and at first was Walther's pupil in playing and in composition; but afterwards this no longer satisfied him, and he continued his studies under Bach.

The fruits of these persevering efforts are very discernible in the few relics of Krebs' compositions which I have been able to collect. There are two chorale arrangements of the most complicated character, but full of genuine musical feeling. One of them, "Christus, der uns selig macht" *per canonem diminutum*, is unfortunately only a fragment. A theme is constructed on the first line—

which is first fugally treated, and remains conspicuous throughout the whole arrangement; elsewhere the material for the counterpoint is derived from the other lines of the chorale. The *cantus firmus* lies in the bass in minims; as soon as the first line is introduced it is associated with it in crotchets. This process is repeated in the following lines, though in a less strictly logical manner. The organ chorale on " Machs mit mir, Gott, nach deiner Gut " is also planned on a canon *per diminutionem*.[225] It is a sufficient proof of the impression that Bach's mastery and skill made on Tobias Krebs, that he intrusted his son, Johann Ludwig (born February 10, 1713),[226] to the same teacher at the early age of thirteen. He, too, grew to be an organist of the first rank; but the genius of the son must not lead us to overlook

---

[225] The authority for these chorales is the volume of works for the organ already spoken of as having belonged to Joh. Lud. Krebs, and now in the possession of Herr F. A. Roitzsch, of Leipzig; the second is also to be found in Frankenberger's autograph by Walther.

[226] Not October 10, as Gerber states, Vol. I., col. 756.

the talent of the father.   He went to Buttstädt in 1721, and was still living there as organist in 1758.[227]

Johann Gotthilf Ziegler, born at Dresden, 1688, remained a shorter time under Bach's tuition.   His talent was early ripe, versatile and restless.   He too, according to Walther, worked at clavier and organ playing under Bach, but in composition followed the guidance of Johann Theile, of Naumburg.   But in the condition of musical science at that time it must have been quite impossible to divide the two branches so sharply; a chorale arrangement, for instance, would fall within the province of organ-playing, but would presuppose a knowledge of the laws of composition.   And Ziegler, at the age of fifty-eight, acknowledges with pride how much he owed to Bach, even in this: "As concerning the playing of chorales, I was instructed by my master, the Capellmeister Bach, who is still living, to play the airs, not only as of the first importance, but according to the tenor of the words."[228]   Ziegler lived at Halle, where he was organist to the church of St. Ulrich, and much sought after as a teacher; and where, too, he had studied theology and jurisprudence about 1715.   Still, after Kirchhoff's death in 1746, he did not succeed in obtaining his post.   He declined all offers of honourable employment elsewhere.[229]

In the year 1715, as it would seem about Easter, Bach took into his house his nephew Bernhard, the second son of his brother at Ohrdruf.   He had not forgotten what he had formerly owed him, and mutual practical help among the members of the family was a traditional custom of all the Bachs.   Bernhard Bach, born November 24, 1700, had studied at first at the Lyceum at Ohrdruf; he himself naïvely

---

[227] Gerber, N. L., III., col. 109.

[228] In his letter of application for the post of organist to the church of the Holy Virgin at Halle, February 1, 1746, given at length by Chrysander, Op. cit., p. 241.

[229] Walther's article on Ziegler is incredibly confused.   In spite of an abundance of chronological data, he never once calculates the time when he was Bach's pupil.   Even the call sent to him from Reval he dates incorrectly, and sets in a wrong light; from documents of the town council of Reval, it was in 1721 that a deputation was sent to Ziegler with an invitation to go there, as my friend Herr O. von Riesemann has obligingly ascertained.

relates that "by reason of his bad memory, father held it to be unadvisable that he should remain at his studies." For this reason he sent him to Weimar to his brother, at that time concertmeister, who was a very famous and skilled *maître*,[230] and there he acquired good proficiency, both on the clavier and in composition."[231] He says nothing of the length of his stay in his uncle's house—still it cannot have extended beyond the year 1717, for if he had moved with him to Cöthen he would certainly have told us so. It is most probably to his industry as a scholar that we owe the greater part of a valuable MS. copy of Sebastian Bach's compositions, which passed into the hands of his brother Andreas Bach, with the post of organist at Ohrdruf, in 1744.[232] Up to this date, when he died, Bernhard had filled this post, which was previously held by their father, who died in 1721. Three MS. works for the clavier exist by him, one of which, a suite in E flat major, betrays an almost comical imitation of Sebastian's methods ; it would be possible to refer its origin almost bar for bar to the six partitas of the first part of the Clavierübung. The second, a sonata in four movements in B flat major,[233] and a third piece, a fantasia in G major, are more independent in style.

Many remembrances of his life in Ohrdruf and Lüneburg must have revived in Sebastian's mind when Georg Erdmann, the companion of his youth, paid him a visit at Weimar some time between 1715 and 1717. Since 1713 Erdmann had had employment in Russia ; he had studied jurisprudence, and in the year 1718 was acting as military law referee to the division under the Russian general, Prince Repnin. He made occasional expeditions from the north to visit his native land, and on one of these occasions he visited Weimar, and had the pleasure of seeing his former school

---

[230] [French words are always French in the original documents.—TRANS.]

[231] In Kromayer's Kirchenbuche, before mentioned as made use of by Brück-ner, Kirchen- und Schulenstaat, Part III., sec. 10, p. 95. It is there expressly stated that he went to Weimar in his fifteenth year.

[232] Compare App. A, No. 18.

[233] The two first are in the possession of Dr. Rust, of Berlin, in an old MS. copy ; the last is owned by Herr Ritter, musical director at Magdeburg.

comrade in the midst of his household and blooming family. Their friendly interchange of sentiments and experiences, begun then by word of mouth, was continued afterwards in a correspondence, and we shall presently have more to say concerning Erdmann.[234]

VI.

CANTATAS WRITTEN AT WEIMAR TO TEXTS BY FRANCK.

WE find Bach at the beginning of the year 1714 court-organist and concertmeister;[235] we have already said that in this latter capacity he must have fulfilled some of the duties of the capellmeister. Samuel Drese was almost incapable of work from his age and infirmities, and his son was a musician of very small pretensions at the best; but Duke Wilhelm Ernst was desirous of establishing at Weimar regular church music on Neumeister's model, incited to the scheme, no doubt, by the example of his cousin at Eisenach. He had not failed to discover the genius for composition of his court-organist, and he therefore issued the order—which indeed had nothing unusual in it—that Bach, as concertmeister, should compose and conduct a certain number of sacred pieces every year,[236] thus concentrating more and more all the most important musical functions in the person of Bach.

The poet who might write the texts was to be found on the spot. Salomo Franck, born March 6, 1659, at Weimar, where his father was private secretary, had probably studied in Jena, where he had published his first volume of poems in 1685; he then spent some time at Zwickau, went to Arnstadt in 1689 in the capacity of secretary to the government of Schwarzburg, and returned to Jena to fill a similar office in that town. He subsequently lived at Weimar as secretary to the Superior Consistory of the Principality of Saxony, and

---

[234] From papers in the imperial archives at Moscow, of which I have copies.

[235] A complete list of the members of the court capelle or band at Weimar, from the years 1714 to 1716, is given in App. B, No. V.

[236] Mizler, Op. cit., p. 163.

died there in 1725. He was also librarian and curator of the ducal collection of coins. He was a member of a society known as the "Association of Ingenious Men" (*Fruchtbringenden Gesellschaft*), and as such enjoyed the epithet of "*Treumeinende*," or, faithful in purpose.[237]

Franck was undoubtedly one of the true poets of his time. In neatness and grace of diction he was equal to Neumeister, and but little his inferior in purity of expression. Added to these he had what Neumeister often lacked, depth and fervour of feeling. This natural bent would of course lead him to lyric poetry, and with this, at that time, sacred verse was synonymous. His masques, his poems written for weddings, on occasions of mourning, and others of the kind, are distinguished by their refined and elegant character, without displaying any great variety or originality of thought. In religious poetry, on the other hand, he revealed a very marked and remarkable individuality. His scope, even here, is limited, no doubt; but his way of seeing and modes of expression are neither borrowed nor absorbed from others; they are the genuine offspring of his own mind. Grandeur and a soaring flight he has not, but a very picturesque vein of rhapsody and tender melancholy. He likes to dwell on the sorrows and sufferings of human life; he lingers by the grave, and muses on death and the inspiring and hopeful images of heavenly joys. In treating of this he displays a very uncommon wealth of fancy, and he soon formed for himself a distinct style for the adequate expression of his ideas and feelings. A certain amount of familiarity with his mode of treatment makes it almost impossible not to recognise it at once; in it he reminds us of Eichendorff, as well as in a certain key of mystical dreaminess, when due allowance is made for the difference of their periods, and in some degree of their subject-matter. Certain turns of language and figures of speech he is apt to repeat frequently, and in the same way he is fond of using intricate metres, artificial schemes of rhyme, and a mixture of long and short lines; he likes, too,

---

[237] Schauer, Vorrede zu Salomo Francks geistlichen Liedern (preface to S. F.'s hymns). Halle: J. Fricke, 1855.

to frame in a verse, as it were, by repeating the first lines at the end of it.

The subjective character of his poems did not hinder their extensive use for church purposes. Franck is a very conspicuous witness to the fact that the transfusion of the objective catholic church sentiments into personal religious feeling met an universal predisposition half-way as it were, even outside the special circle of the Pietists. A reader of his poems, whose knowledge of the conditions under which they were written was merely superficial, would certainly attribute them to a pietistic writer. But that he was far indeed from this is sufficiently proved by his friendship with Olearius, the superintendent at Arnstadt, and by the position of esteem he held at the court of Wilhelm Ernst; there is still further evidence in his numerous texts for cantatas, arranged in the manner of Neumeister. Of his hymns the best known is " So ruhest du, O meine Ruh," although its want of simplicity, and particularly an incessant seeking to play upon words, show that it is a youthful work; and indeed it is contained in his first collection.[238]   Twelve years later he brought out at Arnstadt a collection of *Madrigals* on the Passion; we may sympathise with the fervent feeling of these poems, but cannot overlook the want of taste in much of the expression, and the turgid or lame character of the images.   However, as he went on he succeeded better in finding natural and touching expression for his ideas.   His sacred and secular poems (Geist und Weltlichen Poesien), which came out in two parts in 1711 and 1716, mark the highest level of his works in the sacred lyrics it contains;[239] indeed these volumes include most of what he had produced in the way of occasional poems up to the year when the second part was published, excepting some sacred cantatas, which we must now study more closely.

Franck's earliest cantatas were written in the old form, and consist of Bible texts and hymns in verses.   One whole

---

[238] This appeared (in 1685) under the title Salomon Frankens aus Weimar Geistliche Poesie—Sacred Poetry, &c.

[239] Schauer has published a pleasing selection in his little volume, and in the preface has given a list of Franck's works, so far as they can be identified.

series[240] is included in the sacred and secular poems 94
to 210; a rhythm adapted to recitative is introduced only
into two dialogues, for the second day of Christmas-tide and
the first day of Easter, and in both cases unhesitatingly
given to the chorus. In the second part of the same collection there is likewise a series of hymns for the year
under the title Singende Evangelische Schwanen—Gospel
Songs of the Swan (pp. 2 to 86),—on the subject of death
and the life to come. While these are all, without exception, simple arias—that is to say, hymns in verses—in
pp. 132, 134, and 190 we find the first of his cantata texts
in the complete form as devised by Neumeister. Between
these again there are several poems, intermediate in character, which are devoid of recitative, consisting only of a
string of arias of modern style and of various metres, interspersed with short ejaculations or axioms. This attempt
to reconcile the forms of the older and the newer cantata
—by no means advantageous from the musical point of
view—was evidently the result of the fact that Franck did
not become acquainted with the new style till he was a
man of fifty, and could not at once make up his mind to
give up the old form that he knew and loved. Of the
three series of cantatas for the year which he wrote, and
which have come down to us, the second only consists
of poems of this older character; while in the other, recitatives after the Neumeister model are also introduced. So far
as I have been able to discover he was alone in his experiment. It seems clear too, from the fact that these new
methods were not used by him before he wrote the second
part of his sacred and secular poems, that the idea of adopting the new form of sacred cantatas had been suggested
from Eisenach, and chiefly by the third and fourth cycles of
Neumeister.

All these poems must have been written after 1711; and it
is very possible, indeed probable, that Bach composed music
for one and another of them—indeed he may have used some

---

[240] Evangelische Seelen-Lust über die Sonn-und Festtage durchs ganze Jahr
(Gospel joys for the soul for every Sunday and holy day throughout the year).

of the older texts by Franck as well. None of them are to be
found, it is true, among those of his cantatas which remain
to us; still it is incontestable that he took a great interest in
Franck's poetry, and composed music for it, and not merely
by the desire of his sovereign. Superior as he must have
been to the poet in vigour, spirit and originality, they had
one feature in common—their transcendental mysticism—
and a disposition to regard the actualities of all earthly
things as utterly gloomy and unsatisfying in comparison
with the glorious visions of celestial bliss. And though
he must have told himself that Franck was far from
equalling Neumeister in the incisiveness and point of his
expressions—that in his arias even, his lack of sympathy
with the scope and structure of the grander forms of music
renders his texts inadequate—on the other hand, he cannot
have been insensible to the melodious flow of his verses.
Even when in Leipzig he often returned to Franck's poetry;
and though this was less the case as regards his cantata
texts—which nevertheless were far superior in poetic merit
to Picander's insipid patchwork—others of his hymns
pleased him so much that he endeavoured to find a place
for them in his compositions. It will be shown in the
proper place that one of the noblest pieces of the Passion
according to St. Matthew rests on a modification of a poem
by Franck, which can hardly be attributed to any hand but
that of Bach himself. It would even seem that he made
use of a number of Franck's verses in the Passion according
to St. John. There is no direct evidence that the two were
ever personally acquainted; still it is credible. At the same
time it must not be forgotten that Franck was the elder by
twenty-six years.[241]

A regular use of Franck's texts in the ducal chapel, and
at the same time of a corresponding series of compositions
by Bach, was not begun till the Easter of 1715. It is not
possible now to ascertain what order had previously been

---

[241] In the Geist und weltlichen Poesien, I., p. 529, we find a wedding song,
" Bey der Unruh-Bachischen Ehe-Verbindung vorgestellet " (on the occasion
of the marriage of Unruh and Bach). Was this "maiden Bach" a relative of
Sebastian's ? The church registers afford no information on this point.

observed in the services in the castle chapel, nor what share Bach had taken in them as a composer. It must even remain unknown whether a regular production of certain compositions for church use was required of him from the time when he was first appointed to the post of concert-meister, or not until the following year. But the composition of two of Franck's poems certainly falls within this period; and if we add to these the cantatas by Neumeister, previously discussed, we have the proofs of no small amount of labour in this department even at that early date.

These two cantatas belong to the third Sunday after Trinity, June 17, 1714, and Palm Sunday in 1714 (March 25) or 1715 (April 14).[242] The first, "Ich hatte viel Bekümmerniss"—"My spirit was in heaviness,"[243]—is one of the best known of his works. It refers directly to the epistle for the day, but is of such general application that Bach himself wrote over it "*Per ogni tempo*"—for any season. It may perhaps have been composed for some special occasion, for the treatment is unusually broad and rich. It begins with a very beautiful *sinfonia* in C minor, common time, which has the form of Gabrieli's sonatas. The oboe and first violin have imitative passages full of melody and of even passionate expressiveness, while the second violin, viola, organ and basses support them with majestic harmonies. The vocal portion consists of four choruses set to Bible words—the third being underlaid throughout by a chorale melody—three arias, two recitatives and a duet.

The first chorus, "My spirit was in heaviness" (arranged from the words of Ps. xciv. 19) goes through the theme—

Ich hat - te viel Be - küm - mer - niss

with incisive close treatment (the response enters on the fifth note of the theme) for the first eighteen bars, ascending diatonically, with constant suspensions of the seventh and the second; then for a time at the interval of a fourth; then

---

[242] App. A, No. 25.
[243] B.-G., V., 1, No. 21. Peters, 41. Published, with English words, by Novello, Ewer & Co.

again with gradual ascent and much richer harmonies, which are shared in by all the orchestra. Then a long-drawn "But, Lord," leads into the *vivace*, "Thy consolations have my soul restored," a brilliant upward and downward movement of all the voices and stringed parts in semiquavers, with a predominance of the major key; the last bars grow calmer, while a most ingenious polyphony is developed, and it closes on C major. Then follows an aria for the soprano with oboe obbligato, in which fear and sorrow find utterance with all the impressive vehemence characteristic of Bach. A very melodious recitative for the tenor—the lament of one forsaken by God—leads to the second aria, in F minor. The text compares the woes of humanity to the floods of the sea which threaten to wreck the frail vessel of life; but some of the images are not very clear. The movement here given to the quartet of strings is derived from this figurative idea; the aria is almost unequalled for harmonic depth and fulness, and lends an enhanced effect to that which has preceded it. The voice, which is here treated only as an instrument, though the first among others, is never associated with another for support, and wherever it is accompanied the result is a five-part harmony.

As a contrast to these images of woe, painted as they are in the deepest hues, we have a peculiarly touching commencement to the chorus "Wherefore grievest thou, O my spirit?" (Psalm xlii. 6), sung at first by a few voices, and then emphatically repeated by all. At the words, "and art so unquiet in me," it is vivified into a tone-picture of marvellous art; four motives of the most distinct rhythmical individuality are given to the voices; these subjects pursue each other in canon, and then are all sung together, while an accompaniment in six parts is brought in which is founded on a totally new motive, and which does not combine with the chorus till afterwards. Genius can go no further in depicting the restless hopes and fears of the human soul. Then comes a new section full of tender peace and fervent joyful impetus, "Hope thou in God," which passes into the exquisite closing fugue in C minor. This whole movement is a sort of echo or reminiscence of the past emotions, such as we find in the music to Psalm cxxx., and in certain parts of the "*Actus tragicus*." In technical treatment the fugue reminds us of Bach's earlier period: a single instrument glides in with the theme among the voices in the four-part subject; then for a time the instruments alone treat it fugally, and finally the voices join once more in the intricate maze, beginning the whole fugal structure afresh.

The second part of the cantata begins with a dialogue in recitative for the soprano and bass, representing the Soul and Christ. This, too, is highly musical, and the accompanying strings often have an independent passage. The very first bars contain a most subtle touch. To these words, spoken by the Soul: "Lord Jesus, my repose, my light, where art Thou gone?" the violins work upwards on soft chords of the dominant, thus giving a very graphic image of spiritual longing; then when, after Christ's answer, "Behold, O spirit, I am with thee," the Soul cries out "With me? but here is only night!" the violins quit their hold of the long-drawn high chord, and sink abruptly, an octave and a half at a time, to the very depths, and on the word "night" strike on a brooding and ominous long-sustained chord which is not resolved till Christ speaks His words of comfort. The next number is a duet between the same two allegorical figures with an accompaniment on the organ only (E flat major, at first in common time, then in 3-4, and at the end in common time again); and then comes a great chorale chorus (on the second and fifth verses of "Wer nur den lieben Gott lässt walten"—"He only waits on God who submits to God"). The three other parts work contrapuntally on an independent motive in scale passages up and down to these words, adapted from Psalm cxvi. 7: "Now again be thou joyful, O my spirit: thy reward is of God."

This cantata of Bach's offers us the first example of the transfer of a whole organ chorale in Pachelbel's form to a vocal chorus, but it is far superior to Pachelbel in *technique*, from the logical adoption (musically speaking) of a counterpoint especially its own. The *cantus firmus* lies first in the tenor, with only solo voices in contrast, and all the instruments are silent except the organ; in the other verses the soprano carries on the melody while the whole chorus are employed with all the instruments, reinforced by the addition of trombones; a second scheme of counterpoint is introduced, the former one undergoes new treatment, and the whole proceeds with renewed vigour. It is all worked out with supreme technical knowledge.

A happy flight of song for the tenor—" Rejoice, O my spirit, in thy consolation; for now from thy sorrow thou findest salvation "—bridges over the transition to the last chorus, in C major, common time, which is indeed " the end that crowns the work," and crowns it brilliantly.[244] It is with justice that this hymn of triumph (from Rev. v. 12 and 13) has become so famous; it is unwontedly popular in style for Bach, and reminds us of Handel. This may be explained by supposing that in this instance the sentiment of Bach's older church cantatas once more powerfully asserted itself in him, though subsequently it was driven into the background by the sterner temper of his maturer mind. His youthful frankness and soaring ardour are, as it were, the obverse—the outer face—of that rapturous fervency and tender dreamy spirit which are so peculiarly his own. As regards its construction the fugue has much resemblance to the closing fugue of the " Rathswechsel " cantata of 1708.[245] Here again solo parts begin which, from bar 15 onwards, gradually become merged in the choral mass.

When they have gradually worked up to the top, the trumpets, in three parts, carry on the theme, then the body of violins with the oboe, while the voices have a jubilant imitation in semiquavers. Up to this point we have had no chords but those of the tonic and dominant; now, however, the voices take up the theme with all the weight of homophony in four parts in D minor, and again, after an interlude, in imitation, in F major. The close is marked by an almost wilful audacity after the trumpets have once more rung out the theme in their triumphant tones. Little attention

---

[244] The text of the aria is clearly in two verses; Bach must have had some reason for not making use of the first line of the second verse.

[245] See page 352.

is paid to profound treatment in the development of this fugue, but much to its elaboration in breadth and effect. The counterpoint is always the same, only varying as to the register and part to which it is given. When the orchestra comes in, an imitative treatment of the theme in canon, with a postponement of a quarter bar, is begun, and henceforth each time the theme recurs this recurs also ; thus bars 47-50 are the same as bars 15-18, except that they are sung *tutti*. A constantly repeated figure—

I have often met with in motetts of about 1700. It has a very brilliant effect in a high register, but it is not very melodious, and Bach subsequently discarded it.

In details of style and manner the first chorus keeps to the motett form. Were it not for the short interlude at bar 48 we could well dispense with the whole body of instruments. The vocal parts make up a self-contained, progressive whole ; even the instrumental bass, though it renders the harmonies fuller and clearer, can scarcely be called an essential feature. A characteristic of the motett composers of the time is the use of introductory chords (in the voices) at the beginning, in which means the character of the text is often little regarded. These occur, for instance, in Michael Bach's motett, "Nun hab ich überwunden."[246] Mattheson, who probably became acquainted with this cantata in the year 1720, when Bach was at Hamburg, in blaming Zachau's practice with regard to this, casts reproof on Bach also.[247] "The worthy Zachau," he says, "has a companion in this, and does not stand alone in it, for we find an otherwise excellent *Practicus hodiernus*, which at least does not repeat the words like this : "Lord, Lord, Lord, my spirit was in heaviness, my spirit was in heaviness and deep affliction, and deep affliction. My spirit was in heaviness :|: and deep affliction :|: :]: My spirit was in heaviness :[: and deep affliction :]: My spirit was in heavi-

---

[246] See ante, p. 69.   [247] Critica Musica, II., p. 368.

ness :]: and deep affliction :⌈: :]: :⌈: :]:⌈: My spirit was in heaviness :⌈: and deep affliction :]:" &c. And afterwards : "Sighing, weeping, sorrow, need (pause), sighing, weeping, anxious longing, fear of death (pause), rend the guilty heart in twain," &c. And then, too : "Come, my Saviour, and restore me (pause), shed Thy grace and gladness o'er me (pause), come, my Saviour (pause), come, my Saviour, and restore me, shed Thy grace . . . and gladness o'er me, that this spirit," &c.

With reference to the "Lord, Lord, Lord," at the beginning, this censure is justifiable, seeing that to arrest the attention by means of chords is the duty of the orchestra, and even in a motett they would not be considered good. But Mattheson only refers to this by the way; and as to his other criticism, one is at a loss to know what he means. He had previously laid it down as a rule for setting words that no conclusion of a sentence should be repeated without its beginning—a rule which was evidently laid down with reference to an existing example. Zachau, indeed, had written a fugue on the half of a sentence : "Und den du gesandt hast, Jesum Christum, erkennen"—"And to know Jesus Christ, whom Thou hast sent." There is no example whatever of this kind in Bach; in the first chorus one complete and concise musical idea is formed on the words : "My spirit was in heaviness and deep affliction" (German : "in meinem Herzen"—"within my heart"), an idea of which the central thoughts are the pathetic words : "heaviness" and "heart" and for this reason these words are repeated with their context. In the air the predicate of the sentence alone is treated, while the subject is insisted on in the duet, because here, particularly in the air, almost every word is full of a sentiment which requires to be clearly brought out. It is only from the dry logician's point of view that such beginnings are incomplete, and even then they are hardly so; since he who hears the words, "Sighing, weeping, sorrow, need," sung to a lovely melody, has all that is necessary for intelligibility, and Mattheson must have known this. And yet he himself sets words in this manner, and with much less excuse : "Ah ! (pause), how hungereth my spirit, how hungereth my spirit, Friend of man (pause), Friend of man, joy to inherit,"[248] and certainly would have held it blameless according to his view. It is clear that he only seeks an opportunity to pick a hole in Bach, and to vent the unfriendly feeling he had cherished towards his great contemporary since the year 1720.

If there were nothing else against this cantata, we might proclaim it without hesitation to be the most perfect of its kind existing perhaps anywhere. But there are two weak points. For these indeed the poet is chiefly in fault, but yet the composer must bear the blame of having followed his lead too closely. The general plan of development in the work consists in the contrast between the deepest anguish of spirit and the redemption from that state by Christ's mediation; so it falls naturally into two contrasted states of feeling and two chief divisions. The first chorus, especially after the impassioned and wailing symphony, ought only to give expression to the feeling which pervades the whole first part until the final chorus, in which deliverance is anticipated, but still only anticipated. It does not do this, but contains in itself the contrast which lies at the root of the whole cantata. This is perplexing, for we have to return to pain and sorrow after the joyful soaring up of the end of the chorus, and go slowly through the whole process again. In this respect the cantata is decidedly inferior to the Advent music of the same year. Franck ought to have chosen another chorus text.

The second weak point is in the duet, which is indeed a very extraordinary number. Solo-singing may be introduced into church music, provided that it is cast in such a form that the individual is forgotten. In the same way use may be made of duets and trios, if the parts devote themselves unselfishly to the artistic expression of a common emotion, or an idea of general import. There is also little to be said against it when, in the so-called "dialogues," the Soul and Christ, Fear and Hope, or some other easily intelligible

---

[248] In his Passion Music, to words compiled by Brocke. Winterfeld, Ev. Kirchg., III., 50.

allegorical figures are introduced, and relieve one another
with their characteristic parts, which represent only different
aspects of the same religious feeling.   But all church music
comes to an end as soon as two individuals, as is here the
case, converse with one another in the form of petition and
answer, or of contradiction and agreement.   There is no
longer any question of general feeling, in representing which
the two persons stand for all; for, sentence after sentence, it
is only the individual interests that, with their alternate relations, animate the piece and preserve its flow.   The duet
is what no piece of church music should be—dramatic.
Bach, it must be confessed, not only did nothing to soften
down this fault in the poetry, but increased it by his musical
treatment.   He employed no instrument in the accompaniment whose melodic interweaving might have laid claim to
a share of the interest.   Led by his delight in contrapuntal
part-writing, he, without doubt unintentionally, intensifies
the dramatic element in an almost painful way, when the
voices throw unceasingly from one to the other the ejaculations: "Ah nay!" "Ah yea!" "Thou hatest me!" "I
care for thee!"   Apparently, too, this alternating dialogue
was not Franck's idea at all; it is tolerably clear that he
intended first the "Spirit" and then the bass voice to have
a consecutive solo.   It may be alleged as a mitigating
circumstance that at that time the soprano was sung by
a boy, which in some degree lessens the impression now
inevitably produced, that the piece is a charming love duet.

For these reasons it has not been favourable to the spread
of a sound judgment of Bach's works that the cantata " Ich
hatte viel Bekümmerniss " should be so widely known, while
a number of other works of its class, not inferior to it, and
belonging to it in date, are not known at all.   In this one
there is an apparent justification for the reproach which is
so often brought against him, that his church music contains
theatrical and pietistic elements.   But in truth there is,
besides this duet, only one single movement of a similar
nature (dating from the year 1715).   Franck was very fond
of this form, and Bach accommodated himself to him.
Subsequently he never introduced any piece of the kind

into his cantatas, so far as my knowledge of them extends up to the present time. When similar tasks were given him in the setting of words, he succeeded in giving the voices that carry on the dialogue a higher unity, and in wrapping them in a network of instrumental polyphony in such a way that no doubt remains that by this time he knew what was essential to his style.[249] Error of this kind was so much the easier to fall into as all the other church composers were only too ready to accept the theatrical forms, and Bach had to go on his way apart from and in opposition to them.

We may treat the cantata for Palm Sunday very briefly.[250] The text is in the regular Franck form, which consists of a series of verses intended for arias one after another in different metres and without recitatives, for a bass *arioso* of eight bars on Ps. xl. 8, 9, can hardly be called so. Both the opening and the final chorus are set to aria verses, and we here meet, for the first time in Bach, with the *da capo* form in choral writing. This cantata seems to me in no respect inferior in merit to the foregoing one, with which it has great similarity of plan. It shows, however, the certainty with which Bach's genius could grasp contrasting mental situations, and how thoroughly he entered into the spirit of this particular Sunday. Even in the symphony (G major) the keynote of feeling which permeates and preserves the unity of the whole is struck; it has a tender, solemn, and yet joyful character, like a breath of spring. The lovely interlacing passages on the high violins or the wood wind, supported by the harp-like *pizzicatos* of the lower body of strings, represent the wreathed flowers and leaves with which the gates are decked for the arrival of a beloved one. Then the words, "Himmelskönig, sei willkommen"—"King

---

[249] It is most interesting to compare in this respect the dialogues in the cantatas, "O Ewigkeit, du Donnerwort" (B.-G., XII., 2, No. 60), and "Erfreut euch, ihr Herzen" (ibid., XVI., No. 66). Even the duets in "Wachet auf, ruft uns die Stimme" are differently treated.

[250] "Himmelskönig sei willkommen." Published by J. P. Schmidt in Kirchengesänge für Solo- und Chor-Stimmen mit Instrumental-Begleitung von Johann Sebastian Bach. Berlin : Trautwein, Heft. II.; Autograph in the Royal Library at Berlin.

of heaven, with joy we greet Thee; let our hearts be still Thine home. Hither come; as with joy we run to meet Thee "—are treated in a florid and beautiful fugal chorus. In the course of the three lovely "aria" verses, the feeling is brought out in a masterly way; in contemplating the approaching death of Christ it becomes grave and sad, and at last bitter and piercing, but is relieved and brightened by a wonderful chorale chorus :—

> Jesu, deine Passion
> Ist mir lauter Freude,
> Deine Wunden, Kron und Hohn
> Meines Herzens Weide.
> Meine Seel auf Rosen geht
> Wenn ich dein gedenke;
> In dem Himmel eine Stätt'
> Uns deswegen schenke.[251]

> Jesu, Lord, Thy Passion
> Is my deepest gladness,
> Thy sore wounds, and crown of scorn
> Take away my sadness.
> Oh, my soul is full of joy,
> At Thy contemplation;
> Grant me when my hour shall come
> Full and free salvation.

After that the solemn festal feeling is brought back again in the last chorus, and in the second part takes a splendid flight, remarkable for its grand and artistic working-out.

In the meantime Franck's first year of cantatas was completed, and brought out in two forms; collected together in a small volume with a dedication to the duke, and also printed separately for distribution amongst the congregation, that they might follow. The title was Evangelisches Andachts-Opfer. The compositions contributed to the work by Bach[252]

---

[251] Verse 33 of the hymn, "Jesu Leiden, Pein und Tod," by Paul Stockmann.

[252] Evangelisches | Andachts-Opffer | Auf des | Durchlauchtigsten Fürsten und | Herrn, HERRN | Wilhelm Ernstens, | Herzogens zu Sachsen, Jülich, | Cleve und Berg, auch Engern und | Westphalen, &c., &c. | Unsers gnädigsten regierenden Landes | Fürstens und Herrns | Christ-Fürstl. Anordnung, | in geistlichen | *CANTATEN* | welche auf die ordentliche | Sonn- und Fest-Tage | in der F. S. ges. Hof-Capelle zur | Wilhelmsburg *A.* 1715, zu *musici*ren, | angezündet | von | Salomon Francken, | Fürstl. Sächss. gesamten Ober-*Consistorial-*

are for the most part preserved, but certainly not all of them. The vice-capellmeister, Strattner, had been charged with the duty of composing an anthem for every fourth Sunday. Certain groups of Bach's cantatas—for example, those for the Sixteenth, Twentieth, and Twenty-third Sundays after Trinity, or those for the Fourth Sunday in Advent, Sunday after Christmas, and Second Sunday after Epiphany—show that a similar obligation had been laid upon him. There are nine cantatas of this year, from Easter, 1715, to Easter, 1716.[253] We will review them in their chronological order.

1. Cantata for Easter-Day (April 21, 1715), "Der Himmel lacht, die Erde jubiliret"—"The heavens laugh, the earth itself is joyful!"[254] It was afterwards revised throughout by the composer, and it is only in this improved form that it now exists. In the opening chorus a vocal part is added, and the instruments are strengthened; and the last aria seems to have been altered, not indeed in plan, but in the setting. Thus something must be subtracted from our high estimate of Bach's work in Weimar, so far as this cantata is concerned. The poetry is, for the most part, very successful. It springs out of the joy of the festival itself, but at the same time brings in with exquisite taste the feeling of Spring and re-awakening nature. In the solo texts there is a good deal that is too didactic, but this was often very hard to avoid. The end, however, is as appropriate for music as it is characteristic of Franck. Our thoughts are led from Christ's resurrection to the resurrection of all flesh, and the attainment of ever-lasting bliss, and this is followed (not quite logically) by a wish that death may come soon, to lead us to a speedy union with Christ—every line in this is full of fervent feeling. Bach

---

Secretario in Weimar. | Daselbst gedruckt mit Mumbachischen Schrifften|' —" The offering of Christian devotion. To his serene highness Prince and Lord, Lord Wilhelm Ernest, Grand Duke of Saxony, Julich, Cleve, and Berg, also of Eugern and Westphalia, &c., &c. To be performed, by the command of our most gracious Prince and Lord regnant, as sacred cantatas on the ordinary Sundays and holy-days, in the ducal court chapel at Wilhelmsburg, suggested by Salomon Franck, secretary to the ducal united Upper Consistory at Weimar. Printed there with Mumbach's types." Preserved in Count Stolberg's library at Wernigerode (not in Weimar, as Schauer says, p. cit., Op. xxxix.).

[253] See Appendix A, No. 25.   [254] B.-G., VII., No. 31.

begins with a magnificent sonata (C major, 6-8), the structure
of which in the entry of the instruments agrees with that of
the cantata for Sexagesima, " Gleichwie der Regen," only
that in the combination of the chaconne form with that of
the Italian concerto, with a leaning to the latter, he goes
a step farther, and the first subject does not appear as
the dominant idea throughout the whole. The master unceasingly created new forms, but always within the bounds of
reason. Thus the chorus of rejoicing which follows, again
exhibits a combination of fugue-form and song-form (Liedform), and besides this shows a trace of the Italian aria.
Its first portion is divided into two equal parts, like the first
section (Aufgesang) of a chorale; this is succeeded by a
second portion in another time, and consisting of essentially
homophonic passages; this last, however, consistently with
the character of the whole, flows into a new fugue, and when
it ends the orchestra takes up the opening phrases again.
In the first aria the ingenuity must not be overlooked with
which five questions following one another are musically expressed; the piece is constructed on a freely treated *basso
ostinato*, and is difficult to accompany in a worthy manner.
In the tenor air we meet, for the first time, with one of
those sets of words which express no emotion, but are of
purely dogmatic import. Just as the older church composers
in certain doctrinal portions of the Mass give expression
simply to their general ecclesiastical character, so Bach also
in such cases gives us independent compositions, moving
within that circle of feeling which limits his stricter church
style. But at the same time he expresses a more definite
sentiment, for as the various feelings in his cantatas are
usually developed in gradual progression, so the purport of
such portions is essentially adapted to their position in the
work. And if a rational coherence subsists between the
sections of the text, then text and music ought to fit
each other; the music, it is true, is not the outcome
of the text, but they combine to form a third unit higher
than either by itself. Such is the case here. The opening
part of the cantata is taken up with the objective fact
of Christ's resurrection; from the recitative of this aria

onwards the attention is directed to its prophetic bearing on the life of the Christian, the crowning point of which is the resurrection at the last day. The music serves to bridge over the interval between the joy of the festival and the mystic contemplation of the last scenes. What it says could not be conveyed in words, and that is the true purpose of music. But that this feeling was dear to Bach's heart is shown by the extraordinary vocal and instrumental beauty of the aria. It is like a song of spring pervaded by a soft breath of longing. In form it resembles the bass aria in the cantata for Palm Sunday, which was probably performed eight days before it, and here and there it is like the second aria of "Ich hatte viel Bekümmerniss." The strings are often employed simply to fill up the harmonies, except the first violin, which has many concerted passages with the voice alone; short instrumental interludes are freely interspersed. Such particular features are not to be overlooked, for they are the waymarks in the history of Bach's growth. It is also worthy of remark that the melodic subject of the ritornel is different from the opening phrase for the voice, into which the ritornel comes independently after one bar—the ritornel-subject, too, provides the accompaniment throughout the whole aria.[255] A short recitative, remarkable for its ecstatic flight, leads to the last aria :—

> Letzte Stunde, brich herein,
> Mir die Augen zuzudrücken!
> Lass mich Jesu Freudenschein
> Und sein helles Licht erblicken!
> Lass mich Engeln ähnlich sein,
> Letzte Stunde, brich herein.

> Day of death, O dawn on me,
> With kind hand mine eyelids sealing;
> Let me soon my Saviour see,
> All His glorious light revealing.
> Let me like an angel be ;
> Day of death, O dawn on me.

---

[255] I take this occasion to remark that in the foregoing recitative a mistake in the text has been made, which has not been corrected even in the Bach Society's edition, viz., the words should be : "Auf! von den todten Werken ! Lass, dass dein Heiland in dir lebt, An deinen Leben merken !'

Bach shows us by his treatment how congenial this conclusion is to him.　But is it not strange to conclude an
anthem for Easter—the festival of victory and triumph—
with the contemplation of death and the unknown future,
with vague and anxious longing?　But such is the musician's
nature.　As a true church composer he views everything in
the light of eternity; still, it is not the majestic glory that
the sun sheds from the vast vault of heaven upon all crea-
tures; it is a stray beam of light, falling through a half-open
door into a world of darkness, to let it dimly perceive how
much it lacks of light.　Even those festivals of the Church
which call forth the greatest joy in existence cannot entirely
withdraw him from his natural bent.　He loves the blossoms
of spring, but never so well as when they are illumined by
the evening glow.

The tender and affecting passage for the soprano has an
oboe obbligato; then there comes in the melody of " Wenn
mein Stündlein vorhanden ist "—"When my last hour is
drawing nigh,"—given out quietly and broadly in unison
on the two violins and violas, in a low register.　We are
familiar with the form from the *Actus tragicus*.　Its characteristic is, that the chief factor, the chorale, is brought
in without words, and that the subsidiary factors are set
to words, by which means the natural order of things is
reversed.　The feeling of solo singing is thus drawn within
the sphere of church music, but as ample opportunity is
given for subjectivity in the interpretation of the chorale by
the instruments, an undefined and romantic character pervades the whole.　As in the *Actus tragicus* this form was
found to be admirably suited to the representation of a particular frame of mind, so it is here; but the character of this
cantata would not allow of such a sustained abstraction into
transcendental feeling.　So at the end we find verse 5 of the
same chorale, but sung by the whole choir, and appearing with
distinct outlines from out of the dim twilight that has gone
before.　This verse is introduced by the poet; Bach's genius
consisted in anticipating its melody in the former number, in
such a way as to prepare the way for the final chorale, as
the flower prepares the way for the fruit.　Here again he

has created a new form which he afterwards turned to
account, and always with fresh ingenuity, and producing the
most striking effects. The harmonising of the chorale corresponds to that of the foregoing one ; a feeling of beatitude
is poured through it, so that we seem to feel a breath ot
beings from the other world. The leading idea is derived by
Bach from the opening lines :—

> So fahr ich hin zu Jesu Christ,
> Mein' Arm' thu ich ausstrecken.

> I go to be with Jesus Christ,
> Mine arm to Him uplifting.

The violins and trumpets progress above the vocal parts in
melodies and rhythms which irresistibly call up the idea ot
a soul being borne heavenwards, and stretching out its arms
to the beatific vision; an unspeakable impressiveness is
given by the suspended discord on the fermatas, which is
never resolved until the second quaver. The trumpet, with
its tender, silvery tone, which is carried up very high, must
have had a most magical effect.[256]

Franck's text served for a second composition by Freislich,
the Capellmeister of Sondershausen, who must have known
Bach's work, since his beginning reminds one distinctly of
it.[257] The work is pleasant, but unimportant; it is interesting to us only by the fact that at the end of verse 10
of the Easter hymn, " Früh morgens, da die Sonn aufgeht "
—" At daybreak, when the sun doth rise,"—is introduced,
with its joyful " Hallelujah." To make the usual ending
with such materials was an easier task, and more intelligible
to the multitude.

2. Cantata for the Fourth Sunday after Trinity (July 14,
1715) : " Barmherziges Herze der ewigen Liebe "—" All merciful heart of the love everlasting."[258] It concludes with
the chorale, " Ich ruf zu dir, Herr Jesu Christ "—" I call on
Thee, Lord Jesu Christ." Bach introduces it, too, in the

---

[256] Winterfeld, Ev. Kircheng., III., p. 378, seems to me to misunderstand this
movement, as also does Mosewius, Op. cit., p. 8.

[257] In parts, in the library of the castle church of Sondershausen.

[258] Published by J. P. Schmidt, Op. cit., Book III., from the autograph in the
Royal Library at Berlin.

first number (F sharp minor, 6-4) and gives it to a trumpet
or oboe, accompanying a duet, the figured bass being in
quavers.[259]   By this means he makes a new use of the combination spoken of above, so that the whole cantata is
spanned, as with a widespread arch, by the chorale.   The
fundamental thought of the whole chorale is the bitter lament
over human frailty, beside which, merely as a secondary idea,
there is a prayer to Christ for assistance in leading a life that
shall be pleasing to God.   The introduction of the melody,
even in the first number, naturally proclaims its character,
which, it is true, is quite a different one from that which
appears in the first words of the text :—

> Barmherziges Herze der ewigen Liebe,
>   Errege, bewege mein Herze durch dich,
> Damit ich Erbarmen und Gütigkeit übe,
>   O Flamme der Liebe, zerschmelze du mich!

> All-merciful heart of the love everlasting,
>   O stir up my heart with desires from above,
> That the works which I do may be worthy and lasting,
>   Inflame me and quicken, thou fire of love!"

The idea of divine love inflaming the cold heart of man, and
quickening it to Christian activity, would, no doubt, according
to the poet's idea, rather have demanded warm and glowing
music.   But that would have suggested an emotion which,
however it might be toned down, would be out of keeping
with the purport of the chorale.   This could not be thought
of by Bach, to whom the chorale was the highest form of
church music.   If Franck were in error to choose this hymn,
it gave Bach opportunity for a deeply felt combination, and
is to us a new evidence of his great formative power, even in
the domain of dramatically musical poetry.   As the cantata
stands, it is a complete work of art, perfectly rounded off.
The duet moves in canonic imitations, but the voices (soprano
and tenor) sometimes get too far apart in height and depth.

---

[259] That the trumpet was employed for it, even in Weimar, is shown by the
existence of a trumpet part in G minor, to correspond to the pitch of the cornet
stop on the Weimar organ, for the trumpets always stand in the "chorus" pitch.
The piece is entitled *Duetto*. Thus much in correction of Schmidt's edition,
which is unsatisfactory in other places.

Certain harsh chords are indeed inserted intentionally, but
the melodies are lovely throughout.

For the subject-matter of the recitatives the poet has
adhered to the didactic Gospel for the day ; hence they are
very subdued in tone. Bach has succeeded, however, in
raising them from this by his musical treatment. The first,
for alto, turns into an *arioso*, followed by the instrumental
bass in canon. The same method is also to be found in
the Easter cantata, and again in the Advent and. Oculi
(Third Sunday in Lent) cantatas, and in the cantata for the
Sunday after Christmas in the same year, and may be
regarded as a peculiarity of the master's style at this
period. An aria for alto (A major, 2-4) depicts the feeling
of rapturous expectation of an eternal reward for Christian
works done in this life. The idea presented in the text—of
the sheaves gathered in hereafter, the seeds of which have
been sown in this world—provides the subject of the composition. A happy serenity, the effect of which is doubled
by the troubled music that has gone before, pervades this
charming composition, even in its smallest details ; the strict
polophony is handled with a loveliness like that of Mozart ;
the flood of melody is full and happy, and in the most flowing
style of writing. A new instance of his genius for making
new forms is given by the next aria—B minor, common time
—set to the following words by Franck :—

Das ist der Christen Kunst:	The Christian's task is this :
Nur Gott und sich erkennen,	God and his own heart knowing,
Von wahrer Liebe brennen,	With pure devotion glowing,
Nicht unzulässig richten,	To cease from evil doing,
Noch fremdes Thun vernichten,	All ways of sin eschewing ;
Des Nächsten nicht vergessen,	In faithfulness to labour
Mit reichem Masse messen.	And duly love his neighbour,
Das macht bei Gott und Menschen Gunst,	With God and man to be at peace—
Das ist der Christen Kunst.	The Christian's task is this.

It was far from easy to make a regular composition out
of this material. The form of the Italian aria could not
be used, for the chief point of the thought lies not in the first
line, although that is repeated at the end, but in the lines
that follow ; so that it was impossible to give the chief

musical subject to the first line. Neither could the strophic song-form be turned to account; at most could he adopt the *arioso*, and that could not be used in this place. There was nothing for it but that the composer should create a new form. He therefore took each pair of the lines 2-7 by themselves, inclosing them with the first line, which was repeated for the last, and so made three verses of four lines each. Still the purport of the text would not allow of his using the same music for each and so making a hymn of it; so he treated lines 2-7 as a consecutive whole, closing them again with a repetition of the first. The last two lines he turned into two phrases of four bars each by repeating the words. So we see that a structure was raised which was to give rise to musical ornamentations in the style of the Italian concerto. This is the chief (or concerto-tutti) subject—

Das　ist　der Chris-ten　Kunst,

and this the tributary (or concerto-solo) theme:—

Nur　Gott　und　sich　er-ken-nen, .. Von　wah-rer　Lie-be　bren-nen, ..

The development from these two contrasting themes now follows in quite a regular manner through the related keys. After B minor there comes D major, then A major, and then —for the longer passage, in which the second theme is amplified and prolonged—E minor, and at last B minor again, where the first theme is given out only by the instrumental bass, which in general is treated very independently. Thus the build of the Italian instrumental form is turned to account for Bach's solo treatment. Viewed from the side of feeling, the aria expresses an ardent zeal for a warmly cherished religious conviction, with an impressiveness and stalwart energy which are quite characteristic of Bach. The final chorale, which expresses the emotion of lamentation with the greatest harmonic vigour, is accompanied by an independent instrumental part of most beautiful structure.

3. Cantata for the Sixteenth Sunday after Trinity (October 6), 1715, " Komm, du süsse Todesstunde "—" Come, sweet

hour of my departure."[260]   The gospel for the day narrates
the raising of the widow's son at Nain (Luke vii. 11-17),
which gives the poet an opportunity for treating his favourite
theme of a blessed death and everlasting life, in three arias
and two recitatives.   Bach once more introduces the final
chorale ("Herzlich thut mich verlangen," verse 4) into the
opening number, giving it to the organ on a prominent stop,[261]
during an aria for alto (C major, common time) accompanied
by two flutes and figured bass. The character of the whole cantata is so celestial and suprasensual that we sometimes feel
as though it were no earthly music that we hear, but that we
are moving among spiritual beings.   The airy semiquaver passages on the flutes are a distinct anticipation of the sublime
last chorale in the first part of the St. Matthew Passion; they
float above us like cloudlets in the pure ether, and between
them moves the lovely and lucid form of the solo melody :—

Komm, du sü - sse To - des - stun - de, da mein Geist Ho - nig
speist aus des Lö - - - - - - - - - wen Mun - de

[Come, sweet hour of my departure,
For my soul honey takes from the lion's body.] [262]

---

[260] An old score is preserved in the Royal Library at Berlin. It was probably
written out at Leipzig by an unknown copyist, under Bach's superintendence,
February 2, 1735. (See also Vol. III., App. A, No. 2, near the end.) The complete title is, "*Dom:* 16 *p. Trin:* Kom. du süsse Todes Stunde," on the right the
sign *a* ‖ *ω*, and on the left *a. ω*; and underneath, in another handwriting, "*item
Festo Purific. Mariæ*," and on the right, in the corner, "*di Bach.*" That the
cantata was written in Weimar is seen at a glance by its entire agreement in
plan with the others.

[261] The MS. directs the Sesquialtera to be used. In a later copy the chorale
is given to a soprano voice, with Gerhard's words, "Wenn ich einmal soll
scheiden,"&c. That the instrumental method is to be considered as the original
need scarcely be mentioned after all that has been said above.

[262] A somewhat far-fetched conceit from the history of Samson. See Judges,
chap. xiv.

And all this is covered as with broad wings by the melody (without words) of the old death-bed hymn. The second aria (A minor, 3-4), separated from the first by a recitative, is of a more sombre character, the flutes are replaced by the more impassioned string quartet, and it is sung by a tenor voice. In the former number the voice seemed to proceed from a beatified spirit, but here a human being speaks, longing for death in tones in which pain and bliss are wonderfully blended. After a grand recitative which reconciles these two differing mental conditions, the last aria (C major, 3-8) again proceeds with a tender ecstasy. It is in four parts, reminding us of the older church cantatas; and, except for some simple canonic imitations between the upper and lower pairs of voices, is quite homophonous. It is accompanied by the strings and flutes, to which are given combinations noteworthy alike for excellence of substance and style; especially certain demi-semiquavers on the flute which have a strangely weird effect; they sound like the whisperings of spirits. The crowning point of the chorus is the chorale that immediately follows; above the four-part movement the flute wanders with strange and mysterious passages, giving rise to marvellous harmonies; the whole sounds as though heard in a dream.

Finally, the two recitatives are among the loveliest of Bach's writings. They are also highly characteristic of his own peculiar manner, and are everywhere full of deeply felt musical melody and yet of admirable and vivid declamatory accent. The first is accompanied only by the figured bass, and the second by the whole band, which intensifies and renders all the prominent pathetic portions more impressive, not by preludes and postludes, but in the genuine Bach manner, by richly interwoven subsidiary subjects.[263] The close is particularly remarkable. The subject here is the tolling of the last hour of a man's life, and all the instruments are made to sound a bell-like peal; the basses solemnly swinging to and fro from CC to C, the

---

[263] In bars 4-14 the text of the score differs slightly from the printed poem; Bach seems to have altered it arbitrarily, because the musical declamation was not so well fitted to the original words.

violins in the middle like a vesper-call to prayer, and the
two flutes above in shriller chime.[264]   Surrounded with these
tones, the solo voice enters like an earthly pilgrim on his
last sad journey :—

[Strike, then, oh strike, thou latest hour of life !]

264 In North Germany a bell " tolls the knell of parting " day at six in the

Whether such tone-painting is justifiable or not may indeed be asked. Music cannot, of course, be unconditionally forbidden to imitate and assimilate tones and phrases of musical instruments—and such surely must bells be considered—that are closely associated with certain circumstances of life, so long as such things are treated in an artistic way. Trumpets and horn-tunes occur naturally in battle or hunting pieces, as do pastoral passages on the oboe in representations of shepherd life. Nor is it by accident that these instruments and certain of their characteristic phrases have been brought into combination with those circumstances of life; there is an inner connection between them; they reveal the innermost germ of the living feeling which pervades and animates those circumstances, and the musician in using them only avails himself of the materials which offer themselves to his hand. Inasmuch as it is easy by means of these tone-paintings to call up certain adequate and distinct ideas in the imagination, they are by no means to be despised for dramatic compositions. They may also be employed in purely lyrical work, only it is indispensable that they should be modified and refined into ideal subjects. It is also evident that the simpler and more limited the powers and phrases of the instrument, the more carefully must it be refined and modified, since it the more easily gives the disturbing impression of realism. How well Bach could adhere to this condition, even in imitating the pealing of bells, is shown by the first aria of his cantata " Liebster Gott, wann werd ich sterben," [265] where, to a text precisely similar to the one before us: "Was willst du dich, mein Geist, entsetzen, Wenn meine letzte Stunde schlägt?"— " Why should'st thou tremble, O my spirit, when my last hour on earth shall strike?"—the instrumental basses throughout imitate pealing bells, but so thoroughly transforming them into a musical subject that it is quite of a piece with the rest of the organism. This is not the case here; in the recitative we hear the sound of bells for a few

---

evening; it is the close of man's labour, and he is invited to prayer. Shortly before a smaller warning bell is rung, represented here by the flutes.

[265] B.-G., I., No. 8, P. 1199.

bars, and on a few harmonies, without any preparation in the music, and then again it ceases.

The composer's intention is of course plain; by a reminiscence of the death-peal he means to arouse in us the feeling that steals over us on such occasions; it is a poetic intensifying of the thought, like what he achieves by the introduction of chorale melodies without words. But is it correct or artistic to gain his effect by such external and foreign means? In general, assuredly it is not; and certainly the effect on the hearer of to-day may very possibly be painfully realistic. The question however has a somewhat different aspect when we try to view it in the light of Bach's individuality. As a natural result of his inclination to pure music, he abstained from sound-pictures on the whole. Though in the last recitative of the Advent cantata, "Nun komm, der Heiden Heiland," a piece of tone-painting in the voice part strikes us as strange, it is developed from an accentuation on the words, formed quite naturally on Bach's principle of combining declamatory and musical passages; and in that particular place it has a sublime effect, since it brings out the contrast between the narrowness of the things which belong to the senses and the infinitude of those above them. Other scattered passages of this kind will be accounted for in their own place.

The imitation of pealing bells was, however, an effect of which Bach was very fond, and which occurs in a large number of his works, as for instance in the beginning of the cantata just mentioned, in an aria in the cantata, "Herr, wie du willst, so schicks mit mir,"[266] in a majestic conception in the second recitative of the funeral ode for Queen Christiana Eberhardine,[267] and in the funeral aria "Schlage doch, gewünschte Stunde,"[268] of which, by the way, the poem is easily recognisable as Francke's. Here, however, he has employed it with quite a different view; Bach's relations with the Church and its usages were so close and deep that to him the sound of bells did not seem

---

[266] B.-G., XVIII., No. 73, P. 1676.   [267] B.-G., XIII., 3.
[268] B.-G., XII., 2, No. 53. Also contained in Peters' "Alt-album."

unworthy to be employed in any musical form whatever. If this is considered too naïve and narrow, we reply that true genius must be narrow, and that it is only an exclusive and blind devotion to the object aimed at that has in all times succeeded in creating works of true greatness. Musical history presents one other precisely similar case ; the imitation of the nightingale, the quail, and the cuckoo, in the andante of Beethoven's Pastoral Symphony. It is very easy to see that Beethoven there overstepped the bounds of the ideal, and yet how could he have written this symphony had he not felt the magic charm and the sublimity of Nature so deeply as to regard all her works as sacred ? As we have already pointed out, that which Nature was to the one of these two equally great and nearly allied souls, the Church was to the other.

4. Cantata for the Twentieth Sunday after Trinity (November 3, 1715) : " Ach ich sehe, jetzt da ich zur Hochzeit gehe," &c.[269]—" Ah, I tremble, as the favoured guests assemble." The subject of the Gospel is the parable of the king who made a marriage for his son, and when the guests refused to come, called guests in from the streets, but expelled again those who were unworthy (Matt. xxii. 1-14). Accordingly the chief emotions in the cantata are : fear and anxiety to be found worthy ; longings of the poor human soul to be quickened by the supper of the Lord ; rejoicing at being admitted to it. These are represented in three arias connected by recitatives. The bass begins (A minor, common time) with a masterpiece of polyphony and episodical sequence ; the figure—

goes through the whole like a gnawing anxiety. The second aria, for soprano (D minor, 12-8), breathes out urgent supplication, and is again quite different to anything we have hitherto met with in Bach ; and the exclamation "Jesu!"

---

[269] The score (from the Fischhoff bequest) is in the Royal Library at Berlin, and must have been copied from the original parts in Von Voss's collection. These I have never seen.

thrice repeated is most remarkable in its expression. But when, indeed, was this stream of novelty ever exhausted?

The last aria, a duet between alto and tenor, again opens out an unknown territory. In it there is what we are almost tempted to call a Dionysic rejoicing, as the parts move now in joyful semiquavers, now in long-held shouts of joy, while below them the bass has the following passage, as if for a festal dance :—

&c.

The piece, with its broad treatment and noble freedom, has the form of the Italian aria, and the road by which Bach leads back to the first part is particularly fine. The two voices are now in homophony like a two-part song, and now break into an animated polyphony which reveals its origin in the organ; it is not yet quite in the special Bach form of duet, but there is no trace of the duets of Steffani, which were the pattern at that time, and which were the examples that Handel copied. This exuberant joy is toned down in the final chorale to correspond to the opening; the seventh verse of the hymn "Alle Menschen müssen sterben," is sung to a melody in A minor, which is not known elsewhere. It cannot be decided at present whether it was composed by Bach or no.

5. Cantata for the Twenty-third Sunday after Trinity (November 24, 1715), "Nur jedem das Seine"—"Let all be paid duly."[270] Referring to the Gospel, which treats of the tribute money (Matt. xxii. 18-22), Franck wrote a set of words which are for the most part absolutely devoid of sentiment. The last is alone really fit for musical treatment—the beginning may serve as an example of the rest :—

Nur jedem das Seine!	Let all be paid duly—
Muss Obrigkeit haben	A tithe to thy pastor,
Zoll, Steuern und Gaben,	A tax to thy master;
Man weigre sich nicht	Let no man refuse
Der schuldigen Pflicht!	To any their dues—
Doch bleibe das Herze dem	To God give thy heart, ever
Höchsten alleine!	serving Him truly—
Nur jedem das Seine!	Let all be paid duly!

[270] Autograph score in the Royal Library at Berlin. Comp. App. A., No. 25.

In spite of these dreadfully prosaic rhymes Bach threw
himself into the work with especial interest. He chose his
favourite key of B minor, wrote out the score with careful
neatness, and brought all his art and subtlety to bear on the
music itself. It is easy to perceive that he did not make a
purely ideal piece of music, but that he was really incited by
the words. In order to understand this we must consider
that he viewed them in the idealising light of the Church
and of Scripture; and it must not be forgotten how easily
satisfied the general taste for poetry was at that time, and
how little progress it had made. Bach has displayed his
lofty poetical feeling in so many ways when the matter in
hand was the conception of a general idea, as founded on
the basis of music, that it in no respect detracts from his
greatness that he should have stood no higher than the level
of his time as regards the fitness of special subjects for
poetic treatment. The way in which he conceived the first
aria shows that he saw through the outer husk to the kernel
of the subject. It was the idea of order and obedience
to law and morality that suggested itself to him from the
words, and which he represented in a piece of music which
stands firm, as though hewn out of stone. Another composer would probably not have known even how to set about
treating these words, and that Bach took them up with such
warmth is a beautiful contribution to the knowledge of his
personal characteristics : steadfastness, morality, and a wonderful feeling for order—these were the qualities that pervaded
his whole nature. I cannot describe the piece more fully ;
the full effect lies in the keen and strong general picture—

is the germ from which it grows without break or interrup-
tion. In the following aria, which compares the heart of the
Christian to a worn-out coin, not worthy to be brought to
Christ, the words—

Komm ! arbeite, schmelz, und präge,	Come and melt me ! then, refin- ing,
Dass dein Ebenbild in mir	Stamp me fresh, that I may live
Ganz erneuert werden möge—	Newly with Thine image shining—

give the direction to the bold imagination of the master; the
bass voice (E minor, common time) carries on its earnest
daily toil, while two busily working violoncellos cast a
twilight effect over the piece. A beautiful contrast of tone
is next given by a two-part recitative, between the soprano
and the alto, in imitation, and ending in a long *arioso*.
This bold innovation was only completely possible with
Bach's conception of the recitative. It is followed by a
pure and childlike duet for the same voices (D major, 3-4)
on a poetic text, the subject of which is devotion to the Saviour. Meanwhile the violins and tenors in unison play the
melody of "Meinen Jesum lass ich nicht"—"I will never
leave my Lord,"—the whole constituting a fabric of marvellous delicacy. But the close is not furnished by this chorale,
but by the eleventh verse of Heermann's hymn, "Wo soll
ich fliehen hin," to Pachelbel's melody in the major, used
before this by Michael Bach in a motett, which Sebastian
probably became acquainted with through his near relations
with the latter, or through Walther. It seemed to him
unsuitable for interweaving with the preceding duet; but,
in order not to sacrifice the impression produced by the
other, he has bestowed upon it only the simplest possible
harmonies.[271]

6. Cantata for the Fourth Sunday in Advent (Dec. 22),
1715: "Bereitet die Wege, bereitet die Bahn,"—"Prepare ye
the way, and make ready the road."[272] Without ever betraying a trace of formalism, the master goes on pouring out
new treasures from his inexhaustible fancy. The number
and order of the movements in this cantata are the same
as in the preceding one. The first aria (A major, 6-8) is full
of idyllic festivity. It begins with an exquisite passage for
the oboe, accompanied only by harmonies in chords :—

---

[271] In the autograph, under the title "*Choral semplice stylo*," there is only the
figured bass without words. But it is easy, by means of the printed text, to
know what melody is intended.

[272] Autograph score in the Royal Library at Berlin. *Vide* App. A, No. 27.

When it gets to *e'* it soars joyfully up an octave, over-
shadowing the melody—which now comes in on the violins—
with a brilliant shake, and then gaily interweaving the subject
with the voice part, which busily hastens up and down in
semiquavers, to level every obstacle and to make its way.
The second part is quite charming; the bass first plays the
principal subject in F sharp minor, and the voice comes in
with it afresh with the following—

be - rei - tet die We - ge und ma - chet die Ste - ge

and for the third part the oboe has this passage—

after which the parts go through different keys in three-part
counterpoint, and then, after a repetition, are suddenly
silenced in their busy course, while the soprano alone gives out
the loud and joyful cry, " Messias kommt an !"—". Messiah
is come!"   The way, too, in which the second part leaves off in
D major, and the instruments begin the *da capo* again without
pausing to take breath, is of characteristic charm. Gradually
—in the first recitative—graver thoughts begin to make
themselves felt;[273] and as the priests and Levites in the
Gospel asked John the Baptist, " Who art thou?" so now,
as he goes to meet his Lord, there occurs to the mind of the
Christian the soul-searching question, " Wer bist du ? Frage
dein Gewissen"—"Who art thou ? Ask it of thy conscience,"
—bass aria (E major, common time).   The voice is accompanied only by the organ and figured bass for the violoncello,
which are entwined together in an intricate way, and often
in a curiously low register.   Even if we take into consideration the high pitch of the Weimar organ, and take it for
granted that the figured bass was played very lightly, and
that the bass voice was very powerful, the fact remains that

---

[273] As to the remarkable unison passage between the voice and the bass in
bars 28 and 29 to symbolise the "unison of the soul with Christ," I shall mention it again when speaking of the E minor fugue in Part I. of the Wohltemperirte Clavier.

the effect must have been gloomy and ugly in detail. In several places, too, there are certain harmonic peculiarities. Bach is fond of bringing in, underneath sustained harmonies, whether in the form of firm or broken chords, melodic passages which are to be understood only as a series of passing-notes to some far-off harmonic goal; and until this is reached the ear is of necessity kept in suspense. Though it is not difficult to accustom the ear to these passages (instances of the "inverted pedal," as it is called), they are still further complicated by the circumstance that he does not shrink from making the passing-notes serve as the groundwork of independent harmonies which come into inevitable collision with the chief harmonies. I refer especially to the passage in bars 42 and 43—

where the voice is supported by the lowest notes of the bass, while the chief harmony consists of the third *e*, *g* sharp. Compare also bars 14 to 26. The continuation of bar 43 is still bolder :—

Here, indeed, only the *e* is left, but this makes no difference theoretically, and the progression of the chord is the same as if *e* were not there at all, even in a suspended form—compare bars 16 and 28. That such hazardous passages already appear in Bach, is another proof of how early his musical character was clearly stamped. Their effect is at first repulsive, but when we begin to see the *rationale* and sequence in them, they have a wonderful charm, and especially when the expression of the words is heightened by them, as in this case. As even the gloomy quality of

the tones contributes to this end, we finally quit this aria
with the impression of a stern but imposing whole.

All that need be noticed in the third aria is that it has a
pathetic tone in remembrance of what mankind has gained
by Christ's passion; the recitative has formed a bridge
between the two sentiments. It is set for alto and solo
violin, and in a kind of anticipation of that sublime song of
woe in the "Matthew Passion," "Have mercy upon me, O
Lord!" The prominence which is given in all these cantatas
to the alto voice is due to the excellent quality of the voice
of the alto in the chapel, whose name was Bernhardi. The
chorale "Herr Christ, der einge Gottes-Sohn" — "Lord
Christ, the only Son of God,"—forms a worthy and sublime
conclusion.

7. Cantata for the Sunday after Christmas (December 29,
1715), "Tritt auf die Glaubensbahn"—"Walk in the way
of faith." [274] This has no choruses or chorales, is only written
for two solo voices, and is altogether one of the most remarkable of Bach's productions. It does not derive much of its
origin from the Gospel for the day. That narrates the pro-
phecies of Simeon and of Anna, that Christ " is set for the
fall and rising again of many in Israel," and for a stone of
foundation to some, and of stumbling to others. Franck
has turned this subject into dull verses, comprising two
arias and two recitatives, and for the close a duet between
Christ and the Soul. Bach went beyond the text to the
feeling attributed to the Sunday by the Church; the germ
of his music is the echo of Christmastide, which vibrates
gently on in the soul until new and solemn religious festivals
occupy its attention. He begins with a long orchestral piece,
given to a most exquisite combination of instruments, namely,
to a flute, oboe, viola d'amore, viol da gamba, and organ.
The root of the form is the French overture, but the slow
first section is more in the style of the Gabrieli sonata, and,
although only four bars in length (E minor, common time),

---

[274] The autograph score is in the Royal Library at Berlin, and in the colour,
texture, and watermark of the paper, agrees exactly with the autograph of the
Advent cantata, "Nun komm der Heiden Heiland."

reminds us strongly of the *sinfonia* at the beginning of the
"Ich hatte viel Bekümmerniss." Then follows a fugue, on
a theme of such charm that Bach afterwards used it again in
a modified form for the organ :[275]—

Here all the characteristics of the overture are preserved,
even the typical pedal on the dominant, only that instead of
an organism through the arteries of which runs hot blood, a
tender, soft, and transparent vein is spread out before us,
treated with supreme mastery and tender depth of feeling
(139 bars). The vocal portion of the work begins with a
mild and grave bass aria, in daring, but happily conceived
combination with an oboe, accompanied by the figured bass ;
the bass voice also has the beautiful recitative with *arioso*,
which follows next. The Hofcantor Wolfgang Christoph
Alt seems to have been the principal bass singer in this
chapel, and he must have possessed a magnificent organ, to
judge from the parts written for him by Bach. Even the E
major aria in the proceding cantata is inconceivable without
this ; and here we find, besides others, the following gigantic
leaps :—

in Is - ra - el zum Fall und Auf - er - ste - hen

Although we know Bach's inclination to represent external movement by a solo voice, this seems almost like a
joke. The crowning point of the cantata is the aria for
soprano, in G major, which follows next, which is a very
jewel among all the other airs of Bach. It is, although such
is not the express idea of the text, a lullaby sung at the
cradle of the infant Saviour. The resemblance between this
and the exquisite slumber song in the Christmas oratorio[276]
is evident, but that is the more full and contenting, while
the character of this one is more tender and airy, like a

[275] P. S. V., Cah. II. (241), No. 3.
[276] B.-G., V., 2, p. 68.

sweet and dreamy memory. A graceful charm smiles from
each note, from the rocking passages of the single flute and
viola d'amore, from the silvery tones of the long-held notes,
the tenderness of the melody and its close on the third, from
the caressing sixths of the two instruments above the slow
swing of the bass notes. The final duet, like the duet for
soprano and bass in " Ich hatte viel Bekümmerniss"
(see ante, p. 537), is too dramatic, and inconsistent with
the church style. Besides this the dance rhythm of the
gigue goes through it from beginning to end, but this
indeed was almost necessitated by Franck's poem. On the
other hand the lyrical principle is more adhered to in this
than in the other duet, by the introduction, though but
rare, of independent instrumental passages. As a piece of
music it is sufficiently charming, as scarcely need be said.

8. Cantata for the second Sunday after the Epiphany,
January 19, 1716, " Mein Gott, wie lang, ach lange?"—
" How long, Lord, will thou tarry?"[277]   Nothing is taken
from the Gospel (of the marriage in Cana) except the thought
that God will at last send help in trouble, though He tarry
long. This prescribes the simple psychological course of
the cantata. While the bass persists in monotonous and
never-ending quavers on D, the soprano has a recitative-like
movement, lamenting that no end is seen amid looming
troubles ; the end is very graphic, where the voice soars
upwards on the words " Freudenwein !"—" wine of joy !"—in
demi-semiquavers, and then sighing out the words "mir
sinkt fast alle Zuversicht "—" all confidence is gone from
me,"—sinks wearily down between the two violins in
imitation.

The duet which comes next, between alto and tenor
(A minor, common time), and the words " Du musst
glauben, du musst hoffen "—" Still believing, ever hoping,"
has a feeling of quiet consolation ; with the vocal parts of
this a bassoon part is interwoven in a consummately skilful
manner, consisting partly of broad broken harmonies, partly
of independent passages, partly too of imitations of the

---

[277] Autograph in the Royal Library at Berlin.   Comp. App. A, No. 25.

voice parts. A further step towards perfect consolation
is taken by the bass recitative, " So sei, o Seele, sei
zufrieden "—" Thus, O my spirit, be thou happy,"—till, in
absolute confidence of faith, there sounds out a beautiful
soprano aria (F major, common time), " Wirf, mein Herze,
wirf dich noch in des Höchster Liebesarme!"—" O my
heart, now cast thyself on the Saviour's arms so loving !"—
one of those pieces by Bach that, with their strongly marked
rhythm, their incessant chords of the seventh, and the happy,
victorious expressions of the melody, make us feel we never
could tire of hearing them. Here also we meet with instances of the inverted pedal, those great ventures of harmony, to the flight of which we commit ourselves with
perfect confidence, trusting to the certain aim of the master's
hand. A great effect and an indescribable expression is
given by the alternations between major and minor, which
are introduced with the boldness of Schubert in the middle
and at the end of the aria. As far as regards the combination of quaver triplets with dotted quavers (*i.e.*, ♪. ♪) let it
be understood once for all that the semiquaver in this
rhythmical figure in such cases should always coincide with

the last quaver of a triplet (♩ ♩ ♩). This broad and dignified

rendering, though not quite strict, was the only one in use
until the overweening restlessness of more modern instrumental music came into vogue.[278] The twelfth verse of the
chorale, " Es ist das Heil uns kommen her," forms the close
of this beautiful composition.

9. Cantata for " Oculi " Sunday (Third Sunday in Lent),
(March 15, 1716). " Alles was von Gott geboren "—" All that
is of God's creation." This work was subsequently embodied
in the cantata, " Ein feste Burg ist unser Gott,"[279] which is
made up of it and two chorale choruses, numbers 1 and 5.
The trace still remains of its existence in its original form.
The two choruses must clearly have been composed later,

---

[278] P. E. Bach, Versuch über die wahre Art das Clavier zu spielen, Part I., p.
98 (third edition, Leipzig, 1781). Comp. B.-G., XXII., p. 123, bars 3 and 4.
[279] B.-G., XVIII., No. 89, P. 1012.

while the rest of the work agrees entirely with the other cantatas of this year (1715-1716).[280]   Thus in the first aria (D major, common time) the melody of the final chorale is brought in on the instruments; it is a war-song for the bass, surrounded by the violins and violas in unison, which beat the ground like chargers thirsting for battle under valiant horsemen.   The second aria, introduced by a bass recitative, " Komm in mein Herzenshaus, Herr Jesu, mein Verlangen " —" Come and dwell within my heart, Lord Jesus, my salvation,"—and sung by the soprano with only figured bass accompaniment (B minor, 12-8), is a touching and childlike prayer, in striking contrast to the martial strains that went before. After another recitative for the tenor there comes a duet for tenor and alto, accompanied by the violin and oboe da caccia (G major, 3-4).   The Gospel for the day relates that after one of our Lord's most important discourses a woman from the people lifted up her voice and said, " Blessed is the womb that bare Thee, and the paps which Thou hast sucked," and how He answered, " Yea, rather, blessed are they·that hear the word of God, and keep it."   Accordingly Franck begins his text thus: " Wie selig ist der Leib, der, Jesu, dich getragen!   Doch selger ist das Herz, das dich in Glauben trägt "—" How blessed is the womb that bare Thee, O my Saviour!   But happier still the heart that Thee by faith receives."   This narrative, so touching in its simplicity, was taken by Bach for the groundwork of the duet.   We feel in this a particular kind of softness, quite distinct from other tender pieces by Bach, so that we might almost say it has something feminine and motherly in it.   Even the cradle song in the cantata " Tritt auf die Glaubensbahn " is different, although in some places it is like it.   The homophonous thirds, the immediate modulation into the key of the sub-dominant, and even the bringing in of the F—like a tearful glance from a mother's eyes—all these are very unusual things in the opening of a work by Bach.   Directly after this opening the vocal parts are treated in skilful imitation, surrounded by the oboe and the violin in fantastic and mysterious semi-

---

[280] *Vide* App. A, No. 28.

quavers. Farther on, where Christ's answer is given, the first subject comes in again, but is treated fugally in four parts with the assistance of the instruments—a wonderfully successful amplification by simple means. To each couplet that follows there is a new and fresh image in the music; thus the believer's victory over all his enemies is expressed by a movement of bold and animated character, with reminiscences of the figures in the first aria—his final victory even over death, by imitations which struggle valiantly for a time, and then seem to lose their way in strange and gloomy harmonies. The idea of Death, with his terrors, makes itself felt for a moment; it is then overpowered by the return of the calm ritornel, and finally is completely vanquished by the closing chorale. We could in former cases perceive a reflex of Bach's character in the way in which he conceived the text of an aria. The intensity with which he has here grasped the feeling of the Bible narrative seems to me to reveal more clearly the pure depth of his German heart than any outward incident of his life could do.

We have come to the end; the reader, on glancing back, will observe that elaborate choruses are almost entirely lacking in the works that remain of this year. The chief reason lies in the poems by Franck, for at this time he abstained altogether from employing Bible words; and Bach was well aware of what was required in a text for a chorus. But this is not the only reason. Up to this time, however admirable his productions of a choral kind are here and there, yet the time of his full perfection in that form had not yet arrived. The Weimar period was the flowering-time of his achievements on and for the organ, particularly in the form of the chorale; and this height had to be gained before he could take a further stride and condense into vocal forms the more subjective and dramatic aspects of the instrumental forms. His greatest productions in the way of choral music are indeed his chorale choruses, and these too constitute the crown of his art as applied to the purposes of the Church. The strength of these Weimar cantatas consists in the solos, of which the wealth of ideas, the variety and perfection of form, compel our amazement. Each melody bears its peculiar stamp, in each piece an individual emotion is thoroughly treated, and even in the most dissimilar the composer has succeeded with marvellous versatility in doing full justice to the subjects. The music flows so untiringly and spontaneously that it is utterly inconceivable that such power should ever decay; the most complicated technical problems are solved with such a quiet certainty that they never occur to us as such. The conception of the words shows an intensity of feeling entirely devoted to the Church, and utterly free from any blemish of secular shallowness. His idea is always concentrated on the whole solemnity of meaning of each separate Sunday; and if the text is in-adequate to the thorough bringing-out of the chief thought, he grasps it in its deepest meaning, and gives it its right form by means of his music. The aim and end of the can-tatas, which is the bringing-out of devotional feeling, is here greatly helped by the skilful employment of the chorale. If it were not for the sparing use of chorus-writing these can-tatas might well be considered as the ideal of Bach's church music.

In this first year there comes, by way of interlude, a secular cantata. Duke Wilhelm Ernst, as we have before said, was in the most friendly relations with Duke Christian of Saxe-Weissenfels. This latter personage had inaugurated a grand hunting festival in celebration of his thirty-fifth birthday (February 23, 1716). In order to take his share in the fes-tivities, Duke Wilhelm Ernst commanded a cantata to be produced, in the ducal hunting-lodge, by way of " table-music," and this was to be written by Salomo Franck, and composed by Sebastian Bach.[281] Its form, of course, was allegorical and dramatic, but the merit of the poetry was so slight that it would scarcely repay the trouble of analysing it. The characters, as was customary, were taken from ancient mythology. Diana comes on, and declares that her delight is exclusively in the chase, and Endymion reproaches her with having neglected him. To this the goddess replies that it came about because she must give her whole attention

---

[281] Autograph in the Royal Library at Berlin. *Vide* App. A, No. 27.

to-day to "dear Christian," and so her lover is satisfied, and sings a congratulatory duet with her. Pan, the god of nature, comes in with similar sentiments, and at last Pales, the goddess of flocks and herds, offers her attestation of devoted loyalty. Since there is now a quartet of characters, there is nothing to prevent a proper musical production; so first they sing in four parts, then there is a duet for Diana and Endymion, followed by an aria for Pales and Pan; and the whole closes with a general chorus.

The cantata is rather lengthy, containing ten numbers, besides the connecting recitatives. Bach took a great interest in the composition, as it was probably his first work of the kind, and it contains much charming music. He referred back to it several times as opportunity occurred, and even used separate pieces from it in a later church cantata. It first came into use again for the celebration of the birthday of Prince Ernst August (April 19), the nephew of Duke Wilhelm Ernst, and elder step-brother to the musical Johann Ernst, who succeeded the Duke as Regent in 1728.[282] It was afterwards performed in Leipzig for the anniversary of the name day of King Friedrich August of Saxony (whether the first or second is not stated), "in unter-thänigster Ehrfurcht aufgeführet in dem *Collegio musica* durch *J. S. B.*"[283]—"performed with the most submissive reverence in the musical college, by Johann Sebastian Bach." Probably a part of it at least was performed at another time in honour of Duke Christian and his consort Louise Christine, a princess of the house of Stolberg.[284] Lastly, in

---

[282] In the score, wherever the name "Christian" occurs, Bach has written "Ernst August" above or below it.

[283] As it is stated in a copy of the words written on purpose.

[284] On the last page of the book of words, in which is preserved the original version (but not in Bach's own writing), this is written across the other writing as a parody of the words of the last chorus, by a second hand:—

Die Anmuth umfange, das Glück bediene
Den Hertzog u. seine *Louyse Christine*
Sie weyden in Freuden auf Blumen u. Klee
Es prange die Zierde der Fürstlichen Eh';
   Die andre *Dione*
   Fürst Christians Crone!
Die Anmuth umfange, &c., D.-C.

the year 1735, two arias out of this work were transferred in
an amplified and enriched form to the Whitsuntide cantata,
"Also hat Gott die Welt geliebt"[285]—"So God the Father
loved the world." One of these is the first song of Pan (C
major, common time), in which Bach solved the problem of
setting such unthankful words, by writing a powerful polyphonic movement with the least possible regard to the
subject. In its altered form the treatment becomes broader
and more finished, and the music is made with a masterly
facility to fit the different requirements of the new text in
details; as a whole, however, this would have well repaid
the trouble of another composition. The two arias of Pales
and the second of Pan give the composer a true poetic inspiration, and we see how his heart delighted in the thought
of the free open-air life of shepherds and husbandmen. The
first aria of Pales, "Schafe können sicher weiden"—"All
the flocks may feed in safety,"—accompanied on two flutes
and figured bass (B flat major, common time) is a charming little piece of the most perfect finish.

Bach felt that the second aria (F major, common time)
could be remodelled to something still more beautiful. It
is thirty-six bars long, and lies over a free *basso ostinato*, like
that of the bass aria in the Easter cantata of 1715. This
was retained, but the melody is replaced by another of a
much bolder and freer character, which, with its happy
breath of spring, has even won its way to the hearts of the
musical world of the present day. The piece is enlarged to
fifty-two bars, and the modulations are altered. Not yet
satisfied with this, the master carries on the bass theme in
a postlude of twenty-six bars at the end. The words, "Mein
gläubiges Herze, frohlocke, sing, scherze"—"My heart ever
faithful, sing praises, be joyful,"—were exactly fitted to the
transferred form; and still more was the general feeling of
Whitsuntide, the festival of May.

If such transference from one work to another of a different
kind is possible, there can be no difference in style between
Bach's sacred and secular compositions. And no such

---

[285] B.-G., XVI., No. 68, P. 1287.

difference does actually exist. Bach's style was sacred, and the sacred style was Bach's. He does not put it on and off like a vestment, but uses it always without thinking of it, because his style of composition had developed naturally with his growth, and he could not express himself in any other way. In some details of the secular cantatas he attempts to gird himself somewhat more loosely, and indeed a greater degree of grace is there perceptible. But on the whole his pure polyphonic style is retained in both to an equal degree.

The singers of Weissenfels, so long accustomed to the outward showiness of the opera, must have pulled long faces at this' music, although Bach took the trouble for a moment, in the first aria for Diana, of writing something brilliant and effective. One of the ornaments of the opera at that place was at this time (from what year is not certain) Christiane Pauline Kellner, who may have taken the part of Diana. She made a great effect at the Brunswick Opera at the end of the seventeenth century, and subsequently at Cassel, and gained a great name as a vocalist. Mattheson praises her improvisations, and "her vocal fantasias without a single word." She was also well known in Hamburg.[286] Instances of Bach's having written for female singers are of the rarest occurrence in his life. In his time there were no female singers at the Court of Weimar, either in church or chamber music, and they were first introduced there at the end of 1720.[287]

The second series of Franck's cantatas extended from the first Sunday in Advent of 1716 to the same day in 1717.[288] Thus there were no new poems for the time from Easter till Advent, 1716. Bach, as we have seen, composed for the

---

[286] Mattheson, Das Besch. Orch., p. 137. Walther, pp. 338 and 229. Chrysander, Jahrbücher, I., pp. 188, 190, 200, 202, and 265.

[287] Walther, p. 450, at the bottom.

[288] "Evangelische | Sonn- und Fest- | Tages | Andachten, | Auf | Hochfürstl. Gnädigste Verordnung | Zur | Fürstl. Sächsis. Weimarischen | Hof-Capell-*Music* | In Geistlichen *Arien* | erwecket | Von | Salomon Francken, | Fürstl. Sächs. Gesamten Ober-*Con|sistorial-Secretario* in Weimar.|Weimar und Jena,| Bey Johann Felix Bielcken. | 1717. | " It is in the Grand-Ducal Library at Weimar, without a preface. See App. A, No. 30.

festival of Whitsuntide a cantata to a text of Neumeister,
and we cannot point to any other works of that time.
Indeed, we possess only two cantatas out of the whole of
the second annual series of poems, both of which must
certainly have been written in Weimar. Whether he set
no others, or whether the rest have been lost, remains
uncertain. These two are for the second and the fourth
Sundays in Advent, December 6 and 20, 1716. The
circumstance that one was written so soon after the other
is obviously connected with the death of Drese, the old
Capellmeister, which took place at that time. In this
series, Franck had again altogether avoided the use of
recitative; Bach worked up these cantatas afterwards at
Leipzig, inserting recitatives which were written on purpose,
and dividing each into two sections by introducing a chorale
in the middle. They have only come down to us in this
extended form; but it is easy to restore them to their
original state, excepting perhaps certain improvements
in the details which must have been made in any case.
Each consisted of a chorus, four arias, and a chorale.

The Gospel for the Second Sunday in Advent treats of
Christ's coming to judgment, and affords an opening into
that realm of mysticism in which Bach's genius was so
eminently at home, and in this cantata he spreads his
wings for a mightier flight than we could have dared to
expect even from all that he had done before.[289] The chorus
at the beginning, which is cast in the mould of the Italian
aria, has eighty bars (C major, common time). "Wachet,
betet!"—"Watching, praying!"—these are the words which
serve as the germ for the mighty growth of sound. It is
already a living thing in the instrumental introduction, for
this contains the statement, as it were, of every motive
which is afterwards used by the instruments throughout
the work. Among these the most significant are the
resonant signal call—

---

[289] B.-G., XVI., No. 70, P. 1666.

and a solemn rolling figure in a succession of broad chords,
like that of the C major prelude in the Wohltemperirte
Clavier, through which we hear alternately the soft but
rousing tones of the trumpets and oboes; for even in prayer
we must keep watch! The number for the chorus is worked
upon quite different motives; the materials consisting of hasty
snatches of semiquavers, energetic shouts, bold challenges,
and, as a contrast, devotional streams of harmony, such
as this:[290]—

The four arias constitute so many distinct pictures of astonishing vividness.

Beautiful as the recitatives are (the last, in which the
chorale "Es ist gewisslich an der Zeit"—"It certainly is
now the time,"—peals forth from the trumpets as if its call
were sounding from the clouds, while a powerful picture is
at the same time given of the destruction of the earth, being
especially grand and startling), and absolutely justified as
this means of utterance is on general grounds of art, in the
present instance they cannot be considered necessary. It
seems to me that I can throughout perceive quite clearly
that they were not originally intended by Bach. The
psychological development is followed up with such uninterrupted vigour through the four arias to the final chorale
that the master himself could insert nothing more without disturbing its continuity. The composition was too
thoroughly a spontaneous stream flowing from the very
depths of his being, and in such creations there is no opening for remodelling afterwards; they come into existence
at once, and complete. The first aria, for an alto voice
(A minor, 3-4 time), resembles the tenor song of the Advent

---

[290] The fervent declamation of the last passage reminds us of a similar one in
the *Kyrie* of Beethoven's *Missa Solemnis*.

cantata of 1714; it contains the earnest warning to prepare
for the last day before it is too late and the judgment falls
upon us with terror and dismay, as the fire fell upon guilty
Sodom.   The warning is associated with a tone of deep sadness, as though to convey the feeling that it will be all in
vain to most men.   They will not believe that the end is
near, but the word of Christ shall abide, and He shall
appear in the clouds to judge them; this is the second aria
for soprano (E minor, common time).   In it the expression
of firm conviction on one hand, and on the other of being
appalled by a stupendous vision, is mingled with a mysterious dread.   How majestic are the veins of melody from
bars 7 to 12! and again from 14 to 20, how powerful their
swell!   Does not this broad, deliberate subject—

with its echo-like *diminuendo* to *piano* and *pianissimo*, sound
as if it had been born of space and died away again, shud-
dering into infinitude?

But yet the pious may hold up their heads and be confi-
dent they will "bloom in Eden, and ever serve God."   This
is the sentiment expressed in the following air for the tenor
(G major, common time).[291]   Its free form is similar to that
of the duet of the cantata, "Ach, ich sehe!"—"Ah! I
see!"   The leading theme comes in unexpectedly out of
the obscurity of the sub-dominant in bar 34, a subtle and
poetical illustration of the words, "Hebt euer Haupt
empor"—"Lift up your heads on high."   The melody,
which is beautiful in its construction, is more exclusively
conspicuous throughout the piece than in the other arias;
it is constantly recurring with its consoling sweetness, and
it proves itself truly consolatory, for the last aria for the

---

[291] In Franck's text the third and fourth lines are as follows: " Der jüngste
Tag wird kommen Zu eurer Seelen Flor"—"The last day will come to your
soul's spring-time." Bach has simply ignored the third line, and the verbal
idea is consequently somewhat obscure; still, the omission is a fresh proof of
how completely his mind was directed solely to the illustration of the main
sentiment.

bass (C major, 3-4 time) pours out a flood of eager longing
for that last and blessed day which shall see the translation of the righteous to the realms of joy. Rarely indeed
has Bach written a melody of so pure and self-dependent a
kind, or one which stands out so perfectly from its surroundings, as the twenty-four bars *adagio* which constitute
the beginning of this song. No instrument intrudes; the
voice flows on in a steady and unbroken stream of feeling,
supported only by the solemn tones of the organ in calm and
restful harmony. Suddenly the end of the world bursts
in: the instruments storm, the organ surges, trumpet-calls
sound through the tumult, all the foundations of the earth
quake and fall; but high above the terror of desolation
shines the celestial glory of that new heaven and new earth,
of which it is written that in them there shall be no more
death, and that God shall wipe away all tears (Rev. xxv. 4).
In this the music not only transcends everything earthly in
the expression of feeling, but all consideration for the commonly received rules of form are set aside; after this wild
middle movement Bach returns to the *adagio* of the beginning, and the song goes on to the end in a strain of transcendental rhapsody.

The chorus comes in with the fifth verse of the chorale,
"Meinen Jesum lass ich nicht"—"I will never leave my
Lord." Usually the four-part vocal subject has above it but
one single independent instrumental part, but here this has
failed to satisfy the composer. The violins soar up in a free
vein of melody in three parts; it is the harmony of the
spheres! There is no cantata which gives us, with more
directness and force, the impression that the whole course
of the sentiment it conveys flows undeviatingly to its goal in
the closing chorale. We only feel that we have reached the
end we confidently expected, which our ears had anticipated;
that now the last veil is lifted, and the glory of the heavens
revealed.

The eye that has gazed on the sun turns, dazzled and
indifferent, to the things of earth. Thus it is a disadvantage
to the second cantata, "Herz und Mund und That und

Leben "[292]—" Heart and mouth, and soul, and spirit,"—that it should come under review in chronological order after that just discussed; otherwise we might be delighted with the really fresh and splendid opening chorus (C major, 6-4), with the highly expressive first aria, and indeed with much that is very stirring throughout the work.

We may regard the cantata, "Wachet, betet" as the key-stone of his sacred compositions at Weimar. Even if the master should have found, in other poems of this "Christian Year," an opening for other important compositions—if one or another of these should some day be thrown up by the tide of time—we yet could hardly find in them clearer marks of the marvellous individuality of his genius, which loved to dwell in the gardens of the blest, rising above and beyond the joys and woes of humanity—whose lips were touched by the finger of God, that they might declare His glory to the darkened minds of men.

VII.

AT MEININGEN: JOHANN LUDWIG BACH.   AT DRESDEN: ORGAN WORKS OF THE LATER WEIMAR PERIOD.

WE have no certain record of any journey undertaken by Bach in the years 1715-16, but it can scarcely be doubted that during this period he once paid a visit to Meiningen, and the court of Saxony residing there.[293] The reader may remember that at that time the Capell-Director there was Joh. Ludwig Bach, a descendant of Veit Bach's second son, whose musical gifts reached the highest fruition in this Bach of Meiningen. Up to this time we have no traces of

---

[292] The autograph score is in the Royal Library at Berlin.

[293] If we might regard a copy of the E minor mass by Nikolaus Bach—now in the possession of Messrs. Breitkopf and Härtel—as being in Sebastian's handwriting, this would be a proof that he was in Meiningen in September, 1716, for at the end it has the date, "Meiningen, d. 16 7ᵇʳ 1716." But it was not till a later date that Sebastian Bach wrote some of it in; and, besides, it is not in his hand. Indeed, I cannot read the name under the date as J. S., but as J. L. Bach. Probably it is an autograph of Johann Ludwig Bach.

any intercourse between the two branches, but we find them again as soon as Sebastian had re-established it; for in the year 1717 the eldest son of his brother at Ohrdruf was called "by recommendation" to be court cantor to the foundation at Gandersheim, where Joh. Ludwig's brother was already in office, and where the abbess was the sister of the Duke of Saxe-Meiningen.[294] That these two, the most gifted representatives of the two branches, should have made these advances is a new and pleasing token of the fraternal feeling which pervaded all the members of the great clan. It is still more important to recognise the warm and lasting interest taken by Sebastian in Joh. Ludwig's compositions, and to observe to what extent he benefited in this case again from the rising tide of gradual improvement and advancement in the talents of his family. Joh. Ludwig, it is true, could not contribute any qualifying influence to his cousin's development, for they did not come into contact till Sebastian was already quite independent of it; but he always found ample room and disposition to derive something from the methods of his cousin—more, indeed, it would seem, than from any other composer. There is no other writer whose works he copied to so great an extent at a later period. In this we see something of the same feeling as when he married a daughter of his own race; for, since in him all its gifts and characteristics were most perfectly concentrated and developed, and no further improvement was possible in another generation, he instinctively drew to himself other members of his family for the further fostering of his own individuality —partly, too, from their community of life, and partly for the sake of an exchange of ideas in matters of art.

Of course Joh. Ludwig's talent is in no respect comparable to Sebastian's. Even Joh. Christoph (of Eisenach) ranks higher as to inventiveness and profundity; still he must be regarded as an artist of great originality and many-sided culture. In the first place it is to be observed that he was animated by a totally different spirit to that which characterised the most prominent individuals of the main branch of

---

[294] See *ante*, p. 11. Brückner, Part III., sec. 9, p. 35.

the family. His features even had hardly any resemblance to the face we are accustomed to imagine as typical of the Bachs, from the portraits of Sebastian, his father, and his sons. A pastel portrait, which represents him as a man of nearer forty than thirty, shows us a smooth, roundish face, with soft and delicate outline, and fine arched eyebrows. In a miniature portrait in oil, taken when he was a youth, or quite a young man, the features are, indeed, of remarkable, but almost feminine beauty.[295] And his compositions are equally lacking in breadth, depth, and imaginative power. He never seems to have occupied himself in writing for the organ, and this is certainly significant. His character directed him to what was sweet and pleasing in invention; at the same time he had a natural facility in every line of his art. However, he seems at least to have been diligent in instrumental music.

There is a suite for orchestra by him, of the year 1715, consisting of an overture, air, minuet, gavotte, air, and bourrée;[296] of which the overture is certainly the best section, powerful in the first movement, very flowing and smooth in the second, and rendered effective by the favourite method of introducing pedal points. The first air is very peculiar, consisting almost entirely of semiquavers, and beginning thus :—

The chirping figure (in a bracket), appearing alternately on the solo oboe and in the *tutti*, plays an important part in it. The other dance-movements are sturdy and vigorous, rather than joyous. A rich selection remains of his motetts and

---

[295] The portrait in pastel is in the Royal Library at Berlin. The oil-picture, painted on copper, is in the possession of Herr Dreysigacker, Post-director at Meiningen, who in the politest manner has permitted me to see it. In consequence of some obscure tradition it passed for a portrait of Sebastian Bach, but this was immediately proved to be an error. External and internal evidence alike point to its being the likeness of Johann Ludwig.

[296] In the Royal Library at Berlin, with the following title: "*Ouverture à* 4. | *en G. h.* | *del* | *Joh. Ludwig Baach.* | " In the left-hand lower corner is the date: "*Mens: Febr.* 1715."

church cantatas. Sebastian Bach alone transcribed with his own hand the score of eighteen of the cantatas.[297]

These works stand about midway between the older and the newer cantata forms. The texts contain madrigal verses for recitative, and, side by side with these, Bible texts for solo voices; and, on the other hand, original lines for the choruses. In the Bible texts the *arioso* is retained with those older characters discarded by Sebastian Bach; for instance, the bass solo in the closing cadences is frequently in unison with the bass instruments. The recitatives, strictly speaking, are not yet rendered sufficiently prominent as an independent form by due lightness and freedom of declamation. The arias are for the most part of the *da capo* form, but are meanly proportioned. Sometimes the construction is ill-defined; for instance, an aria for the alto in the cantata " Ja mir hast du Arbeit gemacht " (for Quinquagesima Sunday) begins in 3-2 time with a fine broad melody, but after twenty bars glides off without any visible reason into pure recitative. The choruses are in imitation, but generally not much worked out. Finally, in the treatment of the chorale he prefers a homophonic vocal subject, accompanied by all the violins in a repetition of quavers; occasionally, however, the violins rise above the voice in free and vigorous figures. The general expression of sentiment commonly holds a medium pitch, equally remote from the emotional style of the older cantatas, and the vapid flatness of Telemann, Stölzel, and their fellows. A genuine vein of original invention is everywhere discernible, and often startles us by its vivid imagery. In the cantata just mentioned the bass *arioso* at the beginning is introduced by this subject for the instruments—

[297] Twelve of them are bound together in a volume in the Royal Library at

which admirably depicts Christ's aching prescience of His approaching sufferings; it predominates throughout the *arioso*, and reappears, very cleverly adapted, in the closing chorus with the same idea.[298]

We know that Italian singing was much approved at the Court of Meiningen, and it is therefore pretty obvious that Joh. Ludwig owed the particularly *singable* character of his vocal music in great measure to his studies of the Italian method. It is particularly conspicuous in the motetts. The real originality and superior importance of these works is not fully revealed till we compare them with the mongrel and flaccid motetts by other composers of the period. After Sebastian Bach, I know of none worthy to stand by the side of his Meiningen cousin. We must not, of course, seek in them for such extension and development as is indispensable in the modern type of motett, where Joh. Christoph still held the first place. But it has frequently happened in the history of art that though none but a transcendent genius has been able to reach the highest level attainable at the time, some feebler talents have still succeeded in obtaining a place near it. Then certain elements, which in the process of transition to a different standard of ideal have been somewhat neglected, come to the front again, and with increased boldness, and yet succeed in combining very delightfully with the newer and fresher ones. Joh. Ludwig Bach stood in much nearer relationship to the Italian vocal style of his day than any of his contemporaries, who, when composing motetts, could never emancipate themselves from the idea of concerted music. The true essence of choral singing had been more fully revealed to him, and he had what was lacking to most of the composers of northern and central Germany, an adequate sense of the glowing and satisfying beauty of the pure tones of the

---

Berlin, with a title-page written by Ph. Em. Bach. Besides these, I have seen there the parts of four others transcribed by Sebastian Bach.

[298] Mosewius, by an inexplicable oversight, has quoted this ritornel and the chorale that follows it as a composition of Sebastian Bach's, in Supplement 7 to his essay on that composer's church cantatas and chorale hymns. We have in it an instance of Joh. Ludwig's treatment of a closing chorale.

human voice. Since he had formerly held the post of Court
Cantor he had himself, perhaps, been a good singer. Besides
this he was a highly educated contrapuntist ; indeed it may
safely be said that he was master of all that at that time had
been produced in Italy in this branch ; and as he brought to
it a strong inventive individuality the results are to a certain
extent intelligible.

It is a significant token of his inclination to revel in pure
choral effects that his motetts are of such enormous length.
One for double choir, on Isaiah ix. 6, 7 : " Uns ist ein Kind
geboren," &c., contains no less than 346 bars in common
time, and without any subdivisions into subjects, such
as are usual in Sebastian Bach's motetts; short breathing-
space only is allowed by fermatas in bars 63, 133, 164, 228,
and 275. This gigantic work begins in a simple and deliberate manner, but at bar 64 an image is worked out of
surprising originality; all the basses and tenors lift up their
voices in unison, as if chanting a psalm :—

Then the other four parts come in higher up, in canon-like
imitation—

repeating the motive in D major, then in A minor, then in
two parts again in G major, closing on the dominant. It is
singularly touching when, during the pauses which succeed
the cadences in the upper parts, the basses and tenors carry
on the melody with its firm fulness of tone and deliberate
movement—the whole subject has such an unmistakably
Catholic stamp as to seem quite strange as the composition
of a Protestant musician. After this the two sopranos take
up the long-drawn phrase, then the basses alone, then the
tenors, then the basses again, and now the fabric of the
upper parts becomes firmer and richer. At bar 228 begins
an eight-part fugue : " Solches wird thun der Eifer des

Herrn Zebaoth "—" And the zeal of the Lord of Hosts shall
do this " :—

We should seek long, indeed, perhaps in vain, to find a
piece of equal importance and more admirable of its kind.
It is full of that playful facility, that glowing fusion of
parts, that revelling in sweet sounds, which can only result
when the whole " sings itself," as we say. With different
words this fugue might pass for the work of an Italian
master—we might guess of Leonardo Leo.

Another motett, " Gott sei uns gnädig und segne uns "
(Psalm lxvii.), is a work of perhaps even higher·value.[299] It
is for three choirs, so far at least as that two choirs each
consist of four parts, while the third is represented by a bass
part only. This proceeds independently of the other masses
of voices, and is clearly brought out in a passage in minims
rising from B through the scale to c', and then falling again
to F. Then follows a phrase in which the bass chorus
lingers persistently on the f, with the words " dass wir auf
Erden erkennen seinen Weg, unter allen Heiden sein Heil "—
" That Thy way may be known upon earth," &c. The
beginning is then repeated to the words " Es danken dir,
Gott, die Völker, es danken dir alle Völker "—" Let the
people praise Thee, O God," &c. And the bass chorus pours
out a current of semiquavers in the sharpest contrast—

[299] Amalien-Bibliothek, Vol. xc., piece 2. In this there are to be found
several other remarkable motetts by this master.

while the other two choruses dance round in quavers. Towards the end all the three basses unite to sing semibreves and minims in opposition to the crotchets and quavers of the other parts, using the melody of the Magnificat to these words " Es segne uns Gott, unser Gott; es segne uns Gott und alle Welt fürchte ihn "— " God, even our own God, shall bless us; and all the ends of the world shall fear Him." After which the motett goes on to the end in rich polyphony. These brief indications must suffice in this place; Joh. Ludwig Bach must always hold a prominent position in the history of purely vocal music.

Duke Ernst Ludwig of Saxe-Meiningen left no happy memory behind him, for his administration was selfish, his outlay on his court extravagant, and he encouraged favouritism. But he was a warm friend to the arts which made his court splendid, and above all to music. So early as in 1713 Ludwig Bach had conducted a " Passion Music " in the castle-chapel, and at the same time a whole series of church cantatas in the new form were printed, which were all or many of them by him; by 1719 a third edition of these had been demanded.[300] It is interesting to note here how the different characters of the two courts of Weimar and Meiningen were reflected in the compositions of the two Bachs; in one gravity and severity, in the other brilliancy and sweetness; the character of the reigning prince in each case guided the inspiration of the musician. Concert music was also performed at court, both at the midday meal and in the evening; this last indeed was principally called for when some royal visitor was in the place. The Duke also liked to see foreign artists appear at his soirées.[301] He himself wrote a good deal of sacred poetry, particularly at the time when, after a gay and careless life, graver thoughts began to stir his mind. One of his sisters was the abbess at Gandersheim, another was canoness there;

---

[300] Brückner, Landeskunde des Herzogthums Meiningen, I., p. 65, and certain private documents referring to it.

[301] From data in a document of the court-marshal's office of May 12, 1721. in which a musician of the band complains of having been degraded by the capell-meister.

and if we remember that Freylinghausen's hymn-book was dedicated to this lady abbess, with her deaconess and canoness, and hence that pietism had found its way within the convent walls, we may suppose that the Duke's poetical attempts had also some pietistic bias. He had selected for the text of his own funeral sermon Psalm cxvi. 16, 19, and had written a hymn on it, of which the first verse runs, " Ich suche nur das Himmelleben " :—

> I seek alone the joys of heaven,
>   Thy faithful servant would I be ;
> My heart and soul be wholly given
>   To Him who gave His life for me :
> Thy kingdom come, O Son of God,
> And guide me in the heavenward road.

When he died in 1724, Joh. Ludwig made use of the verses of the psalm and of this hymn as the text of a grand funeral composition in three sections. It would seem that he also availed himself of a melody written by the Duke himself, for an air something like the following lies at the foundation of the second section :—

From all this it is clear that Sebastian might reckon on a very friendly reception at court, and on a delightful interchange of ideas on art with his cousin when he betook himself to Meiningen. And his expectations were fulfilled in every respect; he formed a life-long intimacy with Ludwig; the copies of cantatas before spoken of were not made till he was in Leipzig. It is no doubt an afterglow of the impression made in the ducal family by his artistic powers when we see him, a few years later, entering into relations with the Markgraf Christian Ludwig of Brandenberg, whose sister, Elizabeth Sophia, was the Duke of Meiningen's second wife.

---

302 The score of this funeral music is in the Royal Library at Berlin.

The autumn journey of 1717 had a much more famous outcome. Dresden was now his destination, and in that city both music and the theatre were at that time flourishing greatly under the extravagant rule of Friedrich August I. Bach had some acquaintances among the band, and one of these was the concertmeister Jean Baptiste Volumier, who filled this position at the court of Berlin till 1709 ;[303] possibly also there was Pantaleon Hebestreit, who had been called thither in 1714, and who before that had been at Eisenach with Telemann. Hebestreit was distinguished by his executive skill on an instrument resembling a dulcimer, invented by himself; but he was also an efficient violin-player, and familiar with the French style of music. Volumier was a Frenchman by education if not by birth, and highly esteemed for his performance of the compositions of his countrymen. Other capital artists were also employed there—the organist Petzold, the church composer Zelenka, the violonist Pisendel—so that a stay there must have been very interesting to any musician, and it must have seemed highly desirable to become known in such a circle.

It happened too, quite by chance, that Bach met at Dresden the French clavier and organ-player, Jean Louis Marchand, the private organist to the King of France, and organist also to the church of Saint Benedict at Paris. Marchand was born at Lyons in 1671, and thus was by fourteen years Bach's senior ; he possessed in a high degree both the faults and the merits of his nationality. He was highly gifted in qualities of *technique*, his art was thoroughly elegant, and he well knew how to turn these talents to the best account; but he was at the same time full of vanity, arrogance, and petty caprice. Paris society swore by him, and pupils crowded round him from all parts ; but the disfavour of the King drove him for a time into Germany, and his fame followed him.[304]

---

[303] At any rate he was still there, according to a document in the archives of the Principality of Hesse at Marburg, in 1708 ; his appointment at Dresden dates from June 28, 1709 (Fürstenau, II., p. 65).

[304] A portrait of Marchand, engraved on copper, of the first half of the eighteenth century, now in my possession, bears the inscription : " Organiste du

His playing was greatly admired at the court at Dresden, and procured for him a gift of two medals worth one hundred ducats, and, it is said, a command to remain there permanently. Bach, it is true, did not play before the King, but he had ample opportunity for making himself heard by artists and the friends of art; and a violent dissension arose as to which of the two was the greatest musician. One powerful party consisted of the court circle, for the King was very fond of French music; these took the side of Marchand, while most of the German artists forming the band stood up for Bach. The question finally resolved itself into a battle of opinions as to the greater or less value of French or German music on general grounds, and Bach was urged by his friends to challenge Marchand to a competitive performance. This he did after an opportunity had been contrived for him secretly to hear his antagonist play at court; he wrote to him declaring himself ready to go through any musical ordeal Marchand might choose to impose, provided only that he on his side would undertake the same. Marchand accepted the challenge; a musical jury was selected; the scene of the tournament was to be the salon of a powerful minister, probably of Count Flemming, who had been prime minister since 1712, and who had considerable knowledge of music; out of love of the art he even kept a private band of his own.[305]

Curiosity and excitement rose to a high pitch, and at the appointed hour a large and brilliant assembly of both sexes had met. Bach and the umpires were punctual, but Marchand came not. The company waited awhile; then the count sent to remind him of his appointment, and received in reply the information that he had set out that very morning by the fast coach, and had disappeared from Dresden. With certain prescience of defeat he had abandoned the field;

Roy, né à Lion, mort à Paris le 17 Février, 1732. Agé de 61 ans." Further information as to his life and singular caprices is to be found in Gerber, L., I., col. 870, and in Hilgenfeldt, p. 23. A little-known anecdote is in Caecilia II., p. 85 (Mainz: Schott and Co.). [See article "Marchand," in Grove's Dictionary of Music.]

[305] Fürstenau, Loc. cit., p. 7.

Bach played alone. It is evident that Marchand must have heard him somewhere or other, and have convinced himself that the German musician was infinitely his superior; and not only in organ-playing, in which no doubt he would have declined to compete with him, but on the clavier as well, in which, according to the general opinion of the time, the French school had the advantage and preference. The glory was all the greater for Bach, as he had beaten his opponent on his own special ground. He had long been familiar with Marchand's works, as with those of all the other important French masters, and then and later fully recognised their merits.[806] All that I myself have seen of Marchand's works quite deserve this recognition, and are not inferior to Couperin's clavier works in variety and grace. They offer, no doubt, too thin a pabulum to the more solid German taste, and are besides, like everything French, excessively difficult to play. Adlung, who inquired elaborately into the details of Bach's challenge, said with regard to Marchand's suites: " They never really pleased me but once, namely, when I once spoke to the Capellmeister Bach of his challenge, when he was staying here [at Erfurt], and told him I had these suites by me; and he played them to me in his manner, that is to say, very smoothly and artistically."[807] Of course from such a centre as Dresden the news of an event so glorious to German art could not fail to spread in all directions; the belief in the superiority of French clavier music began to fail, and Bach's fame was greatly enhanced and extended.

After such a success, he might well be indifferent to the fact that no distinction was awarded him on the part of the court. How this could happen remains unexplained. Perhaps the royal interest was exclusively directed to the newly engaged Italian opera company, which arrived at Dresden from Vienna just in the same month, namely, September, when Bach was visiting the capital. Its director was no less a man than Antonio Lotti. At the same time it is not probable that he

---

[806] A suite by him is in Andreas Bach's book, and another, dated 1714, in one of the volumes of Ludwig Krebs' collection.

[807] Adlung, Anl. zur Mus. Gel., p. 719, note 8.

should have met Bach there, or have found the opportunity of making his acquaintance in the midst of all the business in which his new position must have involved him, interesting as it would be to think that the greatest sacred composers of Germany and Italy at that time should once in their lives have stood face to face.[308]

Bach cannot have remained absent from Weimar later than the beginning of October, for extensive preparations were being made there for a jubilee to commemorate the two hundredth anniversary of the Reformation, and the Duke's composer had of course his part in this. The festival lasted three days, from October 31 to November 2, and on the eve of the second day the Duke solemnly established a fund, investing a sum of which the interest was to be distributed annually on his birthday.[309] For this, as well as for the first day of the jubilee, new cantatas were composed and performed; Franck probably wrote the texts,[310] and Bach certainly composed the music for at least one.

He must have been in the midst of all this work when the event occurred which was destined to turn the course of his life into a different channel. Prince Ernst August had married, on January 24, 1716, Eleonore Wilhelmine, a sister of the reigning Prince Leopold, of Anhalt-Cöthen. This young prince, who was devoted to music, had thus come to know Bach, and his former capellmeister having left him a short time previously, he called Bach to the post. We are safe in venturing to assume that Bach at the moment was no longer particularly comfortable at Weimar. After Samuel Drese's death no man had a better right than he to his vacant place. But first of all a project was entertained of making Telemann—a man of very various accomplishments and propor-

---

[308] See App. A, No. 31.

[309] The court organist was to receive three gulden yearly out of this fund (Gottschalg, noté to p. 270).

[310] The proclamation concerning this festival (in the archives at Weimar) speaks in general terms only of the performance of these two cantatas, without mentioning either the poet or the composer. However, we know from a notice in MS. that Franck superintended the printing of the festival programme. The texts themselves I have been nowhere able to find.

tionately respected—capellmeister-general to Duke Ernst of Saxony,[311] and when nothing came of this, Drese's son was appointed, and Bach was simply passed over, without regard to his far more various qualifications, as shown in his eminent artistic industry. Now, notwithstanding that the post offered to him would take him out of the path of art he had hitherto trodden, he did not hesitate to accept it. His move to Cöthen must have taken place at once, in November, for already during the Advent season we find Schubart, his faithful disciple and worthy successor, filling his place at the organ of the castle chapel.[312]

Bach's labours as an officially appointed organist ended for ever with his departure from Weimar. We therefore must here direct our attention to one more aspect of them : his mode, namely, of accompanying congregational singing and his independent treatment of the chorale on the organ. This, indeed, constitutes almost the most important element of all his labours as an artist, and that which proved most fertile in results; and it was in Weimar that he pursued it with the greatest energy. Still the list of his organ compositions is by no means exhausted by those already discussed. He was indefatigable in producing fugues and works of a kindred nature, setting himself a still higher mark, which he did not fail to reach. A certain group of these compositions has a stamp in common which is distinct from the former, and we may consider them as forming a second Weimar period, as opposed to the first. Conspicuous in them above all is the desire to repress mere external brilliancy, and to attain the calmness of depth. It will be permissible to consider these compositions at once.

It will be remembered that we regarded Buxtehude's chaconnes and passecailles as models in their way, which even Bach has not improved on in any essential respect; for which reason he generally held aloof from this particular class of music. The only piece of the kind is a passecaille

<hr />

[311] Mattheson, Ehrenpf., p. 364. The Duke of Weimar is there called Ernst August, a slip of memory on Telemann's part.

[312] Walther, Lexicon, p. 557.

in C minor.[313] Though this has been regarded as a work of Bach's later period, this must have been because his peculiar relations to Buxtehude were not known, for the composition clearly reminds us of him in its details and as a whole; because also its origin from a distinct source was not understood, and finally because the high level of Bach's productions at Weimar, particularly in organ music, was under-estimated.[314] The piece in question, universally and justly admired, is no doubt too mature for the earlier years of this period, and distinctly marks the progress made by Bach between these and his later time at Weimar. It appears as though he had grasped with one clutch all that Buxtehude had laboriously won. Indeed, according to Buxtehude's category, it is not strictly a passecaille, but rather a chaconne; for the theme reappears in the upper and inner parts, and not always unchanged, but often in an ornamented form, while sometimes a mere suggestion is given. Still, on the other hand, the theme is at times insisted on in the bass with so much logical consistency that we cannot venture to call it simply a chaconne; it is rather a combination of the two forms. Just as Buxtehude was wont to consolidate a fugue into a chaconne towards the end, Bach here by a reverse process relaxes the rigidity of this form and passes into the free flow of a fugue. Each musician has an æsthetic feeling, but each shows plainly to which of the two forms he attaches the greater importance. Even the length of the piece betrays the endeavour after an exhaustive amalgamation; it consists of 293 bars, 168 of which belong to the passecaille.

Among the details which most remind us of Buxtehude are the resolution of the harmony in bars 113 to 128, and

---

[313] B.-G., XV., p. 289.   P. S. V., C. 1 (240), No. 2.   An autograph, formerly in the possession of Capellmeister Guhr of Frankfort a. M., has disappeared. But the passecaille is also to be found, beautifully written, in Andreas Bach's collection, which proves its origin. It is singular that none of the editors have paid any attention to this MS.

[314] W. Rust has in this instance given evidence of his feeling for the differences in Bach's style, for he has attributed this passecaille to the Cöthen period at the latest.

the chords which come in with the passage in semiquavers, bars 80 to 88, and, above all, the beginning as far as bar 32, which is wonderfully beautiful, revelling as it were in its anxious longing.   Here the genuine Buxtehude sentiment, in all its rhapsodic youthfulness, predominates over Bach's— which was in a certain sense its opposite—too evidently for us to doubt that the alliance was intentional.   But Bach's sterner tones are rendered all the more expressive as the piece proceeds, and by the time we have reached the fugue, in which the theme of the passecaille is contrasted with another and a new one, all resemblance has vanished.[315]

An organ fugue with a prelude in A major is remarkable, not only for its artistic beauty, but psychologically with reference to the composer.   Its theme—

is, as it were, the "wraith" (or "Doppelgänger") of that on which the instrumental fugue is constructed which serves to introduce the cantata "Tritt auf die Glaubensbahn" —"Walk in the way of faith."   They are different in the gender of the key—so to designate the difference between major and minor—in the key itself, and even in the actual order of the notes, but we see how in spite of all this the idea may nevertheless remain the same.   We may assume that this composition originated soon—or perhaps immediately — after the other, because a later and more perfect remodelling of the organ piece exists; thus it must in any case be attributed to an early time, since Bach never worked up again any organ piece of his Leipzig period.[316] The alterations in the fugue, however, extend only to this : that the time is changed from 3-8 to 3-4 in consideration for the increase in the tone-material, the three closing bars are omitted, and in two places a pedal of high pitch is used which

---

[315] This passecaille has been recently arranged for an orchestra, with a very skilful imitation of organ effects, by H. Esser, and its beauties are thus rendered more accessible to the general public.

[316] B.-G., XV., p. 120.   P. S. V., C. 2 (241), No. 3.   It appears in the original form as a variant.

was probably lacking to the Weimar organ. The fugue is
quite unique among Bach's organ pieces: contrary to the
conditions of the instrument, as it would seem, he has given
it something of a peculiarly feminine character, and this runs
through every thread of it with pure depth of feeling. Broken
harmonies in the counterpoint, soft sixths and passages of
thirds, breathe into it something of the temper of the G major
aria in the cantata just mentioned; the playful suggestions
of stretto are quite delightful, till at last one is fully developed
with infinite grace. From bar 153 the feeling acquires a wonderful intensity; the counterpoint seems to cling in a loving
embrace to the theme, which from bar 161 appears again in
smiling beauty. The alterations in the prelude are more
important; it was recast, not merely fuller in tone, but more
complete in organic structure. Its form still reminds us
of Buxtehude, but the composer soon forsook this entirely.

In the rest of the works to be mentioned here he had
already opened out new paths. These are two fugues in C
minor, one in F minor, and one in F major, and they are so
nearly related in both external and internal structure that—
when we recall Bach's principle of exhausting a certain
vein of form-treatment, when once he had opened it, in a
succession of works—they must have been written at the
same time. The preludes with which two of them (F major
and C minor) are furnished in their present state[317] were
not originally written on purpose, but substituted later for
the original preludes; their grander structure offers too great
a contrast to the fugues, and betrays the period of Bach's
highest mastery. The others, however,[318] evidently form
with their preludes each a complete piece conceived of as a
whole; indeed, the rejected prelude to the C minor fugue
seems to have been preserved separately.[319] The improvements made upon it consist in the utmost possible elimina-
tion of all inorganic ornament, the utmost possible adherence
to a certain distribution and number of parts, and above all

317 B.-G., XV., pp. 155, 218. P. S. V., C. 3 (242), No. 2, and C. 2 (241), No. 6.
318 B.-G., XV., pp. 104, 129. P. S. V., C. 2 (241), No. 5, and C. 3 (242), No. 6.
319 P. S. V., C. 4 (243), No. 12. See, too, Griepenkerl's remarks in the preface.

in the use of a real theme in the place of the secondary motive. The treatment of the theme is imitative, so that the free entrances of the other parts constitute an essential difference from the strict fugue, and allows a wider variety in the development.[320] The F minor prelude, however, does not show this form in all its purity; it includes some strongly marked ideas, but works them out for the most part episodically. The C minor preludes, on the other hand, leave us in no doubt as to the meaning of the composer. They are as like to each other as twin sisters, both in details of structure and in the noble elegiac feeling they express; one and the same spirit fills their inmost being, though in one it is more veiled, more reserved than in the other—ebbing and flowing restlessly, and yet with hardly perceptible movement, over the immutable persistency of a mysterious pedal point; the other is animated with a richer vitality, which blossoms out into a more intense elaboration of harmony from the foundation of two principal motives.

In the fugues we are first struck by the very different stamp of the themes as compared with earlier ones; the stir and bustle of the northern masters, which had left their mark on Bach, is done away with, and has given way to a dignified moderation, moving in well-considered intervals. Here once more that element has clearly asserted its rights which influenced Pachelbel's fugue themes, but which could not produce the most beautiful possible results till it was combined, in Bach's music, with the best feature of the northern masters: namely, that calm, melodic structure, like that of the chorales, whose essence the master had not studied so long in vain. Common to them all is a development from the broad beginning to a constantly increasing agitation; only one of the C minor fugues[321] starts at once with some considerable degree of animation, and produces the enhanced effect rather by harmonic means. Common to them again is the introduction in the middle, usually

---

[320] The two C minor preludes are called *Fantasias* in the MS. Compare with this what has been said *ante*, p. 436.

[321] B.-G., XV., 129.   P. S. V., C. 3 (242), No. 6.

after a perfect cadence, of an episode which then either is
made use of as an answering theme, or else gives way for
the entrance of the leading theme. The least good is the
fugue in F minor, in which also the episode never assumes
a regular form. It has, so far as was possible with Bach, a
somewhat irregular growth; many new figures of counterpoint are brought in, but in a short time seem to lose their
vitality, so that the theme is constantly feeling about for
new support; in spite, therefore, of very great beauties,
something is lacking to our full enjoyment. In the other
fugue, in C minor, from bar 121 to 140, a passage comes in
of very remarkable homophony, which, though it is superficially connected with the rest by the continuous quavers,
in its purpose is quite foreign to it; no similar passage is to
be found in any other organ piece of Bach's, nor is it possible to detect any objective reason for it.

The fugue in F major is that which displays the grandest
development to a regular double-fugue treatment throughout;
but the first, in C minor, has the greatest vigour and fling.
Its theme alone—

reveals that robust and conquering force which was Bach's
alone, and which he most loved to display in his instrumental
fugues.

In estimating Bach's attitude towards congregational
singing as a part of the church services, we must before all
things bear in mind that we have to do with a genius of the
supremest type, with a power of invention which has never
been surpassed in the province of instrumental music, and
in that of organ music has never been even most remotely
approached. At the time of the Reformation organ music
formed no integral constituent in the ideal of Protestant
worship; it served only to support congregational psalmody.
Even under these conditions it is no doubt more essential
than in the Catholic Church, since a more active part is
taken by the congregation in Protestant than in Catholic
worship. But I have already endeavoured to indicate the

undreamed-of importance acquired by the organ after the native freshness of the early evangelical hymns had faded, and men's spirits, no longer capable of a vital and common religious sentiment, had fallen back on a subjective piety which indeed is not foreign to the nature of Protestantism. Here they found in instrumental music the fittest means for giving utterance to their inner life ; and in the organ chorale they found the form which combined for them the Personal element with the Congregational. The natural result was that the organ assumed greater importance than the singing; the instrument strove to display all its wealth and power, the voices became more and more silent. Thus it might well happen that the organist, even where he ought to have accompanied modestly, would not refrain from embroidering on the melody an arbitrary ornamentation, altering its organism by interposing his own fancies. The congregation were content, for the true value of the simple chorale was lost to them. Bach grasped it again in all its richness and depth, and he also detected that if the true art of sacred music were ever to become an accomplished fact, it must be evolved from organ music, and principally from the organ chorale. It was for this very reason, and precisely because he turned this soil in every direction with incredible energy, that he would never resign himself to make his playing a mere useful support for the singing of the congregation—he who, whenever he sat at his instrument, was drinking of the main spring of the Church music of his time. No, infinitely narrow as this province must have seemed, here he always would be the living and creative artist. He had learnt in Arnstadt the limits of this territory, and made use of the experience he had obtained there. He had already reverted to his more general methods of development from the phase of overloaded colouring and too imaginative digressions; and indeed, in the orthodox town of Weimar, he must certainly have had a congregation that understood the nature of the chorale, with a competent cantor and a trustworthy choir of boys.

There is no need to appeal to Bach's example for a decision of the question as to how an organist ought to accompany the hymns. In our time the answer is a simple one, because, unfortunately, we are now far enough from the genetic evolution of Protestant Church music. Our only task now is to keep those treasures of chorale melody that we possess untampered with. From this point of view the admissibility of interludes does not deserve the discussion which, even now, is sometimes wasted on it. They are mere empty vehicles for the display of ignorance and barbarism, and can at most be endured between the separate verses. But the case was then far otherwise, though honest judges could not shut their eyes to the fact that tasteless exuberance in organ music entirely destroyed congregational singing. It was Adlung's opinion that " when so many play as loud as they can, to perform whole passages, intermingled with regular closes, beginning quickly, and then again leaving off slowly, so that either the congregation sing on all out of order, or else must wait too long—it can hardly be said to be the finest performance in this best of worlds."[322] Nikolaus Bach of Jena would have nothing to say to interlude-playing, " because he believed that a steady grasp could control the congregation better without such run-work," and in the castle chapel of Weissenfels they were actually forbidden.

We are not left entirely to guess-work to form an idea of Sebastian Bach's practice in this matter. In the collections of chorales made by his pupils and by Walther a few compositions are to be found which supply us with hints on the subjects in hand. They are arrangements for the organ of the chorales: "Gelobet seist du, Jesu Christ," "*In dulci jubilo*," "Lobt Gott ihr Christen, allzugleich," and " Vom Himmel hoch da komm ich her."[323] Every one who is at all

---

[322] Anleit. zur Musik. Gel., p. 683.

[323] P. S. V., C. 5 (244), Appendix. Nos. 2 and 5 of this appendix are not under consideration here. The first, " Jesus, meine Zuversicht," is a three-part clavier piece with a very ornate subject. This of itself betrays its origin, namely, the little clavier-book planned for his second wife in 1722. It was undoubtedly intended, at the same time, for practice in the *fioriture*, which, it may be incidentally remarked, are not accurately reprinted in Griepenkerl's edition. No. 5, " Liebster Jesu, wir sind hier," is remarkable for being treated as an independent chorale for two manuals. With reference to No. 4, the same melody will be given in the Musical Supplement to Vol. III. of this work.

familiar with the type proper to the organ chorale, sees that
these movements are not of that type.   They all carry on the
melody line by line in broad harmonies, observe the fermatas
as they occur, and introduce passages between the lines, with
individual exceptions, which do not, however, contradict
their fundamental character.   The purpose is evident of
leaving the separate members of the melody in clear relief.
The endeavour to transfer the chorale as a homogeneous
composition to the province of pure music is thrust into the
background, though this is the proper function of the organ
chorale.   Add to this the disconnected character of the
structure, which is in several parts, and in which sometimes
four, sometimes five or more, notes are employed to produce
a really impressive combination of sound, without any particular care being given to the progression of the individual
parts.

The plainest evidence lies, however, in the passages which
have no intrinsic connection with the harmonic structure,
and which were what was then regarded as an interlude.[324]
There can be no doubt that we have here full proof of
the way in which Bach accompanied congregational singing
and chose that his pupils should accompany, since he must
have given them these movements with that view.   If we only
compare them with the organ subject—mentioned previously
to illustrate his custom at Arnstadt [325]—on " Wer nur den
Lieben Gott lässt walten," we shall observe that the upper
part is almost devoid of ornament, that it always goes on
calmly and grandly in its own way, and is only once concealed for a moment by a part rising over it (in "Lobt Gott,
ihr Christen," bars 6 and 7).   The interludes have no independent existence, either of melody or otherwise ; they
are merely ornamental passages.   But within these limits,
which he established out of pious consideration for the uses
of congregational singing, he displays his artistic and
creative genius with wonderful freedom and breadth.   By
these grand harmonies, these glorious bursts of tone, this
bold progression of the parts, he infused a semblance of

---

[324] Adlung, Loc. cit.   [325] *Ante*, p. 313.

poetic exaltation into the simple hymn sung by the people ; and by his deep consciousness of its dramatic significance he lent something of that tendency towards individualisation which is peculiar to Protestantism as opposed to the Romish Church. In the second line of " Lobt Gott, ihr Christen allzugleich "—" Oh praise the Lord with one consent,"—at the words, " To-day His gates are opened wide," one part rises above the melody and soars triumphantly heavenwards. In the harmonising of the melody, " Vom Himmel hoch da komm ich her "—" From highest heaven behold I come,"— the rising and falling passages in semiquavers give a mystical image of the angelic hosts soaring to and from heaven.[326] And even in their more general aspect the character of their purpose in the church service is plainly stamped on these choral settings. Singularly enough they are all Christmas hymns.

The hymn, " *In dulci jubilo*," displays the most genius and grandeur, and in this form it may perhaps have served as an accompaniment to the last strophe. The first lines are brought out in majestic five-part harmony below the notes of the melody. But from the third line the flood of ornate passages which is poured in among these can no longer be restrained; it spreads out under cover of the upper part, becomes visible during the pauses between the sections, sometimes makes its way to the highest part, over-spreading the melody for a little space ; then hurried on into triplets—it surges from the depths with added force, and returns to calm only on the last line but one, where the master restores the peace that ruled at the beginning, and builds up at last a seven-part harmony on the tonic pedal, which is held through several bars. As we contemplate such a piece as this, some dim idea steals over us of the form it must have assumed under Bach's fingers, when, wrapt in the ecstasy of religious inspiration, he called up visions of celestial palaces, appearing and vanishing in an

---

[326] The intention is unmistakable, particularly when we compare it with the organ chorale "Vom Himmel kam der Engel Schaar," in the Little Organ Book.

instant, and golden cloud-castles—the sublime and visionary birthplace of those sacred voices and pious melodies.

Many of these chorale accompaniments may have borne some outward resemblance to the real organ chorale. But a quite distinct principle of structure governed the two forms and must always be ultimately discernible; in the mere accompaniment the centre of gravity, as it were, lay outside the instrument; in the true organ chorale, on the other hand, it lay within it, even though it might claim the co-operation of extra-musical factors. In the organ chorale the melody, as it is played, is the focus from which everything radiates; in the accompaniment it is only one member of the harmonic structure which must throw a halo round the congregational song, and to which, consequently, the composer must direct his chief interest. Hence there can be no doubt that another composition, derived from the same source as those above mentioned, "Liebster Jesu, wir sind hier," is no more than a chorale accompaniment, though the interludes are altogether wanting.[327] The harmonies are so heavy and broad that the counterbalance of a massive unison of voices is indispensable to give a proportionate effect. And, if we still hesitate to decide, we have only to compare with it another organ study on the Te Deum, in which the length alone, 258 bars, at once must exclude all idea of its being an independent organ piece.[328] At any rate it must have been written down in order to give greater value and charm to the repetition of the melody by its carefully considered variety of harmony. Its character agrees perfectly with that of the first chorale setting; and in order to be amply convinced of the difference between this and an organ chorale, we need only compare it with any melody treated contrapuntally throughout that we may choose out of the Little Organ-Book.

This work, the Orgelbüchlein, must serve as a starting

---

[327] P. S. V., C. 5 (244), App., No. 4. Possibly also the setting, from Krebs' collection, P. S. V., C. 5 (244), No. 36, though in this case it is difficult to recognise the special purpose of the piece. The simple chorale which follows this I do not regard as Bach's.

[328] P. S. V. C. 6 (245), No. 26.

point for forming an estimate of Bach's labours as a composer of organ chorales while at Weimar.   It is a collection
of forty-five arrangements, planned by him for beginners in
organ-playing, and in the first instance for his eldest son,
Wilhelm Friedemann, to be a manual of good models in the
arrangement and playing of chorales.[329]   Whether he ever
had thought of publishing it is unknown, but it is certain
that he never completed the work as he intended.   Most of
the leaves and pages of the Little Organ-Book remain blank,
and only bear on the upper stave the beginning of the hymn
of which he intended that the page should contain the
arrangement.   Its modest aspect, and its being destined in
the first instance for a lesson-book, lead us hardly to suspect
the importance of the contents.   But the narrower the circle
in which Bach had to turn, the deeper he went ; and that he
loved to devote himself to young artists, from whom he might
expect a loving insight into his deepest purposes, is shown by
two of his most important clavier works : the Inventionen and
the Wohltemperirte Clavier.   Ziegler describes the tendency of Bach's teaching as being " to set organ chorales,
not merely superficially, but according to the emotion expressed by the words."   In taking this view Bach had
entered into Pachelbel's inheritance ; but he had succeeded
equally well in availing himself of the works in this department of other illustrious artists, more particularly Buxtehude.

---

[329] The whole title, as it stands in the autograph copy in the Royal Library
at Berlin, is as follows : " Orgel-Büchlein | Worinne einem anfahenden Organ-
isten | Anleitung gegeben wird, auff allerhand | Arth einem *Choral* durchzufüh-
ren, an- | bey auch sich im *Pedal studio* zu *habi-* | *litiren*, indem in solchen
darinne | befindlichen *Choralen* das *Pedal* | gantz *obligat* tractiret wird. | Dem
Höchsten Gott allein zu Ehren, | Dem Nechsten, draus sich zu belehren.
*Autore | Ioanne Sebast. Bach | p. t. Capellæ Magistro | S. P. R. Anhal-
tini- | Cotheniensis*" (" A Little Organ-Book, in which it is given to the
beginning organist to perform chorales in every kind of way, and to perfect
himself in the study of the pedal, inasmuch as in the chorales to be found in it
the pedal is treated as quite obbligato.   Inscribed in honour of the Lord Most
High, And that my neighbour may be taught thereby").   92 leaves, oblong
quarto, in boards, leather back and corners.   On the first page, upper right-hand
corner, are these words : "*ex collectione G. Pölchau.*"   P. S. V., C. 5 (244 ,
Sec. 1.   Compare also Griepenkerl's Preface.   B. G. XXV., 2.   Sec., App. A.,
No. 32.

He has profited most from Pachelbel on the ideal side, from Buxtehude on that of form; and now, standing on a commanding eminence, he addressed himself with all the originality and force of his genius to the elaboration of this particular kind of music. His power of inventing combinations is inexhaustible, his ingenuity in working out dramatic sentiments by instrumental means is marvellous, refining them to the utmost tenderness and deepening them almost to infinitude.

In the Little Organ-Book he prescribed to himself certain limits by its instructive purpose, and though it was intended that a " beginning " organist should find the opportunity for performing a chorale " in every kind of way," still the multiplicity here contemplated is to be understood as referring to details rather than to general treatment. Not one of these chorales has that grand form in which each line of the chorale is introduced by a preparatory interlude, and which we have attributed emphatically to Pachelbel. In all, with a single exception, the melody is contrapuntally treated in a continuous flow, and this is even done—with three exceptions again—without an attempt at any striking colouring of the melody. The counterpoint runs on, evolved throughout from one motive, the golden kernel of the chorale tune entangled in its silver tissue. The consistent adherence to this principle is an advance on Bach's part on the practice of his predecessors, and it always rouses our sense of something great and homogeneous. At the same time the counterpoint is in every case full of such vast musical significance that it immediately opens to us a realm of feeling of its own—a realm of feeling which, it is true, was pre-existent in the melody itself, so that it is as though a veil were suddenly lifted, and we looked into the mysterious depths behind. What tender melancholy lurks in the chorale " Alle Menschen müssen sterben "—" All mankind alike must die,"—what an indescribable expression, for instance, arises in the last bar from the false relation between c sharp and c', and the almost imperceptible ornamentation of the melody! It would be perversity to insist on always finding in such features the representation of certain *poetical* images, line for line; it is the general *musical* idea that Bach endeavours to enhance and elaborate by these means.[330] The Christmas melody " Der Tag der ist so freudenreich "—" On this most joyful day of days,"—is beautified by a joyful soaring rhythm; a fresh vitality as of the rising sun flows with constantly increasing power through all three stanzas of the old Easter hymn " Christ is erstanden "—" Jesus is risen,"—and fervent longing is marked in every line of the exquisite labyrinth of music in which the master has involved one of his favourite melodies, "Jesu, meine Freude "—"O Jesu, joy of joys."

Though the motives of the counterpoint are for the most part independently devised, in three of these chorales they are evolved out of the first line of the tune, and in this way they have an inherent organic connection with the chorale itself. These three are: " Dies sind die heilgen zehn Gebot" —"These ten are God's most holy laws,"—" Helft mir Gott's Güte preisen"—"Help me to praise God's goodness,"— " Wenn wir in höchsten Nothen sein "—"'Tis when we are in direst need." In the two last the counterpoint is confined to the four first notes, which are then either set out afresh and independently, or are further developed as episodes or by inversion. Bach is particularly fond of treating the tune in canon, a favourite exercise of skill in which his Weimar contemporary, Walther, was often his competitor. No less than nine of the melodies are thus treated, four of them in canon on the fifth or twelfth, without the strictness of the rest of the counterpoint being in any degree relaxed. And it is in these very pieces that the most powerful general effect goes hand in hand with the most learned harmonic art. For instance, there is a piece of sixteen bars on "Christe du Lamm Gottes"; in the three first bars the three-part counterpoint is given out, then the tenor brings in the melody, the soprano follows a bar later on the fifth, and then begins a fabric—a chain—of peculiar and melancholy

---

[330] In these chorales the fermatas only indicate the end of the lines, and not a real pause. This is quite clear from the canonic treatment, where no pause is possible.

harmonies. At first their strangeness strikes us, perhaps even repels us, but by repeated hearing they grow upon us more and more, and we end by finding them unforgettable, so profound and so truly musical is the interpretation they engraft on to the chorale.

The same canon treatment is applied to the Passion-chorale, "O Lamm Gottes, unschuldig." The expression is here less stern and dry; the anguish, compressed into one cry of need, presently ceases, and the music grows soft and mild just as the words of the hymn also enter more profoundly into the subject. The parts are but four; the swinging passages given to the contrapuntal parts are an anticipation of the accompaniment to the chorale for chorus which closes the first portion of the "Passion according to St. Matthew."

In the arrangement of "Hilf, Gott, dass mirs gelinge"— "Help, Lord, that I may conquer,"—we have again a canon on the fifth carried on by the soprano and alto. Meanwhile the left hand, on the second manual, keeps up an incessant stream of triplets of semiquavers, which sometimes lead below the canon, sometimes mix in with it, and sometimes rise high above it; and here it is very evident that Bach understood how to combine the characteristics of the northern school with the achievements of Pachelbel. It is also very instructive to compare with it Walther's arrangement, which in the same way works out a canon on the fifth, but, as we have seen, in such a way that we were forced to criticise his want of taste. While Bach imitates the melody in notes of the same value, but at an interval of half a bar later he forces the imitating part into accord with the upper part, and yet makes them quite independent of each other. Only an outline of the melody falls upon our consciousness—a silhouette, like the shadow thrown behind a solid body.

In five arrangements Bach has restricted himself to the simple canon on the octave, and in every instance he has given it to the upper manual part and to the pedal. This not unfrequently goes up above the manual bass part, an effect of tone of which Buxtehude and his pupils were also very fond; for instance, in "Gottes Sohn ist kommen" and "*In dulci jubilo*" the pedal part is carried up to *f'* or even *f'* sharp, whence we may infer that Bach must have used the four-feet cornet stop on the pedals which the Weimar castle chapel organ possessed, for a pedal of so great a natural compass could at that time hardly have existed anywhere. Once, in the chorale "Herr Jesu Christ, dich zu uns wend," we find traces of Böhm's influence; his treatment of this chorale has already been analysed (see *ante*, p. 207). Here the bass in canon carries on the melody in diminution as an episode. The other peculiarities of this chorale, however, are not to be referred to the example of the Lüneberg master, but to the influence of the chaconne; in two places a definite bass theme re-enters after short pauses.

A further step towards perfecting this form was taken by Bach when he made the contrapuntal elements in his music a means of reflecting certain emotional aspects of the words. Pachelbel had not attempted this; he lacked the fervid feeling which would have enabled him thus to enter into his subject. And it is *entering into it*, and not a mere depicting of it. For, once more be it said, in every vital movement of the world external to us we behold the image of a movement within us; and every such image must react on us to produce the corresponding emotion in that inner world of feeling. Bach's treatment, then, is simply a deeper penetration into the emotional purport of the poem. "Ach wie flüchtig, ach wie nichtig ist der Menschen Leben!" wrote Michael Franck; and Bach accompanies the melody with restless, gliding semiquavers, hurrying by like misty ghosts. "From heaven came down the angelic host," Luther begins in his well-known Christmas hymn, and Bach's music rushes down and up again like the descending and ascending messengers of heaven (worked out in the left hand, followed by the pedal in double augmentation). "Through Adam's fall the human race has lost its grace by nature" is the first line of a hymn on the atonement; and the pedal indicates the fall of man by an episode in leaps of sevenths. Let us not blame this as being a mere trivial illustration of the first line, for the image it contains of a fall from a condition of innocence to the state of sin governs the whole poem; it was only such images as these that Bach was ever wont to set in music. This is proved, for instance, by the setting of the death-bed hymn, "Herr Gott, nun schleuss den Himmel auf"—"Lord, open now the gates of heaven,"—in which the crabbed counterpoint continues to puzzle us until, half-way through the first verse, we come to the lines, "Hab gnug gelitten Müh und gestritten"—"I have encountered trouble and sorrow,"—and then the meaning is shown to be an image of the turmoil and weariness of the life of man; or consider the organ chorale ·"Da Jesus an dem Kreuze stund"—"When Jesus hung upon the cross,"—the verses are a paraphrase of the seven words spoken from the cross. The fact of His hanging on it is represented by the heavy, syncopated notes—an evidence of a wonderfully true æsthetic feeling, for that enforced quietude of direst anguish was no real calm.

It is, comparatively speaking, very seldom that Bach gives colour to the melody—the Little Organ-Book offers but three examples—but where he does he rises far above his predecessors, even in their finest works, by the culmination of subjects and the depth and boldness of his harmonies. In the chorale, "Das alte Jahr vergangen ist"—"The fleeting year has passed away,"—the gloom and solemnity of the words and air are intensified to the utmost by the chromatic counterpoint; "O Mensch, bewein dein Sünde gross"—"Oh man, thy heavy sin lament,"—has a passage full·of imagination and powerful feeling; the composer was inspired by the miracle of Christ's advent upon earth.

Once we even come upon a free handling of the chorale in the manner of Böhm and the northern composers; from its brilliant executive requirements this piece hardly seems to belong to the collection, and it undoubtedly is of an earlier date; this is the chorale, "In dir ist Freude"—"In Thee is gladness."

Turning now from the small but comprehensive form of the compositions in the Little Organ-Book, we will consider some larger works. So much material here lies before us

that a subdivision into groups will be necessary. As regards
the greater or lesser merits of his compositions Bach
himself has indicated a division; for when at Leipzig he
wrote out with his own hand a selection of the best organ
chorales of his earlier time, and took that opportunity of
working them up again where he thought it necessary; I shall
add to these a few others of equal importance that have come
to us from other sources. Besides these there is a rich mine
in the other chorales, which will serve in the first place to
enable us to get a general idea of the world of form in which
Bach's genius moved, and though we cannot venture to
derive from them a definite chronological arrangement of
the chorales, it may give us the opportunity of determining,
at least in a general way, the limit between his earlier and
his later work.

The earliest chorale arrangements we have had occasion
to study were two series of variations (*ante*, p. 211). To
these we may now add a third in " Sei gegrüsset, Jesu
gütig "—" Hail, O Jesu, gracious Saviour,"—in eleven Partitas. It can at once be detected that these are of different periods; the four first and the seventh resemble
those earliest works, not merely in being restricted to the
manual, but in their whole style and character, particularly
in their resemblance to Böhm; and they show the true
variation type by the melody being completely or partially
absorbed by the ornamental figures, and (in the first) by
its being extended by episodes. Numbers 5, 6, 9, 10, and
11, on the other hand, are regular organ chorales, and
with one exception have an obbligato pedal; their form is
the same as that which predominates throughout the Little
Organ-Book; the tenth variation only, with its fully harmonised interludes—which serve as a rich and prolonged introduction to each line—reminds us of Buxtehude's manner;
we shall presently have to speak more fully of the signs
of this manner in Bach's works of the Weimar period.
Number 8 stands alone, somewhat superior to the first
group, but inferior to the second. The simple chorale
which opens the series has not the awkward clavier style
of harmony shown in the earlier partitas, but is a model of

four-part writing. We are soon brought to the conclusion that Bach worked at this arrangement at three different times; its first state may have been contemporaneous with the two other chorales, and may even have resembled them in the beginning chorale. Later he would have added the beautiful four-part setting, have revised the first variation especially—for this, when compared with the corresponding portion of the other series, is far more regular in style though identical in design—and have concluded with the fourth variation. Subsequently he must have written the whole second group, have mixed up two older variations to fill the seventh and eighth places, revising the eighth, however, and probably supplementing it with the short pedal notes. It is thus that the whole must have grown up —a composition in which we find a remarkable mixture of mature work with what was originally immature and influenced more or less by other minds.[331]

The most primitive form of organ chorale, namely, contrapuntal writing, without any fixed subject or episodic interludes, occurs in only two cases; and in both a few introductory bars begin with an imitation on the first line. The source whence we derive them to a certain extent betrays their early origin; but, simple as they are, they contain much beautiful harmony.[332]

A number of examples are before us in which Pachelbel's form is followed, from the closest adherence to it and through every stage of independent development up to its highest ideal. An arrangement, "Durch Adams Fall ist ganz verderbt"[333] bears the unmistakable stamp of youth; every line is carefully preceded by a fugal interlude, but the melody is not sufficiently prominent, and the counterpoint is naturally not episodical. An arrangement of "Gelobet seist du, Jesu

---

[331] P. S. V., C. 5 (244), Sec. II., 3. A certain degree of corroborative evidence as to the stages of writing and revising this work is to be found in the fact that in one of J. L. Krebs' books the four-part chorale is preserved with only the four first partitas.

[332] These are "Gottes Sohn ist kommen," P. S. V., C. 6 (245), No. 25, and "Vater unser im Himmelreich." Ibid., C. 7 (246), No. 53.

[333] P. S. V., C. 6 (245), No. 21.

Christ"[334] is similar in form, but in this the prominence given to the melody answers to the requirements of the ideal.

An arrangement of "Vom Himmel hoch" is of considerable length; the melody lies in the pedal, but, considering that it occurs without augmentation, the interludes are much too long; and though it is very distinctly brought out by the shades of tone—the pedal ceasing in order to exhibit it more clearly—still the idea is not sufficiently worked out. The *cantus firmus* in "Valet will ich dir geben" is given to the pedal without augmentation, but the interludes are of moderate extent, and the counterpoint is interwoven and blended with delightful grace. Walther loved this piece, and copied it several times; and the composer himself liked it so well that he revised and polished it at a subsequent period.[335]

Pachelbel gave his own ideal the fullest expression when he prefaced a chorale, treated with brilliant counterpoint, by a fugue constructed on the first line of it. Bach seized upon this form, wrote a fugue on the two first lines of "Allein Gott in der Höh," one after the other, and then used them to crown the whole at the close as a *cantus firmus* in the pedal.[336] And, as if this were a mere fragmentary illustration of the principle, he has left us a model of it in a grand arrangement of the Magnificat,[337] which begins with a fugue of ninety-seven bars for the manual, a bold and ambitious structure, below which lie the ponderous foundation-stones of the *cantus firmus*, with its stately tones. Simple chorale fugues, on the other hand, we scarcely ever meet with; in this he followed the example of Buxtehude, who, when he wanted to write a fugue, preferred to invent his own theme. However, Bach has once used "Vom Himmel hoch" in this way, perhaps only because he wished to introduce the two middle lines in diminution as the answering themes; at any rate the form has been essentially altered by this process.[338]

It was inherent in Bach's nature as an artist that the

---

[334] P. S. V., C. 6 (245), No. 23.

[335] P. S. V., C. 7 (246), No. 50, in its revised form. The original form is given in the same volume as a variorum copy.

[336] P. S. V., C. 6 (245), No. 11.   [337] P. S. V., C. 7 (246), No. 41.

[338] P. S. V., C. 7 (246), No. 54.

method of counterpoint hitherto in use—without distinct motives in each part—could soon no longer satisfy him, for it was always his aim to give organic vitality to every part of his material. Just as in the Little Organ-Book each of the parts which accompanied the chorale was derived from a more or less plainly revealed germ, so it was now in the form he borrowed from Pachelbel. This seemed difficult, since this form demands the insertion of interludes, each of which should be formed of the material of the line following it ; but Bach seems to have hit at once on the right methods, without much search. At one time he thought out certain figured subjects of so pliable a nature that it was easy in each to touch the main points of the fundamental subject. Another time he brought in, simultaneously with the ornate episode, the thematic preparation for the *cantus firmus*, so that both were firmly united. We can perceive from several works how he grew more and more skilled in the employment of this device. A *fantasia*, so called, on "Christ lag in Todesbanden" still clings to the old method, but each of the two sections of the time is introduced by a prelude formed on a single motif from their first lines, and this motif is so constructed as to be equally available for counterpoint in four ways.[339] The newer method, however, reigns supreme in an arrangement of "Ich dich hab ich gehoffet, Herr,"[340] only that in this case the ornamental figures are too comprehensive, involving even the *cantus firmus*, which is not brought out by any other means; besides this, the impetus fails at the end of each line, and comes to a standstill, so that the piece falls into so many fragments. The close alone is perfectly satisfactory; the vivacity of the counterpoint is suitably increased, and, after the *cantus firmus* has spoken its last word in the upper part, the pedal once more takes hold of the simple phrase of melody, while the upper parts carry on a very happy accompaniment. "All's well that ends well."

A setting in three parts, for the manuals only, stands out in contrast to this by its evident fulfilment of the composer's

---

[339] P. S. V., C. 6 (245), No. 16.
[340] P. S. V., C. 6 (245), No. 34. Incorrectly called a *Fughetta*

intention; it is on "Allein Gott in der Höh"; in this initial subject—

we not only hear at once the melody of the first line, but each succeeding one is more or less distinctly reproduced, and the substance of all the counterpoint is also contained in it, though it unceasingly renews itself by inversions, extensions, and transformations.[341] The *cantus firmus* goes on steadily above it in half-bar notes.

Sometimes a chorale melody was so constructed in its separate sections that the episode derived from its first line served for all with some slight alterations: for instance, "Ach Gott und Herr," in which this motive—

can be made to answer almost every purpose, as Bach has proved by doing it.[342]

With regard to Buxtehude's works and those of his school, more use could be made of their subtle effects of tone and ingenious devices than of the type as a whole. Still, when in Weimar, Bach not unfrequently trod in Buxtehude's steps in writing small organ chorales, though no doubt he always produced something quite different to anything that master could have created, still the starting-point is plainly recognisable. In later years he altogether quitted this path, into which he had probably been tempted by some external cause. The only example we need mention at present is an arrangement of Clausnitzer's hymn "Wir glauben all an einen Gott."[343] The characteristics of Buxtehude's form were purely musical—an elegant ornamentation of the melody, and delightful additions as to harmony and tone; for the latter he constantly used two manuals, to one of which the melody was given; he also was fond of using the double pedal, and the whole school followed him in this. The more

---

341 P. S. V., C. 6 (245), No. 4.   342 P. S. V., C. 6 (245), No. 1.
343 P. S. V., C. 7 (246), No. 62.

negative characters were his indifference to the due independence of the counterpoint, to giving any prominence to
the *cantus firmus* but that derived from quality of tone, and
to any regular plan in writing interludes, in which the succeeding line was sometimes used, but sometimes not. All
these peculiarities are recognisable in Bach's chorale, but he
could not help compensating as far as possible for the
defects. The first line of melody is given complete to the
tenor, and then, before the entrance of the *cantus firmus*,
there are four bars more of free prelude; the second line
comes in without an introductory interlude, while the first
line of the second section, on the other hand, is fugally
treated with an accompaniment in several parts; the last,
again, has a simple one. The *cantus* is brought out in
notes of the same value on the manual, without any particular ornamentation, but with an unmistakable Buxtehude
coda of rapid passages at the close. But the whole body of
counterpoint is far more coherent, held together not by mere
artistic imitation and episodic treatment, but by the unbroken unity of the movement, which is enlivened by the
free and melodious progression of the separate parts.
Bach has with good reason set aside Buxtehude's fugal
additions, which come to nothing and only hinder the flow,
and he has laid the greatest stress on what is most important to the piece, *i.e.*, the contrast of tones, colour, and
richness of harmony. To this end he has used a double
pedal part throughout the piece, and this gives rise to the
most interesting combinations with the two-part progress
of the acompanying manuals. With an effective arrangement of stops the result must be enchanting.

Knowing that Bach was thus striving after a higher and
new ideal, by the amalgamation of Pachelbel's form with
a contrapuntal treatment which should aim at episodical
treatment in each part, we might expect to find him endeavouring to make more of this last method—which might be
termed especially his own, even if he had not at once impressed on it the stamp of his genius—than he had given
proof of in the Little Organ-Book. The next obvious step
was to work out an original composition on independent

ideas, a piece which should present in music the purport of the chorale it treated, and at the same time receive enlightenment from the poetic sentiment of the chorale tune that was woven in with it. Bach had no hesitation in taking this step, and so again displaying the marvellous continuity and consistency of his development, and the inseparable oneness of his creative utterances in all the various departments of his art. Pachelbel had grasped the idea of the chorale in its relations to the Church as an instrumental work of art; Bach, in the new form, which I will henceforth term the chorale fantasia, expressed almost exclusively those feelings which filled him, personally, when he heard a chorale melody.

The next step in this road must have been either to abandon the *cantus firmus* and to write the beginning of the chorale at the head of the piece, simply to suggest its purport, or else to seek for some means of restoring the chorale to its prominent position without forfeiting the acquisitions made in the department of instrumental music. Bach chose the latter alternative. A direct outcome of this form are those most glorious chorales for chorus and orchestra in which the instruments work out their own structure of parts, while the hymn comes in in the chorus of voices, controlling everything by its high moral significance, and ruling in its own sphere. Bach went to the utmost limits of absorbed subjectivity in treating the organ chorale, but he never set foot in the quicksand beyond them. As a high-minded priest of his art, he diligently strove to impart and interpret to the outer world the divine visions revealed to him in deep solitude. As compared to the chorales for voices designed on this plan, the number of chorale *fantasias* dwindles to nothing. Of course we are not to think of the process of evolution as though Bach, after he had clearly conceived of the transition to the vocal through the instrumental form, had flung this last aside as worthless. On the contrary, even in his later years, he wrote organ chorales, not only in a general way, but especially of this type. For this form bore within it its own justification, like all others that have had their natural place in history, and could

penetrate certain depths of life which remained inaccessible
to all others, even to some which are æsthetically higher.
Thus in the development of art those forms which are
derived from each other always to a certain extent exclude
their parents, and the spirit that has struck all its vital
fibres into the old soil will not generally thrive in the new
one.   There are but a few geniuses, and those the elect, that
are comprehensive enough to effect such an evolution—to
follow out the new without quitting grasp of the old.

The fantasia in three parts on " Jesu, meine Freude "[344]
belongs to the earlier works in the style described above ; it
is a fugal movement on this theme—

with which the chorale is interwoven, in the upper, middle,
or lowest part, as the case may be.   This is very skilfully
managed—still in the first half of the tune only—while the
second section has independent variations in Böhm's manner,
and is thus weakened in effect.   There is also an arrangement of " Nun freut euch, lieben Christen g'mein," in which
a running subject in semiquavers is worked out into a
complete piece, while the *cantus firmus* is carried on by the
pedal in the tenor part.[345]

Finally there are those organ chorales collected by Bach
at a later period, in which we may recognise the very quint-
essence of all he elaborated in Weimar in this field of art.
In making a survey of all his works, to classify them according to their several types, two other works of a similar
character may here be mentioned.   These are two simple
chorales with episodical counterpoints ; indeed, the smaller
half of one of them, " Komm, Gott Schöpfer, heiliger
Geist,"[346] is also to be found in the Little Organ-Book.   The

---

[344] P. S. V., C. 6 (245), p. 29.   [345] P. S. V., C. 7 (246), No. 44.

[346] The shorter form of this chorale cannot be regarded as the original, for
the reason that the pedal has hardly anything to do in it, and so it does not correspond to the object of the Little Organ-Book.   The complete piece is written
out in the collection made by Bach's pupil Altnikol. P. S. V., C. 7 (246), No. 35,
with the abridgment as a variant.

melody is gone through twice—first in the upper part and in crotchets or dotted quavers, with counterpoint chiefly in quavers, and then in augmentation in the pedal with a grandiose effect, after which the accompaniment is spurred on to semiquavers.   The setting in reiteration has not here any relation, as it usually has, to the number of verses in the poem ; in the second instance, on the contrary, this is the case : " O Lamm Gottes, unschuldig." [347]   This sublime composition is of masterly construction.   The first time the *cantus firmus* is given to the upper part, the second time to the middle part, and the third time to the pedal, which up to that moment has been silent.   The counterpoint changes with every verse, and becomes more interesting at every change.   Before the close there is a break, the beginning of the line, " All Sünd hast du getragen "—" Thou hast borne all transgressions,"—being delayed by the introduction of a subject figurative of bearing sin, while the *cantus firmus* proceeds slowly in the lower part ; then, on the words, " Sonst müssten wir verzagen "—" Else must we quake and tremble,"—there is a wailing chromatic passage through four bars in 3-2 time, and the suspense of a half-close : " Gieb uns deinen Frieden, O Jesu "—"Give us thy peace, O Lord."   The mighty waves of sound roll on one after another up and down, not resting till long after the melody is ended, and only the last note of it lingers on, supporting the *agitato* sounds above it, and audible through them all.   It is indeed a marvel of profoundly religious art !

The arrangement of " Nun danket alle Gott " [348] is strictly on Pachelbel's pattern, and without a flaw to mar it, to the very last note.   The jubilant shout that rises to the very clouds, and which Bach alone could raise, is here wanting ; but in many places he has enhanced the beauty of the form by his tuneful counterpoint.

---

[347] P. S. V., C. 7 (246), No. 48, in its revised form ; the earlier form of which I am here speaking is also given among the variants.   But the deviations are unimportant so far as my present purpose is concerned.   The same holds good also with regard to the following chorales, where no special observation is added.

[348] P. S. V., C. 7 (246), No. 43.

Of the two arrangements of the communion hymn, "Jesus Christus, unser Heiland,"[349] the part of the manual betrays itself as a work which can only have been written, at latest, in the first years of Bach's residence at Weimar, by the pedal point which comes in at the close. It is a stroke of genius to have made the passage thrown in at bar 10—and which belongs, as an interlude, to the congregational hymn —reappear in the second half of the chorale as a new contrapuntal subject. The second arrangement is one of the grandest and profoundest creations of this most admirable master. Upon the leading idea of the first verse—

> Jesus Christus, unser Heiland,
> Der von uns den Zorn Gottes wandt,
> Durch das bitter Leiden sein
> Half er uns aus der Höllenpein—
>
> Jesus Christ, our Lord and Saviour,
> Who freed us from the wrath of God;
> By his death and anguish sore
> Redeemed us from the pains of hell—

he constructs three movements. The two first lines are full of solemn agitation, as though tinged with a memory of the Last Supper, and as yet unaffected by any special considerations. From this characteristic subject —

he develops the details of the accompaniment directly, and in inversions. On the third line we come upon chromatic semiquavers rushing past and against each other in a bold *agitato*, indicative of the "anguish sore" (compare bar 37). This contrapuntal motive on the line—

lifts us triumphantly out of this dejection, and culminates in a close full of dignified gravity. Here, as elsewhere, what is most worthy of note is the perfect adaptation of the con-

---

[349] P. S. V., C. 6 (245), No. 32.   The other arrangement, No. 31.

structive requirements of the musical composition to the
impulse roused by the purport of the words. Indeed, Bach
only yields to such an impulse when it can find a justification in the organic structure of the composition; hence,
when he does so, it is all the more impressive. It was impossible to him to mangle the work, as a whole, by introducing petty descriptive details; thus in the short chorales
of the Little Organ-Book we never find him going into the
meaning of each line separately. It was only when the
conditions of the case demanded an artistic treatment of
multiplicity in unity that he allowed his inventive faculty to
be guided by the poetical images, line by line. We find
these conditions here: a tide of sentiment flows through the
whole as strong as we can meet with anywhere. How profound is the impression produced each time, when, after the
entrance of the *cantus firmus*, the melody is repeated in the
upper part!

The chorale, "Von Gott will ich nicht lassen"—"From
God will I not wander,"—is permeated by fervent feeling
and unutterably deep and trustful devotion.[350] The *cantus
firmus* lies constantly in the pedal, and the parts wind around
and above it like a luxurious garland of amaranth. It is not
too much to say that this masterpiece is, in its way, quite
incomparable.

A second arrangement of the deathbed hymn, "Valet
will ich dir geben"—"Farewell I now am saying"—also
belongs here,[351] but how different in this case is the fundamental feeling! A sublime and soul-felt peace soars on
mighty pinions far above the bustle of the "false, deceitful
world"—a representation of the sentiment conveyed in the
words:—

> 'Tis good to dwell in heaven
> The goal of my desires.

Bach has also succeeded in combining the Pachelbel chorale
in a very ingenious manner with the independent organ trio.

---

[350] P. S. V., C. 7 (246), No. 56.
[351] P. S. V., C. 7 (246), No. 51. This is not in the MS. collection, but is undoubtedly genuine.

The older master had been wont to treat the first line fugally, and then to allow the whole melody to come in with brilliant counterpoint, so the younger one constructed a trio on a theme derived from the first phrase of the tune, developed this thoroughly to due proportions, and towards the end brought in the *cantus firmus* almost imperceptibly in the pedal. The melodies, " Allein Gott in der Höh " and " Herr Jesu Christ dich zu uns wend," have both experienced this mode of treatment.[352]

Bach assimilated Buxtehude's type of treatment, not merely for the sake of the opportunities it afforded for the display of a special kind of skill and of a selective feeling for qualities of tone—to both of which Bach attached greater importance at his Weimar period than he did later ; he evidently found a charm in the difficulty of making anything of this style of work which could satisfy his strict requirements. He did not here use any definite method, but proceeded in accordance with the characteristics of the individual melodies, and his own feelings at the moment. Hence these chorales are as unlike each other as possible, and from that very cause are peculiar to eccentricity. That which is nearest to the model form is " Komm, heiliger Geist, Herre Gott," though the lines are worked out with greater breadth, and the parts of the counterpoint are kept in stricter order.[353] But it is proved that the form was far from satisfying Bach by his never having made use of it a second time.

An arrangement of "Allein Gott in der Höh," is of a more original and hybrid form ; on the one hand we have broad and careful interludes in imitation with episodical counterpoint, and on the other the *cantus firmus* in the tenor part in a manual by itself, richly adorned and with the phrases somewhat extended—a tropical luxuriance of foliage with many-

---

[352] P. S. V., C. 6 (245), Nos. 7 and 27. Two variants exist of the latter, but the deviations in one are unimportant, while the other is shorter by more than half, and hardly consists of more than a two-part counterpoint to the air, the subject being derived from the first line. The type is therefore altogether different; compare what is said (*below*, p. 618) concerning "Nun komm der Heiden Heiland."

[353] P. S. V., C. 7 (246), No. 37.

coloured blossoms. The art of combining different qualities of tone is brought to a remarkable pitch, and yet is controlled throughout by a healthy taste. Yet another arrangement of this favourite melody resembles this one in nothing but its extreme complication.[354] It has all the showy colouring of its class, and is divided into separate classes of tone. Besides this, it is arranged as follows : All that stands out in contrast to the melody grows out of a theme derived from the first line of the tune—

and the passage, moving downwards in three intervals of thirds, is again made use of as a motive; thus it comes very near to the chorale fantasia, that ultimate issue of Bach's type of organ chorale. But, as far as regards fulness of tone and harmony, the parts are always kept full throughout, in accordance with the model on which it is founded. Finally, and to mark the beginning of the second section, the first line of this portion comes in, as preparatory, on the pedal. The result is the production of a triumphant and masterly creation, but also of a musical composition which is quite unique.

Equally remarkable, and to the utmost extent in the spirit of Buxtehude, both in form and feeling, and in the words and music alike, is " An Wasserflüssen Babylon." The melody is given to the tenor, and the compact body of contrapuntal parts works on incessantly on the two first lines. Among many subtly conceived embellishments the first line is very remarkable—

for it shows us how much even these means could contribute to determining the sentiment of the piece. I doubt whether this piece can have been written later than 1712. Bach subsequently remodelled it, skilfully adding a fourth part to the accompaniment by a constant use of the double pedal, in

---

[354] P. S. V., C. 6 (245), No. 9. The first is No. 8.

consequence of which the *cantus firmus* lay in the upper part. The piece in this form has acquired a resemblance to the arrangement spoken of above, of " Wir glauben all." An occurrence in Bach's life can be very naturally supposed to be connected with this revision, his journey, namely, to Hamburg, where his composition on the hymn " An Wasser-flüssen Babylon " won high praise from the venerable Reinken. The inference is obvious that he was desirous of meeting this master on his own ground ; he was now nearly a century old, and could have but small sympathy with the new roads struck out by Bach ; his views indeed were essentially those of Buxtehude, and for this reason Bach would have remodelled his earlier work on a basis which would be particularly intelligible to Reinken, developing the combination of different tones and the use of the pedal.[355]

Similar again in general design, but just as unique in other respects, is the setting of " Schmücke dich, o liebe Seele." The accompaniment in three parts consists of figures on the first line of the first section, and afterwards on the first line of the second section, and forms a cycle by returning at the close to the passages introduced at the beginning ; the melody is carried on with many expressive embellishments of the upper part. The strange and mysterious charm of this piece has long occupied the minds of the best students of Bach's work ; a step at least towards its explanation becomes possible from an investigation of the history of its origin. The chief mystery of course must still remain hidden in the creative depths of Bach's genius, which regarded the external characteristics of musical form merely as touches of light and colour by which he might bring before us more vividly a mental image, though solemn and subdued, of heavenly ecstasy. By comparing this chorale with that previously discussed, " Jesus Christus, unser Heiland," we shall imme-

---

[355] P. S. V., C. 6 (245), No. 12. The first form is to be found as a variant in the Appendix ; the arrangement with double pedal is 12 A, and the still later arrangement of the first form with a single pedal part, which was probably a second revision at the time of its insertion in the large MS. volume, is 12 B of the same volume.

diately become conscious of the widely different spheres of feeling in which they dwell.[356]

Bach has left us three arrangements of the old Advent chorale, "Nun komm, der Heiden Heiland," which were evidently thought out as a connected whole.[357] The first is in the Buxtehude form, but this time, setting aside the little imitative introduction, it has hardly any thematic accompaniment, also it extends the highly adorned melody beyond the strict limits of its phrases, and is of remarkable beauty of form. The second appears as a trio, the counterpoint being carried out by a manual and the pedal bass, the melody in the treble on another manual; or in reverse order, the accompaniment being given to the manuals and the *cantus firmus* to the bass. The first line provides the thematic material for the whole, with added figures in semiquavers, and the parts follow each other in canon. A piece is thus evolved which needs nothing but a freely invented theme to take it out of the class of chorales. Such compositions form a bridge over the gap that divides Pachelbel's chorales from the chorale fantasia; and yet they must not be regarded as amalgamating those with the independent organ trio, since the early entrance of the *cantus firmus* leaves no time for independent development. The composition now in question is almost unapproachable in the abruptness of its character and the startling recklessness of the effects of tone, especially in

---

[356] P. S. V., C. 7 (246), No. 49. The reader will here be glad to be reminded of Schumann's fine words concerning this chorale, when a composer almost of our own time was enabled to follow just such a flight as Sebastian Bach's. He says (Schriften, Vol. I., p. 219, first ed.) : " Then, soon after, you, Felix Meritis [Mendelssohn]—man of the noble heart and brow—played one of his chorale arrangements. The text was 'Schmücke dich, o meine Seele'; round the *cantus firmus* clung garlands of golden foliage, and a strain of beatitude was poured into it, for you yourself confessed to me that ' if all hope and faith were taken out of your life, this chorale alone would be enough to restore them to you.' But I was silent, and answered not. I went away, almost mechanically, into the churchyard, and felt a keen pang of regret that I could lay no flower on his urn."

[357] Walther indeed wrote them out in one of the Berlin autographs as one composition. P. S. V., C. 7 (246), Nos. 45, 46, 47. Walther gives the second with the *cantus firmus* in the pedal (Variant II.); hence it must have been left in this form also by Bach, which otherwise would be difficult to believe from bar 33.

the first form.   There are a few other works of the kind by
Bach in which the presentment of a spiritual meaning is
followed up with complete indifference to external effect.
But no purely artistic work can originate in this way, for
that which is beautiful to the senses is an indispensable
condition of form, though not the most important.   The ear
accommodates itself reluctantly and by slow degrees to this
sort of vague suggestion only after we have completely
identified it with the idea and plan of the composition.
Still, this feature could not be absent from the totality and
completeness of Bach's character as an artist; it was that
exaggerated idealism of a true German nature which, walking with its head in the clouds, takes no heed of the earthly
thorns that entangle its feet.

   In the third arrangement of this same chorale the fantasia
form comes prominently forward.   If we add to this powerful
work the even more powerful one on " Komm, heiliger Geist,
Herre Gott," we have completed the whole list of chorale
fantasias composed at this time.   This form was a favourite
one with Bach at a later period, and he expanded this last
work into one of considerable length—nay, we might say he
had never completed it till he did this, for in its first state
it works up only the first four lines of the chorale.[858]   With
regard to the general meaning, hardly anything remains to
be said, but that it is as majestic as the instrument whose
grandeur it was intended to display; the themes in both
cases are very animated and ornate, and present an imposing
contrast to the grandiose calmness of the *cantus firmus* on
the pedal.

   Here we finish our consideration of Bach's organ chorales,
though only indeed for the present.   The master continued
his labours in this department till the close of his life, and
the last and fairest blossoms of his genius have been preserved to us.   But we shall have no more new forms to deal
with; this province of his art he had now fully explored, and

---

   [858] P. S. V., C. 7 (246), No. 36.   The variants in the Appendix.   An old
written copy in the possession of Dr. Rust corresponds with that left by Krebs
in the smallest particular.

it could not be otherwise, for it was on his unbounded possession of it that his further development was based. In concluding this analysis of Bach's labours in organ chorale writing, we at the same time close the most important period of his life, which contains the key to all the others—the first ten years, namely, of his independent mastership. It was not in Bach's nature to contemplate the retrospect of what he had done, or he might have been satisfied with himself. He stood on a supreme eminence as an organ and clavier player, and had early reaped the fruits of his executive skill, which ripens sooner than the intellectual seed, to such an extent that he was known far and wide through central and northern Germany, and was universally famous as the victorious champion of German as opposed to foreign art. And what is more, by his unfaltering progress, his indefatigable utilisation of every element of art that came within his ken, his incessant cultivation of his own amazing gifts, he had produced a multitude of glorious works, differing in kind, it is true, but all bearing more or less relation to a common centre. German, Italian, and French instrumental music, by earlier and contemporary composers—for the organ, clavier, and violin, and of the most various types—old and new forms of the art, both sacred and secular—we have marked them all as they have come within reach of the great whirlpool of Bach's own organ music, seen them drawn into it only to be flung up again in renewed youth, and inspired with fresh vigour and vitality: a picture of many aspects, but withal consistent and complete.

APPENDIX (A, TO VOL. I.)

1 (p. 6). **Hans Bach the Elder.** The genealogy is here incorrect in many respects : the town piper is said to have lived in the tower of the castle of Grimmenstein ; Hans Bach to have lived there till the castle was destroyed, and then to have returned to Wechmar, where, meanwhile his father had died. But the castle of Grimmenstein had been ruined as early as 1567, and Hans Bach was certainly not then born. After this Gotha possessed no castle until the present castle of Friedenstein was constructed in 1646. But the town-hall was so grand and spacious that in 1640 it was made ready as a temporary residence for Duke Ernst the Pious (Beck, Geschichte der Stadt Gotha, p. 422). Veit Bach was still living some time after his son had settled in Wechmar.

2 (p. 9). **Hans Bach the Younger.** This is clear from the following facts : Johann Bach, who according to the register was married in 1635, is there called the *senior ;* on June 7 of the previous year our Hans, No. 3, had been married ; the *senior* is evidently, therefore, to distinguish them. If they had been only cousins, and a distinction had been needed, some other token would surely have been hit upon, while, as between brothers, it is perfectly natural, particularly when one was married so soon after the other. I attach no importance to this question, and only mention it for the father's sake.

3 (p. 10). **The Bach Genealogy.** It is evidently from a confusion with Hans Bach that the father is called a carpet-maker ; and when we find here again three musical sons, it casts a suspicion on the credibility of the statement, and gives it the air of a subsequent invention. With regard to what the genealogy afterwards says as to the further ramification of this branch, it is for the most part guess-work, which is the less valuable because the compiler knew nothing of the existence of the Bach family in Thuringia, reaching back far beyond Veit. The fact that among the Bachs of Bindersleben the tradition still exists that their ancestors were immigrants from Bohemia or Hungary, without their acknowledging any relationship with Seb. Bach, might dispose us for a moment to derive this line from Veit's second son. But the late and spurious character of this tradition—which certainly originated in a desire to connect the Molsdorf-Bindersleben line with the great Sebastian—is evident from the fact that it makes the first Bach settle at once at Molsdorf; and it is still clearer when we remember that its accuracy is very doubtful, even as regards Sebastian's forefathers.

4 (p. 10). **Jakob Bach.** These statements are principally based on a pedigree begun by Veit Bach, and which was in the possession of

Jakob Bach's great-grandson, Joh. Philipp Bach, of Meiningen ; a copy of it came into the hands of Fräulein Emmert, of Schweinfurt. All that the genealogy and its addenda say on the subject agrees with this pedigree, only by an oversight, the year of Jakob Bach's birth is given as that of his death. Gelbke's Kirchen und Schulenverfassung des Herzogthums Gotha, gives 1654 as the date of his birth. In Brückner's Kirchen- und Schulenstaat we find a notice that in 1631 Jakob Bach was installed as usher (Schuldiener) at Thal, near Ruhla, and according to a document of the Visitation of 1642 he is called Schoolmaster of Ruhla. The dates do not fit, but this may be a misprint.

5 (p. 84). **Motett by Christoph Bach.** The only MS. known to me is preserved in the Royal Library at Berlin. It is evidently transcribed from parts, and full of errors. From bar 116 onwards it has become perfect nonsense, from the copyist having overlooked a repeat mark in the alto, by which bars 106 to 119 should have been repeated, and then have gone on to the following passages. A beginning of a similar confusion is to be traced in the same place, in the bass part. In bar 131 the copyist has again overlooked a pause of two bars in the alto, and erroneously transcribed bars 125, 126, 127 a second time (128, 129, 130). The correction of some other inaccuracies is more obvious ; the text is wanting to the last bars. This motett has never been published.

6 (p. 94). **"Ich lasse dich Nicht."** The Royal Library at Berlin possesses this motett in an ancient MS., which, after repeated investigation, I feel assured is an autograph of Sebastian Bach's. The watermark, which I shall fully discuss in Note 27 to this volume, proves it to be of the Weimar period. The character of the writing is very similar to that of the Mühlhausen Rathswechsel Cantata (see p. 340) ; hence the MS. may date from about 1710. The name of the composer is not given, so it cannot be denied that the possibility that this motett is not a work of Joh. Christoph Bach, but of his nephew, Sebastian, has a certain foundation in external circumstances ; and the early period at which Sebastian must have composed it would account for all that seems strange in the peculiarities of style. It appears, too, that throughout the last century it was sung by the Thomasschule choir at Leipzig as a composition of Sebastian Bach. For Rochlitz, himself a chorist of the Thomasschule, and a singer of Bach's motetts, expresses himself as *first* convinced of its spuriousness by Philipp Emanuel's catalogue (see his Sammlung Vorzüglichen Gesangwerke, Vol. III., Part I., p. viii. of the preface), while in his book Für Freunde der Tonkunst, II., p. 144 (third edition), he still lets it pass as a composition of Seb. Bach. The cantor of St. Thomas, too, in 1802, T. G. Schicht, published the motett as a work by Sebastian (Leipzig: Breitkopf und Härtel) ; and in his own MS. copy, now in the Royal Library at Königsberg in Prussia (press-mark 13,583), he appended verses seven and eight of Hans Sachs' poem with a harmonised setting by Seb. Bach, which

is also preserved by L. Erk (Joh. S. Bach's Choralgesänge, I., 121). Still, due consideration must be given to the fact that Ph. Em. Bach seemed not to have acknowledged the motett as a work by his father, though in his catalogue, p. 85, he does not designate it as by Joh. Christoph, but only classes it among the compositions of his Bach ancestors. A final decision cannot indeed be arrived at unless an autograph of Sebastian Bach were to come to light in which he signs himself as the composer. It was first published as a work of Joh. Christoph, by Naue, Part III., p. 9, with a supplementary bass—afterwards by Bote and Bock, of Berlin; Breitkopf and Härtel, of Leipzig; and others.

7 (p. 141). **Friedrich Bach.** A most bewildering blunder has been perpetrated by Gerber in the Lexicon I., col. 491. He says: "The only musical genius living there was a drunken organist, who, when sober, could do as little as his fellow-citizens of the Bach family"; the last four words are misplaced. What Gerber manifestly intended to say was this: " A drunken organist of the Bach family, who when sober," &c. When it is said farther on that the scholars were forced to go to another church than that where Bach played, we need not infer that they abandoned the church of St. Blasius on account of his bad example. They probably had places assigned to them in the Marien-kirche.

8 (p. 174). **J. S. Bach's Mother.** There were at that time—as may be seen from the register for 1666, preserved in the archives of the town-council of Erfurt—no less than three Valentin Lämmerhirts in the city, who all had daughters named Elisabeth. But that it was this particular Elisabeth Lämmerhirt that Ambrosius married is proved by the documents, to be alluded to presently, referring to the "Lämmerhirt will case," from which we learn the name of her brother, Tobias. By this clue it is possible to find our way through the labyrinth of the parish register. Two of the three Lämmerhirts were furriers, and lived side by side in the Junkersande, one in the house known as " The Three Roses," the other as " Zur Jungfrawen "—" The Virgin,"—now No. 1284. But as Tobias Lämmerhirt subsequently had a house in the Breiten-strasse with the same name, "The Three Roses," and as it was customary when people changed their residence to transfer the name of the house, No. 1285, as has been said, is no doubt the house where Sebastian's mother was born. The genealogy speaks of Ambrosius Bach's father-in-law, and of the father of Hedwig Lämmerhirt, as " Raths-Verwandte" —the title given to persons related to a family of which a member had become a town-councillor; but this was premature. The first Lämmerhirt (Valentin also) who is to be found in the lists of the town-council occurs in 1658 and 1663—a younger relative, therefore, of the one now under discussion.

9 (p. 221). **Bach's Residence in Weimar.** A chronological difficulty arose here, for the genealogy and Mizler's Necrology—and,

following them, almost all the later biographies—date the move to
Arnstadt in 1704, while the deed of installation makes it 1703, and that
in so many places that any error of transcription is out of the question.
The error lies therefore in the first-named authorities; and there might
seem to be a doubt whether Bach's residence in Lüneburg should not be
shortened, and his move from thence ascribed to the year 1702, since a
slip of the memory seems more natural which could confound a "2"
with a "3" than one which should extend a few months to a year
and a quarter. But I was so happy as to find among the private papers
of the Grand Duke's court at Weimar a list of the whole band for the
year 1702, and Bach's name is not in it. Now it is certain that
Sebastian quitted Lüneburg about Easter, because there were no profits
from processional singing by the school choir during the summer half-
year. Thus the list could only be rejected as evidence under the
supposition that it was drawn up before Easter, which is very unlikely.
It is also to be observed that this seems to give a disproportionate
length to his residence in Weimar. The whole course of his development could not have tended to his holding such a position; he must
as soon as possible have looked about for a more suitable sphere
of labour, and it might be supposed that he was as likely to have had
the appointment of organist at Arnstadt—which at that time was held
by the incompetent Börner—in 1702 as in 1703. For these reasons,
and because the biographical records of Sebastian Bach in the genealogy
were not written down directly from his statements, and contain other
small oversights—the whole genealogy, indeed, not having been drawn
up under his supervision—in spite of its importance generally as the
oldest authority we possess, I must regard 1704 as an error. Since the
Necrology says the same, no doubt one at least of the hands employed
was the same in both. In 1703 Easter fell on April 8. Thus, in any
case Bach did not remain more than four months in Weimar.

10 (p. 227). **The Treibers' Operetta.** A copy of the text, printed
at Arnstadt in 1705, exists in the Ministerial Library at Sondershausen,
and was in great part reproduced by K. Th. Pabst in 1846 (in the
Gymnasial-Programm, Arnstadt). It may be inferred with certainty
that the elder Treiber (rector of the college) supervised the text at
any rate, since the operetta was performed by the Arnstadt Lyceum
scholars, and the names of the *dramatis personæ* would not have been
so ingeniously devised by any one not perfectly familiar with Latin
and Greek. Thus two drawers of beer are Modulius and Cantharinus;
a cooper's apprentice is Doliopulsantius; the brewer's wife, Eulalia;
a barmaid, Bibisempria. The music was probably written by the
son, or they may have worked at it together. In Arnstadt a legend
grew up that Bach was the composer, but, so far as I can see, without
any foundation but the circumstance that he was organist there at
the time. If it had only been considered how musical both the
Treibers were, and that the son was then staying in Arnstadt, such

a theory would have been impossible. It has even found its way into a novel by E. Marlitt. Bach, like all his family, had occasional impulses to satire and buffoonery, but he certainly would never have worked upon a text so devoid of all life and humour as this. Besides he was by no means always on the best terms with the pupils of the college.

11 (p. 231). "Denn du wirst meine Seele," Easter, 1704. The autograph score and the autograph parts (both in the Royal Library at Berlin) beyond a doubt owe their existence to the Leipzig period of Bach's career, as can be proved both by the paper and the writing; and they also bear unmistakable marks of having been written from an already complete copy. All those corrections and alterations of which Bach's autographs of the cantatas are generally so full are wholly wanting, as well as the letters "S. D. G.," which the master never omitted to sign at the end of a first score ("Soli Dei gloriæ"—"To the glory of God alone"), and as well as letters "J. J." ("Jova" or "Jesu Juva") at the beginning, excepting when making a copy or unimportant rearrangement. The fact that the score runs on without a break, and that the division into sections is not yet indicated, is still further evidence that this was a combination of two works. In this state it is much too lengthy to be performed all at once, under any conditions; and if this was the original form, Bach must have already intended to divide it. But then it would be quite incomprehensible how the divisions should be wanting in this score.

12 (p. 231). In 1748 Johann Sebastian Brunner, at that time cantor of the principal church at Weimar, composed the text and music of a whole cycle of cantatas, in which he partly worked up in an extraordinary manner the sacred verses of some of the older Weimar poets—weaving them together, turning them about, and then printing the result as his own composition. A copy exists in the grand ducal library at Weimar. Thus the cantata text by Salomo Franck, of the year 1716, to which Bach composed his splendid music, "Wachet, betet, seid bereit," was maltreated by him in this way, as may be seen at once by a comparison of the different versions; and a similar fate befel the verses used in the Easter cantata. It is certain that Brunner availed himself of none but Weimar prototypes, since one of the best sacred poets of the time, Salomo Franck, was at that time living and writing in Weimar, and, on the other hand, the demand for cantata verses was at that time very considerable, and Brunner was certainly not fastidious. Hence it follows that the text of Bach's Easter cantata was written in Weimar, and it must also have been within the first twelve years of the eighteenth century, for after that the new cantata form was elaborated there. But the hypothesis that Bach composed the work in question during his second residence in Weimar—that is to say, after 1708—is proved untenable when we compare it with the Mühlhausen "Rathswechsel" cantata and other works dating from that time. In those we

already see the hand of a master, in this only a highly gifted beginner. It only need be supposed that Bach became acquainted with the text during his first stay in Weimar. It is proved that poetical efforts of this kind were already produced there, since a collection of texts for cantatas had been published there by Georg Theodor Reineccius, at that time town cantor, under the title of " Wohlklingendes Lob Gottes," &c.—" Sweet-sounding Praise of God, from the Gospels appointed for Sundays, sung in the parish church of St. Peter and St. Paul, at Weimar, from the First Sunday after Trinity, of the year 1700, with pleasing *concertos*, to the honour of God and the awakening of the congregation." The form which prevails among these is precisely similar to that on which Bach chiefly based his cantata. This composition cannot have been brought out at Weimar, because Bach never spent an Easter there; but we cannot attribute it to the later Arnstadt period, since it is authentic that Bach quarrelled with his choir, took no more trouble about them, and performed none of his compositions with their aid. In itself, too, it is more probable that he should have made use of a text imported from another town at a time when its memory was fresh in his mind. Finally, the composition strikingly betrays the influence of the northern masters, which Sebastian must have retained from his residence in Lüneburg. Since, moreover, in Brunner's text the altered words for the duet are followed by the hymn in seven verses, this is a fresh confirmation of my hypothesis that it originally belonged to a cantata for the Second Sunday after Easter. The two texts were in the same collection, and Brunner took something from the second to eke out the first.

13 (p. 291). **Buxtehude's Abend-Music.** This MS., consisting of eighty-seven leaves, in upright folio, is in the town library at Lubeck. It contains twenty sacred pieces in German *tabulatur*, with an index, and is arranged with admirable neatness and precision. In some places we find a different and certainly more rapid and practised writing, and it is easy to conclude that this must be that of Buxtehude himself. He is only named as the author of Nos. 1, 3, 5, 7, 8, 9, and 12. It can, however, hardly be doubted that all twenty are by him. Wherever the name occurs, excepting to the twelfth, it is added by the second hand; and this has also been more or less busy in Nos. 2, 4, and 6, which have no com-poser's name. In No. 2, indeed, more than two folio pages are in this writing, which displays a steadiness and certainty which could only be the composer's. It would be vain to inquire how a third person could have chanced to interfere with a very competent copyist, and write out a whole section in the midst of a cantata in a different and not particularly good hand. But it is easy enough to imagine that Buxtehude may have been dissatisfied with the movement as it stood in the original copy, and, wishing to remodel it in the handsome folio, found it the simplest plan to write it out himself. Moreover, the un-acknowledged pieces are so perfectly of the same stamp and style as the

signed ones that, if Buxtehude were not their author, he must have had a second self who understood his business as well as he, or better. I have written out the first seven pieces in the modern notation, and tried them note for note. Nos. 1 to 9 and No. 12 are beyond a doubt Buxtehude's work, and so I believe the others to be, from both internal and external evidence. This grand folio copy was evidently made in honour of a highly esteemed master. Buxtehude himself supervised the first part, and probably died soon after. Even where his interference is visible it is but fitful. An instance of this occurs in a remark appended to the fifth movement, where the trumpet parts are written in D, as they are to sound. He has remarked: "N.B.: should be written in C." Now the trumpets have been employed from the beginning and written throughout in D. This note therefore ought to have been at the beginning of the cantata. Judging from this, we need not be surprised at the omission of the name and the irregular interpolations, least of all where we trace the work of the master's own hand. Authors were not so eager in asserting their rights then as they are now.

14 (p. 310). **A Cantata by Buxtehude.** We know from Moller's *Cimbria Litterata* that Buxtehude wrote a composition on the death of his father, " Fried- und Freudenreiche Hinfahrt des alten *Simeons*"; but we cannot assume that it is this one, on account of the addition " in zwey *Contrapuncten musical*isch abgesungen "—" to be sung in double counterpoint,"—which can only refer to a double arrangement, the hymn " Mit Fried und Freud ich fahr dahin." Walther (in the Lexicon, under "Buxtehude") has an obscure remark as to this composition, from which it is not possible even to make out whether the arrangement of the chorale was set for voices or for instruments. He also mentions it once in his MS. work on music.

15 (p. 324). **Froberger and Bach.** Any one who has the opportunity of studying Bach's composition can convince himself of the accuracy of these remarks by a comparison with Froberger's *Diverse Curiose e Rarissime Partite* (Moguntiæ, MDCXCV.), which are published in Commer's *Musica Sacra*, No. 45. The Royal Library at Berlin possesses a small MS. volume of Chaconnes and Canzones, bearing the signature " *Di J. S. Bach*." They certainly show no trace whatever of Bach's style; on the contrary the pieces bear the stamp of Froberger. It is of course possible that the copyist had before him a MS. which bore the name of Bach as its owner, or which may have been made by him, and so came to be erroneously regarded as his composition.

16 (p. 324). **Grand Toccata in C major.** This piece occurs in various old MSS. under very different titles. That of *Toccata*, given by W. Rust in the edition of the Bach-Gesellschaft, is at least so far historically justified that it was applied by Reinken to a work of the same form. The key is sometimes C major and sometimes E major; from certain pedal points in the first and middle movements C major seems to me to be the original one. On the organs of the time, which

were sometimes tuned so high as to be about a third higher than "chamber" pitch, the full chords in the lowest part would not have sounded so heavy as they would now.

17 (p. 380). **Pitch and Key.** The wind instruments alone naturally determine the compromise between the "chorale" and the "chamber" pitch. In the autograph score of the cantata "Tritt auf die Glaubensbahn," composed at Weimar in 1715, of which the key is E minor, the flutes and oboes are in G minor. The score of the cantata "Nach dir, Herr, verlanget mich," written in the early years of his residence at Weimar, has the bassoon in D minor, to the key of B minor. "Barmherziges Herze der ewigen Liebe," written in 1715, is in F sharp minor, and a trumpet part exists in autograph in G minor; since the natural pitch of the trumpet was already a whole tone higher than "chamber" pitch, we have here the difference of a minor third. The Easter cantata, "Der Himmel lacht, die Erde jubiliret," 1715, is in C major, the parts for the bassoons and oboes in E flat major. The Advent cantata for the same year, "Bereitet die Wege," has the oboes, contrary to Bach's usual custom, in the soprano clef; it was only necessary to substitute for this the violin (G) clef, and to strike out the three sharps in order to keep the same proportion. I think that these examples make the matter quite clear. If in other scores of the Weimar period the wind instruments are written in the true key, this proves nothing to the contrary, since it was doubtless for the sake of convenience in reading and uniformity. Bach wrote the wind parts in a score, in a key agreeing with the pitch of the organ only when he was prevented from writing the parts out himself, and would intrust the work of transposing to no one else. And he might also improvise a transposed version of the organ part in performance. Furthermore, by this evidence for the Easter cantata just named, a number of difficulties are cleared away (see B.-G., VII., Preface to Cantata 31) and a new criterion of some value is gained by which to test general chronological details.

It may be asked whether the two versions of the great organ composition in Buxtehude's style (P. S. V. C. 3 [vol. 242], No. 7; B.-G., XV., p. 276), which is found both in C major and E major, do not prove that the work was first written in C for the high-pitched organ at Weimar, and afterwards transposed a major third higher for an instrument of lower pitch. But we know nothing as to the pitch of the Arnstadt organ, and very weighty internal evidence goes to prove an earlier date of composition; and finally it is very remarkable that among all the rest of the Weimar organ compositions no one other is found in a similar transposition. I incline to believe that the transposing of the piece into E major was done in order to make it right for an exceptionally low organ, rather than that it was done to bring it from an exceptionally low key to a suitable average pitch. The new organ, which was built in the year 1756, was tuned to "chamber" pitch (Adlung, *Musica Mech.*

Organ. I, 282), which would perhaps not have been the case had not the inconvenience of a " cornet " pitch been long felt.

18 (p. 397). **Andreas Bach's MS. Volume.** An important aid in the chronological arrangement of Bach's organ and clavier compositions is supplied by the MS. volume of Andreas Bach so often mentioned, which contains, besides compositions by Kuhnau, Polaroli, Reinken, Buxtehude, Böhm, Pachelbel, Buttstedt, Ritter, W[itt], Pestel, Marchand, Telemann (Melante), Marais, J. C. F. Fischer, Küchenthal, and some anonymous pieces, fourteen by Sebastian Bach, namely: 1, Fugue in A major (P. S. I., C. 13 [vol. 216], No. 9) ; 2, Toccata in F sharp minor (P. S. I., C. 4 [vol. 210], No. 4); 3, Overture, &c., in F major (P. S. I., C. 13 [vol. 215], No. 4) ; 4, Passacaglio in C minor (P. S. V., C. 1 [vol. 240], No. 2) ; 5, Toccata in C minor (P. S. I., C. 4 [vol. 210], No. 5) ; 6, Toccata in G major (P. S. I., C. 13 [vol. 215], No. 3) ; 7, Fugue in G minor (P. S. V., C. 4 [vol. 243], No. 7) ; 8, Aria variata, in A minor (P. S. I., C. 13 [vol. 215], No. 2); 9, Fantasia in C major (P. S. V., C. 8 [vol. 247], No. 9) ; 10, Organ chorale, " Gott, durch deine Güte " (P. S. V., C. 6 [vol. 245], No. 25) ; 11, Fugue on a theme by Legrenzi (P. S. V., C. 4 [vol. 243], No. 6) ; 12, Fantasia in B minor (P. S. I., C. 13 [vol. 216], No. 7) ; 13, Fantasia with fugue in A minor (P. S. I., C. 4, No. 2) ; 14, Prelude in C minor (unpublished, pages 71*b* and 72*a* of the MS.). Andreas Bach, born in 1713, was the fifth son of Sebastian's eldest brother, but closer investigation reveals the fact that he cannot have been the original owner of this book, and consequently cannot have written or selected the pieces. His name and the date 1754 are written only on the last page, indistinctly, and evidently at a later period ; but what is decisive is that he was neither a pupil of Sebastian Bach's, nor in any special degree a player on the organ or clavier. His life lay in quite a different direction ; he lived at Ohrdruf till his twentieth year, and then, in 1733, entered a Gotha regiment of Dragoons as oboe-player, and followed it during a campaign on the Rhine ; he was then for five years steward to the Count von Gleichen, and subsequently, through his protection, obtained the post of organist to the church of the Holy Trinity at Ohrdruf; in 1744, on the death of his brother Bernhard, he held the same office in the church of St. Michael. This same Bernhard, on the contrary (born in 1700), had trained himself to considerable eminence as an organist and composer of sacred music, and between the years 1715 and 1717 he had been under the tuition of Sebastian Bach at Weimar. Of course he there did what all the other pupils did, wrote out a number of the best of his master's compositions, with others recommended by him, for his own use. Nothing can seem more obvious than that this book is the result of these labours, and that it should, at the death of Bernhard Bach, have passed into his brother's hands, with the office he had held. The fact that all the pieces by Sebastian Bach, with one exception, and many of the others are in the same even handwriting is an additional proof that it was all

written at the same time; and the fair, clear writing—which is somewhat
florid and cramped—may very well be that of a boy of sixteen or seventeen, a pupil who desired to do the compositions all the honour of a
careful copy. If these conclusions are correct—as I make no doubt—
we may infer that these compositions must have been written at latest
in Weimar, as is probable indeed on internal grounds in most cases, and
certain for other reasons as to one. It is easy to build up further inferences on so broad a foundation, and it gives importance and certainty
to many minor indications. The first notice of this valuable book, a
very superficial one, is in an appendix by C. F. Michaelis to Busby's
History of Music, translated by him (Vol. II., p. 599. Leipzig, 1822).

19 (p. 415). **A Composition by Prince Johann Ernst.**
Though the last-named piece bears, in a MS. by J. P. Kellner, the
title, " *Concerto dell' illustrissimo Principe Giovanni Ernesto, Duca di
Sassonia, appropriato all' Organo a 2 Clav. e Fedale da Giovanni Sebastiano
Bach,*" he here stands in contradiction with himself, since in another
MS. copy he attributes the movement, with the two others belonging
to it, to Vivaldi. I have made many vain attempts to discover Johann
Ernst's published concerto, and particularly with reference to this discussion. Still, as Kellner's manuscripts always betray great haste, and
he gives another concerto of Vivaldi's as Telemann's—since, too, the
concerto in question has the unmistakable stamp of Vivaldi's work—I
remain for the present of opinion that it is a mistake to attribute it to
Johann Ernst. But that such a mistake was possible shows more plainly
than anything would the close connection between the prince and the
production of these concerti.

20 (p. 487). **Neumeister's Texts for Three Cantatas, 1711-13.**
The texts must have been given to the composer some time before
the beginning of the church year, in order that he might have time
to set them to music. Thus the third series must have reached
Eisenach by the end of the summer or in the early autumn of
1711. It is not wholly impossible that Bach should have become
acquainted with the poems earlier in the year, through Telemann, and
have used them. At any rate, the works of the famous poet would have
been regarded as a precious possession, and it is hardly probable that
he would have given them out of his keeping before they had been used
for their original purpose. A simultaneous composition by Bach is
almost certainly out of the question, because in the Christmas cantata
" Uns ist ein Kind geboren " Bach's text is different from that printed
by Tilgner, and used by Telemann. The recitative of fifteen lines is
compressed by Bach into six, the second verse of the hymn is omitted,
and at the close, instead of the last verse of the chorale, " Gelobet
seist du, Jesu Christ," the last verse of " Wir Christenleut hab'n jetzund
Freud " is inserted. In the first cycle of Neumeister's " Fortgesetzten
fünffachen Kirchenandachten " (Hamburg, 1726) we find a cantata
introduced by the same Bible text, and of almost precisely similar

arrangement, ending, too, with the same chorale verse. From this resemblance I think it may be inferred that the text used by Bach was obtained directly from the writer. Why and when the alterations were made can no longer be ascertained, but it was, at any rate, after the distribution of the first edition. Hence it follows that Bach cannot have composed this cantata before Christmas, 1712 ; and since we find him already at work on the fourth series by Advent, 1714, it must have been then or at the same season of 1713. The composition of the music for Sexagesima, " Glechwie der Regen und Schnee," must consequently be ascribed to the spring of 1713 or 1714, for it is to be supposed that Bach, when he began on a series, went on in regular order, and did not first compose a cantata for the Lent season, and then go back to the Christmas festival. This hypothesis would allow a much wider interval for the Easter cantata " Ich weiss, dass mein Erlöser lebt," which is taken from the first series, if it were not so evident that Bach only came to know the first series through the third, and if the composition were not so similar in style to the rest. In technical practice, particularly in the recitatives, it is to a certain extent superior even to them. For these reasons I cannot admit that it was written before the Christmas cantata, but imagine it must have been composed for the Easter festival of either 1713 or 1714.

21 (p. 493). " Gleichwie der Regen und Schnee." The flutes were certainly added subsequently at Leipzig. They are written in A minor, and in the French violin (G) clef, and are not autograph, but only revised by Bach. The way in which they are written appears to me quite explicable ; on this plan all that was needed was to copy the two viola parts, with the necessary alteration of a few accidentals. Then the organ was played in G minor, which was equivalent to A minor of the " chamber " pitch ; and in point of fact we find only one figured organ part, in G minor, and not a second in F minor. The bassoon likewise played in A minor, and an unfigured bass part exists in that key. I therefore cannot comprehend Herr M. Hauptmann's statement in the preface to the cantata, that the flutes must have sounded a ninth lower down, being intended to agree in pitch with the violas. If it had been intended for tenor flutes, neither the violin clef nor the key of A minor would have been used.

22 (p. 511). " Wer mich liebet der wird mein Wort halten." Besides the autograph score and parts, now in the Royal Berlin Library, there is also there an old copy of the score which bears at the beginning in the right-hand corner the date 1731. This caused Zelter to write on the margin of the autograph score this note : " *di* | *J. S. Bach.* | 1731.|" In another and—as a comparison of the style shows at the first glance—a much later cantata for Whit Sunday, Bach has adopted the duet and the bass aria out of this one, working up the duet with his own peculiar mastery as an introductory chorus with additional accompaniment, transferring the bass air to the soprano in F

major, substituting an *oboe da caccia* for the violins, and adopting a
different text.   To the movement thus transformed he has given the
second place; then the remaining six numbers are new (B.-G., XVIII.,
No. 74).   We might be tempted to imagine that the date 1731 indicated
that of the composition of this second cantata, and that by mistake it
had been inscribed on the wrong manuscript.   It will, however, appear
later that the second cantata was written in 1735.   There is still further
evidence that the older cantata was composed at Weimar, since in
the blank lines at the end of the autograph score we find a hasty
indication of the first bars of the final chorus of a cantata for the
Second Day of Whitsuntide, "Also hat Gott die Welt geliebt" (B.-G.,
XVI., No. 68).   (In Bach's manuscripts we frequently come upon traces
of his having hastily noted down a motive that might suggest itself to
him while he was composing, on any vacant sheet that was at hand;
as, for instance, again in the cantata, "Ach lieben Christen, seid
getrost.")   This cantata ("Also hat Gott") is the one which contains
the beautiful aria "Mein gläubiges Herze," which, as is well known,
is a remodelled version of a song from the secular cantata "Was mir
behagt, ist nur die muntre Jagd."   This cantata, however, was written
in 1716 (as will presently appear in the text).   The whole process
then is clear: Bach had to compose two pieces for the Whitsuntide
festival of 1735, and, as he lacked either time or inclination to compose
two perfectly new ones, he adopted, for the first, parts of an older work.
While busied with this a suitable theme for the fugue of the second
cantata occurred to his mind, and he noted it down at once on the score
of the older music, which lay before him.   However, his revived interest
in this aroused his recollection of the time when it was written, and of
his work and experiences then; his thoughts reverted to the duke's
birthday at Weissenfels in 1716, and the music written for that festival,
and he found he could adapt part of it for the second Whitsuntide cantata.
But if the older cantata, "Wer mich liebet," was composed in Weimar, it
can only have been for Whitsuntide of 1716, for in 1715 and 1717 other
texts occur, arranged for his music by the duke (see Nos. 27 and 32 of this
appendix).   Moreover, there are in the copy, which is dated 1731,
other deviations from the original.   In the duets and recitative a tenor
is put in instead of a soprano, and the chorale "Komm, heiliger Geist"
is postponed to the end; but in the parts written by the composer himself, and which, from the character of the paper, ink, and writing, seem
to belong to a later date, these deviations are not attended to.   A
proof that Bach meant to let a chorale follow the bass aria lies in the
words added to the bass part, "*Chorale Segue.*"   In the score, to be sure,
there is no sign of it, though six lines remain vacant on the last page.
Still this is not the only instance in which Bach left out the last chorale;
it is wanting, too, in the Advent cantata for 1715, "Bereitet die Wege,
bereitet die Bahn," and must have been written on a separate sheet.   If
Bach meant to give the trumpets and drums independent employment,

a space of six lines no doubt seemed insufficient; he wrote the chorale on an independent sheet, and the separate parts in the same way, so it might very easily be all lost. The chorale, at any rate, must have been in A minor, and that the beginning and end should be in different keys will surprise no one after the Advent cantata of 1714. In performing it, it suits very well to use the similar movement from the cantata " Bleib bei uns, denn es will Abend werden " (B.-G. I., No. 6).

23 (p. 513). **A Cantata attributed to Bach.** In the Amalien-Biblothek of the Joachimsthaler Gymnasium at Berlin, Vol. No. 43, last portion, there is a MS. with the following title : *Cantata.* | " *Herr Christ der einge u. s. w.* | *a* | 2 *Violini* | *Viola* | *Soprano, Alto,* | *Tenore, Basso* | *e* | *Fondamento.* | *del Sign. J. S. Bach.*" | This composition—which must not be confounded with the great cantata beginning with the same words which Bach wrote for the Eighteenth Sunday after Trinity, and which begins with an imposing chorale in chorus—is founded on a text composed by Neumeister for the Feast of the Annunciation, in his fourth series. But, notwithstanding that the MS. names Bach as the author, and notwithstanding that it was mentioned so early as in Breitkopf's list, Michaelmas 1761, under Bach's name, I am perfectly convinced that it was not he but Telemann who composed it. Bach may possibly have copied it out, just as the cantata " Machet die Thore weit," is still extant in the Royal Library at Berlin in Bach's own writing; or his friend may have given it to him, and then by an oversight it passed under Bach's own name. Nor would this be the only instance of a production of Telemann's passing under the protection of Bach's name. In the list of property left by Philipp Emanuel Bach is a motett for double choir in C major, " Jauchzet dem Herrn alle Welt," designated as Bach's work, and it is still quoted as his, though it belongs to Telemann, and is ascribed to Bach for no other reason than because some one has inserted into the middle of it the grand chorale for chorus out of the last cantata, " Gottlob nun geht das Jahr zu Ende " (B.-G. V., 1, No. 28). Still what Fischhoff observes in the MS. which formerly belonged to him is quite correct : that on a MS. copy in the Conservatorium at Vienna, Bach *and* Telemann are named as the authors. But it will not be requisite to recapitulate the arguments that prove that Bach cannot have written the cantata for the Annunciation. For instance, he never wrote a vocal fugue on such a theme as here serves for the closing movement :—

It does once happen that an undoubtedly genuine cantata by Bach,

" Schau lieber Gott, wie meine Feind " begins as this does, with a simply set chorale. Still, peculiarities enough remain to weigh decisively against the genuineness of the cantata " Herr Christ der ein'ge Gotts-Sohn." The two airs and the recitative can scarcely be called Bach-like ; the former are too shallow and pretty, and the latter is too exclusively declamatory. Any one, however, who is familiar with Telemann's style of composition will easily detect his hand throughout, particularly in the theme here quoted, and in the management of the parts in the chorale.

24 (p. 515). **Bach's Visit to Cassel.** The only person who mentions Bach's journey to Cassel is Constantin Bellermann, some-time Rector of Minden, a native of Erfurt. He published in 1743 a pamphlet, now very rare, with the following title: " *Programma* | *in quo* | *Parnassus* | *Musarum* | *voce, fidibus, tibiisque resonans,* | *sive* | *musices,* | *artis divi-* | *næ, laudes, diversæ species, singulares effectus,* | *atque primarii auctores succinte* | *præstantissimique melopoetæ cum* | *laude enarrantur ;* | *simul et illustres civitatis Mundæ proceres,* | *sum-mique patroni, bonarum artium* | *fautores, atque amici* | *ad audiendas quasdam orationes scholasticus,* | *submisso animi cultu,* | *debitaque reverentia, et humanitate* | *in Lyceum Mundense invitantur* | *a* | *Constantino Beller-manno,* | *P. L. C. et Rectore ibidem CIƆDCCXXXXIII* | *cum censura.* | " In a quarto of 47 leaves, a copy of which is shown in the Royal Library at Berlin, on p. 39 are the following sentences referring to Bach : " *BACHIUS Lips. profundæ Musices auctor his modo commemoratis* [Mattheson, Keiser, Telemann] *non est inferior, qui, sicut HAEN-DELIUS apud ANGLOS, Lipsiæ miraculum, quantum quidem ad Musicam attinet dici meretur, qui, si Viro placet, solo pedum ministerio, digitis aut nihil, aut aliud agentibus, tam mirificum, concitatum, celeremue in Organo ecclesiastico mouet vocum concentum, ut alii digitis hoc imitari deficere videantur. Princeps sane herditarius Hassiæ FRIDERICUS BACHIO tunc temporis, Organum, vt restititutum ad limam vocaret CAS-SELLAS Lipsia accersito eademue facilitate pedibus veluti alatis transtra hæc, vocum gravitate reboantia, fulgurisque in morem aures præsentium terebrantia, percurrente, adeo Virum cum stupore est admiratus, ut annulum gemma distinctum, digitoque suo detractum, finito hoc musico fragore ei dono daret. Quod munus, si pedum agilitas meruit, quid quæso daturus fuisset Princeps (cui soli tunc hanc gratiam faciebat), si et manus in subsidium vocasset.*" By this it appears that Bach went from Leipzig to Cassel. But Bellermann must have been in error as to this point, for no time is conceivable when this can have taken place. The Here-ditary Prince Frederick, from the end of 1714, when he went by way of Stralsund to Stockholm, there to take for his second wife Ulrica Eleanora, sister of Charles XII. of Sweden, in the year 1715, was absent from Germany till the year 1731, when he became Landgrave of Hesse, his father having died a year before. He soon returned to his kingdom of Sweden, leaving Hesse to be ruled by his brother.

Whether he ever returned to Germany (and it must have only been for
a short time, if at all) I am not able to say. It is, however, unimportant, and Bellermann, who must have heard the story from his relations
at Erfurt, or perhaps from Bach himself, who sometimes went there,
cannot have confused Frederick, the King and Landgrave, with Frederick,
the Hereditary Prince. S. Bach can only have been in Cassel before
the last month of the year 1714. The Hereditary Prince was a commanding general in the Spanish War of Inheritance, and was out of the
country until the Peace of Utrecht, in 1713. But he used to reside in
Hesse in the winter, so that we may conclude with certainty that
Bach's going to Cassel can only have taken place in the year 1713-14.
If it was the organ in the Hofkirche which was renewed, there is no
support to be got from this for a more certain proof, since in the documents in the state archives from which all my information is got, there is
no trace of such occurrence. Possibly some other organ is meant.
Bellermann's mistake is easily accounted for; only consider that in
the latter part of his life, Bach was always called " Bach of Leipzig,"
and it might easily be forgotten, even if it were generally known that
he had ever been in Weimar. However, Bellermann's narrative is
mentioned by Adlung. (Anl. z. Mus. Gel., p. 690, Note 1.)

25 (p. 531, 555, 562). **Texts and Watermarks in 1714-15.** The
first independent series of Franck's cantata texts (the full title is given
in note 256, p. 540) is dated 1715, and at the end of the dedication to the
duke the more exact date is given of June 4, 1715. It begins with the
First Sunday in Advent and ends with the Twenty-seventh Sunday after
Trinity; an appendix contains five more cantatas for special occasions.
A doubt may now exist between the years 1714-15 and 1715-16, but we
possess Bach's autograph scores for the Fourth Sunday in Advent and
the Fourth Sunday after Trinity, and as both are dated 1715, the series
of performances cannot possibly have begun with the Advent season.
Still, the beginning cannot be dated later than the Fourth Sunday after
Trinity, 1715. For, from this Sunday till the Annunciation inclusive,
the separate copies of the words were kept, and are now preserved
in the Grand Ducal Library at Weimar—each on two leaves small
octavo, the first bearing the title—and these give us the dates of the
performances with all the precision we could desire. The text for
Cantata Sunday, Fourth after Easter, has the following title page:
"*CANTATA* | Auf den Sonntag CANTA- | TE 1715. in der Fürstl.|
Sächsischen Hof-Capelle zur | Wilhelms-Burg zu *mu* | *sici*ren." Further
evidence is afforded by a notice in the general private accounts for
Michaelmas 1714-15, where, under the heading " Printing, &c.," we find
the following entry : " 13 fl. 15 ggr. for 6 reams of writing paper and 12
reams of printing paper for the church cantatas. July 9, 1715." This
proves that not long previously, at any rate within the second quarter of
the year, Mumbach, the printer, had obtained paper by the duke's order
from a maker, since the account came in on July 1, and was paid on the

9th from the ducal purse. The quantity of paper is accounted for by the preparation of separate sheets printed for each Sunday to be distributed to those who came to church, that they might read them and follow. The date of the dedication, too, indicates the second quarter, for Franck could not possibly have dedicated to his patron a work which had already been some time in use by his band ; and it is quite intelligible that the printing of the collection may not have been ready till a few weeks after the separate sheets printed at once for the requirements of the congregation. Now, did the year begin, in fact, with Cantate Sunday (Fourth after Easter) ? I believe not. Easter fell on April 21, and it would be too singular if some festival had not been chosen for bringing before the world the new institution. Thus then the annual cycle would have extended from Easter to Easter. This would explain the otherwise unaccountable fact that there is no annual series of cantatas for the ecclesiastical year from 1715-16, while we find them again for 1716-17 and 1717-18. To the interval belongs the Whitsuntide cantata, "Wer mich liebet," on Neumeister's text, and at other times they put up with ordinary music ; and during the seasons between the festivals had no special or regular music. The question as to whether Franck may not previously have written a series of cantatas for the court church in Neumeister's place—for the year 1714-15 perhaps—must be answered in the negative, when we remember the dedication to Wilhelm Ernst, printed at the beginning of the " Evangelischen Andachts-Opffer." That he should have dedicated this work to the prince, and have omitted to do so in the succeeding years, indicates that it was the first of its kind. No doubt an earlier one, also dedicated to him, may have been lost ; but then he would hardly have avoided mentioning it, and would not simply have written, as he has done, "Your most gracious and serene highness has been graciously pleased to permit that I should dedicate with the deepest submission, and to inscribe to your highness these evangelical cantatas, prepared by your humble servant (meine Wenigkeit) to the glory of God and the awaking of pious devotion, by the gracious commands of your most Christian highness in all Christian singleness of purpose." It is also worthy of note that in the private accounts of the previous year no trace of a similar outlay for writing and printing paper is to be found. However, it is plain from the terms of the dedication that the duke must previously have interested himself in the employment of music in the castle chapel ; for Franck particularly says, after lauding the many virtues of Wilhelm Ernst: " Among the beautiful Divine services performed to the Lord in your highness's royal court chapel is the devout and heart-stirring music, a foretaste of the heavenly joys, and worthy of perpetual praise." The chief part of this praise is certainly due to Bach, but it would be surprising indeed if, with Franck's poetic gift, he had not before this laboured in co-operation with the great composer.

We must reconcile ourselves to the reflection that we have many losses to bewail. For instance, on November 6, 1713, the dedication of the new church of St. James at Weimar took place with magnificent solemnity. A detailed programme in folio was printed, of which a copy still exists in the archives at Weimar, and which contains the complete text of a cantata composed for the occasion. The text, beginning with a chorus—

> " Hilff, lass alles wohl gelingen,
> Hilff! Herr GOtt wir loben dich "—

> " Help, O Lord, and bless our labours ;
> Help, O Lord, the God we praise,"—

and constructed on the plan of the cantatas of the transition period—as has been described—must for this very reason have been Franck's work, and also betrays itself as his by certain peculiarities of style. Under these circumstances, what can be more probable than that Bach wrote the music for it.

Still, two important cantatas remain to us of the period before April 21, 1715—" Ich hatte viel Bekümmerniss," for the Third Sunday after Trinity, and " Himmelskönig, sei willkommen," for Palm Sunday. The first alone bears the date 1714, but it can be proved that the second was composed at the same time. The texts are not to be found in any of the collections of Franck's poems, but they are his nevertheless. The metre alone proves this; he is fond of short lines, with unexpected introduction of longer ones. The cantatas in the second part, especially of the " Geist- und weltlichen Poesien," contain a great number of such irregular metres. Franck was also very fond of using a verse consisting of four lines in four feet of three syllables each, the first two of which lines ended with a feminine, the last two with a masculine rhyme, such as those of the last aria of " Ich hatte viel Bekümmerniss " :—

> " Erfreue dich Seele, erfreue dich Herze,
> Entweiche nun Kummer, verschwinde du Schmerze,
> Verwandle dich Weinen in lauteren Wein,
> Es wird nun mein Aechzen ein Jauchzen nur sein."

> " Rejoice, O my spirit, in this consolation,
> For now from thy sorrow thou findest salvation;
> The water of grief God hath changed into wine,
> All sadness is over, and gladness is mine."

The character of the recitative, the fondness for introducing a dialogue between Christ and the soul, and many similar or identical passages in these verses and the cantatas known to be his, remove every possible doubt that they are by Franck. The similes are his too, and so is the arrangement of the numbers in the cantata. We know the date at which the cantata "Ich hatte viel Bekümmerniss" was written from Bach's autograph note, for, according to Bach's usual practice, the date on the cover of the parts can mean nothing else than the time of composition. Hence the cantata cannot be that which was written for Halle in the autumn of 1713, as has been supposed (Chrysander, Händel, I., p. 22). Still less can it be so if Franck wrote the words, for Bach composed his trial piece for Halle without any preparation, and undoubtedly to words which were laid before him there and then. Indeed this hypothesis can only have arisen in some measure from the fact that until lately nothing was known of Bach's having already worked so abundantly at that time as a composer of cantatas.

The time when "Himmelskönig sei willkommen" was written can only be approximately calculated. It was written in Weimar—this can be proved to a demonstration by the character of a part of the original MS. The autograph of the score and of one flute and one violin part are in the Royal Library at Berlin; the remaining parts have been written out by a copyist. Of the whole body of parts a small portion was written in Weimar—that is to say, besides the two autograph parts, one soprano part, one alto, one tenor and one bass, as is proved by the watermark in the paper. We know from Bach's own MS. that the Advent cantata "Bereitet die Wege, bereitet die Bahn" was composed in 1715. The paper on which this is written has a very conspicuous watermark, resembling an M with two oblique upward strokes added to its right line, something like this:— **M**

This watermark also occurs in the paper of the autograph of the cantata "Mein Gott, wie lang, ach lange" from Franck's "Evangelischem Andachts-Opffer," and there, on the other side of the sheet, another no less distinct mark is visible—the ox-head of Ravensburg, a sort of two-pronged fork, in this shape:— **U**

These two signs recur again in the cantata "Nur jedem das Seine," which also is derived from the "Evangelischen Andachts-Opffer"; and even the colour of the paper is identical. Finally they occur in an autograph by Walther, who always lived in Weimar—a copy by him of two of Froberger's Toccatas, now in the Royal Institute for Church Music at Berlin. Hence it is quite certain that paper with this mark was used in Weimar at that time. I have investigated the watermarks of every autograph by Bach that has come under my hand, and have convinced myself that this paper was not used either in Cöthen or in Leipzig. In the only instances in which I have detected it, other indications also point to Weimar, and in all the autographs which can either be proved to have been written in Leipzig or which by their calligraphy and contents seem to indicate it, the watermarks are entirely different. In these we frequently find a crescent or the initials M.A.; here and there a fanciful figure :—

Sometimes a stag, or simply an eagle, not to mention other stamps. The smaller portion of the parts as above-mentioned has then this Weimar watermark very plainly, and it is thus proved decisively that the cantata was written in Weimar. And the character of the other parts of the MS. plainly reveal the further fate of the composition. The remaining and larger portion of the parts has been written by a copyist of whose services Bach frequently availed himself in Leipzig, and the watermarks—a crescent, M.A., and cornucopia—also bear witness to their origin; they have a separate wrapper. The autograph score finally is to be ascribed to the Leipzig period by having the cornucopia watermark (on the first leaf of the two beginning sheets we find instead of it a rather large W), but the beautifully careful writing, the bars marked almost throughout with a ruler, the nearly total absence of any alterations or corrections, and finally the absence of the letters *J. J.* at the beginning and *S. D. G.* at the end, suffice to show any one who is familiar with Bach's scores that this, though an autograph, is a second copy. Thus the work must have been composed and performed in Weimar, and then the master must have looked it out again at Leipzig, have had the number of parts multiplied as was there requisite, and have written the score out fair, the work evidently being one that he liked. In the two autograph part copies the last chorus in 6-8 time was written out again at Leipzig; apparently the instrumentation was at first different. Supposing, then, that the cantata was composed at Weimar, the question is, in which year? It cannot have been after the Easter of 1715, since we have the complete annual series by Franck after that time, nor can it have been before 1712, since the text proves an acquaintance with Neumeister's cantatas, and these had not reached Weimar from Eisenach before 1712. Its great resemblance, too, to the cantata "Ich hatte viel Bekümmerniss" would place it near to it in date. Common to them both are the symphonies, composed on the same principle, with a certain broad arrangement of the chorale, equally admirable in both, and holding very much the same position in each. Considerable similarity is observable, too, in the fugal treatment of the other choruses. Both cantatas have three arias, one of which in each has an unfigured bass accompaniment with one instrument *concertante*, and accompanied by a quartet of strings. We may therefore assume that it was written either for March 25, 1714, or April 14, 1715.

26 (p. 541). **Leipzig Cantatas on Franck's Texts.** Bach also composed on the text for the festival of the Trinity, out of the "Evangelischen Andachts-Opffer," "O heilges Geist- und Wasser-Bad"; on that for the Ninth Sunday after Trinity, "Thue Rechnung! Donnerwort, das die Felsen selbst zerspaltet"; for the Thirteenth Sunday after Trinity, "Ihr, die ihr euch von Christo nennet"; and for the Third Sunday after Epiphany, "Alles nur nach Gottes Willen" (B.-G., XVIII., No. 72). The score of the first cantata, written out by Bach's second wife, Anna Magdalena, is in the Amalien Library of the Joachimsthaler Gymnasium at Berlin (No. 105). The original scores of the others are in the Royal Library, Berlin, and the autograph parts of the two last are also preserved there. Neither of these four cantatas was composed in Weimar. Their broad and deeply considered form indicates the Leipzig period. There are also external evidences. In the first there is the crescent watermark in the paper, and a peculiar elegance in the writing which distinguishes several of the later cantatas—for instance, "O ewiges Feuer," and "Weinen, Klagen, Sorgen," and the copy, made in Leipzig, of "Himmelskönig, sei willkommen." In the second the introduction of the oboe d'amore is decisive, for this instrument was unknown in Weimar in Bach's time, as we learn from Walther (under the word "oboe"); so is the hasty writing, full of corrections, by which the greater part of Bach's Leipzig cantatas are distinguished. The same marks hold good for the two last cantatas. We have already seen, when considering Neumeister's poems, that the master, under some circumstances, went back to older texts; and this is very easy to understand in the case of Franck's poems, of which he was very fond.

27 (p. 557). **Cantata, "Bereitet die Wege."** I have spoken in detail in No. 25 of the character of the autograph. Here I must add, however, that it is not perfect. The final chorale is wanting. From a comparison with the printed text, it was the fifth stanza of the hymn : "Herr Christ, der ein'ge Gotts-Sohn" ("Ertödt uns durch dein Güte"). Since the autograph, as it stands, fills three sheets in such a a way that only two lines are left empty on the last page, the chorale must have been written on a separate sheet. But that it did actually at one time exist is proved by the circumstance that at the end of the aria the usual *S. D. G.* is wanting. To complete it the final chorale from "Jesus nahm zu sich die Zwölfe" may be used (B.-G., V., 1, No. 22),

or the simple four-part movement, published by Erk (I., 47), either of them transposed to A major.

28 (p. 564). "**Alles was von Gott geboren.**" In a catalogue of written musical works of the publishing firm of Breitkopf, of Leipzig, for the year 1761, the title of the cantata is quite accurately given, with the Sunday for which it was written and the list of vocal and instrumental parts. The statement, which has been extensively repeated from Winterfeld (Ev. Kir., III., p. 328), that Bach wrote the cantata "Ein feste Burg" for the Reformation Jubilee of the year 1717, is a complete mistake. It is only in his later years that we find Bach rearranging or making use of his early works; and that he should, in Weimar, and for so important an occasion, have worked back on a composition written only two years previously is incredible, even if it were not expressly called "a newly composed piece" in the printed account of the festival (in the archives of Weimar). Indeed, Franck, who wrote two new series of church cantatas for the years 1716-18, would not have permitted a mere *rechauffé* of old verses on such an occasion. Finally—and this is not the least decisive argument—a composition such as the introductory chorus to this cantata lay certainly quite beyond Bach's powers at that time. This chorale chorus, in its grand proportions and vigorous flow, is the natural and highest outcome of Bach's progressive development, and he never wrote anything more stupendous. When it was that the Weimar cantata was expanded cannot at present be accurately determined : I should think for the Reformation Festival of 1730. In June of that year the two hundredth anniversary of the delivering of the Confession of Augsburg was celebrated, and for this occasion Bach composed three cantatas. It was quite natural that the Reformation Festival should be held with special splendour, and equally natural that Bach should be exhausted by so many festal compositions, and feel no further inclination to compose anything altogether new. Besides this, just in this month he was in a particularly depressed and unpropitious frame of mind. From the alterations which he made on this occasion in the old materials, one point at any rate is clear : the chorale melody of the first aria, worked up in Buxtehude's manner, was originally given only to the instruments (probably the oboe and organ), a method Bach was fond of employing throughout this annual series. The words given to the second verse Franck had intended for the closing chorus, and they no doubt originally stood there in Bach's composition. When he extended the work it occurred to him to use all four verses, so he gave the fourth to the final chorale and the second to the first aria, and composed new choral subjects for the first and third. Indeed it is perceptible at once that the voice part is merely a simplification of the oboe part, and much that is characteristic has to this end been suppressed—for instance, the truly Buxtehude-like attack, with a rolling, ascending scale in bar 23. He has given it little of any special character, excepting a few closing cadences. The alteration of the

text, however, in the beginning of the duet can hardly be Bach's own doing. Instead of the original words: " Wie selig ist der Leib," &c.— " Blessed is the womb that bare Thee, but still more blessed is the heart that bears Thee in faith"—we find, " Wie selig sind doch die, die Gott in Munde tragen "—" How blessed are the lips that bear God's holy name !" &c.—which has no special sense in itself, and entirely destroys the image which is called up by the music. No autograph exists to settle the question. Some petty prudishness may have prompted the alteration. But there are inaccuracies in other parts of the text.

29 (p. 566). **Secular Cantata, " Diana and Endymion."** The poem is to be found in the appendix to the second part of the Geist- und weltlichen Poesien (pp. 436 to 440), and has the following heading: "Diana, Endymion, Pan, and Pales, performed for the birth-day festival of his Highness the Duke Christian, at Saxe-Weissenfels as banquet-music, in the Prince's hunting-lodge after a hunt of wild beasts." The date is not given, but it can be calculated. The order of the poems dedicated on special occasions to illustrious personages is chronological. On page 235 is a congratulatory cantata to Wilhelm Ernst for the new year 1714; before this are the festal verses used on the consecration of Saint James' Church, November 6, 1713; before these again, a New Year's cantata, for 1713. Franck evidently was first prompted to add an appendix while the book was being printed, when he saw that there still would be room. In it are two birthday poems to Wilhelm Ernst—written, therefore, in October, 1714 and 1715—and then comes the Weissenfels birthday cantata, February, 1716. The book was brought out in 1716, so a later date is out of the question. An earlier year might be assumed, since Franck may have given the poems to the duke the first place in his arrangement. However, the many and striking similarities between this work and the church cantatas composed at that time seem to argue decisively for 1716. The first aria for Diana reminds us in bars 19 and 20 of certain passages in the D minor aria of the cantata for the Twentieth Sunday after Trinity ; the bass in the second aria of Pales is like the duet of that same cantata; the close on the subdominant in the aria for Diana (bar 27), with its reversion to the principal key, reminds us of a similar point in the first aria of " Bereitet die Wege "; finally, the first aria for Pales is like the G major aria in the cantata "Tritt auf die Glaubensbahn." All this points to the year 1716 as the date of this composition, because this would seem to account for his remembering it when rearranging the Whitsuntide cantata of 1716 in the year 1735 (see *ante*, No. 22 of this appendix).

30 (p. 569). **The Evangelische Sonn- und Festtags-Andachten** are dated 1717. It is obvious that this cannot mean that they belong to the ecclesiastical year of 1717-18. The separate sheets were the first printed—none, however, have been preserved—and as this took place towards the end of the civic year it is scarcely possible that

the collection should have been printed within the same year, particularly if it was to be done so carefully and elegantly, as we see was the case. Moreover, in December, 1717, Bach was no longer in Weimar. None of the cantatas composed on texts from this series remain to us in their original form—we only know them in their later arrangements of the Leipzig period, which are recognisable in the first place by the introduction of recitatives and chorales, as well as by their division into two portions. Franck used no recitative in his Evangelischen Andachten; he invariably begins with a text for chorus of his own composition, follows it with verses of different metres for three—or at most four—arias, and closes with a chorale. Indeed, he did not call these poems *cantatas*, but *sacred arias*. And that these are actually rearrangements is easily proved. I may spare myself the trouble with regard to the cantata for the second Sunday in Advent, "Wachet, betet, seid bereit," since the keen eye of the editor has already detected the evidence without any reference to the date when the text was written (B.-G., XVI., preface, p. xx.). Here the additions consist of the recitative (pp. 343, 349, 354, and 360), and the chorale (p. 354). The increased length necessitated the division into two portions, and the cantata in its altered form was given to the Twenty-sixth Sunday after Trinity. Other changes are not discoverable. I have already mentioned a cycle of cantatas written by Johann Sebastian Brunner, the cantor of Weimar for the year 1748, in which he made a singular use of the poems of former writers (see No. 12 of this appendix). He availed himself of the text, and mixed up its different lines in a really ingenious manner, not always escaping making nonsense of them.

The autograph score of the cantata for the Fourth Sunday in Advent, "Herz und Mund und That und Leben," is in the Royal Library at Berlin. The very form of it tells the history of its origin. The autograph consists of six sheets; judging from the watermarks the four first are of Weimar paper, the two last of Leipzig. That it is a fair copy is proved by the great elegance and neatness of the writing—the bars are marked with a ruler in the first chorus, and carefully drawn all through; there are hardly any corrections, and there is no heading, nor the usual *J. J.* The whole aspect of the MS. is precisely similar to that of the autograph of "Himmelskönig, sei willkommen"—both seem to have taken their present form at about the same time. When Bach was about to remodel the cantata, he first wrote separately the pieces to be inserted, and then copied the whole out fair. In the roll of score and parts he had brought from Weimar, he found a few sheets of music-paper still blank. With the economy which characterised him in these matters, he made use of them, and, as they were not sufficient, took two sheets of fresh paper. The alterations in the text are here more considerable. Irrespective of the fact that the cantata is intended for a different occasion—the Feast of the Visitation of the B.V.M.—and that three recitatives were added, above all the closing chorale was altered. In Franck's text it originally consisted of the sixth verse of " Ich dank dir, lieber Herre " ("Dein Wort lass mich bekennen "); in remodelling it Bach inserted at the first portion the sixth verse of the hymn by Janus, "Jesu, meiner Seelen Wonne," with the melody of " Werde munter, mein Gemüthe," by which arrangement the two last notes of the last two lines had to be sung in a slur together : a licence the master also allowed himself in the Passion according to Matthew (B.-G., IV., p. 173), with an ornate instrumental accompaniment, and a repeat at the end of the whole. In this way the chorale subject of the first *state* is altogether lost. Then the arias 2 and 3 had had to change places; a few changes in the words are unimportant, but it is worthy of note that the first aria is now accompanied by the oboe d'amore, which it cannot have been in the first instance. Finally, a new text is given to the fourth aria, as these words originally used did not suit the Festival of the Visitation. The rearrangement of the numbers is precisely similar to that which I thought must be supposed to have taken place in the remodelling of the Easter cantata for 1704, and this I desire particularly to note, to protect myself against criticism in that instance.

The composition for the Third Sunday in Advent is also still extant, " Aergre dich, o Seele, nicht"; the original score is in the Royal Library at Berlin. Dr. Rust was so obliging as to investigate it carefully by my request, as I had not the time to do so. It is a copy written in Leipzig, revised by Bach, with additions in his own hand, and the heading written inside : " *J. J. Dominica 7 post Trinitatis di J. S. Bach aō* 1723." This distinctly fixed date will not allow me to venture to call this cantata a rearrangement, much as there is to be said for the assertion that, at the time when the elder Drese died, and his son was hindered by mourning from carrying out his duties as a composer, Bach would have set all three cantatas one after another. Besides, there are many passages where the music fits very well with the remodelled text, and very badly with the original. The recitative and the chorale in the middle are again interpolated ; the final chorale, verse 8 of the hymn "Von Gott will ich nicht lassen " ("Darum ob ich schon dulde hier Widerwärtigkeit"), is wholly absent from the score.

31 (p. 586). **Bach and Marchand at Dresden.** I must relate this oft-told incident in much plainer words, that there may be no confusion between the picturesque and fanciful legend and historical truth. An incontestable authority is the report of " Magister" Johann Abraham Birnbaum, as given in his Vertheidigung seiner unparteyischen Anmerkungen über eine bedenkliche Stelle in dem sechsten Stücke ben critischen Muskus, wider Johann Adolph Scheibens Beantwortung derselben (Leipzig, 1739), reprinted in the new revised and extended edition of Scheibe's Kritische Musicus (Leipzig, Breitkopf, 1745), p. 899 —A defence of his unprejudiced observations on an important passage in the Criticus Musicus, &c.—Birnbaum wrote this in defence of Bach,

and under his supervision, dedicating it also to him. There can therefore be nothing in it which Bach himself can have thought inaccurate
or unfair. Birnbaum tells us (p. 981): "He who, if I were to name
him, would be regarded as the greatest master of his time on the
clavier and organ in all France, and against whom the court composer [Bach] not long since fully vindicated his honour and that of
Germany. This was *Mons. Marchand*, who, being in Dresden, and
the court composer being also there, was by the desire and command of a great personage at court challenged in a polite letter
to a trial and competition of their respective skill on the clavier,
and pledged himself to appear as required. The hour came when
the two great performers were to measure their strength. The court
composer, with those who were to be the umpires in this musical
contest, both on his side and on the other, anxiously awaited the
opponent, but in vain. At last the information was brought that he
had vanished from Dresden at break of day by the swift post. Beyond
a doubt the Frenchman had found his boasted skill too feeble to stand
against the mighty attack of his experienced and bold antagonist.
Otherwise he would not have sought safety in such rapid flight." The
trustworthiness of this account is enhanced by the fact that Adlung,
who in the same way had it from Bach's own lips, agrees almost exactly
with it. He says (Anleit. zur Mus. Gel. p. 690, § 345): "Marchand, a
Frenchman, must be mentioned, who at one time found himself in
Dresden with our capellmeister; and by various discussion it came to
be suggested that the two men should compete, in order to see whether
the German nation or the French could produce the best master of the
clavier. Our countryman at the appointed time performed in public, but
his opponent had proved his disinclination to measure himself against
him by making himself scarce. When at one time Herr Bach was with
us in Erfurt, I was prompted by a desire to know exactly all about it, to
ask him, and he then told it me all; but partly there is no room for it
here, and partly I have forgotten it again." The occurrence is related
with much greater detail in Mizler's Necrology, written by Ph. Em.
Bach and Agricola, p. 163: "The year 1717 gave Bach, who was
already so famous, a new opportunity of acquiring fresh honours.
The clavier and organ player *Marchand*, who was celebrated in France,
had come to Dresden, had played before the king with particular appro-
bation, and was so successful that a place in the king's service was
offered him at a high salary. The concertmeister in Dresden at that
time, *Volumier*, wrote to Bach, whose merits were not unknown to him,
and invited him to come without delay to Dresden to compete with the
haughty *Marchand* for the advantage. Bach willingly accepted the
invitation, and went to Dresden. *Volumier* received him with joy, and
arranged an opportunity for him to be hidden to hear his antagonist.
Bach then invited *Marchand* by a polite note, in which he offered to play
at sight any musical task that *Marchand* might set him, and demanded

of him an equal readiness for the contest.   Great audacity, no doubt !
The day and place were fixed—not without the king's knowledge.   Bach
at the appointed time betook himself to the house of a distinguishec
minister, where a large company of persons of high rank and of both
sexes were assembled.   *Marchand* kept them waiting a long time; at last
the master of the house sent to *Marchand's* lodgings to remind him, in
case he had forgotten, that now was the time to prove himself a man.
But with great surprise they received the information that *Monsieur
Marchand* that selfsame day, very early, had set out from Dresden by
extra post.   Bach, who was now master of the field, had consequently
ample opportunity for showing the skill with which he was armed
against his antagonist, and this he did to the admiration of all.   The
king had intended him to have a present of 500 thalers, but by the dis-
honesty of a certain servant, who thought he could make a better use of
this gift, he was robbed of it, and had to carry home the honour he had
earned as his sole remuneration, &c.   However, Bach always willingly
paid *Marchand* the tribute of praise for his beautiful and very neat
execution."   An equally detailed account is given by F. W. Marpurg
(Legende einiger Musikheiligen.   Cöln, 1786, p. 292); he, too, says he
had his information from Bach himself, but his account does not agree
with that in the Necrology in many particulars.   According to him
Bach was admitted to a court concert by the king's permission,
stood by Marchand while he played variations on a French air, and
when called upon to play took up Marchand's thema and played new
and endless variations on it.   He then invited him to compete *on the
organ*, and gave him a theme on a sheet of paper to work out at sight;
but Marchand did not come to the struggle, but disappeared from
Dresden.   The fact that the two last accounts agree neither with each
other, nor with Birnbaum and Adlung, makes them both suspicious ;
indeed by analysing them duly we can plainly detect the process by
which a historical myth is gradually developed.   Birnbaum and Adlung
agree in making Bach's presence in Dresden accidental, which seems
quite natural, knowing as we do his habit of making yearly journeys
for the purposes of his art.   In the Necrology and in Marpurg he is
appealed to as a champion in need, which is highly improbable, because
correspondence and travelling were at that time far more difficult than
now, and it is perfectly senseless to imagine that the request can
have emanated from Volumier, a Frenchman, who can hardly have
had an interest in seeing his countryman vanquished by a German;
while it is, on the other hand, very credible that Bach should have
had an earlier correspondence with Volumier regarding a journey to
Dresden, and have been encouraged by him to undertake it.   In the
older accounts we do not find a word of the king's participation in the
matter, and in Mizler it is smuggled in in such a way as to give the
contest the effect of a brilliant whim.   In that case the conditions of the
affair have no sense ; if the king really interested himself in it it would

have taken place at court, and not at Count Flemming's house. Marpurg goes even further: Bach did not hide himself to hear Marchand, but was admitted to a court concert. The interest in the clavier competition being thus diminished, the challenge is supposed to be to play the organ, which in itself is to the last degree improbable, even if exterior circumstances were more trustworthy; and a performance *impromptu*, which is to be based on a theme, ceased to be impromptu. Indeed, the papers of the court and household accounts for 1718 (in the Royal archives at Dresden) prove that Bach did not play before the king. In fol. 32 (under "Nach *specificirte* auf allergnädigste mündliche Königl. Verordnung im Jahre, 1717, bey dero Ober Cämmerey *Casse* bezahlte Posten ")* ve find the following note, " 528 Kfl. [Kaiser-gulden] $7\frac{1}{2}$ Kr., or 130 ducats, at 2 thlr. 17 ggr., in the form of three medals, of which one of 30 ducats value is graciously presented to the violinist Frühwirth, who played at Carlsbad, and the two others of 100 ducats to the organist Marchand, who played in the *Capelle* band." Since the affair between Bach and Marchand had attracted so much attention, it is incredible that if he too had had a gift it should not have been mentioned with Marchand's. If he had played before the king his Majesty would certainly never have allowed him to depart empty-handed. It farther follows that he cannot have been cheated of his reward by a court servant, since under any circumstances the account must have been entered. Moreover, the sum of 500 thls. is much too high an estimate if Marchand only received 100 ducats $=$ 270 thlr. 20 gr. Handel, too, had no more when, two years later, he played at court (*see* Chrysander, II., p. 18). It is very possible that such smuggling-in was common enough at court; perhaps it was the discovery of such an instance at a later period which gave rise to a supposition in the Bach family which, by frequent repetition, as is not uncommon, gradually assumed the aspect of a fact. The entry given above has no date. However, from the place in which it occurs, we may conclude that Marchand was in Dresden at some time about September; the accounts are generally arranged chronologically, and this would correspond with the time of year when Bach usually made his journeys.

32 (p. 598). **The Little Organ Book,** as may be seen by the title-page, was written at Cöthen. But if all the contents were also composed in Cöthen, it would be difficult to explain in any satisfactory manner the following note: "*p. t.* [*pro tempore*] *Cappellæ Magistro S.*[*erenissimi*] *P.*[*rincipis*] *R.*[*egnantis*] *Anhaltini-Cotheniensis.*" Bach could only have written " *pro tempore* " with reference to some earlier time, of course that at Weimar, when most, if not all, of the chorales here copied out were composed. And this is only compatible with the difference in his duties there and in Cöthen. Here he had not the smallest direct connection with the organ and organ-playing; in Weimar, on the contrary, it

---

* Posts paid out of the household purse by the special order of the king.

was the main feature of his duties. Adlung says expressly (Anleitung, p. 690) : " He set some beautiful chorales when he was court organist at Weimar." But of course he does not mean to limit his labours to the organ. Added to this, most of his organ chorales which are to be found in Walther's collections occur in the Little Organ Book, particularly those in the three collections at Berlin (in the Royal Library) : " Das alte Jahr vergangen ist," "Gelobet seist du, Jesu Christ," "Herr Gott, nun schleuss den Himmel auf," "Heut triumphiret Gottes Sohn," "Jesu, meine Freude," " Mit Fried und Freud ich fahr dahin," "*Puer natus in Bethlehem*," " Von Himmel hoch da komm ich her "; those in the Frankenberger autograph : " Es ist das Heil uns kommen her," " Herr Christ, der ein'ge Gott'ssohn." The last two occur, too, in the Königsberg autograph. I have already shown how Walther's intimacy with Bach grew up gradually, and that their intercourse came to a standstill and ceased altogether, at any rate after Bach's departure, and probably during the last years of their residing in the same town; it is therefore plain enough that Walther must have obtained those of Bach's chorales which he inserted in his collections from the composer, between 1708 and 1717, probably nearer the former than the later year. It is further evidence that most of the chorales of the Little Organ Book were written during the time when Walther and Bach had common views of their art, and that they show a conspicuous predilection for canon treatment, which was a speciality of Walther's, and which Bach subsequently abandoned.

But the accuracy of the opinion that most of the chorales of the Little Organ Book were written in Weimar is still more conclusively proved by the following considerations. In the beginning of the year 1879 I found in the possession of Herr Ernst Mendelssohn-Bartholdy, of Berlin, a second autograph of the Little Organ Book. It had belonged to Felix Mendelssohn-Bartholdy in his time, and he had supplied it with a cover and title-page written in his own hand. It was in his possession in 1836. Two leaves out of it he gave to his betrothed for her album. A third leaf he subsequently gave to Madame Clara Schumann. These donations are noted on the cover. They are still extant, the former in the possession of Frau Wach, wife of Professor Wach, of Leipzig ; the latter is still in the hands of Madame Clara Schumann at Frankfort-on-the-Maine. This autograph which has lost its original title, consists, as it now exists in Herr Ernst Mendelssohn-Bartholdy's hands, of fourteen elegantly and clearly written leaves in small oblong quarto ; the pages are not numbered, and contain the following chorales :—

" Das alte Jahr vergangen ist " (14).
" In dir ist Freude " (13).
" Mit Fried und Freud ich fahr dahin " (15).
" Christe, du Lamm Gottes " (19).
" O Lamm Gottes unschuldig " (16).
" Da Jesus an dem Kreuze stund " (20).

"O Mensch, bewein dein Sünde gross " (18).
"Christus, der uns selig macht " (17).
"Wir danken dir, Herr Jesu Christ " (21).
"Hilf Gott, dass mirs gelinge " (23).
"Herr Gott, nun schleuss den Himmel auf " (24).
"Christ lag in Todesbanden " (28).
"Jesus Christus, unser Heiland " (25).
"Christ ist erstanden " (29).
"Erstanden ist der heilge Christ " (26).
"Heut triumphiret Gottes Sohn " (27).
"Erschienen ist der herrliche Tag " (30).
"Es ist das Heil uns kommen her " (34).
"Ich ruf zu dir, Herr Jesu Christ " (36).
"In dich hab ich gehoffet Herr," *alio modo* (22).

The two unnumbered leaves in Frau Wach's possession contain :—
"Liebster Jesu wir sind hier "* (31).
"Dies sind die heilgen zehn Gebot " (35).
"Vater unser im Himmelreich " (37).
"Durch Adams Fall ist ganz verderbt " (38).

The leaf in Madame Schumann's possession has :—
"Komm, Gott Schöpfer heiliger Geist " (32).
"Herr Jesu Christ dich zu uns wend " (33).

Thus this autograph contained altogether twenty-six chorales. A later hand, for the convenience of copying, has arranged it differently. He has added numbers to the chorales, inserted in brackets above and after the first lines of each. The new arrangement did not follow that of the more ample Cöthen autograph, as we may see by comparing them ; for the order of the pieces, with one exception (" Christ ist erstanden "), is quite different in the two copies. Still the circumstance that it only begins at No. 13 leads us to the conclusion that when it was made it contained twelve chorales more. This we may also infer from the fact that while the order of the chorales in the Mendelssohn autograph follows, on the whole, that of the ecclesiastical year, those for Advent and Christmas are wanting. We are therefore justified in supposing that Mendelssohn's autograph originally included thirty-eight chorales : eight less than the Cöthen copy.

From an examination of both we infer that the Mendelssohn copy must be a good deal the older. In the first place we find the chorales "Christus, der uns selig macht " and "Komm, Gott Schöpfer heiliger Geist " in an older reading. These are not unknown in this form. Griepenkerl has given them as a variorum reading in his edition of Bach's organ chorales. As his authorities he names, for the first,

---

* On three sets of lines ; the second version in the Cöthen Autograph.

Schübler's collection, and for the second simply this autograph. Now, as the two variants do not occur in the Cöthen copy, this older autograph must have been before him, and must have been then in Schübler's possession; Mendelssohn may have had it from him. Thus we have here rediscovered an authority which since Griepenkerl's time had been lost.

The earlier date of the Mendelssohn autograph is further proved by the chorales " Hilf Gott, das mirs gelinge " and " In dich hab ich gehoffet Herr." The former, which in the Cöthen autograph is copied fair, while in the Mendelssohn copy it is full of corrections, has here been written at first on two staves. When Bach had written as far as the fourth bar he perceived that he should not have room enough. He therefore has drawn, freehand, a third stave for the pedal, which runs on to the end of the piece. In the Cöthen autograph it is written on three staves from the first, that is to say the pedal part is written in German " tabulatur " notation below the second stave. The chorale " In dich hab ich gehoffet " Bach wished to introduce in two different arrangements when he put together the chorales in the Mendelssohn copy. One was ready done; this he copied in, wrote over it " alio modo," and left a leaf free for the arrangement still waiting to be composed. When he arranged the more extensive Cöthen collection, intended to contain a larger number of chorales, this arrangement was still not composed, but he had not given up the intention ; here again he left a place for it. If the contents of the Little Organ Book, as it was first written out, exist in the Cöthen MS. we must conclude that the Mendelssohn autograph is an extract; but, if so, how comes it that Bach should have left a space for a piece not yet composed? No composer ever undertakes the rearrangement of an earlier work of his own until it is removed by some lapse of time, which enables him to form an unprejudiced estimate of it, or until he has reached a standpoint conspicuously in advance of the former. And many years certainly had intervened between the time when these two copies, the Cöthen and the Mendelssohn autographs, were made. And the former was not written all at once, but, as may be plainly seen from the difference in writing, added to by degrees during the years of his residence at Cöthen. Consequently the Mendelssohn autograph confirms what, on other grounds, seems probable, that the contents of the Little Organ Book were in great part not composed in Cöthen. At least 26—but presumably 38—of the 46 chorales were written before the Cöthen period.

We can go farther still. Supposing the Mendelssohn autograph to have been written in his later years at Weimar, the MS. still bears unmistakable traces in a great part of its contents of being only a transcript of a still older work. On page 611, note 346, I have alluded to this, and I consider the statement as quite incontrovertible that the chorale in the Little Organ Book, " Komm, Gott Schöpfer," as it stands there, cannot have been originally written for that book. Correctly speaking, it is not at all suited to it. In the Little Organ Book Bach himself says, "the pedal is to be treated exclusively as obbligato," and here we find it almost entirely the reverse. This piece has been conceived of as an introduction to a much grander organ chorale, which in fact we actually possess. It is only in its original connection that we can at all understand those short pedal notes which only serve to mark the progression of the harmony; after this the pedal must of course have taken up the *cantus firmus,* and in order that it might do so with the more effect Bach is as sparing as possible in the first use of the pedal. Thus the longer organ chorale was already in existence before Bach inserted this fragment of it in the Mendelssohn autograph. It is also remarkable that, setting aside the two complete rearrangements, the chorales of the Mendelssohn copy deviate only in minute particulars from the Cöthen autograph. The chief differences are in "Mit Fried und Freud," bar 13, alto; the last crotchet:—

(the *c′* in the third note is quite clearly intended); In " Herr Gott nun schleuss den Himmel auf," bar 21, alto—

and in the last bar of the same, and the last beat of the bar in the tenor part:—

In "O Lamm Gottes, unschuldig," the upper part in bar 6 is :—

In " Hilf Gott, das mirs gelinge," in the last bar the pedal part is—

but afterwards the low F sharp was added. But, on the other hand, there are many calligraphic errors, and in not a few pieces ties, single notes, and even whole sets of notes are left out altogether through carelessness. Thus, in " In dir ist Freude," bars 3 and 4, both the lower parts are omitted; in " Herr Gott nun schleuss," bar 1, the two last notes, and in bar 13 from the second to the sixth notes, in the pedal part; in " O Mensch bewein," bar 8, the first half-bar in the tenor in bar 10, the first three-quarters of the bar in the pedal; in " Wir danken dir," bar 1, the first note in the tenor; and in "Christ ist erstanden " and " Heut triumphiret Gottes Sohn" there are omissions; in this last instance alone the gaps were filled up by Bach himself at a later date. Such a thing never happened, I should think, to any composer who writes a complete work fairly out, or at least when, as was done by Bach, the greatest care is bestowed even upon the characteristics of style. These chorales are not written in a hurry, but somewhat thoughtlessly and mechanically, and this could only be done by Bach when he was engaged in the mere copying of an old or long-finished piece. We shall not venture too much in putting back the date of the chorales in the Mendelssohn autograph to the earlier years of the Weimar period.

Since the body of this work was written Rust has edited for the Bach Gesellschaft the Orgelbüchlein (Little Organ Book), and the six grand organ chorales of the Schübler MS., with eighteen others (B.-G., XXV., 2). In the first volume of this book (published in 1873) I expressed for the first time an opinion that, irrespective of his very early attempts, all Bach's organ chorales were the fruits of the Weimar period, with the exception of the third part of the Clavierübung, the six chorales in Schübler's copy, and the partitas on "Vom Himmel hoch." In Rust's preface he puts forward a contrary view. He attributes the chorales of the Orgelbüchlein—with the exception of "Liebster Jesu, wir sind hier"—to the Cöthen period, and the eighteen great chorales to the Leipzig time. The Mendelssohn autograph was not known to him. He has dealt somewhat cavalierly as to refuting the reasons I adduced for my opinion, simply ignoring them. I will here bring forward one point more. In the Necrology, p. 163, it is said that Bach composed *most* of his organ pieces in Weimar. It is obvious to any one who has studied the course of Bach's development that this refers particularly to the organ chorales, and to them above all. Of these we possess between 120 and 130, besides the three early partita arrangements. But if the forty-six (or forty-five) chorales in the Little Organ Book, the eighteen large ones edited by Rust, the sixteen in the Clavierübung, the six in Schubler's collection, the five pieces in canon on "Vom Himmel hoch" —altogether about ninety pieces—were all composed in Cöthen and Leipzig, what remains for him to have done in Weimar? Rust's evidence is not satisfactory. Where he says that Walther's MSS. seems to be of later date than the Cöthen autograph, I do not know on what he takes his stand. Walther's writing—and this would afford a moderately accurate standard—remained remarkably uniform throughout his life; I myself possess an autograph of some extent by him, written as early as 1708, in which the writing is just the same as that of his chorale collections. But, even if Rust were right, this—in the face of all critical method—would not prove his assertion that Walther's MS. could not therefore be referred to older original copies. In point of fact, Walther did not by any means always have recent copies when making his various collections of chorales; on the contrary, he liked to write them out himself, and would take the opportunity of inserting emendations of his own—a fact which deserves to be considered when variorum readings are under discussion (see Spitta's edition of Buxtehude's organ compositions: critical notes to Vol. II., p. viii.). The allusion to the organ in the Lutheran church at Cöthen cannot be regarded as decisive. If the chorales " Gottes Sohn ist kommen" and "*In dulci jubilo*" really could have only been played upon it, all that this would prove is that *they* must have been composed in Cöthen, and would in no way hinder that the rest should have been written in Weimar. But the premise is defective ; the high pedal notes *f'* and *f'* sharp would be brought out very well on the Weimar castle organ by the aid of the four-foot cornet stop. The note added to the chorale " Gottes Sohn ist kommen," in the Cöthen autograph—"*Ped. Tromp.* 8 *F* "—merely renders it highly probable that Bach played the chorale on the organ of the Lutheran church; if he played it at Weimar he would only have to use different combinations of stops.

I must go at rather greater length into a third course of evidence which Rust has attempted to make use of. Chorale melodies, or, as we should call them, hymn-tunes, like popular song-tunes, go through a variety of small modifications in the course of transmission, which then become concrete in the use of certain congregations. Thus, for instance, a melody would be somewhat differently sung in Nuremberg and in Leipzig, or Gotha, or Hamburg, and many other similar variations would have originated in other places. Rust assumes that Bach in his organ chorales and arrangements for church use would always have adhered strictly to the form of the tune commonly in use in the town where he might be writing the piece. He adduces a list of melodies which he maintains were in use among the congregations of Weimar; and when he finds that a chorale in the Little Organ Book does not exactly correspond with these he concludes that the piece in question cannot have been composed in Weimar. This method is very applicable for chronological calculations if it is used as an auxiliary to others of greater value; but it proves a broken staff when we attempt to rely upon it alone. One example will suffice: The melody of " Komm, heiliger Geist, Herre Gott " was used in identically the same form in the cantata written at Weimar, " Wer mich liebet," and the motett written at Leipzig, " Der Geist hilft unsrer Schwachheit auf." But this form does not coincide with that which, as we may infer from Vopelius' Gesangbuch and Vetter's Musicalischer Kirch- und Hauss-Ergötzlichkeit, was in use among the Leipzig congregations. The chorale, " O Lamm Gottes unschuldig," is different in Vopelius and in Vetter to the form used in the Passion music (St. Matthew). The tune, " Meinen Jesum lass ich nicht," again is different in the same Passion music, and in the cantata, " Mein liebster Jesus," which was also written in Leipzig (1724). One only of the two, however, can have been in congregational use. Thus this once, at least, Bach did not recur to the same form. " Helft mir Gott's Güte preisen " exists in two forms, which differ rather conspicuously; both occur in Leipzig cantatas—the one in " Herr Gott dich loben wir," the other in " Herr, wie du willt." Indeed, the final chorale of the Ascension oratorio shows yet a third form, and Vetter gives a fourth. " Jesu meine Freude " occurs in the Leipzig cantatas : " Jesus schläft, was soll ich hoffen," " Sehet, welch eine Liebe," and " Bisher habt ihr nichts gebeten," and in each with certain differences in the tune ; and a fourth form, in the turn of the last line, is to be found in the second verse of the chorale of the motett of the same name. In all these instances—and I could easily add to their number —where do we find an adherence to the form in congregational use ?

Rust's assumption rests, in my opinion, on a false idea of Bach's attitude towards congregational singing. The master always recognised it as the central point of his church duties, but still he went to the task with a certain Protestant independence. Though he considered himself bound by it on the whole, still in detail he must of necessity bend the chorale to his own subjective needs. The only rule he acknowledged was to keep the chorale melody in the same form throughout when once he had used it in a composition. To this rule the exceptions are extremely rare, but beyond this his selection of this or that form of melody is entirely subordinate to his own artistic standard. This he regarded as his right, and in the same way he adopted the words of hymns of which the tunes were well known to other melodies, fitting them together. The Christmas oratorio affords an example. It is unnecessary to go into any further items of Herr Rust's argument; its conclusion is worthless so soon as the premise is shown to be false, and it is clear from what has been said why I consider it so.

Since we concluded, from the fact that certain chorales occur in Walther's collections, that they must have been composed in Weimar, we have an equal right to assign the rest of Bach's chorales which are in Walther's collection, but not in the Little Organ Book, to the Weimar period. These are in the Berlin autographs : " Komm, Gott Schöpfer " (P. S. V., C. 7, v. 246, No. 35), and " Nun komm, der Heiden Heiland " (P. S. V., C. 7, v. 246, Nos. 45-47)—two copies ; in one of these the quavers for the right hand in the third verse are written as semiquavers. In the Frankenberger autograph we have (excluding the " Ein feste Burg ist unser Gott," which has been already mentioned) " Herzlich thut mich verlangen " (P. S. V., C. 5, v. 244, No. 27, with some small deviations which prove the excellence of Griepenkerl's edition), " Valet will ich dir geben " (P. S. V., C. 7, v. 246, and a variant in No. 50, which differs in three places from Griepenkerl's edition), " Vater unser im Himmelreich " (P. S. V., C. 7, v. 246, No. 53). The Königsberger autograph includes the same chorales and two more : " Ach Gott und Herr " (B minor, common time, *see* Themat. Cat., App. I., Series V., No. 10), thus proving their genuineness, and " Wer nur den lieben Gott lässt walten." This last is nothing more than the chorale accompaniment previously mentioned in illustration of

Bach's methods of playing in Arnstadt, with the omission of the pre-post and interludes, and a few trifling differences. The arrangement is undoubtedly by Bach. As the subject recurs in the Clavierbüchlein (P. S. V., C. 5, v. 244, Nọ. 52) in a still more ornate form, and evidently intended for the practice of embellishments, we can trace the proceṣs by which Bach gradually grew into a conviction of what the sole use of such settings could be. Finally, in Andreas Bach's book we find the organ chorale on " Gott, durch deine Güte " (P. S. V., C. 6, v. 245, No. 25) in " Tabulatur " notation ; but, unlike Griepenkerl's edition, it is 3-2 time. Any direct chronological data for further labours in this direction are wanting, but we need only utilise those we already possess, and compare all the organ chorales that remain to us, remembering at the same time the ṡtatement of the Necrology that *most* of Bach's organ pieces were written at Weimar to acquire the conviction that the list of those about which we are certain is quite insufficient. We must seek for further traces. In the Berlin Library is a MS. of Bach's organ chorales, containing the following sixteen numbers in the master's own hand: 1. Fantasia on " Komm, heiliger Geist" (P. S. V., C. 7, v. 246, No. 36) ; 2. " Komm, heiliger Geist " (Ibid., No. 37) ; 3. " An Wasser-flüssen Babylon " (Ibid., v. 245, No. 12b) ; 4. " Schmücke dich, O liebe Seele (Ibid., v. 246, No. 29) ; 5. Trio on " Herr Jesu Christ, dich zu nus wend " (Ibid., v. 245, No. 27) ; 6. " O Lamm Gottes unschuldig " (Ibid., v. 246, No. 48) ; 7. Nun danket alle Gott " (Ibid., No. 43) ; 8. " Von Gott will ich nicht lassen " (Ibid., No. 56) ; 9-11. " Nun komm der Heiden Heiland " (Ibid., Nos. 45-47) ; 12. " Allein Gott in der Höh " (Ibid., No. 9) ; 13. " Allein Gott in der Höh " (Ibid., No. 8) ; 14. Trio on the same (Ibid., No. 7) ; 15. " Jesus Christus, unser Heiland" (Ibid., No. 31) ; 16. Variations in canon on " Vom Himmel hoch " (C. 5, v. 244, II., No. 4). Among them there are a few more pieces written out by Altnikol, his pupil, and subsequently his son-in-law. By this and by the character of the paper we see it is of the Leipzig period ; at the same time it is a fair copy.

We have already learnt to regard the three arrangements of " Nun komm, der Heiden Heiland " as probably produced at Weimar. The chorale " Komm, Gott Schöpfer, heiliger Geist," of which the same view is the probable one, is to be found in this same copy in Altnikol's hand. But it is very remarkable that we should find that variants exist of all the chorales contained in it, with only three exceptions (" Schmücke dich, o liebe Seele," " Nun danket alle Gott," and " Allein Gott in der Höh," No. 12), and that when compared with them all of these appear to have been remodelled later. An exact examination leads us to the conviction that Bach was accustomed to revise in later years all his instrumental compositions written in Leipzig, because at the close of the Cöthen period his instrumental purview had been finally extended and his technical skill brought to the utmost perfection. The inference is almost inevitable. In this MS. Bach collected the more worthy of his earlier works, and took the opportunity of subjecting them once more to a thorough revision. Nor is this probability excluded even though some of them were composed in Cöthen. Only we must always remember that his position there led him to quite other work. He had no immediate reason for playing the organ there—nay, it was a very poor instrument; so that it can only have been with a view to his journeys that he can ever have felt moved to compose anything great and worthy of himself for his favourite instrument. Finally, if, after sifting out all the organ chorales published by Bach himself in Leipzig, we compare, from the standpoint offered by this collection, all the rest of his works of this kind remaining to us, we perceive at once that scarcely one of them can belong to a later time; most must be ascribed to an earlier. On the whole—this is the final result—we are not likely to err if we estimate Bach's work as a setter of chorales from the total mass of the organ chorales, with the exception of the third part of the Clavierübung, the six edited by Joh. Georg Schübler and published at Zella (the rest are in part arrangements of cantatas), and the variations in canon on "Vom Himmel hoch." These are all contained in the edition by Griepenkerl, with the exception of a few pieces which are doubtful, and it is based on the best authorities, so far as they were at that time attainable. I have already pointed out an error in it. The chorale "Gott der Vater wohn uns bei" (P. S. V., C. 6, v. 245, No. 24) is by Walther. I also regard the chorale "Ich hab mein Sach Gott heimgestellt" (v. 245, No. 28) as undoubtedly spurious, though only on internal evidence, it is true; its extraordinary canon treatment is a pendant to the former, and must also be of Walther's composition. I am doubtful as to the two-part arrangement of "Allein Gott in der Höh" (v. 245, No. 3). Bernhard Bach wrote somewhat in this style; still, a few important features warn us to be careful.

END OF VOL. I.